D1823115

Microsoft®

Windows® 2000
Server
Operations
Guide

IT Professional

PUBLISHED BY
Microsoft Press
A Division of Microsoft Corporation
One Microsoft Way
Redmond, Washington 98052-6399

Library of Congress Cataloging-in-Publication Data
Microsoft Windows 2000 Server Resource Kit / Microsoft Corporation.
        p. cm.
    Includes index.
    ISBN 1-57231-805-8 (Resource Kit)
    ISBN 0-7356-1796-1
    1. Microsoft Windows 2000 Server.   2. Operating systems (Computers).   I. Microsoft
Corporation.
QA76.76.O63 M5241328   2000
005.4'4769--dc21   99-045616

Printed and bound in the United States of America.

1 2 3 4 5 6 7 8 9   QWT   7 6 5 4 3 2

Distributed in Canada by Penguin Books Canada Limited.

A CIP catalogue record for this book is available from the British Library.

Microsoft Press books are available through booksellers and distributors worldwide. For further information about international editions,
contact your local Microsoft Corporation office or contact Microsoft Press International directly at fax (425) 936-7329. Visit our Web site a
www.microsoft.com/mspress. Send comments to *rkinput@microsoft.com*.

Acquisitions Editor: Juliana Aldous Atkinson
Project Editor: Aileen Wrothwell

Body Part No. X08-78661

Thank you to those who contributed to this book:

Department Managers: Paul Goode, Ken Western
Documentation Managers: Laura Burris, Martin DelRe, Peggy Etchevers
Resource Kit Program Managers: Chris Hallum, Martin Holladay,
Louis Kahn, Ryan Marshall, Paul Sutton

Server Operations Guide

Technical Writing Lead: Sybil Wood
Writers: Rick DeJarnette, James Klima, Brian Roberts, Audrey Wehba

Editing Leads: Deborah Annan, Jennifer Hendrix, Kate O'Leary
Book Editing Leads: Kristen Gill, Paulette McKay
Copy Editors: Kate McLaughlin, Mary Rose Sliwoski
Scott Somohano, Thelma Warren
Glossary: Daniel Bell

Resource Kit Tools Software Developers: Dan Grube,
Michael Hawkins, Darryl Wood, Zeyong Xu
Documentation Tools Software Developers: Amy Buck, Tom Carey,
Ryan Farber, Mark Pengra, Fred Taub

Production Leads: Sandy Dean, Jane Dow, Keri Grassl, Jason Hershey
Production Specialists: Michael Faber, Dani McIntyre, Lori Robinson

Indexing Leads: Jane Dow, Veronica Maier
Indexer: Kumud Dwivedi, Diana Rain

Lead Graphic Designer: Flora Goldthwaite
Designers: Chris Blanton, Siamack Sahafi

Art Production: Blaine Dollard, Jenna Kiter, Amy Shear, Gabriel Varela

Test Lead: Jonathan Fricke
Testers: Brian Klauber, Jeremy Sullivan

Windows 2000 Lab Manager: Edward Lafferty
Administrators: Deborah Jay, Grant Mericle, Dave Meyer,
Dean Prince, Robert Thingwold, Luke Walker, Joel Wingert, Frank Zamarron
Lab Partners: Cisco Systems, Inc., Compaq, Inc.,
Hewlett-Packard Corporation, Intel Corporation

A special thanks to the following technical experts who contributed to and supported this effort:

Brian Andrew, Reza Baghai, Eugene Baucom, Maurizio Bellassai, June Blender, Bill Blomgren, Roger Bruist, Felipe Cabrera, Phillip Carver, Ben Christenbury, Marion Cole, Arren Conner, Buddy Cox, Joseph Dadzie, Steve DeVos, Brian Dodd, Bo Downey, David Everett, David Fields, Patrick Franklin, Jee Fung Pang, David Golds, Darrell Gorter, Scott Graff, Glenn Grant, Karen Greaves, Tim Green, Rob Greenwell, Rich Hagemeyer, Renee Hall, Scott Hallock, Jeff Heffner, Martin Holladay, Michael Jacquet, Babak Jahromi, Romano Jerez, Peter Johnston, Nikhil Joshi, Keith Kaplan, Steven Kiraly, Rama Koneru , Tom Kufeldt, Norbert Kusters, Bruce Langworthy, Patrick Lewis, Daniel Lovinger, Mark Lucovksy, Tim Lytle, Ryan Marshall, Aaron Massey, Michael McCartney, Randy McLaughlin, Ed McLees, Chris McKitterick, Michael Miele, Brett Miller, Loren Moore, Paul Moore, Alan Morris, Jackie Mounts, Steven Munk, Erik Odenborg, Steve Olsson, Michael Peterson, Ravisankar Pudipeddi, Kartik Raghavan, Aaron Reynolds, Lynn Roe, Robert Rosa, Maher Saba, Derick Schaefer, Stuart Sechrest, Joseph Seifert, Kathy Sestrap, Art Shelest, Dale Sinnott, Bob Snead, Kent Somerville, Christy Sutton, Albert Ting, Rob Trace, Tom Van Baak, Catharine Van Ingen, Landy Wang, Brad Waters, Bob Watson, Dan Weston, Steve Wilson, David Winkler, Rick Winter, Wesley Witt, Jon Wojan, Bruce Worthington, Wade Yamauchi

Contents

Part 2   Performance Monitoring

Part 4   Troubleshooting

Introduction

Welcome to the *Microsoft® Windows® 2000 Server Resource Kit Server Operations Guide.*

The *Microsoft® Windows® 2000 Server Resource Kit* consists of seven volumes and a single compact disc (CD) containing tools, additional reference materials, and an online version of the books. Supplements to the *Windows 2000 Server Resource Kit* will be released as new information becomes available, and updates and information will be available on the Web on an ongoing basis.

The *Server Operations Guide* provides the information you need to understand and maintain your server installations. This guide includes descriptions of the disk, file system, storage, printing, troubleshooting, and system recovery features that are included with Microsoft® Windows® 2000. Particular attention is given to the new storage features, such as Removable Storage and Remote Storage, and characteristics new to NTFS, such as reparse points and disk quotas. This guide also covers troubleshooting and system recovery tools, strategies, and recommendations. With the exceptions of printing and performance monitoring, the information in this guide pertains to stand-alone computers. See the other volumes in the *Windows 2000 Server Resource Kit* for information about networked systems.

Document Conventions

The following style conventions and terminology are used throughout this guide.

Element	Meaning
bold font	Characters that you type exactly as shown, including commands and switches. User interface elements are also bold.
Italic font	Variables for which you supply a specific value. For example, *Filename.ext* could refer to any valid file name for the case in question.
`Monospace font`	Code samples.
`%SystemRoot%`	The folder in which Windows 2000 is installed.

Reader Alert	Meaning
Tip	Alerts you to supplementary information that is not essential to the completion of the task at hand.
Note	Alerts you to supplementary information.
Important	Alerts you to supplementary information that is essential to the completion of a task.
Caution	Alerts you to possible data loss, breaches of security, or other more serious problems.
Warning	Alerts you that failure to take or avoid a specific action might result in physical harm to you or to the hardware.

Resource Kit Compact Disc

The *Windows 2000 Server Resource Kit* companion CD includes a wide variety of tools and resources to help you work more efficiently with Windows 2000.

Note The tools on the CD are designed and tested for the U.S. version of Windows 2000. Use of these programs on other versions of Windows 2000 or on versions of Microsoft® Windows NT® can cause unpredictable results.

The *Resource Kit* companion CD contains the following:

Windows 2000 Server Resource Kit Online Books An HTML Help version of the print books. Use these books to find the same detailed information about Windows 2000 as is found in the print versions. Search across all of the books to find the most pertinent information to complete the task at hand.

Windows 2000 Server Resource Kit Tools and Tools Help Over 200 software tools, tools documentation, and other resources that harness the power of Windows 2000. Use these tools to manage Active Directory™, administer security features, work with the registry, automate recurring jobs, and many other important tasks. Use Tools Help documentation to discover and learn how to use these administrative tools.

Windows 2000 Resource Kit References A set of HTML Help references:

- **Error and Event Messages Help** contains most of the error and event messages generated by Windows 2000. With each message comes a detailed explanation and a suggested user action.

- **Technical Reference to the Registry** provides detailed descriptions of Windows 2000 registry content, such as the subtrees, keys, subkeys, and entries that advanced users want to know about, including many entries that cannot be changed by using Windows 2000 tools or programming interfaces.

- **Performance Counter Reference** describes all performance objects and counters provided for use with tools in the Performance snap-in of Windows 2000. Use this reference to learn how monitoring counter values can assist you in diagnosing problems or detecting bottlenecks in your system.

- **Group Policy Reference** provides detailed descriptions of the Group Policy settings in Windows 2000. These descriptions explain the effect of enabling, disabling, or not configuring each policy, as well as explanations of how related policies interact.

Resource Kit Support Policy

The software supplied in the *Windows 2000 Server Resource Kit* is not supported. Microsoft does not guarantee the performance of the *Windows 2000 Server Resource Kit* tools, response times for answering questions, or bug fixes to the tools. However, we do provide a way for customers who purchase the *Windows 2000 Server Resource Kit* to report bugs and receive possible fixes for their issues. You can do this by sending e-mail to rkinput@microsoft.com. This e-mail address is only for *Windows 2000 Server Resource Kit* related issues. For issues relating to the Windows 2000 operating system, please refer to the support information included with your product.

PART 1

Storage, File Systems, and Printing

Microsoft® Windows® 2000 provides significant enhancements to data storage, NTFS and FAT32 file systems, and network printing. Part 1 describes the storage, file system, and printing features and tools in Windows 2000 and provides information that can be used during troubleshooting.

In This Part

CHAPTER 1

Disk Concepts and Troubleshooting

Understanding the organizational structure of information on hard disks, as well as being familiar with disk terminology, is key to diagnosing and troubleshooting disk problems. When troubleshooting system problems, you can refer to this chapter for detailed descriptions of the master boot record (MBR) and boot sector, two disk sectors that are critical to the startup process.

In This Chapter

Related Information in the Resource Kit

- For more information about startup, see "Startup Process" in this book.

- For more information about file systems, see "File Systems" in this book.

- For more information about preparing for and performing recovery, see "Repair, Recovery, and Restore" in this book.

Basic and Dynamic Disks

Microsoft® Windows® 2000 offers two types of disk storage configurations: basic disk and dynamic disk. Basic disk is similar to the disk structures used in Microsoft® Windows NT®. Dynamic disk is new to Windows 2000. By default, Windows 2000 initializes hard disks as basic disk.

The Disk Administrator tool found in Microsoft® Windows NT® version 4.0 and earlier has been replaced in Windows 2000 with the Disk Management snap-in for Microsoft Management Console (MMC). Disk Management supports both basic and dynamic disks. You can use the upgrade wizard in Disk Management to convert hard disks to dynamic disks.

You can use both basic and dynamic disks on the same computer system, and with any combination of file systems (file allocation table [FAT], including FAT16 and FAT32, and NTFS file system). However, all volumes on a physical disk must be either basic or dynamic.

You can upgrade from basic to dynamic storage at any time. Any changes made to your disk are immediately available in Windows 2000—you do not need to quit Disk Management to save them or restart your computer to implement them. However, if you upgrade the startup disk to dynamic, or if a volume or partition is in use on the disk that you are upgrading, the computer must be restarted for the upgrade to succeed.

Terms

To help you understand the differences between basic disk and dynamic disk, a set of definitions are provided.

Basic Disk

A basic disk is a physical disk that contains primary partitions and/or extended partitions with logical drives used by Windows 2000 and all versions of Windows NT. Basic disks can also contain volume, striped, mirror, or redundant array of independent disks (RAID) Level 5 (also known as striped with parity) sets that were created using Windows NT 4.0 or earlier. As long as a compatible file format is used, basic disks can be accessed by Microsoft® MS-DOS®, Microsoft® Windows® 95, Microsoft® Windows® 98, and all versions of Windows NT.

Since Windows 2000 automatically initializes disks as basic, you can troubleshoot partitions and volumes using the same methods as in Windows NT.

Note FAT32 is new in Windows 2000. Disk troubleshooting tools from Windows NT will likely not recognize FAT32 boot sectors and may cause problems with FAT32-formatted volumes. If FAT32 is used on your computer, be sure to use a disk troubleshooting tool designed for Windows 2000 that recognizes this file format.

New or empty disks can be initialized as either basic or dynamic after the hardware installation is complete. However, to set up a new fault-tolerant (FT) disk system, you must upgrade to dynamic disk.

Basic Volume

A basic volume is a volume on a basic disk. Basic volumes include primary partitions, logical drives within extended partitions, as well as volume, striped, mirror, or RAID-5 sets created using Windows NT 4.0 or earlier. You cannot create basic volumes on dynamic disks.

Note Creating new FT sets, such as mirrored and RAID-5 volumes, is only available on computers running Windows 2000 Server. The disk must be upgraded to dynamic disk before these volumes can be created. You can, however, use a computer running Windows 2000 Professional to create mirrored and RAID-5 volumes on a remote computer running Windows 2000 Server.

Dynamic Disk

A dynamic disk is a physical disk that has been upgraded by and is managed with Disk Management. Dynamic disks do not use partitions or logical drives. They can contain only dynamic volumes created by Disk Management. Only computers running Windows 2000 can access dynamic volumes.

Note Disks that have been upgraded from basic to dynamic disk still contain references to partitions in the partition table of the MBR. However, the MBR's reference to these partitions identifies the partition types as dynamic, indicating to Windows 2000 that the disk configuration data is now maintained in the disk management database at the end of the disk. Furthermore, any new changes made to the disk, such as deleting existing or creating additional volumes, are not recorded in the partition table.

Dynamic disks use dynamic volumes to subdivide physical disks into one or more drives enumerated by letters of the alphabet. Disk configuration data is contained in a disk management database stored in the last 1 megabyte (MB) of space at the end of the disk. Since dynamic disks do not use the traditional disk organization scheme of partitions and logical volumes, they cannot be directly accessed by MS-DOS, Windows 95, Windows 98, or any versions of Windows NT. Disk shares on dynamic disks, however, are available to computers running all of these operating systems.

Dynamic Volume

A dynamic volume is a logical volume that is created on a dynamic disk using Disk Management. Dynamic volume types include simple, spanned, striped, mirrored, and RAID-5, although only Windows 2000 Server supports the FT volume types (mirrored and RAID-5). You cannot create dynamic volumes on basic disks. Dynamic volumes are not supported on portable computers or removable media.

Note Dynamic volumes that were upgraded from basic disk partitions cannot be extended. This specifically includes the system volume, which contains hardware-specific files needed to start Windows 2000, and the boot volume, which contains the Windows 2000 system files required for startup. Only volumes created after the disk was upgraded to dynamic can be extended.

Partitions and Volumes

When you upgrade to dynamic disk, existing partitions and logical volumes are converted into dynamic volumes. Table 1.1 illustrates the translation of terms between basic and dynamic disk structures.

Table 1.1   Translation of Terms Between Basic and Dynamic Disk

Basic Disk Organization	Dynamic Disk Organization
Primary partition	Simple volume
System and boot partitions	System and boot volumes
Active partition	Active volume
Extended partition	Volume and unallocated space
Logical drive	Simple volume
Volume set	Spanned volume
Stripe set	Striped volume
Stripe set with parity	RAID-5 volume
Mirror set	Mirrored volume

Features of Basic Disk

You can use partitions on a basic disk just as you did with Microsoft® Windows NT® Server version 4.0, but you do not need to commit changes to save them or to restart your computer to make the changes effective. Changes made by Disk Management are implemented immediately. Unless you are making a change that affects existing files on the disk, the system executes your change without confirmation.

You can create up to four partitions in the free space on a physical hard disk; one of these can be an extended partition. You can use the free space in the extended partition to create one or more logical drives. You cannot use basic disk to create any kind of multiple volume sets or FT volumes.

You can perform the following tasks only on a basic disk:

- Create and delete primary and extended partitions.
- Create and delete logical drives within an extended partition.
- Format a partition and mark it as active.
- Delete volume, striped, mirror, or stripe sets with parity.
- Break a mirror from a mirror set.
- Repair failed legacy FT volumes such as mirror sets or stripe sets with parity.

Certain legacy functions are no longer available on basic disks because multiple-disk storage systems need to use dynamic disks. Disk Management supports legacy volumes that exceed a single partition on more than one hard disk, but it does not allow you to create new ones. For example, you cannot create volume, striped, mirror, or RAID-5 sets or extend volumes and volume sets on a basic disk.

While you cannot create new multiple disk sets on basic disks, you can delete them. Be sure to back up all the information on the set before you delete it.

To establish a new spanned, striped, mirror, or RAID-5 set, first upgrade the disk to dynamic disk. To convert an existing volume, striped, mirror, or RAID-5 set, upgrade the physical disks on which the set resides to dynamic disk.

Features of Dynamic Disk

Disk Management is very flexible. The number of volumes that you can create on a physical hard disk is limited only by the amount of available free space on the disk. You can also create volumes that span two or more disks and that, if you are running Windows 2000 Server, are fault tolerant.

You can perform the following tasks only on a dynamic disk:

- Create and delete simple, spanned, striped, mirrored, and RAID-5 volumes.
- Extend a simple or spanned volume.
- Remove a mirror from a mirrored volume or break the mirrored volume into two volumes.
- Repair mirrored or RAID-5 volumes.
- Reactivate a missing or offline disk.

Dynamic disks are not supported on portable computers. If you are using a portable computer and right-click a disk in the graphical or list view in Disk Management, you will not see the option to upgrade the disk to dynamic.

Note On some older and non-Advanced Configuration and Power Interface (ACPI)–compliant portable computers, you might be able to upgrade to dynamic disk, but it is neither recommended nor supported.

The limitations of dynamic volumes occur in the following situations:

When installing Windows 2000 If a dynamic volume is created from unallocated space on a dynamic disk, you cannot install Windows 2000 on that volume.

The setup limitation occurs because Windows 2000 Setup uses BIOS calls that only recognize volumes listed in the partition table. Only basic disk partitions, as well as simple and mirrored volumes of dynamic disks that were upgraded from basic disk partitions, appear in the partition table. Dynamic disk does not use the partition table to manage its volumes, so new dynamic volumes are not registered in the partition table as they are created. Windows 2000 must be installed on a volume that is correctly represented in the partition table.

When extending a volume You can install Windows 2000 on a dynamic volume that was upgraded from a basic disk partition, but you cannot extend either the system volume or the boot volume. Neither can be part of a spanned volume, since Windows 2000 considers extended volumes to be the same as spanned volumes.

Windows 2000 cannot extend a dynamic volume that was a basic volume before the dynamic disk upgrade, and the system and boot volumes (which might be one and the same) are likely the same volumes that existed under basic disk. The upgraded simple volume must match the listing found in the partition table. Extending the dynamic volume changes its size, but the partition table's registration of that volume is not updated to reflect the change. The only dynamic volumes on which you can install Windows 2000 are simple and mirrored volumes, and since these volumes must be registered in the partition table, they must be upgraded from basic to dynamic.

Features Common to Both Basic and Dynamic Disks

You can perform the following tasks on both basic and dynamic disks:

- Check disk properties such as capacity, available free space, and current status.
- View volume and partition properties such as size, drive-letter assignment, label, type, and file system.
- Establish drive-letter assignments for disk volumes or partitions, and for CD-ROM devices.
- Establish disk sharing and security arrangements for a volume or partition.
- Upgrade a basic disk to dynamic or revert a dynamic disk to basic.

Disk Sectors Critical to Startup

The two sectors critical to starting your computer are the master boot record (MBR), which is always located at sector 1 of cylinder 0, head 0, the first sector of a hard disk, and the boot sector, which resides at sector 1 of each volume. These sectors contain both executable code and the data required to run the code.

Note The use of basic or dynamic disk does not affect where the MBR is located on disk and only minor differences exist between the two for how the partition table is configured. However, as the Disk Management database contains the information where dynamic volumes begin and end, the method of walking, or navigating, partition tables to find the start and end of partitions and logical volumes, as well as finding volume boot sectors, does not work on dynamic disks. Disk editing tools, such as DiskProbe and third-party tools, can walk the partitions as expected with basic disks. Also, many disk editor tools that work with Windows NT and NTFS are not currently compatible with FAT32 boot sectors and volumes.

Master Boot Record

The MBR, the most important data structure on the disk, is created when the disk is partitioned. The MBR contains a small amount of executable code called the master boot code, the disk signature, and the partition table for the disk. At the end of the MBR is a 2-byte structure called a signature word or end of sector marker, which is always set to 0x55AA. A signature word also marks the end of an extended boot record (EBR) and the boot sector.

The disk signature, a unique number at offset 0x01B8, identifies the disk to the operating system. Windows 2000 uses the disk signature as an index to store and retrieve information about the disk in the registry subkey:

HKEY_LOCAL_MACHINE\SYSTEM\MountedDevices

Master Boot Code

The master boot code performs the following activities:

1. Scans the partition table for the active partition.
2. Finds the starting sector of the active partition.
3. Loads a copy of the boot sector from the active partition into memory.
4. Transfers control to the executable code in the boot sector.

If the master boot code cannot complete these functions, the system displays one of the following error messages:

- Invalid partition table
- Error loading operating system
- Missing operating system

Note There is no MBR on a floppy disk. The first sector on a floppy disk is the boot sector. Although every hard disk contains an MBR, the master boot code is used only if the disk contains the active, primary partition.

For more information about troubleshooting MBR problems, see "Damaged MBRs and Boot Sectors" later in this chapter.

Partition Table

The partition table, a 64-byte data structure used to identify the type and location of partitions on a hard disk, conforms to a standard layout independent of the operating system. Each partition table entry is 16 bytes long, with a maximum of four entries. Each entry starts at a predetermined offset from the beginning of the sector, as follows:

- Partition 1   0x01BE (446)
- Partition 2   0x01CE (462)
- Partition 3   0x01DE (478)
- Partition 4   0x01EE (494)

Note Only basic disk makes use of the partition table in Windows 2000. Dynamic disk uses the Disk Management database located at the end of the disk for disk configuration information. The partition table is not updated when volumes are deleted or extended after the dynamic disk upgrade, or when new dynamic volumes are created.

The following example shows a partial printout of an MBR revealing the partition table from a computer with three partitions. When there are fewer than four partitions on a disk, the remaining partition table fields are set to the value 0.

```
000001B0:                                           80 01            ..
000001C0: 01 00 07 FE BF 09 3F 00 - 00 00 4B F5 7F 00 00 00   ......?...K.□...
000001D0: 81 0A 07 FE FF FF 8A F5 - 7F 00 3D 26 9C 00 00 00   ........□.=&....
000001E0: C1 FF 05 FE FF FF C7 1B - 1C 01 D6 96 92 00 00 00   ...............
000001F0: 00 00 00 00 00 00 00 00 - 00 00 00 00 00 00         .............
```

Table 1.2 describes the fields in each entry in the partition table. The sample values correspond to the first partition table entry shown in the preceding example. The Byte Offset values correspond to the addresses of the first partition table entry. There are three additional entries whose values can be calculated by adding 10h to the byte offset value specific for each additional partition table entry (for example, add 20h for partition table entry 3 and 30h for partition table entry 4).

Table 1.2   Partition Table Fields

Byte Offset	Field Length	Sample Value	Field Name and Definition
0x01BE	BYTE	0x80	**Boot Indicator**. Indicates whether the volume is the active partition. Legal values include: 00. Do not use for booting. 80. Active partition.
0x01BF	BYTE	0x01	**Starting Head**.
0x01C0	6 bits	0x01 *	**Starting Sector**. Only bits 0-5 are used. The upper two bits, 6 and 7, are used by the Starting Cylinder field.
0x01C1	10 bits	0x00 *	**Starting Cylinder**. Uses 1 byte in addition to the upper 2 bits from the Starting Sector field to make up the cylinder value. The Starting Cylinder is a 10-bit number, with a maximum value of 1023.
0x01C2	BYTE	0x07	**System ID**. Defines the volume type. See Table 1.3 for sample values.
0x01C3	BYTE	0xFE	**Ending Head**.
0x01C4	6 bits	0xBF *	**Ending Sector**. Only bits 0-5 are used. The upper two bits, 6 and 7, are used by the Ending Cylinder field.
0x01C5	10 bits	0x09 *	**Ending Cylinder**. Uses 1 byte in addition to the upper 2 bits from the Ending Sector field to make up the cylinder value. The Ending Cylinder is a 10-bit number, with a maximum value of 1023.
0x01C6	DWORD	0x3F000000	**Relative Sectors**. The offset from the beginning of the disk to the beginning of the volume, counting by sectors.
0x01CA	DWORD	0x4BF57F00	**Total Sectors**. The total number of sectors in the volume.

A BYTE is 8 bits, a WORD is 16 bits, a DWORD is 32 bits, and a LONGLONG is 64 bits. Sample values marked with an asterisk (*) do not accurately represent the value of the fields, because the fields are either 6 bits or 10 bits and the data is recorded in bytes.

Numbers larger than one byte are stored in little endian format, or reverse-byte ordering. Little endian format is a method of storing a number so that the least significant byte appears first in the hexadecimal number notation. For example, the sample value for the **Relative Sectors** field in the previous table, 0x3F000000, is a little endian representation of 0x0000003F. The decimal equivalent of this little endian number is 63.

Boot Indicator Field

The first element of the partition table, the **Boot Indicator** field, indicates whether or not the volume is the active partition. Only one primary partition on the disk can have this field set.

It is possible to have different operating systems and different file systems on different volumes. By using disk configuration tools such as the Windows 2000-based Disk Management or the MS-DOS-based Fdisk to designate a primary partition as active, the **Boot Indicator** field for that partition is set in the partition table.

System ID Field

Another element of the partition table is the **System ID** field. It defines which file system, such as FAT16, FAT32, or NTFS, was used to format the volume and the FT characteristics of the volume. The **System ID** field also identifies an extended partition, if one is defined. Windows 2000 uses the **System ID** field to determine which file system device drivers to load during startup. Table 1.3 identifies the values for the **System ID** field.

Table 1.3   System ID Values

Partition Type	ID Value
0x01	FAT12 primary partition or logical drive (fewer than 32,680 sectors in the volume)
0x04	FAT16 partition or logical drive (32,680–65,535 sectors or 16 MB–33 MB)
0x05	Extended partition
0x06	BIGDOS FAT16 partition or logical drive (33 MB–4 GB)
0x07	Installable File System (NTFS partition or logical drive)
0x0B	FAT32 partition or logical drive
0x0C	FAT32 partition or logical drive using BIOS INT 13h extensions
0x0E	BIGDOS FAT16 partition or logical drive using BIOS INT 13h extensions
0x0F	Extended partition using BIOS INT 13h extensions
0x12	EISA partition
0x42	Dynamic disk volume
0x86	Legacy FT FAT16 disk *
0x87	Legacy FT NTFS disk *
0x8B	Legacy FT volume formatted with FAT32 *
0x8C	Legacy FT volume using BIOS INT 13h extensions formatted with FAT32 *

Partition types denoted with an asterisk (*) indicate that they are also used to designate non-FT configurations such as striped and spanned volumes.

When a mirrored or RAID-5 volume is created in Windows NT 4.0 or earlier, the high bit of the **System ID** field byte is set for each primary partition or logical drive that is a member of the volume. For example, a FAT16 primary partition or logical drive that is a member of a mirrored or RAID-5 volume, has a **System ID** value of 0x86. A FAT32 primary partition or logical drive has a **System ID** value of 0x8B, and an NTFS primary partition or logical drive has a **System ID** value of 0x87. Volumes that have the high bit set can only be directly accessed by Windows 2000 and Windows NT. Disk shares on FT disks, however, are also available to computers running MS-DOS, Windows 95, and Windows 98.

Note MS-DOS can only access volumes that have a **System ID** value of 0x01, 0x04, 0x05, or 0x06. However, you can delete volumes that have the other values listed in Table 1.3 using MS-DOS tools such as Fdisk. If you use a low-level disk editor, such as DiskProbe, you can read and write to any sector, including ones that are in NTFS volumes.

Starting and Ending Cylinder, Head, and Sector Fields

The **Starting** and **Ending Cylinder**, **Head**, and **Sector** fields (collectively known as the **CHS** fields) are additional elements of the partition table. These fields are essential for starting the computer. The master boot code uses these fields to find and load the boot sector of the active partition. The **Starting CHS** fields for non-active partitions point to the boot sectors of the remaining primary partitions and the EBR of the first logical drive in the extended partition as shown in Figure 1.1.

Knowing the starting sector of an extended partition is very important for low-level disk troubleshooting. If your disk fails, you need to work with the partition starting point (among other factors) to retrieve stored data.

Note To have a written record of the starting and ending sectors of the partitions on your hard disk, as well as other useful disk configuration data, use the DiskMap tool. For more information about DiskMap, see the documentation provided on the *Windows 2000 Resource Kit* companion CD.

Figure 1.1 shows the MBR, partition table, and boot sectors on a disk with four partitions. The definitions of the fields in the partition table and the extended partition tables are the same.

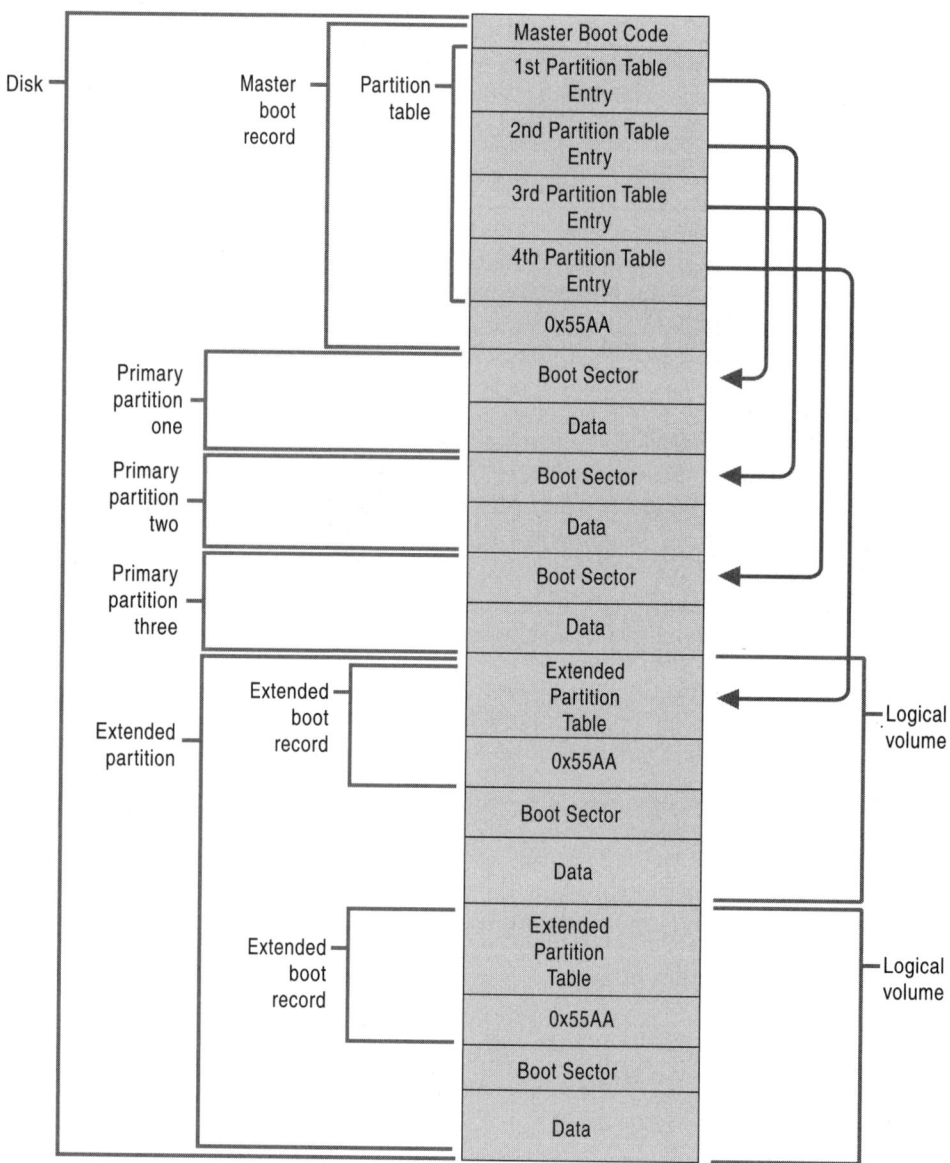

Figure 1.1   Detail of a Basic Disk with Four Partitions

The **Ending Cylinder** field in the partition table is 10 bits long, which limits the number of cylinders that can be described in the partition table to a range of 0–1,023. The **Starting Head** and **Ending Head** fields are each one byte long, which limits the field range to 0–255. The **Starting Sector** and **Ending Sector** fields are each six bits long, which limits the range of these fields to 0–63. However, the enumeration of sectors starts at 1 (not 0, as for other fields), so the maximum number of sectors per track is 63.

Because all hard disks are low-level formatted with a standard 512-byte sector, the maximum disk capacity described by the partition table is calculated as follows:

```
Maximum capacity = sector size x cylinders (10 bits) x heads (8 bits) x
sectors per track (6 bits)
```

Using the maximum possible values yields:

```
512 x 1024 x 256 x 63 (or 512 x 2^24) = 8,455,716,864 bytes or 7.8 GB
```

The calculation results in a maximum capacity of slightly less than 8 gigabytes (GB). Before BIOS INT 13h extensions drive geometry translation (also known as logical block addressing, or LBA) were introduced, the active, primary partition could not exceed 7.8 GB, regardless of the file system used.

Important When using the standard 512-byte sector, the maximum cluster size that you can use for FAT16 volumes while running Windows 2000 is 64 kilobytes (KB). Therefore, the maximum size for a FAT16 volume is 4 GB.

If you use a multiple-boot configuration with Windows 95, Windows 98, or MS-DOS, FAT16 volumes must be limited to 2 GB to be accessed from these operating systems. In addition, a Macintosh computer that accesses volumes on a computer running Windows 2000 cannot access a FAT16 volume that is larger than 2 GB. If you try to use a FAT16 volume larger than 2 GB when running MS-DOS, Windows 95, or Windows 98, or try to access such a volume from a Macintosh computer, you might get a message that zero bytes are available.

The maximum FAT16 volume size that you can use on a computer depends on the disk geometry and the maximum values that fit in the partition table entry fields. Table 1.4 shows the typical FAT16 volume size when LBA is enabled or disabled. The number of cylinders in both cases is 1,024 (0–1,023). When a primary partition or logical drive extends beyond the 1,023rd cylinder, all fields described in this section contain the maximum values.

Table 1.4   FAT16 Volume Size When LBA Is Enabled or Disabled

Translation Mode	Number of Heads	Sectors per Track	Maximum Size for System or Boot Partition
Disabled	64	32	1 GB
Enabled	255	63	4 GB

Warning Do not change the LBA setting on any hard disk containing data. You can adversely affect the process in which the system translates the disk attributes for storing data and corrupt all the files and partitions on the physical disk. Refer to your computer owner's manual before modifying this BIOS setting.

To accommodate sizes larger than 7.8 GB, Windows 2000 ignores the values in the **Starting** and **Ending Sector** fields of the partition table in favor of the **Relative Sectors** and **Total Sectors** fields.

Relative Sectors and Total Sectors Fields

The **Relative Sectors** field represents the offset from the beginning of the disk to the beginning of the volume, counting by sectors, for the volume described by the partition table entry. The **Total Sectors** field represents the total number of sectors in the volume.

Using the **Relative Sectors** and **Total Sectors** fields (resulting in a 32-bit number) provides eight more bits than the CHS scheme to represent the total number of sectors. This allows partitions containing up to 2^{32} sectors to be defined. With a standard sector size of 512 bytes, the 32 bits used to represent the **Relative Sectors** and **Total Sectors** fields translates into a maximum partition size of 2 terabytes (or 2,199,023,255,552 bytes).

This addressing scheme is only used in Windows 2000 with NTFS and FAT32.

Note In addition, the Format tool of Windows 2000 limits the maximum size of FAT32 volumes it can create to 32 GB. However, Windows 2000 can directly access larger FAT32 volumes created by Windows 95 OSR2 or Windows 98.

Windows 2000 uses the fields in the partition table entries to access all partitions. A partition that is formatted while Windows 2000 is running puts data into the **Starting** and **Ending CHS** fields to have compatibility with MS-DOS, Windows 95, and Windows 98, and to maintain compatibility with the BIOS INT 13h for startup.

Extended Boot Record

An EBR, which consists of an extended partition table and the signature word for the sector, exists for each logical drive in the extended partition. It contains the only information on the first side of the first cylinder of each logical drive in the extended partition. The boot sector in a logical drive is usually located at either Relative Sector 32 or 63. However, if there is no extended partition on a disk, there are no EBRs and no logical drives.

Note This information applies only to disks configured with basic disk.

The first entry in an extended partition table for the first logical drive points to its own boot sector. The second entry points to the EBR of the next logical drive. If no further logical drives exist, the second entry is not used and is recorded as a series of zeroes. If there are additional logical drives, the first entry of the extended partition table for the second logical drive points to its own boot sector. The second entry of the extended partition table for the second logical drive points to the EBR of the next logical drive. The third and fourth entries of an extended partition table are never used.

As shown in Figure 1.2, the EBRs of the logical drives in the extended partition are a linked list. The figure shows three logical drives on an extended partition, illustrating the difference in extended partition tables between preceding logical drives and the last logical drive.

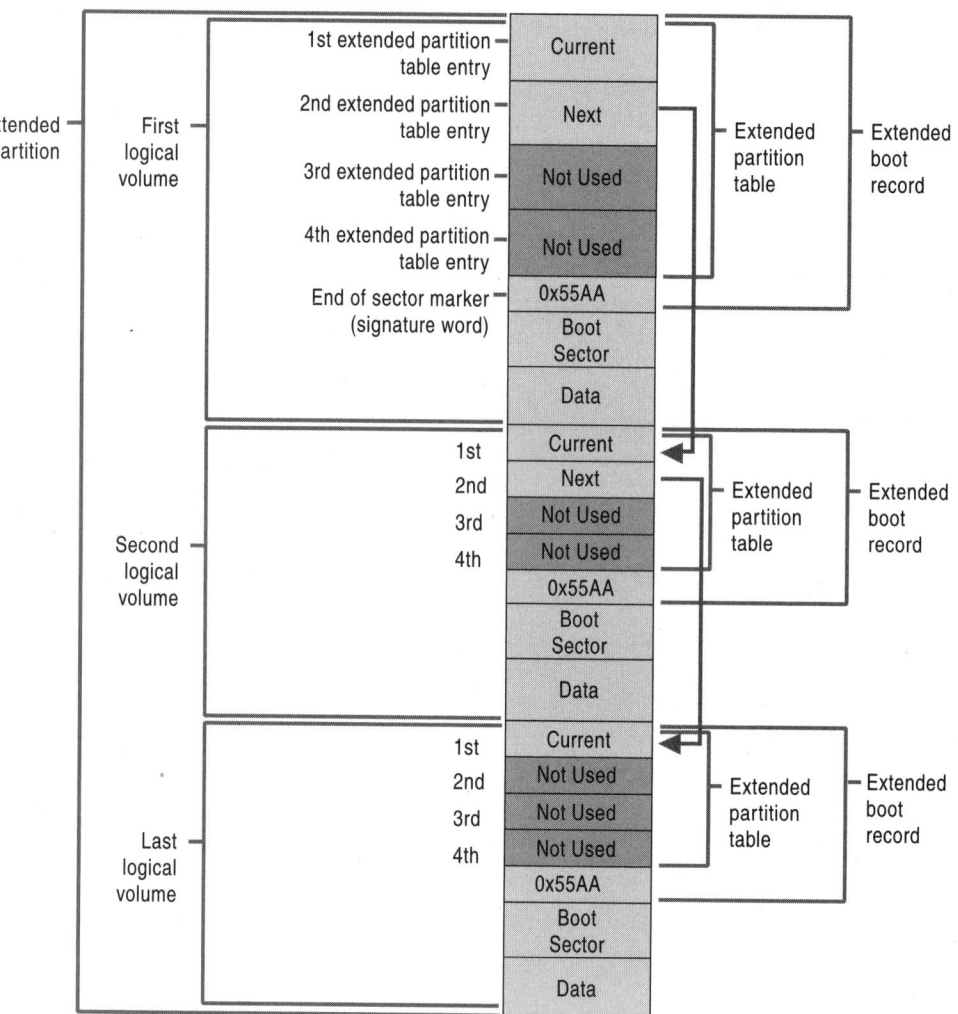

Figure 1.2   Detail of an Extended Partition

With the exception of the last logical drive on the extended partition, the format of the extended partition table, described in Table 1.5, is repeated for each logical drive: the first entry identifies the logical drive's own boot sector and the second entry identifies the next logical drive's EBR. The extended partition table for the last logical drive has only its own partition entry listed. The second through fourth entries of the last extended partition table are not used.

Table 1.5   Contents of Extended Partition Table Entries

Extended Partition Table Entry	Entry Contents
First	Information about the current logical drive in the extended partition, including the starting address for data.
Second	Information about the next logical drive in the extended partition, including the address of the sector that contains the EBR for the next logical drive. If no further logical drives exist, this field is not used.
Third	Not used
Fourth	Not used

The fields in each entry of the extended partition table are identical to the MBR partition table entries. See Table 1.2 for more information about partition table fields.

The **Relative Sectors** field in an extended partition table entry shows the number of bytes that are offset from the beginning of the extended partition to the first sector in the logical drive. The number in the **Total Sectors** field refers to the number of sectors that make up the logical drive. The value of the **Total Sectors** field equals the number of sectors from the boot sector defined by the extended partition table entry to the end of the logical drive.

Because of the importance of the MBR and EBR sectors, it is recommended that you run disk-scanning tools regularly as well as regularly back up all your data files to protect against losing access to a volume or an entire disk.

Boot Sector

The boot sector, located at sector 1 of each volume, is a critical disk structure for starting your computer. It contains executable code and data required by the code, including information that the file system uses to access the volume. The boot sector is created when you format a volume. At the end of the boot sector is a two-byte structure called a signature word or end of sector marker, which is always set to 0x55AA. On computers running Windows 2000, the boot sector on the active partition loads into memory and starts Ntldr, which loads the operating system.

The Windows 2000 boot sector consists of the following elements:

- An *x*86-based CPU jump instruction.
- The original equipment manufacturer identification (OEM ID).
- The BIOS parameter block (BPB), a data structure.
- The extended BPB.
- The executable boot code (or bootstrap code) that starts the operating system.

Note All Windows 2000 boot sectors contain these elements. However, the NTFS boot sector, the FAT16, and the FAT32 boot sectors are all formatted differently.

The BPB describes the physical parameters of the volume: the extended BPB begins immediately after the BPB. Due to differing types of fields and the amount of data they contain, the length of the BPB is different for FAT16, FAT32, and NTFS boot sectors.

The information in the BPB and the extended BPB is used by disk device drivers to read and configure volumes. The area following the extended BPB typically contains executable boot code, which performs the actions necessary to continue the startup process.

Boot Sector Startup Processes

Computers use the boot sector to run instructions during startup. The initial startup process is summarized in the following steps:

1. The system BIOS and the CPU initiate the power-on self test (POST).
2. The BIOS searches for a boot device (typically a disk).
3. The BIOS loads the first physical sector of the boot device into memory and transfers CPU execution to that memory address.

If the boot device is on a hard disk, the BIOS loads the MBR. The master boot code in the MBR loads the boot sector of the active partition, and transfers CPU execution to that memory address. On computers that are running Windows 2000, the executable boot code in the boot sector finds Ntldr, loads it into memory, and transfers execution to that file.

Note Windows 2000 cannot start up from a spanned, striped, or RAID-5 volume that is running dynamic disk. These disk structures cannot be registered into the MBR's partition table, so a system partition using these structures is not startable. Windows 2000 must be fully loaded into memory before they can be used.

If there is a floppy disk in drive A, the system BIOS loads the first sector (the boot sector) of the disk into memory. If the disk is startable—formatted by MS-DOS with core operating system files applied—the boot sector loads into memory and uses the executable boot code to transfer CPU execution to Io.sys, a core MS-DOS operating system file. If the floppy disk is not bootable, the executable boot code displays an error message such as:

```
Non-System disk or disk error
Replace and press any key when ready
```

Note This error will not appear on normally functioning systems that are configured to look for the startup files on drive C first. On many computers, an option in the CMOS setup program allows the user to set the sequence of installed disks that the system searches for the startup files.

If you get similar errors when trying to start the computer from the hard disk, the boot sector might be corrupted. For more information about troubleshooting boot sector problems, see "Damaged MBRs and Boot Sectors" later in this chapter.

Initially, the startup process is independent of disk format and operating system. The unique characteristics of operating and file systems become important when the boot sector's executable boot code starts.

Components of a Boot Sector

The MBR transfers CPU execution to the boot sector, so the first three bytes of the boot sector must be valid, executable x86-based CPU instructions. This includes a jump instruction that skips the next several nonexecutable bytes.

Following the jump instruction is the 8-byte OEM ID, a string of characters that identifies the name and version number of the operating system that formatted the volume. To preserve compatibility with MS-DOS, Windows 2000 records "MSDOS5.0" in this field on FAT16 and FAT32 disks. On NTFS disks, Windows 2000 records "NTFS."

Note You may also see the OEM ID "MSWIN4.0" on disks formatted by Windows 95 and "MSWIN4.1" on disks formatted by Windows 95 OSR2 and Windows 98. Windows 2000 does not use the OEM ID field in the boot sector except for verifying NTFS volumes.

Following the OEM ID is the BPB, which provides information that enables the executable boot code to locate Ntldr. The BPB always starts at the same offset, so standard parameters are in a known location. Disk size and geometry variables are encapsulated in the BPB. Because the first part of the boot sector is an x86 jump instruction, the BPB can be extended in the future by appending new information at the end. The jump instruction needs only a minor adjustment to accommodate this change. The BPB is stored in a packed (unaligned) format.

FAT16 Boot Sector

Table 1.6 describes the boot sector of a volume formatted with the FAT16 file system.

Table 1.6 Boot Sector Sections on a FAT16 Volume

Byte Offset	Field Length	Field Name
0x00	3 bytes	Jump Instruction
0x03	LONGLONG	OEM ID
0x0B	25 bytes	BPB
0x24	26 bytes	Extended BPB
0x3E	448 bytes	Bootstrap Code
0x01FE	WORD	End of Sector Marker

The following example illustrates a hexadecimal printout of the boot sector on a FAT16 volume. The printout is formatted in three sections:

- Bytes 0x00–0x0A are the jump instruction and the OEM ID (shown in bold print).

- Bytes 0x0B–0x3D are the BPB and the extended BPB.

- The remaining section is the bootstrap code and the end of sector marker (shown in bold print).

```
Physical Sector: Cyl 0, Side 1, Sector 1
00000000: EB 3C 90 4D 53 44 4F 53  - 35 2E 30 00 02 40 01 00   .<.MSDOS5.0..@..
00000010: 02 00 02 00 00 F8 FC 00  - 3F 00 40 00 3F 00 00 00   ........?.@.?...
00000020: 01 F0 3E 00 80 00 29 A8  - 8B 36 52 4E 4F 20 4E 41   ..>...)..6RNO NA
00000030: 4D 45 20 20 20 20 46 41  - 54 31 36 20 20 20 33 C0   ME    FAT16   3.
00000040: 8E D0 BC 00 7C 68 C0 07  - 1F A0 10 00 F7 26 16 00   ....|h......&..
00000050: 03 06 0E 00 50 91 B8 20  - 00 F7 26 11 00 8B 1E 0B   ....P.. ..&.....
00000060: 00 03 C3 48 F7 F3 03 C8  - 89 0E 08 02 68 00 10 07   ...H........h...
00000070: 33 DB 8F 06 13 02 89 1E  - 15 02 0E E8 90 00 72 57   3.............rW
00000080: 33 DB 8B 0E 11 00 8B FB  - 51 B9 0B 00 BE DC 01 F3   3.......Q.......
00000090: A6 59 74 05 83 C3 20 E2  - ED E3 37 26 8B 57 1A 52   .Yt... ...7&.W.R
000000A0: B8 01 00 68 00 20 07 33  - DB 0E E8 48 00 72 28 5B   ...h. .3...H.r([
000000B0: 8D 36 0B 00 8D 3E 0B 02  - 1E 8F 45 02 C7 05 F5 00   .6...>....E.....
```

```
000000C0: 1E 8F 45 06 C7 45 04 0E  - 01 8A 16 24 00 EA 03 00   ..E..E.....$....
000000D0: 00 20 BE 86 01 EB 03 BE  - A2 01 E8 09 00 BE C1 01   . ..............
000000E0: E8 03 00 FB EB FE AC 0A  - C0 74 09 B4 0E BB 07 00   .........t......
000000F0: CD 10 EB F2 C3 50 4A 4A  - A0 0D 00 32 E4 F7 E2 03   .....PJJ...2....
00000100: 06 08 02 83 D2 00 A3 13  - 02 89 16 15 02 58 A2 07   .............X..
00000110: 02 A1 13 02 8B 16 15 02  - 03 06 1C 00 13 16 1E 00   ...............
00000120: F7 36 18 00 FE C2 88 16  - 06 02 33 D2 F7 36 1A 00   .6........3..6..
00000130: 88 16 25 00 A3 04 02 A1  - 18 00 2A 06 06 02 40 3A   ..%.......*...@:
00000140: 06 07 02 76 05 A0 07 02  - 32 E4 50 B4 02 8B 0E 04   ...v....2.P.....
00000150: 02 C0 E5 06 0A 2E 06 02  - 86 E9 8B 16 24 00 CD 13   ............$...
00000160: 0F 83 05 00 83 C4 02 F9  - CB 58 28 06 07 02 76 11   .........X(...v.
00000170: 01 06 13 02 83 16 15 02  - 00 F7 26 0B 00 03 D8 EB   ..........&.....
00000180: 90 A2 07 02 F8 CB 42 4F  - 4F 54 3A 20 43 6F 75 6C   ......BOOT: Coul
00000190: 64 6E 27 74 20 66 69 6E  - 64 20 4E 54 4C 44 52 0D   dn't find NTLDR.
000001A0: 0A 00 42 4F 4F 54 3A 20  - 49 2F 4F 20 65 72 72 6F   ..BOOT: I/O erro
000001B0: 72 20 72 65 61 64 69 6E  - 67 20 64 69 73 6B 0D 0A   r reading disk..
000001C0: 00 50 6C 65 61 73 65 20  - 69 6E 73 65 72 74 20 61   .Please insert a
000001D0: 6E 6F 74 68 65 72 20 64  - 69 73 6B 00 4E 54 4C 44   nother disk.NTLD
000001E0: 52 20 20 20 20 20 20 00  - 00 00 00 00 00 00 00 00   R       .........
000001F0: 00 00 00 00 00 00 00 00  - 00 00 00 00 00 00 55 AA   ..............U.
```

Tables 1.7 and 1.8 illustrate the layout of the BPB and the extended BPB for FAT16 volumes. The sample values correspond to the data in the preceding example.

Table 1.7   BPB Fields for FAT16 Volumes

Byte Offset	Field Length	Value	Field Name and Definition
0x0B	WORD	0x0002	**Bytes Per Sector**. The size of a hardware sector. Valid decimal values for this field are 512, 1024, 2048, and 4096. For most disks used in the United States, the value of this field is 512.
0x0D	BYTE	0x40	**Sectors Per Cluster**. The number of sectors in a cluster. Because FAT16 can track only a limited number of clusters (up to 65,536), large volumes are supported by increasing the number of sectors per cluster. The default cluster size for a volume depends on the volume size. Valid decimal values for this field are 1, 2, 4, 8, 16, 32, 64, and 128. Values that lead to clusters larger than 32 KB (**Bytes Per Sector * Sectors Per Cluster**) can cause disk and software errors.
0x0E	WORD	0x0100	**Reserved Sectors**. The number of sectors preceding the start of the first FAT, including the boot sector. The value of this field is always 1.

(continued)

Table 1.7   BPB Fields for FAT16 Volumes   *(continued)*

Byte Offset	Field Length	Value	Field Name and Definition
0x10	BYTE	0x02	**Number of FATs.** The number of copies of the FAT on the volume. The value of this field is always 2.
0x11	WORD	0x0002	**Root Entries.** The total number of 32-byte file and folder name entries that can be stored in the root folder of the volume. On a typical hard disk, the value of this field is 512. One entry is always used as a Volume Label, and files and folders with long names use multiple entries per file. The largest number of file and folder entries is typically 511, but entries run out before you reach that number if long file names are used.
0x13	WORD	0x0000	**Small Sectors.** The number of sectors on the volume represented in 16 bits (< 65,536). For volumes larger than 65,536 sectors, this field has a value of zero and the **Large Sectors** field is used instead.
0x15	BYTE	0xF8	**Media Descriptor.** Provides information about the media being used. A value of 0xF8 indicates a hard disk and 0xF0 indicates a high-density 3.5-inch floppy disk. Media descriptor entries are a legacy of MS-DOS FAT16 disks and are not used in Windows 2000.
0x16	WORD	0xFC00	**Sectors Per FAT.** The number of sectors occupied by each FAT on the volume. The computer uses this number and the number of FATs and hidden sectors, to determine where the root directory begins. The computer can also determine where the user data area of the volume begins based on the number of entries in the root directory (512).
0x18	WORD	0x3F00	**Sectors Per Track.** Part of the apparent disk geometry used on a low-level formatted disk.
0x1A	WORD	0x4000	**Number of Heads.** Part of the apparent disk geometry used on a low-level formatted disk.
0x1C	DWORD	0x3F000000	**Hidden Sectors.** The number of sectors on the volume before the boot sector. This value is used during the boot sequence to calculate the absolute offset to the root directory and data areas.
0x20	DWORD	0x01F03E00	**Large Sectors.** If the value of the **Small Sectors** field is zero, this field contains the total number of sectors in the FAT16 volume. If the value of the **Small Sectors** field is not zero, the value of this field is zero.

Table 1.8   Extended BPB Fields for FAT16 Volumes

Byte Offset	Field Length	Value	Field Name and Definition
0x24	BYTE	0x80	**Physical Drive Number**. Related to the BIOS physical drive number. Floppy disk drives are identified as 0x00 and physical hard disks are identified as 0x80, regardless of the number of physical disk drives. Typically, this value is set prior to issuing an INT 13h BIOS call to specify the device to access. The value is only relevant if the device is a boot device.
0x25	BYTE	0x00	**Reserved**. FAT16 volumes are always set to zero.
0x26	BYTE	0x29	**Extended Boot Signature**. A field that must have the value 0x28 or 0x29 to be recognized by Windows 2000.
0x27	DWORD	0xA88B3652	**Volume Serial Number**. A random serial number created when formatting a disk, which helps to distinguish between disks.
0x2B	11 bytes	NO NAME	**Volume Label**. A field once used to store the volume label. The volume label is now stored as a special file in the root directory.
0x36	LONGLONG	FAT16	**File System Type**. A field with a value of either FAT, FAT12 or FAT16, depending on the disk format.

FAT32 Boot Sector

Table 1.9 describes the boot sector of a volume formatted with the FAT32 file system.

Note   The FAT32 boot sector is structurally very similar to the FAT16 boot sector, but the FAT32 BPB contains additional fields. The FAT32 extended BPB uses the same fields as FAT16, but the offset addresses of these fields within the boot sector are different than those found in FAT16 boot sectors. Drives formatted in FAT32 are not readable by operating systems that are incompatible with FAT32.

Table 1.9   Boot Sector Sections on a FAT32 Volume

Byte Offset	Field Length	Field Name
0x00	3 bytes	Jump Instruction
0x03	LONGLONG	OEM ID
0x0B	53 bytes	BPB
0x40	26 bytes	Extended BPB
0x5A	420 bytes	Bootstrap Code
0x01FE	WORD	End of Sector Marker

The following example illustrates a hexadecimal printout of the boot sector on a FAT32 volume. The printout is formatted in three sections:

- Bytes 0x00–0x0A are the jump instruction and the OEM ID (shown in bold print).

- Bytes 0x0B–0x59 are the BPB and the extended BPB.

- The remaining section is the bootstrap code and the end of sector marker (shown in bold print).

```
Physical Sector: Cyl 878, Side 0, Sector 1
00000000: EB 58 90 4D 53 44 4F 53 - 35 2E 30 00 02 08 20 00   .X.MSDOS5.0... .
00000010: 02 00 00 00 00 F8 00 00 - 3F 00 FF 00 EE 39 D7 00   ........?....9..
00000020: 7F 32 4E 00 83 13 00 00 - 00 00 00 00 02 00 00 00   □2N............
00000030: 01 00 06 00 00 00 00 00 - 00 00 00 00 00 00 00 00   ...............
00000040: 80 00 29 8B 93 6D 54 4E - 4F 20 4E 41 4D 45 20 20   ..)..mTNO NAME
00000050: 20 20 46 41 54 33 32 20 - 20 20 33 C9 8E D1 BC F4     FAT32   3.....
00000060: 7B 8E C1 8E D9 BD 00 7C - 88 4E 02 8A 56 40 B4 08   {......|.N..V@..
00000070: CD 13 73 05 B9 FF FF 8A - F1 66 0F B6 C6 40 66 0F   ..s......f...@f.
00000080: B6 D1 80 E2 3F F7 E2 86 - CD C0 ED 06 41 66 0F B7   ....?.......Af..
00000090: C9 66 F7 E1 66 89 46 F8 - 83 7E 16 00 75 38 83 7E   .f..f.F..~..u8.~
000000A0: 2A 00 77 32 66 8B 46 1C - 66 83 C0 0C BB 00 80 B9   *.w2f.F.f.......
000000B0: 01 00 E8 2B 00 E9 48 03 - A0 FA 7D B4 7D 8B F0 AC   ...+..H...}.}...`
000000C0: 84 C0 74 17 3C FF 74 09 - B4 0E BB 07 00 CD 10 EB   ..t.<.t.........
000000D0: EE A0 FB 7D EB E5 A0 F9 - 7D EB E0 98 CD 16 CD 19   ...}....}.......
000000E0: 66 60 66 3B 46 F8 0F 82 - 4A 00 66 6A 00 66 50 06   f`f;F...J.fj.fP.
000000F0: 53 66 68 10 00 01 00 80 - 7E 02 00 0F 85 20 00 B4   Sfh.....~.... ..
00000100: 41 BB AA 55 8A 56 40 CD - 13 0F 82 1C 00 81 FB 55   A..U.V@........U
00000110: AA 0F 85 14 00 F6 C1 01 - 0F 84 0D 00 FE 46 02 B4   .............F..
00000120: 42 8A 56 40 8B F4 CD 13 - B0 F9 66 58 66 58 66 58   B.V@......fXfXfX
00000130: 66 58 EB 2A 66 33 D2 66 - 0F B7 4E 18 66 F7 F1 FE   fX.*f3.f..N.f...
00000140: C2 8A CA 66 8B D0 66 C1 - EA 10 F7 76 1A 86 D6 8A   ...f..f....v....
00000150: 56 40 8A E8 C0 E4 06 0A - CC B8 01 02 CD 13 66 61   V@............fa
00000160: 0F 82 54 FF 81 C3 00 02 - 66 40 49 0F 85 71 FF C3   ..T.....f@I..q..
00000170: 4E 54 4C 44 52 20 20 20 - 20 20 20 0D 0A 4E 54 4C   NTLDR      ..NTL
00000180: 44 52 20 69 73 20 6D 69 - 73 73 69 6E 67 FF 0D 0A   DR is missing...
00000190: 44 69 73 6B 20 65 72 72 - 6F 72 FF 0D 0A 50 72 65   Disk error...Pre
000001A0: 73 73 20 61 6E 79 20 6B - 65 79 20 74 6F 20 72 65   ss any key to re
000001B0: 73 74 61 72 74 0D 0A 00 - 00 00 00 00 00 00 00 00   start..........
000001C0: 00 00 00 00 00 00 00 00 - 00 00 00 00 00 00 00 00   ...............
000001D0: 00 00 00 00 00 00 00 00 - 00 00 00 00 00 00 00 00   ...............
000001E0: 00 00 00 00 00 00 00 00 - 00 00 00 00 00 00 00 00   ...............
000001F0: 00 00 00 00 00 00 00 00 - 00 7B 8E 9B 00 00 55 AA   .........{....U.
```

Tables 1.10 and 1.11 illustrate the layout of the BPB and the extended BPB for FAT32 volumes. The sample values correspond to the data in the preceding example.

Table 1.10   BPB Fields for FAT32 Volumes

Byte Offset	Field Length	Value	Field Name and Definition
0x0B	WORD	0x0002	**Bytes Per Sector**. The size of a hardware sector. Valid decimal values for this field are 512, 1024, 2048, and 4096. For most disks used in the United States, the value of this field is 512.
0x0D	BYTE	0x08	**Sectors Per Cluster**. The number of sectors in a cluster. Because FAT32 can only track a finite number of clusters (up to 4,294,967,296), extremely large volumes are supported by increasing the number of sectors per cluster. The default cluster size for a volume depends on the volume size. Valid decimal values for this field are 1, 2, 4, 8, 16, 32, 64, and 128. The Windows 2000 implementation of FAT32 allows for the creation of volumes only up to a maximum of 32 GB. However, larger volumes created by other operating systems (Windows 95 OSR2 and later) are accessible in Windows 2000.
0x0E	WORD	0x0200	**Reserved Sectors**. The number of sectors preceding the start of the first FAT, including the boot sector. The decimal value of this field is typically 32.
0x10	BYTE	0x02	**Number of FATs**. The number of copies of the FAT on the volume. The value of this field is always 2.
0x11	WORD	0x0000	**Root Entries (FAT12/FAT16 only)**. For FAT32 volumes, this field must be set to zero.
0x13	WORD	0x0000	**Small Sectors (FAT12/FAT16 only)**. For FAT32 volumes, this field must be set to zero.
0x15	BYTE	0xF8	**Media Descriptor**. Provides information about the media being used. A value of 0xF8 indicates a hard disk and 0xF0 indicates a high-density 3.5-inch floppy disk. Media descriptor entries are a legacy of MS-DOS FAT16 disks and are not used in Windows 2000.
0x16	WORD	0x0000	**Sectors Per FAT (FAT12/FAT16 only)**. For FAT32 volumes, this field must be set to zero.
0x18	WORD	0x3F00	**Sectors Per Track**. Contains the "sectors per track" geometry value for disks that use INT 13h. The volume is broken down into tracks by multiple heads and cylinders.
0x1A	WORD	0xFF00	**Number of Heads**. Contains the "count of heads" geometry value for disks that use INT 13h. For example, on a 1.44-MB, 3.5-inch floppy disk this value is 2.

(continued)

Table 1.10   BPB Fields for FAT32 Volumes   *(continued)*

Byte Offset	Field Length	Value	Field Name and Definition
0x1C	DWORD	0xEE39D700	**Hidden Sectors**. The number of sectors on the volume before the boot sector. This value is used during the boot sequence to calculate the absolute offset to the root directory and data areas. This field is generally only relevant for media that are visible on interrupt 13h. It must always be zero on media that are not partitioned.
0x20	DWORD	0x7F324E00	**Large Sectors**. Contains the total number of sectors in the FAT32 volume.
0x24	DWORD	0x83130000	**Sectors Per FAT (FAT32 only)**. The number of sectors occupied by each FAT on the volume. The computer uses this number and the number of FATs and hidden sectors (described in this table), to determine where the root directory begins. The computer can also determine where the user data area of the volume begins based on the number of entries in the root directory.
0x28	WORD	0x0000	**Extended Flags (FAT32 only)**. The value of the bits in this two-byte structure are:
			Bits 0–3: Number of the active FAT (starting count at 0, not 1). It is only valid if mirroring is disabled.
			Bits 4–6: Reserved.
			Bit 7: A value of 0 means the FAT is mirrored at run time into all FATs. A value of 1 means only one FAT is active (referenced in bits 0-3).
			Bits 8–15: Reserved.
0x2A	WORD	0x0000	**File System Version (FAT32 only)**. The high byte is the major revision number, whereas the low byte is the minor revision number. This field supports the ability to extend the FAT32 media type in the future with concern for old FAT32 drivers mounting the volume. If the field is non-zero, back-level Windows versions will not mount the volume.
0x2C	DWORD	0x02000000	**Root Cluster Number (FAT32 only)**. The cluster number of the first cluster of the root directory. This value is typically, but not always, 2.
0x30	WORD	0x0100	**File System Information Sector Number (FAT32 only)**. The sector number of the File System Information (FSINFO) structure in the reserved area of the FAT32 volume. The value is typically 1. A copy of the FSINFO structure is kept in the Backup Boot Sector, but it is not kept up-to-date.
0x34	WORD	0x0600	**Backup Boot Sector (FAT32 only)**. A non-zero value indicates the sector number in the reserved area of the volume in which a copy of the boot sector is stored. The value of this field is typically 6. No other value is recommended.
0x36	12 bytes	0x000000000 00000000000 0000	**Reserved (FAT32 only)**. Reserved space for future expansion. The value of this field should always be zero.

Table 1.11   Extended BPB Fields for FAT32 Volumes

Byte Offset	Field Length	Value	Field Name and Definition
0x40	BYTE	0x80	**Physical Drive Number**. Related to the BIOS physical drive number. Floppy disk drives are identified as 0x00 and physical hard disks are identified as 0x80, regardless of the number of physical disk drives. Typically, this value is set prior to issuing an INT 13h BIOS call to specify the device to access. It is only relevant if the device is a boot device.
0x41	BYTE	0x00	**Reserved**. FAT32 volumes are always set to zero.
0x42	BYTE	0x29	**Extended Boot Signature**. A field that must have the value 0x28 or 0x29 to be recognized by Windows 2000.
0x43	DWORD	0xA88B3652	**Volume Serial Number**. A random serial number created when formatting a disk, which helps to distinguish between disks.
0x47	11 bytes	NO NAME	**Volume Label**. A field once used to store the volume label. The volume label is now stored as a special file in the root directory.
0x52	LONGLONG	FAT32	**System ID**. A text field with a value of FAT32.

NTFS Boot Sector

Table 1.12 describes the boot sector of a volume formatted with NTFS. The bootstrap code for an NTFS volume is longer than the 426 bytes, as shown in Table 1.12. When you format an NTFS volume, the format program allocates the first 16 sectors for the boot sector and the bootstrap code.

Table 1.12   Boot Sector Sections on an NTFS Volume

Byte Offset	Field Length	Field Name
0x00	3 bytes	Jump Instruction
0x03	LONGLONG	OEM ID
0x0B	25 bytes	BPB
0x24	48 bytes	Extended BPB
0x54	426 bytes	Bootstrap Code
0x01FE	WORD	End of Sector Marker

On NTFS volumes, the data fields that follow the BPB form an extended BPB. The data in these fields enables Ntldr to find the master file table (MFT) during startup. On NTFS volumes, the MFT is not located in a predefined sector, as on FAT16 and FAT32 volumes. For this reason, the MFT can be moved if there is a bad sector in its normal location. However, if the data is corrupted, the MFT cannot be located, and Windows 2000 assumes that the volume has not been formatted.

The following example illustrates the boot sector of an NTFS volume formatted while running Windows 2000. The printout is formatted in three sections:

- Bytes 0x00–0x0A are the jump instruction and the OEM ID (shown in bold print).

- Bytes 0x0B–0x53 are the BPB and the extended BPB.

- The remaining code is the bootstrap code and the end of sector marker (shown in bold print).

```
Physical Sector: Cyl 0, Side 1, Sector 1
00000000: EB 52 90 4E 54 46 53 20 - 20 20 20 00 02 08 00 00   .R.NTFS    .....
00000010: 00 00 00 00 00 F8 00 00 - 3F 00 FF 00 3F 00 00 00   .......?...?...
00000020: 00 00 00 00 80 00 80 00 - 4A F5 7F 00 00 00 00 00   ........J.□.....
00000030: 04 00 00 00 00 00 00 00 - 54 FF 07 00 00 00 00 00   ........T......
00000040: F6 00 00 00 01 00 00 00 - 14 A5 1B 74 C9 1B 74 1C   ...........t..t.
00000050: 00 00 00 00 FA 33 C0 8E - D0 BC 00 7C FB B8 C0 07   .....3.....|....
00000060: 8E D8 E8 16 00 B8 00 0D - 8E C0 33 DB C6 06 0E 00   ..........3.....
00000070: 10 E8 53 00 68 00 0D 68 - 6A 02 CB 8A 16 24 00 B4   ..S.h..hj....$..
00000080: 08 CD 13 73 05 B9 FF FF - 8A F1 66 0F B6 C6 40 66   ...s......f...@f
00000090: 0F B6 D1 80 E2 3F F7 E2 - 86 CD C0 ED 06 41 66 0F   .....?.......Af.
000000A0: B7 C9 66 F7 E1 66 A3 20 - 00 C3 B4 41 BB AA 55 8A   ..f..f. ...A..U.
000000B0: 16 24 00 CD 13 72 0F 81 - FB 55 AA 75 09 F6 C1 01   .$...r...U.u....
000000C0: 74 04 FE 06 14 00 C3 66 - 60 1E 06 66 A1 10 00 66   t......f`..f...f
000000D0: 03 06 1C 00 66 3B 06 20 - 00 0F 82 3A 00 1E 66 6A   ....f;. ...:..fj
000000E0: 00 66 50 06 53 66 68 10 - 00 01 00 80 3E 14 00 00   .fP.Sfh.....>...
000000F0: 0F 85 0C 00 E8 B3 FF 80 - 3E 14 00 00 0F 84 61 00   ........>.....a.
00000100: B4 42 8A 16 24 00 16 1F - 8B F4 CD 13 66 58 5B 07   .B..$......fX[.
00000110: 66 58 66 58 1F EB 2D 66 - 33 D2 66 0F B7 0E 18 00   fXfX.-f3.f.....
00000120: 66 F7 F1 FE C2 8A CA 66 - 8B D0 66 C1 EA 10 F7 36   f......f..f....6
00000130: 1A 00 86 D6 8A 16 24 00 - 8A E8 C0 E4 06 0A CC B8   ......$.........
00000140: 01 02 CD 13 0F 82 19 00 - 8C C0 05 20 00 8E C0 66   ........... ...f
00000150: FF 06 10 00 FF 0E 0E 00 - 0F 85 6F FF 07 1F 66 61   ..........o..fa
00000160: C3 A0 F8 01 E8 09 00 A0 - FB 01 E8 03 00 FB EB FE   ...............
00000170: B4 01 8B F0 AC 3C 00 74 - 09 B4 0E BB 07 00 CD 10   .....<.t........
00000180: EB F2 C3 0D 0A 41 20 64 - 69 73 6B 20 72 65 61 64   .....A disk read
00000190: 20 65 72 72 6F 72 20 6F - 63 63 75 72 72 65 64 00    error occurred.
000001A0: 0D 0A 4E 54 4C 44 52 20 - 69 73 20 6D 69 73 73 69   ..NTLDR is missi
000001B0: 6E 67 00 0D 0A 4E 54 4C - 44 52 20 69 73 20 63 6F   ng...NTLDR is co
000001C0: 6D 70 72 65 73 73 65 64 - 00 0D 0A 50 72 65 73 73   mpressed...Press
000001D0: 20 43 74 72 6C 2B 41 6C - 74 2B 44 65 6C 20 74 6F    Ctrl+Alt+Del to
000001E0: 20 72 65 73 74 61 72 74 - 0D 0A 00 00 00 00 00 00    restart........
000001F0: 00 00 00 00 00 00 00 00 - 83 A0 B3 C9 00 00 55 AA   ..............U.
```

Table 1.13 describes the fields in the BPB and the extended BPB on NTFS volumes. The fields starting at 0x0B, 0x0D, 0x15, 0x18, 0x1A, and 0x1C match those on FAT16 and FAT32 volumes. The sample values correspond to the data in the preceding example.

Table 1.13   BPB and Extended BPB Fields on NTFS Volumes

Byte Offset	Field Length	Sample Value	Field Name
0x0B	WORD	0x0002	Bytes Per Sector
0x0D	BYTE	0x08	Sectors Per Cluster
0x0E	WORD	0x0000	Reserved Sectors
0x10	3 BYTES	0x000000	*always 0*
0x13	WORD	0x0000	*not used by NTFS*
0x15	BYTE	0xF8	Media Descriptor
0x16	WORD	0x0000	*always 0*
0x18	WORD	0x3F00	Sectors Per Track
0x1A	WORD	0xFF00	Number Of Heads
0x1C	DWORD	0x3F000000	Hidden Sectors
0x20	DWORD	0x00000000	*not used by NTFS*
0x24	DWORD	0x80008000	*not used by NTFS*
0x28	LONGLONG	0x4AF57F0000000000	Total Sectors
0x30	LONGLONG	0x0400000000000000	Logical Cluster Number for the file $MFT
0x38	LONGLONG	0x54FF070000000000	Logical Cluster Number for the file $MFTMirr
0x40	DWORD	0xF6000000	Clusters Per File Record Segment
0x44	DWORD	0x01000000	Clusters Per Index Block
0x48	LONGLONG	0x14A51B74C91B741C	Volume Serial Number
0x50	DWORD	0x00000000	Checksum

Protecting the Boot Sector

Because a normally functioning system relies on the boot sector to access a volume, it is highly recommended that you run disk scanning tools such as Chkdsk regularly, as well as back up all of your data files to protect against data loss if you lose access to a volume.

Troubleshooting Disk Problems

There are various causes of disk problems and means of recovering from them. The following are tools that you can use to troubleshoot disk problems:

- DiskProbe can be used to examine and change information on individual disk sectors.
- DiskMap can be used to display the layout of partitions and logical volumes on your disk.

Neither of these tools is designed for use with dynamic disks because they cannot read the dynamic Disk Management database. DiskProbe can change the values of individual bytes in any sector on a dynamic disk, but it cannot navigate the structure of a dynamic disk, so it might be impossible to find the sector you want to view or edit. Therefore it is generally recommended that these tools only be used on basic disks.

DiskProbe is part of the Support Tools collection and can be installed from the Support\Tools folder of the Windows 2000 product CD. For more information about using DiskProbe, see the document Dskprtrb.doc in the folder Program Files\Support Tools.

DiskMap is a tool included on the *Windows 2000 Resource Kit* companion CD and is installed with the rest of the Resource Kit tools. For more information about DiskMap, see the document Diskmap.doc in the folder C:\Program Files\Resource Kit.

Warning Be extremely cautious about making any changes to the structures of your hard disk! DiskProbe does not validate the proposed changes to records. Incorrect values in key data structures can render the hard disk inaccessible or prevent the operating system from starting.

You can easily make changes that have serious consequences, resulting in the following error messages:

```
You cannot start any operating system.
A volume is no longer accessible.
You have to recreate and reformat all of the partitions and logical
volumes.
```

DiskProbe displays a messages asking you to verify any change that you want recorded to disk. Please carefully consider any changes before accepting them.

With careful use of the disk tools, you can solve problems whether they occur through human error, hardware problems, power outages, or other events. It is a good idea to familiarize yourself with these tools in a test situation. Testing is especially important if your configuration has spanned, striped, mirror, or RAID-5 sets.

Note   Using DiskProbe, you can save, restore, find, examine, and change the bytes of any sector on the disk, including the MBR and the boot sector. The MBR of disk 0 is used to start Windows 2000–based computers, and the system and boot volumes of disk 0 must be defined in the partition table, making the boot sectors easily located, regardless of the disk configuration used. As a result, DiskProbe can be used to back up and restore these disk structures on computers using dynamic disk.

Viruses

It is always important to take precautions to protect your computer and the data on it from viruses. Many computer viruses exploit the disk structures that your computer uses to start up by replacing, redirecting, or corrupting the code and data that start the operating system.

MBR Viruses

MBR viruses exploit the master boot code that runs automatically when the computer starts up. MBR viruses are activated when the BIOS activates the master boot code, before the operating system is loaded.

Many viruses replace the MBR sector with their own code and move the original MBR to another location on disk. Once the virus is activated, it stays in memory and passes the execution to the original MBR so that startup appears to function normally. Some viruses do not relocate the original MBR, causing all volumes on the disk to become inaccessible. If the active, primary partition's listing in the partition table is destroyed, the computer cannot start. Other viruses relocate the MBR to the last sector of the disk; if that sector is not protected by the virus, it might be overwritten during normal use of the computer, preventing the system from being restarted.

Boot Sector Viruses

As with the master boot code, the boot sector's executable code also runs automatically at startup, creating another vulnerable spot exploited by viruses. Boot sector viruses are activated before the operating system is loaded and run when the master boot code in the MBR identifies the active, primary partition and activates the executable boot code for that volume.

Many viruses update the boot sector with their own code and move the original boot sector to another location on disk. Once the virus is activated, it stays in memory and passes the execution to the original boot sector so that startup appears normal. Some viruses do not relocate the original boot sector, making the volume inaccessible. If the affected volume is the active, primary partition, the system cannot start. Other viruses relocate the boot sector to the last sector of the disk. If that sector is not protected by the virus, it might be overwritten by normal use of the computer, rendering the volume inaccessible or preventing the system from restarting, depending upon which volume was affected.

How MBR and Boot Sector Viruses Affect Windows 2000

A computer can contract an MBR or boot sector virus by one of two common methods: by starting up from an infected floppy disk; or by running an infected program, causing the virus to drop an altered MBR or boot sector onto the hard disk.

The function of an MBR or boot sector virus is typically contained once Windows 2000 has started. If a payload is not run during system startup and the virus preserved the original MBR or boot sector, Windows 2000 prevents the virus from self-replicating to other disks.

Windows 2000 is immune to viruses infecting these disk structures during normal operation, because it only accesses physical disks through protected mode disk drivers. Viruses typically subvert the BIOS INT 13h disk access routines, which are ignored once Windows 2000 has started. However, Windows 2000 computers that are multiple-booted with MS-DOS, Windows 95, or Windows 98 can become infected when Windows 2000 is not running the computer.

If a multiple-boot computer on which Windows 2000 has been installed becomes infected by an MBR or boot sector virus while running another operating system, Windows 2000 is vulnerable to damage.

Once the protected mode disk drivers have been activated, the virus cannot copy itself to other hard disks or floppy disks because the BIOS mechanism on which the virus depends is not used for disk access. However, viruses that have a payload trigger that executes during startup are a threat to computers that are running Windows 2000 because the trigger process is initiated before the control during the computer startup process passes to Windows 2000.

Treating an MBR or Boot Sector Virus Infection

To remove a virus from your computer, use a current, well-known, commercial antivirus program designed for Windows 2000, and update it regularly. In addition to scanning the hard disks in your computer, be sure to scan all floppy disks that have been used in the infected computer, in any other computers, or with other operating systems in an infected multiple-boot computer. Scan them even if you believe they are not infected. Many infections recur because one or more copies of the virus were not detected.

If the computer is already infected with a boot sector virus when Windows 2000 is installed, standard antivirus programs might not completely eliminate the infection because Windows 2000 copies the original MS-DOS boot sector to a file called Bootsect.dos and replaces it with its own boot sector. The Windows 2000 installation is not infected, but if the user chooses to start MS-DOS, Windows 95, or Windows 98, the infected boot sector is reapplied to the system, reinfecting the computer. Antivirus tools that are not specifically designed for Windows 2000 do not know to check Bootsect.dos for viruses.

AVBoot

Microsoft provides a customized antivirus tool that can be used for these types of viruses. AVBoot is located in the \Valueadd\3rdparty\Ca_antiv folder of the Windows 2000 Setup CD. Insert an empty, high-density, 3.5-inch floppy disk, and use Windows 2000 Explorer to locate and double-click Makedisk.bat to create a startup floppy disk that automatically runs AVBoot.

AVBoot scans the memory as well as the MBR and all boot sectors of every locally installed disk. If a virus is found, it offers to remove the virus.

Important   Whether you use a third-party antivirus program or AVBoot, be sure to regularly update the virus signature files. Once you install an antivirus program, immediately update the signature files, usually through an Internet connection. Check with the software manufacturer's documentation for specific instructions. AVBoot includes update instructions in the installation folder and on the AVBoot floppy disk.

It is extremely important that you regularly update your antivirus program. In most cases, antivirus programs are unable to reliably detect and clean viruses of which they are unaware. False negative reports can result when using an out-of-date virus scanner. Most commercial antivirus software manufacturers offer monthly updates. Take advantage of the latest download to ensure that your system is protected with the latest virus defenses.

Fdisk /mbr

Do not depend on the MS-DOS command **Fdisk /mbr**, which rewrites the MBR on the hard disk, to resolve MBR infections. Many newer viruses have the properties of both file infector and MBR viruses, and restoring the MBR does not solve the problem if the virus immediately reinfects the system. In addition, running **Fdisk /mbr** on a system infected by MBR viruses that do not preserve or encrypt the original MBR partition table permanently prevents access to the lost partitions. If the disk was configured with a third-party disk management program, running this command eliminates the program overlay control and you cannot start up from the disk.

Important Running **Fdisk /mbr** overwrites only the first 446 bytes of the MBR, the portion known as the master boot code, leaving the existing partition table intact. However, if the signature word, the last two bytes of the MBR, has been deleted, the partition table entries are overwritten with zeroes. If an MBR virus overwrites the signature word, access to all partitions and logical volumes is lost.

Fixmbr command

The Recovery Console, a new troubleshooting tool in Windows 2000, offers a feature called **Fixmbr**. However, it functions identically to the **Fdisk /mbr** command, replacing only the master boot code and not affecting the partition table. For this reason, it is also unlikely to help resolve an infected MBR.

For more information about the Recovery Console, see "Repair, Recovery, and Restore" in this book.

Damaged MBRs and Boot Sectors

When you start a computer from the hard disk, the system BIOS code identifies the startup disk and reads the MBR. The master boot code in the MBR searches for the active, primary partition on the hard disk. If the first hard disk on the system does not contain an active partition, or if the master boot code cannot locate the system partition's boot sector to start the operating system, the MBR displays one of the following error messages:

```
Invalid partition table.
Error loading operating system.
Missing operating system.
```

There might not be an active partition on the hard disk that you want to use to start the computer, or the wrong partition might be identified as the active partition. In this case, use an MS-DOS startup floppy disk to start the computer and use the MS-DOS tool Fdisk to set or change the active partition.

Note   Fdisk can only set primary partitions as the active partition. If MBR corruption prevents Fdisk from setting or changing the active partition, you might need to use a third-party, low-level disk editor that can work under MS-DOS to make this change manually. The partition table field that needs to be changed is the **System ID** field. For more information about the fields in the partition table, see "Master Boot Record" earlier in this chapter.

Using an Emergency Repair Disk

If the boot sector cannot find Ntldr, Windows 2000 cannot start. This can be caused by moving, renaming, or deleting Ntldr, corruption of Ntldr, or corruption of the boot sector. Under these circumstances, the computer might not respond to input or might display one of the following error messages:

```
A disk read error occurred.
NTLDR is missing
NTLDR is compressed.
```

If Ntldr is damaged or missing, or if the boot sector is corrupted, you can resolve either problem by starting the Emergency Repair Disk (ERD) and following the prompts for repairing the installation. For more information about the ERD, see Windows 2000 Server Help.

Using the Recovery Console

If the system cannot start due to a corrupted MBR or boot sector, you can recreate either of these disk structures by using the Recovery Console.

To start the Recovery Console, start the computer from the Windows 2000 Setup CD or the Windows 2000 Setup floppy disks. If you do not have Windows 2000 Setup floppy disks and your computer cannot start from the CD, use another Windows 2000–based computer to create the setup disks. For information about creating the Windows 2000 Setup floppy disks, see Windows 2000 Server Help.

Start the computer and enter Windows 2000 Setup. Press ENTER at the **Setup Notification** screen to go to the **Welcome to Setup** screen. Press R to repair a Windows 2000 installation, and then press C to use the Recovery Console.

The Recovery Console displays all valid installations of Windows 2000 on the computer. To access the hard disk, press the number key representing the Windows 2000 installation you want to repair (typically represented as 1: C:\WINNT), and then press ENTER.

Note If you press ENTER without typing a number, the Recovery Console quits and restarts the computer.

The Recovery Console may also show valid installations of Windows NT. However, as the Recovery Console was not specifically designed to work with Windows NT, the results of attempting to access a Windows NT installation can be unpredictable.

The Recovery Console then prompts you for the Administrator password.

Note To access the hard disks with Recovery Console, you must know the password for the local Administrator account. If you do not have the correct password, or if the security database for the installation of Windows 2000 you are attempting to access is corrupted, Recovery Console does not allow access to the local disks.

To replace the MBR, at the Recovery Console command prompt, type:

fixmbr

Verify if you want to proceed because depending upon the location and the cause of the corruption within the damaged MBR, this operation can cause the data on the hard disk to become inaccessible. Press Y to proceed, or N to cancel.

Important Running **Fixmbr** overwrites only the master boot code, leaving the existing partition table intact. If the corruption in the MBR affects the partition table, running **Fixmbr** may not resolve the problem.

To have the Recovery Console replace the boot sector, at the Recovery Console command prompt, type:

fixboot

If you do not specify a particular drive, the Recovery Console replaces the boot sector of the boot partition. If another volume's boot sector is corrupted, enter the **Fixboot** command, followed by a space, and then specify the drive letter with a colon immediately afterward.

You can also use DiskProbe to edit these disk structures. Because DiskProbe only runs under Windows 2000 and Windows NT, you can only use it to fix errors on a boot sector, a non-startup partition, or an MBR on a non-startup disk. For more information about using DiskProbe to edit boot sectors and MBRs, install the Support Tools from the Windows 2000 Setup CD and see the document Dskprtrb.doc.

For more information about the Recovery Console, see "Repair, Recovery, and Restore" in this book.

Other Disk Problems

Disk problems can occur that do not involve the MBR, partition table, extended partition table, or boot sector. Typically, the Windows 2000 disk tools cannot be used to troubleshoot these disk problems.

Stop 0x0000007B — Inaccessible Boot Device

This Stop message, also known as Stop 0x7B, indicates that Windows 2000 lost access to the system partition during the startup process.

This error can be caused by a number of factors, including the failure of the boot device driver to initialize, the installation of an incompatible disk or disk controller, an incompatible device driver, disk cabling problems, disk corruption, viruses, or incompatible logical block addressing (LBA).

The system BIOS allows access to fixed disks that use fewer than 1024 cylinders. Many later disks, however, exceed 1024 cylinders. LBA is used to provide support for these disks. Such support is often built into the system BIOS. However, there are potential problems with LBA, such as:

- If partitions are created and formatted with LBA disabled, and LBA is subsequently enabled, a STOP 0x7B can result. The partitions must be created and formatted while LBA is enabled.

- Some LBA schemes are not compatible with Windows 2000. Check with your vendor.

Warning Changing LBA modes from one scheme to another can force you to recreate and reformat the partitions.

For more information about Stop message 0x7B, see "Windows 2000 Stop Messages" in this book.

Volume Displays as Unknown

If you create and format a volume with NTFS, FAT16, or FAT32, but you cannot access files on it, and Disk Management displays the volume as Unknown, the boot sector for the volume might be corrupted. For NTFS volumes, there are two other possible causes for a volume to display as Unknown:

- Permissions for the volume have been changed.
- The master file table (MFT) is corrupted.

The boot sector can be corrupted by viruses. For more information about cleaning an infected computer, see "Viruses" earlier in this chapter.

Permission problems can occur when you perform the following tasks:

- Create a second volume.
- Remove the group Everyone from the access control list (ACL).
- Grant access to a specific user.

The single user has normal access, but if other users log on, or if Windows 2000 is reinstalled, Disk Management shows the drive as Unknown. To correct this problem, log on as an administrator and take ownership of all folders, or return full control to the group Everyone.

If the MFT file is corrupted, there is no general solution, and you need to contact Microsoft Product Support Services.

CMOS Problems

The CMOS typically stores configuration information about the basic elements of the computer, including RAM, video, and storage devices. If the CMOS is damaged or incapable of retaining its configuration data, the computer might be unable to start.

Each manufacturer and BIOS vendor can decide what a user can configure on the CMOS, and what the standard configuration is. You can access the CMOS by using either a keyboard sequence at startup or a software tool, depending on the manufacturer's specifications. It is recommended that you record or print all CMOS information.

The computer uses the CMOS checksum to determine if any CMOS values have been changed other than by using the CMOS Setup program. If the checksum is not correct, the computer cannot start.

After the CMOS is correctly configured, any CMOS problem is usually caused by one of the following problems:

- A weak battery, which can happen when the computer has been turned off for a long time.
- A loose or faulty connection between the CMOS and the battery.
- A damaged CMOS caused by static electric discharge.

Cables and Connectors

Another source of disk problems can be cabling and connectors. Cables can go bad, but if the cable works initially, it is likely to work for a long time. When new disks are added to the computer, check for cabling problems. New problems might stem from a previously unused connector on an existing cable or from a faulty, longer cable used to connect all the disks that might have replaced the working original. Also check the connections to the disk themselves. If the cables are tightly stretched, one or more connectors may work themselves loose over time, resulting in intermittent problems with the disks.

If your system has small computer system interface (SCSI) adapters, contact the manufacturer for updated Windows 2000 drivers. Try disabling **sync negotiation** in the SCSI BIOS, checking the SCSI identifiers of each device, and confirming proper termination. For enhanced integrated drive electronics (EIDE) devices, define the onboard EIDE port as **Primary only**. Also, check each EIDE device for the proper master, slave, or stand-alone setting. Try removing all EIDE devices except for hard disks.

To make sure that any new disks and disk controllers are supported, see the Microsoft Windows 2000 Hardware Compatibility List (HCL) link on the Web Resources page at http://windows.microsoft.com/windows2000/reskit/webresources.

Additional Resources

- For more information about basic and dynamic disks, see Windows 2000 Server Help.
- For more information about troubleshooting disk problems, see Windows 2000 Server Help.

C H A P T E R   2

Data Storage and Management

Data storage and management innovations in Microsoft® Windows® 2000 include Removable Storage and Remote Storage. The overall storage architecture changes provided with Windows 2000 allow users more manageable storage flexibility. They also allow users to take advantage of current storage concepts, including bulk media changers and libraries, data-vaulting managers, and fault-tolerant storage subsystems that are being introduced by a variety of vendors.

In This Chapter

Related Information in the Resource Kit

- For more information about NTFS and file systems, see "File Systems" in this book.

- For information about backing up data to Remote Storage, see "Backup" in this book.

- For more information about restoring data from Remote Storage, see "Repair, Recovery, and Restore" in this book.

Overview of Data Management

Significant changes have been made to the storage feature set in Windows 2000. These factors support growing storage requirements in large environments, scalability requirements of mission-critical applications, and support for innovation in the storage market. To address these needs, Windows 2000 features an improved NTFS file system and an extensive list of new storage features and applications.

Current Trends

The quantity of data stored in distributed systems has increased exponentially over the last decade. Migration of mission-critical systems to distributed environments, increases in the number of Internet and intranet applications, and general growth in the enterprise end-user community are all contributing factors. The result is that the number of storage devices in an organization increases in direct proportion to the number of client/server systems.

Recent advances in both the hardware and software required to meet the growing demands of client and server computing include new storage devices, media types, data transfer protocols, and management standards. Storage concepts, such as Remote Storage, bulk media changers and libraries, data vaulting managers, and fault-tolerant storage subsystems are being introduced by a variety of vendors.

Storage requirements continue to increase. As storage becomes more complex, administrators must be able to manage it effectively to accomplish their computing goals, both short term and long term.

Storage Features

Windows 2000 introduces several new storage and storage-related features. These features, available to users and administrators, provide better flexibility, enhanced administrative control, and more efficient usage of resources. Some of the features are enhanced versions of previous Windows applications; others are new. Correct use of these features can help to improve security and reduce management costs associated with storage.

Removable Storage

Removable Storage is a new core Windows 2000 service that manages removable storage media and robotic storage libraries. Removable Storage eliminates the need for independent software vendors (ISVs) to support these devices on a per-device basis. More importantly, Removable Storage enables multiple applications to share expensive removable media storage devices. This allows storage applications to concentrate on customer features rather than hardware issues.

As shown in Figure 2.1, Removable Storage provides a single set of application programming interfaces (APIs) that allows applications to catalog all removable media (except floppy disks and similar small capacity media), such as disk, tape, and optical media, which are either stored on shelves (offline) or in libraries (online). Also, by disguising the complexities of underlying robotic library systems, Removable Storage both lowers costs of developing and operating storage applications and provides consistency to customers who purchase these applications.

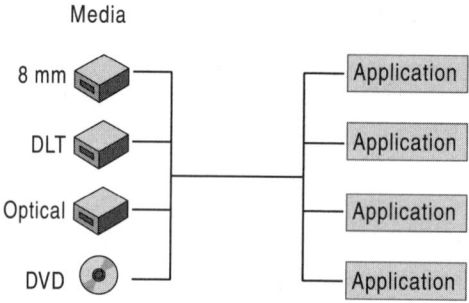

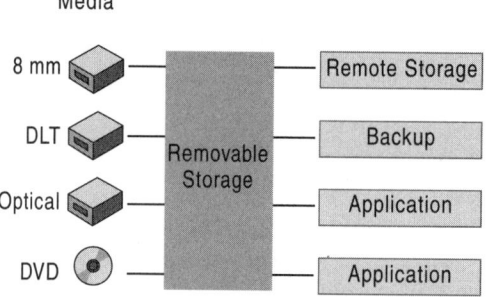

Figure 2.1   Removable Media with and Without Removable Storage

Removable Storage uses media pools to organize media. Media pools have several functions in the management of a media server, such as controlling access to media and grouping media by their use. Media pools allow media to be shared across applications, and they allow such sharing to be tracked.

Remote Storage

Remote Storage is a hierarchical storage management application that migrates data from primary storage to secondary storage. Hierarchical storage management makes sure that data is stored in the most cost-effective method possible. Frequently accessed data is stored on high-performance disks, while data that is not accessed as often is migrated to less expensive media until it is needed again.

Regardless of where the data is stored, the file system namespace continues to provide users with access to the file. When the file is accessed, Remote Storage retrieves the file from its storage location and restores it to the file system. Supported secondary storage in Windows 2000 is limited to tape, such as digital audio tape (DAT) and digital linear tape (DLT).

Remote Storage helps manage the cost associated with large quantities of data that must be accessible. Figure 2.2 illustrates the architecture of Remote Storage.

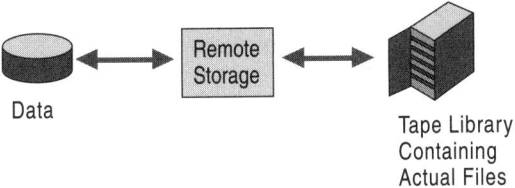

Figure 2.2   Remote Storage

Disk Management

The Disk Management function is enhanced in Windows 2000. Disk Management introduces new disk layouts that provide better manageability and recoverability. Enhancements to Disk Management include a remote administration Microsoft Management Console (MMC) snap-in and an expanded fault tolerance feature set. Moreover, most volume configuration changes do not require restarting the computer.

Disk Quotas

Disk quotas are a new feature in NTFS that provide more granular control of disk storage. Quotas allow administrators to limit the amount of disk space that a user can consume on an NTFS volume.

Disk quotas provide system administrators with a powerful tool for managing storage growth. Administrators can set both soft and hard limits: when a user exceeds a warning level (soft limit), an event is logged; when a user exceeds the hard limit, they receive an Out of Disk error.

Removable Storage

Windows 2000 Removable Storage provides services to applications and system administrators that facilitate the use, sharing, and management of the removable media devices attached to a computer running Microsoft® Windows® 2000 Professional or Windows 2000 Server. Using Removable Storage services allows applications to share local robotic media libraries and tape and disk drives. Removable Storage is not in the media data path, so managing media content is left to Removable Storage client applications, which are referred to as data-mover applications. For example, backup applications use Removable Storage to keep track of the identity of the tapes they use. Removable Storage mounts tapes when needed by the backup application, but the backup application itself keeps track of the backup sets stored on that media.

Removable Storage includes a Windows 2000 service program which runs as part of the service host program (Svchost.exe), the Removable Storage database, and the Removable Storage snap-in.

Removable Storage Service

Using low-level services provided with Windows 2000, Removable Storage acts on requests made by client applications, including:

- Mounting and dismounting media
- Cleaning drives
- Adding and removing media
- Library inventory
- Enabling and disabling libraries, drives, and media
- Accessing media and library attributes

Removable Storage provides these services to client applications by means of an API. This API, and the services provided through it, hide the details of the various drives and libraries. Removable Storage implements a generic changer model which incorporates all essential aspects of libraries and drives. Removable Storage drivers map real drives and changers to this model.

Moving media within a robotic-based library is one example of how Removable Storage is used. The media-moving hardware (usually referred to as a transport) on the hundreds of robotic libraries available today varies widely. Some robotic libraries have hands that grab media and move them from a home storage location (usually referred to as a slot) to a drive. Other types of robotic libraries move a magazine containing some number of media and then push one medium from the magazine into a drive. A mount request from a Removable Storage application mounts media of either description. Figure 2.3 shows the Removable Storage components.

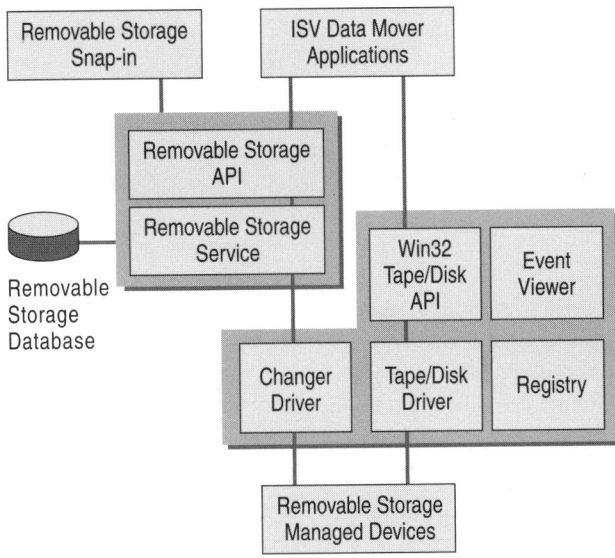

Figure 2.3   Removable Storage Components

Removable Storage Database

The Removable Storage database is the mechanism used by Removable Storage to track media-related system components, including the identity of media known by the system. It stores the status of these system components and maintains media inventories. The Removable Storage database includes the following information:

- The configuration and state of the library, drive, and media
- Media pool configuration and contents
- Library work list
- Operator requests

The Removable Storage database stores the properties of the objects (for example, libraries, drives, and media) that Removable Storage manages. Removable Storage maintains the data in the database and updates it whenever an administrator or an application makes a change in a computer running Removable Storage. For example, if an administrator wants to mount a medium in an online library, Removable Storage mounts the medium and updates the database to reflect the change.

Note   The Removable Storage database is used internally by Removable Storage and is not directly available to applications or administrators.

Removable Storage Snap-in

The Removable Storage snap-in is an administrative interface to Removable Storage. It allows administrators to add Removable Storage objects, view and modify properties of Removable Storage objects, insert and eject media, perform inventories, mount and dismount media, and check status information.

Basic Concepts

Removable Storage can be described in terms of five basic concepts: media, physical locations, media pools, work queue items, and operator requests. The last four of these are the top level nodes in the Removable Storage snap-in. The first, media, is the most fundamental concept and affects all the others.

Media

Units of media store information. Each unit of media (or medium, also referred to as a "cartridge") is of a certain type, such as 8mm tape, magnetic disk, optical disk, or CD-ROM.

Most types of media have a single side. For example, a tape must always be oriented in a certain way. When the tape is placed in a drive, all of its data is accessible. Some types of media, such as magneto-optic (MO) disks, have two sides. An MO disk has an "A" side and a "B" side. When an MO disk is placed in a drive with the "A" side up, then the "A" side is accessible and the "B" side is not. To access the "B" side, the disk must be inserted with the "B" side up.

Removable Storage represents media physically and logically. Physical media are the tangible media that are inserted and removed from libraries and mounted in drives.

When an application wants to access data on a medium, Removable Storage generates a logical identifier (ID) that allows the application to request the data on that medium. Since access to the data occurs only through that ID, Removable Storage can manage the physical location of the data. For example, if the original medium begins to fail, Removable Storage can move the data to a new medium without having to notify the application.

Physical media and the sides they contain are tracked in Removable Storage and can take on various states as they are entered into a library and used. For more information about media and side states, see "Media Handling and Usage" later in this chapter.

Removable Storage provides the infrastructure necessary to share media among various applications. Removable Storage ensures that all media are used in such a way as to preserve the data they contain. Removable Storage accomplishes this by identifying and verifying the identity of each medium. For more information about how Removable Storage verifies the identity of media, see "Media Identification and Naming" later in this chapter.

Physical Locations

Removable Storage manages two classes of physical locations: libraries and the offline media physical location. Libraries include both media and the means to read and write them. The offline media physical location is a special holder for media that is cataloged by Removable Storage, but does not reside in a library.

The set of all physical locations includes the libraries and the offline media physical location.

Libraries

In its simplest form, a library is composed of data storage media and a means to read and write the media. A CD-ROM drive with a disc inserted is a simple library with one drive, no slots, and no transport. A more complex example of a library is a robotic-based tape library, which holds several (up to several thousand) tapes, has one or more tape drives, and has a mechanical means to move tapes into and out of the drives.

Specifically, libraries are composed of the following:

Slots   Slots are storage locations in the library. For example, a tape library has one slot for each tape that the library can hold. A stand-alone drive library has no slots. However, most libraries have at least four slots. Sometimes slots are organized into collections of slots called magazines. Magazines are usually removable.

Drives   A drive is a device that can read or write to a medium. An Iomega Jaz drive, for example, can read and write to a Jaz cartridge which is inserted into it. A library has at least one drive.

Transports   A transport is the robotic device that moves a medium from its slot to a drive and back again. Robotic libraries usually have only one transport.

Bar Code Readers   A label with a bar code is attached to the outside of a cartridge that is both human readable and computer readable. Libraries that hold media with bar codes attached might have a bar code reader. There is only one reader, which is usually mounted on the transport.

Doors   A door is a means to gain unconstrained access to the media in a library. On larger libraries a door might resemble an actual door. When the door is open, an administrator can add and remove media from the library. Doors on smaller libraries might not always look exactly like doors, but they still provide the same functionality. For example, some small changers have all their slots in a magazine. When an administrator instructs Removable Storage to open the door, the changer pushes the magazine out through the front. The administrator can add, replace, or remove media and then reinsert the magazine into the changer. When an administrator adds media to a library, the media are placed directly into a slot. Some libraries have no doors, while others have several.

Insert/Eject Ports   While doors provide unconstrained access to the media in a library, an insert/eject (IE) port provides very controlled access. When an administrator adds media to a library through an IE port, the media are not placed directly into a slot. Instead, the media are placed in the IE port and then the library uses the transport to move the media from the IE port to a slot. Some libraries have no IE ports, while others have several. Also called "mailslots," some IE ports handle only one cartridge at a time, while others may handle several.

Types of Libraries   A robotic library can have any of the components described above. At a minimum, a robotic library has some media, slots to hold the media, one or more drives, a transport, and either a door or an IE port. Robotic libraries are sometimes referred to as changers or jukeboxes. No human intervention is required to place a medium in a library in one of its drives.

A stand-alone drive library or stand-alone drive is a special kind of library. A medium must be manually placed in a drive. The CD-ROM drive found on most desktop computers is a stand-alone drive library. Removable Storage treats stand-alone drives as libraries with one drive and an IE port. Removable Storage models these drives as libraries to make its program interfaces simpler. For this reason, an application need not know whether a medium is mounted by a transport or a human.

Offline Media Physical Location

The offline media physical location is where Removable Storage lists media that are not in a library. The physical location of media in an online library is the library in which it resides. Media that are not in any of these libraries, such as archived backup tapes on a shelf, are offline media and reside in the offline media physical location. When a user or administrator moves an offline medium into a library, Removable Storage changes its physical location to be the library into which it was placed. When a medium is taken out of an online library, Removable Storage notes that it now resides in the offline media physical location.

Media Pools

A media pool is a logical collection of media that share some common attributes. A media pool contains media of only one type, but media in the media pool can be in more than one library. Each medium is in a media pool. There are two classes of media pools: system and application. System media pools are created by Removable Storage for its own use and include the free, import and unrecognized pools. Application media pools are created by applications to group media. Grouping media is especially important if several applications are sharing the libraries attached to a system and the media they contain.

Each media pool has access permissions that control access to the media that belong to it. While these permissions do not control access to the data contained on the media, they do control the manipulation of the media, including an application's ability to move media from the pool or to allocate it for its own use.

Media pools can be used hierarchically. A media pool can be used to hold other media pools, or it can be used to hold media. An application that needs to group media of several types into one collection can create an application media pool for the whole collection and additional media pools within it, one for each media type. Removable Storage actually uses this technique for its system pools. Within the free pool, for example, is a media pool for each media type. Both sides of a two-sided medium are always in the same pool.

System Pools

The system pools are used to hold media that are not currently being used by an application. The free pool holds unused media that are available to applications, and the unrecognized and import pools are temporary holding places for media that have been newly placed in a library. For more information on how Removable Storage uses these pools, especially the unrecognized and import pools, see "Media Handling and Usage" later in this chapter.

Free Pools   The free pools support sharing media among applications. They contain media that are freely available to any application, and they hold no useful data. An application can draw media from the free pools when it needs additional media, and it can return media to the free pools when the media are no longer needed and should be made available to other applications.

Unrecognized Pools   When a medium is placed in a library, Removable Storage tries to identify it. If it has not seen this particular media before nor discerned its format or the application which last wrote data on it, Removable Storage places the medium in the unrecognized pool for its media type. Blank media are treated this way. Media in the unrecognized pools might have data on them, but they are not cataloged by Removable Storage nor is Removable Storage able to read any data on these media.

Import Pools If Removable Storage can identify the format or application associated with a medium that has just been placed in a library but has never been seen before, it places the medium in the import pool. For example, if an administrator placed a tape written by Backup on one system into a library attached to a second system, the instance of Removable Storage on the second system recognizes that the tape was written using Microsoft Tape Format (MTF) and places it in the proper media type import pool.

Application Pools

Each application that uses media managed by Removable Storage uses one or more application pools. Applications can create these pools, or they can be created using the Removable Storage snap-in. Permissions on application pools can be set up to allow applications to share pools, or to assign each application its own set of pools.

As mentioned earlier, a pool can either be created to hold other pools or it can be created to hold media. A pool created to hold media has additional properties that specify the actions to be taken when an application allocates or deallocates media.

The following example shows one way in which media pools might be configured to support the needs of several client applications. The example system contains two libraries—one optical disk library and one tape library—and two data mover applications—a backup application and a document management application.

Table 2.1 shows how the two applications use the two media types.

Table 2.1   Media Type and Data Mover Applications

Media Type	Backup Application	Document Management Application
Tape media	Full backup Incremental backup	Engineering archive documents
Optical disk media	Catalog storage	Accounting documents Engineering documents

Work Queue

When applications make a library request , Removable Storage places these requests in a queue and processes them as resources become available. For example, a request to mount a tape in a library results in a mount work queue item, which might wait until a drive is available.

Table 2.2 describes the states that a work queue item can have while it is being handled by Removable Storage.

Table 2.2   Work Queue States

State	Description
Queued	A work item is queued from the time an application issues a request until Removable Storage examines the request.
In Process	A work item is in process while Removable Storage is actively working on completing it.
Waiting	If Removable Storage examines the request and finds that one or more of the resources needed to satisfy the request is busy (for example, the requested drive is being used by another application), the request enters the waiting state.
Completed	When Removable Storage completes the request, the work queue item for that request enters the completed state.
Failed	If Removable Storage is unable to complete the request, the work queue item for that request enters the failed state.

Operator Requests

Note "Operator" as used here, is synonymous with "administrator."

Sometimes, even with robotic libraries, manual assistance is needed to complete a request or perform maintenance or support. If an application requests that a medium in the offline media physical location be mounted, the medium must be manually entered into an online library, generating a request to the operator to enter the cartridge.

Operator requests can be presented to an administrator through the Windows 2000 Messenger Service or the system tray. An administrator can refuse or complete the request. Definitions of the operator request states are shown in Table 2.3.

Table 2.3   Operator Request States

State	Description
Submitted	Removable Storage or an application has submitted a request for administrator action. This operator request is waiting for the operator to complete the requested operation.
Refused	An operator has indicated that the requested action will not be performed.
Completed	An administrator has indicated that the action was completed, or Removable Storage has detected that the action was completed.

Media Identification and Naming

As a manager of shared resources, Removable Storage ensures that client applications do not corrupt each other's data. Placing permissions on media pools prevents an application from modifying the data of another application. Another way to accomplish this is to assign each medium a unique name which applications can use to refer to it, and to track the identities of all media in a system, ensuring that the mapping between the unique name and the physical media is always accurate.

A library management system could simply use a media's home slot as its identity. A request to mount a medium in a drive could be as simple as "Mount the medium in slot 6 of drive 2." There are problems with this minimalist approach, however. An administrator could exchange the medium in slot 6 for that in slot 7 during a door access. An application executing the request might get a medium it did not expect and not know it. To prevent this, Removable Storage assigns each medium a unique name, which is used to refer to the medium programmatically. In keeping with Windows 2000 naming conventions, Removable Storage uses globally unique identifiers (GUIDs) as the form for these names.

Removable Storage identifies each medium side by reading its label. At various times, Removable Storage reads the label to ensure that the name it has for a medium maps correctly. Consider a refinement of the example given earlier. If the name of a medium simply referred to the medium in slot 7, an administrator could change the contents of slot 7 during a door access and the next time an application used the name it would get a different medium. Removable Storage prevents this by associating information stored in the medium's label with its name. Each time a medium is mounted, for example, Removable Storage reads the label to ensure that the medium it mounted is correct. An inventory is an operation that an administrator can request or that Removable Storage can initiate, which verifies the labels associated with each named medium in a library.

Since administrators also need to identify media uniquely, and since GUIDs are difficult to read in printed form, Removable Storage also assigns each medium a display name. These names are changeable so if an administrator has a naming scheme for media, a display name can be assigned that is different from the one Removable Storage initially assigned.

On-media Identifiers

On-media identifiers (OMIDs) are electronically recorded labels on each medium side in a Removable Storage system. Each label is composed of at least two parts: a type and an ID. A label type identifies the format used to record information on the medium. A label ID is an identifier that uniquely identifies each medium.

Different media types have different types of labels. Media sides with file systems (optical disk and Jaz cartridges, for example) have file system labels. An NTFS-formatted Jaz cartridge, for example, has an NTFS label type, and the ID is the volume serial number. Tapes using MTF have a label type of MTF and the ID is derived from various fields in the MTF header.

On-media identifiers are handled somewhat differently for CD-ROM and DVD-ROM media. Serial numbers for instances of these media might not be unique—a library can hold multiple copies of the same CD-ROM title, for example, with each having the same serial number—so Removable Storage allows non-unique label IDs in this case. This doesn't degrade the media identification objectives of Removable Storage; any of the CD-ROMs with identical IDs can be used interchangeably since their contents are identical and cannot be changed.

Duplicate Copies of Media

Although Removable Storage tries to uniquely identify each cartridge that it manages, it also handles media duplicates. It treats identical media as separate media that are identical in every way and can be used interchangeably. For example, if a user has two copies of the Windows 2000 Server Setup CD and places both in a changer, Removable Storage shows both media and each can be mounted, ejected, and so on, separately. Since each has its own record in the database, it is possible to attach different attributes to each media. You can give each a different display name, for example, although this is discouraged because there is no guarantee that these differing attributes will always be associated with the same cartridge. If both are ejected, the attributes may be reversed when both are inserted again.

Bar Codes

Bar code labels on physical media, in libraries with bar code readers, are used as a shortcut to determine the identity of physical media and its sides. Reading an on-media label can be time consuming since it requires reading data on the media, which requires that the medium be placed in a drive if it's not already there. With unique bar codes, a bar code scan is a much faster way of identifying a physical medium and the sides it contains.

Media Names

When new physical media are placed into a library, Removable Storage assigns an initial display name to the media that an administrator can use to visually identify the media. This name is derived from several sources, including the on-media label and the bar code. The rules include the following:

1. If the media has a bar code label, its alphanumeric value is used as the display name.

2. If the media is single-sided and has a recognized label type on its single side, the name is taken from the label. If the format is MTF, the label is taken from information in the MTF header. If the format is a file system, the name is taken from the volume name.

3. The sequence number is used.

Media Change Detection

Many removable media devices, including all those connected to the system by means of SCSI and IDE, cannot themselves report when media are entered or removed. Instead the host system must notice such changes either by querying the device specifically for this information or when performing some other operation on the drive.

Since Removable Storage controls changers and knows when media enter and leave drives, this is not a problem for drives in changers. It is an issue, however, for stand-alone drives. The information that Removable Storage has about the contents of a stand-alone drive might be incorrect if the state of the drive has changed. For example, the snap-in might show that a drive is empty for a period of time after a tape is inserted into a tape drive. An inventory operation on the stand-alone drive library brings the state up-to-date.

Some applications need to have current information. For these applications Removable Storage provides a media change detection mechanism that can be turned on and controlled through Removable Storage API calls. With media detection turned on for a stand-alone drive library, the state of the drive that Removable Storage presents to applications is updated almost immediately after the physical state of the drive changes.

Media Handling and Usage

Most of what Removable Storage does involves both moving media around within and between libraries, and controlling access to that media. While Removable Storage is handling them in these ways, the media in a Removable Storage system have states associated with them. These states determine which operations are permitted and which are prevented. While a medium is available, for example, any application can claim it for its own use, but a medium already in use by one application cannot be claimed by another.

There are two sets of media-related states that govern most of the handling and usage by Removable Storage and its applications: media states and side states.

Media States

The states associated with physical media reflect that the operations performed on them mostly involve movement.

Table 2.4 describes the Removable Storage media states.

Table 2.4   Physical Media States in Removable Storage

Physical Media State	Description
Idle	Medium is in a slot if in a library, or on a shelf if in the offline physical location.
In Use	Removable Storage is in the process of moving the medium.
Mounted	Medium is in a drive, but might not be accessible yet.
Loaded	Medium is in a drive, and the contents of one of its sides are accessible.
Unloaded	Medium is still in a drive, but the contents of the side that was loaded are no longer accessible.

A side is accessible if an application can perform I/O on it. This distinction is most marked in the case of certain tape drives. Inserting a tape into one of these drives does not make its contents accessible. A portion of the tape must be pulled out of the cartridge and wrapped around the tape drive head, a process sometimes referred to as *loading*.

Side States

Since data is stored on a medium side, states associated with sides reflect usage rather than physical location. Table 2.5 lists and describes the Removable Storage media states.

Table 2.5   Side States in Removable Storage

Side State	Description
Allocated	A side that has been claimed for use by an application. The side is not available to any other application.
Available	A side that is available to be claimed and used by any application.
Completed	A side that is in use, but can no longer be used for write operations. The side is physically or logically full.

(continued)

Table 2.5   Side States in Removable Storage   *(continued)*

Side State	Description
Decommissioned	A side that can no longer be used because it has crossed a usage threshold. It has reached its allocation maximum (specified by the administrator or an application) and cannot be used again.
Unrecognized	A side whose label types and label IDs are not recognized by Removable Storage.
Imported	A side whose label type is recognized by Removable Storage, but whose label ID is not. It is a new side that Removable Storage has never seen before, but whose format it recognizes.
Inaccessible	A side of a multi-sided cartridge that is in a drive, but not the accessible side.
Incompatible	A side that is not compatible with the pool in which its medium was identified. The medium containing the side needs to be immediately ejected from the library.
Reserved	The second side of a two-sided medium. It is unavailable for allocation to all but the application which already has the first side allocated.
Unprepared	Side that is not claimed or used by any application, but which does not have a free label on it. Applications cannot allocate unprepared media. This is a temporary state. See the following discussion on the interplay between media states and pools.

State Transitions

The state a physical medium or side is in determines what can happen to it next. The transitions for physical media are fairly straightforward. A medium starts off idle and goes to in use when it's being moved to a drive or IE port. Once in a drive, it goes from mounted to loaded. When it is dismounted it goes from unloaded, to in use, and then to idle when it is back in its slot.

More interesting and complex are the state transitions associated with sides.

When a medium is inserted into a library, Removable Storage tries to identify it by reading the labels on its sides. If Removable Storage recognizes an OMID (both the label type and ID) this medium is reentered into a library. Removable Storage notes the change in location, and its sides keep the same state they had when the medium was ejected from the library. If Removable Storage does not recognize the label type, it sets the side's state to unrecognized. If Removable Storage recognizes the label type but not the label ID, Removable Storage sets the side's state to imported.

If a medium is found to not be compatible with the current library, Removable Storage sets its states to incompatible. This might happen if a medium with a form factor (size and shape) identical to that supported by a library, but different in the way information is recorded, is inserted into that library. For example, there are several tape media types that use an 8mm form factor. Since all attempts to read the medium fail, it is incompatible with the library. Media in the incompatible state cannot be changed to another state, and needs to be ejected from the library.

Removable Storage initially sets the state of inserted CD-ROM media to imported.

Sides that are unrecognized can only be changed to available. Generally, unrecognized sides are either on media that have never been used before or were used in a way that is unrelated to any of the Removable Storage client applications and so the contents are not useful. Figure 2.4 describes the legal state transitions for a side.

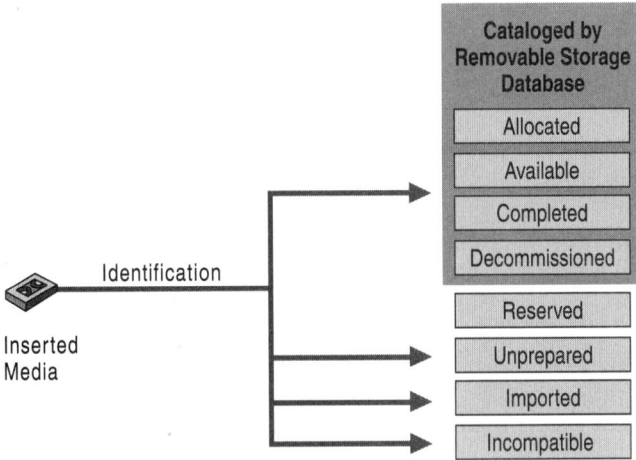

Figure 2.4   Media States

Free Media

Sides that are freely available for any applications to use are in the free pool in the available state. Removable Storage writes a special label (called a free label) on these media so that it can clearly identify these media as holding no useful data. While Removable Storage is in the process of writing a free label, it marks the side as unprepared. This is usually a transitory state, but can persist if, for example, the medium with the side being labeled is in the offline physical media location. Such a side stays in this state until inserted into a library. Any transition into the available state results in writing a free label and therefore passes through the unprepared state.

Application-Specific Media States

When an application needs to claim a side for its use it allocates an available side. This process changes the state of the side from available or imported to allocated. An application allocates a medium that is in the imported state when it recognizes that the new side has data that it needs. When it no longer needs any of the data stored on the side, the application deallocates the side, changing its state back to available.

When a medium is full in some sense—either the side can hold no more data or the application can write no more—an application can mark the medium as complete.

Removable Storage keeps track of the number of times a side is allocated. When this count crosses a threshold, the side is decommissioned. Sides in this state are past their useful life. This count is checked when a side is deallocated.

Since the sides of a two-sided medium are allocated separately, it is possible for an application to try to allocate both sides, or to have the second side claimed by a different application. Having two separate applications allocate the sides of a medium can be problematic, especially in circumstances where media are moved between systems. Removable Storage provides a mechanism that applications can use to eliminate this problem. When an application allocates the first side of a two-sided medium the second side is placed in the reserved state. Only the application that allocated the first side can allocate the reserved second side. If the application determines that it does not need the second side, it can change the state of the second side back to available.

When an application deallocates one side of a medium that contains reserved sides, Removable Storage changes the state of all reserved partitions to available.

Relationship Between Media Pools and States

There are relationships between the various system and application media pools and the states of the sides they contain.

The import pool can hold only media in the import state. Sides in the unrecognized pool can only be in the unrecognized state. In fact, these pools hold sides in these states until applications need them (for example, to move them to application pools). A side in the import state which is moved to an application pool remains in the import state until the application writes a new label on the side and informs Removable Storage.

Sides in the free pools are always in the available state (or the transitional unprepared state). Sides moved into one of the free pools automatically have free labels written on them. Application pools can hold media in any state, except reserved, decommissioned, and unrecognized.

Removable Storage provides a few shortcuts to move sides among pools while changing their state. Normally, an application allocates a side that is in its application pool. However, an application pool property allows Removable Storage to move a side into an application pool when an application tries to allocate a side. If the application tries to allocate a side in a pool in which there are no available sides, Removable Storage moves a side from the appropriate free pool into the application pool and puts it into the allocated state. Conversely, another application pool property indicates that when allocated sides in the pool are deallocated they need to be returned to the appropriate free pool along with the change to the available state.

Administering Removable Storage

Systems with a few stand-alone drives and a single Removable Storage-aware application typically require no Removable Storage administration. Systems with more complex configurations, such as those with tape or optical disk libraries or multiple Removable Storage-aware applications, do require administration, however. There are also rare cases in which a Removable Storage-aware application does require some administration on a system with a simple configuration.

Device Support

There are many drives and robotic libraries available, and not all of them can be supported. See the Microsoft Windows 2000 Hardware Compatibility List (HCL) link on the Web Resources page at http://windows.microsoft.com/windows2000/reskit/webresources.

Each of the supported robotic libraries has its own configuration method and options. In order for them to work correctly with Removable Storage you must configure your robotic libraries with certain settings of these options. Please consult the HCL for the proper configuration settings for all supported drives and robotic libraries.

Installing and Configuring Removable Storage-Aware Applications

Under normal circumstances, Removable Storage-aware client applications can perform any Removable Storage configuration or setup that they need at the time they are installed. If such an application requires an application media pool, for example, then the pool needs to be created when the application is installed and the permissions need to be set accordingly at that time.

Some applications use their own format or labeling scheme. In order for Removable Storage to correctly process OMIDs on the sides written by these applications, it needs a special dynamic-link library (DLL) that can read the label and determine the OMID. Such a DLL is called a media label library (MLL), and client applications that use them must install them.

Preparing Media

Most applications draw available media from the free pool. Placing media in the free pool is also called "preparing" the media, and must be done either by a Removable Storage-aware application or by an administrator. If your Removable Storage-aware applications do not automatically prepare media, you might have to use the Removable Storage snap-in. You can prepare media in the unrecognized pool, and you can prepare media in the import pool if you are certain that the media contains no useful data. Available media in application pools can also be prepared, but Removable Storage does not prepare allocated media.

To prepare a tape, for example, in the Removable Storage snap-in, right-click the media in the details pane, and then click **Prepare**.

Using Operator Requests in Removable Storage

A Removable Storage operator request is a request for an administrator to perform a task. Operator requests can be issued by Removable Storage or by Removable Storage client applications. Removable Storage generates operator requests in the following situations:

- Media must be moved online because an application has initiated a mount request for a medium that is offline.

- There are no available media online. An application has asked for available media and there are none online in the specified application media pool or the appropriate free media pool. The administrator can supply new media or available media that is offline to satisfy the request.

- A device failed and requires service.

- A drive needs to be cleaned and there is no usable cleaner cartridge available in the library unit.

Operator requests are displayed in the Removable Storage snap-in. Administrators can satisfy or cancel operator requests. After satisfying an operator request, the administrator must acknowledge the request in the Removable Storage snap-in. When an administrator cancels an operator request, Removable Storage notifies the application that generated the request. Removable Storage saves operator requests for less than one hour after they have been satisfied or canceled.

Security

Removable Storage provides security for itself, media pools, and libraries. It contains an access control list (ACL) that controls who can connect to the service and who can work with operator requests. To edit this ACL, right-click the root node in the Removable Storage snap-in. Each library has an ACL that governs who can perform specific tasks, and each pool also contains an ACL. Table 2.6 describes what permissions are required for specific snap-in operations.

Table 2.6   Permissions Required For Removable Storage Snap-in Operations

Function	Media Pool			Library			Service		
	Use	Modify	Control	Use	Modify	Control	Use	Modify	Control
Connect to the service							X		
Create media pools		X							
Delete media pools			X						
Dismount media	X			X					
Mount media	X			X					
Move media from pool to pool		X							
Open the library door						X			
Delete a library					X				
Dismount a drive						X			
Eject media						X			
Insert media						X			
Inventory a library						X			
Cancel an operator request									X
Satisfy an operator request									X
Clean a drive						X			
Insert/eject a cleaner						X			

Controlling the Service

Removable Storage is configured in Windows 2000 to start automatically when you start your computer. It is possible to change the service to be manually started, but this is highly discouraged. Disabling the service breaks several applications that are included with Windows 2000, such as Backup and Remote Storage.

As with other Windows 2000 services, Removable Storage can be stopped, started, and restarted by means of the service control manager.

Service Startup Tasks

Removable Storage performs several tasks when it starts. During some of these tasks Removable Storage is unavailable to administrators and client applications. At other times during startup it can accept requests; however, execution might be delayed while Removable Storage completes this initialization. The following steps outline the process performed by Removable Storage during startup:

Note It is important to note that the process is the same whether Removable Storage is starting after a system start or simply restarted while the system is running.

---

1. Cancel all work items that are still in queue from the last time the service ran.
2. Configure libraries, including associating drives with changers and identifying stand-alone drives.
3. Inventory the contents of each library. Removable Storage performs an inventory in each library according to its set default. At this point Removable Storage determines which slots have media and which media need identification. It also empties the drives, if possible. If the drives are currently in use, Removable Storage leaves the media in the drive and examines the media in the drive at a later time.
4. Start accepting requests from applications.
5. Complete the default inventory work, identifying media as needed.

Device Configuration

Because Removable Storage manages removable media devices, it relies on Plug and Play to tell it which devices are attached to a system, but Removable Storage must match drives with robotic libraries. If Plug and Play indicates that a robotic library is attached to a system, Removable Storage must go through the list of drives that are also attached and detect which ones are actually inside the robotic library and which are stand-alone drive libraries. If certain rules are followed, Removable Storage can do this mapping entirely on its own. If these rules cannot be followed, you must manually map drives to robotic libraries.

Auto-Configuration

Removable Storage auto-configures robotic libraries if the following are true:

- Robotic library hardware units support drive element address reporting with the **ReadElementStatus** SCSI command. Consult the manufacturer to find out if your library hardware unit supports this feature.

- All drives inside a robotic library are on the same SCSI bus as the library.

Manual Configuration

Because not all library hardware units and system configurations support the Removable Storage auto-configuration feature, Removable Storage provides a method for manually configuring library hardware units. However, only use this method when it is necessary, because Removable Storage cannot detect manually configured changes. In general, manually configure Removable Storage only when it detects a robotic library that it cannot configure. After it is set for manual configuration, a changer does not participate in auto-configuration even if its configuration is changed.

In most cases, Removable Storage starts auto-configuration after hardware is installed, moved, or removed. This happens automatically when you restart after adding the device. For changers that cannot be auto-configured, Removable Storage adds incomplete registry entries and generates an operator request to manually configure such changers. The following procedure can be used to manually configure Removable Storage.

▶ **To manually configure Removable Storage**

You must complete all of the following steps to manually configure Removable Storage:

Caution Do not use a registry editor to edit the registry directly unless you have no alternative. The registry editors bypass the standard safeguards provided by administrative tools. These safeguards prevent you from entering conflicting settings or settings that are likely to degrade performance or damage your system. Editing the registry directly can have serious, unexpected consequences that can prevent the system from starting and require that you reinstall Windows 2000. To configure or customize Windows 2000, use the programs in Control Panel or Microsoft Management Console (MMC) whenever possible.

---

1. Stop Removable Storage.
2. Back up the Removable Storage database by copying the files in %SystemRoot%\System32\ntmsdata\ to a secure temporary directory.

3. Restart Removable Storage. Note all the drives that appear as stand-alone drive libraries. Removable Storage displays all drives that are not mapped to a changer as stand-alone drive libraries, including ones that are actually in the changer but are unmapped.

4. Empty all drives on your system.

5. Place a medium in a drive in the library you are trying to configure, either by opening the library door or through a front panel and IE port (see your changer's documentation for details about how to do this). Click **Refresh** in the snap-in for each of the stand-alone drives, and then find the one that now shows that it has media in it. Open the property sheet for that drive and note the device name on the **Device Info** property page. Complete this step for each drive in the changer that you are trying to configure.

6. From the **Start** menu, click **Run**, type **regedt32.exe** or **regedit.exe**, and then click **OK**.

7. In the Removable Storage configuration information in the registry subkey HKEY_LOCAL_MACHINE\System\CurrentControlSet\Services\NtmsSvc \Config, create a REG_DWORD entry called **AutoCfg** and set the value to **0**.

8. Stop Removable Storage.

9. In the registry editor, navigate to HKEY_LOCAL_MACHINE\System \CurrentControlSet\Services\NtmsSvc\Config. The Config subkey contains a subkey for each changer (such as Changer0) and a subkey for each stand-alone drive. Each changer subkey contains an entry for each drive bay in the changer, such as **DriveBay0.**

10. For each drive bay entry that has the value "???", replace that value with the device name (without any initial "\" or "." characters, such as "Tape3") of the drive in that bay.

11. Close the registry editor.

12. Restart Removable Storage. Removable Storage reads the new configuration information and initializes the devices.

13. Using the snap-in, mount a medium in each drive in the library after Removable Storage is initialized. If any of the configurations are incorrect, Removable Storage generates an error message either during initialization or the mount.

14. If the manual configuration was unsuccessful, stop the Removable Storage process. Copy your backup version of the Removable Storage database files back to the %SystemRoot%\System32\ntmsdata\ directory to restore the database and restart the manual configuration process.

If Removable Storage does not generate any error messages, the manual configuration was successful, and you have completed the manual configuration process.

Database Backup and Recovery

Removable Storage stores its catalog of media in a database on disk. While
Removable Storage can recover some of the information by inventorying the
attached libraries, all of the application-oriented information might be lost if the
database is lost. For this reason, the Removable Storage database must be backed
up regularly. For more information about backing up the Removable Storage
database, see "Backup" in this book.

Maintaining a Consistent Database

The default location for the Removable Storage database is
%SystemRoot%\System32\ntmsdata, which normally contains four files and a
folder. Unless you change the location where the database is stored Backup takes
the proper steps to create a consistent backup of the database when ntmsdata is
selected for backup.

If you decide to move the database or if you do not use Backup, you are
responsible for ensuring that you get a consistent database when you do a backup.

Important   The backup application that you use is responsible for backing up
Removable Storage. If you do not use Backup, which is part of Windows 2000,
and you do use Removable Storage, verify that the backup application backs up
Removable Storage.

The database must be internally consistent to produce a backup that can be
restored successfully. There are two ways of doing this: shutting down Removable
Storage and *exporting* the database. The latter is what Backup does if you have
not changed the location of the Removable Storage database and you select
ntmsdata. If you can shut down Removable Storage while backing up the
database, your backup operation can simply make copies of the database files
themselves. If shutting down the service is not an option (for example, because a
Removable Storage–aware application must remain running), you must provide a
way for Removable Storage to export a consistent copy of the database for
backup. You can also create a small Removable Storage–aware application that
calls the **ExportNtmsDatabase** API. For more information about this API and
about writing Removable Storage–aware applications, see the Microsoft Platform
Software Development Kit (SDK) link on the Web Resources page at
http://windows.microsoft.com/windows2000/reskit/webresources.

Tracking the Backup Media

The administrator must always know the location of the most recent Removable
Storage database backup. To help identify the backup during disaster recovery,
the administrator needs to record and maintain the medium display name and the
on-media identifier in a safe place.

You might need this information to help the backup application identify the media from which to restore the database. You can get the display name from the property page for the medium, and the on-media identifier from the property page on the property sheet for the medium side.

Recovering the Database Files

Note The information in this section assumes that there has been no change to the system configuration that affects Removable Storage since the backup was made.

To allow the recovery application to access media, it must be mounted in a drive. If you are going to restore the database using Backup, then Removable Storage must be running and you can use Removable Storage to mount the media, but without the full database you'll have to get Removable Storage running with enough of a database to mount the database backup tape for Backup. To do this, delete any files that might be in ntmsdata and start Removable Storage. Removable Storage then inventories each of the libraries attached to the system.

Tip For large libraries, this might take hours. To minimize the time for this process, perform standard backups often.

Tapes made with Backup show up in the import pool. Start Backup and have it move these tapes to its own application pool. Select the ntmsdata directory and start a restore process. Backup will store the database files and set Removable Storage to run on the recovered database after the next service restart.

If you are not using Backup, you need to use other means to mount the media, restore the files, and recover the database. Most libraries have doors or front panels that you can use to mount media manually. Next, copy or restore the database files to disk. If Removable Storage is not running, you can copy the database files to a directory that holds the Removable Storage database (%SystemRoot%\system32\ntmsdata is the default directory). Then start Removable Storage. If you must have Removable Storage running while you are restoring the database files, copy or restore the database files to the directory \Export, which is a subdirectory of the one that contains the database, and run a utility that calls **ImportNtmsDatabase**. For more information about creating this utility, see the Microsoft Platform Software Development Kit (SDK) link on the Web Resources page at http://windows.microsoft.com/windows2000/reskit /webresources. For more information about recovering Removable Storage, see "Repair, Recovery, and Restore" in this book.

Updating the Restored Database

The recovered database might not be synchronized with the state of media when the database was lost. Table 2.7 describes some reasons why the Removable Storage database might not be synchronized and how Removable Storage-aware applications can resolve each problem.

Table 2.7   **Synchronizing Restored Database Files**

Problem	Solution
A medium is deallocated by an application after the backup but before the disaster and remains in the application media pool. Removable Storage recognizes this medium as allocated and puts it in the application media pool.	The application can deallocate this medium again.
A medium is allocated by an application after the backup but before the disaster. Removable Storage puts the medium in the import media pool.	The application can allocate this medium directly out of the import pool.

Note   An application can recover the Removable Storage database when it has been lost,there is no backup copy, and the application has not lost the database that refers to the lost Removable Storage database. This process requires significant knowledge on the part of the administrator of the application.

Using the Removable Storage Snap-in

The Removable Storage snap-in allows you to perform several tasks. The snap-in can be found beneath the storage node in the Computer Management snap-in. It can also be started directly from the command line, by running Ntmsmgr.msc.

Inserting and Ejecting Media

Removable Storage uses a library's IE port, if it has one, for inserting and ejecting media, or it uses the door. Selecting an insert task on a library with a door but no IE port results in the same behavior as if you selected a door access.

When using a door access to enter or remove media, make sure that you consult the property page for the library and the document for the changer to determine the proper slot numbers. Most changers label each slot clearly, but some do not.

Caution   If during a door access you exchange media in libraries without bar codes, you need to run a full inventory after completing the door access. The change is not detected by a fast inventory and an identity mismatch occurs the next time media in the slot is mounted.

Tables 2.8, 2.9, and 2.10 show the results of moving CD media, tape media, and optical/rewritable media among media pools.

Note Because CD media are read-only, Removable Storage does not allow each medium to be placed in the free pool.

CD media appear in the unrecognized pool only if they are formatted with a file system that Windows 2000 does not recognize.

Table 2.8   Moving CD Media Among Media Pools

From/To	Import Pool	Unrecognized Pool	Application Pool
Import		Not Allowed	OK
Unrecognized	Not Allowed		Not Allowed
Application	OK	Not allowed	

Table 2.9   Moving Tape Media Among Media Pools

From/To	Free Pool	Import Pool	Unrecognized Pool	Application Pool
Free		Not Allowed	Not Allowed	Retains Free Label until application writes new label.
Import	Write Free Label		Not Allowed	Not Allowed
Unrecognized	Write Free Label	Not Allowed		Not Allowed
Application	Write Free Label	Not Allowed	Not Allowed	Retains current Label

Table 2.10   Moving Optical/Rewritable Media Among Media Pools

From/To	Free Pool	Import Pool	Unrecognized Pool	Application Pool
Free		Not Allowed	Not Allowed	Retains Free Label until application writes new label.
Import	Write Free Label		Not Allowed	Retains label already on media.
Unrecognized	Write Free Label	Not Allowed		Not Allowed
Application	Write Free Label	Not Allowed	Not Allowed	Retains current Label. Both sides are moved.

Inventories

There are two types of inventories, fast and full. You can set which is to be used as the default inventory method in the **Library** property page in the Removable Storage snap-in.

A fast inventory only checks for slot state changes between full and empty. If the Removable Storage database indicates that a slot has a cartridge in it, but the fast inventory shows that it no longer has a cartridge, Removable Storage marks the cartridge that was in the slot as offline. If a slot was empty and is now full, Removable Storage identifies the cartridge in the slot. Slots that remain full are assumed to contain the same cartridge. Full inventory actually identifies each medium. This can take a while, unless the media has bar code labels. A full inventory of bar code–labeled media only reads the bar codes. Full inventories of media that are not bar coded read the on-media identifier on each medium in the library.

Cleaning Drives

Some drives, especially tape drives, require periodic cleaning. Usually there is a light on the front of the drive that indicates that a drive is dirty, and in this state most I/O operations fail. Under most circumstances a drive detects that it is dirty while a Removable Storage client application is running. How the client application handles this situation is typically described in the documentation for that application, but for some changers Removable Storage can automatically clean the drive for you after the application is finished using the drive.

In the Removable Storage model of device maintenance, each library unit can contain one cleaner cartridge. There is a wizard available through the snap-in, which you can use to insert a cleaning cartridge into each library that supports automatic cleaning.

Removable Storage maintains a usage count for each cleaner cartridge. When a cleaner reaches its maximum usage count, Removable Storage generates an operator request. If the administrator ejects a cleaner cartridge before it has reached its maximum usage count, Removable Storage displays the usage count information.

Caution Problems occur if Removable Storage attempts to identify a cleaning cartridge as a regular medium. Most drives treat cleaning cartridges differently from regular media, and this different behavior can result in Removable Storage error messages that might appear as if Removable Storage or the library is malfunctioning. Never start Removable Storage for the first time with a cleaning cartridge in the library, or attach a new library with a cleaning cartridge inside. In both these cases Removable Storage performs a full inventory of the library, which includes trying to identify each cartridge. In addition, never insert a cleaning cartridge using the same mechanism used for ordinary media. If there is any doubt about the Removable Storage database's consistency, please remove the cleaning cartridges from the attached libraries. These problems might appear if the database becomes inconsistent or is restored from an old backup.

Work Queue Items

You can use the property page about the work queue item to control how long completed and failed work queue items are retained. If you are having problems you might set the work queue to retain failed items so that you can investigate. The property page for each failed item shows the reason that it failed.

On startup you might see a number of canceled work queue items. When Removable Storage is shut down there might be work queue items still queued. These are canceled the next time Removable Storage starts up.

Operator Requests

Use the property page on the root node of the Removable Storage snap-in to set a method to receive notification of outstanding operator requests. The two available methods are Windows 2000 Messenger Service and a system tray icon. When the messenger service is selected, an application message appears whenever there is an operator request. Make sure that the Messenger Service is running if this option is selected, and then start the Removable Storage snap-in to view the operator request queue and determine what Removable Storage is asking you to do.

If the system tray method is selected, a system tray icon appears whenever there is an outstanding operator request. Clicking on the system tray icon displays a snap-in of operator requests, making it easier to mark them refused or complete. All operator requests must be completed or refused.

The property page of the operator request node in the Removable Storage snap-in lets you set how long to retain completed and failed (including canceled) operator requests. It also provides buttons that can be used to process deleted, completed, and failed operator requests immediately. The **Default** button deletes all requests specified by the controls on the properties sheet, while the **Delete all now** button deletes all completed and failed requests.

Library and Drive States

A library is online while it is operating and connected to the computer that is running Removable Storage. A library is not present if it is not operating or if it is disconnected from the computer. Both robotic and stand-alone libraries can be either online or not present. If a library is removed, the administrator must manually delete the library from Removable Storage. Removable Storage does not automatically delete libraries to avoid deleting information that might still be valuable if the library was disconnected inadvertently or temporarily.

Drives in offline libraries are offline, but media in offline libraries are considered online since they reside in a library. Offline media physical locations, then, are different from offline libraries.

Scripting

You can create command scripts to perform routine or automated activities using the Removable Storage command-line program Rsm.exe. You can use this program to have Removable Storage perform a number of activities, such as ejecting tapes, creating medial pools and so on.

Troubleshooting

Problems with Removable Storage can be caused by hardware or software. The information required to help you resolve either type of problem is contained in the following paragraphs.

Configuration

If you are having problems with Removable Storage correctly configuring your devices, please consult the HCL to make sure your device is supported. If it is, make sure you have configured the device according to the guidelines listed for your device on the HCL. Many changers support many operational configurations, while Removable Storage requires certain settings of these configurations.

Make sure that the hardware is configured correctly. If the device is attached to the host by means of a SCSI bus, ensure that the bus is configured correctly, with no SCSI ID collisions, with proper termination and in accordance with all cable length and SCSI controller parameters, and so on. IDE devices need to be properly configured as master or slave devices and the like.

If all the hardware is configured properly, make sure that Windows 2000 has found the devices and loaded the drivers for them. Make sure you should see your changer under **Media Changers** in the Device Manager, and any drives under **Disk drives** or **Tape drives**. If a driver is loaded, check the system Event Log to see if the driver encountered an error while initializing the device.

If all the devices are working properly, but Removable Storage is still unable to configure them automatically, try manually configuring the devices.

Operation

If you are getting failed work queue items, the property sheet gives a reason for the failure, which can help you diagnose the problem.

If your library is configured correctly but begins malfunctioning, the first place to look for the cause is the system log. Look for Removable Storage messages, but also look for change, drive, and controller error messages. If these devices are experiencing errors, take appropriate actions to clear the errors, such as power cycling or resetting the device.

Operations can begin failing if the system runs low on system resources, such as memory and disk space. You can determine if this is the case by checking the system Event Log.

If the devices and the rest of the system appear to be operating normally, stopping and restarting Removable Storage might clear problems.

If media that are associated with client applications known to Removable Storage are always placed in the unrecognized pool when inserted, or mount requests fail because of an OMID mismatch, the MLL might be missing or installed incorrectly. Information about MLLs is contained in the registry entry HKEY_LOCAL_MACHINE\SYSTEM\CurrentControlSet\Control\NTMS\OMID\Tape.

Typically, the directory %SystemRoot%\System32 contains all media label library DLLs and is accessible only by administrators.

Remote Storage

Remote Storage runs on computers running Windows 2000 Server. There are two layers to the storage hierarchy. The higher layer, local storage, is made up of the local NTFS volumes of the Windows 2000 file server hosting the Remote Storage software. NTFS volumes are managed at the root of the physical volume. The lower layer, remote storage, stores the data that has been copied from local storage.

Important   Remote Storage is available on computers running Windows 2000 Server. It is not part of Windows 2000 Professional.

Remote storage uses a single or multiple tape library. Within a single library, two drives at most are used at a particular time; one for managed data entering remote storage, and one for recalled data leaving remote storage.

Basic Concepts

Remote Storage manages data in local storage, moving less-used data to remote storage, making local storage available for new data. Remote Storage automatically manages the movement of data between local storage and remote storage according to administrator-defined guidelines set for each local storage volume. The administrator-defined guidelines consist of:

- Desired Free Space. The amount of free space specified to be kept on the managed volume.

- File Selection Criteria. Criteria that determine which data is eligible for movement to remote storage.

To prepare for the need to free space on local storage, Remote Storage regularly premigrates (copies) the unnamed data attribute of all eligible NTFS files on local storage to remote storage making these files premigrated files. The last access time of the file does not change when a file is premigrated. When free space on local storage is less than the Desired Free Space, premigrated files are automatically and immediately converted to placeholders until the desired amount of free space is available. A placeholder is an NTFS file which points to the copy of its unnamed data attribute in remote storage and has its unnamed data attribute truncated (removed) from local storage. The placeholder is marked with FILE_ATTRIBUTE_OFFLINE. Even though Remote Storage has changed the physical size of the file on local storage, the logical size and the date/time (create, last modified, last accessed) of the file remains unchanged. Users or applications (for example, disk quotas) that utilize file size are not affected by Remote Storage data migration. Users see all files regardless of storage location, as shown in Figure 2.5.

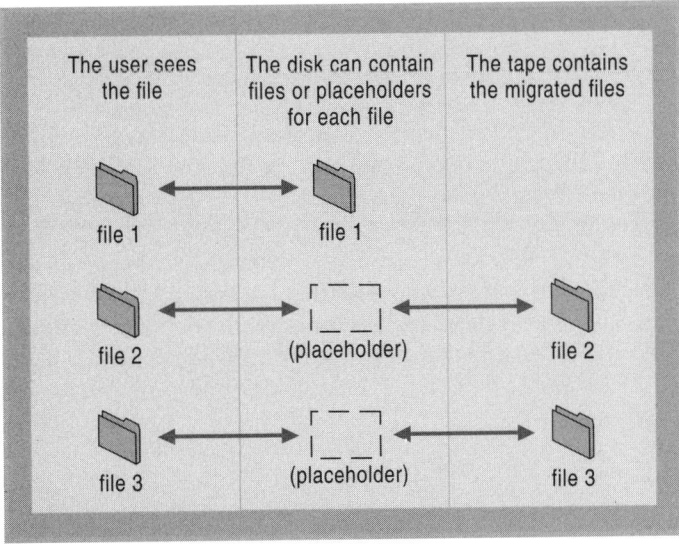

Figure 2.5   File Migration Representation

If a user or application reads, writes, or memory maps a placeholder that was opened using the normal NTFS open request (with no special flags), the unnamed data attribute of the file is automatically recalled from remote storage to local storage, returning this file to the premigrated file status, and the request completes. The latency of the first read, write, or memory map depends on the following criteria:

- The type of remote storage (random access or serial access).
- If remote storage is removable media, whether or not the media is mounted.
- The speed of the device accessing the data (drives or head speed).
- The availability of the devices in remote storage.
- Whether or not there is space to recall the file on local storage.

Notification can be issued to the user when the recall takes a while to complete. If remote storage is inaccessible, the open request fails.

Note FILE_FLAG_OPEN_NO_RECALL is a new flag supported for Windows 2000. If the open request is issued with the new FILE_FLAG_OPEN_NO_RECALL flag, the requested amount of data is read and cached internally and returned to the caller. However, the file remains truncated. The file is read-only, and the data is placed directly into the read buffer, bypassing local storage. The file remains truncated.

If the open request is issued with the FILE_FLAG_BACKUP_SEMANTICS flag, the unnamed data attribute of the file is not recalled. This allows backup programs prior to Windows 2000 to interact with Remote Storage. FILE_FLAG_OPEN_ NO_RECALL is added for the legacy backup programs so that the file can be backed up without being recalled.

If you do not want legacy backup applications to back up Remote Storage files, you can set the registry value HKEY_LOCAL_MACHINE\SYSTEM \CurrentControlSet\Services\RSFilter\Parameters\SkipFilesForLegacyBackup to 1. Restarting or stopping and starting Remote Storage is required for this change to take effect.

Placeholders and premigrated files can be renamed without affecting the management of the data. When placeholders or premigrated files are copied, the file is recalled and the entire file contents are copied to the new file. The original file remains a premigrated file, while the new file is neither a placeholder nor a premigrated file.

Remote Storage provides disaster prevention and recovery features, including:

- The ability to generate multiple media copies of removable media.
- The ability to replace damaged removable media while Remote Storage is running.
- The ability to recover from loss of Remote Storage metadata.

Remote Storage interfaces are integrated with Windows 2000 Explorer and the Disk Management snap-in. The Remote Storage snap-in allows an administrator to:

- Allocate and configure Remote Storage remote storage devices and media.
- Set Remote Storage systemwide feature options.
- Configure Disk Management settings for Remote Storage–managed volumes.
- View information about Remote Storage activity.
- Recover from media disasters.
- Create and submit jobs.

Remote Storage restricts the number of data paths accessing remote storage. Objects are copied into remote storage using one data path while objects are recalled to local storage using the second data path. Data might be entering and leaving remote storage at the same time, but multiple data paths in the same direction are not allowed.

Note The maximum size of data managed is equal to the amount of media within a storage pool.

The minimum size of managed data is the size which results in space being reclaimed in local storage. This is equal to the amount of space used in the master file table (MFT) record for the file to hold the placeholder data.

Benefits

Remote Storage provides the following benefits to its users:

- A virtual expansion of local storage space using lower cost remote storage.
- Transparent automatic access to data in remote storage.
- Automation of the labor-intensive overhead associated with daily manual data management operations.
- Centralized sharing of remote storage for multiple volumes.

- Integration with the following features of the Windows 2000 operating system:
    - MMC interface
    - Windows 2000 Explorer
    - Windows 2000 Disk Management
    - Event logs
    - Windows 2000 Security
    - NTFS
    - Job Scheduler
    - Microsoft® Systems Management Server
    - Active Directory™ directory service
    - Indexing Services

Local Storage Management

Remote Storage manages NTFS volumes on a computer that is running Windows 2000 Server. Remote Storage does not support clustering.

Remote Storage manages free space on a logical volume. Management begins at the root of the physical volume.

NTFS volumes that reside on removable media can be managed. However, the placeholders on the removable media are not recallable if the volume is plugged into any computer other than the original computer being managed.

Disk Management Attribute

Remote Storage provides a single, system wide, Desired Free Space setting that can be applied to each managed volume. This setting establishes a threshold that triggers an automatic file truncation to free storage on the managed volume when free space is too low. The Desired Free Space setting can be specified by the administrator.

When you initially configure the Desired Free Space for a new managed volume, a reasonable predetermined default value is displayed. Separate from the default value, the system allows an administrator to set a new Desired Free Space for several different managed volumes all at the same time.

The single, system wide, Disk Management attribute is used for truncating premigrated files. The Disk Management attribute is not used to determine how much data is premigrated at a time.

Files are selected for Remote Storage based on the following criteria:

- Path name.
- File names, including wildcard characters in names.
- Inclusion or exclusion of specifications.

The following criteria can be applied to an entire volume but not at an individual file level:

- Last access date or inactivity period
- Owner
- File size
- System and hidden files

By default, the Windows 2000 system files or any files marked with the system attribute are excluded from premigration by Remote Storage.

The administrator uses these criteria to specify the eligible files. The inclusion and exclusion rules are applied such that the more specific a rule is to a file, the higher its priority. For example, the rules of "Exclude *.*" and "Include \PROG*.EXE" causes the file "\Prog\Test.exe" to be included and "\Test.exe" to be excluded.

The implementation of the selection criteria decision engine is extensible using a Component Object Model (COM) interface, so that it can be enhanced in the future and can allow user modifications.

Manage Files

The administrator schedules the management of files based on the specified file selection criteria. All files which meet the criteria are premigrated. The Desired Free Space is not used to determine how many files to premigrate. Premigrated files are tracked to allow rapid file truncation.

Even though Remote Storage changes the physical size of the file on local storage, the logical size and the date/time (create, last modified, last accessed) of the file remains unchanged.

Remove Volume From Management

This action removes the volume from management, and can optionally recall all files from Remote Storage.

Automatic File Truncation

Remote Storage initiates Automatic File Truncation whenever a managed volume's free space level is less than the Desired Free Space. Eligible premigrated files are truncated to free space on local storage. The premigrated files are quickly identified and truncated, based on the last access date. If the premigrated file has not been modified, then the file is truncated and becomes a placeholder. If the premigrated file has been modified, the file is not considered premigrated any longer and is returned to "normal file" status. Additionally, the capacity flow meter is decremented and the data for the premigrated file in remote storage is marked as "deleted" to facilitate space reclamation. Reclamation is the process of deleting from the Remote Storage media pool files that are no longer of interest or are no longer necessary, thereby making that storage space available for reuse.

The automatic file truncation continues until the free space on the volume is greater than the Desired Free Space.

Scheduled File Truncation

Scheduled File Truncation can be scheduled by the administrator to force the truncation of premigrated files to placeholders. The premigrated files that meet the selection criteria are truncated regardless of the free space level of the volume. Premigrated files are checked to make sure that they have not been modified since they were premigrated. If the premigrated file has been modified, then the file is not considered premigrated and the file is returned to "normal file" status. Additionally, the data for the premigrated file in remote storage is marked as "deleted" to facilitate space reclamation.

This action allows proactive space management by an administrator. The action can be scheduled to reduce volume usage in advance of a known volume-intensive event, such as the installation of a very large application.

Validate Managed Files

Validate Managed Files can be scheduled by the administrator to validate placeholders and premigrated files that meet the selection criteria. Validation includes detecting placeholders moved among volumes, disconnected placeholders and modified premigrated files. Corrective actions are taken immediately to synchronize the placeholders and premigrated files with remote storage.

Validate Managed Files is used after restoring files to a volume or after disk errors on a volume. It can be scheduled to run on a regular basis (once a month) to validate the local storage and correct any inconsistencies.

Note   Recalls are logged in the Windows 2000 Event Log.

Local Storage

The unnamed data attribute of an NTFS file has the information being tracked by NTFS that is needed to manage the data. The modification time, logical size, physical size, and access time of the file are all kept relative to the unnamed data attribute. The modification time and logical file size are never changed for the file even when it is a placeholder.

First Read, Write, and Memory Map

The file is recalled if necessary on the first read, write, or memory map request. If the data is in remote storage but is not in the library, the recall does not succeed. Automatic recall of data that is not in the library is not available and fails with the message STATUS_FILE_IS_OFFLINE. The administrator needs to manually insert the media into the library and then try the recall again.

If a request is made against a premigrated file, it is not affected by Remote Storage. The data for the file exists locally on the NTFS volume and is accessed normally.

The client making the request on the server might time out. Client computers have their own configured time-out which is independent of Remote Storage, and if recalling the data takes longer than the time-out, the input/output request fails on the client. In Windows 2000, the time-out for accessing off-line Remote Storage files is 15 minutes.

Note   Changing attributes or ACLs or named streams in a file does not recall the file.

NTFS "File Open"

By default, when a placeholder is opened on an NTFS volume, the data is copied directly from remote storage to local storage and the file is considered a premigrated file. The last access time of the file is changed. Specific error cases arise because of the state of the system or the location of the data in remote storage. When the data cannot be brought back to local storage, the open request *always* fails with the message STATUS_FILE_IS_OFFLINE.

The FILE_FLAG_OPEN_NO_RECALL flag is honored if the file is opened for read access only, or if the open fails.

If the open request is made with the FILE_FLAG_OPEN_NO_RECALL flag the data is recalled at read time, cached, and placed directly into the application's read buffer. This allows backup systems to get an image of the file that appears (and restores) as a premigrated file but that was not recalled by the backup application.

Note The migrated data appears only briefly and is not actually copied to local disk storage.

Runaway Recall Detection and Prevention

Runaway recalls can be prevented by specifying that no more than a certain number of files can be recalled by a user from a volume in an hour. This is an administrator-defined setting, both in terms of enabling or disabling the feature, and in specifying the number of recall requests that are handled in a particular period of time.

Administrators can select exemption from any recall limit.

Deletion of a Premigrated File or Placeholder

No action is taken upon the deletion of a placeholder or premigrated file. It is not possible to synchronously determine when a file is going to be deleted.

Renaming, Moving, or Copying Placeholders and Premigrated Files

Files cannot be renamed across volume boundaries. Placeholders and premigrated files can be renamed only on the same volume. Renaming a file does not cause the data in remote storage to be recalled. Truncation and recall of these files are not affected.

Copying or moving placeholders between volumes causes the data to be recalled and the entire file, including all migrated data, is copied. At the end of a move operation the original placeholder file is deleted. Copying a file has the same behavior within a volume or across volumes. Moving placeholders on the same volume is a rename operation.

A placeholder can be moved to another volume within the same system by using Backup to back up and restore the placeholder to another volume. In this case, the moved placeholder points to remote storage and is valid to initiate a recall. A user-defined action to validate placeholders corrects any potential inconsistencies between the placeholder and remote storage. Even without the validation of a placeholder, opening the moved placeholder recalls the correct data; however, a volume decommission does not work properly.

Table 2.11 summarizes the results of the specific actions when the destination of the action is the same or a different volume.

Table 2.11   Results of Premigrated File Actions

Action	Destination Same Volume	Destination Different Volume
Copy File	Recall	Recall
Cut File	Recall and delete original	Recall and delete original
Move File	No Recall (is a Rename)	Recall and delete original
Rename File	No Recall	N/A

Volume Decommission

When a managed volume is decommissioned, the physical volume is not accessible. All information needed to decommission the volume is already known. Any data associated with the volume that is in remote storage is treated as available during space reclamation.

If placeholders are moved between volumes, the placeholders must be validated so that correct volume information is known about the placeholders. If the placeholders have not been validated, the volume decommissioning can cause incorrect data within remote storage to be treated as available during space reclamation. For more information about validating volumes, see "Local Storage Management" earlier in this chapter.

Restoring Placeholders from Backup and Disconnected Placeholders

A primary storage backup application, such as Backup, protects placeholders. If the placeholder is deleted, lost, or destroyed the only recourse is to retrieve a copy from the backup media. This is the same mechanism that must be used if any other file on the volume is deleted, lost, or destroyed.

The data in remote storage is accessible only through a placeholder. If the placeholder is deleted, that data is inaccessible. If a placeholder is restored from backup, the placeholder is reconnected to that data.

Disconnected placeholders are placeholders whose file contents have been removed from remote storage. These placeholders might have been restored from backup after the space in remote storage was reclaimed or the data within remote storage might be physically unavailable because of media failures. Disconnected placeholders do not point to valid locations in remote storage and are cleaned up by validating placeholders. If the placeholders are disconnected, they are removed from the system to synchronize the remaining placeholders with remote storage.

Interaction with other Reparse Point Types

Volume mount points and symbolic links cannot be changed into placeholders. The system explicitly ignores these types of files.

Any file system scan that encounters a mount point or symbolic link does not follow the link: physical volume space is the scarce resource and mount points and symbolic links are virtual concepts that extend the directory view.

Placeholders Binding to a Specific Remote Storage

Placeholders identify the specific remote storage system which contains the managed data, tying a placeholder to a specific Remote Storage Engine. Placeholders cannot be moved between multiple remote storage systems.

Windows 2000 Security Integration

Remote Storage supports NTFS security features. Remote Storage only recalls files if the user has valid access to a placeholder. A placeholder is identified as a special remote storage reparse point. The security of the placeholder is determined by the security of the reparse point mechanism.

Administrators and regular users go through normal Windows 2000 user security checks. The Remote Storage Administrative user interface uses Windows 2000 permissions to grant or deny access to the user interface. Only user accounts in the Administrators group are allowed access to the user interface functions.

File Collocation

Files are grouped together by their volume and by the time that they were originally premigrated. The files remain grouped during all remote storage operations. No other grouping of files is supported.

Replication

Files that are being replicated can be excluded from the Manage Files action by the administrator using the file selection criteria.

Remote Storage Engine

Remote storage is the part of the system that holds the copies of the data. The Remote Storage Engine consists of the media used to store the data, libraries, and drives.

The Remote Storage Engine service runs on computers that are running Windows 2000 Server. Only one Remote Storage Engine can exist on a server. The Remote Storage Engine does not run on Windows 2000 Professional.

Flow Meter Capacity Metric

Remote Storage maintains a flow meter capacity metric monitoring the amount of data that is contained in remote storage, including overflowed and shelved data. Copying data from local storage to remote storage increases the value of the capacity metric. Removing local storage references to data in remote storage decreases the value of the capacity metric. The change in the capacity metric is immediate, but some operations are not immediately detected.

Remote Storage increments the value of the flow meter capacity metric whenever one of the following occurs:

- A new file is managed.
- A previously deleted placeholder is restored to a volume and reconnected to remote storage.

Remote Storage decrements the value of the flow meter capacity metric whenever one of the following occurs:

- A premigrated file is modified.
- A placeholder or premigrated file is deleted.
- A file is unmanaged.

There might be a latency associated with the decrementing of the flow meter capacity metric since the detection of these conditions can happen at a later time.

Storage Pool

All remote storage in Remote Storage exists in a single storage pool: there is no storage pool management required.

Relocation is the movement of data from one remote storage pool to another. Since Remote Storage only supports a single remote storage pool, relocation is not supported in Remote Storage.

Remote Storage supports one storage library within the single tape storage pool. The library must have at least one drive, and two or more drives to support media copies. When multiple drives exist within a library, all drives must be identical in type (for example, density or firmware).

Handling of Physically Full Remote Storage

Remote Storage provides the following options for handling physically full remote storage situations:

- Stop managing new files. Remote Storage becomes a recall-only system; this mode is invoked only after any possible space reclamation is performed.
- Shelf Storage. Remote Storage cycles removable media to "shelf"; recalls of files stored on shelved media require administrator interaction.

Remote storage is considered full either when there is not enough scratch media or when the scratch media are not online. In either case, the administrator must provide manual intervention.

A notice is issued when physical remote storage utilization reaches the administrator-defined warning level.

Shelf Media

Shelf media for Remote Storage are media that are not currently accessible by the system. The medium with the data on it can be removed from the device and the media management subsystem tracks its location. Shelf media allow a system to have more data in remote storage than the device can physically contain.

For removable media, the administrator can remove media and optionally replace them with blank media. Remote Storage continues to premigrate data using the new media, and the removed media are considered shelf media. If a user needs access to data on shelf media, the administrator must place the shelf media in the library, and the new media become shelf media. Media do not need to be full to be shelf media.

Media Status and Location

When a medium is marked as having errors, the administrator is notified of the reason for the status change; the information is also kept in the Windows 2000 Event Log for later reference.

Media within a library are not tied to specific locations or slots. The system adjusts to media being in different locations, so media can be shuffled in a library.

Upgrading Remote Storage Libraries

Removable Storage provides Remote Storage with the ability to replace a library with another library containing identical media and data read/write mechanisms. The administrator must physically move the media from the old library to the new library, that is, physically replace the library, and then use the user interface to register configuration changes within Remote Storage.

Remote Storage Device Support

Remote Storage supports all 4mm, 8mm, and DLT tape devices supported by Removable Storage. Because Remote Storage supports only a single media type, a device cannot be a mixed media device.

Kernel-Level Drivers

Remote Storage utilizes Windows 2000 kernel-level drivers to support the management of tape devices. The Microsoft Certified device drivers provide the backbone of device support for Remote Storage.

Sharing Libraries with External Applications

Remote Storage cooperatively shares storage libraries with external applications using a common media management facility such as Removable Storage. A simple media management facility exists within Remote Storage that is usable by other applications.

Minimally, Remote Storage supports nonconcurrent library sharing with external applications. Specific device slots can be designated as in use by an external application.

User Interfaces

The Remote Storage snap-in presents a hierarchical view of the Remote Storage system. Each node in the hierarchy represents a different component of the Remote Storage system. This allows the system administrator to configure the components of the Remote Storage by invoking their corresponding configuration screens or property sheets.

The top level component of the Remote Storage hierarchy is the Windows 2000 Server hosting remote storage. All other components in the Remote Storage snap-in are descendants of the Windows 2000 Server hosting remote storage.

The Remote Storage user interface (UI) is comprised of four parts: the Remote Storage Administrative user interface; the Recall Notification user interface; Windows Explorer integration; and Disk Management integration. The Remote Storage snap-in runs on Windows 2000 Server and Windows 2000 Professional. The nonadministrative UIs (Recall Notification, Windows Explorer integration, and Disk Management integration) run on the same platforms.

Remote Storage Snap-in

The Remote Storage snap-in provides the following components:

- Snap-in registration and initialization
- Namespace node enumeration
- Command architecture action enumeration
- Toolbar and toolbar button enumeration
- Menu and menu item enumeration
- Drag-and-drop registration and negotiation
- Persistent storage handling

The characteristics of the Remote Storage snap-in include the following:

- A two-paned representation of the system in which the console tree contains a hierarchical view of the objects in an administered system, and the right view contains information, properties, and images describing the objects.
- Easy access to frequently used features; features used less often don't clutter the interface.
- Direct manipulation of objects (drag-and-drop, inserting, deleting with single keystrokes, or mouse movements).
- Use of visual metaphors: similar actions have similar interfaces.
- Minimal intervention by the administrator when the Remote Storage is behaving correctly. However, when a problem arises, the Remote Storage snap-in provides very clear and unambiguous notification of the problem.
- All administrative functionality housed in the user interface. No separate, stand-alone administrative utilities exist, although distributed end-user user interface tools exist outside the Remote Storage snap-in.
- Integration of system configuration and monitoring in a single tool.

Recall Notification

On Windows 2000 recall notification can monitor currently active client initiated recalls. The name of the file is shown to the user when a recall is in progress.

This application allows the administrator to cancel the recall. This has the effect of freeing the application (the read, write, or memory map request fails) but, if data transfer has started, the file is still recalled.

Windows Explorer Integration

Placeholders in Windows Explorer are visually different from normal (untruncated) files, but premigrated files appear the same as normal files. Remote Storage integration with Windows Explorer requires adding a new property page to both the file and directory property sheets (accessible through Windows Explorer) to represent storage management properties. The new storage management pages provide information on migration status, premigrated file data location in remote storage, premigrated date and time, and possibly other relevant information. Users have read-only access to the new Remote Storage property pages, though they can force immediate premigration of individual files or entire directories by setting a **Premigrate Now** option on the Remote Storage page.

Specific integration areas include (in order of priority):

1. Windows Explorer does not open the unnamed data stream of placeholder files unless the user needs access to the file data. For less essential tasks, such as showing the icon in the file list, Windows Explorer must use a default icon or an alternative storage location.

2. Windows Explorer must preserve the last access date when a file is opened for behind-the-scenes use (for example, preserving the last access date when searching files for content indexing or when finding a string to satisfy a user query).

3. Content indexing or search operations needs to skip placeholders unless the user has been made aware of the consequences (such as the extended wait to fetch the data from remote storage) and wants to proceed. If the search includes placeholders, use FILE_OPEN_NO_RECALL on the open request. This open mode allows the file to be read without recalling it to primary storage.

4. When a list of files is displayed, the application needs to indicate which files are placeholders.

5. When showing file properties, those that are contained in the unnamed data stream are not be shown by default if the file is a placeholder. When the file is a placeholder, the user is alerted to this fact and made to take extra steps to retrieve this information.

6. Defer the read, write, or memory map of a placeholder until the last moment to avoid unnecessary recall in case the user aborts the operation. For example, do not open the file when Copy or Cut is selected; wait until the Paste operation is performed.

Remote Storage introduces a new property page into the property sheet for managed volumes, which shows statistics and graphics indicating the amount of free space, used space, space taken up by placeholders, and a representation of how much virtual disk space the placeholders represent.

Disk Management Integration

Windows 2000 Disk Management allows the user to bring up a property sheet for each volume on a computer. This property sheet is the same property sheet accessible through My Computer. The Remote Storage property sheet shows total used space, free space, premigrated file space, truncated files (placeholders), untruncated file disk usage, premigration space savings, truncated file compression ratio, percent of files that are placeholders, and other volume report information. The property sheet used by Windows 2000 Disk Management (and by My Computer) is Remote Storage–aware, but the Remote Storage snap-in is not required to use Disk Management.

Miscellaneous Windows 2000 Shell Integration

In addition to integration with Windows Explorer and the Windows 2000 Disk Management snap-in, the Remote Storage snap-in also integrates with the Windows 2000 shell in the following ways:

- Major Remote Storage system events are logged with and reported from the Windows 2000 Event Log.

- Controls, dialogs, and property pages are consistent with Microsoft® Windows® 95 and Microsoft® Windows® 98.

Local Storage Configuration and Management

Remote Storage supports the configuration and management of volumes for local storage. Volumes can be managed individually or in groups.

Disk Management (All Volumes Being Managed)

Disk Management, a subfolder of Remote Storage Computer in the snap-in, deals with the administration and configuration of all managed volumes.

Single Managed Volume

Individual managed volumes are controlled at the Disk Management level.

Directories and Files on a Single Managed Volume

Inside each managed volume are directories and files. Placeholders are shown differently from normal, untruncated files. If you are viewing the file in Windows Explorer, it appears with an overlay icon. From the command prompt, the **Dir** command displays the file size in parentheses.

Single Unmanaged Volume

The administrator has configuration control over volumes that have Remote Storage installed, but which are not currently managed by Remote Storage. Although a volume might not be currently managed, it can still have placeholders on it that can be recalled.

Local Storage Management Monitoring

Remote Storage supports the monitoring of local storage system activity by means of the Remote Storage snap-in. This monitoring occurs at the Disk Management level, the single managed volume level, for directories and files on a single managed volume, and for single unmanaged volumes.

Remote Storage Configuration and Management

Remote storage administration involves managing and configuring the storage devices and media that make up remote storage. The ability to configure and manage remote storage requires administrator privileges.

Remote Storage Management Monitoring

Remote Storage supports monitoring remote storage system activity by means of the Remote Storage snap-in. This monitoring occurs at the overall remote storage level and the volume level or libraries level.

Job Management and Monitoring

The Remote Storage snap-in provides wizards to create and define jobs.

The Remote Storage snap-in provides monitoring of jobs currently running in the system. This provides visual feedback of current system activity. All currently running jobs can be viewed in one monitor screen.

Setup, Installation, and License Management

System installation and setup are integrated with Microsoft® BackOffice® setup and license management. Remote Storage provides Systems Management Server extensions to improve distributed administration. The installation procedure provides an acceptable default configuration of the Remote Storage system that can be run in batch or interactive mode. The installation addresses the following areas:

- Provides instructions and warnings on how the installation proceeds.
- Explains license agreement.
- Gathers user information (such as name and company).
- Allows installer to select components to install.
- Allows installer to specify location of Remote Storage server, UI administration tool, and other tools.
- Selects premigrate volumes.
- Selects media copying policy.

- Selects program folder.
- Copies files and installing, setting up the registry, and performing other tasks.
- Sets up licensing defaults.
- Reboots the system, if desired.

Remote Storage and Windows 2000

Remote Storage is integrated closely with Windows 2000. Table 2.12 provides details of this integration and describes the interfaces between Remote Storage and Windows 2000.

Table 2.12   Remote Storage and Windows 2000 Integration

Interface	Description
Placeholder format and reparse points	A placeholder has the system-defined $REPARSE_POINT attribute set with information that can identify and retrieve the unnamed data attribute from remote storage. The unnamed data attribute is in remote storage and its length is zero bytes. The reparse point type is Remote Storage.
	The recall mechanism is based on the reparse point being identified by NTFS and is an efficient mechanism that uses this information when recalling a file.
File size of a placeholder	The logical file size of the unnamed data attribute of a placeholder is the size of the unnamed data attribute as it was before it was truncated. The physical size of the unnamed data attribute of a placeholder is zero bytes.
Disk quotas and remote storage	Disk quotas do not change. Disk quotas are based on the logical file size which is not changed by Remote Storage, therefore the amount of space in use on a volume is not reduced or changed by having data in remote storage.
Remote Storage stage change	Remote Storage supports a Distributed Component Object Model (DCOM) interface–based mechanism that can change the system status.
Event Log usage	Major Remote Storage system events are logged in the Windows 2000 Event Log. The Windows 2000 Event Viewer is used to see the logged events.
	The following events are optionally logged in the Windows 2000 Event Log: • Files being recalled • Files being managed • Files being truncated • Media being mounted • Jobs being run • Files being scanned

(continued)

Table 2.12   Remote Storage and Windows 2000 Integration   *(continued)*

Interface	Description
Windows 2000 Job Scheduler	Remote Storage uses the Windows 2000 Job Scheduler to schedule Remote Storage jobs. Job status can be monitored from within the Remote Storage snap-in.
	Depending on the Job Scheduler, a job window can be specified that limits the amount of time spent in a single scan. This is useful because the system might have a large amount of data to manage and the scan might initially take too much time. A bookmark is kept where the scan stopped so the scan can continue from that point the next time it is run.
Windows 2000 registry usage	Remote Storage uses the registry to keep persistent information about startup, including the programs needed to initialize setup.
Windows 2000 client time-out on recall	The registry entry HKEY_LOCAL_MACHINE\SYSTEM \CurrentControlSet\Services\LanmanWorkstation\parameters \OfflineFileTimeOutIntervalInSeconds controls the time-out period that the client uses when sending requests to a server. The default is value is 900 (or 15 minutes). You can increase this value on all Windows 2000 clients that open files on the volumes managed by Remote Storage.

Multiple Remote Storage Interactions

A Remote Storage installation is limited to a single system running Windows 2000 Server in terms of hosting, Disk Management, and Remote Storage. There is no limit, however, to the number of stand-alone Remote Storage instances that can run on a homogeneous Windows 2000 network.

Moving Data Between Instances of Remote Storage to Another Remote Storage

To move managed data from one Remote Storage installation to another, the administrator recalls managed data and moves the data to another volume managed by Remote Storage that manages the data.

Recalling Across Remote Storage Instances

Remote Storage does not support recalling placeholders from a volume which has been managed at different times by two different Remote Storage instances.

Version Compatibility

Remote Storage does not provide an upgrade path for those running third-party remote storage products. Remote Storage provides a subset of features provided in previous remote storage products and is therefore not sufficient for upgrading the system. For example, an existing system with more than one device cannot upgrade to Remote Storage.

Remote Storage–Aware Products

Because Remote Storage manages data transparently for applications and users, there is no absolute requirement that other applications running on NTFS be Remote Storage–aware, that they contain specific code to recognize that Remote Storage is running. However, products that regularly open many files might cause a great deal of data to be recalled and reduce the benefits provided by Remote Storage. For best results, use Remote Storage-aware applications.

Important Although the features included with Windows 2000 are Remote Storage–aware, many other applications are not and may result in time-outs or runaway recalls. In all cases, it is best to check with your ISV to see if they provide a version that is Remote Storage-aware.

Backup Programs

A Remote Storage–aware backup product must have the following abilities:

- A guarantee that a full backup of the file is kept. The backup product must understand the difference between backing up the placeholder and the full data of the file, and must keep the full backup copy.

- Backup a placeholder (reparse point) correctly.

- Use of the FILE_FLAG_OPEN_BACKUP_SEMANTICS parameter when opening a file to back it up.

- Understanding and proper use of FILE_FLAG_OPEN_NO_RECALL.

Backup applications that open placeholders to read and copy without using the FILE_FLAG_OPEN_BACKUP_SEMANTICS parameter cause the data for the file to be recalled. If these products are performing a full system backup, all placeholders are replaced with recalled data.

Remote Storage relies on the primary backup to protect placeholder data. The administrator must be aware of when placeholder backups occur. Specifically, if the backup rotations are used, the administrator must know when the primary backup databases contain a complete copy of the data and when they contain placeholder data.

Backup applications that are Backup-enabled protect placeholder data and do not cause recalls.

Antivirus Programs

Antivirus programs typically open files to check for infection by viruses. These products cause migrated data to be recalled. Remote Storage–aware antivirus programs can operate in one of the following manners:

- Detect placeholders and skip the check on such files. This assumes that the data was checked by the scanner before being premigrated. This might be risky since Remote Storage manages the unnamed data stream and does not manage named data streams. Since data in remote storage remains unchanged, the check for a virus is unnecessary.

- Open the file with the FILE_OPEN_NO_RECALL parameter. This allows the scanner to check the unnamed data stream using local storage without recalling the data. This assumes a linear search of the file data, which might not always be the case.

- Don't update the last access date/time.

Document Management Programs

Many document management products open the data that they are managing, scan for key data, and then store references in additional files or alternate data streams leaving the original data unchanged. A document management product that is Remote Storage–aware opens placeholders with the FILE_OPEN_NO_RECALL parameter allowing the migrated unnamed data to be read but not recalled.

In addition, once the index files are generated, some document management products provide a file viewer much like Windows Explorer. As a Remote Storage-unaware product opens each file, it experiences synchronous recalls of each file and any associated delay. The Remote Storage-aware product indicates which files are migrated, and allows the user to issue asynchronous recalls of the data, while exhibiting improved performance.

Policies for managing files of the document management system exclude index files and other special files so they are quickly accessible to the document management system.

Note The Indexing Service that is included with Windows 2000 is Remote Storage-aware.

Remote Storage Protection and Recovery

Media in remote storage are copied to protect data. Copies are updated as the original media are updated to ensure that a current backup of data is available. For more information about recovering data from Remote Storage, see "Repair, Recovery, and Restore" in this book.

Remote Storage Media Copies

Remote storage media (tape cartridges) are protected by media copies. Media copies are replicas that can be substituted for the original media. Data is migrated only to the original media, but can be recalled from an original or a copy. Copies are made before the original media are completely filled and are updated as the original is updated. When a media copy is completed, it can be removed from the library located with other media in the copy set, and a new media copy is started. Media copies are only created if two or more drives are available to Remote Storage in the library. Other media must be protected by outside sources. Replacing an original with a copy requires administrator intervention. Media copies can be uniquely identified.

When a media copy is used to replace damaged or lost remote storage media, Remote Storage automatically replicates the media again to ensure copy set completeness.

Partial media copies are made by the system to protect the data. These partial copies can be removed from the library and are updated when reinserted in the library. If the source of the media copy is on the shelf, the source media must be reinserted in the library for the completion of the media copy.

Remote Storage Media Copy Sets and Set Rotation

As many as three copy sets of remote storage media are supported. Media for the additional sets can be moved to shelf storage when they are in synch. The administrator can view the status of media copies.

Media for Media Copies

For tape libraries having two or more drives available to Remote Storage, scratch media are used for making a media copy. An administrator can remove the updated media copies on a certain day after several new media copies have been made. This is especially useful for a weekend, during vacations, or initial startup. Once a copy is started, it must be returned to the library to be updated.

Remote Storage Metadata Protection

Remote Storage metadata exists in files which can be protected by the Windows 2000 primary backup system. Only the account used by Remote Storage has access to the metadata, by using Windows 2000 file security. Any operations requiring multiple metadata updates are transactional.

Metadata protection is provided by the Microsoft® Jet database.

Disk Management

Disk Management in Windows 2000 is responsible for creating, deleting, altering, and maintaining storage volumes in a system. Windows 2000 features significant improved manageability and recoverability of volumes in a Windows 2000 environment. This is achieved by the introduction of dynamic disks and a new snap-in. Windows 2000 supports two volume managers: basic disks and legacy Ftdisk volume sets are managed by FTDisk and the Ftdisk.sys driver; dynamic disks and all new volume sets are managed by Logical Disk Manager (LDM) and the Dmio.sys driver. Figure 2.6 shows the Disk Management architecture.

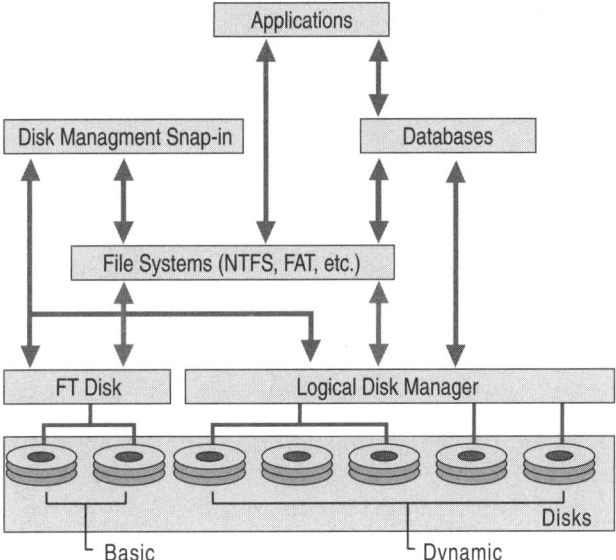

Figure 2.6   Disk Management Architecture

Important   Unlike in Microsoft® Windows NT® version 4.0 and earlier, volume set configuration metadata is stored and replicated with other Disk Management metadata and is not stored in the registry.

Fault-Tolerant Disk Management

Ftdisk was used in Windows NT to manage partitions and all fault-tolerant volumes. In Windows 2000, FTDisk is used to manage basic partitions and fault-tolerant volumes from Windows NT 4.0.

Ftdisk manages basic disks. Basic disks can be partitioned with and recognized by Microsoft® MS-DOS®, Windows 95, Windows 98, and Windows NT. A basic partition does not provide fault tolerance or multiple disk volume functionality. Basic partition configuration is recorded in a few kilobytes of data at the beginning of the disk. Existing fault-tolerant volumes (Ftdisk sets) configured on Windows NT 4.0 can still be used on computers running Windows 2000 or converted to dynamic volumes.

Dynamic Disks

As shown in Figure 2.6, Logical Disk Manager manages dynamic disks, which can only be used on Windows 2000. Dynamic disk configuration uses a private database at the end of the disk in addition to the same kilobytes at the beginning of the disk that are used by basic disks. Any disk containing a volume managed by Disk Management contains this database. The database is replicated among all dynamic disks in the system. Dynamic disks can contain simple volumes, concatenated volumes, stripe volumes, mirrored volumes, and redundant array of independent disks (RAID) level 5 volumes. Dynamic volumes offer features, such as volume extension and fault tolerance configurations. Disk Management user interfaces, such as the Disk Management snap-in included with Windows 2000, interact with both Ftdisk and Disk Management functionality.

For more information about basic and dynamic disks, see "Disk Concepts and Troubleshooting" in this book.

Disk Quotas

Windows 2000 supports disk quotas for volumes formatted as NTFS. You can use disk quotas to monitor and limit disk-space use.

Disk quotas are tracked on a per-user, per-volume basis, and users are charged *only* for the files they own. Quotas are tracked independently for different volumes, even if the volumes are different partitions on the same physical drive. However, if you have shares on the *same* volume, the quotas assigned to that volume apply to all of these shares collectively, and users' utilization of both shares cannot exceed the assigned quota on that volume.

System administrators can use the **Quota** tab of the **Properties** dialog box to perform the following tasks:

- Enable or disable disk quotas on a volume.
- Prevent users from saving new data when their disk quota is exceeded.
- Set the default disk quota warning level and disk quota limit assigned to new volume users.
- View disk quota information for each user using the **Quota Entries** view.

Disk quotas track and control disk space usage for volumes. System administrators can configure Windows 2000 to perform the following tasks:

- Prevent further disk space use and log an event when a user exceeds a specified disk space limit.
- Log an event when a user exceeds a specified disk space warning level.

When you enable disk quotas, you can set both the disk quota limit and the disk quota warning level. The limit specifies the amount of disk space that is allocated to a user. The warning level specifies when a user is nearing the limit. For example, you can set a user's disk quota limit to 50 megabytes (MB), and the disk quota warning level to 45 MB. The user can store no more than 50 MB of data on the volume, and if more than 45 MB are stored on the volume, you can have the disk quota system log a system event.

When you enable disk quotas for a volume, volume usage is automatically tracked for new users, but existing volume users have no disk quotas applied to them. You can apply disk quotas to existing volume users by adding new quota entries in the **Quota Entries** window.

For more information about setting disk quotas, see Windows 2000 Server Help.

Disk Quotas and Free Space

Disk quotas are transparent to the user. When a user asks how much space is free on a disk, the system reports only the user's available quota allowance. If the user exceeds this allowance, the system indicates that the disk is full.

To obtain more free disk space after exceeding the quota allowance, the user must do one of the following:

- Delete files.
- Have another user claim ownership of some files.
- Have the administrator increase the quota allowance.

The following conditions apply when you use disk quotas:

- Disk quotas set on a volume apply only to that volume.

- Disk quotas cannot be set on individual files or folders.

- Disk quotas are based on uncompressed file sizes. You cannot increase the amount of free space by compressing the data.

- If your computer is configured as a multiple-boot system with Windows 2000 and Windows NT 4.0, you can exceed your limit when you are running Windows NT 4.0. However, when you are running Windows 2000, you must move files to a different partition or delete files until you are under your limit.

- To support disk quotas, a disk volume must be formatted with NTFS. Volumes formatted with previous versions of NTFS are upgraded automatically by Windows 2000 Setup.

- To administer quotas on a volume, you must be a member of the Administrators group on the computer where the drive resides.

- If the volume is not formatted with NTFS, or if you are not a member of the Administrators group on the local computer, the **Quota** tab is not displayed on the volume's **Properties** page.

Disk Quota Limits

The disk space used by each file is charged directly to the user who owns the file. The file owner is identified by the security identifier (SID) in the security information for the file. The total disk space charged to a user is the sum of the length of all data streams, and property set streams and resident user data streams affect the user's quota. Compressing or decompressing files does not affect the disk space reported for the files. Therefore, quota settings on one volume can be compared to settings on another volume.

The following are types of disk quota limits.

Warning threshold   You can configure the system to generate a system log file entry when the disk space charged to the user exceeds this value.

Hard quota   You can configure the system to generate a system log file entry or deny additional disk space to the user when the disk space charged to the user exceeds this value.

NTFS automatically creates a user quota entry when a user first writes to the volume. Entries that are created automatically are assigned the default warning threshold and hard quota limit values for the volume.

Disk Quotas States

The administrator can turn quota enforcement on and off. There are three quota states, as shown in Table 2.13.

Table 2.13   Disk Quota States

State	Description
Quota disabled	Quota usage changes are not tracked, but the quota limits are not removed. In this state, performance is not affected by disk quotas. This is the default state.
Quota tracked	Quota usage changes are tracked, but quota limits are not enforced. In this state, no quota violation events are generated and no file operations fail because of disk quota violations.
Quota enforced	Quota usage changes are tracked and quota limits are enforced.

Administering Disk Quotas

Disk quotas monitor volume use to prevent users from affecting others' use of the volume. For example, if a user saves 50 MB on a volume on which each user has been allocated 50 MB of space, some of this data must be moved or deleted before additional data is written to the volume. Other users can continue to save up to 50 MB of space on that volume.

Note Disk Quotas do not prevent adminstrators from allocating more space than is available on the disk. For example, on a 1 GB volume that is used by 100 users, each user might be allocated 100 MB of space to allow each user a reasonable amount of disk space.

Disk quotas are based on file ownership and are independent of the location of the files on the volume. If a user moves files from one folder to another on the same volume, volume space usage does not change; if the user copies the files to a different folder on the same volume, the volume space usage doubles.

The administrator can set default quotas for the volume or quotas for specific users on a volume. A new user receives the default quota unless the administrator established a quota specifically for that user. The administrator can view the level of quota tracking, the default quota limits, and the per-owner quota information. The per-user quota information contains the user's hard quota limit, warning threshold, and quota usage.

If you do not want to use the default disk space limit and warning threshold values for a particular user, use the New Quota Entry feature to set up quota thresholds and limits before the user actually writes data to the volume.

User quota entries cannot be deleted if a user still owns files on the volume; all files owned by that user must either be deleted or moved to another volume, or ownership of the files must be transferred to another user.

Enabling Disk Quotas

When you enable quotas on a volume that already contains files, the disk space used by all users who have copied, saved, or taken ownership of files on the volume up to that point is calculated. The quota limit and warning level are then applied to all current users and to all new users. You can then disable or set different quotas for specific users. You can also set quotas for specific users who have not yet copied, saved, or taken ownership of files on the volume.

For example, you can set a quota of 5 MB for all users of \\Main\General, while ensuring that two users who work with larger files have a 10 MB limit. If both users already have files stored on \\Main\General, select both users and set their quota limit to 10 MB. However, if one or both users do not have files stored on the server when you enable quotas, use the **Select Users** property sheet to set their quota limit to a value higher than the default for new users.

Local and Remote Implementations

Disk quotas can be enabled on volumes residing on both local computers and remote computers. On local computers, quotas can be used to limit the amount of space available to users who log on to the local computer. On remote computers, quotas can limit volume usage by remote users.

You can use quotas to ensure the following:

- Multiple users can share resources on the same computer.
- Disk space on public servers is not monopolized by one or more users.
- Users do not use excessive disk space on a shared folder on your computer.

To enable quotas on remote volumes, they must be formatted as the version of NTFS included with Windows 2000 and be shared from the root directory of the volume. Also, you must be a member of the Administrators group on the remote computer to enable and manage quotas.

System files are included in the volume usage of the person who installed Windows 2000 on the local computer. When implementing disk quotas on a local volume, make sure to take into account the disk space used by these files. Depending on the free space available on the volume, you might want to set a high quota limit or no limit for the user who installed the operating system.

Auditing Disk Space Use

Enabling quotas causes a slight increase in server overhead and a slight decrease in file server performance. By periodically enabling and then disabling quotas, you can take advantage of the auditing capabilities provided by Windows 2000 disk quotas without reducing the performance of your file server.

To create a record of the audit, save a copy of the data to another application, such as Microsoft® Excel.

Exceeding Disk Quota Limits

When you select the **Deny disk space to users exceeding quota limit** option, users who exceed their limit receive an "insufficient disk space" error and cannot write additional data to the volume without deleting or moving files. Individual programs determine their own error handling for this condition. To the program, it appears that the volume is full.

By leaving this option cleared, you can allow users to exceed their limit. This is useful when you do not want to deny users access to a volume, but want to track disk space use on a per-user basis. You can also specify whether or not to log an event when users exceed either their quota warning level or their quota limit.

When you select the **Log event when a user exceeds their quota limit** option, an event is written to the system log when a user exceeds the limit. Administrators can view these events with Event Viewer, filtering for Disk event types. Unless you set a trigger to do so, users are not warned of this event.

Event Viewer builds a historical, chronological record of which users exceeded their quota warning level and quota limits, and when they exceeded them. However, it does not provide information about which users are currently over their quota warning level.

For more information about enabling disk quotas, see Windows 2000 Server Help.

Additional Resources

- For more information about storing and managing data, see the Microsoft Platform Software Development Kit (SDK) link on the Web Resources page at http://windows.microsoft.com/windows2000/reskit/webresources.

- For more information about Disk Management and disk quotas, see Windows 2000 Server Help.

C H A P T E R 3

File Systems

Microsoft® Windows® 2000 supports the NTFS file system, two file allocation table (FAT) file systems (FAT16 and FAT32), the compact disc file system (CDFS), and the Universal Disk Format (UDF). The structures of the volumes formatted by each of these file systems, as well as the way each file system organizes data on the disk, are significantly different. The capabilities and limitations of these file systems must be reviewed to determine their comparative features. The version of NTFS included with Windows 2000 includes reparse points, the change journal, encryption, sparse file support, and several other new features.

In This Chapter

Related Information in the Resource Kit

- For information about disks, see "Disk Concepts and Troubleshooting" in this book.

- For information about disk storage, see "Data Storage and Management" in this book.

- For information about system recovery, see "Repair, Recovery, and Restore" in this book.

About Windows 2000 File Systems

An operating system's ability to access files on a volume depends on the file system with which the volume was formatted. Table 3.1 shows the file system format used by various operating systems.

Table 3.1   Operating System and File System Compatibility

Operating system	File System Format of Volume
Windows 2000	NTFS
	FAT16
	FAT32
Microsoft® Windows NT®	NTFS
	FAT16
Microsoft® Windows® 95 OEM Service Release 2 (OSR2) and Microsoft® Windows® 98	FAT16
	FAT32
Windows 95 prior to version OSR2	FAT16
Microsoft® MS-DOS®	FAT16

Note   FAT16 and FAT32 are referred to synonymously as FAT unless the differences between them must be noted.

You can use long and short file names in both NTFS and FAT volumes. A long file name can be up to 256 characters long. Short file names contain an eight-letter file name and a three-letter file name extenstion and use the format *xxxxxxxx.yyy*. Short file names are compatible with MS-DOS.

FAT File System

The FAT file system has the file allocation table located at the beginning of a logical volume. FAT was designed for small disks and simple folder structures. Two copies of the file allocation table are stored on the volume. In the event that one copy of the file allocation table is corrupted, the other file allocation table is used.

FAT16 File System

FAT16 is included in Windows 2000 for the following reasons:

- It provides backward compatibility in the form of an upgrade path for earlier versions of Windows-compatible products.
- It is compatible with most other operating systems.

For Windows 2000 and Windows NT, the maximum size for a FAT16 volume is 4,095 megabytes (MB).

A volume formatted with FAT16 is allocated in clusters. The default cluster size is determined by the volume size, and can be as large as 64 kilobytes (KB). The cluster size must be a power of 2 between 512 and 65,536 bytes. Table 3.2 shows the default cluster sizes for FAT16 volumes. You can specify a different cluster size if you format the volume with the **format** command from the command prompt. However, the size you specify must be listed in Table 3.2.

Table 3.2   FAT16 Cluster Sizes

Volume Size	Sectors Per Cluster	Cluster Size
0 MB–32 MB	1	512 bytes
33 MB–64 MB	2	1 KB
65 MB–128 MB	4	2 KB
129 MB–255 MB	8	4 KB
256 MB–511 MB	16	8 KB
512 MB–1,023 MB	32	16 KB
1,024 MB–2,047 MB	64	32 KB
2,048 MB–4,095 MB	128	64 KB

FAT16 is not recommended for volumes larger than 511 MB because, when relatively small files are placed on a FAT16 volume, FAT uses disk space inefficiently. You cannot use FAT16 on volumes larger than 4 gigabytes (GB), regardless of the cluster size.

Note On volumes with fewer than 32,680 sectors, the cluster sizes can be up to 8 sectors per cluster. The format program, whether you format the volume using Disk Management or by typing **format** at the command prompt, creates a 12-bit FAT. Volumes less than 16 MB are usually formatted for a 12-bit FAT, but the exact size depends on the disk geometry. The disk geometry also determines the point at which a larger cluster size is needed because the number of clusters on the volume must fit into 16 bits. Therefore, you might have a 33-MB volume that still has only 1 sector per cluster.

FAT12 is the original implementation of FAT and is intended for very small media. The file allocation table for FAT12 is smaller than the file allocation table for FAT16 and FAT32, because it uses less space for each entry. This leaves more space for data. All 5.25-inch floppy disks are formatted with FAT12, and 1.44-MB 3.5-inch floppy disks are generally formatted with FAT12. Volumes on Iomega Zip and Jaz drives are formatted with FAT16.

Structure of a FAT16 Volume

Figure 3.1 illustrates how FAT maps out clusters on a volume. The file allocation table (areas FAT1 and FAT2 in Figure 3.1) identifies each cluster in the volume as one of the following:

- Unused
- Cluster in use by a file
- Bad cluster
- Last cluster in a file

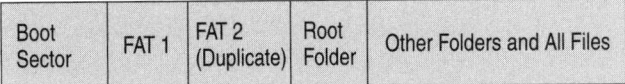

Figure 3.1   Organization of a FAT Volume

The only difference between the root folder and other folders is that the root folder is at a specified location and has a fixed number of entries (for a hard disk). The number of entries on a floppy disk depends on the size of the disk.

Note   Each folder and file in the root folder uses one or more entries. For example, if the fixed number of entries is 512 and you have 100 folders, you can only create 412 files.

Folders have a 32-byte entry for each file and folder contained in the folder. Assuming short file names are used, the entry includes the following information:

- Name (8.3) xxxxxxxx.yyy. (88 bits)
- Attribute byte (8 bits of information, described later in this section).
- One reserved byte.
- Create time (24 bits).
- Create date (16 bits).
- Last access date (16 bits).
- Two reserved bytes.
- Last modified time (16 bits).
- Last modified date (16 bits).
- Starting cluster number in the file allocation table (16 bits).
- File size (32 bits).

In a FAT folder structure, files are given the first available location on the volume. The starting cluster number is the address of the first cluster used by the file. Each cluster contains a pointer to the next cluster in the file, or an end-of-file (EOF) indicator at (0xFFFF) which indicates that this cluster is the end of the file. These pointers and end-of-file indicators are shown in Figure 3.2.

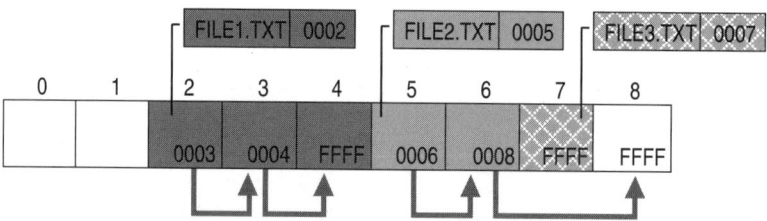

Figure 3.2   Files on a FAT Volume

Figure 3.2 shows three files in a folder. File1.txt is large enough to use three clusters. File2.txt is a fragmented file that also requires three clusters. The third file, File3.txt, fits completely in one cluster. In each case, the folder entry points to the first cluster of the file.

The information in the folder is used by all operating systems that support FAT. Windows 2000 can store additional time stamps in a FAT folder entry. These time stamps show when the file was created or last accessed.

Because all entries in a directory are the same size, the attribute byte for each entry in a directory describes what kind of entry it is. For example, one bit indicates that the entry is for a subdirectory and another bit marks the entry as a volume. Typically, only the operating system controls the settings of these bits.

The attribute byte includes four bits that can be turned on or off by the user—archive, system, hidden, and read-only.

FAT32 File System

Support for FAT32 is new in Windows 2000. FAT16 supports volumes up to 4 GB, whereas theoretically FAT32 can manage volumes up to 2 terabytes. The FAT32 on-disk format and features on Windows 2000 are similar to those on Windows 95 OSR2 and Windows 98.

The size of a FAT32 cluster can range in size from 1 sector (512 bytes) to 64 sectors (32 KB), incremented in powers of 2.

Since FAT32 requires 4 bytes to store cluster values, many internal and on-disk data structures have been revised or expanded. Most programs are unaffected by these changes; however, disk utilities which read the on-disk format must be updated to support FAT32.

Two application programming interfaces (APIs) are disabled on FAT32. Since the BIOS parameter block (BPB) structure grows from 25 bytes on FAT16 to 53 bytes on FAT32, and FSCTL_QUERY_FAT_BPB is defined to return only as much of the boot sector as contains the 25 byte form of the BPB, it is disabled on FAT32. To retrieve the BPB on FAT32, applications should read the volume directly. This also works for FAT16. Extended attributes are disabled on FAT32 since increasing the cluster number to 4 bytes requires the use of the field previously used to index the extended attribute database.

Structure of a FAT32 Volume

The main difference between FAT16 and FAT32 is the logical partition size. FAT32 breaks the 2-GB logical drive limitation of FAT16 volumes by extending a single logical drive capacity to at least 127 GB. If you have a 2-GB FAT16 drive, you must use a 32-KB cluster. With FAT32, the range for a 4-KB cluster, for example, includes drive sizes between 512 MB and 8 GB.

The largest possible file for a FAT32 drive is 4 GB minus 2 bytes. FAT32 uses 4 bytes per cluster within the file allocation table. This differs from FAT16, which uses 2 bytes per cluster within the file allocation table. Table 3.3 shows the default cluster sizes for FAT32.

Table 3.3   FAT32 Cluster Sizes

Partition Size	Default Cluster Size
Less than 8 GB	4 K
Greater than or equal to 8 GB, and less than 16 GB	8 K
Greater than or equal to 16 GB, and less than 32 GB	16 K
Greater than or equal to 32 GB	32 K

A FAT32 volume must have at least 65,527 clusters. Also, the cluster size on a FAT32 volume cannot be such that the file allocation table is greater than (16 MB – 64 KB)/4, or almost 4 million clusters.

FAT16 and FAT32 do not scale well. As the volume gets bigger, the file allocation table gets bigger, which dramatically increases the amount of time it takes Windows 2000 to compute how much free space is on the boot volume when the system is restarted.

For this reason, you may not create a FAT32 volume larger than 32 GB using the Format utility. However, the Windows 2000 Fastfat driver enables you to mount and fully support a FAT32 volume larger than 32 GB.

Use NTFS to format volumes larger than these. For more information about why you should format all Windows 2000 partitions with NTFS, see "Advantages of NTFS" later in this chapter.

File Names on FAT Volumes

Files created or renamed on FAT volumes use attribute bits to support long file names in a way that does not interfere with how MS-DOS gains access to the volume.

Whenever you create a file with a long file name, Windows 2000 creates a conventional 8.3 name for the file and one or more secondary folder entries for the file, one for each 13 characters in the long file name. Each secondary folder entry stores a corresponding part of the long file name in Unicode.

Windows 2000 marks the secondary folder entries as part of a long file name by setting the volume ID, read-only, system, and hidden attribute bits. MS-DOS generally ignores folder entries with all four of these attribute bits set, so these entries are invisible to these operating systems. MS-DOS accesses the file by using the conventional 8.3 file name contained in the folder entry for the file.

Figure 3.3 shows all of the folder entries for the file Thequi~1.fox, which has a long name of The quick brown.fox. The long name is in Unicode, so each character in the name uses 2 bytes in the folder entry. The attribute field for the long-name entries has the value **0x0F**. The attribute field for the short name has the value **0x20**.

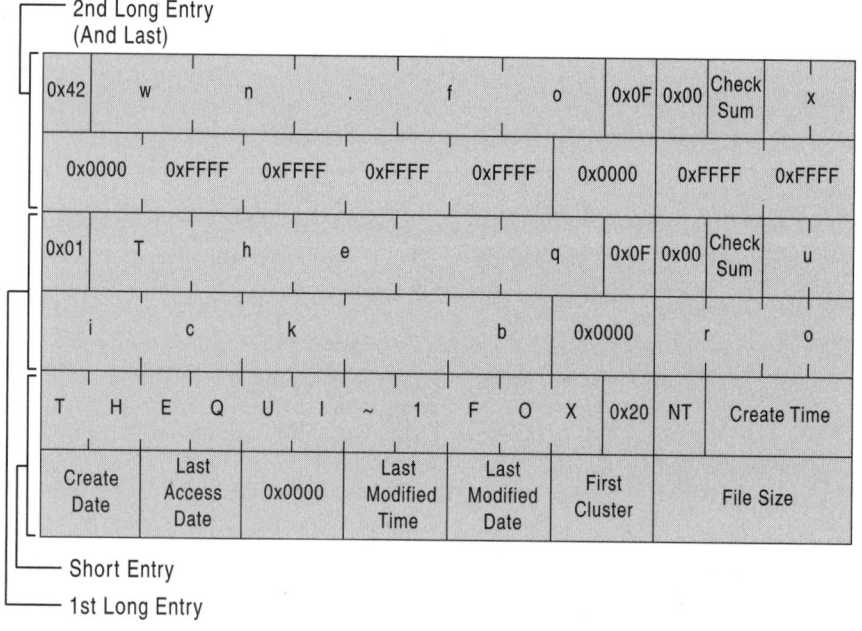

Figure 3.3   Long File Name on a FAT Volume

Note   Windows NT and Windows 2000 do not use the same algorithm to create long and short file names as Windows 95 and Windows 98. However, on computers that multiple-boot these operating systems, files that you create when running one operating system can be accessed when running the other.

For information about how Windows 2000 creates short file names, see "Using Long File Names" later in this chapter.

By default, Windows 2000 supports long file names on FAT volumes. You can prevent a FAT file system from creating long file names by setting the value of the **Win31FileSystem** registry entry (in HKEY_LOCAL_MACHINE\System \CurrentControlSet\Control\FileSystem\Win31FileSystem) to **1**.

Caution   Do not use a registry editor to edit the registry directly unless you have no alternative. The registry editors bypass the standard safeguards provided by administrative tools. These safeguards prevent you from entering conflicting settings or settings that are likely to degrade performance or damage your system. Editing the registry directly can have serious, unexpected consequences that can prevent the system from starting and require that you reinstall Windows 2000. To configure or customize Windows 2000, use the programs in Control Panel or Microsoft Management Console (MMC) whenever possible.

This value prevents Windows 2000 from creating new long file names on all FAT volumes, but it does not affect existing long file names.

Using FAT with Windows 2000

FAT16 works the same way in Windows 2000 as it does in MS-DOS, Windows 3.*x*, Windows 95, and Windows 98. FAT32 works the same way in Windows 2000 as it does in Windows 95 OSR2 and Windows 98. In fact, you can install Windows 2000 on an existing FAT primary partition or logical drive. When running Windows 2000, you can move or copy files between FAT and NTFS volumes.

Note   You cannot use Windows 2000 with any compression or partitioning software that requires disk drivers to be loaded by MS-DOS.

The NTFS File System

Windows 2000 comes with a new version of NTFS. This newest version of NTFS provides performance, reliability, and functionality not found in FAT. Some new features in Windows 2000, such as Active Directory™ directory service and the storage features based on reparse points are only available on volumes formatted with NTFS.

NTFS also includes security features required for file servers and high-end personal computers in a corporate environment, and data access control and ownership privileges important for data integrity.

Multiple Data Streams

NTFS supports multiple data streams, where the stream name identifies a new data attribute on the file. A handle can be opened to each data stream. A data stream, then, is a unique set of file attributes. Streams have separate opportunistic locks, file locks, and sizes, but common permissions.

This feature enables you to manage data as a single unit. The following is an example of an alternate stream:

```
myfile.dat:stream2
```

A library of files might exist where the files are defined as alternate streams, as in the following example:

```
library:file1
       :file2
       :file3
```

A file can be associated with more than one application at a time, such as Microsoft® Word and Microsoft® WordPad. For instance, a file structure like the following illustrates file association, but not multiple files:

```
program:source_file
       :doc_file
       :object_file
       :executable_file
```

You can use the Win32 advanced programming interface (API) **CreateFile** to create an alternate data stream. Or, at the command prompt, you can type commands such as:

```
echo text>program:source_file
more <program:source_file
```

Caution Because NTFS is not supported on floppy disks, when you copy an NTFS file to a floppy disk, data streams and other attributes not supported by FAT are lost without warning.

Reparse Points

Reparse points are new file system objects in the version of NTFS included with Windows 2000. Reparse points have a definable attribute containing user-controlled data and are used to extend functionality in the input/output (I/O) subsystem.

For more information about reparse points, see the Platform Software Development Kit (SDK) link on the Web Resources page at http://windows.microsoft.com/windows2000/reskit/webresources.

Change Journal

The change journal is used by NTFS to provide a persistent log of all changes made to files on the volume. For each volume, NTFS uses the change journal to track information about added, deleted, and modified files. The change journal is much more efficient than time stamps or file notifications for determining changes in a given namespace.

The change journal is implemented as a sparse stream in which only a small active range uses any disk allocation. The active range initially begins at offset 0 in the stream and moves monotonically forward. The unique sequence number (USN) of a particular record represents its virtual offset in the stream. As the active range moves forward through the stream, earlier records are deallocated and become unavailable. The size of the active range in a sparse file can be adjusted. For more information about the change journal and sparse files, see the Platform Software Development Kit (SDK) link on the Web Resources page at http://windows.microsoft.com/windows2000/reskit/webresources.

Encryption

File and directory-level encryption is implemented in the version of NTFS included with Windows 2000 for enhanced security in NTFS volumes. Windows 2000 uses Encrypting File System (EFS) to store data in encrypted form, which provides security when the storage media are removed from a system running Windows 2000. For more information about EFS, see the *Microsoft® Windows® 2000 Server Resource Kit Distributed Systems Guide*.

Sparse File Support

Sparse files allow programs to create very large files, but to consume disk space only as needed. A sparse file is a file with an attribute that causes the I/O subsystem to allocate the file's meaningful (nonzero) data. All nonzero data is allocated on disk, whereas all nonmeaningful data (large strings of data composed of zeros) is not. When a sparse file is read, allocated data is returned as it was stored, and nonallocated data is returned, by default, as zeros in accordance with the C2 security requirement specification.

NTFS includes full sparse file support for both compressed and uncompressed files. NTFS handles read operations on sparse files by returning allocated data and sparse data. It is possible to read a sparse file as allocated data and a range of data without having to retrieve the entire data set, although, by default, NTFS returns the entire data set.

You can set a user-controlled file system attribute to take advantage of the sparse file function in NTFS. With the sparse file attribute set, the file system can deallocate data from anywhere in the file and, when an application calls, yield the zero data by range instead of storing and returning the actual data. File system APIs allow for the file to be copied or backed as actual bits and sparse stream ranges. The net result is efficient file system storage and access. Figure 3.4 shows how data is stored with and without the sparse file attribute set.

Without sparse file attribute set

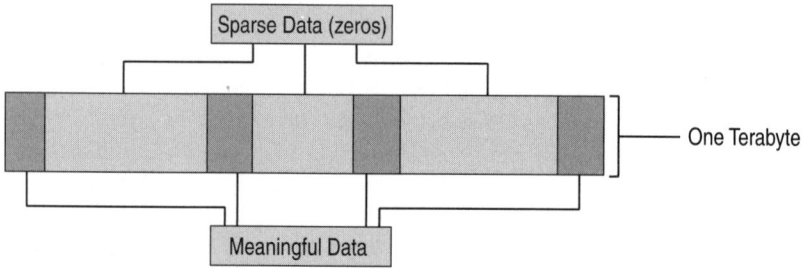

With sparse file attribute set

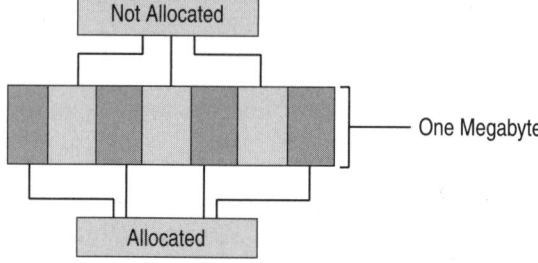

Figure 3.4   Sparse Data Storage

Disk Quotas

Disk quotas are a new feature in NTFS that provide more precise control of network-based storage. Disk quotas are implemented on a per-volume basis and enable both hard and soft storage limits to be implemented on a per-user basis. For more information about disk quotas, see "Data Storage and Management" in this book.

The introduction of distributed file system (Dfs), NTFS directory junctions, and volume mount points also creates situations where logical directories do not have to correspond to the same physical volume. Available disk space is based on user context, and the space reported for a volume is not necessarily representative of the space available to the user. For this reason, do not rely on space queries to make assumptions about the amount of available disk space in directories other than the current one. For more information about Dfs, see the *Distributed Systems Guide*. For more information about volume mount points, see "Volume Mount Points" later in this chapter.

Distributed Link-Tracking

Windows 2000 provides a distributed link-tracking service that enables client applications to track link sources that have been moved locally or within a domain. Clients that subscribe to this link-tracking service can maintain the integrity of their references because the objects referenced can be moved transparently. Files managed by NTFS can be referenced by a unique object identifier. Link tracking stores a file's object identifier as part of its tracking information.

The distributed link-tracking service tracks shell shortcuts and OLE links within NTFS volumes on computers running Windows 2000. For example, if a shell shortcut is created to a text document, distributed link-tracking allows the shortcut to remain correct, even if the target file moves to a new drive or computer system. Similarly, in a Microsoft® Word document that contains an OLE link to a Microsoft® Excel spreadsheet, the link remains correct even if the Excel file moves to a new drive or computer system.

If a link is made to a file on a volume formatted with the version of NTFS included with Windows 2000, and the file is moved to any other volume with the same version of NTFS within the same domain, the file is found by the tracking service, subject to time considerations. Additionally, if the file is moved outside the domain or within a workgroup, it is likely to be found.

Converting to Windows 2000 File Systems

The on-disk format for NTFS has been enhanced in Windows 2000 to enable new functionality. The upgrade to the new on-disk format occurs when Windows 2000 mounts an existing NTFS volume. The upgrade is quick and automatic; the conversion time is independent of volume size. Note that FAT volumes can be converted to NTFS format at any time using the Convert.exe utility.

Important   Performance of volumes that have been converted from FAT is not as high as volumes that were originally formatted with NTFS.

Multiple Booting of Windows NT and Windows 2000

Your ability to access your NTFS volumes when you multiple-boot Windows NT and Windows 2000 depends on which version you are using. (Redirected clients using NTFS volumes on file and print servers are not affected.)

Windows NT Compatibility with the Version of NTFS Included with Windows 2000

When a Windows 2000 volume is mounted on a system running Windows NT 4.0 Service Pack 4, most features of the version of NTFS included with Windows 2000 are not available. However, most read and write operations are permitted if they do not make use of any new NTFS features. Features affected by this configuration include the following:

- **Reparse points.** Windows NT cannot use any features based on reparse points, such as Remote Storage and volume mount points.

- **Disk quotas.** When running Windows NT, Windows 2000 disk quotas are ignored. This allows you to allocate more disk space than is allowed by your quota.

- **Encryption.** Windows NT cannot perform any operations on files encrypted by Windows 2000.

- **Sparse files.** Windows NT cannot perform any operations on sparse files.

- **Change journal.** Windows NT ignores the change journal. No entries are logged when files are accessed.

Cleanup Operations on Windows NT Volumes

Because files on volumes formatted with the version of NTFS included with Windows 2000 can be read and written to by Windows NT, Windows 2000 may need to perform cleanup operations to ensure the consistency of the data structures of a volume after it was mounted on a computer that is running Windows NT. Features affected by cleanup operations are explained below.

Disk quotas If disk quotas are turned off, Windows 2000 performs no cleanup operations. If disk quotas are turned on, Windows 2000 cleans up the quota information.

If a user exceeds the disk quota while the NTFS volume is mounted by a Windows NT 4.0 system, all further disk allocations of data by that user will fail. The user can still read and write data to any existing file, but will not be able to increase the size of a file. However, the user can delete and shrink files. When the user gets below the assigned disk quota, he or she can resume disk allocations of data. The same behavior occurs when a system is upgraded from a Windows NT system to a Windows 2000 system with quotas enforced.

Reparse points   Because files that have reparse points associated with them cannot be accessed by computers that are running Windows NT 4.0 or earlier, no cleanup operations are necessary in Windows 2000.

Encryption   Because encrypted files cannot be accessed by computers that are running Windows NT 4.0 or earlier, no cleanup operations are necessary.

Sparse files   Because sparse files cannot be accessed by computers that are running Windows NT 4.0 or earlier, no cleanup operations are necessary.

Object identifiers   Windows 2000 maintains two references to the object identifier. One is on the file; the other is in the volume-wide object identifier index. If you delete a file with an object identifier on it, Windows 2000 must scan and clean up the leftover entry in the index.

Change journal   Computers that are running Windows NT 4.0 or earlier do not log file changes in the change journal. When Windows 2000 starts, the change journals on volumes accessed by Windows NT are reset to indicate that the journal history is incomplete. Applications that use the change journal must have the ability to accept incomplete journals.

Structure of an NTFS Volume

Like FAT, NTFS uses clusters as the fundamental unit of disk allocation. In the Disk Management snap-in, you can specify a cluster size of up to 4 KB. If you type **format** at the command prompt to format your NTFS volume, but do not specify an allocation unit size using the **/A:<size> switch**, the values in Table 3.4 will be used.

Table 3.4   Default Cluster Sizes for NTFS

Volume Size	Sectors Per Custer	Default Cluster Size
512 MB or less	1	512 bytes
513 MB–1,024 MB (1 GB)	2	1,024 bytes (1 KB)
1,025 MB–2,048 MB (2 GB)	4	2,048 bytes (2 KB)
Greater than 2,049 MB	8	4 KB

Note   Windows 2000, like Windows NT 3.51 and Windows NT 4.0, supports file compression. Since file compression is not supported on cluster sizes above 4 K, the default NTFS cluster size for Windows 2000 never exceeds 4 K. For more information about NTFS compression, see "File and Folder Compression" later in this chapter.

Boot Sector

The first information found on an NTFS volume is the boot sector. The boot sector starts at sector 0 and can be up to 16 sectors long. It consists of two structures:

- The BIOS parameter block, which contains information on the volume layout and file system structures.

- Code that describes how to find and load the startup files for the operating system being loaded. For Windows 2000, this code loads the file Ntldr. For more information about the boot sector, see "Disk Concepts and Troubleshooting" in this book.

Master File Table and Metadata

When a volume is formatted with NTFS, a Master File Table (MFT) file and other pieces of metadata are created. Metadata are the files NTFS uses to implement the file system structure. NTFS reserves the first 16 records of the MFT for metadata files.

Note The data segment locations for both $Mft and $MftMirr are recorded in the boot sector. If the first MFT record is corrupted, NTFS reads the second record to find the MFT mirror file. A duplicate of the boot sector is located at the end of the volume.

Table 3.5 lists and briefly describes the metadata stored in the MFT.

Table 3.5   Metadata Stored in the Master File Table

System File	File Name	MFT Record	Purpose of the File
Master file table	$Mft	0	Contains one base file record for each file and directory on an NTFS volume. If the allocation information for a file or directory is too large to fit within a single record, other file records are allocated as well.
Master file table 2	$MftMirr	1	A duplicate image of the first four records of the MFT. This file guarantees access to the MFT in case of a single-sector failure.
Log file	$LogFile	2	Contains a list of transaction steps used for NTFS recoverability. Log file size depends upon the volume size. It is used by Windows 2000 to restore consistency to NTFS in the event of a system failure. For more information about the log file, see "NTFS Recoverability" later in this chapter.

(continued)

Table 3.5   Metadata Stored in the Master File Table   *(continued)*

System File	File Name	MFT Record	Purpose of the File
Volume	$Volume	3	Contains information about the volume, such as the volume label and the volume version.
Attribute definitions	$AttrDef	4	A table of attribute names, numbers, and descriptions.
Root file name index	$	5	The root directory.
Cluster bitmap	$Bitmap	6	A representation of the volume showing which clusters are in use.
Boot sector	$Boot	7	Includes the bootstrap for the volume if it is a bootable volume.
Bad cluster file	$BadClus	8	Contains bad clusters for the volume.
Security file	$Secure	9	Contains unique security descriptors for all files within a volume.
Upcase table	$Upcase	10	Converts lowercase characters to matching Unicode uppercase characters.
NTFS extension file	$Extend	11	Used for various optional extensions such as quotas, reparse point data, and object identifiers.
		12–15	Reserved for future use.

The remaining records of the MFT contain the file and directory records for each file and directory on the volume.

NTFS creates a file record for each file and a directory record for each directory created on an NTFS volume. The MFT includes a separate file record for the MFT itself. These file and directory records are stored on the MFT. The attributes of the file are written to the allocated space in the MFT. Besides file attributes, each file record contains information about the position of the file record in the MFT.

Each file usually uses one file record. However, if a file has a large number of attributes or becomes highly fragmented, it may need more than one file record. If this is the case, the first record for the file, called the base file record, stores the location of the other file records required by the file. Small files and directories (typically 1,500 bytes or smaller) are entirely contained within the file's MFT record.

Directory records contain index information. Small directories might reside entirely within the MFT structure, while large directories are organized into B-tree structures and have records with pointers to external clusters that contain directory entries that could not be contained within the MFT structure.

NTFS File Attributes

Every allocated sector on an NTFS volume belongs to a file. Even the file system metadata is part of a file. NTFS views each file (or folder) as a set of file attributes. Elements such as the file's name, its security information, and even its data, are all file attributes. Each attribute is identified by an attribute type code and, optionally, an attribute name.

When a file's attributes can fit within the MFT file record for that file, they are called resident attributes. Information such as file name and time stamp are always resident attributes. When the information for a file is too large to fit in its MFT file record, some of the file attributes are nonresident. Nonresident attributes are allocated one or more clusters of disk space and stored as an alternate data stream in the volume. NTFS creates the Attribute List attribute to describe the location of both resident and nonresident attribute records.

Table 3.6 lists the file attributes defined by NTFS, although other file attributes might be defined in the future.

Table 3.6   NTFS File Attribute Types

Attribute Type	Description
Standard Information	Includes information such as time stamp and link count.
Attribute List	Lists the location of all the attribute records that do not fit in the MFT record.
File Name	A repeatable attribute for both long and short file names. The long name of the file can be up to 255 Unicode characters. The short name is the MS-DOS-readable, 8.3, case-insensitive name for the file. Additional names, or hard links, required by POSIX can be included as additional file name attributes.
Security Descriptor	Shows information about who owns the file and who can access the file.
Data	Contains file data. NTFS allows multiple data attributes per file. Each file typically has one unnamed data attribute. A file can also have one or more named data attributes, each using a particular syntax.
Object ID	A volume-unique file identifier. Used by the link tracking service. Not all files have object identifiers.
Logged Tool Stream	Similar to a data stream, but operations on a logged tool stream are logged to the NTFS log file just like NTFS metadata changes. Used by EFS.
Reparse Point	Used for directory junction points and volume mount points. They are also used by file system filter drivers to mark certain files as special to that driver.

(continued)

Table 3.6   NTFS File Attribute Types   *(continued)*

Attribute Type	Description
Index Root	Used to implement folders and other indexes.
Index Allocation	Used to implement folders and other indexes.
Bitmap	Used to implement folders and other indexes.
Volume Information	Used only in the $Volume system file. Contains the volume version.
Volume Name	Used only in the $Volume system file. Contains the volume label.

MS-DOS-Readable File Names on NTFS Volumes

By default, Windows NT and Windows 2000 generate MS-DOS-readable file names on all NTFS volumes. To improve performance on volumes with many long, similar names, you can change the default value of the registry entry **NtfsDisable8dot3NameCreation** (in HKEY_LOCAL_MACHINE\System \CurrentControlSet\Control\FileSystem) to **1**.

Windows 2000 does not generate short (8.3) file names for files created by POSIX-based applications on an NTFS volume, regardless of the value of the **NtfsDisable8dot3NameCreation** registry entry. This means that MS-DOS-based and 16-bit Windows-based applications cannot view these file names if they are not valid 8.3 file names. Use standard MS-DOS 8.3 naming conventions if you want to use files that are created by a POSIX application with MS-DOS-based or Windows-based applications.

Using Long File Names

File names on Windows NT and Windows 2000 platforms can be up to 255 characters, and can contain spaces, multiple periods, and special characters that are forbidden in MS-DOS file names. Windows 2000 makes it possible for other operating systems to access files with long names by automatically generating an MS-DOS-readable (8.3) name for each file. Files are accessible over a network by computers using MS-DOS and Windows 3.*x*, as well as by computers using Windows 95, Windows 98, Windows NT, and Windows 2000 operating systems.

By creating 8.3 file names for files, Windows 2000 also enables MS-DOS-based and Windows 3.*x*–based applications to recognize and load files that have long file names. In addition, when an application saves a file on a computer running Windows 2000, both the 8.3 file name and long file name are retained.

If the long name of a file or folder contains spaces, you must surround the name with quotation marks. For example, if you have a program called Dump Disk Files that you want to run from the command line and you enter the name without quotation marks, it generates the error message "Cannot find the program Dump or one of its components."

You must also use quotation marks when a path typed at the command line includes spaces, as in the following example:

```
move "c:\This month's reports\*.*" "c:\Last month's reports"
```

Use wildcard characters such as the asterisk (*****) and question mark (**?**) carefully in conjunction with the **del** and **copy** command-line commands. Windows 2000 searches both long and short file names for matches to the wildcard character combination you specify, which can cause additional files to be deleted or copied.

Both FAT and NTFS use the Unicode character set for their names, which contain several forbidden characters that MS-DOS cannot read in any file name. To generate a short MS-DOS-readable file name for a file, Windows 2000 deletes all of these characters from the long file name and removes any spaces. Because an MS-DOS-readable file name can have only one period, Windows 2000 also removes all extra periods from the file name. Next, Windows 2000 truncates the file name, if necessary, to six characters and appends a tilde (**~**) and a number. For example, each nonduplicate file name is appended with **~1**. Duplicate file names end with **~2**, then **~3**, and so on. After the file names are truncated, the file name extensions are truncated to three or fewer characters. Finally, when displaying file names at the command line, Windows 2000 translates all characters in the file name and extension to uppercase.

Note You can permit extended characters by setting the value of HKEY_LOCAL_MACHINE\SYSTEM\CurrentControlSet\Control\FileSystem \NtfsAllowExtendedCharacterIn8dot3Name to 1.

When there are five or more files that would result in duplicate short file names, Windows 2000 uses a slightly different method for creating short file names. For the fifth and subsequent files, Windows 2000:

- Uses only the first two letters of the long file name.
- Generates the next four letters of the short file name by mathematically manipulating the remaining letters of the long file name.
- Appends **~1** (or another number, if necessary, to avoid a duplicate file name) to the result.

This method provides substantially improved performance when Windows 2000 must create short file names for a large number of files with similar long file names. Windows 2000 uses this method to create short file names for both FAT and NTFS files.

Table 3.7 shows the short file names for files that were created in the order test 1 through test 6.

Table 3.7   Short File Names Created by Windows 2000 – Example One

Long File Name	Short File Name
This is test 1.txt	THISIS~1.TXT
This is test 2.txt	THISIS~2.TXT
This is test 3.txt	THISIS~3.TXT
This is test 4.txt	THISIS~4.TXT
This is test 5.txt	TH0FF9~1.TXT
This is test 6.txt	THFEF5~1.TXT

If the long file names in Table 3.7 are created in a different order, their short file names are different, as shown in Table 3.8.

Table 3.8   Short File Names Created by Windows 2000 – Example Two

Long File Name	Short File Name
This is test 2.txt	THISIS~1.TXT
This is test 3.txt	THISIS~2.TXT
This is test 1.txt	THISIS~3.TXT
This is test 4.txt	THISIS~4.TXT
This is test 5.txt	TH0FF9~1.TXT
This is test 6.txt	THFEF5~1.TXT

To see both the long and short file names for each file in the folder, type the following on the command line:

dir /x

Compact Disc File System

Windows 2000 provides support for the ISO 9660–compliant CDFS, which supports long file names as listed in the ISO 9660 Level 2 standards.

When creating a CD-ROM to be used on Windows 2000, you must adhere to the following standards:

- All directory and file names must have fewer than 32 characters.
- The directory trcc cannot exceed 8 levels from the root.
- File name extensions are not mandatory.

Universal Disk Format

The UDF is new for Windows 2000. UDF is an ISO 13346–compliant, standards-based file system designed for interchanging data on digital video disk (DVD) and CD-ROM. The primary function of UDF is to support read-only DVD-ROM media.

Note Windows 2000 reads only UDF versions 1.02 and 1.50.

Comparing FAT16, FAT32, and NTFS

You can use FAT16, FAT32, NTFS, or a combination of these file systems on a Windows 2000 system. The choice you make depends on such things as:

- How the computer is used.
- The hardware platform.
- The size and number of hard disks.
- Security considerations.

Important It is recommended that you format all Windows 2000 partitions with NTFS except certain multiple-boot configurations. For more information, see "Advantages of NTFS" later in this chapter.

Comparing FAT File Systems

The numerals in the names FAT16 and FAT32 refer to the number of bits required for a file allocation table entry.

- FAT16 uses a 16-bit file allocation table entry (2^{16} allocation units).
- Windows 2000 reserves the first 4 bits of a FAT32 file allocation table entry, which means FAT32 has a maximum of 2^{28} allocation units. However, this number is capped at 32 GB by the Windows 2000 format utilities.

FAT16 vs. FAT32

Table 3.9 provides a comparison of FAT16 and FAT32 cluster sizes according to drive size.

Table 3.9   Cluster Sizes of FAT16 and FAT32

Drive Size	Default FAT16 Cluster Size	Default FAT32 Cluster Size
260 MB–511 MB	8 KB	Not supported
512 MB–1,023 MB	16 KB	4 KB
1,024 MB–2 GB	32 KB	4 KB
2 GB–8 GB	Not supported	4 KB
8 GB–16 GB	Not supported	8 KB
16 GB–32 GB	Not supported	16 KB
> 32 GB	Not supported	32 KB

There are additional differences between FAT32 and FAT16:

- FAT32 allows finer allocation granularity (approximately 4 million allocation units per volume).
- FAT32 allows the root directory to grow (FAT16 holds a maximum of 512 entries, and the limit can be even lower due to the use of long file names in the root folder).

Advantages of FAT16

Advantages of FAT16 are:

- MS-DOS, Windows 95, Windows 98, Windows NT, Windows 2000, and some UNIX operating systems can use it.
- There are many tools available to address problems and recover data.
- If you have a startup failure, you can start the computer with an MS-DOS bootable floppy disk.
- It is efficient, both in speed and storage, on volumes smaller than 256 MB.

Disadvantages of FAT16

Disadvantages of FAT16 are:

- The root folder can manage a maximum of 512 entries. The use of long file names can significantly reduce the number of available entries.

- FAT16 is limited to 65,536 clusters, but because certain clusters are reserved, it has a practical limit of 65,524. Each cluster is fixed in size relative to the logical drive. If both the maximum number of clusters and their maximum size (32 KB) are reached, the largest drive is limited to 4 GB on Windows 2000. To maintain compatibility with MS-DOS, Windows 95, and Windows 98, a FAT16 volume should not be larger than 2 GB.

- The boot sector is not backed up.

- There is no built-in file system security or file compression with FAT16.

- FAT16 can waste file storage space in larger drives as the size of the cluster increases. The space allocated for storing a file is based on the size of the cluster allocation granularity, not the file size. A 10-KB file stored in a 32-KB cluster wastes 22 KB of disk space.

Advantages of FAT32

FAT32 allocates disk space much more efficiently than previous versions of FAT. Depending on the size of your files, there is a potential for tens and even hundreds of megabytes more free disk space on larger hard disk drives. In addition, FAT32 provides the following enhancements:

- The root folder on a FAT32 drive is now an ordinary cluster chain, so it can be located anywhere on the volume. For this reason, FAT32 does not restrict the number of entries in the root folder.

- It uses space more efficiently than FAT16. FAT32 uses smaller clusters (4 KB for drives up to 8 GB), resulting in 10 to 15 percent more efficient use of disk space relative to large FAT16 drives. FAT32 also reduces the resources necessary for the computer to operate.

- FAT32 is more robust than FAT16. FAT32 has the ability to relocate the root directory and use the backup copy of the FAT instead of the default copy. In addition, the boot record on FAT32 drives has been expanded to include a backup of critical data structures. This means that FAT32 volumes are less susceptible to a single point of failure than FAT16 volumes.

Disadvantages of FAT32

Disadvantages of FAT32 include:

- The largest FAT32 volume Windows 2000 can format is limited in size to 32 GB.

- FAT32 volumes are not accessible from any other operating systems other than Windows 95 OSR2 and Windows 98.

- The boot sector is not backed up.

- There is no built-in file system security or compression with FAT32.

Advantages of NTFS

It is recommended that you format all Windows 2000 partitions with NTFS except multiple-boot configurations where non-Windows 2000 and non-Windows NT startups are necessary.

Formatting your Windows 2000 partitions with NTFS instead of FAT allows you to use features that are available only on NTFS. These include:

Recoverability   The recoverability designed into NTFS is such that a user should seldom have to run a disk repair program on an NTFS volume. NTFS guarantees the consistency of the volume by using standard transaction logging and recovery techniques. In the event of a system failure, NTFS uses its log file and checkpoint information to automatically restore the consistency of the file system. For more information about recovering your system, restoring data, and creating an emergency repair disk (ERD), see "Repair, Recovery, and Restore" in this book.

Compression   Windows 2000 supports compression on an individual file basis for NTFS volumes. Files that are compressed on an NTFS volume can be read and written by any Windows-based application without first being decompressed by another program. Decompression happens automatically during the read of the file. The file is compressed again when it is closed or saved.

In addition, formatting your volumes with NTFS instead of FAT16 or FAT32 provides the following advantages:

- There are some Windows 2000 operating system features that require NTFS.

- Faster access speed. NTFS minimizes the number of disk accesses required to find a file.

- File and folder security. On NTFS volumes, you can set file permissions on files and folders that specify which groups and users have access to them, and what level of access is permitted. NTFS file and folder permissions apply both to users working at the computer where the file is stored and to users accessing the file over the network when the file is in a shared folder. With NTFS you can also set share permissions that operate on shared folders in combination with file and folder permissions.

- Windows 2000 can format volumes up to 2 terabytes in size with NTFS.

- The boot sector is backed up to a sector at the end of the volume.

- NTFS supports a native encryption system called Encrypting File System (EFS), using public-key security to prevent unauthorized access to file contents.

- NTFS functionality can be extended by using reparse points, enabling new features such as volume mount points.

- Disk quotas can be set, limiting the amount of space users can consume on an NTFS volume.

Disadvantages of NTFS

While NTFS is the recommended file system for users of Windows 2000, it is not appropriate in all circumstances. Disadvantages of NTFS include:

- NTFS volumes are not accessible in MS-DOS, Windows 95, and Windows 98. Due to upgrades made to NTFS in Windows 2000, the advanced features of the Windows 2000 implementation of NTFS are not available in Windows NT 4.0 and earlier.

- When very small volumes contain mostly small files, the overhead of managing NTFS may cause a slight performance drop in comparison to FAT.

Formatting the System Partition in Multiple-Boot Configurations

If you want to start another operating system, such as Windows 95, Windows 98, Windows for Workgroups, or MS-DOS, use FAT for your system partition and the boot partitions for the other operating systems. You can use NTFS for your Windows 2000 boot partition and other volumes on the computer, as long as those volumes will not be accessed by an operating system other than Windows 2000.

Which Is Faster – FAT16, FAT32, or NTFS?

For small volumes, FAT16 or FAT32 usually provide faster access to files than NTFS because:

- The FAT structure is simpler.

- The FAT folder size is smaller for an equal number of files.

- FAT has no controls regulating whether a user can access a file or a folder; therefore, the system does not have to check permissions for an individual file or whether a specific user has access to the file or folder. This advantage is minimal because Windows 2000 still has to determine if the file is read-only, or whether the file is on a FAT or NTFS volume.

NTFS minimizes the number of disk accesses and time needed to find a file. In addition, if a folder is small enough to fit in the MFT record, NTFS reads the entire folder when it reads its MFT record.

A FAT folder entry contains an index of the file allocation table, which identifies the cluster number for the first cluster of the folder. To view a file, FAT has to search the folder structure.

In comparing the speed of operations performed on large folders containing both long and short file names, the speed of a FAT operation depends on the operation itself and the size of the folder. If FAT searches for a file that does not exist, it has to search the entire folder—an operation that takes longer on a FAT structure than on the B-tree structure used by NTFS. In mathematical terms, the average time to find a file on a FAT folder is a function of $N/2$, where N is the number of files. On an NTFS folder, the average time is a function of Log N.

Several factors affect the speed with which Windows 2000 reads or writes a file:

- Fragmentation of the file. If a file is badly fragmented, NTFS usually requires fewer disk accesses than FAT to find all of the fragments.

- Cluster size. For both file systems, the default cluster size depends on the volume size, and is always a power of 2. FAT16 addresses are 16 bits, FAT32 addresses are 32 bits, and NTFS addresses are 64 bits.

- The default FAT cluster size is based upon the fact that the file allocation table can have at most 65,535 entries, so the cluster size is a function of the volume size divided by 65,535. Therefore, the default cluster size for a FAT volume is almost always larger than the default cluster size for an NTFS volume of the same size. The larger cluster size for a FAT volume means that there might be less fragmentation in files on a FAT volume.

- Location of small files. With NTFS, small files are entirely contained within the MFT record. The file size that fits in the MFT record depends upon the the number of attributes for the file.

Maximum Volume Sizes

The maximum size of a volume depends on the file system used to format the volume. Windows 2000 allows you to format volumes with three different file systems: NTFS, FAT16, and FAT32.

Windows 2000 has the capability to combine noncontiguous disk areas when creating volume sets and stripe sets, but these volumes have the same maximum size limitations of a single volume.

Maximum Sizes on FAT16 Volumes

FAT16 can support a maximum of 65,535 clusters per volume. Table 3.10 lists FAT16 size limits.

Important For Windows NT and Windows 2000, the cluster size of FAT16 volumes between 2 GB and 4 GB is 64 KB. This cluster size is known to create compatibility issues with some applications. For this reason, it is recommended that FAT32 be used on volumes that are between 2 GB and 4 GB. One of the known compatibility issues involves setup programs that do not compute volume free space properly on a volume with 64 KB clusters and will not run because of a perceived lack of free space. The Format program in Windows 2000 displays a warning and asks for a confirmation before formatting a volume with 64 KB clusters.

Table 3.10   FAT16 Size Limits

Description	Limit
Maximum file size	2^{32} - 1 bytes
Maximum volume size	4 GB
Files per volume	2^{16}

Maximum Sizes on FAT32 Volumes

The FAT32 volume must have at least 65,527 clusters. The maximum number of clusters on a FAT32 volume is 4,177,918. Windows 2000 creates volumes up to 32 GB, but you can use larger volumes created by other operating systems such as Windows 98. Table 3.11 lists FAT32 size limits.

Table 3.11   FAT32 Size Limits

Description	Limit
Maximum file size	2^{32} - 1 bytes
Maximum volume size	32 GB (This is due to the Windows 2000 format utility. The maximum volume size that Windows 98 can create is 127.53 GB).
Files per volume	Approximately 4 million

Important   Windows 2000 can format new FAT32 volumes up to 32 GB in size but can mount larger volumes (for example, up to 127.53 GB and 4,177,918 clusters from a volume formatted with the limits of Windows 98). It is possible to mount volumes that exceed these limits, but doing so has not been tested and is not recommended.

Maximum Sizes on NTFS Volumes

In theory, the maximum NTFS volume size is 2^{32} clusters. However, even if there were hardware available to supply a logical volume of that capacity, there are other limitations to the maximum size of a volume.

One of these limitations is partition tables. By industry standards, partition tables are limited to 2^{32} sectors. Sector size, another limitation, is a function of hardware and industry standards, and is typically 512 bytes. While sector sizes might increase in the future, the current size puts a limit on a single volume of 2 terabytes (2^{32} * 512 bytes, or 2^{41} bytes).

For now, 2 terabytes should be considered the practical limit for both physical and logical volumes using NTFS.

The maximum number of files on an NTFS volume is 2^{32} - 1. Table 3.12 lists NTFS size limits.

Table 3.12   NTFS Size Limits

Description	Limit
Maximum file size	2^{64} bytes - 1 KB (On disk format)
	2^{44} bytes - 64 KB (Implementation)
Maximum volume size	2^{64} allocation units (On disk format)
	2^{32} allocation units (Implementation)
Files per volume	2^{32} - 1

Controlling Access to Files and Folders

On NTFS volumes, you can set file permissions on files and folders that specify which groups and users have access to them, and what level of access is permitted. NTFS file and folder permissions apply both to users working at the computer where the file is stored and to users accessing the file over the network when the file is in a shared folder. With NTFS you can also set share permissions, which operate on shared folders in combination with file and folder permissions. File attributes (read-only, hidden, system) also limit file access. Figure 3.5 shows the permissions listed on the **Security** tab of the **Properties** dialog box.

FAT16 and FAT32 allow you to set file attributes on files but they do not provide file permissions.

The version of NTFS included with Windows 2000 offers an important new feature for managing security—inheritable permissions. The **Security** dialog box offers the option to **Allow inheritable permissions from parent to propagate to this file object** which is enabled by default.

This feature significantly reduces the time and I/O work required to change the permissions of many files and subfolders. For example, suppose a user wants to change the permissions on a tree consisting of several thousand files. With Windows NT 4.0, each file and folder needs to be individually changed. However, with Windows 2000, if the subfolders and files inherit permissions, they only need to be set for the top-level folder.

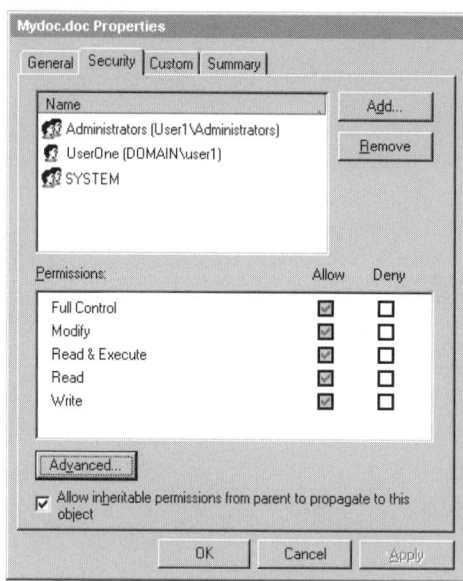

Figure 3.5   Permissions Dialog Box

Figure 3.6 shows the Permissions listed when you select the **Advanced** button on the **Security** tab of the **Properties** dialog box.

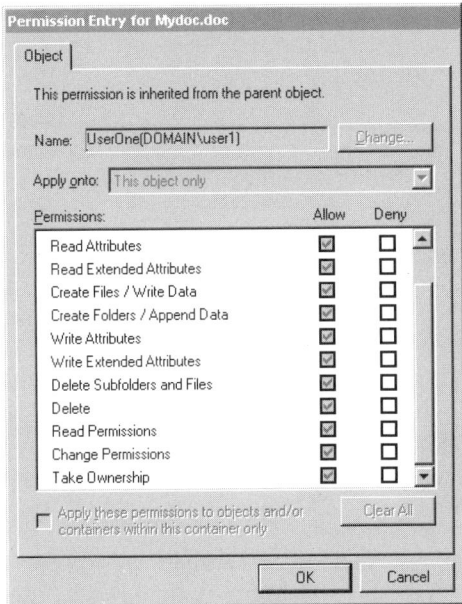

Figure 3.6 Advanced Permissions Dialog Box

Important   To preserve permissions when you copy or move files between NTFS folders, use the Robocopy program on the *Microsoft® Windows® 2000 Resource Kit* companion CD.

You can back up and restore data on FAT and NTFS volumes. However, if you back up data from an NTFS volume and then restore it to a FAT volume, you lose security settings and other file information on the restored copies.

You can restore Remote Storage data only to an NTFS volume. For more information about Remote Storage, see "Data and Storage Management" in this book.

Although NTFS provides access controls to individual files and folders, users can perform certain actions on files or folders even if permissions are set on a file or folder to prevent access to users.

For example, you have a folder (Dir1) containing a file (File1), and you grant Full Control to a user for the folder Dir1. If you specify that the user has No Access to File1, the user can still delete File1. This is because the user's Full Control rights in the folder allow the user to delete the contents (files or subfolders) of the folder.

To prevent files from being deleted, you must set permissions on the file itself, and you must set permissions for the folder containing the file.

Anyone who has List, Read, or greater permissions in a folder can view file properties on any file in the folder, even if file permissions prevent them from seeing the contents of the file.

Note In the **Properties** dialog box, you can use the **Security** tab to deny **Full Control** while leaving **Modify**, **Read & Execute**, **Read**, and **Write** in place.

With FAT volumes, you cannot set any permissions on the individual files and folders. The only security available is the share permissions that are set on the entire share, that affect all files and folders on that share, and that only function over the network. Once a folder is shared, you can protect the shared folder by specifying one set of share permissions for all files and subfolders of the shared folder. Share permissions are set in much the same way file and folder permissions are set in NTFS. But because share permissions apply globally to all files and folders in the share, they are significantly less versatile than the file and folder permissions used for NTFS volumes.

Share permissions apply equally to NTFS and FAT volumes. They are enforced by Windows 2000, not the individual file system. However, when you move or copy a file from an NTFS to a FAT volume, permissions and other attributes unique to NTFS are lost.

POSIX Compliance

If you want POSIX compliance, you must use NTFS. POSIX compliance permits UNIX programs to be ported to Windows 2000. Windows 2000 is fully compliant with the Institute of Electrical and Electronic Engineers (IEEE) standard 1003.1, which is a standard for file naming and identification.

The following POSIX-compliant features are included in NTFS:

- **Case-sensitive naming.** For example, POSIX would interpret README.TXT, Readme.txt, and readme.txt as different files.
- **Hard links.** A file can be given more than one name. This allows two different file names, which can be located in different folders, to point to the same data.
- **Additional time stamps.** These show when the file was last accessed or modified.

Caution   You must use POSIX-based programs to manage file names that differ only in case. POSIX-based programs allow you to create and manage case-sensitive file names.

You cannot use standard commands to manage file names that differ only in case. (Standard commands include those used at the command prompt, such as **copy**, **del**, and **move**, and their equivalents in My Computer.) For example, if you type **del AnnM.Doc** at the command prompt, both annm.doc and AnnM.Doc would be deleted.

File and Folder Compression

Windows 2000 supports compression on individual files and on folders for NTFS volumes. Files compressed on an NTFS volume can be read and written by any Windows-based application without first being decompressed by another program. Decompression occurs automatically when the file is read. The file is compressed again when it is closed or saved. Compressed files and folders have an attribute of **C** when viewed in My Computer.

Only NTFS can read the compressed form of the data. When an application such as Microsoft Word or an operating system command such as **Copy** requests access to the file, NTFS decompresses the file before making it available. For example, if you copy a compressed file from another Windows 2000–based computer to a compressed folder on your hard disk, the file is decompressed, copied, and recompressed.

This compression algorithm is similar to that used by MS-DOS 6.0 DoubleSpace® and MS-DOS 6.22 DriveSpace®, with one important difference—the MS-DOS functionality compresses the entire primary partition or logical drive, while NTFS enables the user to compress individual files and folders within the NTFS volume.

The compression algorithms in NTFS are designed to support cluster sizes of up to 4 KB. When the cluster size is greater than 4 KB on an NTFS volume, none of the NTFS compression functions are available.

Compressing and Decompressing Folders and Files

Files and folders on an NTFS volume are either compressed or decompressed. The compression state of a folder does not reflect the compression state of the files in that folder. For instance, a folder may be compressed, yet all or some of the files in that folder could be decompressed if they were moved from a compressed folder of if you selectively decompressed some of the files in the folder.

You can set the compression state of folders and compress or decompress files by using My Computer or a command-line program called Compact. When using My Computer, you can set the compression state of an NTFS folder without changing the compression state of existing files in that folder. If you have Read or Write permission, you can change the compression state locally or across a network. You have the option of selecting individual folders or files to compress or decompress.

▶ **To set the compression state of a folder**

1. Start **Windows Explorer**. In the left pane, select the folder you want to compress or decompress.

2. On the **File** menu, click **Properties** to display the **Properties** dialog box.

3. On the **General** tab, click **Advanced**.

4. In the **Advanced Attributes** dialog box, select or clear the **Compress contents to save disk space** check box, and then click **OK**.

5. In the **Properties** dialog box, click **OK**.

Windows 2000 then displays the **Confirm Attribute Changes** dialog box. This dialog box gives you the option of either compressing the folder only, or compressing the folder and its subfolders and files. To keep existing files or subfolders in the NTFS folders in their current compression state, click **Apply changes to this folder only**, and then click **OK**.

▶ **To compress or decompress individual files**

1. Start **Windows Explorer**. In the left pane, select the file you want to compress or decompress.

2. On the **File** menu, click **Properties** to display the **Properties** dialog box.

3. On the **General** tab, click **Advanced**.

4. In the **Advanced Attributes** dialog box, select or clear the **Compress contents to save disk space** check box, and then click **OK**.

5. In the **Properties** dialog box, click **OK.**

Note Windows 2000 allows closed page files to be compressed. However, when you restart Windows 2000, the page files automatically revert to an uncompressed state. For information about page files, see the topics about virtual memory in Windows 2000 Server Help.

You can set My Computer to display alternate colors for compressed files and folders with the following procedure:

▶ **To display alternate colors for compressed files and folders**

1. In **My Computer**, select the **Tools** menu.

2. On the **Tools** menu, click **Folder Options**.

3. On the **View** tab, select or clear the **Display compressed files and folders with alternate color** check box.

4. Click **OK** to return to My Computer.

Using the Compact Program

The Compact program is the command-line version of the compression functionality in My Computer. The **compact** command displays and alters the compression of folders and files on NTFS volumes. It also displays the compression state of folders.

There are two reasons why you might want to use Compact instead of My Computer:

- You can use Compact in a batch script.

- If the system fails during compression or decompression, the file or folder is marked as Compressed or Uncompressed. If the operation did not complete, Compact forces the operation to complete in the background.

Note Unlike My Computer, Compact does not prompt you to compress or uncompress files and subfolders when you set the compression state of a folder; it automatically compresses or decompresses any files that are not already in the compression state that you set for the folder.

For more information about the Compact program, at the command prompt, type:

compact /?

or see "File System Tools" later in this chapter.

Effects of Compression on Moving and Copying Files

Moving and copying files and folders in disk volumes can change their compression state. The compression state of these files and folders, and the file system in which they were created, can impact the way they are affected while being moved or copied. The compression state of an NTFS file or folder is controlled by its compression attribute.

Moving Files or Folders on NTFS Volumes

When you move an uncompressed file or folder to another folder, the file remains uncompressed after the move, regardless of the compression state of the folder it was moved to. For example, if you move an uncompressed file to a compressed folder, the file remains uncompressed after the move, as illustrated in Figure 3.7.

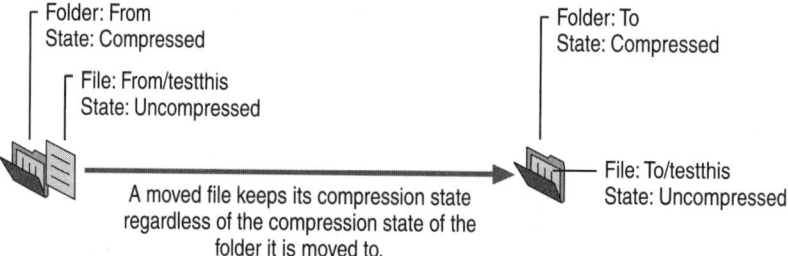

Figure 3.7   Moving an Uncompressed File to a Compressed Folder

When you move a compressed file or folder to another folder, the file remains compressed after the move, regardless of the compression state of the folder it was moved to, as illustrated in Figure 3.8.

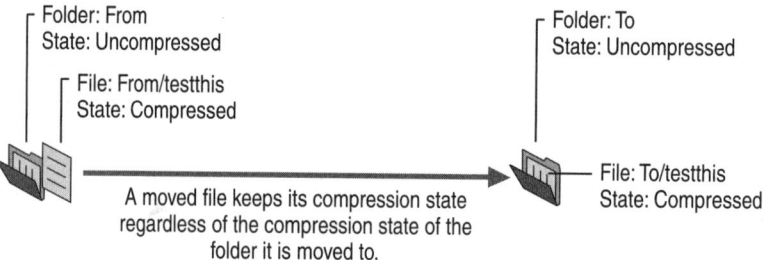

Figure 3.8   Moving a Compressed File to an Uncompressed Folder

Copying Files or Folders on NTFS Volumes

When you copy a file to a folder, the file takes on the compression attribute of the target folder. For example, if you copy a compressed file to an uncompressed folder, the file is automatically uncompressed when it is copied to the folder, as illustrated in Figure 3.9.

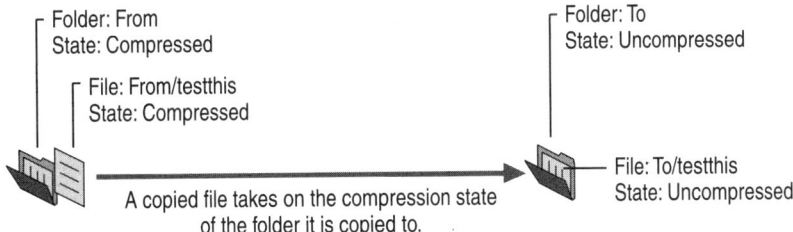

Figure 3.9   Copying a Compressed File to an Uncompressed Folder

When you copy a file to a folder that already contains a file of the same name, the file that is copied takes on the compression attribute of the target file, regardless of the compression state of the folder, as illustrated in Figure 3.10.

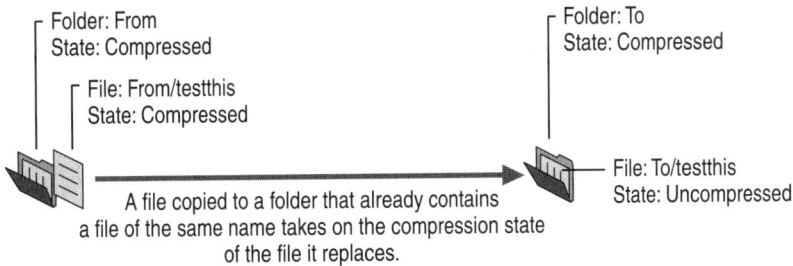

Figure 3.10   Copying a File to a Folder That Already Contains a File of the Same Name

Moving and Copying Files Between FAT16, FAT32, and NTFS Volumes

Like files copied between NTFS folders, files moved or copied from a FAT folder to an NTFS folder always assume the compression attribute of the target folder. Because Windows 2000 supports compression only on NTFS volumes, any compressed NTFS files moved or copied to a FAT volume are automatically decompressed. Similarly, compressed NTFS files copied or moved to a floppy disk are automatically decompressed.

Adding Files to an Almost Full NTFS Volume

When adding files to an NTFS volume that is almost full, you can get error messages that indicate there is not enough disk space to write the entire file if the file cannot be compressed, regardless of the degree of compression in the file when it is opened. For this reason, it is possible to get a read error when you are trying to open a compressed file.

If you copy files to a compressed NTFS folder that does not have enough room for all of the files in their uncompressed state, you will receive a message indicating that there is not enough space on the disk even though the files will all fit when compressed. Because NTFS allocates space based upon the uncompressed size of the file, you can get this error when the uncompressed size of the file exceeds the size of the volume. NTFS does not wait for the compression and writing of one file to complete before it begins work on subsequent files, and the system does not get the unused space back from compression until after the buffer is compressed.

When you are running a program and saving files to a compressed folder on a volume that is almost full, the success of the save depends on factors such as how much the file compresses and whether the beginning of the file compresses well.

If you cannot delete any files or do not have any files that you can compress, you can usually copy all of the files if you first copy the largest or the ones that compress best. You can also try copying them in smaller groups rather than all at once.

NTFS Compression Algorithm

NTFS compression uses a 3-byte minimum search rather than the 2-byte minimum used by DoubleSpace. This search enables much faster compressing and decompressing (roughly two times faster), while sacrificing only two percent compression for the average text file.

Each NTFS data stream contains information that indicates if any part of the stream is compressed. Individual compressed buffers are identified by "holes" following them in the information stored for that stream. If there is a hole, NTFS automatically decompresses the preceding buffer to fill the hole.

NTFS provides real-time access to a compressed file, decompressing the file when it is opened and compressing it when it is closed. When writing a compressed file, the system reserves disk space for the uncompressed size. The system gets back unused space as each individual compression buffer gets compressed.

Note Some programs do not allocate space before beginning a save, and only display an error message when they run out of disk space.

Compression Performance

NTFS compression might cause performance degradation because a compressed NTFS file is decompressed, copied, and then recompressed as a new file, even when copied inside the same computer. Similarly, on network transfers, the file is decompressed, which affects bandwidth as well as speed.

The current implementation of NTFS compression runs more efficiently on Windows 2000 Professional than on Windows 2000 Server. Compression on a computer running Windows 2000 Professional does not seem to produce a substantial performance degradation. Heavily loaded servers with considerable write traffic are poor candidates for data compression, while read-only, read-mostly servers, or lightly loaded servers might not see significant performance degradation.

The two ways to measure the performance of NTFS data compression are size and speed. You can tell how well compression works by comparing the uncompressed and compressed file and folder sizes. For more information about using the DirUse program to see the compressed size of folders see "File System Tools" later in this chapter.

Other Compression Methods

Compression utilities other than NTFS compression are available to compress files on computers running Windows 2000. These utilities differ from NTFS compression in the following ways:

- They usually run only from the command line.
- Files cannot be opened when they are in a compressed state—the file must first be decompressed by using the companion program to the one used to compress the file. When you close the file, it is saved in an uncompressed state, and you must use a program to compress it.

The *Windows 2000 Resource Kit* includes a compress utility, which can only be run from the command line, and two expand utilities: one runs from the command line; the other is a Windows 2000–based program. For more information about these programs, see "File System Tools" later in this chapter.

As mentioned earlier, the DoubleSpace and DriveSpace compression features in MS-DOS cannot be used when running Windows 2000.

NTFS Recoverability

NTFS is a recoverable file system that guarantees the consistency of the volume by using standard transaction logging and recovery techniques. In the event of a disk failure, NTFS restores consistency by running a recovery procedure that accesses information stored in a log file. The NTFS recovery procedure is exact, guaranteeing that the volume is restored to a consistent state. Transaction logging requires a very small amount of overhead.

NTFS ensures the integrity of all NTFS volumes by automatically performing disk recovery operations the first time a program accesses an NTFS volume after the computer is restarted following a failure.

NTFS also uses a technique called cluster remapping to minimize the effects of a bad sector on an NTFS volume. For more information, see "Cluster Remapping" later in this chapter.

Important If either the master boot record (MBR) or boot sector is corrupted, you might not be able to access data on the volume. Recovery from errors with the MBR or the boot sector is discussed in "Repair, Recovery, and Restore" in this book.

Recovering Data with NTFS

NTFS views each I/O operation that modifies a system file on the NTFS volume as a transaction, and manages each one as an integral unit. Once started, the transaction is either completed or, in the event of a disk failure, rolled back (such as when the NTFS volume is returned to the state it was in before the transaction was initiated).

To ensure that a transaction can be completed or rolled back, NTFS records the suboperations of a transaction in a log file before they are written to the disk. When a complete transaction is recorded in the log file, NTFS performs the suboperations of the transaction on the volume cache. After NTFS updates the cache, it commits the transaction by recording in the log file that the entire transaction is complete.

Once a transaction is committed, NTFS ensures that the entire transaction appears on the volume, even if the disk fails. During recovery operations, NTFS redoes each committed transaction found in the log file. Then NTFS locates the transactions in the log file that were not committed at the time of the system failure and undoes each transaction suboperation recorded in the log file. Incomplete modifications to the volume are prohibited.

NTFS uses the Log File service to log all redo and undo information for a transaction. NTFS uses the redo information to repeat the transaction. The undo information enables NTFS to undo transactions that are not complete or that have an error.

Important NTFS uses transaction logging and recovery to guarantee that the volume structure is not corrupted. For this reason, all system files remain accessible after a system failure. However, user data can be lost because of a system failure or a bad sector.

Caching and Data Recovery

The cache is the area of RAM that contains data. When you write data to disk, the lazy-write technique in Windows 2000 indicates that the data is written when, in fact, it is still in the cache. There can also be cache memory on the disk controller or on the disk itself. The following information will help you decide whether you want to enable the disk or controller cache:

- Turning on write caching improves disk performance, particularly if the disk is being heavily written to.

- Control of the write-back cache is a firmware function provided by the disk manufacturer. See the documentation supplied with the disk or disk controller. You cannot configure the write-back cache from Windows 2000.

- Write caching does not impact the reliability of the file system's own metadata. NTFS instructs the disk device driver to ensure that metadata writes get written regardless of whether write caching is enabled. Non-metadata is written to the disk normally, so such data can be cached.

- Read caching in the disk has no impact on file system reliability.

Cluster Remapping

In the event of a bad-sector error, NTFS implements a recovery technique called cluster remapping. When Windows 2000 detects a bad-sector, NTFS dynamically remaps the cluster containing the bad sector and allocates a new cluster for the data. If the error occurred during a read, NTFS returns a read error to the calling program, and the data is lost. If the error occurs during a write, NTFS writes the data to the new cluster, and no data is lost.

NTFS puts the address of the cluster containing the bad sector in its bad cluster file so the bad sector is not reused.

Important Cluster remapping is *not* a backup alternative. Once errors are detected, the disk should be monitored closely and replaced if the defect list grows. This type of error is displayed in the Event Log.

Features Built on Reparse Points

A reparse point is a file or a directory that has user-controlled data stored in the system-administered reparse attribute. The reparse attribute is used by file system filters to enhance the normal behavior of files or directories present in the underlying file system. Thus, a file or a directory that contains a reparse point acquires additional behavior not present in the underlying file system.

For more information about sparse files, see the Platform Software Development Kit (SDK) link on the Web Resources page at http://windows.microsoft.com/windows2000/reskit/webresources.

Remote Storage

Remote Storage uses reparse points to mark files that have some of their state stored remotely. The user accesses a file that is in Remote Storage through a placeholder stored on the local computer. The corresponding file system filter uses the information stored in the reparse point to access the data from the storage location. The reparse point contains the allocation information necessary to identify and retrieve the state of the file that is stored remotely and is needed by NTFS to retrieve the file. For more information about Remote Storage, see "Data Storage and Management" in this book.

Volume Mount Points

Volume mount points are new system objects in the internal namespace of Windows 2000 that represent storage volumes in a persistent, robust manner. This feature allows multiple disk volumes to be linked into a single tree, similar to the way Dfs links remote network shares. You can have many disk volumes linked together, with only a single drive letter pointing to the root volume. The combination of an NTFS junction and a Windows 2000 volume mount point can be used to graft multiple volumes into the namespace of a host NTFS volume. Windows 2000 offers this new mounting feature as an alternative to drive letters so system administrators can transcend the 26-drive letter limit that exists in Windows NT. Volume mount points are robust against system changes that occur when devices are added or removed from a computer.

Important A volume is a self-contained unit of storage administered by a file system. The file system that administers the storage in a volume defines a namespace for the volume. A volume mount point is a directory name in an NTFS file system that denotes the root of an arbitrary volume. A volume mount point can be placed in any empty directory of the namespace of the containing NTFS volume. Because volumes can be denoted by arbitrary directory names, they are not required to have a traditional drive letter.

Placing a volume mount point on an NTFS directory causes the storage subsystem to resolve the directory to a specified local volume. This "mounting" is done transparently and does not require a drive letter to represent the volume. A Windows 2000 mount point always resolves to the root directory of the desired volume. Volume mount points require that the version of NTFS included with Windows 2000 be used because they are based on NTFS reparse points.

File System Tools

The utilities described in this section are available on either the Windows 2000 Setup CD or the *Windows 2000 Resource Kit* companion CD. Table 3.13 shows where to find the utilities.

Table 3.13   Location of File System Utilities

Tool	Location
Cacls	Windows 2000 Setup CD
Compact	Windows 2000 Setup CD
Compress	*Windows 2000 Resource Kit* companion CD
Convert	Windows 2000 Setup CD
DirUse	*Windows 2000 Resource Kit* companion CD
Expand	Windows 2000 Setup CD
Mountvol	Windows 2000 Setup CD

Cacls: Displays and Modifies NTFS Access Control Lists

You can use Cacls to display or modify access control lists (ACLs) of files or folders. Table 3.14 follows the command format and describes the command options. The format of the command is:

CACLS *filename | folder* [**/t**] [**/e**] [**/c**] [**/g** *user:perm*] [**/r** *user* [...]]

[**/p** *user:perm* [...]] [**/d** *user* [...]]

Table 3.14   Cacls Options

Option	Description
file name or *folder name*	Displays ACLs.
/t	Changes ACLs of specified files in the current folder and all subfolders.
/e	Edits an ACL instead of replacing it.
/c	Continues on access-denied errors.
/g *user:perm*	Grants a specified user access rights, where *perm* can be: R (Read) C (Change (write)) F (Full Control)
/r *user*	Revokes a specified user's access rights (only valid with **/e**).
/p *user:perm*	Replaces a specified user's access rights, where *perm* can be: N (None) R (Read) C (Change (write)) F (Full Control)
/d *user*	Denies access to a specified user.

Wildcard characters can be used to specify more than one file in a command. You can also specify more than one user in a command.

If you already have permissions set for multiple users on a folder or file and do not use the **/e** option, all user permissions are removed except for the user and permissions specified on the command line. Use the following syntax when modifying user permissions to include read, change, and full control:

cacls *filename | folder* **/e** **/r** *username*

cacls *filename | folder* **/e** **/g** *username:permission*

cacls *filename | folder* **/e** **/p** *username:permission*

The Cacls tool does not provide a **/y** option that answers automatically with **Y** to the **ARE YOU SURE? Y/N** prompt. However, you can use the **echo** command to pipe the character **Y** as input to the prompt when you are running Cacls in a batch file. Use the following syntax to automatically answer **Y**:

echo y| cacls *filename | folder* **/g** *username***:***permission*

Important Do not enter a space between the **Y** and the pipe symbol (|). If you do, Cacls will not make the permission change.

Compact: Compresses and Decompresses NTFS Files and Folders

Compact is the command-line version of the compression functionality in My Computer. Compact displays and alters the compression of folders and files on NTFS volumes. It also displays the compression state of folders. For more information about this program, at the command prompt type:

compact /?

Table 3.15 describes the options available with Compact. The syntax of the command is:

compact [**/c**] [**/u**] [**/s**[**:***folder*]] [**/a**] [**/i**] [**/f**] [**/q**] [*filename* [...]]

Table 3.15 Compact Options

Option	Description
none	Displays the compression state of the current folder.
/c	Compresses the specified folder or file.
/u	Decompresses the specified folder or file.
/s[**:***folder*]	Specifies that the requested action (compress or decompress) be applied to all subfolders of the specified folder, or to the current folder if none is specified.
/i	Ignores errors.
/f	Forces a specified folder or file to compress or decompress.
/a	Displays files with the hidden or system attribute.
/q	Reports only the most essential information.
filename	Specifies a pattern, file, or folder. You can use multiple file names and wildcard characters.

The following are reasons to use this utility rather than My Computer:

- You can use Compact in a batch script. Using the **/i** option enables you to skip files that cannot be opened when you are running in batch mode, such as files already in use by another program.

- If the system failed during compression or decompression, the file or folder is marked as Compressed or Uncompressed, even if the operation did not complete. You can force the operation to complete by using Compact with the **/f** option (with either the **/c** or **/u** option).

Note Compact automatically compresses or decompresses all of the files and subfolders when you change the compression state of a folder. It does not ask whether you want to change the compression state of the files or subfolders in it.

Volume Compression Requirements

When you attempt to compress a volume that is very low on free space, you might receive an error indicating that there was insufficient space to perform the action.

These errors indicate that the system needs additional free space to perform a compression. The system is not designed to manipulate the data in place on the disk. Additional space is needed to buffer the user data and to hold additional file system metadata. The amount of additional free space required depends on the cluster size, file size, and available space.

Compress: Compresses Files or Folders

Compress is a command-line utility that can be used to compress one or more files. You cannot open a file that has been compressed using this utility until you have expanded it with Expand. To use this program, at the command line type:

compress

with the appropriate options. Table 3.16 describes the options available with Compress. The syntax of the command is:

compress [**–r**] [**–d**] *source* [*destination*]

Table 3.16   Compress Options

Option	Description
–r	Renames compressed files.
–d	Updates compressed files only if out of date.
source	Specifies the source file. The asterisk (*) and question mark (**?**) wildcard characters can be used.
destination	Specifies the destination file or path. The destination can be a folder. If *source* specifies multiple files and the **–r** option is not specified, then *destination* must be a folder.

Note Do not use Compress to compress files or folders on NTFS volumes. Instead, compress NTFS files and folders with Compact or by setting or clearing the **Compressed** attribute in My Computer. For information about using My Computer, see "Compact: Compresses and Decompresses NTFS Files and Folders" earlier in this chapter.

Convert: Converts a Volume from FAT to NTFS

You can use Convert to convert a volume from FAT to NTFS. This utility performs the conversion within the existing volume. You do not need to back up and restore the files when you use this program.

You cannot convert the Windows 2000 boot partition while you are running Windows 2000, so Convert allows you to convert the partition the next time you start Windows 2000. When you convert the partition this way, Windows 2000 restarts twice to complete the conversion process. The syntax of the command is:

convert *drive***: /FS:NTFS [/v]**

To use this utility, at the command line type:

convert

with the appropriate options. Table 3.17 describes the options available with Convert.

Table 3.17   Convert Options

Option	Description
drive	Logical drive that you want to convert.
/FS	Specifies that you want to convert to NTFS.
/v	Runs the tool in verbose mode.

Important   Volumes that are converted from FAT to NTFS, (rather than initially formatted with NTFS) lack some performance benefits. Fragmentation of the MFT might occur and on boot partitions, NTFS permissions are not applied after the partition is converted.

Free Space Required to Convert FAT to NTFS

The conversion of a disk partition from FAT to NTFS requires a sufficient amount of available free disk space in order to build the NTFS disk structures. For information about the process Convert uses to convert FAT to NTFS and the space required for conversion, see the Knowledge Base link on the Web Resources page at http://windows.microsoft.com/windows2000/reskit/webresources.

Converting NTFS and FAT Volumes

FAT and NTFS use very different on-disk structures to represent the allocation of space for files. These structures are often referred to as metadata or file system overhead. Another kind of overhead associated with FAT and NTFS is related to the fact that both file systems allocate disk space in clusters of a fixed size. The exact size of these allocation units or clusters is determined at format time, and the defaults are dependent on the size of the volume.

Like FAT, NTFS has a certain amount of fixed-size overhead and a certain amount of per-file overhead. To support the advanced features of NTFS, such as recoverability, security, and support for very large volumes, the NTFS metadata overhead is somewhat larger than the FAT metadata overhead. However, because NTFS cluster overhead is smaller than FAT cluster overhead, it is often possible to store as much if not more data on an NTFS volume as on a FAT volume, even without using NTFS file compression.

Convert builds the NTFS metadata using space that is considered free space by FAT. Thus, if the conversion fails to complete, the FAT representation of the user files is still valid.

DirUse: Scans a Directory and Reports On Disk Space Usage

You can run DirUse to determine the actual usage of space for compressed files and folders in NTFS volumes. The syntax of the command is:

diruse [/s | /v] [/q:#] [/m | /k | /b] [/a] [/l] [/d] [/o] [/c] [/,] [/*] [*dirs*]

The important option for compressed folders and files is **/c**, which causes the display of compressed file or folder size instead of apparent size. For example, if your D drive is an NTFS volume, type **diruse /s /m /c d:** at the command prompt to get the disk space actually used (in megabytes) and the number of files in each of the folders. To see compression information for an individual file, open My Computer or Windows Explorer, select the file, and, on the **File** menu, select **Properties**.

For more information about DirUse, see the *Windows 2000 Resource Kit* Tools Help, or at the command prompt type:

diruse /?

Expand: Expands Compressed Files

The MS-DOS-based Expand utility runs from the command line. Type the **expand** command with the appropriate options as shown in Table 3.18. The syntax of the command is:

expand [–r] *source* [*destination*]

Table 3.18   Expand Options

Option	Description
–r	Renames expanded files.
source	Specifies the source file. The asterisk (*) and question mark (?) wildcard characters can be used.
destination	Specifies the destination file or path. The destination can be a folder. If *source* specifies multiple files and the **–r** option is not specified, then *destination* must be a folder.

Mountvol: Displays, Creates, and Deletes Volume Mount Points

Mountvol is a utility that enumerates the volumes in your system. Table 3.19 describes the operations Mountvol can perform on a volume mount point.

Table 3.19   Volume Mount Point Operations

Option	Description
Mountvol or Mountvol /?	Displays the name, globally unique identifier (GUID), and location of the volume.
Mountvol [drive:]path VolumeName	Creates a new volume mount point. Specify either a drive letter root directory or an existing empty NTFS directory as the source of the mount point and a volume name as the target.
Mountvol [drive:]path /D	Deletes an existing volume mount point.
Mountvol [drive:]path /L	Lists a volume name for a given volume mount point.

- 'Path' specifies the existing NTFS directory where the mount point will reside.
- 'VolumeName' specifies the name of the volume that is the mount point target.
- '/D' removes the volume mount point from the specified directory.
- '/L' Lists the mounted volume name for the specified directory.

Important A volume can have only one drive letter. Using Mountvol to assign a drive letter fails if the volume already has a drive letter. To avoid this problem, delete the drive letter of the volume before assigning one using Mountvol.

Additional Resources

For more information about transaction logging and NTFS recovery operations, see *Inside Windows NT* by David Solomon (Microsoft Press 1998, ISBN 1572316772).

C H A P T E R   4

Network Printing

By using a computer that is running Microsoft® Windows® 2000 Server as your network print server, you can print from any operating systems that your networked computers use. Computers that are running Microsoft® Windows® 2000 Professional can print easily, even across the Internet. Computers that are running Microsoft® Windows NT® version 4.0 and earlier, Microsoft® Windows® 95, and Microsoft® Windows® 98, do not require manual installation of a printer driver, because print resources are provided automatically from each application. Computers that are running UNIX, NetWare, and Macintosh operating systems can submit print jobs using Print Services for Unix, File and Print Services for NetWare, and Print Server for Macintosh, respectively.

Note This chapter concerns itself primarily with printing across a network and regards Windows 2000 Server as a dedicated print server. For general information about printing, such as creating print jobs and sending them to a printer, see the *Microsoft® Windows® 2000 Professional Resource Kit*.

In This Chapter

Related Information in the Resource Kit

- For information about using a computer that is running Windows 2000 Professional as a peer-to-peer print server for a small LAN (10 or fewer connections), see "Connecting to Microsoft Peer-to-Peer Networks" in the *Microsoft® Windows® 2000 Professional Resource Kit.*

- For more information about using printing resources with Active Directory, see the *Microsoft® Windows® 2000 Server Resource Kit Distributed Systems Guide.*

Introduction to Network Printing

Windows 2000 Server is designed for network printing. Using a variety of platforms, applications send print jobs to printers that are attached to a Windows 2000 print server or are connected to the network by internal network adapters, external network adapters, or another server.

Print Devices, Print Clients, Printers, and Print Servers

A *print device* is a hardware device used for printing. Print device resolution is measured in dots per inch (DPI). The higher the DPI, the finer the resolution.

A print client is an application on a user's computer that submits print jobs to a print device. *Print jobs* are source code that contain both data and commands for print processing. Print jobs are classified into data types based on the modifications that the print server must make to the job to print correctly.

The *printer* is the software interface between a print device and the print clients. It is sometimes called a *logical printer* and typically resides on the print server for remote printing. For local printing or print jobs redirected to a remote print device, the printer software is located on the print client.

The printer software specifies the print device's interface with the operating system and is stored with a unique printer name in the Printers folder. It includes the printer driver. *Printer drivers* are programs that enable applications to communicate properly with specific print devices.

The printer software specifies the port by which a document reaches the print device. A printer port is the software interface through which a computer communicates with the print device by means of a locally attached interface, such as LPT, COM, or universal serial bus (USB) or by means of a network-attached device such as HP JetDirect, Intel NetPort, or Extended Systems Print Server using a network transport protocol like TCP/IP or Data Link Control (DLC).

Multiple printers can be defined for a single print device, allowing clients to use it in different ways. One user might want the device to be widely available; another might want to restrict it; one might want double-sided printing; another might want single-sided printing only. Conversely, as shown in Figure 4.1, a single set of printer software can access multiple print devices. This is called printer pooling.

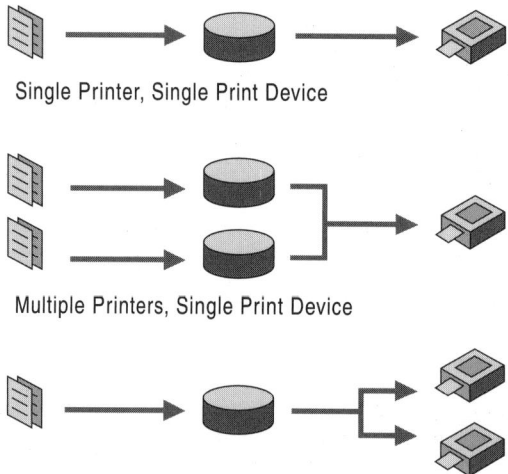

Single Printer, Single Print Device

Multiple Printers, Single Print Device

Single Printer, Multiple Identical Print Devices

Figure 4.1   Printer Software-Hardware Relationships

A *print server* is a computer that manages a queue of print jobs for a shared print device. Computers running Windows 2000 Server or Windows 2000 Professional can function as a print server. However, Windows 2000 Professional limits concurrent connections to 10. If more than 10 clients need to connect to the print server simultaneously, Windows 2000 Server is the better solution.

A print server that is running on Windows 2000 can process remote printing over various network protocols, such as NWLink, TCP/IP, or AppleTalk. The Transmission Control Protocol/Internet Protocol (TCP/IP) is required for Internet communications and is installed with Windows 2000 Server.

The preferred port monitor in Windows 2000 is the Standard TCP/IP Port Monitor (SPM), which uses TCP/IP as the transport protocol. SNMP is used to configure and monitor the printer ports. In addition to SPM, Internet printing adds an hypertext transport protocol (HTTP) port monitor. All other port monitors that were included with Windows NT 4.0 are also present.

Local and Remote Printing

Several combinations of clients, servers, and printers are possible with Windows 2000, depending on whether the print device is *local* (receives data directly from the computer) or *remote* (accessed through a print server), and whether it is networked or directly attached to the computer. A directly attached print device is connected to the computer by a local interface, such as a parallel, serial RS-232/422/IRDA, or USB port. A networked printer is a node on the network: computers send print jobs to it through a network adapter, which might be built-in. A networked printer is also called a network-interface printer.

The following figures show four basic printing configurations. The thin lines represent physical connections, such as network or parallel cables, and the arrows represent the logical print data flow.

Figure 4.2 shows the simplest configuration, a local or stand-alone printer. The print device is plugged into the parallel port of the computer that runs the application. The printer driver and job queue are on that computer, and it sends print data directly to the print device.

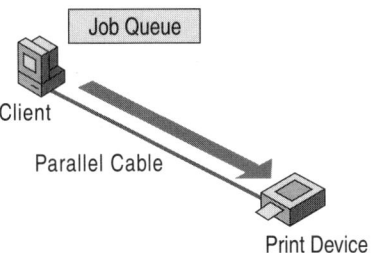

Figure 4.2   Local, Directly Attached Print Device

Figure 4.3 shows a small group of computers sharing a networked print device. This is a peer-to-peer network, where each computer has equal access to the printer, and there is no central control of printing or security. Each computer has its own job queue and cannot see the documents queued on the print device by other computers. If printing halts, the error message does not appear on every client. This is acceptable for small organizations where the users are in frequent contact, but becomes less manageable as traffic increases. Contention among computers submitting documents might cause the print device to time out or reject print jobs.

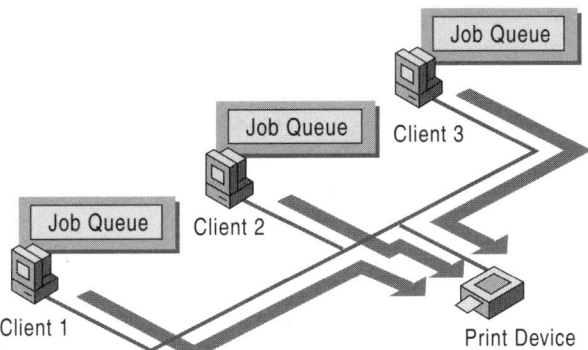

Figure 4.3   Local, Networked Print Device

Figure 4.4 illustrates a network configuration using a central print server. Many clients share access to the print device through the server, which is locally connected to the print device. The job queue resides on the server and is visible to each client.

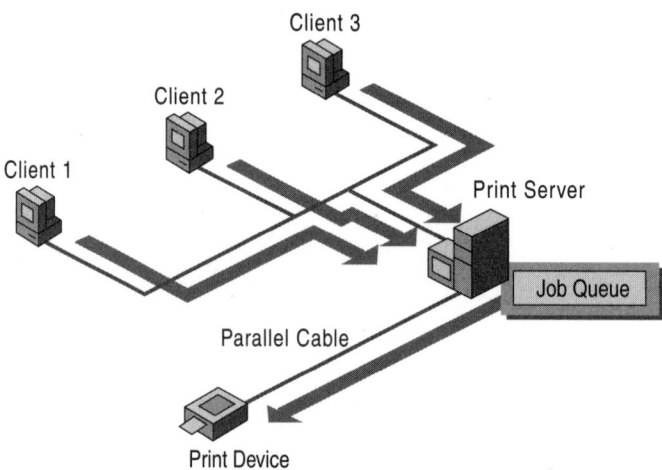

Figure 4.4   Remote, Directly Attached Print Device

Printing is controlled by the server administrator. The administrator defines and enforces a security plan for the network, maintains the printer software, and downloads it to clients when they connect to the printer share. When a client connects to a network print queue, the client checks for new print drivers on the print server and updates older print drivers on the client.

Clients might also be connected to other print devices, and the print server often has several attached print devices. However, the number of parallel ports on the print server limits the number of print devices that can be directly attached to it.

Figure 4.5 shows several clients sharing a print device in a domain managed by a computer that is running Windows 2000 Server; the print device is connected to the server over the network, allowing one print server to manage several print devices.

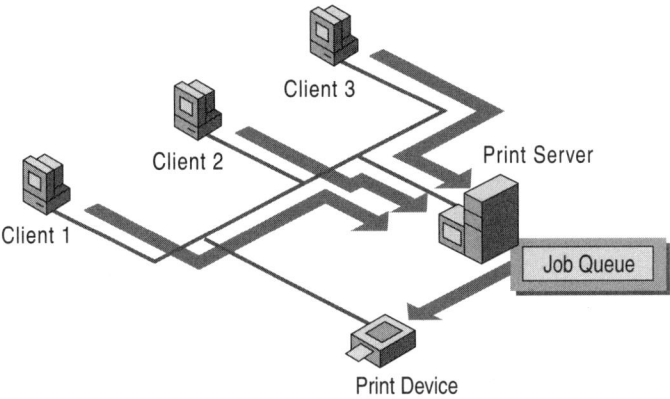

Figure 4.5   Remote, Networked Print Device

Use the Add Printer Wizard to create and share printers so that network clients can connect to them. Regardless of where the print devices are located, the printer software must be located on the print server:

- If the print device is attached locally, the wizard detects it and then attempts to configure the printer software.

- If the print device is attached elsewhere on the network, you must create a port for it when you configure the printer software.

You can also use the Add Printer Wizard to connect to remote print devices. It is important to remember the following:

- *Creating a printer* means installing the print device either directly on a print server or on the network itself, and then configuring the printer software that controls the print device on the print server. Run the Add Printer Wizard and click the **Local computer** option. You must name the printer, install the printer driver, and specify a port.

- *Connecting to a printer* means connecting to the share on the computer that created the printer. To connect to a printer, run the Add Printer Wizard, and click the **Network printer** option. If the print driver for the client platform exists on the print server, it is not necessary to install the printer driver because Windows 2000 downloads it automatically. Otherwise, you will be prompted to install the printer software.

Web Printing

Windows 2000 Server printing is now integrated with the Internet. To install a printer from the Internet, use the printer's Uniform Resource Locator (URL) as the name of the printer. You can also choose to use the URL format within an intranet. For Windows 2000 Server to process print jobs that contain URLs, it must be running Microsoft® Internet Information Services (IIS).

You can view and manage printers from any browser, but you must use Microsoft Internet Explorer version 4.0 or later to be able to connect to a printer using a browser.

For more information about printing over the Internet, see "Internet Printing" later in this chapter.

Architecture

Figure 4.6 shows the processing flow of a document submitted for printing. Some processes, or the software components that perform them, are slightly different for print clients that are not running Windows 2000. For more information about different print clients, see "Working with Other Operating Systems" later in this chapter.

For more information about how Windows 2000 processes print jobs using the Internet or a corporate intranet, see "Internet Printing" later in this chapter.

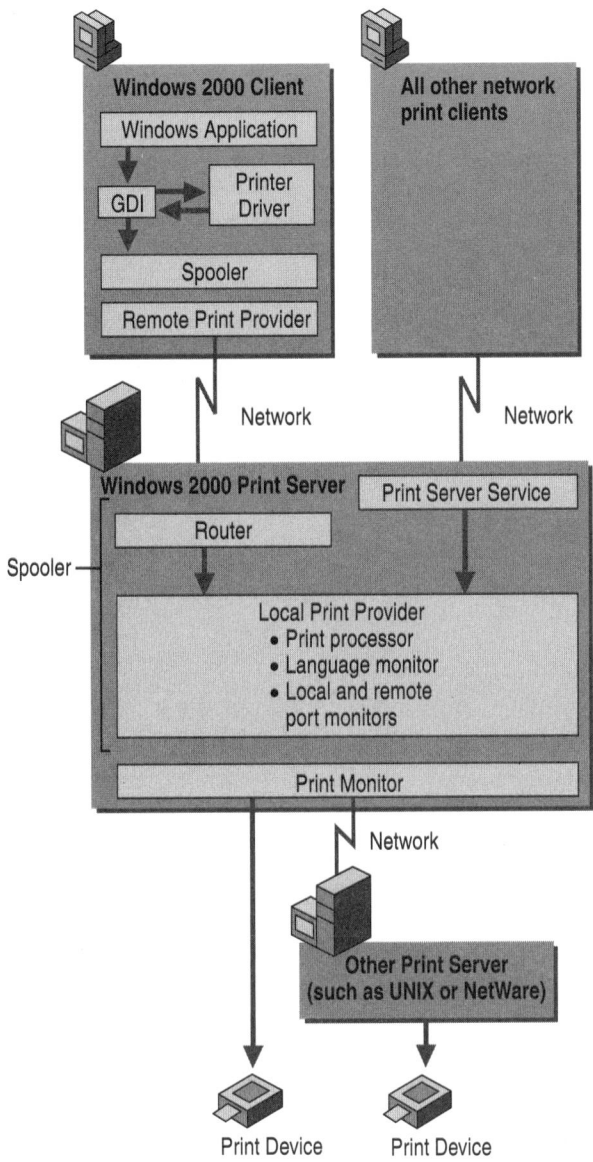

Figure 4.6 Windows 2000 Remote Printing Process

1. A user at a client chooses to print a document.

   If the client is running any Windows-based operating system and is printing from a Windows-based application, the application calls the graphical device interface (GDI), which calls the printer driver associated with the target print device. Using the document information from the application and the print device information from the printer driver, the GDI renders the print job in the printer language of the print device. The application then calls the client side of the spooler (Winspool.drv).

   If the client is running a non-Windows-based operating system or is using a non-Windows-based application on a Windows operating system, another software component replaces the GDI to perform a similar task.

2. The client delivers the print job to the print server.

   If the client is running Windows 2000, the client side of the spooler makes a remote procedure call (RPC) to the server side of the spooler (Spoolsv.exe), which makes a direct application programming interface (API) call to the print router (Spoolss.dll). The print router polls the remote print providers, and the remote print provider (Win32spl.dll) makes an RPC to Spoolsv.exe on the print server, which receives the print job over the network.

   If the client is running another Windows-based operating system or is a Windows 2000 client that created a local printer port and redirected output to a network server (\\Server\Printer), the print job goes to the server message block (SMB) redirector on the client. The redirector delivers the job to the print server service on the print server.

   UNIX or other line printer remote (LPR) clients can print to the Windows 2000 line printer daemon (LPD) service. LPR clients must comply with Request for Comments (RFC) 1179.

   Macintosh clients can print to the Windows 2000 server in two ways:

   - Over AppleTalk if Windows 2000 Server is running Print Server for Macintosh

   - Over TCP/IP if the Macintosh client has an LPR client and Windows 2000 LPD service is running

3. The print router or print server service receives the print job.

   On the print server, print jobs from Windows 2000 clients using Windows applications are enhanced metafiles (EMFs). Some print server services for clients that are not running Windows 2000 assign a data type and others leave the data type blank. Print jobs with no data type assume that the default data type in the **Print Processor** dialog box on the print server. For more information about printer server services, see "Print Processor" later in this chapter.

4. The print router or print server service passes the print job to the local print provider on the server (a component of the spooler), which spools the print job (writes it to disk) in an SPL file.

5. The local print provider polls the print processors. When a print processor recognizes the job's data type, that print processor receives the print job and alters it (or not) according to its data type to ensure that the job prints correctly.

6. The job is despooled to the print monitor.

   If the print device is bidirectional, the job first goes to a language monitor, which handles bidirectional communication with the printer and then passes the job to the port monitor.

   If the print device is not bidirectional, the job goes directly to the port monitor, which transmits the print job to the print device or to another server over a specific communications channel.

7. The print device receives the print job and reproduces the data in the form of the physical medium.

Note For a list of currently supported printers, see the Microsoft Windows 2000 Hardware Compatibility List (HCL) link on the Web Resources page at http://windows.microsoft.com/windows2000/reskit/webresources.

Graphical Device Interface

The GDI calls the printer driver and provides information about the type of printer needed and the data type used. The printer driver responds by sending the GDI the fully qualified path name for the printer and printer escape sequences or Printer Job Language (PJL) which the GDI passes to the spooler.

Windows 3.x-based (16-bit) applications running on Windows 2000 use the Win16-on-Win32 (WOW) layer, which interacts with the applications through the GDI and with printer drivers through the device driver interface (DDI). The WOW layer translates 16-bit print and display APIs to 32-bit Microsoft® Win32® services. The GDI also provides services to the printer driver, including caching, client/server communications, and ANSI-to-Unicode conversion.

Printer Driver

A *printer driver* is a software program that understands how to communicate with printers and plotters. Printer drivers translate the information a user sends from the computer into commands that the printer understands. Various drivers must be installed on the print server to support different hardware and operating systems. For example, an administrator running Windows 2000 Server who shares a printer with clients running Windows 95 and Windows 98 might want to install the appropriate drivers so the users won't be prompted to install the missing drivers.

The printer driver sends the printer-setting information, including the specifications needed to produce each character of the document, to the GDI. It also transmits helper services or utilities required to make the output print correctly.

Windows 2000 provides three generic printer drivers: Universal (Unidriver), PostScript, and HP-GL/2 plotter.

Universal Printer Driver (Unidriver)

The Unidriver is also called the raster driver because it supports raster graphics printing and is compatible with most types of printers. Each printer vendor provides a device-specific data file.

This driver supports color printing at various depths (4 bits per pixel (bpp), 8 bpp, 24 bpp), scalable TrueType and OpenType fonts, device fonts (including double-byte), grayscale printing, font substitution, run length encoding (RLE), Tag Image File Format (TIFF) version 4.0, and Delta Row Compression (DRC). It also has an extension interface that allows printer manufacturers to customize the driver for specific models.

The Unidriver contains the following component files:

- Unidrv.dll is the printer graphics driver file for printer languages based on raster (bitmap) images, including Printer Control Language (PCL), and most inkjet and dot-matrix printer languages.

- Unidrvui.dll is the configuration file. It displays the user interface for Unidrv.dll.

- Raster minidriver (x.gpd) is the data file, also called characterization file. The file name depends on the printer or printer family. For more information, see the documentation included with your printer.

PostScript Printer Driver

The Windows 2000 PostScript driver uses Adobe version 4.3–compatible PostScript printer description (PPD) files. This driver automatically supports key features, including binary transfer compression, resolution, and paper source, for printers reporting as PostScript levels 1, 2, and 3. Its output is device independent because it is fully compliant with Document Structuring Convention (DSC) 3.0.

This driver contains the following component files:

- Pscript5.dll is the driver file.
- Ps5ui.dll is the configuration file. It displays the user interface for the driver file, reports device capabilities to applications, and handles DevMode settings. Ps5ui.dll also allows you to enable TrueType and OpenType font substitution and image color matching, and to determine whether color matching needs to be done on the host or on the printer.

- X.ppd is the data file, also called the characterization file. PPD files are the only printer driver files that are generally binary-compatible across processors and platforms.

HP-GL/2 Plotter Driver

The Windows 2000 plotter driver supports diverse plotters that use the HP-GL/2 language but does not support HP-GL. This driver's output requires a plotting device that can process all of the enhancements built into the HP-GL/2 language.

This driver contains the following component files:

- Plotter.dll is the driver file.
- Plotui.dll is the configuration file. It displays the user interface for Plotter.dll.
- X.pcd is the data file.

If Microsoft does not supply a driver for your printer...

... ask the device manufacturer for compatibility settings. To ensure quality, use drivers that have passed Windows Hardware Quality Labs (WHQL) tests. Microsoft Product Support Services does not support systems with unapproved drivers. For information, see the WHQL link on the Web Resources page at http://windows.microsoft.com/windows2000/reskit/webresources.

You can also e-mail ntwish@microsoft.com to suggest support for a driver or feature. Please include the following information in your request: requester's name, business name, requester's contact information (phone number or e-mail address), printer manufacturer, printer model, and nature of request (feature request or driver request). This does not guarantee that Microsoft will write a driver for your printer.

Client Spooler

The spooler on the client side is not used for network printing. It functions the same as the spooler on the server side when printing locally.

Remote Print Provider

A Windows 2000-based client has three remote print providers. When the server receives a print job from a client, the print router polls the remote print providers and passes the job to the first one that recognizes the printer name. On a Windows-based network, this provider is Win32spl.dll. Win32spl.dll sends jobs to print servers, such as those running Microsoft® Windows NT or Microsoft® Windows for Workgroups.

Win32spl.dll performs specific processing based on the type of target print server:

- For a Windows 2000 print server, Win32spl.dll makes an RPC connection to the spooler on the server (Spoolsv.exe) which makes a call to the print router (Spoolss.dll). The print router receives the job over the network and passes it to the local print provider as if a local client had submitted it.

- For a print server with Windows for Workgroups or OS/2, Win32spl.dll sends a message to the Windows 2000 redirector, which then forwards the job over the network to the server.

Print Router

To submit a document for printing, the application communicates with the client side of the spooler (Winspool.drv). Winspool.drv makes an RPC connection to the server side of the spooler (Spoolsv.exe), which makes a direct API call to the print router (Spoolss.dll), which is also on the server side of the spooler. The print router passes the print job to the local print provider.

Print Server Service

Remote print jobs are intercepted by a print server service before passing to the server spooler. Different services are provided for different clients. A Microsoft® MS-DOS® client running Microsoft Client for Networks, for instance, cannot use the same service as a UNIX client.

The service determines whether the spooler alters the document and how to alter it, and assigns the corresponding data type value to the job. Alternatively, the service can omit the data type and let the print processor component of the spooler apply the default value. Each service supplied with Windows 2000 uses different logic to determine how the document prints. The print server service assigns the RAW (ready to print) data type to all print jobs from clients that are not running Windows 2000 or Windows NT. Print server services, such as Print Services for Unix and Print Server for Macintosh, can also assign the RAW data type to incoming jobs, based on information from the client about the type of printer.

Note This component is used only if the print client has added the printer as a local printer and redirected to a network printer. If the print client has connected to the printer, the job goes directly to the spooler.

The default print server service for Windows 2000 is Windows 2000 Server Service, or Srv.sys. The service receives jobs from print clients that use SMB redirectors. Srv.sys does not set the data type. For more information about the data types used with Windows clients, see "Print Processor" later in this chapter.

Other print server services available with Windows 2000 are listed in Table 4.1.

Table 4.1   Special Print Server Services

Name of Service	Purpose	Availability
Print Services for Unix	Nearly all remote printing using the TCP/IP protocol.	Installed with Windows 2000.
Peer Web Services	Printing to the Internet from Windows 2000 Professional.	*Microsoft® Windows® 2000 Professional Resource Kit* companion CD.
Internet Information Services (IIS)	Printing to and from the Internet using Windows 2000 Server.	Installed with Windows 2000 Server.
File and Print Services for NetWare	Printing from NetWare computers using Windows 2000 Server.	Sold separately as Microsoft Services for NetWare.
Client Service for NetWare	Printing to NetWare servers from Windows 2000 Professional.	Optional component of Windows 2000 Professional.
Gateway Service for NetWare	Printing to and from NetWare print queues using Windows 2000 Server. It also provides a gateway for SMB clients to print to NetWare print queues.	Optional component of Windows 2000 Server.
Print Server for Macintosh	Printing from Macintosh clients.	Optional component of Windows 2000 Server.

Server Spooler

The components below the print router and above the print device are collectively called the spooler. Each component of the spooler uses the services of the component directly below it. The spooler is a series of dynamic-link libraries (DLLs) consolidated in a single architecture, providing smooth background printing by using background thread processing. This means that the spooler passes data to the printer only when the printer is ready to receive more data.

Local Print Provider

The local print provider, Localspl.dll, writes its contents to a spool (SPL) file. It also tracks administrative information, such as user name, document name, and data type, in a shadow (SHD) file. Spooling protects a print job by saving it on disk. If a power failure or other disaster occurs before all jobs in the queue are printed, the SPL and SHD files preserve the documents and prevent loss of data after processing resumes.

Next, Localspl.dll polls the print processors for recognition of the document data type. If no data type has been set, Localspl.dll receives the job and uses the default data type from the **Print Processor** dialog box.

By default, SPL and SHD files are written to the folder %SystemRoot%\System32\Spool\Printers. If the hard disk partition containing Windows 2000 does not have enough space for these files, you can change the location of the folder.

▶ **To change the location of the default spool folder for all printers on a server**

1. In the **Printers** dialog box, on the **File** menu, click **Server Properties**.

2. In the **Print Server Properties** dialog box, click the **Advanced** tab.

3. Type the path and name for the new default spool folder, and then click **OK**.

The change is effective immediately. You do not need to restart your system.

Important Do not attempt to spool to a root (such as D:\). This causes the files to revert to the old default.

▶ **To change the location of the spool folder for a specific printer**

===

Caution Do not use a registry editor to edit the registry directly unless you have no alternative. The registry editors bypass the standard safeguards provided by administrative tools. These safeguards prevent you from entering conflicting settings or settings that are likely to degrade performance or damage your system. Editing the registry directly can have serious, unexpected consequences that can prevent the system from starting and require that you reinstall Windows 2000. To configure or customize Windows 2000, use the programs in Control Panel or Microsoft Management Console (MMC) whenever possible.

===

1. Create a new spool folder.

2. Start a registry editor (Regedt32.exe or Regedit.exe).

3. Add the following entry to the registry:

   Entry name: **SpoolDirectory**

   Path: HKEY_LOCAL_MACHINE\SOFTWARE\Microsoft \Windows NT\CurrentVersion\Print\Printers\<Printer-name>

   Data type: REG_SZ

   Value: <path to the new spool folder>

4. Restart the computer to make the change effective.

Important Do not omit step 1. Adding the **SpoolDirectory** entry to the registry does not create a spool folder. If you do not create a folder, the files spool to the root, which is the default spool folder. For the same reason, never specify a root as the new folder.

By default, SPL and SHD files are deleted after the job prints. However, by enabling spooler event logging, you can use the data they contain to get valuable data about printer traffic, hard disk space, and other printing maintenance issues. See "Auditing Printing Events" later in this chapter.

Print Processor

The print processor tells the spooler to alter a job according to the document data type. It works together with the printer driver to move the spooled print jobs from the hard disk drive to the printer. Localspl.dll is the print processor for all Windows-compatible printing; Sfmpsprt.dll is used to print to Apple devices.

Software vendors can develop their own print processors for custom data types. A printer vendor can also develop a custom print processor if the vendor has its own printer driver or supports a data type other than the five that Localspl.dll supports. Usually, the print processor is installed when the printer driver is installed.

RAW Data Type

For print jobs on computers that are not running Windows 2000 or Windows NT, the spool file's data type is RAW by default. These files are device dependent. The spooled data is destined and formatted for a particular device and does not need to be printed on a different device.

NT EMF 1.00x Data Type

With an EMF file, the GDI releases console control after generating it. The data is then interpreted in the background on a 32-bit spooler thread and sent to the printer driver. Splitting the rendering of a print job in this way is especially useful for very large documents, because the application is not tied up for the whole rendering time. The time gain is greatest if you have connected to rather than added the printer, because the background processing is done on the print server rather than the local computer.

EMF spool files are encoded to provide greater printer independence. For example, a graphic measuring 2 inches by 4 inches on a video graphics adapter (VGA) display and stored in an EMF maintains those dimensions whether it is printed on a 300-dpi laser printer or a 75-dpi dot-matrix printer. The EMF data type also ensures that the print server uses the fonts you specified.

TEXT Data Type

The TEXT data type allows you to send a simple-text print job to a print device (such as a PostScript device) that cannot interpret simple text. The spooler creates a new print job, embedding the text in print instructions derived from the print device's defaults for font, form, and orientation. The spooler uses the resolution setting specified using the **Printing Defaults** button on the **Advanced** tab in the printer's **Properties** dialog box.

Text files consist of ASCII characters. Several character sets are in common use, and text files do not indicate which one to use. The TEXT data type uses the American National Standards Institute (ANSI) character set, so it might print some characters wrong if the application uses a different set. Most character sets are identical for the values 0 through 127, so this problem usually affects only extended characters (values 128 through 255).

Windows operating systems use the ANSI character set. The default PCL character set is called Roman-8. PC-437 and PC-850 are commonly used by MS-DOS-based applications in the United States and Europe, respectively.

Print Monitors

Windows 2000 supports two kinds of print monitors: language monitors and port monitors. Port monitors are further subdivided into local and remote.

Language Monitor

The language monitor provides the common language needed for the client and printer to understand each other in bidirectional communication, so you can configure the printer and monitor printer status. You can request configuration and status from the printer, and the printer can send unsolicited status (such as "Paper tray empty") to the client.

Windows 2000 includes Pjlmon.dll, a language monitor that uses Printer Job Language (PJL) as the language. Any bidirectional printer that uses PJL can use Pjlmon.dll. For example, PJL is the language that implements the bidirectional communication between a Hewlett-Packard LaserJet 5Si and its print server.

If a printer uses a different printer language, the vendor can develop a language monitor for it. A vendor might also develop a language monitor to add data, such as printer-specific control information, to the print stream that is going to a unidirectional printer.

To take advantage of bidirectional printing, you need a bidirectional printer, an IEEE 1284–compliant cable, and a correctly configured port. Some parallel ports are set by default to IBM AT-compatible mode; you need to change the setting to bidirectional.

Local Port Monitor

The local port monitor, Localspl.dll, controls parallel and serial I/O ports where a printer might be attached. It sends print jobs to local devices, including those on familiar ports like LPT1 and COM1.

The FILE port is listed by default on the **Ports** tab of the printer's **Properties** dialog box. When you send a print job to a printer that uses this port, the spooler prompts you for the name of a file where the document needs to be stored.

You can select other local ports by clicking **Add Port** on the **Ports** tab of an existing printer property, selecting **Local Port**, and then clicking **New Port**. The **Port Name** dialog box prompts you for the name of a port to be governed by Localspl.dll. Your entry will be listed as a **Local Port** on the **Ports** tab. Possible entries include:

- A file name, such as C:\dir\file_name. All jobs sent to this port are written to the named file, and each new job overwrites the last one.

- The name of a remote print share, such as \\Server\Printer (URLs are not accepted). Jobs sent to this port are transferred over the network to the named share by the network redirector. This can be useful if you are printing remotely but you want the job to spool locally too (as in network printing on Windows 95 or Windows 98). If your printer is not connected directly to the computer, select **Standard TCP/IP Port** or a remote port monitor other than **Local Port**.

- IrDA. Use this port to connect to infrared-enabled printers meeting Infrared Data Association (IrDA) specifications. If your hardware does not support IrDA, it is not be listed on the Ports tab.

- USB. This specifies the universal serial bus (USB) port, used to connect to cameras, modems, and audio.

- 1394. This specifies the 1394 port designed for Institute of Electrical and Electronics Engineers (IEEE) 1394 bus class drivers.

- NUL. This specifies the null port, which you can use to test whether network clients can send jobs. Jobs sent to NUL are deleted without wasting paper or delaying real print jobs.

▶ **To test client connectivity by using the NUL port**

1. Pause the printer assigned to this port.
2. Send a job from a network client.
3. Look in the queue to confirm that the job arrived.
4. Resume the printer.

A second local port monitor, Usbmon.dll, initially does not appear in the Add Printer Wizard because USB printers are hot-plugging devices. Usbmon.dll is installed automatically whenever you plug in a USB printer to the correct physical port on your computer. If USB has been enabled in BIOS, Windows 2000 detects the device and displays its settings on the screen. You might be required to insert a CD-ROM containing driver files.

Installation opens the USB Root Hub and a generic USB parallel printer port (for example, USB001, 002), and copies the parallel printer point-and-print driver. Scttings for the port can be modified using Device Manager.

Remote Port Monitors

All other port monitors that are supplied with Windows 2000 are remote monitors and enable printing to remote printers. An example is Lanman Print Services Port.

Sharing Printers

To install a printer for use by print clients, you must perform two major tasks:

1. Install and configure the printer on the print server.
2. Share the printer and, optionally, install the drivers for any clients that might be connecting as Plug and Play clients.

By default, the local administrator for a computer can install a printer on that computer. However, as a print server administrator, you can restrict some or all of the local choices for a user through security permissions or, in a Windows 2000 domain, user profiles.

Administering Remote Ports

Windows 2000 Server lets administrators remotely configure and manage ports from any computer running Windows 2000. This feature is applicable to local, Standard TCP/IP, and LPR ports. HP Network and AppleTalk ports must be configured on the Server console.

Local Printing

Local printers can be added from the Printers folder by starting the Add Printer Wizard. However, Plug and Play compatible printers start the Add Printer Wizard automatically when they are connected. Refer to the print device documentation for instructions on connecting the print device to your computer.

Add Printer Wizard

Printing is managed through the Printers folder which contains the Add Printer Wizard, shown in Figure 4.7.

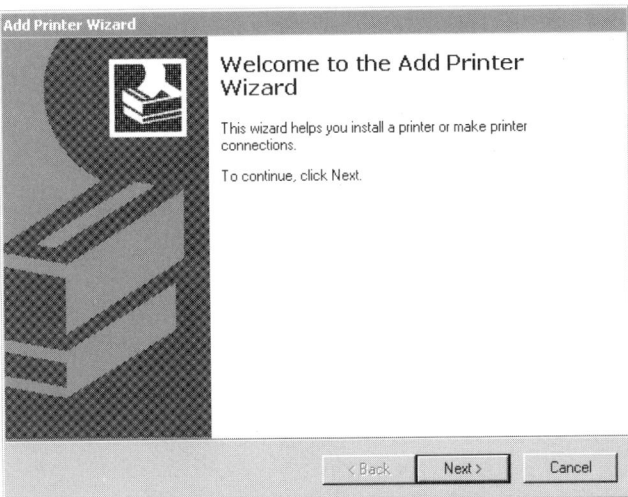

Figure 4.7   Add Printer Wizard

To install a printer under local control, click **Local printer** on the second screen of the wizard. Printer ports can be added and configured in the wizard or at another time. The wizard prompts you to install a printer driver if one is needed; or you can choose to replace the existing driver.

To connect to a printer share controlled by another computer, click **Network printer** in the wizard.

You can also use the wizard to connect to a remote printer share and install its software interface on your computer, assuming that you want local control and have the correct permissions. This bypasses the print server for the remote printer by processing print jobs locally and redirecting the output to a remote printer.

▶ **To install a printer share as a local printer**

1. In the Printers folder, double-click **Add Printer**, and then click **Next**.

2. Click **Local Printer**, and then click **Next**.

3. Click **Create a new port**, select **Local Port**, and then click **Next**.

4. In the **Port name** field, type the address of the network printer share as *server_name**share_name*.

5. On the **Name Your Printer** screen the print device name appears in the input field. Be sure to change the name so that your copy of the printer software cannot be confused with the printer share.

6. Finish the wizard.

   If you choose to share the printer with other network users, the wizard uses the server name and print device name to build a printer share address.

Note Clients on Microsoft 16-bit and UNIX operating systems must always create a printer share as a local printer using the installation commands specific to their systems.

Plug and Play

Plug and Play is a combination of hardware and software that allows Windows 2000 to automate the installation and configuration of new hardware. When a Plug and Play printer is connected to the computer, the printer signals the computer with a Plug and Play identification that Windows 2000 uses to determine the device type and device characteristics (for example, a printer; model 123). The Add Printer Wizard is started and the printer is either configured automatically or the operator is prompted for additional information if all the device characteristics are not known.

Print devices using a USB port or an IEEE 1394 port are detected upon physical connection and are installed automatically. A print device that connects to a parallel port (LPT) cannot be detected when its cable is attached. In this case, you must add the printer using the Add Printer Wizard with **Automatically detect my printer** selected to trigger Plug and Play.

Note When connecting a Plug and Play printer to a Centronix parallel port, the cable must meet the IEEE 1284 standard and the port must be configured as bidirectional in the basic input/output system (BIOS).

If your computer has an IrDA (infrared) port and you have an IrDA-enabled printer, turn them on, and then point the infrared port on the computer at the infrared port on the printer. The appropriate printer driver is installed and the IrDA printer appears in your **Printers** folder. You can also use the Add Printer Wizard to install an IrDA printer by clicking **IRDA** under **Available ports**.

Note Plug and Play print devices are not shared automatically. To share a print device, you must run the Add Printer Wizard.

Forwarding Print Jobs

A null session forwards a print job from one print server to another. This allows job processing to be moved to more protected sites. For example, if you create local printer B that connects to printer share A, you must share local printer B. If a user tries to connect to B and print, access will be denied unless job forwarding is enabled on the computer where printer share A exists.

By default, the null session is disabled, preventing job forwarding, but administrators can edit the registry to enable job forwarding and allow the print server that receives the print job to support null sessions.

Caution Do not use a registry editor to edit the registry directly unless you have no alternative. The registry editors bypass the standard safeguards provided by administrative tools. These safeguards prevent you from entering conflicting settings or settings that are likely to degrade performance or damage your system. Editing the registry directly can have serious, unexpected consequences that can prevent the system from starting and require that you reinstall Windows 2000. To configure or customize Windows 2000, use the programs in Control Panel or Microsoft Management Console (MMC) whenever possible.

▶ **To enable job forwarding**

1. Start a registry editor (Regedt32.exe or Regedit.exe) on the receiving print server, and then find subkey HKEY_LOCAL_MACHINE\SYSTEM \CurrentControlSet\Services\lanmanserver\parameters

2. Change the value of the **NullSessionShares** entry to the share name for the printer.

3. Restart the computer to make the change effective.

Remote Printing

Standard TCP/IP Port Monitor (SPM) is designed for Windows 2000 print servers that communicate with shared printers using TCP/IP. This includes network-ready printers, network adapters like the Hewlett-Packard JetDirect, and external network boxes like the Intel NetPort. SPM can support many printers on one server and is faster and easier to configure than the LPR Port Monitor.

SPM is also compatible with RFC 1759, the standard for the Simple Network Management Protocol (SNMP). As a result, SPM provides much more detailed status than LPR.

For more information about the HPmon print monitor, see "Legacy Network-Interface Printing" later in this chapter. For more information about remote printing to print devices on other platforms, see "Working with Other Operating Systems" later in this chapter.

Prerequisites

To use SPM, TCP/IP must be installed on the print server so it can talk to the print device. Clients do not need TCP/IP; any common network protocol such as SMB, NetWare Core Protocol (NCP), LPR, AppleTalk, or NetBEUI can be used. The transport protocol is not important because only the Windows 2000 print server communicates with the print device.

For example, if both the client and the server have the Internetwork Packet Exchange (IPX) protocol, the client can send the document using IPX. The server can send the document to the printer over TCP/IP. Figure 4.8 illustrates these connections.

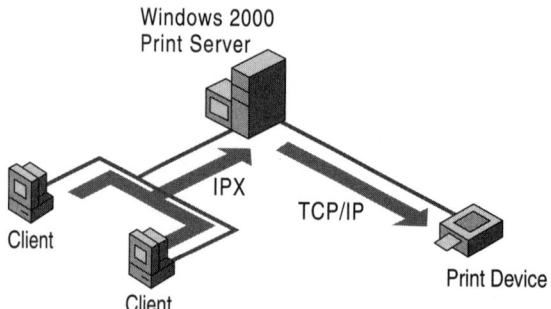

Figure 4.8   Protocol Links for Remote Printing

Print Server Protocols Used

SPM sends documents to a printer using either of two print server protocols, Raw or LPR. Together, these protocols support most current TCP/IP printers. Do not confuse these protocols with the transport protocols such as TCP/IP or DLC.

The Raw protocol is the default for most print devices:

- The print server opens a TCP stream to the printer's port 9100, or another port number, to select connections to multiport external devices. For example, on some devices port 9101 goes to the first parallel port, 9102 goes to the second parallel port, and so on.

- The print server writes to the stream, using normal TCP flow control. The data is raw page description language (PDL), and no protocol is imposed.

- The print server disconnects when it is finished sending data.

SPM uses the LPR protocol if you specify it during port installation or reconfiguration. SPM deviates from the LPR standard in one way: it does not conform to the RFC 1179 requirement that the source TCP port lie between port 721 and port 731. This range is insufficient when a server sends data to more than 11 printers. SPM therefore uses ports from the general, unreserved pool of ports (ports 1024 and above).

Port Installation Procedure

To configure a standard TCP/IP port using SPM, use the following procedure.

▶ **To configure a standard TCP/IP port using SPM**

1. Open the Add Standard TCP/IP Printer Port Wizard by clicking **Standard TCP/IP Port** from the **Add Port** button in either the **Print Server Properties** dialog box or the printer's **Properties** dialog box.

Figure 4.9   Add Standard TCP/IP Printer Port Wizard

2. Type a name or the IP address of a print device in the **Printer Name or IP Address** text box.

3. Type a port name, which can be any character string, in the **Port Name** text box, or use the default name that the wizard supplies, and then click **Next**.

   The system sends an SNMP trap to the device. Using the SNMP values returned from the trap, the device details are determined and the appropriate device options are displayed for further selection (for example, which port on a multi-port print device).

4. If prompted by the **Additional Port Information Required** screen, click **Standard**, and then select one of the listed devices.

   –Or–

   Click **Custom**, and then configure the port by using the **Configure Standard TCP/IP Port Monitor** screen that appears. If you do not know details of the port, try using **Generic Network Card**.

   If the wizard cannot determine the protocol, it prompts you for the information. If you are not prompted, skip to step 6.

5. When prompted for the protocol, select either **Raw** or **LPR**. RAW is preferred.

   If the wizard detects that the device supports multiple ports (indicated in the Tcpmon.ini file), it prompts you to select a port.

6. Select a port from the list and finish the wizard.

   The new port is listed on the **Ports** tab of the **Properties** dialog box.

Reconfiguration

The SPM port can be reconfigured in the printer's **Properties** dialog box. Click the **Configure Port** button on the **Ports** tab. The SPM has its own **Configure** dialog box that appears, as shown in Figure 4.10.

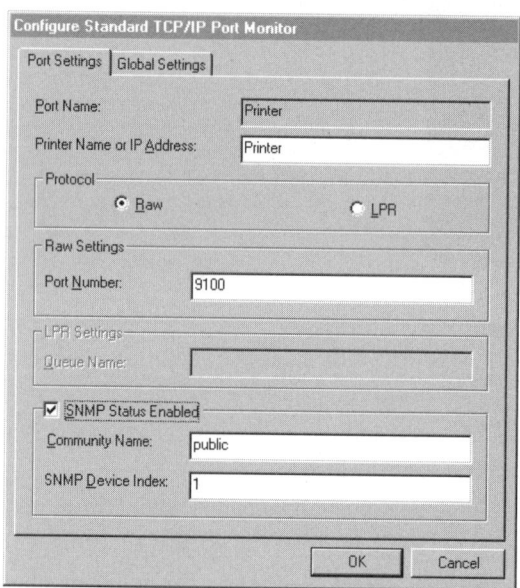

Figure 4.10   SPM Configuration Dialog Box

Warning The dialog box does not verify the settings created in the following procedure. If they are incorrect, the port no longer works. Check with the printer manufacturer to see if the device supports SNMP.

▶ **To reconfigure the Standard TCP/IP Port**

1. In the Add Standard TCP/IP Printer Port Wizard, click either **Raw** (for port 9100) or **LPR** protocol.

2. Depending on which protocol was clicked, select **Raw Settings** or **LPR Settings**.

   For **Raw Settings**, type a port number. For **LPR Settings**, type the LPR queue name specified by the printer vendor.

3. If the print device supports SNMP and RFC 1759, select the **SNMP Status Enabled** check box.

4. If **SNMP Status Enabled** is selected, you can change both the community name and the host device index.

   The device index is used mainly for multiport devices that support several printers; each port on a multiport device has a different device index, specified by the device vendor.

5. When the configuration is correct, click **OK**.

Status Reporting

Printers return status over SNMP. Since SPM is compatible with SNMP, it allows detailed status reporting if the printer provides it. Printers that are not compliant with the SNMP standard do not return status information. When there is an error during printing, the spooler displays a general printing error or does not detect any error at all.

Printer status is returned on a separate thread asynchronously from the print transmission. SPM polls the printers at intervals and sends status updates to the client.

Internet Printing

Installing and configuring a printer from the Internet is like printing on a local port except that the address is a URL. The URL can also be used within an intranet. It makes no difference to the application, which is typically unaware that the printer is accessed through a URL.

If the print server and print client are not within the same intranet, the URL is listed on the client as the printer address.

Figure 4.11 shows the path that print data takes from a client application to a print server spooler when the client prints to a URL-identified job queue.

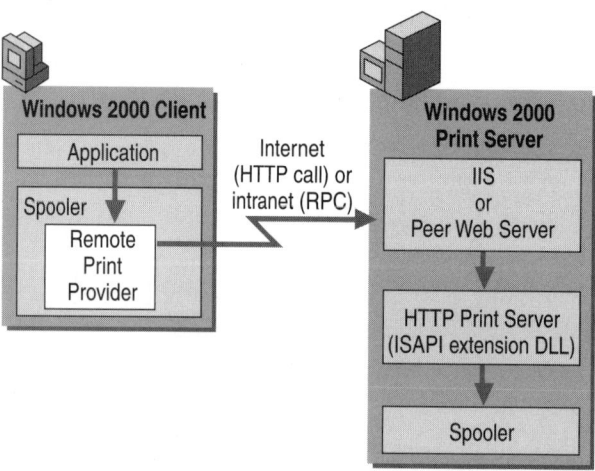

Figure 4.11   Processing Flow when Printing to a URL

Prerequisites

Before a computer running Windows 2000 Professional can print to a printer using a URL address, it must be running Microsoft® Peer Web Services (PWS). A Windows 2000 Server must have Internet Information Services (IIS). The low-level protocol used for job submission is Internet Printing Protocol (IPP) 1.0, which uses the HTTP protocol as a carrier.

Installing a Printer from a Web Page

You can view Web pages to find a URL-identified printer. You can also connect to a printer share via a Web page from clients running Windows 2000, Windows 98, and Windows 95.

Automatic installation begins on the printer's installation page (*share_name* on *server_name*) on the Web. The installation page displays the options your permissions allow you to choose. Click the **Install** option. Windows 2000 downloads the printer software to the client, and the printer is displayed in the Printers folder on the client.

The installation route depends on whether the client and print server are both running Windows 2000 or Windows NT and are within the same intranet. If they are, they communicate via RPCs, and the installed printer will continue to use RPCs to link the client and the server even if HTTP is not specified in the address.

The installation uses HTTP, not RPCs, as the communication medium in the following instances:

- The client and server are not on the same intranet.
- The client is not running Windows 2000, Windows 98, or Windows 95.
- The printer contains an internal network adapter and supports IPP 1.0, and is not connected to a server.

With HTTP, the print server generates and sends the client a cabinet (CAB) file containing the required INF and installation files. On the client computer, the CAB file starts the Add Printer Wizard to complete the installation. A progress report is displayed in HTML while the wizard is working.

Important Installation is not automatic for Web-based printers with internal network adapters. You must start the Add Printer Wizard, enter the printer's URL instead of a universal naming convention (UNC), and finish the wizard manually. This method can be used to install any URL-identified printer by means of HTTP.

Information Displays in HTML

Regardless of the underlying protocol used, the job queue appears in the standard Win32 format when you open the queue window from the Printers folder. When communication is by means of HTTP, however, the job queue is displayed in HTML from http://*server_name*/*share_name*.

If the print server is running IIS or PWS, the Printers folder on the client displays an HTML link to the Web-based printer information page, generated by the print server.

Security for Internet Printing

Print server security is provided by IIS or PWS, which runs on the print server. Basic authentication, which all browsers support, is allowed. To support all browsers and all Internet clients, the administrator must select basic authentication. IIS and PWS also allow the use of Windows NT challenge/response authentication and Kerberos authentication, both of which are supported by Internet Explorer.

The administrator selects the authentication method in IIS or PWS by clicking the **File Security** tab in the **Properties** dialog box for that server. This displays the **File Security** page as shown in Figure 4.12.

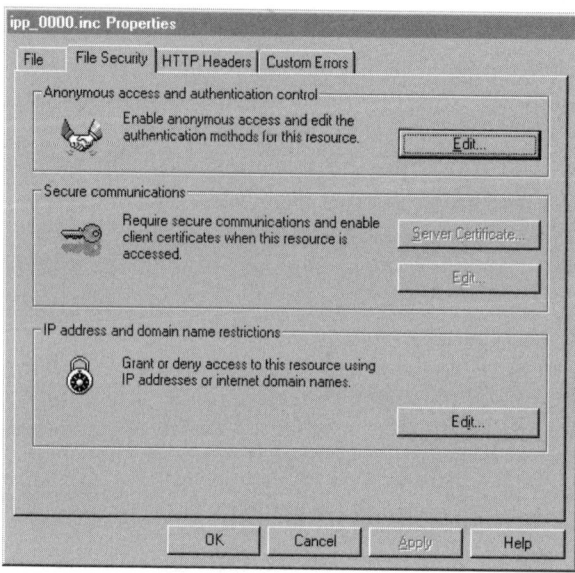

Figure 4.12   File Security Page

▶ **To select an authentication method**

1. In the console tree of the IIS console, expand the node for the server, and then expand the **Default Web Site** node.

2. Click the icon at the Printers node. This node represents a virtual directory that is used to set all security for Internet printing. A list of Web server proxy pages appears in the details pane.

3. Right-click a page icon, click **Properties**, and then click the **File Security** tab. The tab displays three choices for security control: Anonymous access and authentication control, Secure communications, and IP address and domain name restrictions.

4. Click the respective **Edit** button to enable either Anonymous access and authentication control or Secure communications, and then fill in details.

5. Click the **Edit** button under IP address and domain name restrictions to list exceptions to access rights and to toggle the default to either:

   ▪ Grant access to all computers other than the listed exceptions (the initial setting).

   –Or–

   ▪ Deny access to all computers other than the listed exceptions.

6. Click **OK** to save your settings.

Typically, administrators select **Anonymous access**. After clicking the **Edit** button, anonymous access is enabled on the **Authentication Methods** dialog box (Figure 4.13) by clicking the **Anonymous access** check box. Then click the **Basic authentication** check box to select basic authentication.

Note **Integrated Windows authentication** is checked by default and takes precedence over basic authentication if the user's Web browser supports it. To ensure that users are authenticated only with basic authentication, clear all check boxes except **Basic authentication**.

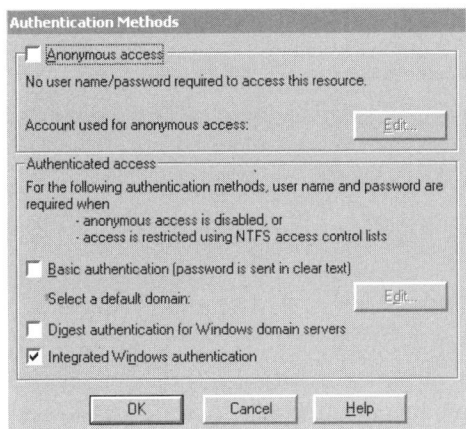

Figure 4.13   Authentication Methods Dialog Box

Checking **Basic authentication** allows all clients to access each server resource by impersonating the Anonymous account IUSR_*computername*. No user action is required. However, if a user attempts to go to another domain or proxy server that does not allow anonymous access, a dialog box appears that asks for the user name and password. If the user closes the box, it does not appear again in the same logon session.

For basic authentication, user names and passwords are not encrypted; they are base-64 encoded and can potentially be intercepted. Integrated Windows authentication is more secure because it does not send the password. IIS applies either challenge/response or Kerberos encryption technology, depending on the capability of the client, when the **Integrated Windows authentication** check box is selected. For more information about IIS security, see the *Microsoft® Windows® 2000 Server Resource Kit Internet Information Services Resource Guide*.

Earlier Network-Interface Printing

The HP Network Print Monitor, Hpmon, is used to send documents to HP network adapters that support only the DLC protocol. Such adapters include both the JetDirect device, which connects a parallel printer to the network, and the network adapters installed in some printers to connect them directly to the network.

Prerequisites

To print to a network adapter by using Hpmon, you must meet the following requirements:

- DLC must be available on the network on which the print device resides.
- The DLC protocol must be installed on both the print server and the network adapter and enabled on the print server.
- Any intervening subnet junctions must be bridged rather than routed. DLC is not routable.
- The hardware address of the network adapter is needed for the print device.
- Install Hpmon on the print server from the Windows 2000 product CD.

Creating a Port

Hpmon is installed when the DLC protocol is installed. You can create a port using the **Port** tab in either the **Print Server Properties** dialog box or the printer's **Properties** dialog box. Double-click **Hewlett-Packard Network Port**.

In the **Name** field, type a logical name for the port. It is used to identify the printer and is associated with the card address (or media access control (MAC) address). In the **Card Address** field, click the network adapter address. If the adapter is not on the network or you are working offline, the address is not listed and you must type it in. If it must be listed but is not, see if the adapter is correctly attached.

Hpmon does not allow more than one print server at a time to access the same network adapter, although each server can access it through more than one port. Configure the Hpmon ports as either a **Job-based connection** or a **Continuous connection**. The default is **Continuous**.

With **Job-based connection**, the print server connects to the adapter, sends a document, and disconnects when the document is printed. The connection is restored when you send another document. This enables other print servers to connect and print.

With **Continuous connection**, the print server stays connected until either it or the adapter is restarted. Security is more centralized because others cannot print to the device unless they manually restart it.

Note If you configure two Windows 2000 print servers to send documents to the same network adapter, set both servers to **Job-based connection**, or one blocks the other from connecting.

Working with Other Operating Systems

Windows 2000 print servers can accommodate a wide variety of computing platforms, operating systems, and network protocols.

Printing from Windows 95 and Windows 98 Clients

Windows 95 and Windows 98 print clients can use Windows 2000 print services without adding software. However, to use the Active Directory™ directory service for a printer search, these clients must have Active Directory Client Upgrade installed. This utility is included with Windows 2000 Server.

Because of the cross-platform point and print functionality in Windows 2000, drivers for clients running Windows 95 and Windows 98 can be installed on the print server; when a client connects, it downloads the drivers from the print server and begins printing. Select the **Sharing** tab from the printer properties on the print server and select the **Additional Drivers** button. From this window, you can select the **Windows 95 or 98** check box. You are then prompted for the location of the Windows 95 or Windows 98 driver files. These files are located on the Windows 2000 Server Setup CD in the directory Printers\win9x. The Add Printer Wizard looks for the printer name in any INF files in the specified location and attempts to install the drivers identified in the INF file.

Printing from Other Microsoft Print Clients

The Windows 3.*x*, MS-DOS, and OS/2 operating systems use their own printer drivers. Clients with these systems can get a list of all available printers in a domain but cannot use Active Directory. These clients can print to a Windows 2000 print server by installing a local printer and redirecting the local port to the network printer share on the Windows 2000-based server. For example, if a printer is installed on LPT1 and you type the following on the command line:

net use lpt1: \\Servername\Sharename

The output to the LPT1 port is redirected by the client network redirector.

Required Redirectors

Network redirectors are required because 16-bit clients print to ports rather than printers and are unaware of the printers in the Printers folder. This limits most 16-bit applications to local ports.

To use remote printers, install Microsoft® LAN Manager Client Version 2.2c (for OS/2) or Microsoft Network Client version 3.0 for MS-DOS (for MS-DOS or Windows 3.*x*). Redirectors are not needed for Microsoft® Windows® for Workgroups (Windows 3.11), which has a built-in redirector.

Note Some 16-bit applications do not print to addresses that are longer than 31 characters; some do not print to any printer if the default printer has a long address. Also some 16-bit applications do not support spaces in addresses.

Output Destination Rules

The rules for directing output differ between 16-bit applications and Windows-based 32-bit applications. Windows 2000 accommodates 16-bit applications in the following ways:

- If the redirector controls the port (as when a **net use** command redirects output to a shared resource), the redirector determines where the document goes.
- If the port is not controlled by a redirector but has a printer assigned to it, the document goes to that printer. That printer's spooling options take effect.
- If the port is not controlled by a redirector and no printer is assigned, the document is sent directly to the port device driver and prints unaltered.

For example, print server \\Server1 has two shared printers defined in its Printers folder. Printer HPV prints to an LPT2 port supplied by a separate I/O card, and printer HPIIISi prints to the FILE port. LPT1 and LPT2 each have one print device attached. Type the **net use** command:

net use lpt3 \\server1\hpiiisi

Copy a file to the parallel ports. In the following results, **/b** is the switch for a binary transfer:

copy test.txt lpt1:/b

The client checks the redirector and finds that it does not manage LPT1. It checks the spooler and finds that neither printer prints to LPT1. The document is sent to the parallel port device driver. To do this, type:

copy test.txt lpt2:/b

The client finds that the redirector does not manage LPT2. It finds that printer HPV prints to LPT2. The job goes to HPV, whose spooling options take effect as the document prints on LPT2. Type:

copy test.txt lpt3:/b

The client finds that the redirector is managing LPT3, so the redirector takes control. The **net use** command has redirected LPT3 output to the print share \\Server1\HPIIISi, where the spooling options of HPIIISi take effect.

Note Although **net use** is typically used to assign a local port to a remote shared resource, it can also assign a local port to a local shared resource. This is useful in testing and troubleshooting.

Printing with UNIX Clients and Servers Using LPR/LPD

A line printer remote (LPR) utility lets an application on one computer print to a spooler on a remote computer. The receiving utility is called a line printer daemon (LPD). The LPR/LPD combination was developed for UNIX computers but is widely used for many operating systems. Both utilities are included in Print Services for Unix.

▶ **To install Print Services for Unix**

1. From the **Start** menu, point to **Settings**, click **Control Panel**, double-click **Add/Remove Programs**, and then click **Add/Remove Windows Components**.

2. Click **Next**.

3. In **Components**, click **Other Network File and Print Services** (but do not select or clear its check box), and then click **Details**.

4. Select the **Print Services for Unix** check box.

5. Click **OK**, and then click **Next**.

Printing Documents Received Through the LPD Utility

The LPD utility, Lpdsvc, receives print jobs from computers that have LPR utilities. Any client that is fully RFC 1179 compliant can use LPR to send printing to Lpdsvc on a printer server that is running Windows 2000. Partially compliant systems might fail.

Note   Windows 2000 also has an emulation subsystem in which you can run and print from UNIX applications written to the POSIX.1 standard. The control commands and processing are the same as in native UNIX systems.

Prerequisites

LPR print clients can print to a print server running Windows 2000 by sending straight text and using the **f** command so that Windows 2000 formats the print jobs properly. The following connections must be in place:

- Both client and server have TCP/IP, and the client has an RFC-compliant version of LPR.

- Print Services for Unix is installed on the print server.

- The printer share name is identified to the LPR software on the client. The share name may differ from the printer name in the Printers folder and in the printer's **Properties** dialog box.

In Windows 2000, the LPD utility is included in Print Services For Unix. When installed, it starts automatically for all shared printers. LPR clients know the printer names as the Windows 2000 share names.

Directing Output

Use the LPR utility on the client to direct the output to a printer on the print server. For example, on a Windows 2000 client, type the following on the command line:

lpr -S servername -P queuename filename

Other LPR clients might use a different command or syntax.

Default Data Types

Print Services for Unix sets the print data type when it sends the document to the spooler. This is derived from the control command included in a print job from an LPR client. It might be necessary to change the default data type at the client to avoid processing PCL or PostScript print jobs as TEXT when they are actually RAW. For more information about the data types, see "Print Processor" earlier in this chapter.

If the control command is **f** or **p**, the data type is TEXT, and the spooler edits the document file to print correctly. If the command is **l**, the data type is RAW and no editing is done. If the command is **o**, the document is already formatted in PostScript code and is assigned the RAW data type.

Some UNIX systems usually send the **f** command by default, resulting in the following symptoms:

- The output includes PCL or PostScript code.
- Extended characters are printed incorrectly.
- The printer's default font is used.
- An extra page is printed at the end.

You can make a registry entry to force Windows 2000 to process the data as RAW. For more information, see the see the Knowledge Base link on the Web Resources page at http://windows.microsoft.com/windows2000/reskit/webresources. Search for the keyword SimulatePassThrough.

Sending Documents Through the LPR Utility

The LPR Monitor (Lprmon) provided with Print Services for Unix acts as the client for printing according to RFC 1179 guidelines and spools to an LPD-enabled target host. The target is usually a UNIX, MVS, or VAX/VMS-based computer but can also be a network adapter, an external network box, a Windows NT–based computer, or a print server running Print Services for Unix or another version of LPD.

Prerequisites

To use Lprmon, the client must have TCP/IP and Print Services for Unix installed. The target server must be running a Berkeley Style Daemons (BSD)–compatible LPD utility according to RFC 1179. If the server is running Windows 2000 or Windows NT, check that Print Services for Unix is started.

Entering the Printer Address

While installing this monitor, the Add Port Wizard asks you to enter the **Name Or Address Of Host Providing LPD** and **Name Of Printer On The Target LPD**. The printer name is defined by the LPD and varies based on the manufacturer. Please refer to the LPD product documentation for the printer names.

Host Name or IP Address

For the host name, enter the DNS name or the IP address. The DNS name of the target computer needs to be defined in the host file on the Windows 2000 print server **hosts** file. You can use the **ping** command to verify the name and address of the target computer. If the connector is a network adapter instead of a computer host, see the documentation provided with it.

Printer Name - Host

If the target host is a UNIX computer and you do not know its name, log on to the UNIX computer that is running a BSD-compatible LPD daemon. To view the target's /etc/printcap file, at the command prompt, type:

cat /etc/printcap

Each entry in a UNIX /etc/printcap file corresponds to a UNIX print queue. The first field of an entry lists names for the print queue (for example, LP, Lablaser, or The_Lab_Printer), separated by "|" characters and ending with a colon. For example, a 9600-baud TTY printer might show a listing such as:

```
lp|lablaser|the_lab_printer:\
:lp=/dev/ttya:br#9600:\
:lf=/usr/spool/lpd/lablaser-err:\
:sd=/usr/spool/lpd/lablaser:
```

The second line tells what kind of printer is used. You can enter any of the names for the print queue in the Add LPR Port Wizard. Alternatively, to display a list of all defined print queue names on the host, type:

lpc stat all

Note This example is for illustration only. Refer to UNIX documentation for information about the /etc/printcap file.

Printer Name - Network Adapter

Because the printer name varies depending on the manufacturer, see the adapter's documentation for details. Typical examples include TEXT, PASSTHROUGH, RAW, P1, P2, and so on.

Changing the Default Control Command

The LPR sends a processing instruction in each print job in the form of a control command: **f**, **l**, **o**, or **p**. The default is **l** for Lprmon and **f** for Lpr.exe, but it can be changed by modifying a registry entry.

Caution Do not use a registry editor to edit the registry directly unless you have no alternative. The registry editors bypass the standard safeguards provided by administrative tools. These safeguards prevent you from entering conflicting settings or settings that are likely to degrade performance or damage your system. Editing the registry directly can have serious, unexpected consequences that can prevent the system from starting and require that you reinstall Windows 2000. To configure or customize Windows 2000, use the programs in Control Panel or Microsoft Management Console (MMC) whenever possible.

▶ **To change the default command for a particular printer**

1. Start a registry editor (Regedt32.exe or Regedit.exe).

2. Add the following entry to the registry:

   Entry name: **PrintSwitch**

   Path: HKEY_LOCAL_MACHINE\SYSTEM\CurrentControlSet\Control\Print \Monitors\LPRPort\Ports\<Port-name>\<IP Address or Host name:Printer-name>

   Data type: REG_SZ

   Value: <control command>

Normally, you would set the default value to **l**, but this can cause a problem when sending an ASCII text file to a PostScript printer on a UNIX computer. The **l** value sets the RAW data type, and the PostScript instructions are ignored. Many UNIX systems add software that scans arriving documents for PostScript code with the **l** value. If it is found, the document goes directly to the printer; otherwise, the software adds PostScript code.

Not all scanners recognize the output of the Windows 2000 PostScript driver as valid PostScript code, and the printer prints PostScript code instead of interpreting it. To correct this, set **o** as the default value for this registry entry.

Respooling

LPR must include an accurate byte count in the control file, but it cannot get it from the local print provider. After Lprmon receives a document from the local print provider, it spools it a second time as a temporary file in the System32 subfolder, finds the size of that file, and sends the size to the LPD print server.

Status Reporting

The LPR protocol does not return a detailed error status report. If there is a problem, the message is always ERROR. To find the specific problem, see Windows 2000 Server Help.

Printing with NetWare Clients and Servers

Microsoft has three products that provide printing compatibility with NetWare systems: File and Print Services for NetWare, Client Service for NetWare, and Gateway Service for NetWare.

Printing Documents from NetWare Clients

A print server that is running Windows 2000 Server can process print jobs from NetWare print clients if the File and Print Services utility is installed. File and Print Services does not run on Windows 2000 Professional. The NetWare clients can be connected to the print server's network directly or through a NetWare server.

Windows 2000 File and Print Services also allows NetWare clients to print to NetWare-compatible printers that are attached directly to the Windows 2000 network.

Prerequisites

You must ensure that communication with NetWare is enabled by means of the NWLink protocol (in full, NWLink IPX/SPX/NetBIOS Compatible Transport). File and Print Services installs NWLink software automatically if it is not already present on the Windows 2000 print server. NetWare connectivity over TCP/IP is not supported.

Printer Search Facility

With File and Print Services, the Windows 2000 print server appears to the NetWare client like a NetWare 3.x-compatible file and print server. File and Print Services presents the same dialog boxes to the client as a NetWare server uses to process a print job from a client. The printers on the Windows 2000 print server are displayed and searched for like NetWare print queues.

Directing Output

To print by means of File and Print Services, NetWare clients must download the printer driver, duplicating the shared printer as a local printer. They cannot use the RPRINTER printing method, although they can use both PSERVER and LDP. Ports must be specified as follows:

- For a printer attached to the Windows 2000 print server, select port LPT1.

- For a networked printer, select either the NetWare_Pserver_0 or NetWare_Pserver_1 port.

Sending Documents to a NetWare Network

Gateway Service for NetWare allows Windows 2000 Server to send print jobs to printers using Novell PSERVER technology on a NetWare network.

When using Gateway Service for NetWare, requests from Microsoft networking clients are processed through the gateway so access is slower than direct access from the client to the NetWare network. Clients that require frequent access to NetWare resources must run Client Service for NetWare to bypass the Windows 2000 print server.

Prerequisites

To use this capability, do the following on the server that is making the connection from the Windows 2000 network:

- Ensure that the NWLink protocol is installed on the computer. Gateway Service for NetWare installs it automatically if it is not already present.

- Install Gateway Service for NetWare on a computer running Windows 2000 Server. To install these utilities, open **My Computer, Control Panel, Network and Dial-up Connections,** and then right-click **Local Area Connection**. Click **Properties**, **Install**, **Client**, **Gateway (and Client) Services for NetWare**, and then click **OK**. Click **Close**.

Note Client Service for NetWare is also installed automatically on the server so you can test your installation by sending a print job from the Windows 2000 server to the NetWare printer.

- Add a NetWare port. This requires you to install the NetWare remote port monitor, Nwmon, which manages communication between the Windows 2000 print server and the print device.

Printer Search Facility

With Gateway Service for NetWare, you can view available NetWare printers in the Add Printer Wizard or by using **net view**.

Connecting to the NetWare Printer Share

Gateway Service lets clients connect to a NetWare printer share the same way they connect to a printer share on the Windows 2000 network. Windows 2000 downloads the printer driver. Printer settings, such as paper size, are not retrievable on a NetWare print server, so you need to adjust them on the client.

Unlike Windows 2000, the NetWare printer driver is not automatically kept current on the client. Use the Add Printer Wizard to update it.

Print Processing

In Novell PSERVER processing, the server grabs the document from a passive print queue, rather than the print server driving the transport of the document.

The Microsoft NetWare print provider, Nwprovau, performs the document transfer. If Nwprovau recognizes the printer name when the print router on the Windows 2000-based print server polls it, it takes control of the print job and sends a message to the NetWare Workstation Service (Nwwks), which in turn passes control to the NetWare redirector. The NetWare redirector sends the print job to the NetWare print server, as shown in Figure 4.14.

Figure 4.14   NetWare Print Provider

Printing with Macintosh Clients and AppleTalk Printers

Print Server for Macintosh allows Macintosh clients to connect to printers shared on computers that are running Windows 2000 Server. The AppleTalk protocol also installs Macintosh Port Monitor (Sfmmon) which allows computers that are running Windows 2000 Professional or Server to print to AppleTalk print devices. Windows 2000 can only send print jobs to a Macintosh computer using AppleTalk when there is third-party software running on the Macintosh.

You only need install the AppleTalk protocol to print to AppleTalk printers on a network. If there are Macintosh clients on the network that need to spool print jobs to the Windows 2000 server, install Print Server for Macintosh on the server.

Printing Documents from Macintosh Clients

Macintosh clients can print to a print server that is running Windows 2000 Server with AppleTalk and Print Server for Macintosh. To the Macintosh client, the Windows 2000–based computer looks like an AppleTalk print device on the network.

Printer Search Facility

Macintosh clients can browse all printers available on the network by using the **Chooser** dialog box. These printers can be distributed over several Windows 2000 print servers. Macintosh users do not have access to Active Directory.

Prerequisites

No reconfiguration of the Macintosh client is required. You must install Print Server for Macintosh to receive the print jobs on the print server. Installing Print Server for Macintosh also installs the AppleTalk protocol.

Print Server for Macintosh is installed from Control Panel. Select **Add/Remove Programs**, **Add/Remove Windows Components**, **Other Network File and Print Services**, and then click **Details**. Click **Print Server for Macintosh**, click the check box, click **OK**, and then click **Next**.

Data Types

Setting up Print Server for Macintosh installs a print processor, Sfmpsprt, that assigns either of two data types, listed in Table 4.2, to a document.

Table 4.2   Data Types for Print Server for Macintosh

Data Type	Instructions to Spooler	Use
RAW	Print the document with no changes.	For all documents targeted to PostScript printers
PSCRIPT1	Convert the document to rasterized images, or bitmaps.	For all documents targeted to non-PostScript print devices

The PSCRIPT1 data type means that the document file is Level 1 PostScript code from a Macintosh client but the target printer is not a PostScript printer. The spooler sends the PostScript code through a Microsoft® TrueImage® raster image processor, which creates a series of one-page, monochrome bitmaps at 300 dots per inch (dpi) maximum. The printer driver returns a print job that prints the bitmaps on the page.

Because the monochrome, 300-dpi limitation is in the raster image processor software, it applies even if the driver supports color or higher resolution. (PostScript printers are not affected.) For those who need a higher-end raster image processor, original equipment manufacturer (OEM) Win32 raster image processor packages are commercially available for Windows NT 3.1 and later versions.

Note Do not send binary PostScript jobs to a server running Windows 2000. Because Windows 2000 is not designed for this type of input, all output is garbled.

User-Level Security

Native Macintosh networking supports security for files but not for printers. AppleTalk has no mechanism supporting client user name or password. Thus Macintosh print clients cannot identify themselves on a Windows 2000 network, and the print server cannot impose user-level security on them. If a Macintosh client is physically able to send a job to the printer, it has implicit permission. However, you can set user-level permissions for all Macintosh print clients as a group.

▶ **To limit user permissions for Macintosh print clients**

1. Create a new user account for the group, to take the place of the System account, giving this account the print permissions that you want the group to have.

    By default, the Macintosh MacPrint service logs on as the System account. That account has print permission on all local printers and thus gives Macintosh clients access to any local printer on the Windows 2000 server.

2. Set the MacPrint service to log on using the new account.

Tip This procedure can be used to bypass a restriction of the System account, that is, the inability of a System account on one computer to access resources on other computers. Thus MacPrint, logging on as System, cannot send print jobs to printers that forward jobs to other print servers. The solution is to give the new user account permission to print on all print servers to which print jobs are forwarded.

Sending Documents over AppleTalk

Windows 2000 has a Macintosh port monitor, Sfmmon, that sends print jobs to remote printers such as the Apple LaserWriter family using the AppleTalk protocol. It also lets you send jobs to AppleTalk spoolers regardless of the printer to which the spooler is attached. This monitor also enables any computer running Windows 2000 to send local print jobs to AppleTalk printers. Macintosh clients can also send local print jobs to AppleTalk printers but might not share these printers with other clients.

Note Some printers misprint non-PostScript documents if these documents are received over AppleTalk; others misprint PostScript documents containing binary data if they arrive over any protocol but AppleTalk. These problems result from restrictions in those printers and do not mean that Windows 2000 is transmitting documents incorrectly.

Prerequisite

For a computer running Windows 2000 to print to a remote Macintosh device, the AppleTalk protocol must be installed on both the sending computer and the receiving print device. If the sending computer running on a Windows 2000 Server configuration has Print Server for Macintosh installed to provide access to Macintosh clients, AppleTalk was installed automatically.

Printer Capture

A captured printer accepts print jobs only from the Windows 2000 print server, thus giving you complete control over the printer. In general, it is best to capture a printer unless another source (such as a Macintosh server) prints to it. If a printer is used only by Windows 2000, it is recommended that you capture it.

Capture ensures that users do not accidentally bypass the print server and send print jobs directly to the printer or reset the printer, which might cause spooler problems. It also prevents job contention caused by the client preparing the printer to accept the same level of PostScript printing that the driver on the client supports. This can cause excessive cycling of the printer, taking up excessive time and stressing the print device.

If a printer is not captured, both Windows 2000 Server and Macintosh users can send print jobs to it. You can enable or disable printer capture by rerunning the Add Printer Wizard and answering **No** or **Yes** to **Do you want to capture this AppleTalk printing device?**

Printing and Active Directory

A directory service needs to make it easy for users to find printers. In Windows 2000, the print subsystem is tightly integrated with Active Directory, making it possible to search across a domain for printers at different locations.

Printing and Directory Service Overview

Active Directory is a distributed database shared by the domain controllers in a network. Information about printer queues, sites, names, and addresses is kept in Active Directory. This information must be sent by individual print servers, as shown in Figure 4.15. It is important to keep the printer information that is stored in Active Directory up-to-date.

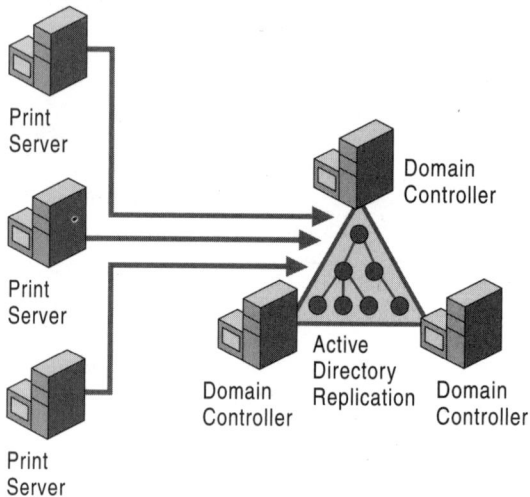

Figure 4.15   Print Servers and Active Directory

Pertinent characteristics of the relationship between print servers and Active Directory include the following:

- Each print server is responsible for publishing its own printers in Active Directory.

- The print server does not have an affinity to any specific domain controller—it dynamically finds a domain controller in the appropriate domain.

- When a printer is updated on the print server, the changes are automatically propagated through Active Directory.

- Printers are published in Active Directory as **printQueue** objects. The published **printQueue** object contains a subset of the information stored on the print server for a printer.

By default, the integration of printing with Active Directory is configured to work without administrative intervention. You only need to make changes if the default behavior is not acceptable. The default behavior includes the following:

- Any printer shared by a print server is published in Active Directory. This still requires administrative access to the host computer to install and share a printer.

- The **printQueue** object is placed in the print server's **Computer** object in Active Directory. To learn more about the information that is propagated into the Active Directory **printQueue** object, see the Platform Software Development Kit (SDK) link on the Web Resources page at http://windows.microsoft.com/windows2000/reskit/webresources.

- When any change occurs in the printer's configuration, the Active Directory object is updated. All the configuration information is resent to Active Directory even if not all of it has not changed.

- If a print server disappears from the network, its printers are removed from Active Directory.

Publishing Windows 2000 Printers

You can only publish printers that are shared. Printer publishing is controlled by the **List in the Directory** check box on the printer's **Sharing** tab.

The Add Printer Wizard does not let you change this setting when you create a printer. Printers that are added using the Add Printer Wizard are published by default. If you do not want a printer published in Active Directory, on the **Sharing** tab of the printer properties, clear the **List in the Directory** check box.

Note For a USB printer that is detected and installed automatically, you must manually share and publish it using the **Sharing** tab.

The printer is placed in the print server's **Computer** object in Active Directory. Once it has been placed in Active Directory, the object can be moved or renamed using the Active Directory Users and Computers console.

Publishing a Printer Manually

To publish a printer in Active Directory manually, you must first set the pruning interval to "never." If you do not do this, the printer you manually add to Active Directory is removed the next time the pruner runs. Then publish the printer using the Add Printer Wizard to permanently create the **printQueue** object.

Publishing Mechanism

The print server sends data asynchronously to Active Directory. Initially it sends the data after a one-second delay. If this fails, the server retries after a longer period and continues until it reaches a delay of two hours. At this point the server retries at this interval until it is successful. During this pending phase, the message "The Directory operation is still in progress" is displayed on the **Sharing** tab of the printer properties.

The printer is published to a random domain controller, so a query might not show the printer until it has been replicated to all the domain controllers. For local domain controllers on the same site, the maximum delay is approximately 30 minutes, but is typically 5 – 10 minutes. For inter-site searches, the delay depends on the replication strategy of your organization.

Pruning Orphans

When a printer is deleted from a print server, the corresponding Active Directory object is removed. However, there can be circumstances where the printer is no longer available. For example, when the print server is being rebuilt or is powered off.

Under these circumstances the orphaned entries must be removed because Active Directory must reflect only the print devices that are currently available. A program called an orphan pruner accomplishes this by running on each domain controller to periodically check for orphaned printers. If a printer does not exist, it is deleted. The pruner only looks at print servers that are in the same site as the domain controller on which it is running.

The orphan pruner is controlled by several policy settings. By default, if the pruner cannot see a printer three times in a row at 8-hour intervals, it assumes that the entry is no longer valid and deletes it.

In some cases, the pruner might remove a printer that still needs to be published. For example, if a print server is down for a few days, its printers need to be removed. Once the server comes back up, its printers need to be republished. To cover this situation, a print server verifies that its printers are published when it restarts and the spooler starts up. You can force a restart by issuing the commands:

```
net stop spooler
```

and

```
net start spooler
```

Alternatively, you can use the "check published state" policy.

Sites Without Domain Controllers

It is unusual but possible to create an Active Directory site that has no domain controllers. If this case, the print servers in the site are never pruned. To resolve this, you can make another domain controller responsible for managing this site. This is also required for users to log on to the network.

▶   **To add a site to a domain controller in another site**

Caution Do not use a registry editor to edit the registry directly unless you have no alternative. The registry editors bypass the standard safeguards provided by administrative tools. These safeguards prevent you from entering conflicting settings or settings that are likely to degrade performance or damage your system. Editing the registry directly can have serious, unexpected consequences that can prevent the system from starting and require that you reinstall Windows 2000. To configure or customize Windows 2000, use the programs in Control Panel or Microsoft Management Console (MMC) whenever possible.

1. Start a registry editor (Regedt32.exe or Regedit.exe).

2. Add the **SiteCoverage** entry to the registry. For its value, list each additional site that the domain controller must cover:

    Path: HKEY_LOCAL_MACHINE\SYSTEM \CurrentControlSet\Services\Netlogon\Parameters\SiteCoverage

    Data type: REG MULTI_SZ

    Value: *<site name>*

Supporting Non-Windows 2000 Printers

Printers that are on print servers running Windows NT 4.0 or Windows NT 3.51 can be published in Active Directory by using the Users and Computers console. Alternately, you can use the Pubprn.vbs script, which is provided in the System32 folder. You can publish all printers on a server or specify single printers to be published.

To run Pubprn.vbs, type:

Cscript c:\winnt\system32\pubprn.vbs <params>

If you don't enter any parameters, the following help message is displayed:

```
Usage: [cscript] pubprn.vbs server "LDAP://OU=..,DC=..."
    server is a Windows NT server name (e.g.: Server) or UNC printer
name (\\Server\Printer)
    "LDAP://CN=..,DC=..." is the DS path of the target container
Example 1: pubprn.vbs MyServer
"LDAP://CN=MyContainer,DC=MyDomain,DC=Company,DC=Com"
Example 2: pubprn.vbs \\MyServer\Printer
LDAP://CN=MyContainer,DC=MyDomain,DC=Company,DC=Com"
```

For instructions about publishing printers on other network operating systems, see the *Microsoft® Windows® 2000 Server Resource Kit Internetworking Guide.*

Group Policy Settings

Table 4.3 lists group policies related to printing. The Computer column indicates whether this policy must be set for the domain controller or for the print server. It is recommended that you have one or more computer groups for the domain controllers and one or more computer groups for the main printer servers to set the policy on those groups.

Table 4.3   Important Group Policy Settings for Printing

Name	Description	Computer	Default
Pruning Interval	The length of time that the pruner waits before starting another Active Directory scan.	Domain controller	8 hours
Pruning Retries	The number of scans after which the pruner deletes the printer from Active Directory if it is missing.	Domain controller	3

(continued)

Table 4.3   Important Group Policy Settings for Printing *(continued)*

Name	Description	Computer	Default
Backward Compatibility Printer Pruning	You might want a different pruning policy for non-Windows 2000 printers. The default is to never prune. Alternately, you can choose to prune only if the print server confirms that the printer is absent.	Domain controller	Never
Allow Pruning of Published Printers	If true, the printers published by this computer are candidates for pruning. If false, the pruner never attempts to prune the printer on this server.	Server	True
Allow Printers to be Published	Disable this option to prevent printers from being published	Server	Yes
Automatically Publish New Printers	Disable this option to prevent the Add Printer Wizard from automatically publishing a new printer when it is added	Server	Yes
Check Publish State	If this is set to any other value than never, the print server checks if its printers are published at regular intervals. (The check is the same as what is performed at system startup).	Server	Never

For more information about Group Policy, see "Group Policy" in the *Microsoft® Windows® 2000 Server Resource Kit Distributed Systems Guide*.

Printer Location Tracking

Printer location tracking in Windows 2000 allows users to search for and find printers at their location or another specified location, according to attributes assigned to printers.

For more information about printer location tracking and procedures for setting it up, see Windows 2000 Server Help.

Group Policy lets you configure printer location tracking for a group of computers. See the "Computer location" and "Pre-populate printer search location text" policies in Computer Configuration\Administrative Templates\Printers. For information about these policies, see the **Explain** tab for each policy or the Windows 2000 Resource Kit Group Policy Reference (Gp.chm) on the *Windows 2000 Resource Kit* companion CD.

Printing and Clusters

The Cluster service is a virtual server that supports mission-critical applications and data by allowing a group of independent computers to work together as a single system. The cluster appears to network clients as a single server. All computers in the cluster are known by a common name—the cluster name. Each computer is a node, and if one node fails, the cluster's resources "fail over"—move over to a node that is still operating.

Cluster service runs only on Windows 2000 Advanced Server. However, after it is set up on Windows 2000 Server computers, it can be administered, including installing and configuring printers, from any computer running Windows 2000 in the network.

Creating the Spooler

Adding printers requires the creation of a spooler for the cluster so the cluster can be used as a print server. Without a spooler, you cannot add printers.

Prerequisites

To create a spooler for a cluster, you must be the administrator of the cluster as well as of each node within the cluster.

You must also have the administration software installed on your computer. Cluster Administrator is the graphical application supplied with the Cluster service package to manage clusters. Alternatively you can use Cluster.exe, a command-line tool, or custom administration tools developed using the Cluster service command interfaces.

Specifying the Resource

The network applications, data files, and other tools installed on the nodes are the cluster resources, which provide services to network clients. The spooler is specified by selecting the **Print Spooler** resource type in the **Cluster Administrator** window or using a Cluster.exe command. Resources are organized into groups, consisting of resources that are interdependent and therefore must fail over together. There can be no more than one Print Spooler resource per cluster group.

The procedure to specify a Print Spooler resource is as follows. It is like the procedure for creating any resource in Cluster service, and more details can be found in other chapters in this book.

▶ **To create a Print Spooler resource**

1. In the **Cluster Administrator** window, start the New Group Wizard, and then create a group for the print spooler.

    This group, called the virtual server, is used to contain all resources necessary to create a printer share.

2. Add an IP Address resource to the group.

    This resource is a prerequisite for the Network Name resource, created next. If the nodes have Print Services for Unix installed and started, clients with the LPR utility can also use this IP address to access the printer.

3. Add a Network Name resource to the group.

    This is the server name (cluster name) that clients will use when connecting to the printer share.

4. Add a Physical Disk resource to the group.

    The Physical Disk resource is where the spooler files for the printer shares will be stored. This resource must be on the SCSI bus that is common to the nodes.

5. Add the Print Spooler resource to the group.

    Ensure that the spool directory is placed on a Physical Disk resource that is part of the group.

6. Configure the possible owners.

7. Add the Physical Disk and Network Name resources as dependencies.

8. On the **Parameters** property sheet for the Print Spooler resource type, configure the following options:

    ▪ **Spool folder**: type a fully qualified path for the spool folder (for example, G:\Spool). The spooler creates the folder if it does not already exist.

    ▪ **Job completion time out**: specify how long the document can take to get from the client to the printer before the printer stops trying to print it.

9. Use Cluster Administrator to bring the Print Spooler resource online.

After you have created and configured the Print Spooler resource, you need to install printer drivers on each node and add printers to the clustered spooler.

Installing Printing Components

This process does not use Cluster Administrator. Instead, perform the following actions. Only TCP/IP and simple LPR ports are supported.

- Go to the Printers folder for each node and ensure that each has the appropriate protocols, port monitors, language monitors, print processors, and forms installed. You can do this remotely, but you must address each node by its node name, not the cluster name. A specification made on one node does not carry over to the other nodes, so ensure that the settings are identical on all nodes.

- On each node install the printer drivers you want to use for the cluster. Each node of the cluster must have the correct printer drivers installed for all clients that connect to the printer share. Otherwise, Point and Print does not work and clients are prompted to install drivers when they connect to the printer the first time.

- Add printer ports from the Cluster virtual computer Printers folder in addition to the cluster node computers.

Adding a Printer to a Cluster

After creating the group, resources, ports, and printer drivers, you can add a printer to the cluster. Each node must have connectivity to the remote print server device (port). A locally connected computer cannot be used in a cluster configuration because the printer is connected directly to the node and does not fail over if that node goes down.

Adding a printer to a cluster is the same as adding it to any other computer, with the following exceptions:

- Never start from the local Printers folder. The cluster always appears remote, even if you are working on the active cluster node. Instead, type the cluster name (for example, \\Cluster-prn) in the **Run** menu. Then click the remote Printers folder that is displayed.

- If the Add Printer Wizard does not appear when the remote Printers folder opens, you cannot continue. One of three things is wrong:

  - You do not have administrator permissions on each cluster node.

  - The spooler service is not started on the current computer (unlikely).

  - The cluster does not have at least one Print Spooler resource online.

What Happens at Failover

When a group containing a Print Spooler resource fails over to another node, the document that is currently being spooled to the printer is restarted from the other node after the failure. When you move a Print Spooler resource or take it offline, Cluster service waits until all documents are finished spooling or until the configured wait time has elapsed. Documents that are spooling from an application to a Print Spooler resource are discarded and must be respooled to the resource (or reprinted) if the group containing the resource fails over before the application has finished spooling.

Monitoring Printer Performance

Windows 2000 provides several features that allow you to assess the performance of your network printing resources.

Using System Monitor

System Monitor allows you to observe counters for printing performance. It also supports setting alert levels for the counters being monitored. Individual counters and objects are present for each instance of a printer that is installed.

The two most critical performance counters for monitoring printing are the following:

- Bytes Printed/sec. The number of RAW bytes per second that are sent to the printer. Low values for this counter can indicate that the printers are underutilized, either because there are no jobs, print queues are not evenly loaded, or the server is too busy. This value varies according to the type of printer. Consult your printer documentation for acceptable values for printer throughput.
- Job Errors. Number of job errors. Job errors are typically caused by improper port configuration. Check your port configuration for invalid settings. A printing job instance will increment this count only once, even if it happens multiple times. Also, some monitors do not support this kind of error, causing the counter to remain at 0.

Collecting baseline data is an important step in monitoring all performance counters. For more information about System Monitor, see "Overview of Performance Monitoring" in this book.

Auditing Printing Events

Auditing is a means of tracking a printer's usage. It's possible to specify which groups or users and which actions to audit for a particular printer, as well as audit both successful and failed actions. Windows 2000 stores the data that is generated from auditing a file, which can be viewed and published in various formats using Event Viewer.

To change audit entries, you use the **Audit Entry for** *printer_name* page of the Printer Properties dialog box (Figure 4.16).

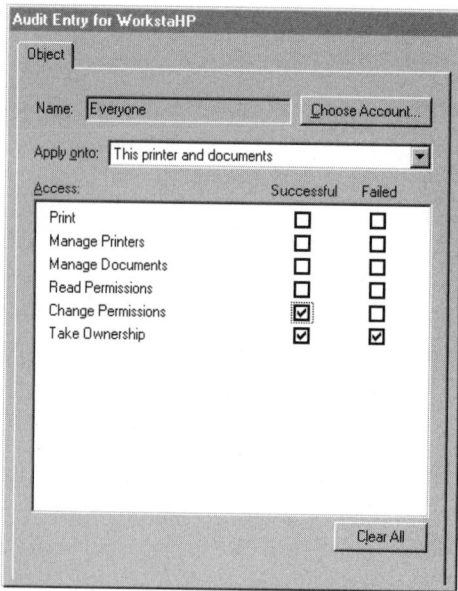

Figure 4.16   Example of an Audit Entry Page

▶ **To add, remove, view, or edit audit entries for a printer**

1. In the **Properties** dialog box for the printer, click the **Security** tab, and then click **Advanced**.

2. Click the **Auditing** tab.

   If the tab is not visible, this means you do not have administrator permissions (Manage Printers, Manage Documents) for the server and you cannot continue.

3. Use the **Add** and **Remove** buttons to specify user names and/or groups to be audited, or the **View/Edit** button to change settings.

   The **Add** and **View/Edit** buttons take you to the **Audit Entry for** *printer_name* page as shown in Figure 4.16.

4. On the **Audit Entry** page, under **Apply onto**, specify whether the auditing should be done by printer, by document, or both.

5. Under **Access**, select check boxes as appropriate to tailor the auditing for the users or groups appearing in the **Name** box:

   ▪ **Successful** means "Audit all successful attempts to perform this action."

   ▪ **Failed** means "Audit all failed attempts to perform this action."

   ▪ **Print**, **Manage Printers**, and **Manage Documents** are the printing permissions. **Read Permissions**, **Change Permissions**, and **Take Ownership** are permissions to control permissions. Table 4.4 shows the associated events that are audited by selecting each permission.

6. To configure another user or group for auditing, click **Choose Account**.

7. When finished, click **OK** to save all your settings.

Note Most printers should not be audited: the Event Log service would fill up with useless information. It is best to limit auditing to select, high-security printers.

Table 4.4   Audit Events Matrix for Printers

	Permission Selected for Auditing					
Event	**Print**	**Manage Documents**	**Manage Printers**	**Read Permissions**	**Change Permissions**	**Take Ownership**
Printing documents	Audited	Not audited	Not audited	Not audited	Not audited	Not audited
Changing document printing preferences	Audited	Not audited	Not audited	Not audited	Not audited	Not audited
Changing document job properties	Not audited	Audited	Not audited	Not audited	Not audited	Not audited
Pausing, restarting, moving, and deleting documents	Not audited	Audited	Not audited	Not audited	Not audited	Not audited
Changing document printing defaults	Not audited	Audited	Audited	Not audited	Not audited	Not audited
Creating a printer share	Not audited	Not audited	Audited	Not audited	Not audited	Not audited

(continued)

Table 4.4   Audit Events Matrix for Printers *(continued)*

Event	Print	Manage Documents	Manage Printers	Read Permissions	Change Permissions	Take Ownership
		Permission Selected for Auditing				
Changing printer properties	Not audited	Not audited	Audited	Not audited	Not audited	Not audited
Deleting a printer	Not audited	Not audited	Audited	Not audited	Not audited	Not audited
Reading printer permissions	Not audited	Not audited	Not audited	Audited	Not audited	Not audited
Changing printer permissions	Not audited	Not audited	Not audited	Not audited	Audited	Not audited
Taking ownership	Not audited	Not audited	Not audited	Not audited	Not audited	Audited

Important   For this procedure to work, the **Audit Object Access** option in Group Policy must be set to audit successful attempts, failed attempts, or both. To access this option, click **Computer Configuration**, **Windows Settings**, **Security Settings**, **Local Policies**, and then click **Audit Policy**.

Logging Spooler Events

Another source of valuable information is the spooler, which can provide data about printer traffic, hard disk space, spooler errors, and other printing maintenance issues. Use the following procedure to enable spooler event logging.

▶ **To enable spooler event logging**

1. In the **Printers** dialog box, click the appropriate printer.

2. On the **File** menu, click **Server Properties**.

3. Click the **Advanced** tab.

4. Verify that the entry in the **Spool folder** field is the path you want; if not, type in the correct path.

5. Select any combination of the three check boxes related to event logging to enable the information that you want, and then click **OK**.

Note   These check boxes also appear in Group Policy under User Configuration.

For more information about the spooler, see "Server Spooler" earlier in this chapter.

Utilities

Windows 2000 provides several utilities to help you administer your network printing resources.

rundll32

Some enterprise configurations require clients to connect to network printers during an unattended setup. Microsoft facilitates this with the **rundll32** command, which allows printers to be installed from the command line. This is particularly useful when you need to add or remove printers from a group of users by means of a logon script.

The **rundll32** command provides greater control than older supplemental utilities such as Con2prt.exe, which allowed only for the addition and deletion of networked printers. For example, the **rundll32** command allows local printers to be modified and deleted. It also allows you to add printer connections by computer rather than by user as the Add Printer Wizard does. The result is that you can control all aspects of the end user's printing experience by running a local or remote batch file or logon script containing **rundll32** commands.

The case-sensitive syntax for the **rundll32** command is:

rundll32 printui.dll,PrintUIEntry *<options>*

Examples of useful options include:

rundll32 printui.dll,PrintUIEntry /il /c\\computer

This installs a printer for the user logged on a remote computer named *computer* by running the Add Printer Wizard. You can also type:

rundll32 printui.dll,PrintUIEntry /ga /c\\computer /n\\print_server\printer

This adds a connection to *print_server/printer* for all users on a remote computer named *computer*.

The available options for **rundll32** are shown in Figure 4.17

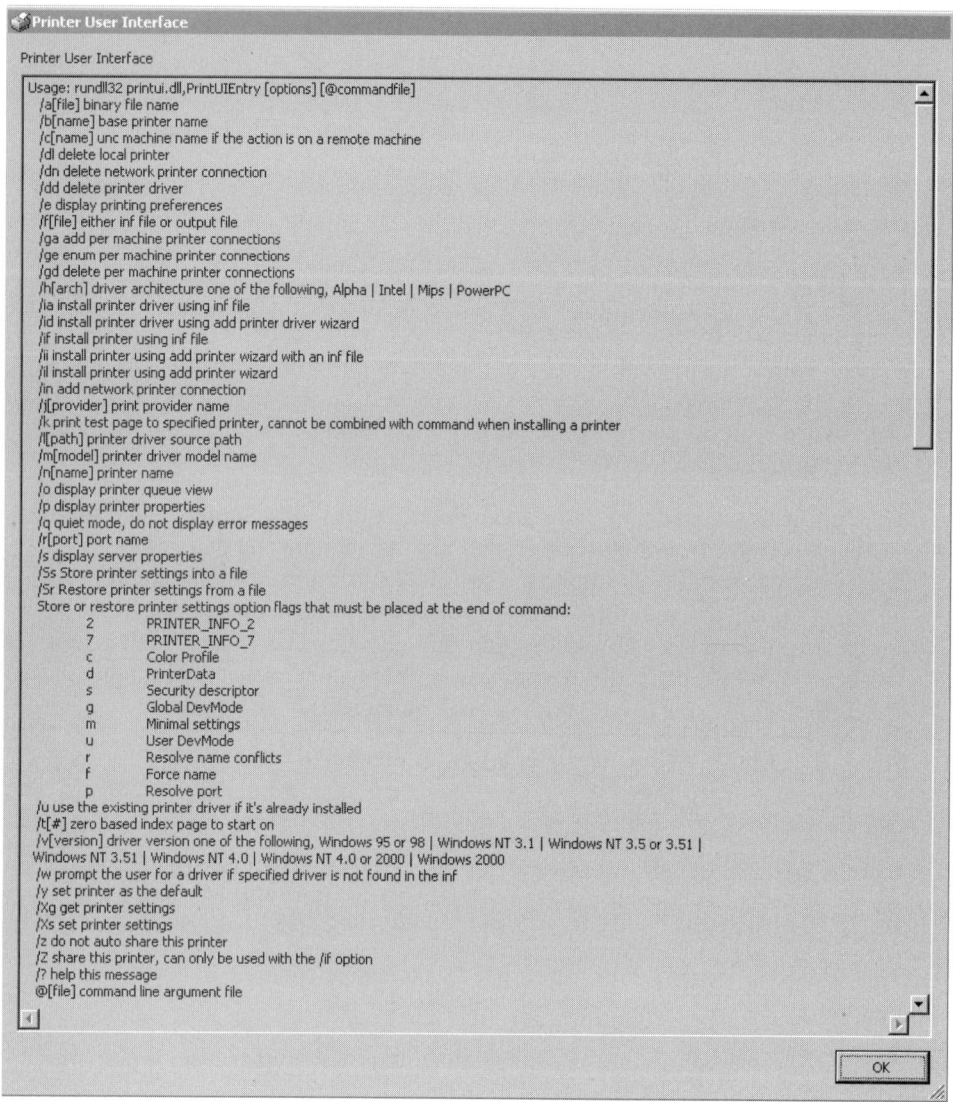

Printer User Interface

Printer User Interface

```
Usage: rundll32 printui.dll,PrintUIEntry [options] [@commandfile]
   /a[file] binary file name
   /b[name] base printer name
   /c[name] unc machine name if the action is on a remote machine
   /dl delete local printer
   /dn delete network printer connection
   /dd delete printer driver
   /e display printing preferences
   /f[file] either inf file or output file
   /ga add per machine printer connections
   /ge enum per machine printer connections
   /gd delete per machine printer connections
   /h[arch] driver architecture one of the following, Alpha | Intel | Mips | PowerPC
   /ia install printer driver using inf file
   /id install printer driver using add printer driver wizard
   /if install printer using inf file
   /ii install printer using add printer wizard with an inf file
   /il install printer using add printer wizard
   /in add network printer connection
   /j[provider] print provider name
   /k print test page to specified printer, cannot be combined with command when installing a printer
   /l[path] printer driver source path
   /m[model] printer driver model name
   /n[name] printer name
   /o display printer queue view
   /p display printer properties
   /q quiet mode, do not display error messages
   /r[port] port name
   /s display server properties
   /Ss Store printer settings into a file
   /Sr Restore printer settings from a file
   Store or restore printer settings option flags that must be placed at the end of command:
        2          PRINTER_INFO_2
        7          PRINTER_INFO_7
        c          Color Profile
        d          PrinterData
        s          Security descriptor
        g          Global DevMode
        m          Minimal settings
        u          User DevMode
        r          Resolve name conflicts
        f          Force name
        p          Resolve port
   /u use the existing printer driver if it's already installed
   /t[#] zero based index page to start on
   /v[version] driver version one of the following, Windows 95 or 98 | Windows NT 3.1 | Windows NT 3.5 or 3.51 |
   Windows NT 3.51 | Windows NT 4.0 | Windows NT 4.0 or 2000 | Windows 2000
   /w prompt the user for a driver if specified driver is not found in the inf
   /y set printer as the default
   /Xg get printer settings
   /Xs set printer settings
   /z do not auto share this printer
   /Z share this printer, can only be used with the /if option
   /? help this message
   @[file] command line argument file
```

OK

Figure 4.17   Rundll32 Options

PrnAdmin

The PrnAdmin utility lets you use scripts that perform administrative printer
functions. You can create your own scripts or modify one of the sample scripts
that is provided with PrnAdmin. Either way you can manage both local and
remote printers using PrnAdmin.

This tool can perform the following functions:

- Add or delete local or remote printers.
- Add or delete printer connections.
- Add or delete local or remote forms.
- Add or delete ports on local or remote printers.
- Add or delete printer drivers on local or remote printers.
- Enumerate ports, drivers, printers, or forms on local or remote printers.
- Pause, resume, or purge a local or remote printer.
- Configure a local or remote printer.

Note To create scripts, you need to know a scripting language such as Microsoft® Visual Basic or JavaScript or be able to make use of the objects provided by PrnAdmin in any language that supports COM programming.

To install PrnAdmin, type the following command:

regsvr32 [Path]PrnAdmin.dll

To use the PrnAdmin sample scripts shown in Figure 4.18, type:

Cscript prnmgr.vbs

```
E:\WINNT\System32\cmd.exe
Microsoft Windows 2000 [Version 5.00.2072]
(C) Copyright 1985-1999 Microsoft Corp.

E:\>cscript prnmgr.vbs -?
Microsoft (R) Windows Script Host Version 5.1 for Windows
Copyright (C) Microsoft Corporation 1996-1999. All rights reserved.

Usage: prnmgr [-adl?][c] [-c server-name][-b printer-name][-m driver-model]
              [-p driver-path][-r port-name][-f file-name]
Arguments:
-a     - add local printer
-ac    - add printer connection
-d     - delete local printer
-dc    - delete printer connection
-l     - list printers
-p     - driver path can be local or network path i.e. a:\ or \\server\share
-p     - driver path can be local or network path i.e. a:\ or \\server\share
-x     - delete all local printers
-xc    - delete all printer connections, cannot be used with the -c option
-?     - display command usage

Examples:
prnmgr -l -c \\server
prnmgr -a -b "foo4L" -m "HP LaserJet 4L" -r "7.7.7.7:7bar"
prnmgr -a -b "foo4L" -m "HP LaserJet 4L" -r "lpt1:"
prnmgr -a -b "foo4L" -c \\server
prnmgr -ac -b "\\server\HP 4L bar1"
prnmgr -dc -b "\\server\HP 4L bar1"
prnmgr -x
prnmgr -x -c, \\server
prnmgr -xc
```

Figure 4.18   PrnAdmin Scripts

P A R T   2

Performance Monitoring

Monitoring server performance involves observing a system both as a whole and as a collection of its individual components. Part 2 describes the tools Windows 2000 provides for assessing system performance, explains how your system uses its hardware resources, and offers strategies for correcting performance problems.

In This Part

CHAPTER 5

Overview of Performance Monitoring

Monitoring performance is a necessary part of preventive maintenance for your computer system. Through monitoring, you obtain performance data that is useful in diagnosing system problems and in planning for the growth in demand for system resources.

In This Chapter

Related Information in the Resource Kit

- For more information about diagnosing system problems, see "Troubleshooting Strategies" in this book.

- For more information about tools for monitoring performance, see *Microsoft® Windows® 2000 Resource Kit* Tools Help.

Performance Monitoring Concepts

Regular performance monitoring ensures that you always have up-to-date information about how your computer is operating. When you have performance data for your system over a range of activities and loads, you can define a baseline—a range of measurements that represent acceptable performance under typical operating conditions. This baseline provides a reference point that makes it easier to spot problems when they occur. In addition, when you are troubleshooting system problems, performance data gives you information about the behavior of system resources at the time the problem occurs, which is useful in pinpointing the cause. Finally, monitoring system performance provides you with data to project future growth and to plan for how changes in your system configurations might affect future operation. Figure 5.1 shows the sequence for monitoring different system resources.

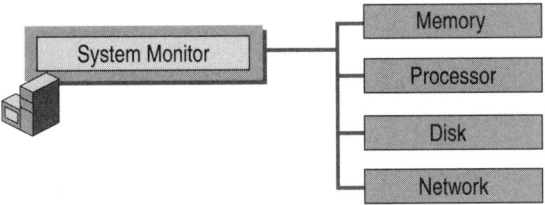

Figure 5.1   Overall Monitoring Sequence

The following sections describe the scope and type of performance data collected, the design of the performance data architecture, and methods of data collection used by the performance tools.

Scope of Performance Data

In general, performance monitoring concentrates on how the operating system and any applications or services that are instrumented for performance-data collection use the resources of the system, such as the disks, memory, processors, and network components. *Throughput*, *queue*, and *response time* are terms that describe resource usage.

Throughput Defined

Throughput is a measure of the work done in a unit of time, typically evaluated from the server side in a client/server environment. Throughput tends to increase as the load increases up to a peak level. It then begins to fall, and a queue might develop. Throughput in an end-to-end system, such as client/server, depends on how each component performs. The slowest point in the system sets the throughput rate for the system as a whole. Often this slow point is referred to as a bottleneck. Performance monitoring tells you where bottlenecks occur in your system. The resource that shows the highest use is often the bottleneck, but not always—it can also mean a resource is successfully handling a lot of activity. As long as no queues develop, there is no bottleneck. Microsoft® Windows® 2000 reports throughput data on resources such as disks and network components.

Queue Defined

A queue can form under a few different circumstances. For example, a queue can develop when requests come in for service by the resource at a faster rate than the resource's throughput, or if requests demand differing, particularly longer, amounts of time from the resource. A queue can also form if requests occur at random intervals—for example, in large batches for a time and then none at all. When a queue becomes long, work is not being handled efficiently, and you might experience delays in response time. Windows 2000 reports queue development on disks, processors, and server work queues, tracking server message block (SMB) calls of the Server service.

Response Time Defined

Response time is the measure of time required to do work from start to finish. In a client/server environment, you typically measure response time on the client side. Response time generally increases as the load increases. You can measure response time by dividing the queue length for the resource over the resource throughput. As an alternative, the new trace log feature in the Windows 2000 performance tools allows you to track units of work from start to finish in order to determine response times.

The following sections describe how performance monitoring tools enable users to collect data about the throughput, queue formation, and response time of different system resources.

Data Collection Architecture

Windows 2000 collects data about system resources, such as disks, memory, processors, and network components. In addition, applications and services that you might be running on your system can also perform data collection. By default, the operating system obtains performance data for system resources using the registry.

When you use performance tools to access registry functions for performance data, the system collects the data from the appropriate system object managers, such as the Memory Manager, the input/output (I/O) subsystem, and so forth.

As an option, Windows 2000 supports collecting data using the Windows Management Infrastructure (WMI) interface by means of the following command syntax typed at the Windows command prompt:

perfmon / WMI

In addition to several of the system performance counter DLLs, the operating system installs managed object files (MOFs) for data collection using WMI instead of the registry. These files reside in System32\Wbem\Mof. The Windows Management service must be running on the monitoring and monitored computer (if different) in order to obtain data using WMI.

Windows 2000 defines the performance data it collects in terms of objects, counters, and instances. Think of a performance object as any resource, application, or service that you can measure. The following sections describe these entities in more detail.

Performance Objects

By default, Windows 2000 installs numerous performance objects corresponding to hardware or other resources in the system. The following table shows the default performance objects installed by the operating system on a Microsoft® Windows® 2000 Professional installation.

Table 5.1   Windows 2000 Performance Objects

Object name	Description
ACS/RSVP Service	Reports activity of the Quality of Service (QoS) Admission Control Service used to manage the priority use of network resources (bandwidth) at the subnet level.
Browser	Reports activity of the Browser service in Microsoft® Windows® 2000 Server that lists computers sharing resources in a domain and other domain and workgroup names across the wide area network (WAN). Windows 2000 provides the Browser service for backward compatibility with clients that are running Microsoft® Windows® 95, Microsoft® Windows® 98, Microsoft® Windows® 3.x, and Microsoft® Windows NT®.
Cache	Reports activity for the file system cache, an area of physical memory that holds recently used data.

(continued)

Table 5.1   Windows 2000 Performance Objects *(continued)*

Object name	Description
Distributed Transaction Coordinator	Reports statistics about activity of the Microsoft Distributed Transaction Coordinator, a part of Component Services (formerly known as Transaction Server) used to coordinate two-phase transactions by Message Queuing.
HTTP Indexing Service	Reports statistics regarding queries run by the Indexing service, a service that builds and maintains catalogs of the contents of local and remote disk drives to support powerful document-search capabilities.
IAS Accounting Clients	Reports activity of the Internet Authentication Service (IAS) as it centrally manages remote client accounting (usage).
IAS Accounting Servers	Reports activity of the Internet Authentication Service (IAS) as it centrally manages remote server accounting (usage).
IAS Authentication Clients	Reports activity of the Internet Authentication Service (IAS) as it centrally manages remote client authentication.
IAS Authentication Servers	Reports activity of the Internet Authentication Service (IAS) as it centrally manages remote server authentication.
ICMP	Reports the rates at which Internet Control Message Protocol (ICMP) messages are sent and received by using the ICMP protocol, which provides error correction and other packet information.
Indexing Service	Reports statistics pertaining to the creation of indexes and the merging of indexes by the Indexing service. Indexing service indexes documents and document properties on your disks and stores the information in a catalog. You can use Indexing service to search for documents, either with the Search command on the Start menu or with a Web browser.
Indexing Service Filter	Reports filtering activity of the Indexing service. Indexing service indexes documents and document properties on your disks and stores the information in a catalog. You can use Indexing service to search for documents, either with the Search command on the Start menu or with a Web browser.
IP	Reports activity at the Internet Protocol (IP) layer of Transmission Control Protocol/Internet Protocol (TCP/IP).
Job Object	Reports the accounting and processor usage data collected by each active, named job object.

(continued)

Table 5.1   Windows 2000 Performance Objects *(continued)*

Object name	Description
Job Object Details	Reports detailed performance information about the active processes that make up a job object.
Logical Disk	Reports activity and usage of disk partitions and volumes.
	Use **diskperf -y** to enable disk counters and **diskperf -n** to disable them. To specify the type of counters you want to activate, include **d** for physical disk drives and **v** for logical disk drives or storage volumes. When the operating system starts up, it automatically sets the **diskperf** command with the **-yd** switch to activate physical disk counters. Type **diskperf -yv** to activate logical disk counters. For more information about using the **diskperf** command, type **diskperf -?** at the command prompt.
Memory	Reports usage of random access memory (RAM) used to store code and data.
NBT Connection	Reports the rate at which bytes are sent and received over connections that use the NetBT protocol, which provides NetBIOS support for the TCP/IP protocol between the local computer and a remote computer.
Network Interface	Reports rates at which bytes and packets are sent and received over a TCP/IP connection by means of the network adapters. Typically the first instance of the Network Interface object (Instance 1) that you see in System Monitor represents the loopback address; however, sometimes the loopback address does not appear. The loopback address is a local path through the protocol driver and the network adapter. All other instances represent installed network adapters (WAN interfaces, remote access modems, and so forth).
Objects	Reports data about system software objects, such as events, and so on.
Paging File	Reports usage of the paging file, used to back up virtual memory allocations.
Physical Disk	Reports usage of hard disks and redundant array of independent disks (RAID) devices.
Print Queue	Reports statistics for print jobs in the queue of the print server. New for Windows 2000.
Process	Reports activity of the process, which is a software object that represents a running program.
Processor	Reports activity of the processor (also called the CPU), the part of your computer hardware that carries out program instructions.
Redirector	Reports activity for the Redirector file system, which diverts file requests to network servers.

(continued)

Table 5.1   Windows 2000 Performance Objects *(continued)*

Object name	Description
Server	Reports activity for the Server file system, which responds to file requests from network clients.
Server Work Queues	Reports the length of queues and objects in the queues for the Server service.
System	Reports statistics for systemwide counters that track file operations, processor time, and so on.
TCP	Reports the rates at which TCP segments are sent and received using the Transmission Control Protocol (TCP).
Telephony	Reports activity for telephony devices and connections.
Thread	Reports activity for a thread (the part of a process that uses the processor).
UDP	Reports the rates at which User Datagram Protocol (UDP) datagrams are sent and received using UDP.

If you are running Windows 2000 Server, Setup automatically installs the Active Server Pages, FTP Service, Internet Information Services Global, and Web Service objects for use with Internet Information Service. In addition, Windows 2000 Server Setup installs the SMTP Server and SMTP NTFS Store Driver objects. Depending on the services you have configured, your system might provide several additional objects, such as the NTDS object, which reports activity of the Active Directory™ directory service, and the DNS object, which reports performance statistics for the Domain Name System (DNS) service. For detailed information about these and other performance objects, see the Windows 2000 Performance Counters Reference on the *Microsoft® Windows® 2000 Resource Kit* companion CD.

For information about writing applications that install performance objects that can be integrated with the performance tools, see the Software Development Kit (SDK) documentation in the MSDN™ Library at http://windows.microsoft.com/windows2000/reskit/webresources.

Performance Counters and Instances

Each object has counters that are used to measure various aspects of performance, such as transfer rates for disks or the amount of processor time consumed for processors. Each object has at least one instance, which is a unique copy of a particular object type, though not all object types support multiple instances. This chapter and the following chapters describe objects, counters, and instances using the following syntax:

\\Computer_name\Object(ParentInstance/ObjectInstance#InstanceIndex)\Counter

The *Computer_name* portion is optional; if you do not include a computer name, the default is the local computer.

Note that the syntax includes a parent instance, object instance, and an instance index. This applies, for example, if the object has multiple instances and these instances might be identifiable by name or number, as defined by the counter developer. (Typically, internal system counters use numeric instance indexes.)

For example, if you are monitoring threads of the Microsoft Windows Explorer process, track the Windows Explorer instance of the Thread object (Windows Explorer would be the parent instance), and then each thread running Windows Explorer (these threads are child instances). The instance index allows you to track these child instances. The instance index for the thread you want might be 0, 1, and so on, for each thread, preceded by the number sign (*#*). The operating system configures System Monitor properties to display duplicate instances by default. Instance index 0 is hidden; numbering of additional instances starts with 1. You cannot monitor multiple instances of the same process unless you display instance indexes.

An instance called _Total is available on most objects, and represents a sum of the values for all instances of the object for a specific counter.

Data Collection and Reporting

Depending on the tools used, you can configure data collection to occur almost immediately or according to a predefined schedule. Performance data reported is sampled, meaning that data is collected periodically rather than traced, whereby data is obtained as events occur. This collection method has the advantage of keeping overhead low, but it might occasionally overestimate or underestimate values when activity falls outside the sampling interval.

If you want more precise performance data, use event tracing, a new capability in Windows 2000. Event tracing can measure activity as it happens, eliminating the inaccuracies of sampling and making it possible to correlate resource usage such as page faults, disk input/output (I/O), and processor time with workload that can include threads, processes, or transactions. This capability supplements counter-based monitoring methods. You can configure trace logs for providers you have or for the built-in system provider that runs traces for the Windows kernel provider using trace logs in **Performance Logs and Alerts**. Because running trace logs of page faults and file I/O data incurs some performance overhead, log this data only for brief periods. Note that an additional program is required to parse the log output into readable form. Developers can create such a tool using APIs provided in the Platform Software Development Kit.

For information about writing a trace provider, see the Platform Software Development Kit (SDK) documentation in the MSDN Library at http://windows.microsoft.com/windows2000/reskit/webresources.

Depending on how a counter is defined, its values might be reported in one of the following ways:

- Instantaneous counters, which might have names containing the word "current," display the most recent measurement. Be aware that instantaneous counters might not provide meaningful data unless you have a steady workload.

- Averaging counters, which typically have names that include "per second" or "percent," measure a value over time and display the average of the last two measurements over the period between samples. (Because counters are never cleared, this is actually an average of the difference between the measurements.) When you start these counters, you must wait for the second measurement to be taken before any values are displayed. For example, Memory\Pages/sec shows the number of pages read over the sample interval, divided by the number of seconds in the interval.

  For averaging counters, the sampling method can result in a slight delay in displaying values as data is collected and computed. In addition, after a single large value is reported, causing spikes in a performance graph, averaging counter values can be artificially high for a while until the average starts to reflect more recent steady-state activity.

Windows 2000 supports other types of counters, such as percentage, difference, and text. Difference counters display the change in value between the last two measurements. By default, counters that display their values as percentages cannot exceed 100 percent.

For information about the preceding generic counter types and their specific subtypes, see the Windows 2000 Performance Counter Reference (Counters.chm) on the *Windows 2000 Resource Kit* companion CD.

Monitoring Tools

The primary monitoring tools in Windows 2000 are the Performance console and Task Manager. Task Manager offers an immediate overview of system activity and performance, and the Performance console provides detailed information that can be used for troubleshooting and bottleneck analysis. The Performance console hosts two tools: System Monitor, and Performance Logs and Alerts. The chapters in this part of the *Server Operations Guide* concentrate on using the Performance console. The following sections describe the utilities that are installed with the operating system.

You can start the Performance console from the **Administrative Tools** menu. To use the **Administrative Tools** menu in Windows 2000 Professional:

Add the **Administrative Tools** menu to the **Programs** menu.

Or, use the **Administrative Tools** menu in Control Panel

Administrative Tools are provided on the **Start** menu by default in Windows 2000 Server.

▶ **To add the Administrative Tools menu to the Programs menu on a computer running Windows 2000 Professional**

1. On the **Start** menu, point to **Settings**, and then click **Taskbar & Start Menu**.

2. Click the **Start Menu Options** tab. Under **Start Menu Settings**, select the **Display Administrative Tools** check box and then click **OK**.

3. Click the **Start** button again, point to **Programs**, and then click **Administrative Tools**.

▶ **To use the Administrative Tools menu in Control Panel**

1. Double-click **My Computer** on the Windows 2000 desktop.

2. Under **My Computer**, double-click **Control Panel**.

3. In Control Panel, double-click **Administrative Tools**.

System Monitor

System Monitor in Windows 2000 extends the functionality provided by Performance Monitor, which shipped in Microsoft® Windows® NT versions 4.0 and Windows 3.51. Features of System Monitor include the following:

- The graph display is much more flexible and configurable. You can modify many attributes of the display, including changing font and color, adding borders, and so on.

- Counter configuration is simplified. You can now copy counter paths and settings from the System Monitor display to the Clipboard and paste counter paths from Web pages or other sources into the System Monitor display.

- Graphs can be printed when performance displays are saved as HTML files using the **Save As** command on the shortcut menu. In addition, you can save reports as tab-separated files (for use with Microsoft Excel) by means of the **Save As** command. To use the shortcut menu, right-click the details pane of System Monitor.

- System Monitor is portable. Because System Monitor is hosted in the Microsoft Management Console (MMC), you can save a console file containing a group of counters that you want to monitor—you can install it on any other computer and be able to monitor the same types of data on that computer. This is useful in monitoring other systems that you administer.

- The functionality of System Monitor chart, histogram, and report views is provided by an ActiveX® control (Sysmon.ocx). This design gives a user the flexibility of including the control in an HTML page (PerfManager on the *Windows 2000 Resource Kit* companion CD is an example) or of programming the control into a Microsoft® Office or Microsoft® Visual Basic® application, as described in "Integrating the System Monitor Control into Office and Other Applications" later in this chapter. In most cases, you work with the control's functionality in the form it is presented in Perfmon.msc, the Microsoft Management Console component that hosts the performance tools.

For information about logging and alert capabilities of the Performance console, see "Performance Logs and Alerts" later in this chapter. Windows NT 4.0 Performance Monitor is provided under the name Perfmon4.exe on the Windows 2000 Resource Kit companion CD. Typing **perfmon.exe** at the command prompt causes the system to launch System Monitor, not Performance Monitor.

Starting System Monitor

If you are running Windows 2000 Professional, you can start the Performance console as follows:

- On the **Administrative Tools** menu, click **Performance**.

  Or, on the **Start** menu, click **Run**, type **perfmon.msc**, and then click **OK**.

  Or, type **perfmon.msc** at the Windows command prompt.

When you start the Performance console, a blank System Monitor graph appears. **Performance Logs and Alerts** appears beneath System Monitor in the console tree, as shown in Figure 5.2.

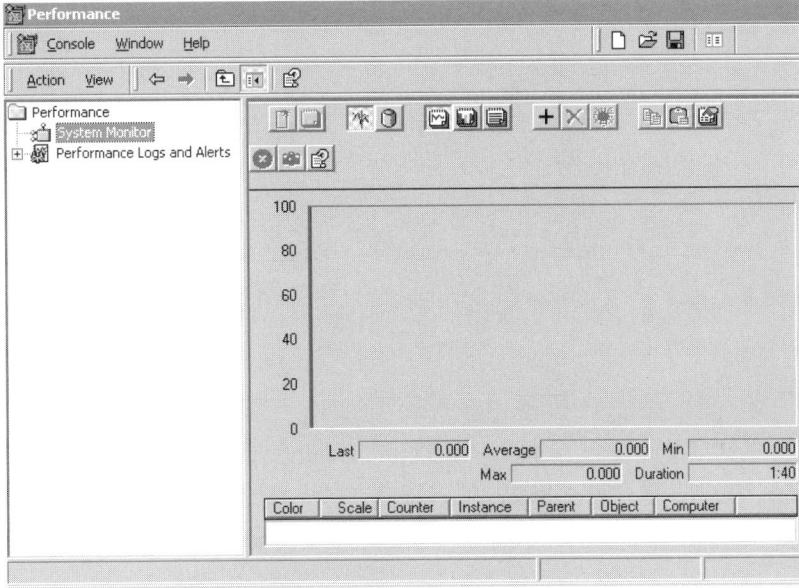

Figure 5.2   Performance Console

The following section describes the user interface for System Monitor and provides tips on how to use it.

Working with System Monitor

With System Monitor you can create graphs, bar charts (histograms), and text reports of performance counter data. System Monitor is designed for short-term viewing of data, troubleshooting, and diagnosis.

The System Monitor display consists of the following elements:

- An optional toolbar with capabilities such as copying and pasting counters, clearing counters, adding counters, and so on. The toolbar buttons provide the quickest way of configuring the monitoring display, but you can also use a shortcut menu to add counters and configure properties.

- The area where counter values are displayed. You can vary the line style, width, and color of these lines. You can also change the color of the window and of the chart within the window.

- A legend showing the selected counters and associated data such as the computer name, parent object, and instances.

- A value bar, where you see the last, minimum, maximum, and average values for the counter that is currently selected. The value bar also shows a **Duration** value that indicates the total elapsed time displayed in the graph (based on the update interval).

- A timer bar that moves across the graph indicates the passing of each update interval. Regardless of the update interval, the view shows up to 100 samples. System Monitor compresses log data as necessary to fit it in the display. For example, if there are 1,000 samples, the display might show every tenth sample.

You can configure System Monitor using either the toolbar or a shortcut menu. Using the shortcut menu offers more control and flexibility in configuring the display. The following sections describe these different configuration methods. To see procedures and a brief overview of System Monitor, click **Help** on the System Monitor toolbar.

Using the Toolbar

The toolbar is displayed by default. Using the toolbar, you can configure the following options:

- **Type of display.** Use the **View Chart**, **View Histogram**, or **View Report** button.

Figure 5.3 shows the different display options.

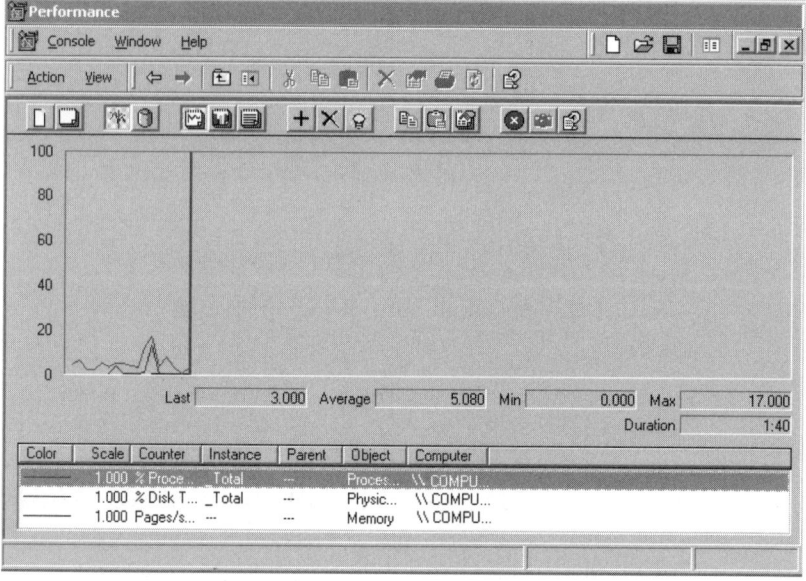

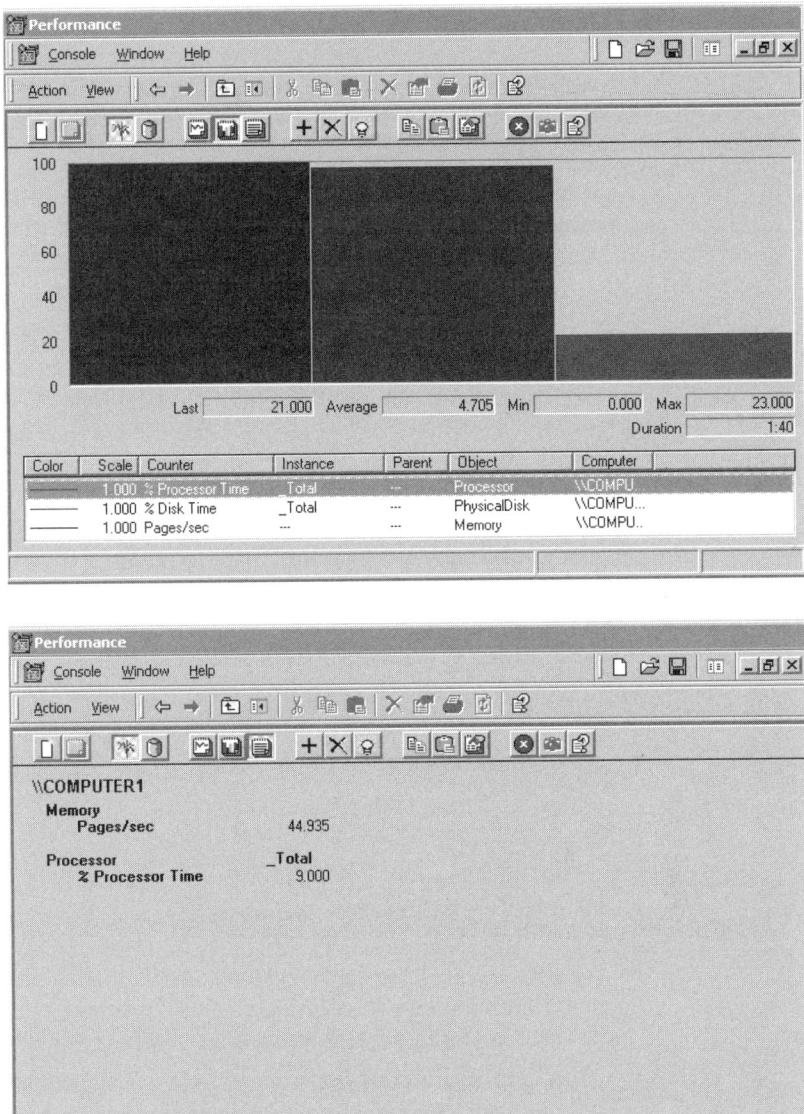

Figure 5.3   Display Type Options for System Monitor

Histograms and reports are useful for simplifying graphs with multiple counters. However, they display only a single value, so they are recommended only when you are charting current activity and watching the graphs as they change. When you are reviewing data logged over time, line graphs are much more informative so that trends can be identified.

- **Data source.** Click the **View Current Activity** button for real-time data or the **View Log File Data** button for data from either a completed or a currently running log.

- **Counters.** Use the **Add** or **Delete** buttons as needed. You can also use the **New Counter Set** button to reset the display and select new counters. Clicking the **Add** button displays the **Add Counters** dialog box, as shown in Figure 5.4. You can also press the DEL key to delete a counter that is selected in the legend.

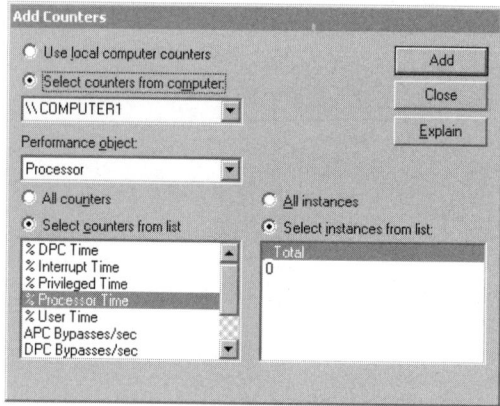

Figure 5.4   Add Counters Dialog Box

- **Data updates.** Click **Clear Display** to clear the displayed data and obtain a fresh data sample for existing counters. To suspend data collection, click **Freeze Display**. Use the **Update Data** button to resume collection.

- **Highlighting chart or histogram data.** To accentuate the line or bar for a selected counter with white (default) or black (for light backgrounds), click **Highlight** on the toolbar.

- **Importing or exporting counter settings.** To save the displayed configuration to the Clipboard for insertion into a Web page, click **Copy Properties**. To import counter settings from the Clipboard into the current System Monitor display, click **Paste Counter List**.

- **Configuring other System Monitor properties.** To access colors, fonts, or other settings that have no corresponding button on the toolbar, click **Properties**.

Using the Shortcut Menu

When you right-click the System Monitor display, a shortcut menu appears with the following options:

- **Add Counters.** Use this option in the same way you use the **Add** button in the toolbar.

- **Save As.** Use this if you want to save the current display configuration under a new name. If you click **Save** on the **Console** menu, the current settings are stored, overwriting the blank version of Perfmon.msc installed by Windows 2000 Setup and altering the default appearance of the tool.

- **Properties.** Click this button to access the five properties tabs that provide options for controlling all aspects of System Monitor data collection and display. The **General** properties tab appears by default, as shown in Figure 5.5.

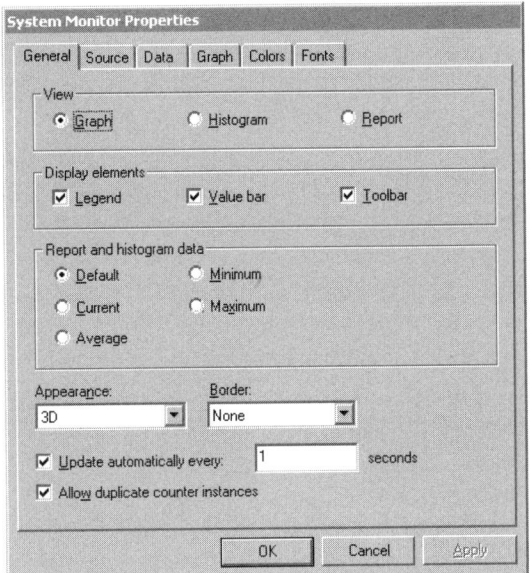

Figure 5.5   General Tab

Many properties can be configured from the toolbar, but some are only configurable using **System Monitor Properties**. The following table lists property tabs alphabetically by name, along with the attributes they control.

Table 5.2   System Monitor Properties

Use this tab	To add or change this
Colors	Background color of results pane surrounding the chart area, color of chart data-display area.
	You can choose each color from a palette (in the **Property Name** list box) or you can base the colors on system colors (screen elements) defined using the **Display** icon in Control Panel. When using the palette, note the following:
	▪ **BackColorCtl** refers to the area surrounding the chart.
	▪ **BackColor** refers to the chart data-display area.
	▪ **ForeColor** refers to the color of the text in the display and legend.
	Grid color, timer bar color.
Data	Color, width, style, or chart line.
	Notice that defining a nondefault line width limits the line styles that are available. Styles can be selected only when you are using the default line width.
	Scale of counter data values.
	Counter values can be scaled exponentially from .0000001 to 1000000. You might want to adjust the counter scale settings to enhance the visibility of counter data in the chart. Changing the scale does not affect the statistics displayed in the value bar.
	Objects, counters, and instances.
Fonts	Font type, size, and style.
General	View type: chart, histogram, or report.
	Update frequency and manual or periodic sampling.
	Histogram or report value type (choose between minimum, maximum, average values for the one displayed in a report view).
	Using report value types other than **Current** when monitoring real-time data incurs substantial overhead because of the need to make calculations across all samples for each value displayed.
	Display of counter legend.
	Display of last, minimum, and maximum values for a selected counter (the value bar).
	Border style, appearance of the entire control. You can include or omit a border, or configure three-dimensional or flat effects for the window.
	Display of toolbar.
	Display of instance indexes (for monitoring multiple instances of a counter).
	The first instance (instance number 0) displays no index; System Monitor numbers subsequent instances starting with 1.

(continued)

Table 5.2   System Monitor Properties *(continued)*

Use this tab	To add or change this
Graph	Title of graph.
	Label on value axis, vertical or horizontal grid lines, and upper and lower limits of graph axes.
Source	Source of data displayed: current data input to the graph, current or archived data input from a log.
	Time range for a log and view time range.

Getting the Most from System Monitor

Windows 2000 Server online Help for System Monitor explains how to perform common tasks. The following list supplements the information provided in online Help to enable you to use System Monitor more effectively.

- **Print data.** You can print performance data in several ways:

  - Copy the current view to the Clipboard (by pressing ALT+PRINT SCREEN), start a paint program, paste in the image from the Clipboard, and then print it.

  - Add the System Monitor control to a Microsoft Office application such as Microsoft® Word or Microsoft® Excel, configure it to display data, and then print from that program. For information about this process, see "Integrating the System Monitor Control into Office and Other Applications" later in this chapter.

  - Save the System Monitor control as an HTML file by right-clicking the details pane of System Monitor and typing a file name for the HTML file to be created. You can then open the HTML file and print it from Microsoft® Internet Explorer or another program.

  - Import a log file in comma-separated (.csv) or tab-separated (.tsv) format into an Excel spreadsheet and print from that application.

- **Learn about individual counters.** When adding counters, if you click **Explain** in the **Add Counters** dialog box for System Monitor or **Performance Logs and Alerts**, you can view counter descriptions.

- **Vary the data displayed in a report.** By default, reports display only one value for each counter. This is current data if the data source is real-time activity, or averaged data if the source is a log. However, using the General properties tab, you can configure the report display to show different values, such as the maximum, minimum, and so on. Notice that monitoring the nondefault value for a report can increase performance-monitoring overhead.

- **Arrange items in the legend.** To sort entries in ascending or descending order for that category, click **Object**, **Counter**, **Instance**, or **Computer** in the counter legend. For example, to sort all counters by name, click **Counter**.

- **Select a group of counters or counter instances to monitor.**
  - To select all counters or instances, click **All counters** or **All instances**.
  - To select specific counters or instances, click **Select counters from the list** or **Select instances from the list**.
  - To monitor a group of consecutive counters or instances in a list box, hold down the SHIFT key and scroll down through the items in the list box.
  - To select multiple, nonconsecutive counters or instances, select the item and press CTRL.

Important   Monitoring large numbers of counters can incur a high amount of overhead, even to the point of making the system unresponsive to keyboard or mouse input. To reduce this burden, display data in report view when collecting from large numbers of counters or direct data to a binary log, and view the data in System Monitor as it is being written to the log.

- **Simplify detailed graphs.** You can maintain two separate instances of System Monitor if you want to monitor a large number of counters while keeping each graph relatively simple and uncluttered. It is also a good way to compare data from different sources.
- **Track totals for all instances of a counter.** Instead of monitoring individual instances for a selected counter, you can instead use the _Total instance, which sums all instances' values and reports them in System Monitor.
- **Pinpoint a specific counter from lines in a graph.** To match a line in a graph with the counter for which it is charting values, double-click a position in the line. If chart lines are close together, try to find a point in the graph where they diverge.
- **Accentuate a specific counter's data.** To draw attention to a particular counter's data, use the highlighting feature. To do so, press CTRL+H or click **Highlight** on the toolbar. For the counter selected, a thick line replaces the colored chart line. For white or light-colored backgrounds (defined by the BackColor property), this line is black; for other backgrounds, this line is white.
- **View data from a running log.** If you are working with a log file that is currently collecting data, you need to click the **Select Time Range** button and keep moving the **Time Range** bar to the right to update the display with new samples.
- **Use Windows NT 4.0 settings files.** You can display legacy alert, report, chart, and log settings files in System Monitor by using the following command at the command prompt:

  perfmon.exe *settings_file_name*

When you open one of these settings files, the system temporarily converts the file for use with System Monitor but discards the converted version after the console starts. If you want to save the settings file for permanent use with System Monitor, type the following command:

perfmon.exe /HTMLFILE:*new_file_name settings_file_name*

Performance Logs and Alerts

Performance Logs and Alerts, a service in Windows 2000, improves the logging and alert capabilities that were provided in Windows NT 4.0. Logging is used for detailed analysis and record-keeping purposes. Retaining and analyzing log data collected over a period of several months can be helpful for capacity and upgrade planning.

Windows 2000 provides two types of performance-related logs—counter logs and trace logs—and an alerting function. The following list describes these new or enhanced tools:

- Performance Logs and Alerts replaces Performance Data Log in the Windows NT Server 4.0 Resource Kit. As a result, data collection occurs regardless of whether any user is logged on to the computer.

- In Windows 2000, counter logs record sampled data about hardware resources and system services based on performance objects and counters in the same manner as System Monitor. When a counter log has been started, the Performance Logs and Alerts service obtains data from the system when the update interval has elapsed.

- Trace logs collect event traces that measure performance statistics associated with events such as disk and file I/O, page faults, or thread activity. When the event occurs, a data provider designed to track these events sends the data to the Performance Logs and Alerts service. The data is measured from start to finish, rather than sampled in the manner of System Monitor. The built-in Windows 2000 kernel trace data provider supports tracing system data; if other data providers are available, developers can configure logs with those providers as appropriate. A parsing tool is required to interpret the trace log output. Developers can create such a tool using APIs provided in the Platform Software Development Kit.

- With the alerting function, you can define a counter value that will trigger actions such as sending a network message, running a program, or starting a log. Alerts are useful if you are not actively monitoring a particular counter threshold value but want to be notified when it exceeds or falls below a specified value so that you can investigate and determine the cause of the change. You might want to set alerts based on established performance baseline values for your system. For information about establishing a baseline, see "Starting Your Monitoring Routine" later in this chapter.

- Viewing logged data is easier and more convenient. Counter logs can be viewed in System Monitor as they are collecting data as well as after data collection has stopped. Data in counter logs can be saved as comma-separated or tab-separated files that are easily viewed with Excel.

- Logs can be circular—that is, recording data until they achieve a user-defined size limit and then starting over. Alternatively, linear logs collect data according to user-defined parameters such as: run for a specified length of time, stop when that parameter is met, and start a new log. A binary file format can also be defined for logging intermittent data (such as for a process that is not running when you start the log but that begins and ends during the logged interval).

- You can save log settings to an HTML file or you can import settings from an HTML page to create new logs. When exported, the resulting HTML page hosts the System Monitor control, an ActiveX control that provides the performance monitoring user interface. If you open this page, you can dynamically observe, from a System Monitor view, the same counters you configured in the log. When imported, a new log or alert is created, based on the settings in the HTML page. This is a convenient way to insert the same settings into both a log and an alert, if appropriate.

- Configuring logs and alerts is flexible and easy to manage. Users can manage multiple logging sessions from a single console window. For each log, users can start and stop logging either manually, on demand, or automatically, at scheduled times or based on the elapsed time or the current file size. Users can also specify automatic naming schemes and stipulate that a program be run when a log is stopped.

Starting Performance Logs and Alerts

In Windows 2000 Professional, the Performance Logs and Alerts component is available in the Performance console and in the Computer Management console. The following procedures describe how to open the component from these locations.

Note This procedure assumes that you have added the **Administrative Tools** option to your **Programs** menu as described in "System Monitor" earlier in this chapter.

▶ **To start Performance Logs and Alerts from the Performance console**

1. Click **Start**, point to **Programs**, and then click **Administrative Tools**.

2. Click **Performance**.

3. Double-click **Performance Logs and Alerts** to display the available tools.

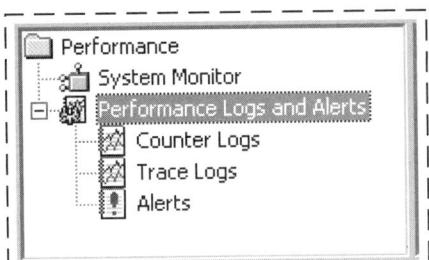

Figure 5.6   Performance Logs and Alerts Console Tree

Working with Logs and Alerts

To begin configuring logs and alerts, click the name of the tool to select it. If any logs or alerts have previously been defined, they will appear in the appropriate node of the details pane. A sample settings file for a counter log named System Overview is included with Windows 2000. You can use this file to see some basic system data such as memory, disk, and processor activity. For information about the types of data to monitor in your own configuration, see "Starting Your Monitoring Routine" later in this chapter.

Right-click in the details pane to create a new log or alert. You can do this in a new file or you can use settings from an existing HTML file as a template.

Note   You must have Full Control access to a subkey in the registry in order to create or modify a log configuration. (The subkey is HKEY_CURRENT_MACHINE\SYSTEM \CurrentControlSet\Services\SysmonLog\Log_Queries.) In general, administrators have this access by default. Administrators can grant access to users by using the Security menu in Regedt32.exe. To run the Performance Logs and Alerts service, you must have the right to start or otherwise configure services on the system. Administrators have this right by default and can grant it to users by using Group Policy. For information about starting and using Group Policy, see Windows 2000 Server Help.

You are prompted to name your log or alert and then to define properties. Figure 5.7 is an illustration of the **General** properties tab for a counter log.

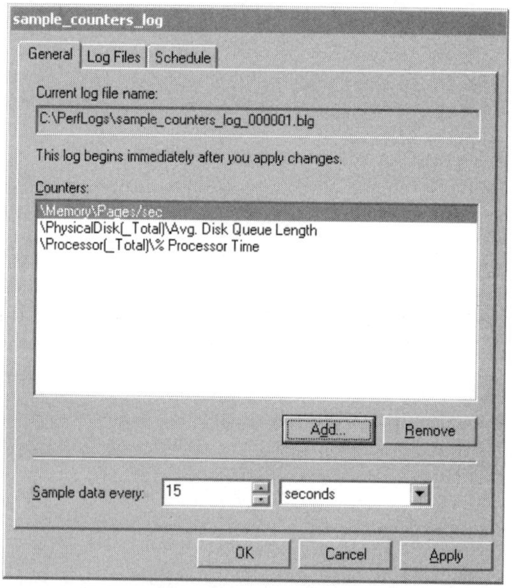

sample_counters_log

General | Log Files | Schedule

Current log file name:

C:\PerfLogs\sample_counters_log_000001.blg

This log begins immediately after you apply changes.

Counters:

\Memory\Pages/sec
\PhysicalDisk(_Total)\Avg. Disk Queue Length
\Processor(_Total)\% Processor Time

Add...   Remove

Sample data every: 15   seconds

OK   Cancel   Apply

Figure 5.7   General Properties Tab for a Counter Log

If you are configuring a counter log or an alert, use the **Add Counters** dialog box to specify objects, counters, instances, and updating. If you are configuring a trace log, use the **General** property tab shown in Figure 5.8.

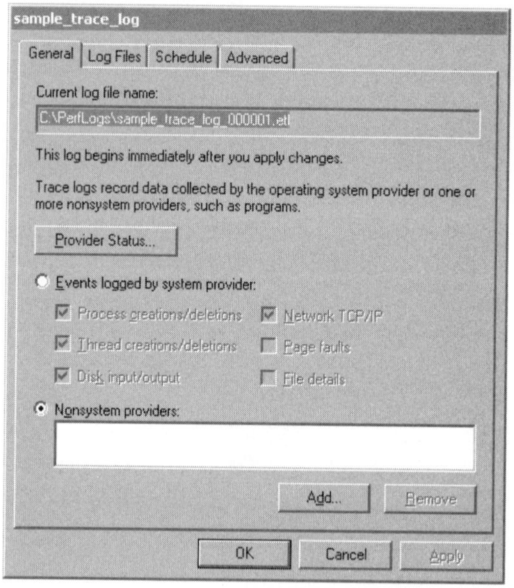

sample_trace_log

General | Log Files | Schedule | Advanced

Current log file name:

C:\PerfLogs\sample_trace_log_000001.etl

This log begins immediately after you apply changes.

Trace logs record data collected by the operating system provider or one or more nonsystem providers, such as programs.

Provider Status...

○ Events logged by system provider:

☑ Process creations/deletions   ☑ Network TCP/IP
☑ Thread creations/deletions   ☐ Page faults
☑ Disk input/output   ☐ File details

● Nonsystem providers:

Add...   Remove

OK   Cancel   Apply

Figure 5.8   General Properties Tab for Trace Log

Each tool offers some unique properties. The ability to configure scheduling is common to logs and alerts, but some options might not be available for all tools. Table 5.3 describes the options available in each tool and the property tab to use to configure it.

Table 5.3   Summary of Log and Alert Properties

For this feature	Use this tab	To configure these settings	Notes
Alerts	General	Counters, sample interval, alert threshold, and alert comment	
	Action	Actions to take when an event occurs	Examples of actions for an alert include running a program, sending a message, starting a counter log, and updating the event log.
	Schedule	Start and stop parameters for alerts	Automated restart is not available if you configure the alert to stop manually.
			You might need to update the Performance Logs and Alerts service properties if you opt to run a program that displays to the screen after the system triggers an alert. Use **Services** under **Services and Applications** in **Computer Management** for this purpose.
Counter Logs	General	Counter log counters and sample interval	
	Log Files	File type, file size limits, path and name, and automatic naming parameters	Counter logs can be defined as comma-separated or tab-separated text files, or as binary linear or circular files.

(continued)

Table 5.3   Summary of Log and Alert Properties *(continued)*

For this feature	Use this tab	To configure these settings	Notes
Counter Logs	Schedule	Manual or automated start and stop methods and schedule	Counter logs can be defined as comma-separated or tab-separated text files, or as binary linear or circular files.
			You can specify that the log stop when the log file is full.
			You cannot configure the service to automatically restart or to run a program if a log is configured to stop manually.
			You cannot configure a log to stop when full if the file is configured on the **Log Files** tab to grow to a maximum size limit.
Trace Logs	General	Trace log providers and events to log	You cannot configure the service to automatically restart if a log is configured to stop manually.
			You can have only one system trace log running at a time. You cannot enable multiple providers simultaneously.
			To obtain disk input/output data from the system provider, you must also select **File details**.
	Log Files	Trace log comment, file type, path and name, and automatic naming parameters	Only two types of trace logs are available: circular and sequential.
	Schedule	Start and stop parameters for a trace log	You cannot configure the service to automatically restart or to run a program if a log is configured to stop manually.
	Advanced	Trace log buffer size, limits, and transfer interval (periodic flushing)	

To start or stop a log or alert, right-click the name in the Performance Logs and Alerts window, point to **All Tasks**, and then click **Start** or **Stop**.

Getting the Most from Performance Logs and Alerts

Windows 2000 Server online Help for Performance Logs and Alerts describes performing the most common tasks with logs and alerts. The following list provides some additional hints about using the tools effectively:

- Export log data to a spreadsheet for reporting purposes. Importing log data into a spreadsheet program such as Excel offers benefits, such as easy sorting and filtering of data. To format the data for easy export, configure the log file type as Text File-CSV or Text File-TSV on the **Log Files** properties tab.

- Record transient data in a log. Not all counter log file formats can accommodate data that is not persistent throughout the duration of the log. If you want to record intermittent data such as a process that starts after you start the log, select the binary linear or circular file format on the **Log Files** tab.

- Limit log file size to avoid disk-space problems. If you choose automated counter logging with no scheduled stop time, the file will grow to the maximum size allowed based on available space on your disk up to 2GB (the largest log file that System Monitor can read). Trace logs have no file-size limit. When setting this option, take into consideration your available disk space and any disk quotas that are in place. Change the file path from the default (the Perflogs folder on the local computer) to a location with adequate space if appropriate. An error might occur if your disk runs out of disk space due to logging.

- Name files for easy identification. Use **File name** and **End file names with** on the **Files** properties tab to make it easy to find specific log files. For example, if you set up periodic logging, such as a log for every day of the week, you can develop different naming schemes with the base name being the computer where the log was run, or the type of data being logged, followed by the date as the suffix. For example, you could have a scheme that generates a file named ServerRed1_050212.blg, meaning it was created on a computer named ServerRed1 at noon, assuming the **End file name with** entry was set at **mmddhh**.

- Determine what trace data providers are available for trace logging. On the **General** properties tab, click **Provider Status** to see all data providers that have been installed. To see only enabled (running) data providers, click the **Show only enabled providers** check box in the **Provider Status** dialog box. For more information about WMI data providers, see the WMI SDK documentation in the MSDN Library at http://windows.microsoft.com/windows2000/reskit/webresources. You can only have one instance of each provider running at the same time.

Task Manager

Task Manager provides information about applications currently running on your system, the processes and memory usage or other data about those processes, and statistics about memory and processor performance.

Comparison with System Monitor

Although useful as a quick reference to system operation and performance, Task Manager lacks the logging and alert capabilities of the Performance console. In addition, although the data displayed by Task Manager comes from the same source as some performance counters, Task Manager does not have access to the breadth of information available from all installed counters. However, Task Manager provides capabilities not available with the Performance console, as described in Table 5.4. For information about these capabilities, see online Help for Task Manager and the chapters identified in Table 5.4.

Table 5.4   Other Chapters on Task Manager

Capability	Server Operations Guide chapter
Stop running processes.	"Analyzing Processor Activity"
Change the base priority of a process.	"Analyzing Processor Activity"
Set affinity for a process to a particular processor (on multiprocessor systems).	"Measuring Multiprocessor System Activity"

Starting Task Manager

To start Task Manager, use any of these methods:

- Press CTRL+SHIFT+ESC.
- Right-click the taskbar, and then click **Task Manager**.
- Press CTRL+ALT+DEL, and then click **Task Manager**.

You can also start Task Manager from the command prompt or the **Run** dialog box.

Working with Task Manager

Task Manager has three tabs: **Applications**, **Processes**, and **Performance**. While Task Manager is running, the status bar always displays the total number of processes, CPU use, and virtual memory use for the system. Note the following display possibilities:

- All Task Manager columns can be resized.
- Clicking a column sorts its entries in ascending or descending order.

- Select **Always on Top** from the **Options** menu to keep the window in view as you switch between applications.
- Press CTRL+TAB to toggle between tabs, or click the tab.

When Task Manager is running, an accurate miniature CPU usage gauge appears on the taskbar on the end opposite the **Start** button. When you place the mouse pointer over this icon, it displays the percentage of processor use in text format. The miniature gauge always matches the CPU Usage History chart on the **Performance** tab, as shown in Figure 5.9.

Figure 5.9   Task Manager CPU Gauge Shown on the Taskbar

To make Task Manager the top window, double-click the gauge, or right-click the gauge and then select **Task Manager** from the menu that appears.

If you run Task Manager frequently and do not want to see its button on the taskbar, click **Hide When Minimized** on the **Options** menu. To open an instance of Task Manager when it is hidden, click the Task Manager CPU gauge on the taskbar.

You can control the rate at which Task Manager updates its counts by setting the **Update Speed** option on the **View** menu.

- **High.** Updates every half-second.
- **Normal.** Updates once per second.
- **Low.** Updates every 4 seconds.
- **Paused.** Does not update automatically. Press F5 to update.

This will reduce Task Manager overhead, but might cause you to miss some data. You can force an update at any time by clicking **Refresh Now** on the **View** menu or by pressing F5.

Monitoring Processes

In **Task Manager**, click the **Processes** tab to see a list of running processes and measures of their performance. The Task Manager process table includes all processes that run in their own address space, including all applications and system services.

To include those in the display, on the **Options** menu, click **Show 16-bit Tasks**. Figure 5.10 is an example of how Task Manager displays process information.

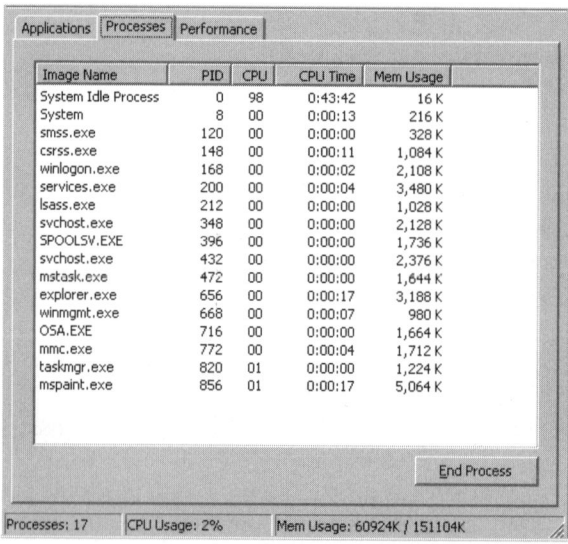

Figure 5.10   Processes Tab in Task Manager

Note System Monitor displays its values in bytes, whereas Task Manager displays its values in kilobytes, which are units of 1,024 bytes. When you compare System Monitor and Task Manager values, multiply System Monitor values by 1,024.

To add to or remove performance measures from the display for the processes listed, on the **View** menu, click **Select Columns**. Table 5.5 briefly describes the measures and their System Monitor counterparts, if any.

Table 5.5   Comparison of Process Data Supplied by Task Manager and System Monitor

Task Manager process measure	Description	System Monitor process object counters
Base Priority	The base priority of the process, which determines the order in which its threads are scheduled for the processor.	Priority Base
	The base priority is set by the process code, not the operating system. The operating system sets and changes the dynamic priorities of threads in the process within the range of the base.	
	Use Task Manager to change the base priority of processes. For more information about changing priority to improve processor performance, see "Analyzing Processor Activity" in this book.	

(continued)

Table 5.5   Comparison of Process Data Supplied by Task Manager and System Monitor *(continued)*

Task Manager process measure	Description	System Monitor process object counters
CPU Time	The total processor time, in seconds, used by the process since it was started.	None
CPU Usage	The percentage of time the threads of the process used the processor since the last update.	% Processor Time
GDI Objects	The number of Graphics Device Interface (GDI) objects currently used by a process. A GDI object is an object from the GDI library of application programming interfaces (APIs) for graphics output devices.	None
Handle Count	The number of object handles in the process's object table.	Handle Count
I/O Other	The number of input/output operations generated by a process that are neither reads nor writes, including file, network, and device I/Os. An example of this type of operation would be a control function. I/O Others directed to CONSOLE (console input object) handles are not counted.	I/O Other Operations/sec For more information about monitoring I/O, see the following chapters in this book: "Examining and Tuning Disk Performance" "Monitoring Network Performance"
I/O Other Bytes	The number of bytes transferred in input/output operations generated by a process that are neither reads nor writes, including file, network, and device I/Os. An example of this type of operation would be a control function. I/O Other Bytes directed to CONSOLE (console input object) handles are not counted.	I/O Other Bytes/sec
I/O Read Bytes	The number of bytes read in input/output operations generated by a process, including file, network, and device I/Os. I/O Read Bytes directed to CONSOLE (console input object) handles are not counted.	I/O Read Bytes/sec
I/O Reads	The number of read input/output operations generated by a process, including file, network, and device I/Os. I/O Reads directed to CONSOLE (console input object) handles are not counted.	I/O Read Operations/sec

(continued)

Table 5.5   Comparison of Process Data Supplied by Task Manager and System Monitor *(continued)*

Task Manager process measure	Description	System Monitor process object counters
I/O Write Bytes	The number of bytes written in input/output operations generated by a process, including file, network, and device I/Os. I/O Write Bytes directed to CONSOLE (console input object) handles are not counted.	I/O Write Bytes/sec
I/O Writes	The number of write input/output operations generated by a process, including file, network, and device I/Os. I/O Writes directed to CONSOLE (console input object) handles are not counted.	I/O Write Operations/sec
Image Name	Name of the process.	The process name in the **Instances** box
Memory Usage	The amount of main memory, in kilobytes, used by the process.	Working Set
Memory Usage Delta	The change in memory use, in kilobytes, since the last update. Unlike System Monitor, Task Manager displays negative values.	None
Nonpaged Pool	The amount of memory, in kilobytes, used by a process. Operating system memory that is never paged to disk. Paging is the moving of infrequently used parts of a program's working memory from RAM to another storage medium, usually the hard disk.	Pool Nonpaged Bytes
Page Faults	The number of times that data had to be retrieved from disk for this process because it was not found in memory. This value is accumulated from the time the process is started.	None Page faults/sec is the rate of page faults over time.
Page Faults Delta	The change in the number of page faults since the last update.	None
Paged Pool	The amount of system-allocated virtual memory, in kilobytes, used by a process. The paged pool is virtual memory available to be paged to disk. Paging is the moving of infrequently used parts of a program's working memory from RAM to another storage medium, usually the hard disk. The paged pool includes all of user memory and a portion of system memory.	Pool Paged Bytes
Peak Memory Usage	The peak amount of physical memory resident in a process since it started.	None

(continued)

Table 5.5   Comparison of Process Data Supplied by Task Manager and System Monitor *(continued)*

Task Manager process measure	Description	System Monitor process object counters
PID (Process Identifier)	Numerical ID assigned to the process while it runs.	ID Process
Thread Count	The number of threads running in the process.	Thread Count
USER Objects	The number of USER objects currently being used by a process. A USER object is an object from Window Manager, which includes windows, menus, cursors, icons, hooks, accelerators, monitors, keyboard layouts, and other internal objects.	None
Virtual Memory Size	The amount of virtual memory, or address space, committed to a process.	Private Bytes

For more information about Task Manager and its use in monitoring processor and memory performance, see the following chapters in this book:

- "Evaluating Memory and Cache Usage"
- "Analyzing Processor Activity"
- "Measuring Multiprocessor System Activity"

Monitoring the System

To see a dynamic overview of system performance, including a graph and numeric display of processor and memory usage, click the Task Manager **Performance** tab, as shown in Figure 5.11.

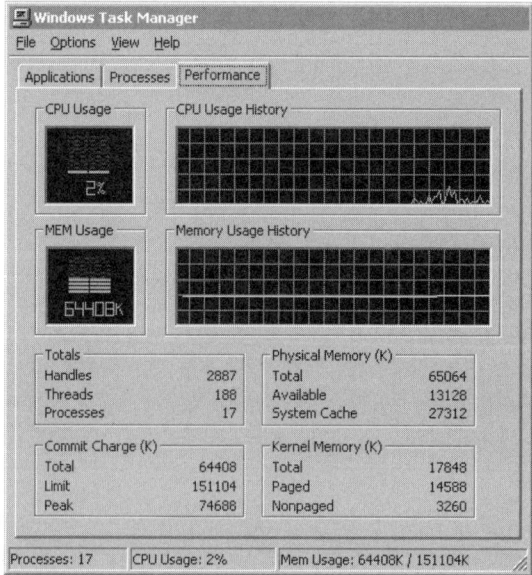

Figure 5.11   Task Manager Performance Tab

To graph the percentage of processor time in privileged or kernel mode, click
Show Kernel Times on the **View** menu. This is a measure of the time that
applications are using operating system services. The remaining time, known as
user mode, is spent running threads within the application code.

Users of multiple-processor computers can click **CPU History** on the **View** menu
and then graph the nonidle time of each processor in a single graph or in separate
graphs.

The following table briefly describes the counts on the Performance tab and their
System Monitor counterparts, if any.

**Table 5.6   Comparison of System Data Provided by Task Manager and System
Monitor**

Task Manager counts	Description	System Monitor counters
CPU Usage	The percentage of time the processor is running a thread other than the Idle thread.	Processor\% Processor Time
MEM Usage	The amount of virtual memory used, in kilobytes.	Memory\Committed Bytes
Total Handles	The number of object handles in the tables of all processes.	Process(_Total)\Handle Count

(continued)

Table 5.6   Comparison of System Data Provided by Task Manager and System Monitor *(continued)*

Task Manager counts	Description	System Monitor counters
Total Threads	The number of running threads, including one Idle thread per processor.	Process(_Total)\Thread Count
Total Processes	The number of active processes, including the Idle process.	Object\Processes is the same, but excludes the Idle process.
Physical Memory: Total	Amount of physical, random access memory, in kilobytes, installed in the computer.	None
Physical Memory: Available	Amount of physical memory available to processes, in kilobytes. It includes zeroed, free, and standby memory.	Memory\Available Bytes
Physical Memory: File Cache	Amount of physical memory, in kilobytes, released to the file cache on demand.	Memory\Cache Bytes
Commit Charge: Total	Size of virtual memory in use by all processes, in kilobytes.	Memory\Committed Bytes
Commit Charge: Limit	Amount of virtual memory, in kilobytes, that can be committed to all processes without enlarging the paging file.	Memory\Commit Limit
Commit Charge: Peak	The maximum amount of virtual memory, in kilobytes, used in the session. The commit peak can exceed the commit limit if virtual memory is expanded.	None
Kernel Memory: Total	Sum of paged and nonpaged memory, in kilobytes.	None (Sum of Pool Paged Bytes and Pool Nonpaged Bytes)
Kernel Memory: Paged	Size of the paged pool, in kilobytes, allocated to the operating system.	Memory\Pool Paged Bytes
Kernel Memory: Nonpaged	Size of the nonpaged pool, in kilobytes, allocated to the operating system.	Memory\Pool Nonpaged Bytes

Resource Kit Performance Tools

The *Windows 2000 Resource Kit* companion CD contains other performance-related tools, such as the following:

- **Ctrlist.exe.** This prints counter descriptions to a file or to the screen.
- **Extctrlst.exe.** This lists all counter DLLs that are running and provides the capability of disabling them. For more information about disabling counters, see "Troubleshooting Problems with Performance Tools" later in this chapter.
- **Perfmtr.exe.** This command-line utility is useful for dynamically monitoring performance statistics relating to memory, processor, and I/O activity.
- **Showperf.exe.** This program is useful for developers who want to see the counter type, index, and the contents of the Performance Data block so they can view and debug the counter's raw data structure.
- **Typeperf.exe.** This is a command-line utility for displaying performance information from individual performance counters.

For information about the utilities listed, see the *Windows 2000 Resource Kit* Tools Help. Programs used in specific bottleneck analysis contexts are described in the chapters to which they apply.

Starting Your Monitoring Routine

Setting up a monitoring routine consists of several steps, including setting up a basic monitoring configuration (sometimes called "overview" settings), testing the limits of acceptable performance under various conditions, and establishing a baseline. The following sections describe how to undertake these steps.

Your Minimum Monitoring Configuration

The minimum performance objects to monitor are those corresponding to the main hardware resources of your system: memory, processors, disks, and network components. Table 5.7 lists the appropriate counters and the categories of information they provide.

Table 5.7   Monitoring the Minimum Objects

Component	Performance aspect being monitored	Counters to monitor
Disk	Usage	LogicalDisk\% Free Space
		LogicalDisk\% Disk Time
		PhysicalDisk\Disk Reads/sec
		PhysicalDisk\Disk Writes/sec
		Use **diskperf -y** to enable disk counters and **diskperf -n** to disable them. To specify the type of counters you want to activate, include **d** for physical disk drives and **v** for logical disk drives or storage volumes. When the operating system starts up, it automatically sets the **diskperf** command with the **-yd** switch to activate physical disk counters. Type **diskperf -yv** to activate logical disk counters. For more information about using the **diskperf** command, type **diskperf -?** at the command prompt.
		The % Disk Time counter must be interpreted carefully. Because the _Total instance of this counter might not accurately reflect utilization on multiple-disk systems, it is important to use the % Idle Time counter as well. Note that these counters cannot display a value exceeding 100 percent.
		For more information about disk performance counters, see "Examining and Tuning Disk Performance" in this book.
Disk	Bottlenecks	LogicalDisk\Avg. Disk Queue Length
		PhysicalDisk\Avg. Disk Queue Length (all instances)
Memory	Usage	Memory\Available Bytes
		Memory\Cache Bytes
		You can also use Memory\Committed Bytes and Memory\Commit Limit to detect problems with virtual memory.

(continued)

Table 5.7   Monitoring the Minimum Objects *(continued)*

Component	Performance aspect being monitored	Counters to monitor
Memory	Bottlenecks or leaks	Memory\Pages/sec
		Memory\Page Faults/sec
		Memory\Pages Input/sec
		Memory\Page Reads/sec
		Memory\Transition Faults/sec
		Memory\Pool Paged Bytes
		Memory\Pool Nonpaged Bytes
		Although not specifically Memory object counters, the following are also useful for memory analysis:
		Paging File\% Usage Object (all instances)
		Cache\Data Map Hits %
		Server\Pool Paged Bytes and Server\Pool Nonpaged Bytes
Network	Usage	Network Segment: % Net Utilization
		Note that you need to install the Network Packet Protocol driver for Network Monitor in order to use this counter.
Network	Throughput	Protocol transmission counters (varies with networking protocol); for TCP/IP:
		Network Interface\Bytes total/sec
		Network Interface\Packets/sec
		Server\Bytes Total/sec or Server\Bytes Sent/sec and Server\Bytes Received/sec
		You might want to monitor other objects for network and server throughput, as described in "Monitoring Network Performance" in this book..
Processor	Usage	Processor\% Processor Time (all instances)
	Bottlenecks	System\Processor Queue Length (all instances)
		Processor\Interrupts/sec
		System\Context switches/sec

If you want to test the limits of your system as part of establishing a baseline, monitor the recommended counters during the following activities:

- Adding base services
- Adding connections
- Running network applications
- Opening a file

- Printing a file
- Copying or writing to a file
- Accessing a database
- Sending a message

Establishing the Baseline

After becoming familiar with System Monitor and the process of configuring graphs and logs, you are ready to incorporate monitoring into your daily routine of system administration. Routine monitoring over periods ranging from days to weeks to months allows you to establish a baseline for system performance.

A baseline is a measurement that is derived from the collection of data over an extended period during varying but typical types of workloads and user connections. The baseline is an indicator of how individual system resources or a group of resources are used during periods of normal activity.

When determining your baseline, it is very important to know the types of work being done and the days and times when the work is being done. That will help you to associate work with resource usage and to determine the reasonableness of performance during those intervals.

For example, if you find that performance diminishes somewhat for a brief period at a given time of day, and you find that at that time many users are logging on or off, it might be an acceptable slowdown. Similarly, if you find that performance is poor every evening at a certain time and you can tell that that time coincides with nightly backups when no users are logged on to the system, again that performance loss might be acceptable. But you can make that determination only when you know the degree of performance loss and its cause.

When you have built up data on performance over a period, with data reflecting periods of low, average, and peak usage, you can make a subjective determination of what constitutes acceptable performance for your system. That determination is your baseline. Use your baseline to detect when bottlenecks are developing or to watch for long-term changes in usage patterns that require you to increase capacity.

Analyzing Monitoring Results

The baseline you develop establishes the typical counter values you should expect to see when your system is performing satisfactorily. The following section provides guidelines to help you interpret the counter values and eliminate false or misleading data that might cause you to set your own target values inappropriately.

When you are collecting and evaluating data to establish a valid performance baseline, consider the following guidelines:

- When monitoring processes of the same name, watch for unusually large values for one instance and not the other. This can occur because System Monitor sometimes misrepresents data for separate instances of processes of the same name by reporting the combined values of the instances as the value of a single instance. Tracking processes by process identifier can help you get around this problem. For information about monitoring processes, see "Analyzing Processor Activity" later in this book.

- When you are monitoring several threads and one of them stops, the data for one thread might appear to be reported for another. This is because of the way threads are numbered. For example, you begin monitoring and have three threads, numbered 0, 1, and 2. If one of them stops, all remaining threads are resequenced. That means that the original thread 0 is now gone and the original thread 1 is renamed to 0. As a result, data for the stopped thread 0 could be reported along with data for the running thread 1 because old thread 1 is now old thread 0. To get around this problem, you can include the thread identifiers of the process's threads in your log or display. Use the Thread\Thread ID counter for this purpose.

- Do not give too much weight to occasional spikes in data. These might be due to startup of a process and are not an accurate reflection of counter values for that process over time. The effect of spikes can linger over time when using counters that average.

- For monitoring over an extended period of time, use graphs instead of reports or histograms because these views only show last values and averages. As a result, they might not give an accurate picture of values if you are looking for spikes.

- Unless you specifically want to include startup events in your baseline, exclude these events because the temporary high values tend to skew overall performance results.

- Investigate zero values or missing data. These can impede your ability to establish a meaningful baseline. There are several possible explanations for this. For more information, see "Troubleshooting Problems with Performance Tools" later in this chapter.

Identifying Potential Bottlenecks

Deviations from your baseline provide the best indicator of performance problems. However, as a secondary reference, the following table describes recommended thresholds for object counters. Use this table to help you identify when a performance problem is developing on your system. If the values listed are consistently reported on your system, consult additional chapters in the Performance Monitoring section of this book for how to investigate and correct the problems causing these values.

Table 5.8   Recommended Thresholds for the Minimum Set of System Counters

Resource	Object\Counter	Suggested threshold	Comments
Disk	LogicalDisk\% Free Space	15 percent	None
Disk	LogicalDisk\% Disk Time	90 percent	None
Disk	PhysicalDisk\ Disk Reads/sec, PhysicalDisk\ Disk Writes/sec	Depends on manufacturer's specifications	Check the specified transfer rate for your disks to verify that this rate does not exceed the specifications. In general, Ultra Wide SCSI disks can handle 50 to 70 I/O operations per second.
Disk	PhysicalDisk\ Current Disk Queue Length	Number of spindles plus 2	This is an instantaneous counter; observe its value over several intervals. For an average over time, use PhysicalDisk\Avg. Disk Queue Length.
Memory	Memory\ Available Bytes	Less than 4 MB	Research memory usage and add memory if needed.
Memory	Memory\ Pages/sec	20	Research paging activity.
Network	Network Segment\% Net Utilization	Depends on type of network	You must determine the threshold based on the type of network you are running. For Ethernet networks, for example, 30 percent is the recommended threshold.
Paging File	Paging File\% Usage	Above 70 percent	Review this value in conjunction with Available Bytes and Pages/sec to understand paging activity on your computer.
Processor	Processor\% Processor Time	85 percent	Find the process that is using a high percentage of processor time. Upgrade to a faster processor or install an additional processor.

(continued)

Table 5.8   Recommended Thresholds for the Minimum Set of System Counters *(continued)*

Resource	Object\Counter	Suggested threshold	Comments
Processor	Processor\ Interrupts/sec	Depends on processor; for current CPUs, use a threshold of 1500 interrupts per second.	A dramatic increase in this counter value without a corresponding increase in system activity indicates a hardware problem. Identify the network adapter or disk controller card causing the interrupts. You might need to install an additional adapter or controller card.
Server	Server\Bytes Total/sec		If the sum of Bytes Total/sec for all servers is roughly equal to the maximum transfer rates of your network, you might need to segment the network.
Server	Server\Work Item Shortages	3	If the value reaches this threshold, consider tuning the InitWorkItems or MaxWorkItems entries in the registry (in HKEY_LOCAL_MACHINE \SYSTEM\CurrentControlSet \Services\lanmanserver\Parameters). For more information about MaxWorkItems, see the Microsoft Knowledge Base link on the Web Resources page at http://windows.microsoft.com /windows2000/reskit/webresources
			Caution Do not use a registry editor to edit the registry directly unless you have no alternative. The registry editors bypass the standard safeguards provided by administrative tools. These safeguards prevent you from entering conflicting settings or settings that are likely to degrade performance or damage your system. Editing the registry directly can have serious, unexpected consequences that can prevent the system from starting and require that you reinstall Windows 2000. To configure or customize Windows 2000, use the programs in Control Panel or Microsoft Management Console whenever possible.
Server	Server Work Queues\Queue Length	4	If the value reaches this threshold, there might be a processor bottleneck. This is an instantaneous counter; observe its value over several intervals.
Multiple Processors	System\Processor Queue Length	2	This is an instantaneous counter; observe its value over several intervals.

Investigating Bottlenecks

Investigating performance problems should always start with monitoring the whole system before looking at individual components. In precise terms, a bottleneck exists if a particular component's limitation is keeping the entire system from performing more quickly. Therefore, even if one or more components in your system is heavily used, if other components or the system as a whole show no adverse effects, then there is no bottleneck.

For example, suppose that a process had 10 threads, each of which used exactly 0.999 seconds of processor time once every 10 seconds. If each thread made a request exactly 1 second after the previous one in perfect sequence, the processor would be 99.9 percent busy, but there would be no queue, no interference between the threads, and, technically, no bottleneck, although the system probably could not support any increased load or variation in its request scheduling without creating one.

Factors involved in the development of a bottleneck are the number of requests for service, the frequency with which requests occur, and the duration of each request. As long as these are perfectly synchronized, no queue will develop and no bottleneck will arise. The device with the smallest throughput ratio is probably the primary source of the bottleneck.

It is difficult to detect multiple bottlenecks in a system. You might spend several days testing and retesting to identify and eliminate a bottleneck, only to find that another appears in its place. Only thorough and patient testing of all elements can ensure that you have found all of the problems.

It is not unusual to trace a performance problem to multiple sources. Poor response time on a workstation is most likely to result from memory and processor problems. Servers are more susceptible to disk and network problems.

Also, problems in one component might be the *result* of problems in another component, not the cause. For example, when memory is scarce, the system begins moving pages of code and data between disks and physical memory. The memory shortage becomes evident from increased disk and processor use, but the problem is memory, not the processor or disk.

If you identify a resource that is out of range for your baseline or based on the recommended thresholds discussed in the preceding section, you need to investigate the activity of that resource in greater detail. This includes the following steps:

- Analyze your hardware and software configurations. Does your configuration match Microsoft recommendations for the operating system and the services you are supporting?

- Review entries in the event log for the time period when you begin seeing out-of-range counter values; these entries might provide information on problems that might result in poor system performance.

- Examine the kinds of applications you are running and what resources they demand, to determine their adequacy.

- Consider variables in your workload, such as processing different jobs at different times. For more efficient analysis, when you are looking for a specific problem, limit your charts and reports to specific events occurring at known times.

- For immediate diagnosis and problem solving of situations such as shutdowns and logon failures, log or monitor for a shorter time. Sampling should be frequent when monitoring over a short period. Similarly, for long-term planning and analysis, log for a longer period and set the update interval accordingly.

- Consider network or disk utilization or other activities occurring at the times that you see increasing resource utilization. Try to understand the usage patterns. Are they associated with specific protocols or computers?

- Approach bottleneck correction in a scientific manner. For example, never make more than one change at a time, always repeat monitoring after a change to validate the results, eliminate results that are suspect, and keep good records of what you have done and what you have learned.

When investigating bottlenecks in specific resources, focus on the performance objects and counters that pertain to the specific resource that appears to be your bottleneck. Your reference for information about these counters and how to detect and correct bottlenecks should be the chapter of this guide that refers to the resource you are investigating. These chapters also discuss how to use other Windows 2000 tools and utilities on the *Windows 2000 Resource Kit* companion CD for bottleneck detection and tuning. The chapters are as follows:

- "Evaluating Memory and Cache Usage"
- "Analyzing Processor Activity"
- "Examining and Tuning Disk Performance"
- "Monitoring Network Performance"
- "Measuring Multiprocessor System Activity"

Troubleshooting Problems with Performance Tools

Occasionally you might have problems obtaining performance data, or you might find that monitoring a process is adding an unnecessary load to a computer you are monitoring. The following sections discuss how to handle some of these problems:

- Investigating Zero Values
- Investigating Other Problems with Tool Usage
- Controlling Performance Monitoring Overhead

Investigating Zero Values

If data for selected counters is consistently reported as zeroes, this might indicate a problem with the counters or the way you are using the performance tools, rather than just the absence of any nonzero data. Following are descriptions of the possible causes and solutions to problems that result in missing or zero counter values.

- The process being monitored has stopped and, as a result, there is no data for the process in the performance tools. If you stopped the process manually, restart it to see the process in System Monitor. Otherwise, check Event Viewer for concurrent entries. You might find an error associated with this process.

- The counter DLL was disabled after you selected the corresponding counters in a log or display. The performance tools will not detect that the counter was removed or disabled, but will report the counter data as zeroes.

- You are attempting to monitor a computer that you don't have permission to access. This might occur if you are using a saved console that specifies a particular computer name. This causes System Monitor to report data as zeroes. It also causes System Monitor to start up slowly. For more information see "Security Issues" later in this chapter.

Investigating Other Issues with Performance Tools

You might occasionally believe that data reported by the performance tools is invalid, that data is incomplete, or that the tools are not operating properly. This section addresses some problems you might encounter with the tools and how to correct them.

Data seems to be missing.

- System Monitor might show gaps in its line graphs because data collection was subordinated to higher-priority processing activity on a system with a heavy load. When the system has adequate resources to continue with data collection, the graphing will resume as usual. A message appears describing this. Note also that you might see delays in display of data for some counters. Counters that display an average must wait for two samples to elapse before displaying a value. For ways to reduce the performance overhead of system monitoring, see "Controlling Performance Monitoring Overhead" later in this chapter.

- Values recorded in a log do not appear in the graph view. This is because the graph is limited to 100 samples. Reducing the size of the Time Window on the **Data** property tab can allow you to see a more complete range of data.

Objects, counters, or instances seem to be missing or invalid.

In some cases you might find that you cannot find an object you want to monitor. This might be caused by the following:

- You have not started or installed the process that starts the object counters. Use Task Manager to verify that the process is running. If so, use Exctrlst.exe on the *Windows 2000 Resource Kit* companion CD to verify that the counter DLL is running.

- You have not enabled the counters (such as with the Network Segment object counters). If you do not see a counter that you want to monitor, make sure that the service or feature that provides the counter has been installed or configured. For information about how to install or configure the service or feature, see online Help for the service or feature.

- If counters have been disabled, then they will not appear in the Add Counters dialog box. There are several reasons that a counter DLL might be disabled:

    - A user disables counter DLLs using Exctrlst.exe on the *Windows 2000 Resource Kit* companion CD.

    - The Performance Library's built-in testing routines have found problems with the counter DLLs and have disabled them to prevent them from interfering with operation of the Performance console. If this has occurred, the Application Log in Event Viewer contains a message to this effect.

To re-enable the counters for debugging purposes, locate the Performance subkey under the subkey for the service (typically, HKEY_LOCAL_MACHINE\SYSTEM\CurrentControlSet\Services *service_name*\Performance\) and change the value for the Disable Performance Counters entry from 1 (disabled) to 0 (enabled). Notice that a counter DLL that the system has automatically disabled is likely to contain errors and may cause the system to slow.

- You lack permissions on the computer being monitored. If you do not have appropriate permissions to monitor the computer, an error message will be displayed when you attempt to select the computer. An administrator must ensure that your user account has permissions to use the performance tools. If you are trying to monitor a remote system, for information about security issues, see "Monitoring Remote Computers" later in this chapter.

- The DLL that installs the counters is generating errors. An example is if the counter does not handle localization functions correctly. Check Event Viewer to see if the counter DLL or the Performance Data Helper (PDH) library reported any errors. If necessary, you can disable counter DLLs that are causing errors by using Exctrlst.exe on the *Windows 2000 Resource Kit* companion CD.

- You are trying to monitor a 16-bit or MS-DOS application. Only 32-bit processes appear in the **Instances** box. Active 16-bit processes appear as threads running in a Windows NT Virtual DOS Machine (NTVDM) process. (Virtual DOS Machine is an environment system for MS-DOS and 16-bit Windows emulation.) If you want to monitor a 16-bit application, see "Monitoring 16-bit Windows Applications" later in this chapter.

Note   When trying to monitor administrative tools hosted in MMC, note that they appear as instances of MMC in the **Add Counters** dialog box.

- The instance you want to monitor is not currently active. If you are configuring System Monitor to collect real-time data, you can only select active instances for data collection. (If you are viewing logged data, you can select inactive instances for which the log contains data.) If you select the process and it stops after you have selected it, it will continue to appear in the list box but the reported data will be zeroes.

- You might see situations where an instance seems inappropriate for the counter—such as the _Total instance for the Process\ID Process counter. All counters for an object have the same instances.

Data seems invalid.

There are several reasons that counters might report unlikely values:

- You sometimes see an extremely high value for one instance and not the other when you are monitoring processes of the same name. This is because the performance tools sometimes misrepresent data for separate instances of processes with the same name by reporting the combined values of the instances as the value of a single instance. Using the instance index and tracking the Process\ID Process and Process\Creating Process ID counters can help you get around this problem.

- Also, when monitoring several threads and one of them stops, the data for one thread might appear to be reported for another. This is because of the way threads are numbered. For example, you begin monitoring and have three threads, numbered 0, 1, and 2. If one of them stops, all remaining threads are resequenced. That means that the original thread 0 is now gone and the original thread 1 is renamed to 0. As a result, data for the stopped thread 0 could be reported along with data for the running thread 1 because old thread 1 is now old thread 0. Again, using the instance index can help you to track these threads.

Problems with System Monitor and MMC

- If you are trying to create a custom console with System Monitor and another tool, you might have a problem because System Monitor is not listed in the **Add Standalone Snap-in** dialog box. This is because System Monitor is not designed as an extension snap-in but as an ActiveX control. To create a custom console containing System Monitor, you select **ActiveX Control** in the **Add Standalone Snap-in** dialog box and select **System Monitor Control** in the **Insert ActiveX Control** dialog box. System Monitor Control will appear as the name of the utility in your custom console; you can change it as needed.

- Help for System Monitor does not appear in MMC; only Performance Logs and Alerts is shown in MMC Help. Because System Monitor is designed as an ActiveX control, it is unlike other MMC snap-ins. For example, System Monitor Help is not available by clicking **Help Topics** on the **Help** menu or by right-clicking **System Monitor** and selecting **Help** in the shortcut menu. Instead, click **Help** on the System Monitor display toolbar.

Problems with logs

- Trace log data is not output as readable text. You must use a parsing utility to interpret the trace log output. Developers can create such a utility with the APIs provided in the Platform Software Development Kit.

- An error message appears if you try to export log data to Microsoft Excel while the Performance Logs and Alerts service is actively collecting data to that log. The service must be stopped because Excel requires exclusive access to the log file. Other programs are not known to require this exclusive access; therefore, in general, you can work with data from a log file while the service is collecting data to that file.

- Data from a running log does not seem to be updating. If you are working in System Monitor with a log file that is currently collecting data, you will need to click **Select Time Range** and keep moving the **Time Range** bar to the right to update the display with new samples.

- Processes that started while a log was running do not appear in my exported log. Logged data can be saved as comma-separated or tab-separated files that are easily viewed with Microsoft Excel. However, some limitations apply when you use this format. Instances that start after the log is started will not be reflected. You need to use the binary log format to see data for these instances.

- Errors occur regarding counter log size. This could be because your counter log has consumed the available space on the hard drive that you specified in the log file path. In addition, counter logs have a maximum size of 2 GB, and a message will appear when the log reaches this limit. Note that logs this size are unwieldy and slow to work with.

- An exported monitoring configuration is collecting data from the wrong computer. This is probably because you selected the **Select counters from computer** option when you saved the console and installed it on another system. Instead, select **Use local computer counters**.

- The Performance Logs and Alerts service stops and does not restart. If a network connection is lost during remote monitoring, or if there is a problem with a counter DLL, this could cause the Performance Logs and Alerts service to shut down. The service is configured to restart only once after the first failure. Thereafter, you need to start the service manually. To avoid recurrence of this problem, modify the startup properties of the services in **Services** under **Administrative Tools**. Also make sure to investigate the cause of the shutdown by reviewing the event log and disabling problem DLLs. To do this, use Exctrlst, a utility included on the *Windows 2000 Resource Kit* companion CD.

- Workspace (.pmw) files that were created with Windows NT 4.0 Performance Monitor are not fully compatible with Windows 2000 System Monitor. Only one of the views saved in the workspace is available in System Monitor. System Monitor can read log files created with earlier versions of Performance Monitor when you use the following syntax at the Windows 2000 command prompt:

perfmon.exe *log_file_name*

This command does not invoke Windows NT 4.0 Performance Monitor, but instead a shell program that starts System Monitor. Windows NT 4.0 Performance Monitor is available as Perfmon4.exe on the *Windows 2000 Resource Kit* companion CD.

Controlling Performance Monitoring Overhead

When you select a counter in any view, the performance tools collect data for all counters of that object, but display only the one you select. This causes only minimal overhead, because most of the tools' overhead results from the display. You can control monitoring overhead in the following ways:

- Use logs instead of displaying a graph. The user interface is more costly in terms of performance.

- Limit the use of costly counters; this increases monitoring overhead. For information about costly counters, see the Performance Counter Reference on the *Microsoft® Windows® 2000 Resource Kit* companion CD.

- Lengthen collection intervals if possible. In general, 600-second (10-minute) intervals are sufficient for ordinary monitoring.

- Collect data during peak activity rather than over an extended interval.

- Reduce the number of objects monitored unless these are critical to your analysis.

- Put the log file on a disk that you are not monitoring.

- Check the log file size when logging multiple servers to a single computer to see how much space the data is taking up.

- Limit to brief periods the trace logs that are monitoring page faults or file I/O. Prolonged trace logging strains system performance.

- Avoid configuring System Monitor reports to display nondefault data. If you choose nondefault data (the defaults are Average value for logs; Last value for graphs) in the Report view, the statistic is calculated at each sample interval. This incurs some additional performance overhead.

Specific Monitoring Scenarios

This section describes various scenarios such as monitoring remote computers and monitoring servers and services.

Monitoring Remote Computers

In general, monitoring remote computers differs little from monitoring local computers. This section discusses some facts to consider when evaluating whether to monitor remotely or locally.

Methods of Monitoring

When monitoring activity on remote computers, you have some options with regard to how to collect data. For example, you could run a counter log on the administrator's computer, drawing data continuously from each remote computer. In another case, you could have each computer that is running the service collect data and, at regular intervals, run a batch program to transfer the data to the administrator's computer for analysis and archiving. Figure 5.12 illustrates these options.

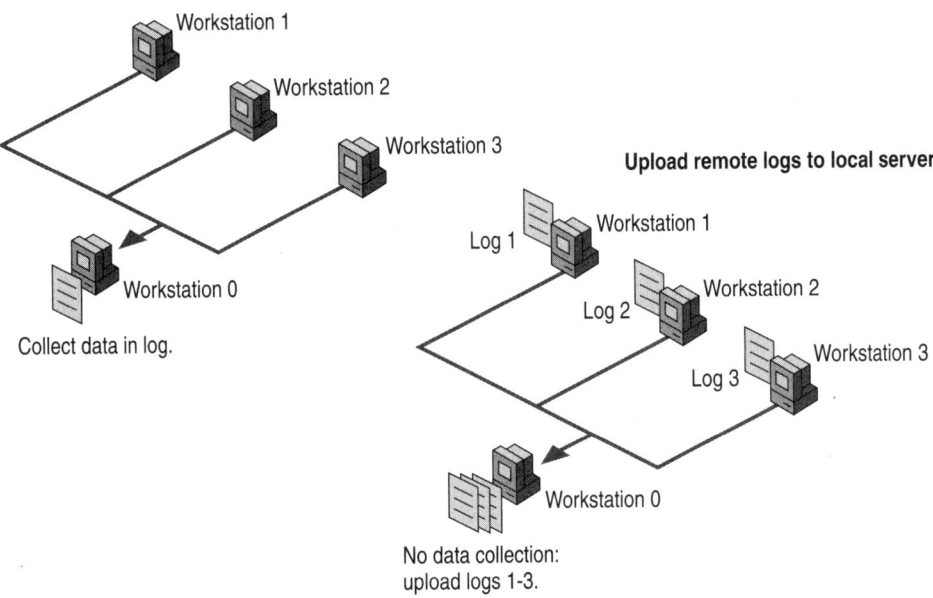

Figure 5.12   Comparison of Performance Data Logging Options

Choose a monitoring method based on your needs from the ones described in the following list:

- Centralized data collection (that is, collection on a local computer from remote computers that you are monitoring) is simple to implement because only one logging service is running. You can collect data from multiple systems into a single log file. However, it causes additional network traffic and might be constrained by available memory on the administrator's computer. Frequent updating also adds to network activity. Centralized monitoring is useful for a small number of servers (25 or fewer). For centralized monitoring, use the **Add Counters** dialog box to select a remote computer while running System Monitor on your local computer.

- Distributed data collection (that is, data collection that occurs on the remote computers you are monitoring) does not incur the memory and network traffic problems of local collection. However, it does result in delayed availability of the data, requiring that the collected data be transferred to the administrator's computer for review. This kind of monitoring might be useful if you suspect the server is part of the problem. It is also useful if you suspect that the network is the cause of performance problems and you are concerned that data packets you want to monitor are being lost, because it isolates the computers from the network during data collection. In general, local monitoring creates more disk traffic on each monitored computer. For distributed monitoring, use **Performance Logs and Alerts** under **Computer Management** to select the computer you want to monitor.

Security Issues

If you are collecting data using the registry, monitoring a remote computer requires the use of the Remote Registry Service. If the service stops due to failure, the system restarts it automatically only once. Therefore, if the service stops more than once, you must restart the service manually on the second and any subsequent failures. To change this default behavior, modify the properties for Remote Registry Service. You can access service properties using **Services** under **Services and Applications** in **Computer Management** or under **Administrative Tools**. Also check the application and system logs in Event Viewer for events that might explain why the service stopped.

In addition, remote data collection requires access to certain registry subkeys and system files. Users need a minimum of Read access to the Winreg subkey in HKEY_LOCAL_MACHINE\SYSTEM\CurrentControlSet\Control \SecurePipeServers to provide remote access to the registry for the purpose of collecting data on remote systems. By default, members of the Administrators group have Full Control access and members of the Backup Operators group have Read access. Users also need Read access to the registry subkey that stores counter names and descriptions used by System Monitor. This subkey is HKEY_LOCAL_MACHINE\SOFTWARE\Microsoft \Windows NT\CurrentVersion\Perflib*LanguageID*, where *LanguageID* is the numeric code for the spoken language for the operating system installation. (For the English language, the subkey is Perflib\009.) By default, members of the Administrators and Creator Owners groups, and the System account, have Full Control access and members of the Interactive group have Read access.

Users might also require read access to the files that supply counter names and descriptions to the registry, Perfc*.dat and Perfh*.dat. (The asterisk is a wildcard character representing the specific language code; for English, these are Perfc009.dat and Perfh009.dat.) If these files reside on an NTFS volume, then, in order to have access to them, the access control lists (ACLs) on these files must specify that the user has such access. By default, members of the Administrators and Interactive groups have sufficient access.

The remote computer allows access only to user accounts that have permission to access it. In order to monitor remote computers, the Performance Logs and Alerts service must be started in an account that has permission to access the remote computers you are attempting to monitor. By default, the service is started under the local computer's system account, which generally has permission to access only services and resources on the local computer. To start this under a different account, start Computer Management, click the plus sign (**+**) beside **Services and Applications**, and click **Services**. Click **Performance Logs and Alerts**, and update the properties under the **Log On** tab. To monitor using counter logs or alerts, you must also have permission to read the HKEY_CURRENT_MACHINE\SYSTEM \CurrentControlSet\Services\SysmonLog\LogQueries registry subkey.) In general, administrators have this access by default. In each case, attempting to use the tools without appropriate permissions will generate an error message.

If you are collecting data remotely by means of WMI, the user must be a member of the Administrators group.

Monitoring Servers and Services

Computers that provide shared resources to users of a network are called servers. This section describes the relationship between a the workload of a server and its resource utilization. This section also covers establishing a baseline for a server, identifying emerging problems, and upgrading.

Characterizing Server Workload

Some servers are characterized by the workload they support, as indicated in Table 5.9. Servers supporting these workloads can have specific resource requirements. These requirements and how to monitor them with performance monitoring tools are described later in this chapter.

Table 5.9   Objects to Monitor Based on Server Workload

Server workload	Heaviest resource usage	Objects to monitor
Application servers	Memory and processor	Cache, Memory, Processor, and System
Servers used for backups	Processor and network	System, Server, Processor, and Network Segment
Database servers	Disks and processor	PhysicalDisk, LogicalDisk, Processor, and System
		If using Microsoft® SQL Server™, see the product documentation for information about installed performance objects.

(continued)

Table 5.9   Objects to Monitor Based on Server Workload *(continued)*

Server workload	Heaviest resource usage	Objects to monitor
Domain controllers	Memory, processor, network, and disk	Memory, Processor, System, Network Segment, Network Interface, protocol counters (TCP, UDP, ICMP, IP, NBT Connection, NetBEUI, NetBEUI Resource, NWLink IPX, NWLink NetBIOS, NWLink SPX), PhysicalDisk, and LogicalDisk
		The NWLink object counters report zero values for frame-related data.
		For Active Directory, also monitor the NTDS and Site Server LDAP Service objects; for Windows 2000 servers, monitor the Browser object. As applicable, monitor DNS or WINS objects.
File and print servers	Memory, disk, and network components	Memory, Network Segment, PhysicalDisk, and LogicalDisk
		For print servers, use the Print Queue object for monitoring queue activity.
Mail/messaging servers	Processor, disk, and memory	Memory, Cache, Processor, System, PhysicalDisk, and LogicalDisk
		If using Microsoft Exchange, see the product documentation for information about installed performance objects.
Web servers	Disk, cache, and network components	Cache, Network Segment, PhysicalDisk, and LogicalDisk

Tip As a general recommendation, servers with major roles should be dedicated to a single purpose rather than shared among multiple purposes. For example, do not have domain servers or database servers do double duty as application or file and print servers because these secondary activities can impede the ability of the server to handle its primary workload.

As a service runs, it makes specific demands on system resources. In addition to the monitoring resource requirements defined by the computer's workload, you can obtain information about the services using performance data made available through the services. Many services running under Windows 2000 Server supply performance counters that can be used to measure service activity and resource utilization. Monitoring these counters provides data you can use to determine how well your server is functioning.

In addition to the standard counters described in "Overview of Performance Monitoring," you can use the System object counters to obtain information of interest on server computers. For example, you might want to examine the values for System\System Up Time. If this value is consistently low, it might indicate frequent failures, meaning that the server remains up only for a short time.

Establishing a Baseline on Server Computers

Monitor the performance of your server at the busiest times of day as well as when it is idle or when activity levels are low. Consider the number of concurrent users as well as the number of inactive connections during the times you are monitoring because the server expends resources tracking inactive as well as active connections. After collecting and reviewing this data, you can set a baseline for the performance of your server. This baseline can be used as a reference point for determining when performance problems exist and for projecting future resource requirements. When data consistently falls outside of the baseline ranges, consider it a signal that the performance of your server is changing—either because the demand is increasing or a bottleneck is developing. You will then want to monitor activity more closely to determine whether your server needs tuning or upgrading.

When you become aware of changes in performance that result in values outside your baseline, monitor the system counters representing the disk, memory, processor, and network components along with the Processor\% Processor Time counter for the services that you are running to see if there is a correlation between service activity and resource usage. If so, you might need to tune the service.

Note Unless you are testing a computer's startup performance, wait until the startup process has concluded before monitoring system performance. Otherwise, you might mistake the high utilization values characteristic of process startup for the process's typical load.

In general, you will want to monitor a server from a different computer so as to minimize the impact of the testing process on the computer being tested. For more information about the advantages and disadvantages of remote versus local monitoring, see "Monitoring Remote Computers" earlier in this chapter.

Upgrading Servers and Capacity Planning

The chapters "Analyzing Processor Activity," "Evaluating Memory and Cache Usage," and "Examining and Tuning Disk Performance" in this book provide information about tuning and planning for upgrades for hardware resources such as memory, processors, or disks when counter values indicate that these are being strained by your workload. In addition, the chapter "Measuring Multiprocessor System Activity" addresses the special considerations for obtaining optimal performance from scaled systems and discusses the benefits of server clustering and load balancing.

The capacity of a server depends on many variables, including the number of work units (such as client requests), the amount of time required for each unit, and the corresponding resource utilization. Because of the many variables of an individual server implementation, it is extremely difficult to arrive at a perfect formula for gauging the capacity of your server.

Monitoring Legacy Applications

For optimal performance, it is recommended that all applications you run under Windows 2000 be 32-bit. However, if you need to continue using 16-bit Windows or MS-DOS-based applications, this section describes how you can monitor their activity.

Monitoring 16-bit Windows Applications

In Windows 2000, by default, all active 16-bit Windows applications run as separate threads in a single multithreaded process called NT Virtual DOS Machine (NTVDM). The NTVDM process simulates a 16-bit Windows environment complete with all of the DLLs called by 16-bit Windows applications.

This configuration poses two challenges for running 16-bit applications:

- It prevents 16-bit applications from running simultaneously, which might impede their performance.

- It makes monitoring a bit trickier because 16-bit applications do not appear by name in the **Add Counters** dialog box for the performance tools; instead, they appear as undistinguishable NTVDM processes.

As a result, Windows 2000 includes an option to run a 16-bit application in its own separate NTVDM process with its own address space. You can monitor 16-bit Windows applications by identifying them by their thread identifier (ID) while they are running, or by running each application in a separate address space.

In addition to the 16-bit applications, each NTVDM process includes a heartbeat thread that interrupts every 55 milliseconds to simulate a timer interrupt, and the Wowexec.exe thread, which helps to create 16-bit tasks and to handle the delivery of the 16-bit interrupt. This thread supports 16-bit Windows applications in a 32-bit Windows environment. The WOW subsystem provides a virtual DOS machine where all Win16 applications run. You will see the heartbeat and Wowexec threads when monitoring 16-bit applications.

Only one 16-bit Windows application thread in an NTVDM can run at one time and, if an application thread is preempted, the NTVDM always resumes with the same thread. This limits the performance of multiple 16-bit applications running in the same NTVDM process, although this limitation becomes an issue only when the processor is very busy.

Although System Monitor can monitor 16-bit applications in Windows 2000 because they run in the same process, the trick to monitoring more than one 16-bit application is to distinguish among the threads of the NTVDM process.

To monitor one 16-bit application, select the NTVDM process in System Monitor. (Other performance tools used to monitor processes can be used for monitoring the NTVDM process. For more information, see "Analyzing Processor Activity" in this book.) If you have multiple 16-bit processes running in NTVDM, you can distinguish them by their thread identifiers (IDs). You might have to start and stop the 16-bit process to determine which ID is associated with which 16-bit process.

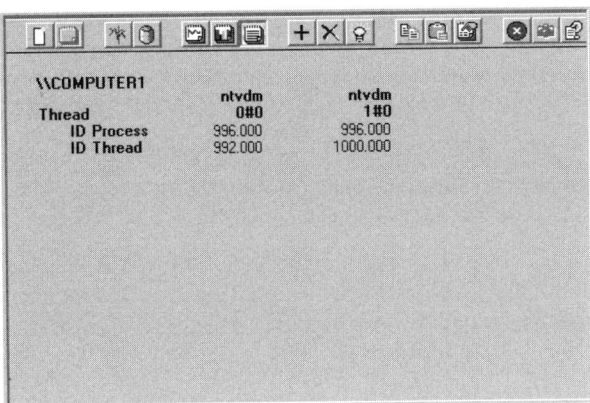

Figure 5.13   NTVDM Threads in System Monitor

Figure 5.13 shows a System Monitor report on a single NTVDM process. The ID Process and ID Thread counters are included to help you distinguish among the threads. One of the threads is the heartbeat thread, one is the Wowexec thread, and one is a 16-bit application.

System Monitor identifies threads by the process name and a thread number. The thread numbers are ordinal numbers (beginning with 0) that represent the order in which the threads started. The thread number of a running thread changes when a thread with a lower number stops, and all threads with higher numbers move up in order to close the gap. For example, if thread 1 stopped, thread 2 becomes thread 1. Therefore, thread numbers are not reliable indicators of thread identity.

Instead, with System Monitor you can track processes and threads using the process IDs and thread IDs. The process ID identifies the process in which the thread runs. The thread ID identifies the thread. Unlike the thread number, which can change over the time the thread runs, the system assigns the thread ID when the thread starts and retains it until the thread stops.

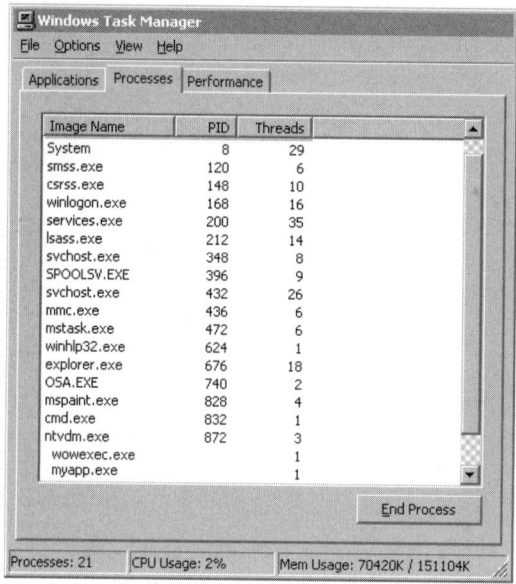

Figure 5.14   MyApp, Wowexec, and Ntvdm on the Task Manager Process Tab

As shown in Figure 5.14, Task Manager makes it easy to identify 16-bit applications because it displays the names of the executable files indented below the NTVDM process name. To monitor 16-bit processes in Task Manager, click the **Processes** tab, and on the **Options** menu, click **Show 16-bit Tasks**.

In this example, you can see the Wowexec (Windows on Windows) and the MyApp threads. The heartbeat thread is not an executable and does not appear as a process in Task Manager. However, the **Thread Count** column on the far right shows that all threads are running in the NTVDM process.

Running 16-bit Windows Applications in a Separate Process

Windows 2000 lets you opt to run a 16-bit Windows application in separate, unshared NTVDM process with its own memory space. This eliminates competition between NTVDM threads in a single process, making the 16-bit application thread fully multitasking and preemptive. It also simplifies monitoring.

▶ **To run a 16-bit application in its own address space**

- At the command prompt, type:

  start /separate *processname*

In Task Manager and System Monitor, two instances of the NTVDM process appear. You can use their process identifiers to distinguish between them. Figure 5.15 shows NTVDM threads with the process identifier.

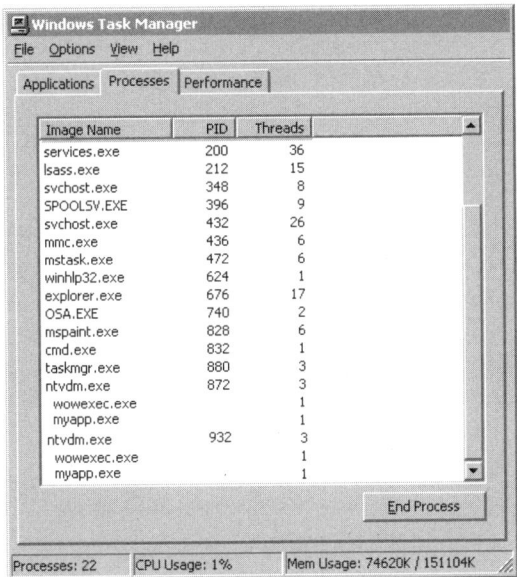

Figure 5.15   NTVDM Instances in Task Manager with Process Identifiers

Figure 5.15 shows Task Manager monitoring two copies of a 16-bit application, each in its own NTVDM process.

Monitoring MS-DOS Applications

In Windows 2000, each MS-DOS application runs in its own NTVDM process, eliminating some of the problems encountered in 16-bit Windows applications. All of the NTVDM processes are called Ntvdm.exe by default, but you can use the following procedure to change the name for easier tracking.

▶ **To create a new process name for an NTVDM process**

1. Copy Ntvdm.exe to a file with a different name.

2. Change the value of the **cmdline** entry in HKEY_LOCAL_MACHINE\SYSTEM\CurrentControlSet\Control\WOW to the name of your copy of Ntvdm.exe. The default value is *systemroot*\System32\Ntvdm.exe.

3. When you start an MS-DOS application, it will run in a process with that name. Figure 5.16 shows how your edited process name appears in Regedt32.

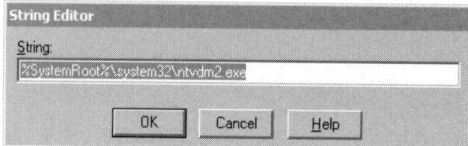

Figure 5.16   New Process Name in Regedt32

Tip You do not have to restart the computer for the registry change to take effect. Thus, you can change the registry between starting different MS-DOS applications and have each start in a uniquely named process. It is also prudent to set the process name back to Ntvdm.exe when you are finished.

If you are not satisfied with the performance of your MS-DOS-based applications in Windows 2000, try changing the following settings, accessed by right-clicking the file in Windows Explorer:

- Under **Usage** in **Screen** properties for the .pif file, select **Full-Screen** to speed up video display performance. Press ALT+ENTER to get in and out of full-screen mode.

- Disable the Compatible Timer Hardware Emulation feature in the _Default.pif or the application's program information file (PIF). To disable it, clear the check box displayed when you click the **Windows NT** button under **Program** properties for the file. Because this feature causes a decrease in performance, use it only if it is required to allow an application to run under Windows 2000.

- If the application is in a window and seems to pause periodically, try reducing idle sensitivity by moving the **Idle Sensitivity** slider to the left in **Misc** properties for the application's .pif.

- If the MS-DOS-based application can be configured for printing, choose LPT1 or LPT2 rather than parallel port. Most of the applications use Int17 to print when configured for LPT. If you select parallel port mode, these applications print directly to printer ports. Parallel mode is significantly slower in Windows 2000 compared to Windows 3.*x*.

Integrating the System Monitor Control into Office and Other Applications

You can host the System Monitor ActiveX control in applications of the Microsoft Office 97 suite or later and in HTML pages. The following sections describe how to integrate and use these controls, including the following:

- Inserting the control into an Office document or on a Web page
- Formatting the control within a document

Placing the Control in an Office Document or on a Web Page

Integration of the Microsoft Office applications with Visual Basic for Applications makes the process of adding the System Monitor control almost identical across these applications. The following procedures describe how to insert the control in applications such as Microsoft Word, Microsoft Excel, and Microsoft PowerPoint®. For purposes of this section, the word "document" is used to refer to PowerPoint slides, Word documents, or Excel spreadsheets.

- Default key settings in Microsoft Word might conflict with the CTRL+H combination used for System Monitor highlighting. You might need to change these to support highlighting when the System Monitor control (Sysmon.ocx in the *systemroot*\System32 folder) is used in Microsoft Word.

In addition, you can add the control to a Web page using an HTML editor that supports insertion of ActiveX controls or using a text editor as described in "To insert the control in an HTML Page."

▶ **To insert the System Monitor control into a Microsoft Office application**

1. Start the application and select **Toolbars** under the **View** menu.
2. Under **Toolbars**, select **Control Toolbox**.

3. With the Control Toolbox displayed, click the **More Controls** icon and select the **System Monitor Control**.

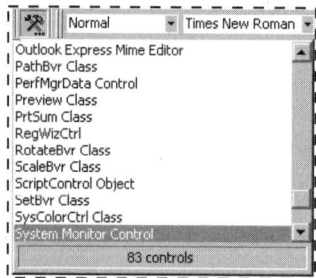

Figure 5.17   System Monitor Control in the Control Toolbox

Figure 5.17 shows the System Monitor control selected in the Control Toolbox.

4. Place the control on the page according to the requirements of the application. See the following differences among applications:

- In a Microsoft Word document, select the insertion point (where the I-beam is flashing) before selecting the control. The control will appear at the position you selected. Design mode is active and you need to exit Design mode before setting control properties or adding counters. Click the **Design Mode** icon to exit.

- In a Microsoft Excel spreadsheet, select the control and then select the insertion point. When the crosshair appears, note that you can create a placeholder for the control by holding down the left mouse button and dragging the mouse pointer across the columns and rows that you want the control to occupy. Releasing the mouse button causes the control to appear in the space you selected.

  If you do not create a placeholder, you can click any location on the spreadsheet and the control will be inserted in the location with a default size. Design mode is active and you need to exit Design mode before setting control properties or adding counters. Click the **Design Mode** icon to exit.

- In a Microsoft PowerPoint slide, select the control and then select the insertion point. With the crosshair visible on the screen, note that you can hold down and drag the mouse button to the size you want and the control will be inserted in the placeholder. Otherwise, you can click anywhere on the slide to place the control in that location with a default size and you can modify the size coordinates later (as described in "To format the control in a document").

The Design mode icon is not displayed after you insert the control although Design mode *is* in effect. To exit Design mode, on the **View** menu, click **Slide Show**.

Note The System Monitor control is not displayed correctly until you exit Design mode.

With the control sited in the document, you can add counters or modify control properties, as described in the System Monitor Help file (Sysmon.chm).

If you select **Graph** for the Display Type and the size you define for the control is insufficient to show the graph data, only a portion of the graph will be displayed (such as the vertical minimum and maximum scale values, and the counter-data graph lines).

If you select **Report** for the Display Type and the size is insufficient to show all the report data, the control includes vertical and horizontal scroll bars so that you can scroll to view the data that does not fit in the display.

If you want to format the control in the application, resume Design mode by clicking the Design mode icon in the Control Toolbox and see the procedure named "To format the control in a document" later in this chapter.

▶ **To insert the control in a Microsoft Visual Basic program**

1. On the **File** menu, choose **New** to open a new project (such as a Standard EXE or an ActiveX Document EXE).

2. On the **Project** menu, click **Components** to show the **Components** dialog box.

   You can also view the **Components** dialog box by right-clicking the Toolbox. If the Toolbox is not displayed, in the **View** menu, select the **Toolbox** command.

3. Under **Controls** in the **Components** dialog box, select the **System Monitor Control Library** check box, and then click **OK**.

   An icon for the System Monitor control now appears in the Toolbox.

4. With the form or the document displayed, double-click the **System Monitor Control** icon to add it to the form or document for your program.

   This places the control in the document, occupying the entire size of the form. If you want to select a size for the control, click the **System Monitor Control** icon *once* and then, when the crosshair appears, hold down and drag the mouse to the size you want the control to occupy on the form.

Immediately after inserting the control, the application is in Design mode, so you can format the control within a document. For more information, see the procedure "To format the control in a document" later in this chapter.

▶ **To insert the control in an HTML page**

- Using a text editor, create a page to include the control. To place the control on the page, insert the <OBJECT> tag and specify the class ID as follows:

```
<OBJECT classid="clsid:C4D2D8E0-D1DD-11CE-940F-008029004347">
</OBJECT>
```

This places the control in the document and, when you view the page in a Web browser, you can add counters or modify control properties as described in the procedures that appear later in this document.

To include functions in your page that automate the setting of properties or addition of counters, use scripts written in Visual Basic Scripting Edition (VBScript), or use Microsoft FrontPage®, as described in the following procedure.

▶ **To insert the System Monitor control into a Web page created with Microsoft FrontPage**

1. In a new or existing FrontPage Web page, on the **Insert** menu, select **Other Components**, and then select **ActiveX Control**.

2. In the **ActiveX Control Properties** dialog box, select **Sysmon Graph Control** in the **Pick A Control** list box.

3. To add VBScript, click **Extended**, and complete the **Extended Attributes** dialog box as needed.

For more information about VBScript, see the VBScript link on the Web Resources page at http://windows.microsoft.com/windows2000/reskit/webresources.

Formatting the Control in a Document

The default appearance of the control can vary based on the document in which it resides. This is because the control takes the ambient properties of the document in which it is running. For example, when placed in Microsoft Word or FrontPage, the graph background, font, and chart background color might be reset to the default color and font used by those documents. Therefore, after you insert the control in a Microsoft Office application, you might want to change its appearance with respect to the document itself.

Using Design mode in Visual Basic or Office documents, you can easily manipulate the control's attributes such as size, position, and so on as you could with any linked or embedded object. In addition, you have access to the control's properties, methods, and events from the Visual Basic editor for programming the control's behavior within the document. (The control's user interface is inactive when the document is in Design mode.) Note that there are slight differences in how some of the Office applications handle formatting the inserted control.

Note When changing the properties of the control, it is possible to set colors for **BackColor**, **ForeColor**, or **GraphBackground**, or to set graph line colors that are not visible. Therefore, make sure to check the appearance of your control display after you make changes to its properties.

In addition, you cannot programmatically format the properties and methods of the control using the Visual Basic editor. Use VBScript or Jscript® in your HTML editor for this purpose.

▶   **To format the control in a document**

1. Resume Design mode and make the changes you want. To resume Design mode in PowerPoint, exit the Slide Show view.

   - To change the position of the control in the document, drag the control to another position in the container.

   - To change the height or width of the control in the document, drag one of the selection handles of the control in the appropriate direction.

2. To access the control properties or the Visual Basic code editor, right-click the control and select **Properties** or **View Code**, as appropriate. In the Visual Basic code editor window, you can view the Object Browser if needed.

    Notice that some commands on this shortcut menu (such as Cut, Copy, or Paste) are designed for other embedded or linked objects in that document; they are not relevant to the control and might be unavailable (dimmed).

Note When you use Microsoft Office applications, it is possible to modify the control in the document so that the control's properties become inaccessible. This occurs because the control is being converted into an embedded object. For example, if you click the **System Monitor Control Object** command in Microsoft Word (by right-clicking the control) and select the **Convert** command, the **Convert** dialog box appears. If you click **OK** in this box, the control's properties and view-code option become unavailable. You will not be able to change the position or the size of the object in Word.

---

3. Exit Design mode before trying to add counters or to edit the control's default properties.

Notice that the appearance of the control might not update properly until you exit Design mode.

For information about the control's objects, properties, and so on, see the Software Development Kit (SDK) documentation in the MSDN Library at http://windows.microsoft.com/windows2000/reskit/webresources.

C H A P T E R   6

Evaluating Memory and Cache Usage

Use the Performance console and other Microsoft® Windows® 2000 tools to assess available memory and to observe the effects of a memory shortage, a common cause of poor computer performance. Examine the effectiveness of the file system cache—an area of physical memory where recently used data read from or written to the disk is mapped for quick access. In addition, use Windows 2000 tools to investigate memory problems caused by applications that have not been optimized.

In This Chapter

Related Information in the Resource Kit

- For general information about performance monitoring, see "Overview of Performance Monitoring" in this book.

- For information about developer tools see the *Microsoft Windows 2000 Resource Kit* companion CD, or see the MSDN link on the Web Resources page at http://windows.microsoft.com/windows2000/reskit/webresources.

Overview of Memory Monitoring

Low memory conditions can slow the operation of applications and services on your computer and impact the performance of other resources in your system. For example, when your computer is low on memory, *paging*—that is, the process of moving virtual memory back and forth between physical memory and the disk—can be prolonged, resulting in more work for your disks. Because it involves reading and writing to disk, this paging activity might have to compete with whatever other disk transactions are being performed, intensifying a *disk bottleneck*. (A disk bottleneck occurs when disk performance decreases to the extent that it affects overall system performance.) In turn, all this work by the disk can mean the processor is used less or is doing unnecessary work, processing numerous interrupts due to repeated *page* CIEBs. (Page faults occur when the system cannot locate requested code or data in the physical memory available to the requesting process.) In the end, applications and services become less responsive.

Figure 6.1 illustrates the sequence in which you conduct the monitoring process. Memory has such an important influence on system performance that monitoring and analyzing memory usage is one of the first steps you take when assessing your system's performance.

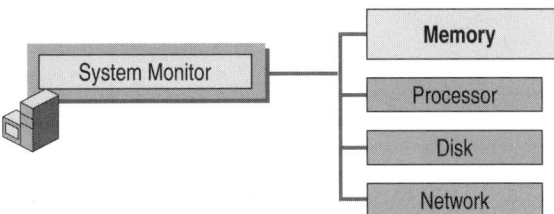

Figure 6.1   Role of Memory Monitoring in Overall Monitoring Sequence

The first phase of analyzing memory usage involves understanding your current memory configuration and your workload, using the steps in the following list:

- Determine the amount of physical memory that is currently installed, and compare it against minimum operating system requirements.

- Read "Understanding Memory and the File System Cache" in this chapter for information about the relationship between system memory and the file system cache.

- Establish a baseline for memory usage on your computer by determining performance ranges for low or idle, average, and peak usage periods.

- Optimize the system memory configuration to the system workload, including verifying cache and paging file sizes.

Focus subsequent monitoring on how your system uses memory and on identifying memory shortages or other problems, using the following steps:

- Look at memory characteristics of processes using the Process\Working Set and Process\Private Bytes counters. The Working Set counter reports the amount of committed memory allocated to the process. This might include shared and private bytes currently resident in physical memory. The Private Bytes counter reports memory allocated exclusively to the process. Working set monitoring is important because, when memory is in short supply, the operating system trims the *working sets* of processes and paging occurs. (The working set of a process is the amount of physical memory assigned to that process by the operating system.)

- Monitor the counters listed in "Investigating Disk Paging" later in this chapter to understand the relationship between the amount of paging and the amount of disk activity and their effect on overall performance. Excessive paging can burden the disk.

- Determine the effectiveness of the file system cache. Your system performs better when it can find requested data in the cache, rather than having to read from the disk.

- Learn how to tune the *working sets* of applications, if you have access to source code. Efficient applications maintain a small working set without generating page faults.

Determining the Amount of Installed Memory

Start your monitoring efforts knowing that you have at least the minimum amount of memory required to run Windows 2000. These requirements are as follows:

- Microsoft® Windows® 2000 Professional: 32 megabytes (MB)
- Microsoft® Windows® 2000 Server: 64 MB

The memory recommendation for Windows 2000 Professional is based on a typical desktop configuration including a business productivity application, such as a word processor or a spreadsheet program, an e-mail application, and a Web browser. The memory recommended for Windows 2000 Server is based on either a dedicated or a multiuse server with a low load, such as a small file-sharing and Web service configuration for a small office. If you are using a database management system such as Microsoft® SQL Server™ or a messaging server such as Microsoft® Exchange, consult the documentation for those products to determine the memory recommended for running them on Windows 2000 Server.

There are a few different ways to determine the amount of memory on your computer. You can find the amount of physical memory installed on your system by clicking the **Performance** tab in Task Manager. Or you can find the amount of available RAM by double-clicking **System** in **Control Panel** and then clicking the **General** tab.

Note   You can see the memory configuration on local or remote systems using System Information. For more information, see Windows 2000 Server Help.

The operating system distinguishes memory usage by applications and services depending on whether the usage involves the paged or the nonpaged pool. The paged pool contains memory for objects used by applications and services that can be paged to disk; objects in the nonpaged pool cannot be paged to disk. The operating system determines the size of each pool based on the amount of physical memory present. Memory pool usage can be an important factor in evaluating memory usage by your applications. For more information, see "Investigating User-Mode Memory Leaks" and "Investigating Kernel-Mode Memory Leaks" later in this chapter.

The file system cache, which is a subset of physical memory used for fast access to data, and the *disk paging file*, which supports *virtual memory*, influence the amount of memory used by the operating system and applications. (The disk paging file, also called a swap file, is a file on the hard disk that serves as temporary, virtual memory storage for code and data.) Virtual memory is the space on the hard disk that Windows 2000 uses as memory. For purposes of monitoring, the most important types of virtual memory are committed memory that the system sets aside for a process in the paging file and available memory that is not in use by a process. (Another type of memory managed by Windows 2000 is reserved memory, which the system sets aside for a process but which might not be entirely used.) The following sections describe the influence of the cache and the paging file on performance and explain how best to adjust these for optimal memory usage.

Understanding Memory and the File System Cache

Windows 2000 allocates a portion of the virtual memory in your system to the *file system cache*. The file system cache is a subset of the memory system that retains recently used information for quick access. The size of the cache depends on the amount of physical memory installed and the memory required for applications. The operating system dynamically adjusts the size of the cache as needed, sharing memory optimally between process working sets and the system cache.

On computers running Windows 2000 Server, the value set for the **LargeSystemCache** registry entry in HKEY_LOCAL_MACHINE\System\CurrentControlSet\Control\Session Manager\Memory Management controls the size of the cache. You should set the value of the **LargeSystemCache** entry using the Windows 2000 Server user interface, rather than by editing the registry. Use the **Server Optimization** tab in the **File and Printer Sharing for Microsoft Networks Properties** dialog box to control memory buffer allocation for network connections and the size of the file system cache working set. Figure 6.2 illustrates the user interface for configuring these settings. Notice that these settings are not available on Windows 2000 Professional.

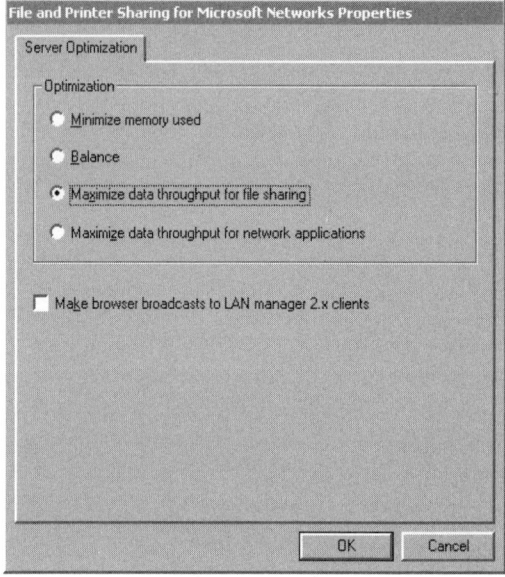

Figure 6.2   File and Printer Sharing for Microsoft Networks Properties Dialog Box

▶ **To view or change Server Optimization settings**

1. From the **Start** menu, point to **Settings**, and then click **Control Panel**.

2. Double-click **Network and Dial-up Connections**.

3. Double-click **Local Area Connection**, and then click the **Properties** button.

4. In the **Local Area Connection Properties** dialog box, double-click **File and Printer Sharing for Microsoft Networks**.

5. Under **Optimization**, if you are running Windows 2000 Server, the **Maximize Data Throughput for File Sharing** option is selected by default.

6. Click **OK**.

The values for the **LargeSystemCache** entry are shown in Table 6.1, along with their corresponding options under **File and Printer Sharing for Microsoft Networks Properties**.

Table 6.1   Settings that Manage Cache Size in the Registry and the User Interface

Registry value	User interface option	Description	Notes
0	**Maximize data throughput for network applications**	Optimizes systems for distributed applications that typically do their own memory caching (such as SQL Server, which sets this option by default). This setting is useful for computers providing application services because it favors the working sets of processes over the working set of the file system cache.	This setting is useful for larger server applications and database servers such as SQL Server that need to maximize process working sets over the file system cache working set.
1	**Maximize data throughput for file sharing**	Optimizes the system for file and printer sharing resources. This is the default set by Windows 2000 Server Setup. If you have at least 128 MB of RAM, this value results in a very high maximum size for the cache working set. The **Maximize Data Throughput for File Sharing** option is useful for computers that typically run the Server service for file sharing.	On Windows 2000 the file system cache working set can be increased by 464 MB of additional virtual address space (up to 960 MB) if the system has less than 16 GB of RAM, is not configured to start with the /3GB Boot.ini switch, and the **PagedPoolSize** entry is set to a value other than 0xFFFFFFFF (or 0 on systems with more than 1 GB of RAM), such as 192000000, the system is not running Terminal Services, and the **SystemPages** entry is not set to 0xFFFFFFFF . For more information about how various memory-management registry entries interact, see "Optimizing Your Memory Configuration" later in this chapter.

To adjust the way memory is allocated on your system, you might want to tune the settings of the preceding registry entries under the Memory Management subkey. The following section describes how to do this.

Optimizing Your Memory Configuration

The default memory-management settings for your system are optimal in most situations and do not need to be changed. However, the system can provide a much larger working set and additional virtual address space for the system cache if some settings are manually tuned. These settings include the following registry entries in the HKEY_LOCAL_MACHINE\System\CurrentControlSet\Control \Session Manager\Memory Management subkey:

- **LargeSystemCache**. A value of 1 maximizes the size of the system cache's working set and, with PagedPoolSize set to 192000000 and SystemPages set to 0, provides a large virtual address space for the cache, provided that Terminal Services and the /3GB switch are not used. In addition, the maximum working set and large virtual address space for the file system cache are unavailable if Driver Verifier, a tool for testing kernel drivers, is enabled with the special pool. For information about Driver Verifier, see the Driver Development Kits link on the Web Resources page at http://windows.microsoft.com/windows2000/reskit/webresources.

- **PagedPoolSize**. Changing this to 0xFFFFFFFF or leaving it at the default of 0 maximizes the size of the virtual address space used for the paged pool. To set aside extended virtual address space for the file system cache, change this value to 192000000, set **LargeSystemCache** to 1, and set **SystemPages** to 0.

- **SystemPages**. Changing this to 0xFFFFFFFF provides an additional 464 MB of system page table entries for the virtual address space. Notice that making this change prevents expanding the system cache by 464 MB (limiting it to 512 MB) and limits the paged pool size to 192 MB, provided **PagedPoolSize** is not set to 0xFFFFFFFF to obtain the maximum virtual address space for the paged pool.

Notice that you have the option of changing the settings for **LargeSystemCache** in the user interface (using the **Server Optimization** tab in **File and Printer Sharing for Microsoft Networks** properties). However, you can only change the settings of **SystemPages**, **PagedPoolSize**, and **NonPagedPoolSize** using a registry editor.

Caution   Do not use a registry editor to edit the registry directly unless you have no alternative. The registry editors bypass the standard safeguards provided by administrative tools. These safeguards prevent you from entering conflicting settings or settings that are likely to degrade performance or damage your system. Editing the registry directly can have serious, unexpected consequences that can prevent the system from starting and require that you reinstall Windows 2000. To configure or customize Windows 2000, use the programs in Control Panel or Microsoft Management Console (MMC) whenever possible.

If you are using Terminal Services or your system is configured to start with the /3GB switch, these features consume the extra virtual address space that you might otherwise allocate to the system cache or the paged pool and that space is unavailable.

Do not change the SecondLevelDataCache entry

Some third-party sources have erroneously reported that modifying the **SecondLevelDataCache** registry entry in HKEY_LOCAL_MACHINE\System\CurrentControlSet \Control\Session Manager\Memory Management can enhance system performance. The second level (L2) cache is recognized by the operating system and is fully utilized regardless of the setting of this parameter.

Adjusting Paging File Size

For virtual-memory support, Windows 2000 creates one paging file called Pagefile.sys on the disk or volume on which the operating system is installed. The default size is equal to 1.5 times the amount of physical memory. A small paging file limits what can be stored and might exhaust your virtual memory for applications. If you are short on RAM, more paging occurs, which generates extra activity for your disks and slows response times for the system.

Note Special considerations apply for sizing the paging file on Windows 2000 Advanced Server when you are using 4 gigabyte RAM tuning (4GT). For more information, see Windows 2000 Advanced Server Help.

Because the size and location of paging files can affect your system's performance, you might want to modify these. Also, because maintaining multiple files on multiple drives can improve performance, you might want to add a paging file. Figure 6.3 shows the **Virtual Memory** dialog box, which you use to change your paging file settings. See Windows 2000 Server Help for specific instructions.

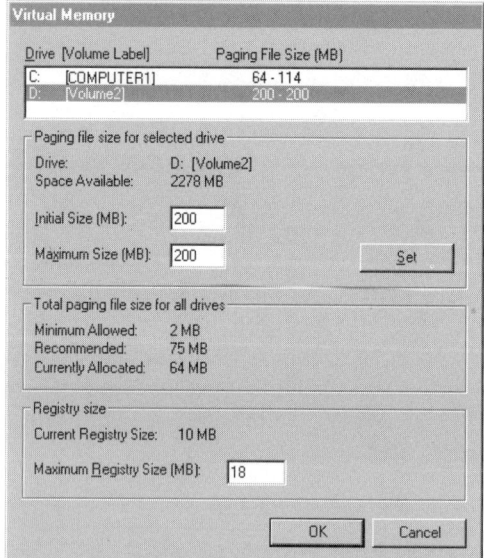

Figure 6.3   Virtual Memory Dialog Box

The following guidelines describe how to optimize the paging file.

Set the Same Initial and Maximum Size

Setting the paging file's initial size and maximum size to the same value increases efficiency because the operating system does not need to expand the file during processing. Setting different values for initial and maximum size can contribute to disk fragmentation.

Expand the Default Size

Expanding the default size of the paging file can increase performance if applications are consuming virtual memory and the full capacity of the existing file is being used. To determine how large your paging file should be based on your system workload, monitor the Process (_Total)\Page File Bytes counter. This indicates, in bytes, how much of the paging file is being used.

You can also determine the appropriate size of a paging file by multiplying the Paging File\% Usage Peak counter value by the size of Pagefile.sys. The % Usage Peak counter indicates how much of the paging file is being used. You should consider expanding the page file whenever this counter reaches 70 percent of the total size in bytes of all paging files or the Memory\% Committed Bytes In Use counter reaches 85%, whichever occurs first.

A large paging file uses disk storage space, so do not create a large paging file on a disk that is very active (for example, one that services heavy application or network activity) or one that has limited space. Change the file size gradually and test performance until you find the optimal balance between paging file and disk space usage. The operating system requires a minimum of 5 MB of free space on a disk. For more information, see "Examining and Tuning Disk Performance" in this book.

Before increasing the file size, make sure you have adequate disk space, particularly on your servers. For more information, see "Monitoring Network Performance" in this book.

Move the Paging File

If disk space on your boot volume is limited, you can achieve better performance by moving the paging file to another volume. However, you might want to leave a smaller paging file on the boot volume and maintain a larger file on different volume with more capacity for the sake of recoverability. Depending on how you have configured your system's startup and recovery options, the configuration might require that you maintain a paging file of a certain size on the boot volume. Therefore, make sure to consider your startup and recovery settings when planning to move the paging file. For information about startup and recovery options such as writing debugging information, see Windows 2000 Help.

Use Multiple Disks

Although Windows 2000 supports a limit of 4,095 MB for each paging file, you can supply large amounts of virtual memory to applications by maintaining multiple paging files. Spreading paging files across multiple disk drives and controllers improves performance on most modern disk systems because multiple disks can process input/output (I/O) requests concurrently in a round-robin fashion.

A mirrored or striped volume is a good candidate for placement of a paging file. Placing the paging file on its own logical partition can prevent file fragmentation. Creating multiple paging files on a single logical volume or partition does not improve performance.

If you find that page writing and disk writing or page reading and disk reading are equivalent on a logical disk, splitting the paging file onto separate volumes is helpful.

Set a Smaller Default Size for Systems Running Windows 2000 Advanced Server

If you are working in an enterprise environment using the 4-GB RAM Tuning (4GT) option and have a system with more than 4 GB of physical memory, you might want to consider changing the default size of your paging file. In Windows 2000, the default paging file size is equal to 1.5 times the amount of physical memory on the system. On a 4-GB computer, this might result in a paging file too large to be effective. A 256-MB paging file might be a more effective use of disk space. However, a smaller paging size affects the size of total committed memory for applications. For best results, review these settings with the independent software vendor (ISV) for your applications that are being run with the 4GT option. For more information about 4GT, see Windows 2000 Advanced Server Help.

Note To see how the paging file is used during memory shortages, start the LeakyApp tool on the *Windows 2000 Resource Kit* companion CD, designed to simulate memory leaks for monitoring purposes. While running LeakyApp, monitor Paging File\% Usage and Process(_Total)\Page File Bytes. Log these counters to get an idea of the rate of growth of the paging file.

Establishing a Baseline for Memory

After determining that you have an adequate amount of physical memory and that your configuration is appropriate, examine your physical memory usage under a normal workload to establish a baseline or reference point for physical memory usage. The baseline is generally not a single value but a range within which physical memory usage can fluctuate and still provide acceptable performance. You can use the baseline to identify trends, such as increasing physical memory demands over time, or to recognize problems that arise from a sudden change.

To determine a baseline for your system, use the following counters to create logs of memory usage over an extended period (from several weeks to a month).

- \Memory\Pages/sec
- \Memory\Available Bytes
- \Paging File(_Total)\% Usage

As you monitor the values of these counters, you might see occasional spikes. Typically, you can exclude these from your baseline because it is the consistent, repetitive values with which you are most concerned; the range of values that seem to appear consistently constitutes your baseline. When values fall outside of these ranges for extended periods, follow the instructions provided in this chapter to investigate the variations.

Virtual Memory Usage

Even if your system exceeds the minimum physical memory requirements for the operating system, you might face situations in which you do not have enough physical memory. For example, if you run several memory-intensive applications or if several users share your computer, the available physical memory of your system could be consumed, affecting your system's performance.

To see how much virtual memory your Windows 2000 Professional–based computer uses, start all applications and use Task Manager to see the Peak Commit Charge value. This value appears in the **Commit Charge** box on the **Performance** tab. Commit charge is the number of pages reserved for virtual memory that are backed by the paging file.

Peak committed memory is the highest amount of virtual memory (in bytes) that has been committed over this sample. To be committed, these bytes must either have a corresponding amount of storage available on disk or in main memory. Compare this value against the size of the paging file to determine if the paging file is sized appropriately.

On a computer running Windows 2000 Server, in addition to total committed memory, you need to consider the number of users sharing a system and the number of files they open to determine memory requirements for your workload.

Under **Computer Management**, use **Shared Folders** under **System Tools** to view this information.

For information about additional recommendations pertaining to memory on server computers, see "Monitoring Network Performance" in this book.

Default Services Memory Consumption

In general, Windows 2000 has been optimized so that only the most commonly used services run by default, and you should not have to turn off any services. However, you can reduce the memory requirements of your system by turning off some of the default services provided by the operating system.

▶ **To stop a service**

1. From the **Start** menu, point to **Programs,** point to **Administrative Tools,** and then click **Services**.

2. Right-click the name of a service, and then click **Stop**.

This procedure stops the service for the current session. To disable the service permanently, you need to change the value for service start-up in the properties dialog box for the service. To use this dialog box, click Services in the Administrative Tools menu or under the Computer Management console. Right-click the service you want to change, select Properties in the shortcut menu, and change the value to Disabled in the Startup type box.

Investigating Memory Problems

After you have observed memory usage under normal conditions and established your memory baseline, you might notice that the memory counters sometimes stray from the typical range. The following sections describe how to investigate conditions that cause memory values to deviate from the baseline.

The following activities help you to learn about and analyze memory usage and memory bottlenecks using System Monitor counters and other tools.

- Investigating memory shortages
- Investigating disk paging
- Investigating user-mode memory leaks
- Investigating kernel-mode memory leaks
- Monitoring the cache
- Resolving memory and cache bottlenecks

Table 6.2 summarizes the most important counters to monitor for analyzing memory usage.

Table 6.2   Counters for Analyzing Memory Usage

To monitor for	Use this *Object\Counter*
Memory shortages	Memory\Available Bytes or Available KBytes (to see the amount in kilobytes) or Available MBytes (to see the amount in megabytes) Process (*All_processes*)\Working Set Memory\Pages/sec Memory\Cache Bytes

(continued)

Table 6.2   Counters for Analyzing Memory Usage *(continued)*

To monitor for	Use this *Object\Counter*
Frequent hard page faults	Memory\Pages/sec Process (*All_processes*) \Working Set Memory\Pages Input/sec Memory\Pages Output/sec
Excess paging with a disk bottleneck	Memory\Page Reads/sec Physical Disk\Avg. Disk Bytes/Read
Paging file fragmentation	PhysicalDisk\Split IOs\sec PhysicalDisk\% Disk Read Time PhysicalDisk\Current Disk Queue Length Process\Handle Count
Memory leaks; memory-intensive applications	Memory\Pool Nonpaged Allocations Memory\Pool Nonpaged Bytes Memory\Pool Paged Bytes Process(*process_name*)\Pool Nonpaged Bytes Process(*process_name*)\Handle Count Process(*process_name*)\Pool Paged Bytes Process(*process_name*)\Virtual Bytes Process(*process_name*)\Private Bytes
Cache Manager efficiency	Cache\Copy Read Hits % Cache\Copy Reads/sec Cache\Data Map Hits % Cache\Data Maps/sec Cache\MDL Read Hits % Cache\MDL Reads/sec Cache\Pin Read Hits % Cache\Pin Reads/sec To identify cache bottlenecks, also use Memory\Pages Input/sec with these counters.

Important The LogicalDisk object counters are not available by default. If you want to monitor the values for these counters, you must first activate the counters by typing **diskperf –yv** at the Windows command prompt.

Investigating Memory Shortages

Your system can develop a memory shortage if multiple processes are demanding much more memory than is available or you are running applications that leak memory. Monitor the following counters to track memory shortages and to begin to identify their causes.

- **Memory\Available Bytes** indicates how much physical memory is remaining after the working sets of running processes and the cache have been served.

- **Process (*All_processes*)\Working Set** indicates the number of pages that are currently assigned to processes. When there is ample memory, then the working set structures can fill with pages that are not currently needed to do work but that were needed in the past and might be needed in the future. Because there is no memory shortage, the working set structures are not trimmed. As a result the working set approximates pages that have been referenced in a longer period of time. However, when memory is in short supply, the working set might be trimmed. As a result, the working set in that case approximates the number of pages referenced in a much shorter period of time.

- **Memory\Pages/sec** indicates the number of requested pages that were not immediately available in RAM and had to be read from the disk or had to be written to the disk to make room in RAM for other pages. If your system experiences a high rate of hard page faults, the value for Memory\Pages/sec can be high.

To maintain a minimum number of available bytes for the operating system and processes, the Virtual Memory Manager continually adjusts the space used in physical memory and on disk. In general, if memory is ample, working set sizes can increase as needed. If the memory supply is barely adequate or very close to the amount required, you might see the operating system trim some working-set sizes when another process needs more memory—at startup, for example. Figure 6.4 illustrates this situation.

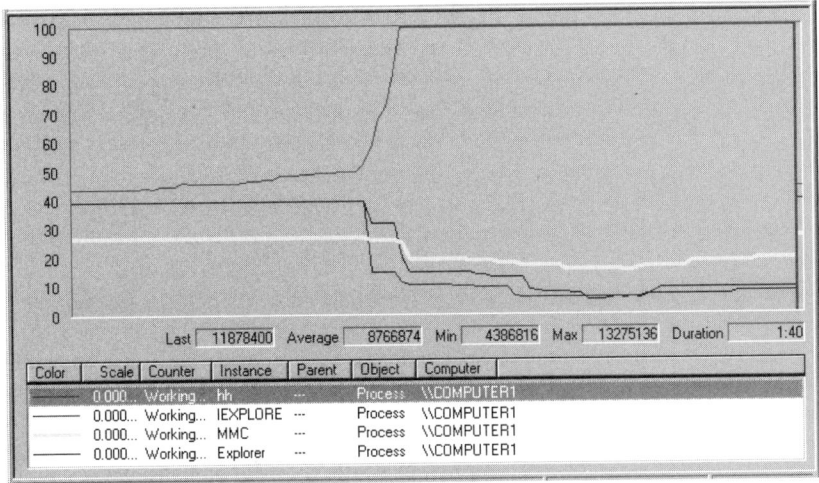

Figure 6.4   Working Set Values of Processes as One Process Starts Up

If the value for Memory\Available Bytes is consistently below the system-defined threshold and the value for Memory\Pages/sec spikes continuously, it is likely that your memory configuration is insufficient for your needs. To confirm that a high rate of paging is related to low memory, see "Investigating Disk Paging" later in this chapter.

Note   You might see a low value for Memory\Available Bytes, which is not caused by a memory shortage, in the following situations:

- During large file-copy operations such as a system backup. In this case, you can verify that the copy operation is the cause by monitoring Memory\Cache Bytes as well. You should see Memory\Cache Bytes rise as Memory\Available Bytes falls. Otherwise, you need to investigate the cause as described in this chapter.

- The **Maximize Data Throughput for File Sharing** option is selected in the **File and Printer Sharing for Microsoft Networks Properties** dialog box. This allocates a large system cache, which might not be appropriate for how your computer is used. For more information about how this setting should be configured, see "Optimizing Your Memory Configuration" earlier in this chapter.

- The working sets of processes have become smaller and there is no demand for pages for other purposes. In this case the number of available bytes might be low but there is no need to trim working sets and there are few if any page faults.

To identify processes associated with low-memory conditions, examine memory usage by specific processes, and determine if a process is leaking memory as described in "Investigating User-Mode Memory Leaks" and "Investigating Kernel-Mode Memory Leaks" later in this chapter.

If available memory is consistently low (2 MB or less), the computer becomes unresponsive because it is occupied exclusively with disk I/O operations. During paging due to low memory, the processor is idle while waiting for the disk to finish. Therefore, it is important, especially on server computers, to investigate and correct the cause of a low-memory condition. Notice which processes are running as well as the sizes of their working sets as you monitor memory counters. The processes might need to be updated or replaced if they are contributing to memory shortages and you do not want to acquire additional memory.

For information about how to address a memory shortage, see "Resolving Memory and Cache Bottlenecks" later in this chapter.

Investigating Disk Paging

Use memory counters that report paging activity to identify memory shortages resulting in disk bottlenecks. Start by monitoring the memory counters and working set values as you did when checking for a memory shortage in the preceding section. Confirm that hard page faults are occurring using the Memory\Pages/sec counter.

If hard page faults are occurring, monitor disk counters to assess how the disk is behaving during paging: whether it is busy with other work or with handling page faults. Monitor disk paging using the following steps and associated counters:

1. To confirm hard page faulting use the following Memory and Process counters:
   - Memory\Pages/sec
   - Process (*All_processes*) \Working Set
   - Memory\Pages Input/sec
   - Memory\Pages Output/sec

2. To understand the impact of page faulting on the disk, compare the number of reads and read bytes measured by the following counters:
   - Memory\Page Reads/sec
   - PhysicalDisk\Disk Reads/sec
   - PhysicalDisk\Avg. Disk Read Bytes/sec

Confirming Hard Page Faults

To confirm hard page faults, examine the hard page fault rate using Memory\Pages/sec and the working sets of active processes using Process(*process_name*)\Working Set, as described in "Investigating Memory Shortages." Memory\Pages/sec is the sum of Pages Input/sec and Pages Output/sec and reports the number of requested pages that were not immediately available in RAM and had to be read from the disk (resulting in hard page faults) or that had to be written to the disk to make room in RAM for other pages. Monitoring processes' working sets enables you to correlate a given application's memory usage with page faulting. When memory is in short supply, working sets are continuously trimmed and page faults are frequent.

Acceptable rates for Memory\Pages/sec range from 40 per second on older laptop computers to 150 per second for the newest disk systems. Use a shorter monitoring period on client computers than on server computers (updating once per second is appropriate) because paging activity can occur in bursts on client computers. Paging activity tends to reach a steady state on server computers; therefore, longer-term monitoring is appropriate.

Note Page Fault Monitor (Pfmon.exe), a tool on the *Windows 2000 Resource Kit* companion CD, lists hard and soft page faults generated by each function call in a running process. You can display the data, write it to a log file, or both. For more information, see Windows 2000 Resource Kit Tools Help (W2rktools.chm) on the *Windows 2000 Resource Kit* companion CD.

You can also monitor page faults and memory management data using Trace Logs in the Performance snap-in. For more information, see "Overview of Performance Monitoring" in this book.

When values exceed the acceptable range for your type of disk, investigate disk activity to determine if the faulting is causing a disk bottleneck. Memory\Pages Input/sec reflects the rate at which pages were read from the disk and thus gives you data on hard page faults. Depending on the capabilities of your disk, high values can indicate a lack of memory sufficient to hurt system performance. See Figure 6.5 for an example of page faulting.

Note You might see high levels of paging with Memory\Pages/sec when pages are read to and from noncached, memory-mapped files. When these files are used in this way, Memory\Pages/sec or Memory\Available Bytes is high but Memory\Paging File\%Usage and Memory\Cache Faults/sec are normal to low.

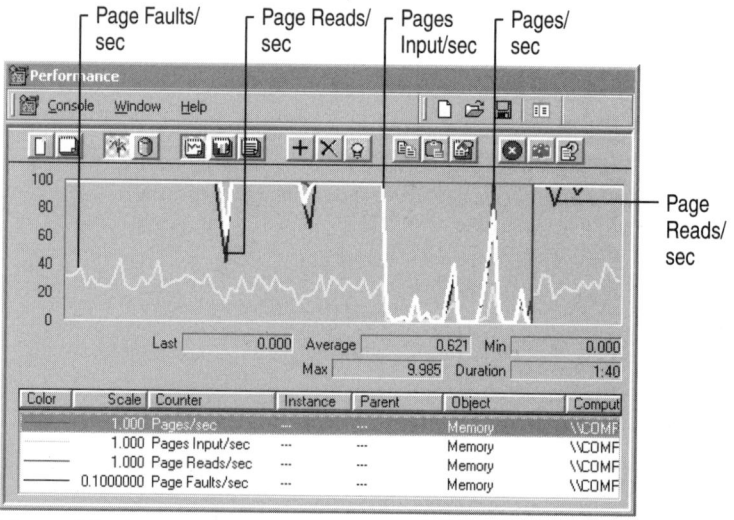

Figure 6.5   Paging Activity on a System with Low Memory

The other component of Memory\Pages/sec, Memory\Pages Output/sec, indicates the rate at which pages were written to the disk. Although this activity does not generate hard page faults, disk-write activity can indirectly reflect a memory shortage and indicates additional disk activity. This is because, as the Virtual Memory Manager needs to trim pages from a working set, it might find that some pages contain changed data. In this case the changed data must be written to disk to free the pages. When memory is in ample supply, Memory\Pages Output/sec is likely to be low because there is less need to free changed pages and write that data to disk. For more information about investigating applications that generate disk-write activity, see "Examining and Tuning Disk Performance" in this book.

Assessing the Effect of Page Faults on the Disk

To understand the impact of page faulting on the disk, examine the number of disk operations that occur as a result of paging. If paging activity dominates your disk's workload, a memory shortage is causing a disk bottleneck. Start by looking at Memory\Page Reads/sec. This counter indicates the number of read operations by the disk that were required to retrieve faulted pages. Compare the number of reads performed with the number of pages faulted to determine how many pages are retrieved per read. A high ratio of reads to faults means a large number of pages are not found in physical memory and are being demanded from the disk, creating a disk bottleneck.

Next, determine what proportion of your disk's overall work is occupied with reading pages from memory. To do this, compare page reads to disk reads. If there is a correlation between the values of Memory\Page Reads/sec and PhysicalDisk\Disk Reads/sec, it is likely that paging activity makes up the majority of your disk activity and could be causing a disk bottleneck.

To see the relationship between paging and disk read operations from a different perspective, monitor the value of PhysicalDisk\Avg Disk Read Bytes/sec or PhysicalDisk\Avg Disk Read Bytes/sec while you are monitoring Page Reads/sec. The Avg Disk Read Bytes/sec counter indicates the rate at which the disk is transferring data during reads. Because this is a measurement of bytes rather than of pages or of the number of reads, you need to convert to identical units. Use the following formula for this purpose: value of PhysicalDisk\Disk Read Bytes/sec ÷ 4096 (number of bytes in a page).

If the result is approximately equal to the value of Page Reads/sec, paging activity is the bulk of your disk read activity, and the memory shortage represented by heavy paging activity could in turn be causing a disk bottleneck. To see if this activity is reaching a rate high enough to cause poor disk performance, see your disk manufacturer's documentation for the number of I/O transactions per second you can expect from your disk. Disks currently available can sustain a transfer rate of 70 I/O operations per second. For more information about locating disk bottlenecks, see "Examining and Tuning Disk Performance" in this book.

Figure 6.6 illustrates disk activity associated with paging activity when memory is low.

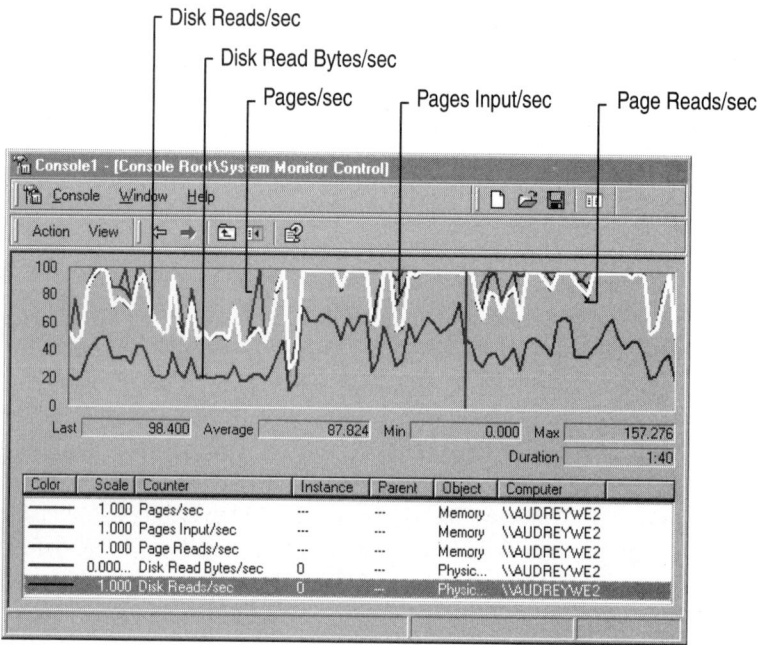

Figure 6.6   Disk and Paging Activity When Memory Is Low

Investigating User-Mode Memory Leaks

A memory leak occurs when applications allocate memory for use but do not free allocated memory when finished. As a result, available memory is used up over time, often causing the system to stop functioning properly. Therefore, it is important to investigate the causes of all memory leaks, particularly on server computers. This section describes how to identify memory leaks, including ones that affect the critical nonpaged memory pool, and where to find tools and information related to working with memory leaks.

Note It is sometimes possible to mistake an increase in system load for a memory leak. To distinguish between these conditions, observe the Memory and Process counters over a number of days. If you see the system first reach a steady state, then attain a level of increased load (usually achieved during some peak portion of the day), and then fall again, it is likely you are seeing variations in load rather than a leak. On network computers, look at user sessions and throughput rates such as transferred bytes per second to eliminate workload as a factor.

Identifying a Memory Leak

The symptoms of a memory leak include the following:

- A gradually worsening response time.

- The appearance of an error message, shown in Figure 6.7, indicating that the system is low on virtual memory. (Another message box might precede this, indicating that virtual memory has been exceeded and that the system has increased the paging file size automatically.)

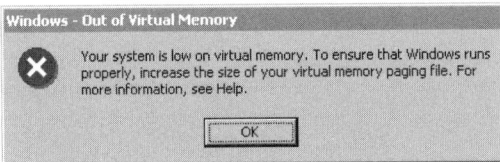

Figure 6.7   Out of Virtual Memory Error Message

- The appearance of error messages indicating that system services have stopped.

If you suspect that a particular application or service is causing a memory leak, investigate the memory use of your applications using the following counters:

- **Memory\Available Bytes** reports available bytes; its value tends to fall during a memory leak.

- **Memory\Committed Bytes** reports the private bytes committed to processes; its value tends to rise during a memory leak.

- **Process(*process_name*)\Private Bytes** reports bytes allocated exclusively for a specific process; its value tends to rise for a leaking process.

- **Process(*process_name*)\Working Set** reports the shared and private bytes allocated to a process; its value tends to rise for a leaking process.

- **Process(*process_name*)\Page Faults/sec** reports the total number of faults (hard and soft faults) caused by a process; its value tends to rise for a leaking process.

- **Process(*process_name*)\Page File Bytes** reports the size of the paging file; its value tends to rise during a memory leak.

- **Process(*process_name*)\Handle Count** reports the number of handles that an application opened for objects it creates. Handles are used by programs to identify resources they must access. The value of this counter tends to rise during a memory leak; however, you cannot rule out a leak simply because this counter's value is stable.

Monitor these counters over a period ranging from two hours to a few days. Logging is recommended, both because of the overhead of monitoring multiple instances of the Process counters and because leaks tend to manifest themselves slowly.

In addition, to isolate the problem and avoid unnecessary overhead, monitor from a remote computer, if possible. Network activity or interaction with other computers can interfere with the results.

Memory Leaks and the Nonpaged Pool

Although any leak is serious, memory leaks are of particular concern when they involve the nonpaged pool. Many system services allocate memory from the nonpaged pool because they need to reference it when processing an interrupt and cannot take a page fault at that time. To identify whether or not a leak affects the nonpaged pool, include the following counters in your monitoring:

- Memory\Pool Nonpaged Bytes
- Memory\Pool Nonpaged Allocs
- Process(*process_name*)\Pool Nonpaged Bytes

Note Because the internal counters used by Task Manager, Process Monitor, and System Monitor to measure the size of the nonpaged pool for each process are not precise, it is recommended that you monitor changes in the overall pool size over time (a few days, for example), rather than rely on the absolute, instantaneous values reported for each process. The counter values are estimates that count duplicate object handles as well as space for the object. Also, because the process pool size counts are rounded to page size, pool space is overestimated when a process uses only part of a page. In contrast, total pool size counts are precise. Therefore, the sum of pool sizes for each process might not equal the value for the whole system.

The counters on the Memory object monitor the total size of the nonpaged pool and the number of allocations of pool space for the whole system. The counter on the Process object monitors nonpaged pool space allocated to each process.

To use System Monitor to monitor the nonpaged pool for leaks, follow these steps:

- Record the size of the nonpaged pool when the system starts. Then log the Memory and Process objects for several days; a 10-minute update interval is sufficient.

- Review the log for changes in size of the nonpaged pool. You should be able to associate any increases in the size of the pool, as indicated by Memory\Pool Nonpaged Bytes, with the start of a process, as indicated by Process\% Processor Time. Also look at individual Process object counters such as Process\Handle Count, Process\Private Bytes, Process\Nonpaged Pool Bytes, Process\Paged Pool Bytes, and Process\Threads. During a memory leak, you might also see rising values for these counters.

  When processes are stopped, you should see a decrease in pool size. Any growth in the nonpaged pool is considered abnormal, and you need to distinguish which process is causing the change in pool size.

  You might also want to monitor the number of active threads before and after running the process (use the **Performance** tab in Task Manager or the Objects\Threads or Process(_Total)\Thread Count counters). A process that is leaking memory might be creating a large number of threads; these appear when the process starts and disappear when the process stops.

- Watch the value of Memory\Pool Nonpaged Bytes for an increase of ten percent or more from its value at system startup to see if a serious leak is developing.

The following additional tools provide information about the paged and nonpaged memory pools as listed in Table 6.3. These tools collect their data from the same sources.

Table 6.3   Tools That Provide Information About Memory Pools

Tool Name	Description	Location
Memsnap (memsnap.exe)[1]	Records system memory usage to a log file.	Windows 2000 Support Tools
Process Monitor (pmon.exe)[1]	Provides total and per process values for nonpaged and paged pool memory. Also monitors the committed memory values shown in the Pmon display for increases; the process with the leak should have an increasing value reported under Commit Charge.	Windows 2000 Support Tools

[1] These tools are useful because they show allocations on a per-process basis.

For information about installing and using the Windows 2000 Support Tools and Support Tools Help, see the file Sreadme.doc in the \Support\Tools folder of the Windows 2000 operating system CD.

For a quick demonstration of a memory leak, start LeakyApp, a test tool on the *Windows 2000 Resource Kit* companion CD, and observe the values of the monitored counters. Notice the steady increase in the following counters: Memory\Pages/sec, Process(LeakyApp)\Working Set, and Process(LeakyApp)\Private Bytes.

Figure 6.8 illustrates counter activity during a memory leak generated by the LeakyApp tool.

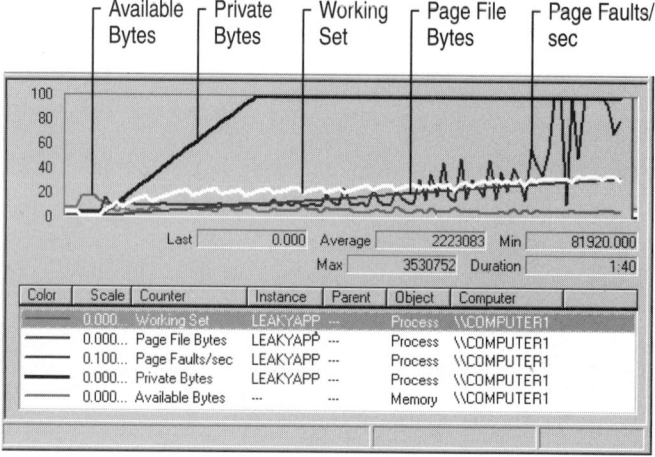

Figure 6.8   Process Memory Activity During a Memory Leak

Although the memory leak illustrated in Figure 6.9 has a systemic effect, the problem can be tracked to a single cause—the leaking application. If you have an application that exhibits similar behavior, it is recommended that you either modify it (if you have access to the source code) or replace it with another program.

Developer tools for analyzing and tuning memory usage by applications are available on the *Windows 2000 Resource Kit* companion CD. For more information about developer tools, see the MSDN link on the Web Resources page at http://windows.microsoft.com/windows2000/reskit/webresources.

The following tools optimize memory-intensive applications.

- **Application Monitor (ApiMon)** on the *Windows 2000 Resource Kit* companion CD monitors page faults caused by an application and reports them by Microsoft® Win32® function calls.

- **The Working Set Tuner (WST)** on the SDK analyzes the patterns of function calls in your application code and generates an improved function ordering to reduce physical memory usage. One objective of tuning your working set is to arrive at the smallest possible working set without causing page faults.

- **Virtual Address Dump (Vadump)** on the SDK creates a list that contains information about the memory usage of a specified process, including address size, total committed memory for the image, the executable, each dynamic-link library (DLL), and heap usage.

The nonpaged pool size and the paged pool size are set by default during Windows 2000 Setup based on your memory configuration. The maximum nonpaged pool size is 256 MB. The maximum paged pool size is approximately 470 MB. The actual size varies depending on your configuration. More physical memory results in less paged pool because the virtual address space must instead be used to contain more critical memory-management structures. The pool sizes are defined in the registry in the HKEY_LOCAL_MACHINE\System\CurrentControlSet\Control\Session Manager\Memory Management subkey.

To extend the file system cache working set from 512 MB to 960 MB, set the value of the **PagedPoolSize** registry entry to 192000000, set **SystemPages** to 0, and make sure that the system is optimized for file sharing with **LargeSystemCache** set to 1. To make the maximum virtual address space available to the paged pool, set the **PagedPoolSize** registry entry to 0xFFFFFFFF , provided your system is not using the /3GB Boot.ini switch.

Typically you do not need to set the **NonPagedPoolSize** entry because on systems with more than 1.2 GB of memory, the system automatically defaults to the maximum nonpaged pool size. If you need to set the **NonPagedPoolSize** value, set it to the value you want (in bytes); do not set it to 0xFFFFFFFF .

Investigating Kernel-Mode Memory Leaks

Kernel-mode processes such as device drivers can also leak memory when bytes are allocated but not freed. Again, you typically track these over a period of several hours or days, but instead of relying on System Monitor counters, use Pool Monitor (Poolmon.exe). For information about Pool Monitor, see Windows 2000 Support Tools Help. For information about installing and using the Windows 2000 Support Tools and Support Tools Help, see the file Sreadme.doc in the \Support\Tools folder of the Windows 2000 operating system CD.

Pool Monitor (Poolmon.exe) shows the amounts of nonpaged and paged memory that were allocated and freed, calculates the difference between these, and associates the data with a function tag to help you identify the process involved. By default, Windows 2000 is configured not to collect pool information because of the overhead. To use Poolmon, you must enable the pool tag signal. Use Gflags.exe to make the change. In Gflags, select the **Enable Pool Tag** check box. For information about using Poolmon and Gflags, see Support Tools Help. For information about installing and using the Windows 2000 Support Tools and Support Tools Help, see the file Sreadme.doc in the \Support\Tools folder of the Windows 2000 operating system CD.

The pool tag is a mechanism for identifying the driver or other part of the kernel allocated to a particular portion of memory. These tags can be examined to reveal memory leaks and pool corruption, and the offending code component can be determined by finding which code component is allocated to which tag. Look for a tag with rapidly increasing byte counts that does not free as many bytes as it allocates, and verify that this tag corresponds to a function for which the increasing memory allocation might be appropriate. If it does not appear appropriate, it might be necessary to debug and tune the application to eliminate the leak.

Monitoring the Cache

The Windows 2000 file system cache is an area of memory into which the I/O system maps recently used data from disk. When processes need to read from or write to the files mapped in the cache, the I/O Manager copies the data from or to the cache, without buffering or calling the file system, as if it were an array in memory. Because memory access is quicker than a file operation, the cache provides an important performance boost to the processes.

Cache object counters provide information about data hits and misses and about file I/O operations that reflect how efficiently their applications access data in the file system cache. However, because the cache counters are based on the views mapped by the Cache Manager and not on data from the Virtual Memory Manager, the cache counter values do not provide definitive information about bottlenecks. In some cases, cache counters can report low rates of hits or high rates of misses, suggesting that the system is accessing the disk when, in fact, the requested data has been retrieved from memory. This can occur if virtual addresses mapped by the Cache Manager no longer exist, for example, because the file has closed. To obtain more accurate data on I/O bottlenecks, use the Memory\Pages Input/sec counter.

The cache itself can never really have a bottleneck because it is just a part of physical memory. However, when there is not enough memory to create an effective cache, the system must retrieve more data from disk, resulting in I/O operations that can impact overall performance. Such a shortage of cache space can be considered a cache bottleneck.

Cache bottlenecks are of greatest concern to administrators of Windows 2000 Server–based computers and to users of Windows 2000 Professional–based computers running CAD/CAM applications or large databases accessing large blocks of multiple files that rely on the cache. Administrators of server computers need to monitor cache counters because these provide indirect indications of the memory supply. Windows 2000 Server defines a large system cache by default to maximize the likelihood that data is found in memory, rather than retrieved from disks. The cache counters can reveal that a small cache (based on a short supply of memory) is hurting system performance.

Note Many Web servers or large database applications, such as SQL Server, maintain a separate cache and do not use the file system cache. In addition, they might have their own cache-monitoring counters.

With memory-mapped file I/O, an entire file can be opened without actually being read into memory. Only the views (smaller portions of the file) are mapped into the process's address space just before I/O operations are performed. Memory-mapped I/O keeps the cache size small. For more information about memory-mapped I/O, see the Software Development Kit (SDK) link on the Web Resources page at http://windows.microsoft.com/windows2000/reskit/webresources.

Developers who want to understand how their programs use the cache for read and write operations might also want to monitor the cache. Data requested by an application is mapped to the cache and then copied from there. Data changed by applications is written from the cache to disk by the lazy writer system thread or by a write-through call from the application. The lazy writer thread in the system process periodically writes changed pages from the modified page list back to disk and flushes them from the cache. When a page is flushed from the cache, changed data is written from the page in the cache to the disk and the page is deleted from the cache. Thus, monitoring the cache is like watching your application I/O. Remember, however, that if an application uses the cache infrequently, cache activity has an insignificant effect on the system, on the disks, and on memory.

Understanding the Cache Counters

Use the following System Monitor Cache and Memory counters to measure cache performance. For instructions based on specific symptoms, see "Interpreting Changes in Cache Counter Values" later in this chapter.

Cache\Copy Read Hits %   Monitor this counter for hit rates and miss rates. Any value over 80 percent indicates that the application uses the cache very efficiently. Compare this counter with Cache\Copy Reads/sec to see how many hits you are really getting. Even though the hit percentage is small, if the rate of operations is high, this might indicate better cache effectiveness than a high percentage with a low rate of operations.

Note   For best results, monitor the Cache\Copy Read Hits % counter using the graph view rather than the report view. Hit percentage rates frequently appear as spikes that are hard to detect in a report.

Cache\Copy Reads/sec   Observe this counter to see the rate at which the file system attempts to find application data in the cache without accessing the disk. This is a count of all copy read calls to the cache, including hits and misses. Copy reads are the usual method by which file data found in the cache is copied into an application's memory buffers.

Cache\Data Flush Pages/sec   Review this counter for the rate at which applications change pages of cached data and the pages are written back to disk. This includes pages that have been written by the system process when many changed pages have accumulated, pages that have been flushed so that the cache can be trimmed, and disk writes that are caused by an application write-through request.

Cache\Data Flushes/sec Monitor this counter for the rate at which cache data is being written back to disk. This counter reports application requests to flush data from the cache and is an indirect indicator of the volume and frequency of application data changes.

Cache\Data Maps/sec Examine this counter for the rate at which file systems map pages of a file into the cache for reading. This counter reports read-only access to file system directories, the file allocation table (FAT) in the FAT file system, and the Master File Table in the NTFS file system. This counter does not reflect cache use by applications.

Cache\Fast Reads/sec Observe this counter for the rate at which applications bypass the file system and access data directly from the cache. A value over 50 percent indicates the application is behaving efficiently. Fast reads reduce processor overhead and are preferable to I/O requests.

Cache\Lazy Write Flushes/sec Review this counter for the rate at which an application changes data, causing the cache to write to the disk and flush the data. If this value reflects an upward trend, memory might be becoming low. Lazy write flushes are a subset of data flushes. The lazy writer thread in the system process periodically writes changed pages from the modified page list back to disk and flushes them from the cache. This thread is activated more often when memory needs to be released for other uses. This counter counts the number of write and flush operations, regardless of the amount of data written.

Cache\Lazy Write Pages/sec Examine this counter value for the rate at which pages are changed by an application and written to the disk. If the counter value is increasing, this can indicate that memory is becoming low. Cache\Lazy Write Pages are a subset of Data Flush Pages.

Cache\Read Aheads/sec Use this counter to monitor the rate at which the Cache Manager detects that the file is being accessed sequentially. Sequential file access is a very efficient strategy in most cases. During sequential file access, the Cache Manager can read larger blocks of data into the cache on each I/O, thereby reducing the overhead per access.

Memory\Cache Bytes Monitor this counter for growth or shrinking of the cache. The value includes not only the size of the cache but also the size of the paged pool and the amount of pageable driver and kernel code. Essentially, these values measure the system's working set.

Memory\Cache Faults/sec Observe this counter for the rate at which pages sought in the cache were not found there and had to be obtained elsewhere in memory or on the disk. Compare this counter with Memory\Page Faults/sec and Pages Input/sec to determine the number of hard page faults, if any.

Note Performance Meter (Perfmtr.exe), a tool on the *Windows 2000 Resource Kit* companion CD and the SDK, lists among other statistics, data about the file system cache. For more information, see the *Windows 2000 Resource Kit* Tools Help (W2rktools.chm) or the SDK documentation.

Interpreting Changes in Cache Counter Values

Administrators need to watch for signs from the cache counters that low memory is causing insufficient cache size and consequently that cache usage is resulting in unnecessary disk I/O, which degrades performance. Monitor for the following conditions, using the counters as described. (Options for improving these conditions include defragmenting the disk and adding memory.)

Reduction in Cache Size

When memory becomes scarce and working sets are trimmed, the cache is trimmed as well. If the cache grows too small, cache-sensitive processes are slowed by disk operations. To monitor cache size, use the Memory\Cache Bytes and Memory\Available Bytes counters. Note that the effect of a smaller cache on applications and file operations depends on how often and how effectively applications use the cache.

Frequent Cache Flushing

Frequent cache flushing might occur if data is written to the disk frequently in order to free pages. Data flush counters reflect cache output. Monitor the Cache\Data Flushes/sec and Cache\Lazy Writes Flushes/sec counters.

Cache\Pin Reads/sec tells you how often the cache is reading data with the intention of writing it. A pin read occurs when data is mapped into the cache just to be changed and is then written back to disk. It is pinned in the cache to be sure the data being changed is not written to disk until the update is complete. Creating a file or changing its attributes results in a pin read. Changing file contents does not result in a pin read. Cache\Pin Reads/sec can predict flushing activity.

High Rates of Cache Misses

High cache miss rates indicate that requested data is not available in physical memory and must be retrieved from the disk. Monitor the Cache object counters that record hit percentages and hit rates (such as Cache\Copy Read Hits % and Cache\Copy Read Hits/sec).

Make sure to review both hit percentage and hit activity counters to ensure that your data gives an accurate picture of cache efficiency. For example, you might notice that your hit percentage is very high (90 percent on average), implying that the cache is highly efficient. However, when you examine hit activity, you might notice that only a few copy reads have occurred during the sample. In this case, relying on the percentages would have given you a false impression of cache effectiveness. Therefore, examining hit percentages over a range of activity rates is recommended.

For computers running Windows 2000 Server, you might also want to monitor MDL Read Hits % and MDL Reads/sec. The Server service might use MDL reads rather than copy reads for large data transfers. MDL reads rely on direct memory access (DMA) for better overall performance.

High Rates of Cache Faults

Although you cannot tell from the Memory\Cache Faults/sec counter value alone, an increase in cache faults might mean that hard page faults are occurring, resulting in disk activity. Memory\Cache Faults/sec reports fault activity for the system working set, including hard and soft page faults. Because the cache counters do not provide conclusive information about this, you must monitor Memory\Pages Input/sec to determine if hard page faults are occurring.

If Cache Faults/sec values increase and hit-percentage counter values decrease, it is likely there is not enough memory to create an efficient cache. When insufficient memory forces the system to maintain a small cache size, disk I/O tends to increase.

You can see the impact of cache and memory activity on the disk by adding Memory\Pages Output/sec to Cache\Data Flush Pages/sec. This total is approximately equal to the page equivalent of Disk Write Bytes/sec for the PhysicalDisk counters. As the Pages Output/sec and Data Flush Pages/sec counter values increase, so does the value of Disk Write Bytes/sec, reflecting the increasing disk writing activity. (Differences in values can be attributed to the sampling behavior of System Monitor.) Similarly, there is a corresponding read impact: look at Memory\Pages Input/sec; this should equal the number of bytes of memory reported under Disk Read Bytes/sec but expressed in pages for the PhysicalDisk counters as described in "Assessing the Effect of Page Faults on the Disk" earlier in this chapter.

Resolving Memory and Cache Bottlenecks

While monitoring your memory and cache resources, you might discover memory and cache bottlenecks in your system. As a result, you might need to optimize cache usage, replace applications, or even add new memory. The following tips can assist you with your decision-making process.

Optimizing Cache Usage

Even though you cannot change the cache itself, there are a few things you can do to make the most of the cache.

- For applications that you develop or maintain, improve the locality of reference in your application's data structures. This improves its cache performance and minimizes its working set so that it uses less space in memory. In addition, it reduces disk access that can slow performance systemwide.

- If you are running Windows 2000 Server, you can direct the Virtual Memory Manager to give the cache higher priority for space than the working sets of processes. See "To adjust Server Optimization settings" earlier in this chapter to change memory management settings. To favor the cache, choose **Maximize Data Throughput for File Sharing**. To favor working sets, choose **Maximize Data Throughput for Network Applications**.

- Change the way work is distributed among workstations. Try dedicating a single computer to memory-intensive applications such as CAD/CAM and large database processors.

- Add memory. When memory is scarce, the cache is diminished and cannot do its job. After the new memory is installed, the Virtual Memory Manager expands the cache to use the new memory.

Resolving a Memory Bottleneck

Although adding memory is the easy solution to a memory bottleneck, it should not be the first solution you undertake. Try the following, more cost-effective alternatives before spending money on additional memory. If you ultimately decide to add memory, note that the maximum amount of memory recommended for a computer running Windows 2000 Server is 4 GB.

- Monitor your applications and replace or correct those that leak memory or use it inefficiently.

- Modify your application to improve the locality of reference. The Working Set Tuner, included in the Platform SDK, recommends an optimal organization of code functions. For more information, see the MSDN link on the Web Resources page at http://windows.microsoft.com/windows2000/reskit/webresources.

- Increase the size of the paging file. In general, the bigger you can make it, the better it is. You can also have multiple paging files, though you should only have multiple paging files per physical drive when the drive is not partitioned into logical drives. Striped volumes can be used. This improves the read-write rates for the paging file because the work is distributed over multiple disks.

- Check the available space on your disks. If you are using a large paging file and space is not available, this can produce the symptoms of a memory bottleneck.

- To conserve memory, avoid using some display and sound features. Features that can drain memory include animated cursors, desktop icons, large-bitmap wallpaper, and some screen saver programs; removing or disabling them can offer some benefit on a memory-constrained system. Reducing display color depth and screen resolution can also save memory but to a lesser degree.

- To free memory, turn off services you do not use. Stopping services that you do not use regularly saves memory and improves system performance. However, make sure you understand the ramifications of stopping a service before you do so.

- Remove unnecessary protocols and drivers. Even idle protocols use space in the paged and nonpaged memory pools. Drivers also use memory. You can see how a driver uses memory with Pool Monitor (Poolmon.exe).

- Replace 16-bit systems with 32-bit systems for better reliability and performance.

- If you have other computers that are underutilized, move memory-intensive applications to those computers.

Additional Resources

For more information about developer tools, see the MSDN link on the Web Resources page at http://windows.microsoft.com/windows2000/reskit/webresources.

C H A P T E R   7

Analyzing Processor Activity

After memory consumption, processor activity is the most important thing to monitor in your system. A busy processor might be efficiently handling all the work on your computer, or it might be overwhelmed. Examine processor activity to tell the difference. Use performance counters and *Microsoft® Windows® 2000 Resource Kit* tools to measure processing activity and to determine how to improve performance if necessary.

In This Chapter

Related Information in the Resource Kit

- For information about using System Monitor graphs and counter logs, see "Overview of Performance Monitoring" in this book.

- For information about implementing and optimizing multiprocessor systems, see "Measuring Multiprocessor System Activity" in this book.

Overview of Processor Monitoring and Analysis

Uniprocessor monitoring and analysis involve many variables. The following steps summarize in-depth monitoring and analysis of processor activity.

- Establish a baseline for processor performance that is reflective of your system's typical workload. Perform this step to characterize your system's workload and identify how applications use the system.

- Examine overall processor usage by viewing processor queue length and processor utilization (also referred to as processor time). Perform this step to obtain an overview of how heavily system resources are used.

- Examine activity that adds to the processing load, such as high rates of interrupts and context switches. Perform this step to determine the efficiency of your system.

- Examine individual processes and their percentage of the overall processor time. Perform this step to learn about the processes on your system.

- Examine the threads—the units of work that make up a process—for each individual process and each thread's processor usage. Perform this step to learn about thread utilization on the system.

- Evaluate thread priorities and change them to see if this provides better performance. (Microsoft does not recommend this is as a long-term solution, but suggests it for testing purposes.) Perform this step to learn how threads interact and to determine which threads are preempting other, lower-priority threads.

Figure 7.1 illustrates the role of processor monitoring in overall system monitoring.

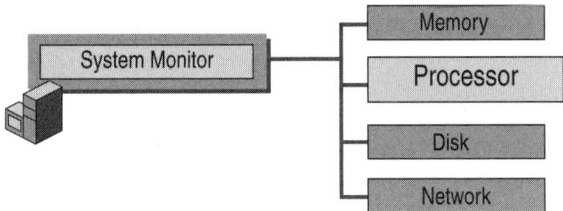

Figure 7.1   Role of Processor Monitoring in Overall Monitoring Sequence

Before you begin the monitoring process, become familiar with the counters designed to measure processor activity and the *Windows 2000 Resource Kit* tools that can give you more information about processor workload and performance. The following sections summarize these counters and tools.

Processor Counters

The System, Processor, Process, and Thread objects contain counters that provide useful information about the work of your processor. Examine the following counters for details about computer processes.

Table 7.1   Processor Counters

Object	Counter	Description
System	Context Switches/sec	The average rate per second at which context switches among threads on the computer. High activity rates can result from inefficient hardware or poorly designed applications. Compare these counters with Processor\% Privileged Time, Processor\% User Time, and Processor\% Interrupt Time. See "Monitoring Interrupts" and "Monitoring Context Switches" later in this chapter.
Processor	Interrupts/sec	The average rate per second at which the processor handles interrupts from applications or hardware devices. High activity rates can indicate hardware problems. Compare these counters with Processor\% Privileged Time, Processor\% User Time, and Processor\% Interrupt Time. See "Monitoring Interrupts" and "Monitoring Context Switches" later in this chapter.
System	Processor Queue Length	An instantaneous count of threads that are in the processor queue. See "Observing Processor Queue Length" later in this chapter.
Processor	% Processor Time	The percentage of time the processor was busy during the sampling interval. This counter is equivalent to Task Manager's CPU Usage counter. See "Examining the Processor Time Counter" later in this chapter. For the value of total processor utilization systemwide, use the Processor(_Total)\% Processor Time counter.
Process	% Privileged Time	The percentage of time a process was running in privileged mode. See "Processes in a Bottleneck" later in this chapter.
Process	% Processor Time	The percentage of time the processor was busy servicing a specific process.
Process	% User Time	The percentage of time a process was running in user mode.
Process	Priority Base	Windows 2000 schedules threads of a process to run according to their priority. Threads inherit base priority from their parent processes. The base priority level of the process can range from lowest to highest: Idle, Normal, High, or Real Time.
Thread	Thread State	A numeric value indicating the execution state of the thread. The system numbers threads from 0 through 5; the states seen most often are 1 for ready, 2 for running, and 5 for waiting. Threads with a state of 1 are in the processor queue.

continued

Table 7.1   Processor Counters *(continued)*

Object	Counter	Description
Thread	Priority Base	The base priority level (from 1 through 31) for the thread based on the priority class of the process. Windows 2000 schedules threads of a process to run according to their priority. Threads inherit base priority from their parent processes.
Thread	Priority Current	The current priority level of a thread. This level can vary during operation.
Thread	Context Switches/sec	The average rate per second at which the processor switches context among threads. A high rate can indicate that many threads are contending for processor time. See "Threads in a Bottleneck" later in this chapter.
Thread	% Privileged Time	The percentage of time a thread was running in privileged mode.
Thread	% User Time	The percentage of time a thread was running in user mode.

Note Because System Monitor samples processor time, the values for processor time counters reported by the Processor, Process, and Thread objects might underestimate or overestimate activity on your system that occurs before or after collection of the sample.

In addition to the preceding list of objects and counters, the Job Object and Job Object Details objects provide information about processor usage. These performance objects are installed by default for monitoring job object performance. The job object makes it possible for developers to manage groups of processes by their processor usage and other factors. For example, job objects make it possible for applications to restrict the amount of processor time a process consumes; this is called process throttling. Process throttling is useful in Web-based administration applications for limiting the amount of processor capacity a site uses over a defined interval, thus avoiding bottlenecks and freeing processor capacity for other tasks. You might also use the job object to manage sharing of CPU time among groups of jobs. In addition to supporting process throttling, job objects help developers control the active number of processes, process identifiers (IDs), priority classes, and processor affinity. For information about creating applications using the job object, see the Platform Software Development Kit (SDK) link on the Web Resources page at http://windows.microsoft.com/windows2000/reskit/webresources. For a discussion of application support and job objects, see Getting Started in Windows 2000 Help.

Resource Kit Tools for Processor Monitoring

The Resource Kit companion CD contains utilities to help you understand and experiment with processor performance, as listed in Table 7.2.

Table 7.2   Performance Utilities

Utility name	Description
CPUStres	Simulates processor workload.
Qslice	Provides a graphical display of processor usage by process.

Establishing a Baseline for Processor Performance

Begin your monitoring routine with an examination of processor usage under your normal workload. By doing so, you can begin to establish a baseline or reference point for processor usage. The baseline is generally not a single value, but a range within which processor usage can fluctuate and still provide acceptable performance. You can use the baseline to identify trends, such as increasing processor demands over time, or to recognize problems that arise from a sudden change.

Selecting Counters for Baseline Monitoring

To determine the baseline, use the following counters to create logs of processor usage over an extended period (from several weeks to a month).

- Processor\% Processor Time
- System\Processor Queue Length

Be aware of the Idle process when monitoring processor usage. The Idle process runs a thread on each processor. This thread runs when the system is not already running the thread of an active user or system process. System Monitor and Task Manager both use the Idle process to calculate time when the processor is not busy. You can see processor time for the Idle process on the **Processes** tab in Task Manager (called the System Idle Process) or by tracking the Process(Idle)\% Processor Time counter in System Monitor. Notice that the Total instance for this counter includes processor time for the Idle process. To measure the Idle process, use the Process(Idle)\% Processor Time counter, or use the **Processes** tab in Task Manager. Zero idle time could mean that the processor is handling a lot of work, but it could also mean that the processor or central processing unit (CPU) is overloaded.

Selecting Times for Baseline Monitoring

To monitor processor activity, log the counters of the System, Processor, Process, Thread, PhysicalDisk, and Memory counters for at least several days at an update interval ranging from 15 minutes to an hour. (Use much shorter intervals for bottleneck detection.) Include network counters such as Bytes Total/sec (on the Network Interface object) if you suspect that network traffic might be interrupting the processor too frequently. Because excessive demand on memory and disk resources can cause bottlenecks that appear to affect your processor's performance, also include disk and memory counters in your monitoring configuration to help you determine the true source of any processor bottleneck.

If any applications running on the computer have counters, use these counters to monitor their activity and monitor these values along with system counter values.

Track the values reported at various times of day—for example, while users are logging on or off, while backups are being done, and so forth. As you are monitoring values for these counters, you might see occasional spikes. Typically, you can exclude these from your baseline; the range of values that seem to appear consistently are the ones that constitute your baseline.

Note   Keep in mind application overhead and disk-space usage when you set your monitoring frequency. Frequent updating demands more work and more file storage capacity from your computer. In general, you should experiment with different update intervals to balance these considerations against the level of detail you require for your monitoring data. For more information about how to monitor performance, see Windows 2000 Professional Help.

The longer you log, the more accurate your baseline will be. Processor use might be a problem only at certain times of the day, week, or month, and you are likely to see patterns in your workload that are correlated with changes in processor activity if you log for a longer duration. You can even use the log service to schedule monitoring at critical times to determine whether your processor is operating efficiently. During these critical times, you might want to log over intervals as short as every two seconds to get an accurate picture of processor usage on your system. This will help you isolate those applications that heavily stress your processor for further investigation and monitoring.

Recognizing a Processor Bottleneck

Processor bottlenecks occur when the processor is so busy that it cannot respond to requests for time. Although a high rate of processor activity might indicate an excessively busy processor, a long, sustained processor queue is a more certain indicator. As you monitor processor and related counters, you can recognize a developing bottleneck by the following conditions:

- Processor\% Processor Time often exceeds 80 percent.

- System\Processor Queue Length is often greater than 2 on a single-processor system.

- Unusually high values appear for the Processor(_Total)\Interrupts/sec or System\Context Switches/sec counters.

The most common causes for processor bottlenecks are insufficient memory or excessive numbers of interrupts from disk or network input/output (I/O). To investigate these possible causes, see the following chapters:

- "Evaluating Memory and Cache Usage" in this book

- "Examining and Tuning Disk Performance" in this book

- "Monitoring Network Performance" in this book

Also, the Processor(_Total)\Interrupts/sec counter value might rise dramatically if you've recently added many new applications or users. During periods of low activity the only source of interrupts might be the processor's timer ticks; these are periodic events that increment a processor hardware timer. These occur approximately every 10 to 15 milliseconds, or about 66 to 100 interrupts per second. Interrupt rates vary depending on system workload, including network packets per second and disk I/O operations per second. Watch for interrupt values that fall out of a normal range (expect these to be in the 1000s of interrupts on Microsoft® Windows® 2000 Server and from 200 to 300 on Microsoft® Windows® 2000 Professional). If Processor\% Interrupt Time exceeds 20 to 30 percent per processor, it might indicate that the system is generating more processor interrupts than it can handle. If this is the case, you might need to upgrade some of your components. For more information, see "Monitoring Network Performance" in this book.

If a processor bottleneck does not exist but you are dissatisfied with system performance, and you have ruled out memory and other hardware factors, consider the following options to improve CPU response time or throughput:

- Schedule processor-intensive applications to run when the system load is low. Use **Scheduled Tasks** in Control Panel or the **at** command to do this.

- Upgrade to a faster processor. Upgrading to a higher-speed processor with a larger L2 cache will expedite processing regardless of your system's workload.

  When upgrading to a faster processor, check with the chip vendor to ensure that you use the correct memory speed for the chip. Incompatible memory speed could cause a computer with a faster processor to appear to run more slowly than a computer with a slower processor.

Note Using multiple processors rather than switching to a faster one might not automatically improve performance in a dramatic manner. For example, a 200-megahertz (MHz) dual-processor computer might not perform equally to a 400-MHz uniprocessor computer with all workloads because of overhead inherent in synchronization. Because scaling can incur some overhead, it is important to be aware of the factors involved and how to manage them. For more information, see "Measuring Multiprocessor System Activity" in this book.

If conditions do not warrant immediate processor replacement, begin monitoring processor activity and system performance as described in the following sections.

Examining the Processor Time Counter

The Processor\% Processor Time counter determines the percentage of time the processor is busy by measuring the percentage of time the thread of the Idle process is running and then subtracting that from 100 percent. This measurement is the amount of processor utilization. Although you might sometimes see high values for the Processor\% Processor Time counter (70 percent or greater depending on your workload and environment), it might not indicate a problem; you need more data to understand this activity. For example, high processor-time values typically occur when you are starting a new process and should not cause concern.

Note The value that characterizes high processor utilization depends greatly on your system and workload. This chapter describes 70 percent as a typical threshold value; however, you may define your target maximum utilization at a higher or lower value. If so, substitute that target value for 70 percent in the examples provided in this section.

To illustrate, consider that Windows 2000 allows an application to consume all available processor time if no other thread is waiting. As a result, System Monitor shows processor-time rates of 100 percent. If the threads have equal or greater priority, as soon as another thread requests processor time, the thread that was consuming 100 percent of CPU time yields control so that the requesting thread can run, causing processor time to lessen. For a discussion of priority and scheduling, see "Threads in a Bottleneck" later in this chapter.

If you establish that processor-time values are consistently high during certain processes, you need to determine whether a processor bottleneck exists by examining processor queue length data. Unless you already know the characteristics of the applications running on the system, upgrading or adding processors at this point would be a premature response to persistently high processor values, even values of 90 percent or higher. First, you need to know whether processor load is keeping important work from being done. You have several options for addressing processor bottlenecks, but you need to first verify their existence.

If you begin to see values of 70 percent or more for the Processor\% Processor Time counter, investigate your processor's activity further, as follows:

- Examine System\Processor Queue Length.

- Identify the processes that are running when Processor\% Processor Time and System\Processor Queue Length values are highest.

Observing Processor Queue Length

A collection of one or more threads that is ready but not able to run on the processor due to another active thread that is currently running is called the processor queue. The clearest symptom of a processor bottleneck is a sustained or recurring queue of more than two threads. Although queues are most likely to develop when the processor is very busy, they can develop when utilization is well below 90 percent. This can happen if requests for processor time arrive randomly and if threads demand irregular amounts of time from the processor. For more information about monitoring and adjusting thread scheduling, see "Threads in a Bottleneck" later in this chapter.

The System\Processor Queue Length counter shows how many threads are ready in the processor queue, but not currently able to use the processor. Figure 7.2 shows a sustained processor queue with utilization ranging from 60 to 90 percent. Notice that the default scale for the Processor Queue Length counter value is 10. Therefore, System Monitor graphs a queue that is two threads long as 20. You can change the scale factor using the **Data** properties tab in System Monitor.

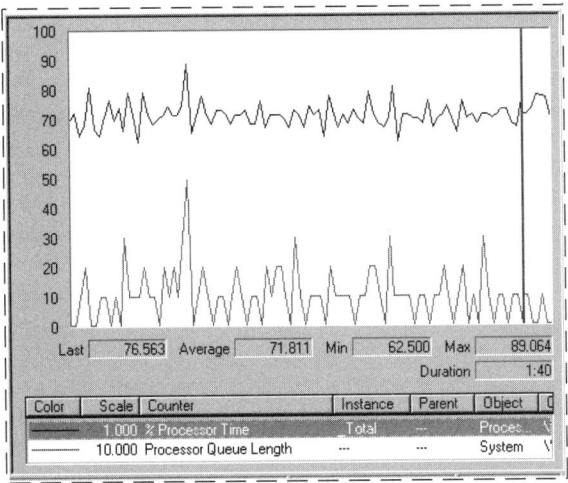

Figure 7.2   Sustained Processor Queue with Rising Processor Usage

In Figure 7.2, the line across the top represents Processor(_Total)\% Processor Time. The lower line is System\Processor Queue Length.

Figure 7.3 shows a sustained processor queue accompanied by processor use at or near 100 percent.

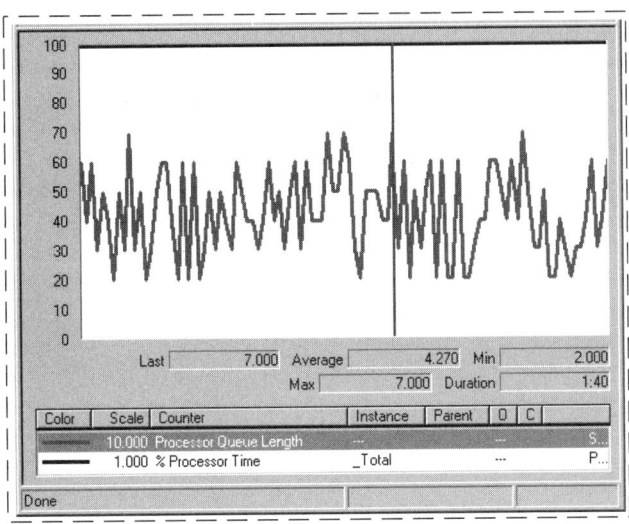

Figure 7.3   Sustained Processor Queue with Maximum Processor Usage

Figure 7.4 illustrates how a processor bottleneck interferes with your computer's performance. It shows that when a processor is already at 100 percent utilization, starting another process does not accomplish more work.

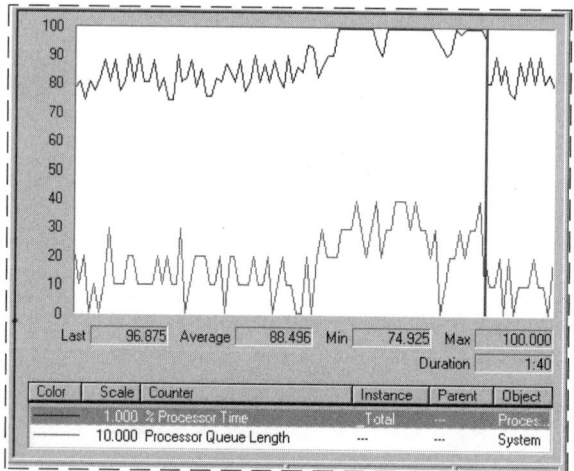

Figure 7.4   Saturated Processor

In Figure 7.4, the dark line running across the top of the graph is Processor(_Total)\% Processor Time. The line below it is System\Processor Queue Length. Midway through the sample interval, a process with three threads was started. The graph illustrates that the queue increased as a result of this added workload. Some of the threads of the added process might be in the queue, or they might be running, having displaced the threads of a lower-priority process. Nonetheless, because the processor was already at maximum capacity, it can accomplish no additional work.

If your system's counter values appear similar to those in Figure 7.4, this indicates a bottleneck. Logging, over time, will reveal any patterns associated with the bottleneck. For example, you might find that bottlenecks occur when certain processes are running or at a certain time of day. In this case, you might be able to eliminate the bottleneck by balancing the workload between computers—that is, running the process on another, less loaded computer.

However, if sustained queues appear frequently, you need to investigate the processes that are running when threads collect in the queue. To determine this:

- Identify the processes that are consuming processor time. Determine whether a single process or multiple processes are active during a bottleneck. Running processes appear in the **Instance** box when you select the Process\% Processor Time counter. For more information, see "Processes in a Bottleneck" later in this chapter.

- Scrutinize the processor-intensive processes. Determine how many threads run in the process and watch the patterns of thread activity during a bottleneck.

- Evaluate the priorities at which the process and its threads run. You might be able to eliminate a bottleneck merely by adjusting the base priority of the process or the current priorities of its threads. However, Microsoft does not recommend this as a long-term solution. Use Task Manager to find the base priority of the process.

Note Different guidelines apply for queue lengths on multiprocessor systems. For busy systems (those having processor utilization in the 80 to 90 percent range) that use thread scheduling, the queue length should range from one to three threads per processor. For example, on a four-processor system, the expected range of processor queue length on a system with high CPU activity is 4 to 12.

On systems with lower CPU utilization, the processor queue length is typically 0 or 1.

There are other objects that track processor queue length. The Server Work Queues\Queue Length counter reports the number of requests in the queue for the processor on the selected server. For more information about monitoring the Server Work Queues object, see "Monitoring Network Performance" in this book.

Monitoring Interrupts

Sharply rising counts for interrupts can affect your processor's performance, and you should investigate their cause. The Processor\Interrupts/sec counter reports the number of interrupts the processor is servicing from applications or hardware devices. You should expect interrupts to range upward from 1,000 per second for computers running Windows 2000 Server and upward from 100 per second for computers running Windows 2000 Professional. This interrupt rate is dependent on the rate of disk I/O operations per second and network packets per second. If your interrupt counter values are out of range, there might be hardware problems such as a conflict between the hard-disk controller and a network adapter. You can use System Information and Device Manager in the Computer Management console to check for problems with the disk controller or network adapter.

You might want to monitor interrupts along with I/O activity involving both disks and network cards. Use the Disk Reads/sec or Disk Writes/sec counters on the PhysicalDisk object to monitor disk I/O as described in "Examining and Tuning Disk Performance" in this book. Use the network transmission counters to monitor network activity as described in "Monitoring Network Performance" in this book. You can tell if interrupt activity is becoming a problem by determining the ratio of interrupts to I/O operations. An optimal ratio is one interrupt to four or five I/O operations. A one-to-one correspondence between these factors indicates poor performance and requires action.

If network or disk I/O is involved, you should consider upgrading to a controller and a driver that support interrupt moderation or interrupt avoidance. Interrupt moderation allows a processor to process interrupts more efficiently by grouping several interrupts to a single hardware interrupt. Interrupt avoidance allows a processor to continue processing interrupts without new interrupts being queued until all pending interrupts are complete. For more information about managing interrupts from network adapters, see "Monitoring Network Performance" in this book.

High values for % Processor Time for threads of the System process can also indicate a problem with a device driver.

Monitoring Context Switches

A context switch occurs when the kernel switches the processor from one thread to another—for example, when a thread with a higher priority than the running thread becomes ready. Context switching activity is important for several reasons. A program that monopolizes the processor lowers the rate of context switches because it does not allow much processor time for the other processes' threads. A high rate of context switching means that the processor is being shared repeatedly—for example, by many threads of equal priority. A high context-switch rate often indicates that there are too many threads competing for the processors on the system.

Note The rate of context switches can also affect performance of multiprocessor computers. For information about how to monitor and tune context-switch activity on multiprocessor systems, see "Measuring Multiprocessor System Activity" in this book.

You can view context switch data in two ways:

- The System\Context Switches/sec counter in System Monitor reports systemwide context switches.

- The Thread(_Total)\Context Switches/sec counter reports the total number of context switches generated per second by all threads.

Although these counters might vary slightly due to sampling, generally they will be nearly equal.

Figure 7.5 plots System\Context Switches/sec during a transient bottleneck.

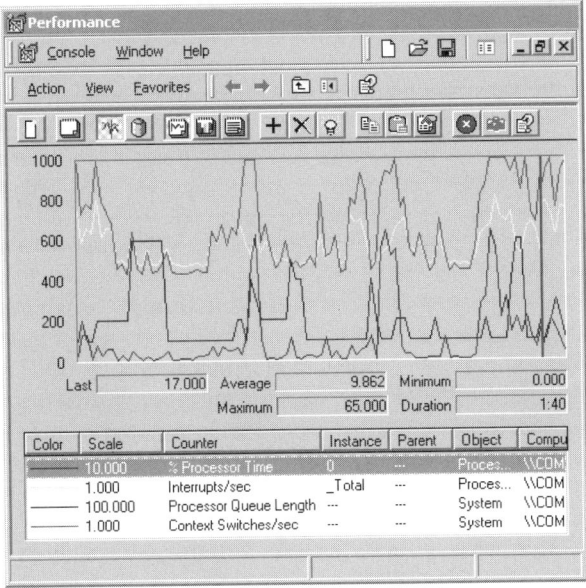

Figure 7.5   Systemwide Context Switches During a Processor Bottleneck

In Figure 7.5, Processor(_Total)\% Processor Time jumps to about 60 percent during the sample interval. System\Processor Queue Length (scaled by a factor of 10), shows that the queue varies from 2 to 6, with a mean near 4. System\Context Switches (shown scaled by a factor of 10), reveals an average of about 750 switches per second. A rate of context switches from 500 to 2,000 per second might indicate a problem with a network adapter or a device driver or that you are using an inefficient server-based application that spawns too many threads.

The Pviewer utility on the on the Windows 2000 operating system CDreports context switch data.For information about installing and using the Windows 2000 Support Tools and Support Tools Help, see the file Sreadme.doc in the \Support\Tools folder of the Windows 2000 operating system CD.

Processes in a Bottleneck

After you have identified a processor bottleneck, you next need to determine whether a single process is using the processor or whether the processor is being consumed by running many processes. To do this, log processor time used by each process running on your computer, as follows:

- Select the Process object.
- Select the % Processor Time counter.
- Select each process instance.

Important All processes that are running will appear in the **Instance** box listed by the name of the associated executable program (for example, Windows Explorer appears as "explorer" in the **Instance** box). Note that if you are running multiple instances of the same executable program, System Monitor lists these under the identical name; thus, you will need to track these by their process identifiers. You can find the process identifier by using the Process\Process ID counter or by adding the PID column in Task Manager. For more information, see "Threads in a Bottleneck" later in this chapter.

For more information about MS-DOS-based (shown as NTVDM for Windows NT Virtual DOS Machine) and Win16-based processes that appear differently in the user interface. See "Overview of Performance Monitoring" in this book.

Identifying Active Processes

To determine the processing load generated by your typical workload, include the instances for the processes that you normally run. If you find that you don't normally use some processes (such as background services) that are already running, stop these processes and measure the impact on your processing load. This might be an easy way to improve your computer's processing efficiency. However, before doing so, make sure you understand the possible effects. To stop a service, complete the following procedure.

▶ **To stop a service**

1. Click **Start**, point to **Programs**, and then click **Administrative Tools**.
2. Click **Computer Management**, and then, in the console that appears, click **Services and Applications**.
3. Under **Services and Applications**, double-click **Services**.
4. Right-click the name of a service, and then click **Stop**.

Isolating Processor-Intensive Workloads

If the threads of a process are using a high percentage of CPU time, the process should be analyzed to determine if the application's performance can be optimized. For information about improving application performance, see the Platform Software Development Kit (SDK) link on the Web Resources page at http://windows.microsoft.com/windows2000/reskit/webresources. If optimization does not yield satisfactory results, you need to add processor resources.

Device driver problems can cause high % Processor Time values for the System process. In addition, if you have screen savers running on your system, note that they use a large amount of processor time, particularly ones that use OpenGL (a software interface that supports production of high-quality, three-dimensional color imaging). Monitor your screen saver executable and, if necessary, change to one that uses less processor time. (Typically this is only applicable to servers.)

If a single process is using the processor, the chart line associated with that process will be the highest one in the graph, such as in Figure 7.6, which is an actual histogram of a processor bottleneck caused by a single process. Running CPU Stress, a utility on the *Windows 2000 Resource Kit* companion CD, produced the results shown in this example.

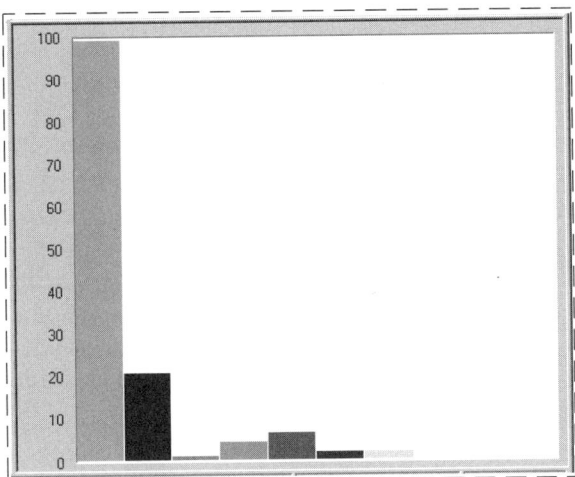

Figure 7.6   Processor Bottleneck Caused by a Single Process

This histogram shows that a single process (represented by the tallest bar) is highly active during a bottleneck; its threads are running for more than 90 percent of the sample interval. If this pattern persists and a long queue develops, it is reasonable to suspect that the application running in the process is causing the bottleneck.

Note that a highly active process is a problem only if a queue is developing. If you are not satisfied with response time and throughput, you can choose to upgrade to a faster processor to achieve better performance.

If you suspect that an application is causing a processor bottleneck, stop using the application for a few days or move it to a different computer. Another option is to schedule the process to run outside of peak operating hours. Then log processor use again. If the problem disappears, it is likely that the application caused it.

Reducing Single-Process Bottlenecks

If you cannot use another computer and you have access to the application source code, you can tune the application to increase efficiency. Start by using a profiler, an analysis tool that you can use to examine the run-time behavior of your programs. Profiling enables you to analyze how the application is spending processor time. The Platform Software Development Kit (SDK) includes tools and methods for profiling and optimizing applications, including instructions for developing performance counters to monitor the inner workings of your application. To tune an application to be less CPU-intensive, use SDK utilities such as Call Attributed Profiler (CAP) or File I/O Synchronization Win32 API Profiler (FIOSAP). You can also use APIMon and Kernprof, which are included on the *Windows 2000 Resource Kit* companion CD.

If tuning efforts do not reduce the application's load on your processor, or if you do not have access to the application source code, you can:

- Consider adding a processor or upgrading the one you have. If your application is multithreaded, adding a processor can alleviate a bottleneck because multithreaded applications can run on multiple processors. However, single-threaded applications will not benefit because the system cannot distribute their thread activity across processors; these applications need faster processors or need to run on a computer with extra processing capacity. In general, a faster CPU will probably result in a greater performance gain than installing additional processors because the management of the work performed by multiple CPUs also consumes processor time.

- Investigate the activity of threads in the process. For more information about examining thread behavior and changing thread scheduling patterns to ensure that the necessary processes get processor time, see "Threads in a Bottleneck" later in this chapter. This section also contains instructions for determining whether a process is single-threaded or multithreaded; this distinction is important in making an upgrade decision.

- If processor use continues to create a bottleneck even without the application that you first suspected, repeat the preceding steps and carefully monitor the processes that are active when the queues are longest.

- Consider replacing the application with one that has been optimized to run under Windows 2000.

Observing Processor Consumption by Multiple Processes

Figure 7.7 shows a histogram of processor time for many active processes. This example was produced by running two instances of CPU Stress, which consumes processor cycles at the priority and activity levels you specify.

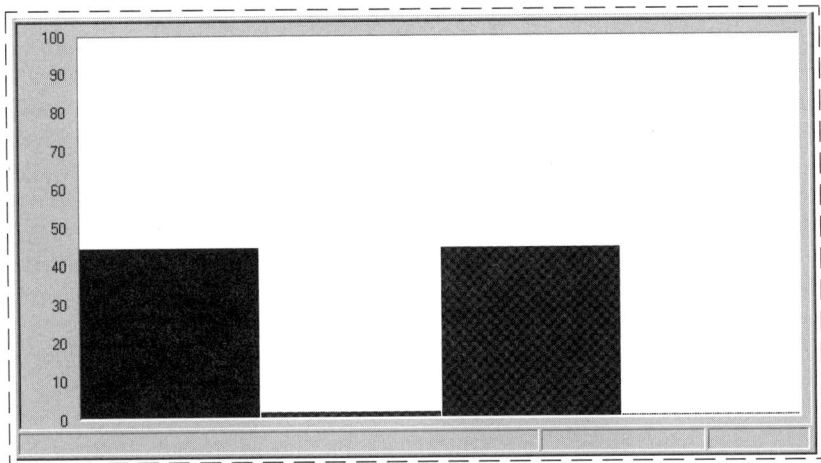

Figure 7.7   Processor Time for Multiple Active Processes

In this example, two processes are consuming the processor while sharing it nearly equally. Although each process is using only 45 percent of the processor, the result is the same as a single process using 90 percent of processor time.

Figure 7.8 shows System\Processor Queue Length during this bottleneck.

\\COMPUTER1				
Process	CPUSTRES	explorer	MyProcess	services
% Processor Time	48.177	2.511	48.177	0.076
System				
Processor Queue Length	6.200			

Figure 7.8   Processor Queue Length During Activity of Many Processes

In Figure 7.8, Processor\% Processor Time for all processes is close to 100 percent during the sample interval. System\Processor Queue Length reveals a long queue, averaging over six threads.

Figure 7.9 shows Task Manager during the same bottleneck. It shows that two CPU Stress processes are each using about half of the time of the single processor on the computer. (Task Manager shows current values, so you need to watch the display to see changes in processor use for each process.)

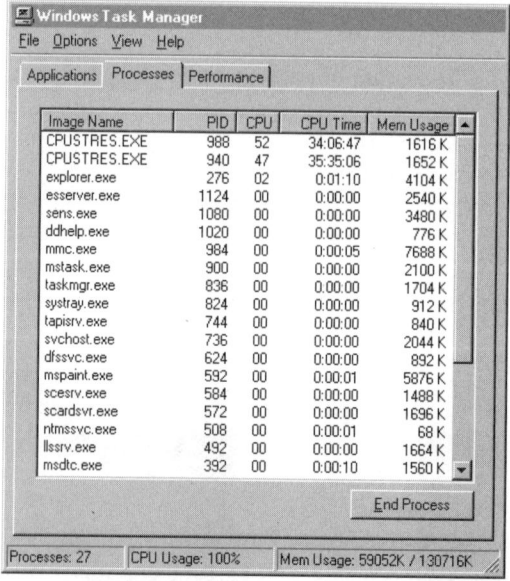

Figure 7.9   CPU Usage for Multiple Processes in Task Manager

At this point, you can choose to add a processor or upgrade the one you have, or you can investigate the activity further by researching thread behavior. Although a faster processor might help this situation somewhat, multiple-process bottlenecks are best resolved by adding another processor. Multithreaded processes, including multithreaded Windows 2000 services, benefit the most from additional processors because their threads can run simultaneously on multiple processors. You might want to partition the processes among the processors for optimal efficiency. For more information, see "Measuring Multiprocessor System Activity" in this book.

To find out more about how a particular process uses the processor, examine the Process\% User Time and Process\% Privileged Time counters, followed by Thread object counters, as described in the following section.

For more information about determining if your application is multithreaded, see "Threads in a Bottleneck" later in this chapter. You might also want to find out whether all threads in a multithreaded process are active during bottlenecks. The benefit of adding processors depends on whether you have a lot of active threads. You could find, as a result of monitoring, that threads in a process are inactive most of the time, so adding a processor to handle these inactive threads is a waste of money and capacity.

For more information about the benefits of adding processors to manage a larger workload (called scaling) and how to determine whether scaling is appropriate, see "Measuring Multiprocessor System Activity" in this book.

Threads in a Bottleneck

Investigate the individual thread or threads of the process or processes running during a bottleneck to understand more about the activity consuming the processor. Monitor the following factors to understand how thread activity is contributing to the problem, whether the cause is a single process or multiple processes:

- The number of threads in each process that is running during a bottleneck
- The amount of processor time a thread is consuming
- The priority level at which threads are scheduled to run
- The amount of time the threads are using the processor in privileged mode

You can use performance counters to analyze thread activity and adjust thread scheduling to allow more processor time for bottlenecked processes.

Apart from adjusting the thread's scheduling priority, you cannot alter thread behavior without changing the program code of the associated application. However, if you have access to application source code, you can write counters to monitor thread activity at a lower level. For more information, see the Platform Software Development Kit (SDK) link on the Web Resources page at http://windows.microsoft.com/windows2000/reskit/webresources.

Single vs. Multiple Threads in a Bottleneck

Bottlenecks can result from activity of multiple threads in a single process, single threads in multiple processes, or multiple threads in multiple processes. Because these problems require different solutions, you need to first distinguish their causes.

To study threads during a bottleneck, log counters of the Processor, Process, and Thread objects for several days at an update interval of 60 seconds. This will allow you to look at thread activity during typical operating conditions and help you associate that activity with processor usage.

> **Important** Performance counter values for threads are subject to error when threads are stopping and starting. Faulty values sometimes appear as large spikes in the data. For more information, see "Overview of Performance Monitoring" in this book.

▶ **To determine whether a process is single-threaded or multithreaded**

1. Right-click the Windows task bar and select **Task Manager**.

2. In **Task Manager**, click the **Processes** tab and, on the **View** menu, click **Select Columns**.

3. In the **Select Columns** dialog box, select the **Thread Count** check box, and then click **OK**.

   This column shows the total number of threads associated with the process.

Figure 7.10 illustrates how Task Manager displays the number of threads running in a process, and the name of the process.

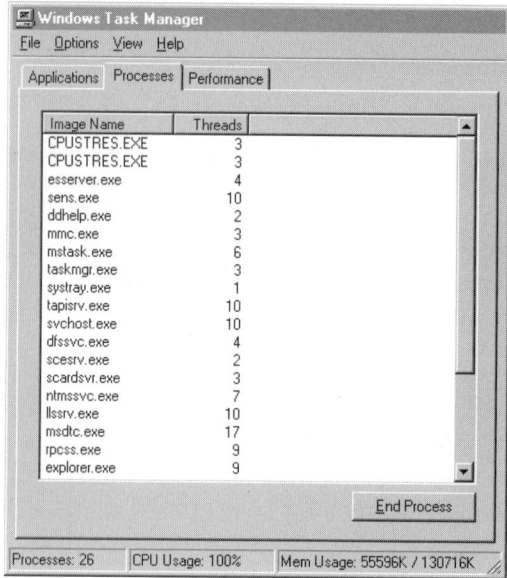

Figure 7.10   Number of Threads Initiated by a Process Shown in Task Manager

In System Monitor or Counter Logs, select the Thread object and look at all instances listed in the **Instance** box. If there are several thread identifiers (IDs) listed, then the process is multithreaded. Figure 7.11 illustrates multiple threads of a process as they are listed in the **Instances** box in the System Monitor user interface.

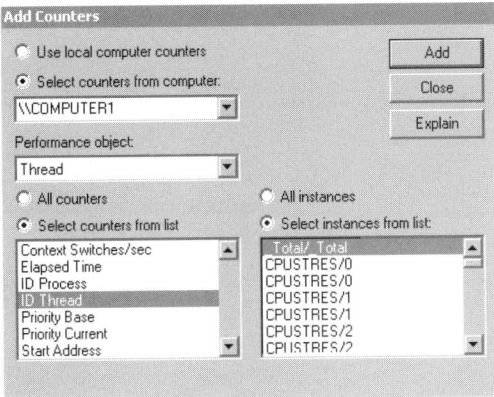

Figure 7.11   Thread Instances Shown When Adding Counters in System Monitor

System Monitor identifies threads by process name and thread number. The order in which the threads appear on the chart depends on the order in which you add them to your chart. The thread number shown in the **Instance** box represents the order in which the threads started, and it can change even as the process runs.

Thread identifiers are valid only during the lifetime of the thread; they are recycled when the thread terminates. Thread numbers can change while running, so it is best to monitor by thread identifier. The Tlist utility provides thread identifier information. For information about Tlist, see Windows 2000 Support Tools Help. For information about installing and using the Windows 2000 Support Tools and Support Tools Help, see the file Sreadme.doc in the \Support\Tools folder of the Windows 2000 operating system CD.

If a process is multithreaded, adding a processor will help improve performance. If it is single-threaded, you can improve performance by using a faster processor. These solutions are more advanced and more relevant to developers who also might want to tune the problem applications.

Charting Processor Usage Per Thread

Observing processor time by threads in a process provides additional information about the activity of the processor during a bottleneck. System Monitor provides the Thread\%Processor Time counter for monitoring processor usage for each thread in a running process. If you have determined that a process is single-threaded, you do not need to track the processor time for the process's thread because this will be nearly identical (except for small variations due to sampling) to the processor time you recorded when tracking the process itself.

Figure 7.12 shows Thread\% Processor Time for all initialized threads during a bottleneck. Each bar of the histogram represents the processor time of a single thread.

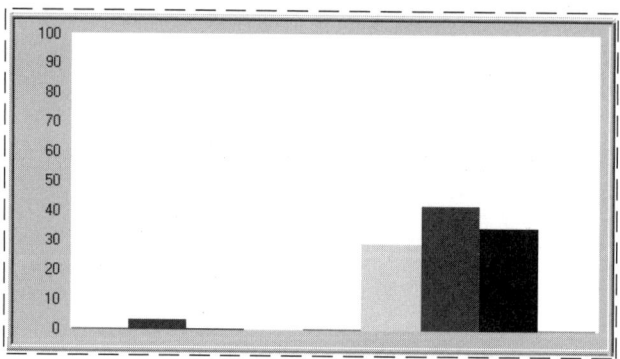

Figure 7.12   View of Threads and Processor Usage

Figure 7.12 shows that the three threads of the CPU Stress process are dominating the pattern of processor use, although a few other threads are getting some processor time.

If your thread activity appears similar to the preceding figure and a long queue is developing, some applications on your system are probably not getting enough processor time to run as efficiently as you would like. To investigate the threads of the process and how they use the processor, monitor context switching and user-mode vs. kernel-mode CPU usage, as described in the following sections.

Context Switches

The Thread\Context Switches/sec counter in System Monitor provides another perspective on how the operating system schedules threads to run on the processor. A context switch occurs when the kernel switches the processor from one thread to another. A context switch might also occur when a thread with a higher priority than the running thread becomes ready or when a running thread must wait for some reason (such as an I/O operation). The Thread\Context Switches/sec counter value increases when the thread gets or loses the time of the processor.

In the course of a context switch, at least two threads are changing their thread state. However, one of the threads may be the idle thread of a given processor. A careful examination of context switch data reveals the patterns of processor use for a thread and indicates how efficiently a thread shares the processor with other threads of the process or other processes.

The System\Context Switches/sec counter that reports systemwide context switches should be close to if not identical to the value provided by the _Total instance of the Thread\Context Switches/sec counter. Monitoring over time should help you determine the range by which the two counters' value might vary.

Interpret the data cautiously. A thread that is heavily using the processor lowers the rate of context switches because it does not allow much processor time for other processes' threads. A high rate of context switching means that the processor is being shared repeatedly—for example, by many threads of equal priority. It is a good practice to minimize the context switching rate by reducing the number of active threads on the system. The use of thread pooling, I/O completion ports, and asynchronous I/O can reduce the number of active threads. Consult your in-house developers or application vendors to determine if the applications you are running provide tuning features that include limiting the number of threads.

A context switching rate of 300 per second per processor is a moderate amount; a rate of 1000 per second or more is high. Values at this high level may be a problem.

You can determine whether context switching is excessive by comparing it with the value of Processor\% Privileged Time. If this counter is at 40 percent or more and the context-switching rate is high, then you can investigate the cause for high rates of context switches.

User Mode and Privileged Mode

You can determine the percentage of time that threads of a process are running in user and privileged mode. User mode is the processing mode in which applications run. Privileged or kernel mode is the processing mode that allows code to have direct access to all hardware and memory in the system. Developers might want to know how much time a process is spending in each mode and what function is using the processor in this way.

I/O operations and other system services run in privileged (kernel) mode; user applications run in user mode. Unless they are graphics-intensive or I/O-intensive (such as file and print services), most applications should not be processing much work in kernel mode.

System Monitor has % Privileged Time and % User Time counters on the System, Processor, Process, and Thread objects. These counters are described in "Processor Counters" earlier in this chapter. System Calls/sec is also a useful indicator of privileged time usage because application calls to the operating system are handled in privileged mode.

In the user time and privileged time counters, System Monitor displays the proportion of total processor time that the process is spending in user or privileged mode.

Figure 7.13 is a System Monitor report on the proportion of user and privileged time for three processes.

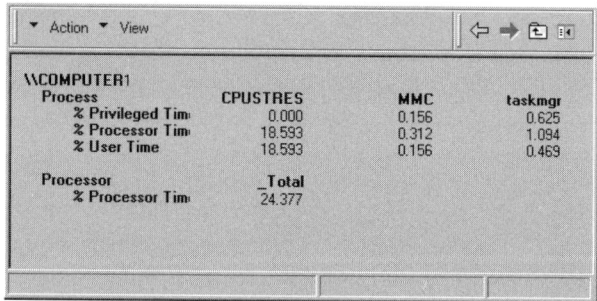

Figure 7.13   User and Privileged Time for Processes

In Figure 7.13, Microsoft Management Console (MMC), the process in which System Monitor is running, is running mainly (80 percent) in privileged mode. Taskmgr, the Task Manager process, is also running mainly in privileged mode (70 percent), though this proportion varies significantly as the process runs. In contrast, CpuStres, the process for the CPU Stress test program, runs entirely in user mode all of the time.

Figure 7.14 shows the proportion of user and privileged time for each thread of the Task Manager process.

```
\\COMPUTER1
  Process                taskmgr
      % Privileged Time    1.875
      % Processor Time     2.031
      % User Time          0.156

                         taskmgr      taskmgr      taskmgr
  Thread                    0            1            2
      % Privileged Time    1.875        0.000        0.000
      % Processor Time     2.031        0.000        0.000
      % User Time          0.156        0.000        0.000
```

Figure 7.14   User and Privileged Time for a Process and Its Threads

The Process Viewer (Pviewer.exe) utility displays the proportion of user and privileged time for each running process and, separately, for each thread in the process. In Process Viewer, the user and privileged mode percentages for each process always total 100 percent because idle time is included. However, in System Monitor the percentages for each process reflect the amount of nonidle processor time actually used in each mode and instead total the amount of nonidle time. Therefore, the value for each process might not total 100 percent. To see the process times add up to 100 percent, combine the percentages for all processes including the Idle process.

For information about Pviewer, see Windows 2000 Support Tools Help. For information about installing and using the Windows 2000 Support Tools and Support Tools Help, see the file Sreadme.doc in the \Support\Tools folder of the Windows 2000 operating system CD.

Advanced Topic: Changing Thread Priority to Improve Performance

After observing the threads that use the greatest amount of processor time, monitor the dispatch states of the threads. This will tell you which threads are running and which threads are ready. Most important, monitoring thread states on your system can help you identify which threads are piling up in the queue and which threads are actively running at various times.

The Thread\Thread State counter provided by System Monitor reports the current execution state (also known as dispatch state) of a thread. System Monitor reports thread state as a numeric value from 0 through 7, corresponding to whether the thread is ready, running, terminated, and so on.

Table 7.3 lists the thread states you will typically see.

Table 7.3   Typical Thread States

Thread state	Description
0	Initialized.
1	Ready. The thread is prepared to run on the next available processor.
2	Running.
3	Standby. The thread is about to use the processor.
4	Terminated.
5	Waiting. The thread is not ready to run, typically because another operation (for example, involving I/O) must finish before the thread can run.
6	Transition. The thread is not ready to run because it is waiting for a resource (such as code being paged in from disk).
7	Unknown. The thread is in an unknown state.

To determine which threads are contending for the processor, track the states of all threads in the system using System Monitor. Figure 7.15 shows a histogram. The vertical maximum for the chart is set to 10 to make it easier to see the values; an alternative for easier viewing is to display the thread-state values in a report view.

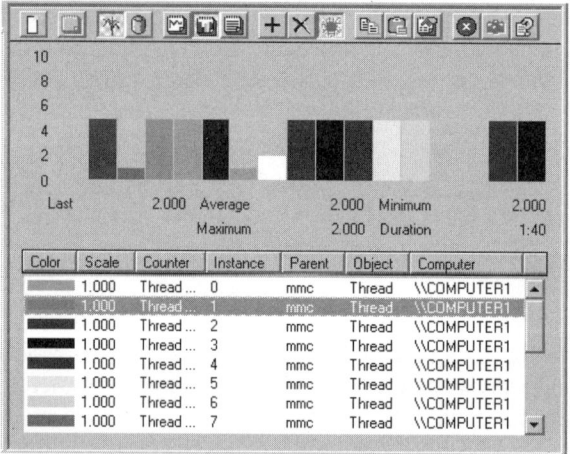

Figure 7.15   Display of Thread States

Notice that the preceding figure plots a thread of the MMC process with the steady value of **2** for running. This is the thread of the System Monitor snap-in that is collecting the data that you are monitoring. As long as System Monitor is running, one of its threads will be shown to be running. Other threads' state values alternate between **1** for ready and **5** for waiting.

Plotting thread-state data in a chart rather than a histogram might make it easier to view the switching of thread states. Note in Figure 7.16 how a process's thread moves from the waiting state (plotted on the chart at 5) to the ready state (plotted on the chart at 1).

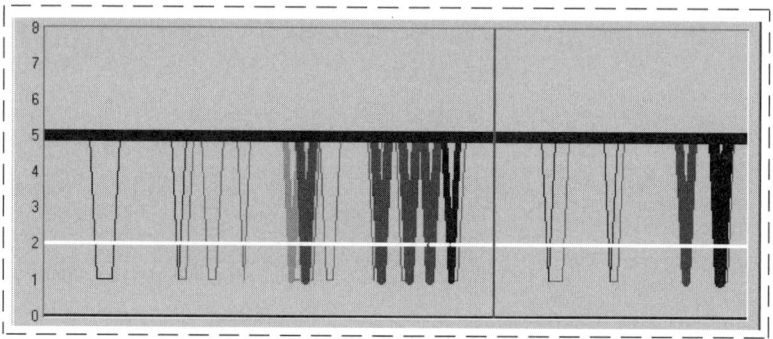

Figure 7.16   Changing Thread States

To find out how long threads remain in a particular state, log Thread\Thread State and, when the log is completed, export it to Microsoft Excel. A sample log is shown in Figure 7.17.

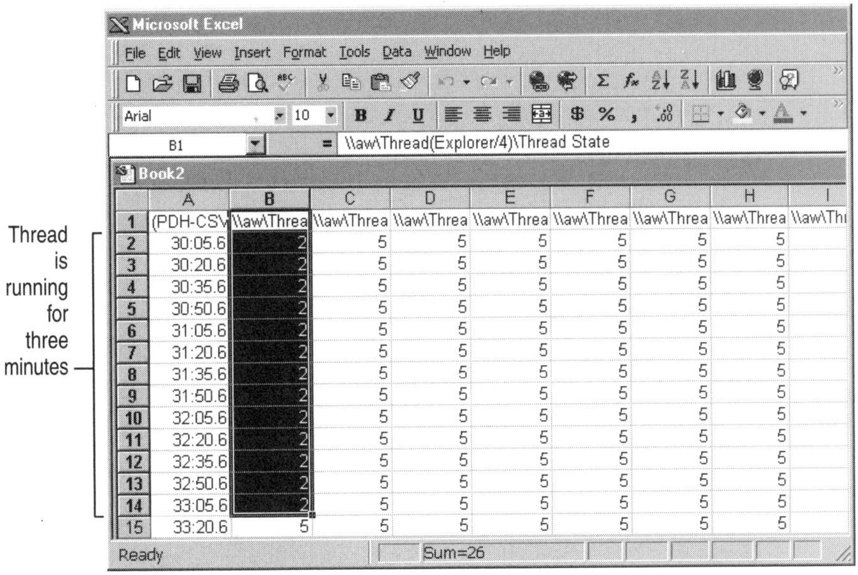

Figure 7.17   Sample Log Output Viewed in Microsoft Excel

By looking at log output, you can get an idea of the length of time that a thread remains in a state by totaling the number of seconds that elapsed until the thread's state changed. However, it is important to note that, due to the fact that sampling omits some data, you might not see all of the state changes that occur.

In addition, the Thread\Thread Wait State counter and Perfmon4.exe on the *Windows 2000 Resource Kit* companion CD give you information about why a thread is in a waiting state.

The value reported for Thread Wait Reason is a code. The Counters Help file on the *Windows 2000 Resource Kit* companion CD provides descriptions for these codes.

Examining and Adjusting Thread Priority

Examining thread context switching and thread state gives you information about when threads in a bottleneck are being scheduled to run by the operating system and when threads are being held in the queue prior to running. Although the operating system is inherently designed to optimize the scheduling of threads, you have some control over this behavior, to adjust for situations in which scheduling behavior on your system is unsatisfactory. This section describes how you can determine a thread's scheduling priority and how you can adjust thread priority to reduce bottlenecks and allow blocked threads to run.

Important To ensure optimum performance on production systems, Microsoft recommends that you adjust priorities of processes first in a test environment. In addition, you should make these adjustments only if you have an in-depth understanding of priority settings and their effect on other processes and the operating system.

Priority Class and Priority

Under the preemptive multitasking strategy built into Windows 2000, threads and processes are assigned a priority for scheduling purposes. A thread's priority determines the order in which it is scheduled to run on the processor.

A thread's priority is based on the priority class of its parent process. The four process priority classes are:

- **Idle.** Screen savers and other processes that periodically update the display typically use the Idle class.

- **Normal.** The default priority class for a process is Normal.

- **High.** Processes that run in the High priority class receive the majority of processor time.

- **Real Time.** Many kernel-mode system processes, such as those that manage mouse and keyboard input and other device operations, run in the Real Time priority class.

Each process's priority class sets a range of priority values (between 1 and 31, where 1 is lowest and 31 is highest), and the threads of that process have a priority value that is within that range. (Priority 0 is reserved for system use.) If the priority class is Real Time (priorities 16 through 31), the thread's priority cannot change while the thread is running. If you have at least one priority 31 thread running, other threads cannot run.

On the other hand, threads running in all other priority classes are variable, meaning that the thread's priority can change while the thread is running. For threads in the Normal or High priority classes (priorities 1 through 15), the thread's priority can be raised or lowered by up to a value of 2 but cannot fall below its original, program-defined base priority. When the base priority is adjusted to optimize scheduling, the resulting value is called the thread's dynamic priority.

Table 7.4 associates each process priority class with relative thread priorities, ranked from highest priority to lowest. Notice that the highest priority class is Real Time and the lowest is Idle.

Table 7.4   Process Priority Classes With Relative Thread Priorities

| Thread priorities | Process priority classes | | | |
	Real time	High	Normal	Idle
Time critical	31	15	15	15
Highest	26	15	10	6
Above normal	25	14	9	5
Normal	24	13	8	4
Below normal	23	12	7	3
Lowest	22	11	6	2
Idle	16	1	1	1

Thread Scheduling

The scheduling routines of the operating system run the highest-priority ready thread uninterrupted during a *quantum* (also known as a time slice—the maximum amount of time a thread can run before the system checks for another ready thread of the same priority to run). If a higher-priority thread becomes ready during the quantum, the lower-priority thread is interrupted and the higher-priority thread is run. Otherwise, threads running at the same priority are scheduled in a round-robin fashion, switching among threads in order, and run until the quantum expires.

In general, Windows 2000 always runs the highest-priority ready thread. However, there are optimization strategies built into the operating system to address situations in which the default scheduling methods would cause problems. The following sections describe these strategies.

Foreground Process Scheduling

The scheduler runs a foreground process at a higher priority, which means it tends to get more time slices than background processes. In addition, the scheduler ensures that those time slices are longer than the ones allocated to background processes. As a result, the foreground process is much more responsive than other processes because it is scheduled more often, and when it is scheduled it continues running longer before being preempted. By default, Windows 2000 Professional defines short, variable quanta for applications and gives a foreground application a priority boost. On the other hand, Windows 2000 Server has longer, fixed quanta with no priority boost for foreground applications, allowing background services to run more efficiently. To see foreground process scheduling in action, monitor the processor time for a process and move its window to the bottom of the stack. Note that the time value allocated to that process falls immediately. Then move the process to the top of the stack and note that the processor time value rises immediately. See Figure 7.18 for an illustration.

Automatic Priority Boost

The operating system automatically boosts the thread's priority enough for the low-priority thread to complete its operation and release the resource. After raising a thread's dynamic priority, the scheduler reduces that priority by one level each time the thread completes a time slice (quantum), until the thread drops back to its base priority.

For information about how you can change thread priority, see "Determining and Tuning Priority" later in this chapter.

Determining and Tuning Priority

If a system has high rate of CPU utilization, it is generally best to add processing power by upgrading to a faster processor or to add a processor for symmetric multiprocessing (SMP). However, if you find that some threads are consistently unable to get processor time, you can adjust the thread's priority to allow them to run temporarily. Adjusting thread priority is not recommended as a long-term solution but is a useful illustration of the effect of thread priority on thread activity. Although this section covers elevating priority to allow a process to run, you can also lower the priority of a process if you want it to run in the background while nothing else is running.

Windows 2000 and the *Windows 2000 Resource Kit* companion CD include several utilities for monitoring the base priority of processes and threads and the dynamic priority of threads. They include:

- In Windows 2000: System Monitor and Task Manager.
- With Support Tools on the Windows 2000 operating system CD: Pviewer.

> **Warning**   Changing priorities might destabilize the system. Increasing the priority of a process might prevent other processes, including system services, from running. Decreasing the priority of a process might prevent it from running, not merely force it to run less frequently. In addition, lowering priority does not necessarily reduce the amount of processor time a thread receives; this happens only if it is no longer the highest-priority thread.

System Monitor

System Monitor lets you watch and record—but not change—the base and dynamic priorities of threads and processes. System Monitor has priority counters on the Process and Thread objects:

- Process\Priority Base
- Thread\Priority Base
- Thread\Priority Current

Figure 7.18 is a chart of the base priorities of several processes. The Idle process (the white line at the bottom of the chart) runs at a priority of Idle (0), so it never interrupts another process.

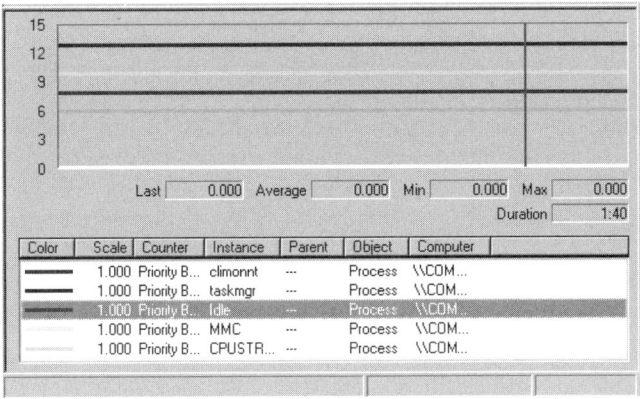

Figure 7.18   Processes and Their Base Priorities

Figure 7.19 is a chart of the dynamic priority of the single thread in the Paintbrush utility (Mspaint.exe) as it changes in response to user actions. The base priority of the thread is 8 (Foreground Normal). During this period of foreground use, the dynamic priority of the thread is 14, but drops to 8 when other processes need to run.

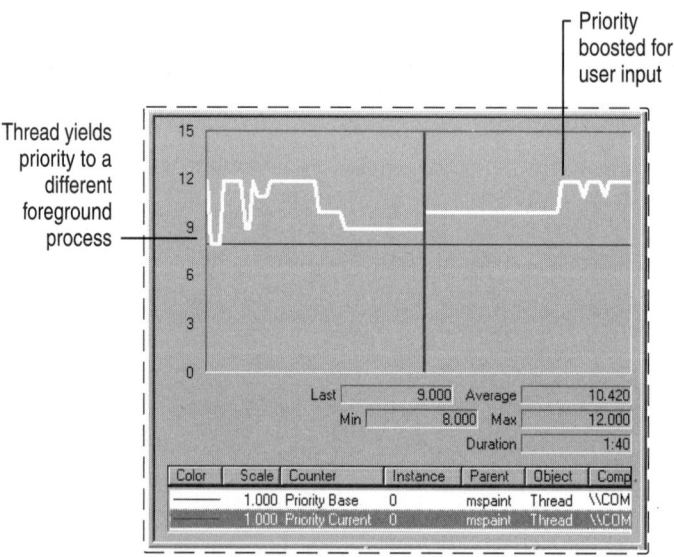

Figure 7.19   Processes Showing Base and Current Priorities

Task Manager

Task Manager presents and lets you change the base priority of a process, but it does not monitor threads. Base priorities changed with Task Manager are effective only as long as the process runs. For more information, see Task Manager online Help or see "Overview of Performance Monitoring" in this book.

Important In order to make this change, your user account must have permission to increase scheduling priority. By default, only user accounts in the Domain Admins or Administrator groups in Windows 2000 Server or Power User groups in Windows 2000 Professional have this permission.

▶ **To change the base priority of a process**

1. In Task Manager, click the **Processes** tab.

2. Right-click a process name. Its menu appears.

3. Click **Set Priority**, and then click a new base priority.

Caution Problems can arise if multiple processes are running at the High priority class level. Avoid setting more than one process to run at this level.

The change in priority is effective at the next Task Manager update; you need not restart the process.

Process Viewer

Process Viewer (Pviewer.exe), one of the Support Tools on the Windows 2000 operating system CD, lets you monitor process and thread priority and change the base priority class of a process. For information about installing and using the Windows 2000 Support Tools and Support Tools Help, see the file Sreadme.doc in the \Support\Tools folder of the Windows 2000 operating system CD.

Start Command

When you begin processes from a command prompt using the **start** command, you can specify a base priority for the processes for that run. To see all of the start options, type **start /?** at the command prompt.

You can change the priority class of a process to Real Time by using **start /realtime** at the command prompt or by using Task Manager. Note that changing the priority from **/normal** to **/high** or to **/realtime** can cause severe degradation of performance of other tasks. Note also that setting a processor-bound application to Real Time priority could cause the computer to stop responding.

Windows 2000 Configuration and Process Priority

Windows 2000 Professional is configured by default to assign variable, short quanta to applications and to boost applications in the foreground. In contrast, Windows 2000 Server is configured to assign long, fixed quanta without any foreground boost to support the efficiency of background services. You can simulate the behavior of one type of operating system when the other type of system is installed—that is, simulate Windows 2000 Server behavior on a Windows 2000 Professional installation, or vice versa. Figure 7.20 shows the interface that you use for changing application response on an installation of Windows 2000 Server.

▶ **To access the Performance Options dialog box**

1. In Control Panel, double-click **System**.

2. Click the **Advanced** tab, and then click **Performance Options**.

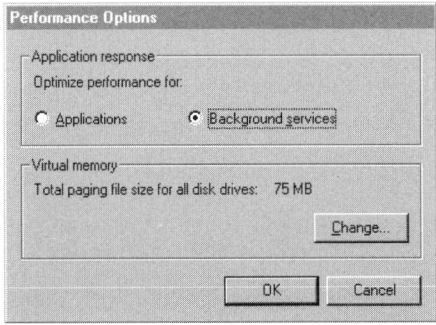

Figure 7.20   Performance Options Dialog Box in System Properties

It is easiest to see a change in thread priority as a result of resetting **Performance Options** if you shut down and then restart the computer. Changes in quantum type and length are so minute they are often undetectable to the user.

Testing Priority Changes

The previous sections described changing thread priority so that, under bottleneck conditions, threads can run more efficiently. Unfortunately, when processor capacity is already stretched to its limit, boosting priorities of blocked threads might not eliminate or reduce processor bottlenecks. In this case, it is best to add processor capacity.

Figure 7.21 shows threads of different priorities contending for processor time. It demonstrates the changing distribution of processor time among processes of different priorities as demand for processor time increases. (This test was conducted using the utility CPU Stress.)

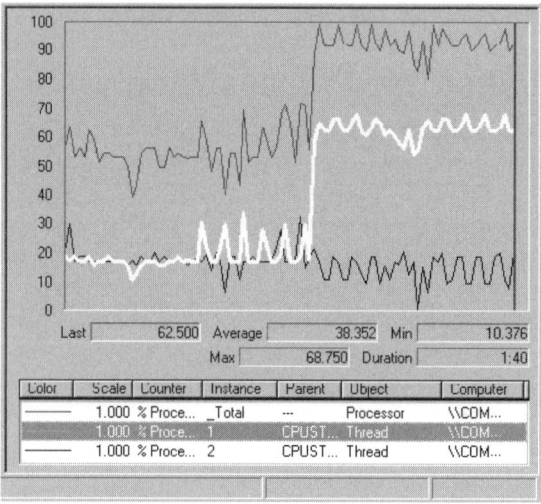

Figure 7.21   CPU Time Allocation to Threads Based on Priorities

This chart shows two threads of the same process running on a single-processor computer. Notice the values for processor time for the _Total instance and for threads 1 and 2.

Figure 7.22 shows two threads of the same process running on a single-processor computer. Figures 7.23, 7.24, and 7.25 provide more detail about how processor usage by threads of CPUStres changed in relation to each thread's priority.

In Figure 7.22, the two threads running CPUStres start out at the same low level of activity and run at the same priority—Normal.

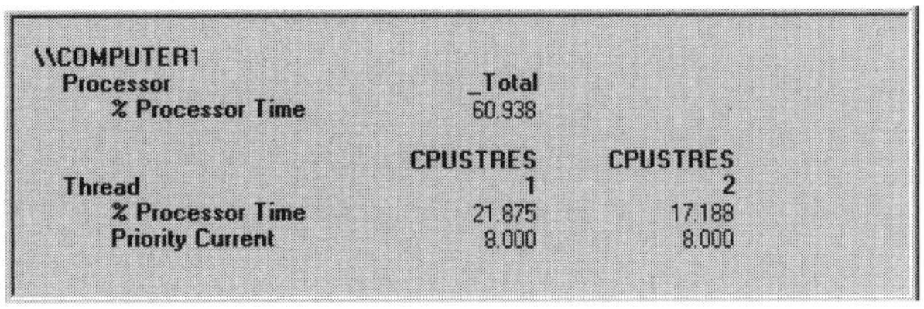

```
\\COMPUTER1
   Processor                           _Total
      % Processor Time                 60.938

                                       CPUSTRES     CPUSTRES
   Thread                              1            2
      % Processor Time                 21.875       17.188
      Priority Current                 8.000        8.000
```

Figure 7.22   Comparison of Threads at Normal Priority

Then, if you increase the priority of Thread 1 to Above Normal, and increase its activity level to moderate, you should notice a slight drop in CPU time for Thread 2, as shown in Figure 7.23.

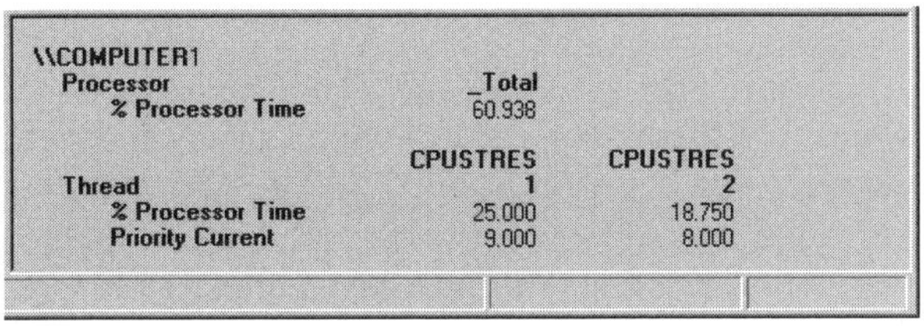

```
\\COMPUTER1
   Processor                           _Total
      % Processor Time                 60.938

                                       CPUSTRES     CPUSTRES
   Thread                              1            2
      % Processor Time                 25.000       18.750
      Priority Current                 9.000        8.000
```

Figure 7.23   Comparison of Threads at Normal and Above Normal Priority

Resetting priority for both threads to Normal while running at a higher rate of activity causes each process to consume a large share of processor time, as shown in Figure 7.24. Total processor usage is consistently and extremely high.

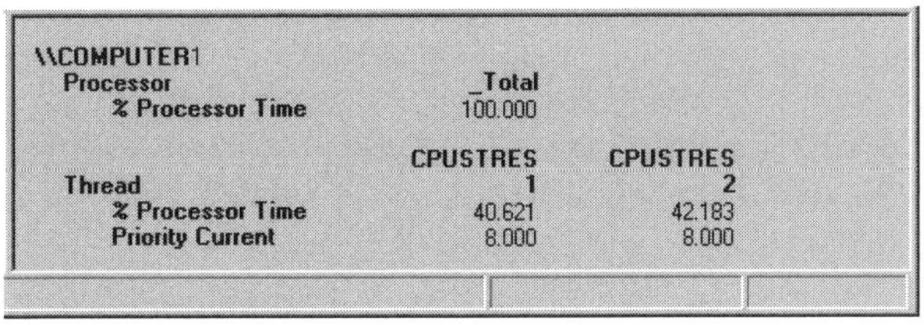

```
\\COMPUTER1
   Processor                           _Total
      % Processor Time                 100.000

                                       CPUSTRES     CPUSTRES
   Thread                              1            2
      % Processor Time                 40.621       42.183
      Priority Current                 8.000        8.000
```

Figure 7.24   Comparison of Normal-Priority Threads Under Slightly Different Loads

Finally, raising the priority level of Thread 1 to Above Normal while maintaining its heightened level of activity results in a much greater allocation of processor time to the higher-priority thread and a dramatic drop in processor time for Thread 2, as shown in Figure 7.25.

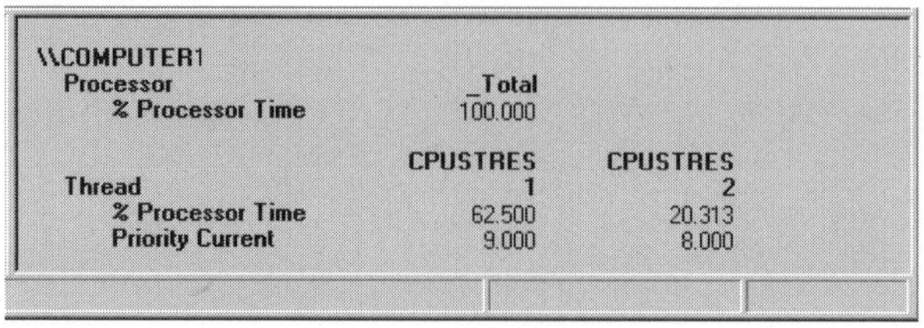

```
\\COMPUTER1
    Processor                           _Total
        % Processor Time                100.000

                                 CPUSTRES      CPUSTRES
    Thread                           1             2
        % Processor Time            62.500        20.313
        Priority Current             9.000         8.000
```

Figure 7.25   Normal Threads Under Substantially Different Loads

These results demonstrate that when the processor has extra capacity, increasing the priority of one thread has little effect on the processor time allotted to each of the competing threads. However, when the processor is at its busiest, increasing the priority of one of the threads, even by one priority level, causes the higher-priority thread to get the vast majority of processor time.

In fact, when all processor time is consumed, Thread 2 might not have been scheduled at all were it not for priority boosts. Windows 2000 uses priority boosts to give processor time to lower-priority ready threads that would not otherwise be able to run. This is especially useful when a thread in low priority is waiting for an I/O operation.

Eliminating a Processor Bottleneck

If you determine that you do have a processor bottleneck, some of the following steps can shorten the processor queue and reduce the burden on your processor. Monitor processor usage and processor queue length after every change to determine the impact on resource usage and overall system operation.

- Upgrade to a faster processor. A faster processor improves response time and throughput for any type of workload.

  Make sure to use a processor with the largest processor cache that is practical. The size of the processor cache is important for your system's performance. You can typically choose from 512 KB to 2 MB for the L2 cache. (The primary cache is determined by what type of processor is installed.)

- Add another processor. If the process you are running has multiple, active threads that are processor-intensive, then it is a prime candidate for a multiprocessor system. It is important that most of the threads be active while the process is running; otherwise, the additional processing power might be wasted. To be certain the process will benefit from an additional processor, verify that most threads are active (that is, consuming a moderate to high amount of processor time). You can see this by monitoring thread state.

  For more information on upgrading to multiple processors, see "Measuring Multiprocessor System Activity" in this book.

- Analyze the application and optimize it if necessary by using the performance utilities in the Platform SDK.

- Upgrade your network or disk adapters. In general, 32-bit, intelligent adapters are recommended. Intelligent adapters provide better overall system performance because they allow interrupts to be processed on the adapter itself, relieving the processor of this work.

  Try to obtain adapters that have optimization features such as interrupt moderation and features for networking, such as card-based TCP/IP checksum support.

Additional Resources

- For more information about how Windows 2000 manages processes and threads, including a discussion of its scheduling strategies, see *Inside Windows NT, Second Edition*, available from Microsoft Press.

CHAPTER 8

Examining and Tuning Disk Performance

The disk system handles the storage and movement of programs and data on your system, giving it a powerful influence on your system's overall responsiveness. The Performance console provides disk-specific counters that enable you to measure disk activity and throughput, and instructs you on strategies to improve disk performance. In addition, it also covers tools found on the *Microsoft®* *Windows® 2000 Resource Kit* companion CD that can assist you in determining which programs are putting the greatest demand on your disk system.

In This Chapter

Related Information in the Resource Kit

- For more information about disks and file systems, see "Disk Concepts and Troubleshooting" and "File Systems" in this book.

- For more information about system monitoring, see "Overview of Performance Monitoring" in this book.

- For more information about evaluating memory usage, see "Evaluating Memory and Cache Usage" in this book.

Disk Monitoring Concepts

You need to observe many factors in determining the performance of a disk system. These include the level of utilization, the rate of throughput, the amount of disk space available, and whether a queue is developing for their disk systems. It is also important to monitor other types of activity that arise from disk operations, such as interrupts generated by the disk system and paging activity, because of their influence on other resources, such as processor or memory.

Figure 8.1 illustrates the importance of monitoring disk systems in relation to the overall performance of your system.

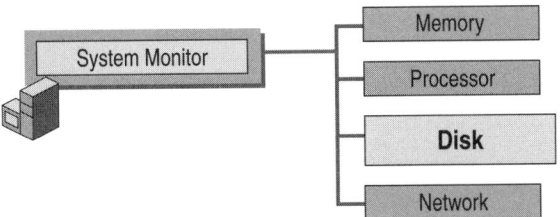

Figure 8.1 Role of Disk Monitoring in System Monitoring

Many of these factors are interrelated. For example, if utilization is high, transfer rates (*throughput*) might peak, and a queue might begin to form. These conditions might result in increased response time and cause performance to slow. Although disk space doesn't directly affect the disk's transfer rate, when extremely low, disk space can also have an influence on response time because applications that read and write data can't do so as efficiently. Detect these performance issues through monitoring before they cause problems.

This chapter covers the following stages of a disk-monitoring strategy:

- Configuring the disk and file system for best performance
- Working with disk counters to monitor your disk space and disk efficiency
- Establishing a baseline for disk performance
- Investigating performance problems

Configuring the Disk and File System for Performance

The type of file system you are using affects your disk performance. The way in which the disk aligns tracks and sectors during format also affects performance. You should configure the file system and the disk's track and sector alignment for optimal performance.

Configuring Your File System

In general, the NTFS file system is the recommended file system for its advantages in terms of reliability and security, and it is required for large drive sizes. However, these advantages come with some overhead. You can disable some functionality to improve NTFS performance as follows:

- Disable creation of short names. By default, NTFS generates the style of file name that consists of eight characters, followed by a period and a three-character extension for compatibility with MS-DOS and Microsoft Windows 3.*x* clients. If you are not supporting these types of clients, you can turn off this setting by changing the default value of the **\NtfsDisable8dot3NameCreation** registry entry (in HKEY_LOCAL_MACHINE \SYSTEM\CurrentControlSet\Control\Filesystem) to 1.

- Disable last access update. By default NTFS updates the date and time stamp of the last access on directories whenever it traverses the directory. For a large NTFS volume, this update process can slow performance. To disable automatic updating, change the value of the **NtfsDisableLastAccessUpdate** registry entry (in HKEY_LOCAL_MACHINE\SYSTEM\CurrentContolSet\Control \Filesystem)\ to 1.

- Reserve appropriate space for the master file table. Add the
  NtfsMftZoneReservation entry to the registry as a REG_DWORD in
  HKEY_LOCAL_MACHINE\SYSTEM
  \CurrentControlSet\Control\FileSystem. When you add this entry to the
  registry, the system reserves space on the volume for the master file table.
  Reserving space in this manner allows the master file table to grow optimally.
  If your NTFS volumes generally contain relatively few files that are typically
  large, set value of this registry entry to 1 (the default). Typically you can use a
  value of 2 or 3 for moderate numbers of files, and 4 (the maximum) if your
  volumes tend to contain a relatively large number of files. However, make sure
  to test any settings greater than 2 because these higher values cause the system
  to reserve a much larger portion of the disk for the master file table.

Caution Do not use a registry editor to edit the registry directly unless you
have no alternative. The registry editors bypass the standard safeguards
provided by administrative tools. These safeguards prevent you from entering
conflicting settings or settings that are likely to degrade performance or
damage your system. Editing the registry directly can have serious, unexpected
consequences that can prevent the system from starting and require that you
reinstall Windows 2000. To configure or customize Windows 2000, use the
programs in Control Panel or Microsoft Management Console (MMC)
whenever possible.

For information about changing the registry, see Windows 2000 online Help.

Bypassing I/O Counts

By default, Task Manager continuously measures data for process I/O operations
that you can select and display under the Processes tab in Task Manager. In a
multiprocessor environment, this data is shared by the processors on which the
process runs. When a process that generates considerable disk and network I/O,
such as a database service, runs on several processors, updating the shared
measurements of process I/O and global I/O operations can slow the system. You
can improve the performance of I/O-intensive operations on SMP systems if you
configure the system to bypass the global I/O counters and Task Manager process
I/O counters. To do so, add the **CountOperations** entry to the registry as a
REG_DWORD in HKEY_LOCAL_MACHINE\SYSTEM\CurrentControlSet
\Control\Session Manager\I/O System\. Set the entry value to 0. When so
configured, Task Manager no longer provides per-process I/O measurements. For
more information about Task Manager, see "Overview of Performance
Monitoring" earlier in this book.

Configuring Disk Alignment

Windows 2000 has an internal structure called the *master boot record* (MBR) that limits the maximum number of hidden sectors to 63. (For more information about the master boot record, see "Disk Concepts and Troubleshooting" in this book.) This characteristic of the MBR causes the default starting sector for disks that report more than 63 sectors per track to be the 64th sector. As a result, when programs transfer data to or from disks that have more than 63 sectors per track, misalignment can occur at the track level, with allocations beginning at a sector other than the starting sector. This misalignment can defeat system optimizations of I/O operations designed to avoid crossing track boundaries.

Additional disk-design factors make proper alignment even more difficult to achieve. For example, track information reported by disks is not always accurate. In addition, many disks have different numbers of sectors on different tracks (as might be the case with the outer bands versus the inner bands). Diskpar.exe, a sample program on the *Windows 2000 Resource Kit* companion CD, shows how you can use Windows 2000 APIs to obtain and set partition information. By applying the same functions used in this tool, you can avoid performance loss due to disk misalignment on disks with large track sizes and alignment optimizations.

Working with Disk Counters

Windows 2000 includes counters that monitor the activity of physical disks (including removable media drives) and logical volumes. The PhysicalDisk object provides counters that report physical-disk activity; the LogicalDisk object provides counters that report statistics for logical disks and storage volumes. These counters measure disk throughput, queue length, usage, and other data. The interrelationships between different aspects of disk performance make it useful to monitor them simultaneously. The operating system enables a driver called Diskperf.sys to activate the disk monitoring counters. By default, the operating system activates only the PhysicalDisk performance counters. Users must activate the LogicalDisk counters manually using the **diskperf** command. See the following procedure for activating disk counters with the **diskperf** command.

▶ **To use the diskperf command to enable LogicalDisk object counters**

- At the command prompt, type **diskperf −yv**

The **diskperf** command takes the following syntax:

diskperf [−y[d|v] | −n[d|v]] [*computer_name*]

Use **−y** to enable counters and **−n** to disable counters. To specify the type of counters, include **d** for physical disk drives or **v** for logical disk drives or storage volumes. When the operating system starts up, it automatically sets the **diskperf** command with the **−yd** switch to activate physical disk counters. For more information about using the **diskperf** command, type **diskperf −?** at the command prompt.

The PhysicalDisk object counters provide data on activity for each of the physical disks in your system; the LogicalDisk object counters provide data on logical volumes in your system. The System Monitor user interface identifies physical disks by number starting with 0. If you are monitoring logical disks, it identifies these by drive letter. For logical disks consisting of multiple physical disks, the disk instances might appear as 0 C and disk 1 C, where logical drive C: consists of physical drives 0 and 1.

When monitoring logical volumes, remember that they might share a physical disk and your data might reflect contention between them. If you have a *spanned*, *striped*, or *mirrored* volume with disk controllers that support hardware-enabled redundant array of independent disks (RAID) volumes, the counters report physical disk data for all disks in the stripe or mirror as if they are a single disk. For disks with controllers that use software-enabled RAID, the counters report disk data for each physical disk.

Use the counters described in Table 8.1 to measure disk space, disk throughput, and disk utilization.

Table 8.1 Performance Objects and Counters for Disk Monitoring

Counter	Description
LogicalDisk\% Free Space	Reports the percentage of unallocated disk space to the total usable space on the logical volume. When calculating the _Total instance, the %Free Space counters recalculate the sum as a percentage for each disk.
	There is no % Free Space counter for the PhysicalDisk object.
LogicalDisk\PhysicalDisk \Avg. Disk Bytes/Transfer	Measures the size of input/output (I/O) operations. The disk is efficient if it transfers large amounts of data relatively quickly.
	Watch this counter when measuring maximum throughput.
	To analyze transfer data further, use Avg. Disk Bytes/Read and Avg. Disk Bytes/Write.

(continued)

Table 8.1   Performance Objects and Counters for Disk Monitoring *(continued)*

Counter	Description
LogicalDisk|PhysicalDisk \Avg. Disk sec/Transfer	Indicates how fast data is being moved (in seconds). Measures the average time of each data transfer, regardless of the number of bytes read or written. Shows the total time of the read or write, from the moment it leaves the Diskperf.sys driver to the moment it is complete.
	A high value for this counter might mean that the system is retrying requests due to lengthy queuing or, less commonly, disk failures.
	To analyze transfer data further, use Avg. Disk sec/Read and Avg. Disk sec/Write.
LogicalDisk|PhysicalDisk \Avg. Disk Queue Length	Tracks the number of requests that are queued and waiting for a disk during the sample interval, as well as requests in service. As a result, this might overstate activity.
	If more than two requests are continuously waiting on a single-disk system, the disk might be a bottleneck. To analyze queue length data further, use Avg. Disk Read Queue Length and Avg. Disk Write Queue Length.
LogicalDisk|PhysicalDisk \Current Disk Queue Length	Indicates the number of disk requests that are currently waiting as well as requests currently being serviced. Subject to wide variations unless the workload has achieved a steady state and you have collected a sufficient number of samples to establish a pattern.
	An instantaneous value or snapshot of the current queue length, unlike Avg. Disk Queue Length, Avg. Disk Read Queue Length, and Avg. Disk Write Queue Length, that reports averages.
LogicalDisk|PhysicalDisk \Disk Bytes/sec	Indicates the rate at which bytes are transferred and is the primary measure of disk throughput.
	To analyze transfer data based on reads and writes, use Disk Read Bytes/sec and Disk Write Bytes/sec, respectively.
LogicalDisk|PhysicalDisk \Disk Transfers/sec	Indicates the number of read and writes completed per second, regardless of how much data they involve. Measures disk utilization.
	If value exceeds 50 (per physical disk in the case of a stripe set), then a bottleneck might be developing.
	To analyze transfer data based on reads and writes, use Disk Read/sec and Disk Writes/sec, respectively.
LogicalDisk \Free Megabytes	Reports the amount of bytes on the disk that are not allocated.
	There is no Free Megabytes counter for the PhysicalDisk object.

(continued)

Table 8.1   Performance Objects and Counters for Disk Monitoring *(continued)*

Counter	Description
LogicalDisk|PhysicalDisk \Split IO/sec	Reports the rate at which the operating system divides I/O requests to the disk into multiple requests. A split I/O request might occur if the program requests data in a size that is too large to fit into a single request or if the disk is fragmented. Factors that influence the size of an I/O request can include application design, the file system, or drivers. A high rate of split I/O might not, in itself, represent a problem. However, on single-disk systems, a high rate for this counter tends to indicate disk fragmentation.
LogicalDisk|PhysicalDisk \% Disk Time	Reports the percentage of time that the selected disk drive is busy servicing read or write requests. Because this counter's data can span more than one sample, and consequently overstate disk utilization, compare this value against % Idle Time for a more accurate picture.
	By default this counter cannot exceed 100 percent; however, you can reset the registry to allow System Monitor to display percentages exceeding 100 percent if appropriate. For information about this adjustment and other aspects of performance data collection and reporting, see "Performance Objects" in "Overview of Performance Monitoring" in this book.
LogicalDisk|PhysicalDisk \% Disk Write Time	Reports the percentage of time that the selected disk drive is busy servicing write requests.
LogicalDisk|PhysicalDisk \% Disk Read Time	Reports the percentage of time that the selected disk drive is busy servicing read requests.
LogicalDisk|PhysicalDisk \% Idle Time	Reports the percentage of time that the disk system was not processing requests and no work was queued. Notice that this counter, when added to % Disk Time, might not equal 100 percent, because % Disk Time can exaggerate disk utilization.

When working with the disk-time or disk-queue length counters, be aware of the following limitations that might yield unlikely counter values.

- The % Disk Read Time and % Disk Write Time counters can exaggerate disk time. This is because they report busy time based on the duration of the I/O request, which includes time spent in activities other than reading to or writing from the disk. It then sums up all busy time for all requests and divides it by the elapsed time of the sample interval. If multiple requests are in process at a time, the total request time is greater than the time of the sample interval; as a result, reported disk utilization can exceed actual utilization.

- Counter values that report sums can be misleading for multidisk systems. When you look at the _Total instance for the % Disk Time or disk-queue counters on a multidisk system, the counters report values totaled for all disks and do not divide these totals over the number of disks in use. Therefore, in a system with one idle disk and one disk that is 100 percent busy, it can appear as if all disks are 100 percent busy.

The following sections describe how you can use disk-monitoring counters to observe available space on the disk and to observe the efficiency of disk operations as you become acquainted with your system's disk performance.

Monitoring Disk Space

It is important to monitor the amount of available storage space on your disk because programs might fail due to an inability to allocate space. In addition, low disk space might make it impossible for your paging file to grow to support virtual memory. Fragmentation also has this effect. For information about setting the paging file size for optimal performance, see "Evaluating Memory and Cache Usage" in this book.

Use the % Free Space and Free Megabytes counters to monitor disk space. If the available space is becoming low, you might want to run Disk Cleanup in the Disk Properties dialog box, compress the disk, or move some files to other disks. Notice that disk compression incurs some performance loss.

Another option is Remote Storage, which enables you to create virtual disk storage out of tape or optical drives. When you use this service, infrequently accessed files are moved to tape or to other media storage. Remote Storage volumes are well suited for data that you need to access only at certain intervals, such as quarterly reports. For more information about remote storage options, see "Data Storage and Management" in this book.

If you are using NTFS and you want to restrict the amount of space allocated by individual users, use the Quota tab in Disk Properties. Notice that using quotas results in a small performance loss. If you are not using NTFS, you can set an alert on the % Free Space counter to track dwindling disk space.

Note Free space on a Distributed file system (Dfs) share can change as you move from one directory to another within a Dfs share namespace. Thus, when accessing network shares, do not assume that the amount of free space you see at the root is available throughout the entire tree.

Even if you are not currently short on disk space, you need to be aware of the storage requirements for applications you are running. Complete the following procedure to determine whether your disk has adequate space for your needs.

▶ **To evaluate the adequacy of your system's disk capacity**

1. For best results, start with 1 GB (although the minimum disk size required to install the operating system might be lower).

2. Add the total size of all applications.

3. Add the size of the paging file (this depends on the amount of memory; this size should be at least twice that of system memory).

4. Add the amount of disk space budgeted per user (if a multiuser system), multiplied by the number of users.

5. Multiply by 130 percent to allow room for expansion (this percentage can vary based on your expected growth).

The result is the size of disk you need.

Note Although not exactly a disk-storage issue, disk fragmentation slows the transfer rate and seek times of your disk system and you should monitor for increasing disk fragmentation. On single-disk systems, you can use the Split IO/sec counter to determine the degree of fragmentation of your disks. Defragment the disk if this counter rate is consistently high and run Disk Defragmenter periodically to keep stored data organized for best performance.

Figure 8.2 shows a graph of disk counters including % Free Space. Notice that the % Free Space counter begins to rise approximately half way through the graph. This illustration shows changes that result from deleting files on the disk.

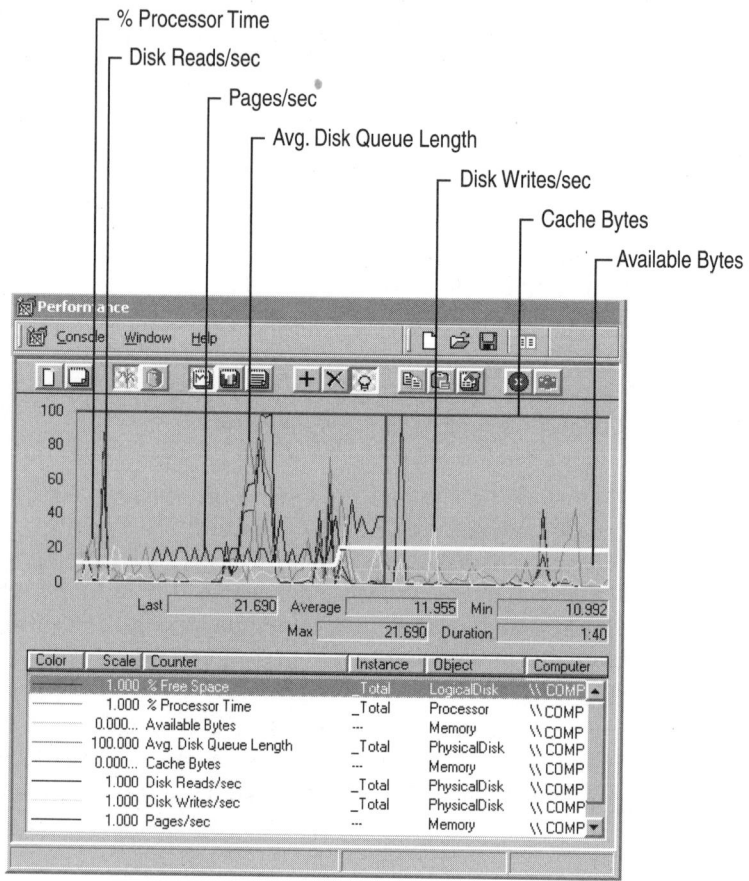

Figure 8.2   Increase in % Free Space Counter

Monitoring Disk Efficiency

Along with disk capacity, you should consider disk throughput when evaluating your starting configuration. Use the bus, controller, cabling, and disk technologies that produce the best throughput that is practical and affordable. Most workstations perform adequately with the most moderately priced disk components. However, if you want to obtain the best performance, you might want to evaluate the latest disk components available.

If your configuration contains different types of disks, controllers, and buses, the differences in their designs can have an influence on throughput rates. You might want to test throughput using these different disk systems to determine if some components produce less favorable results overall or for certain types of activity, and replace those components as needed. In addition, the use of certain kinds of volume-set configurations can offer performance benefits. For example, using stripe sets can provide better performance because they increase throughput by enabling multiple disks to service sequential or clustered I/O requests. System Monitor supports monitoring volume sets with the same performance objects and counters provided for individual disks. Notice that hardware-based RAID devices report all activity to a single physical disk and do not show distribution of disk operations among the individual disks in the array. For more information about using striped volumes, see Windows 2000 online Help.

Be aware of the seek time, rotational speed, access time, and the data transfer rate of your disks by consulting manufacturer documentation. Also consider the bandwidth of cabling and controllers. The slowest component determines the maximum possible throughput, so be sure to monitor each component.

To compare the performance of different disks, monitor the same counters and activity on the disks. If you find differences in performance, you might want to distribute workload to the better performing disk or replace slower performing components.

Preparing for Comparison Testing

If you want to know more about the volume and rate of activity through the disk system, monitor the reading and writing activity as described in the following sections. Before you begin to test disk efficiency, complete the following steps to ensure valid results:

- When testing disk performance, log performance data to another physical disk or computer so that it does not interfere with the disk you are testing. If you cannot do this, log to another logical volume on the drive, or measure monitoring overhead during an idle period and subtract that overhead from your data to ensure your results include only disk-specific data and not overhead from other activity.

- Monitor individual instances whenever practical. Summed values and the _Total instance can provide overstated values. For more information about interpreting counter data, see "Working with Disk Counters" earlier in this chapter.

- Remember to defragment your disk before testing. If your disk is nearly full, the remaining free space is likely to be fragmented, which adds to the seek time of I/O write operations as the disk looks for each sector of free space.

- Ensure that disks being monitored are not compressed or encrypted, to avoid having these features add overhead during monitoring. However, if you plan to use these features, testing performance with the features deployed can yield results that are more representative of your production environment.

The following are suggested tests to perform to learn about your disk system's performance.

Testing Maximum Throughput

A maximum throughput test tells you about one of the limits of your system. To conduct a maximum throughput test, you can use one of the request-generation programs that are publicly available on the World Wide Web. Use the following counters on the PhysicalDisk and LogicalDisk objects for this test:

- Avg. Disk Read Queue Length
- Avg. Disk Bytes/Read
- Avg. Disk sec/Read
- Disk Read Bytes/sec
- Disk Reads/sec

Figure 8.3 illustrates a test of maximum throughput. Notice that the values for Disk Read Bytes/sec and Avg. Disk Read Queue Length become extremely high in this graph.

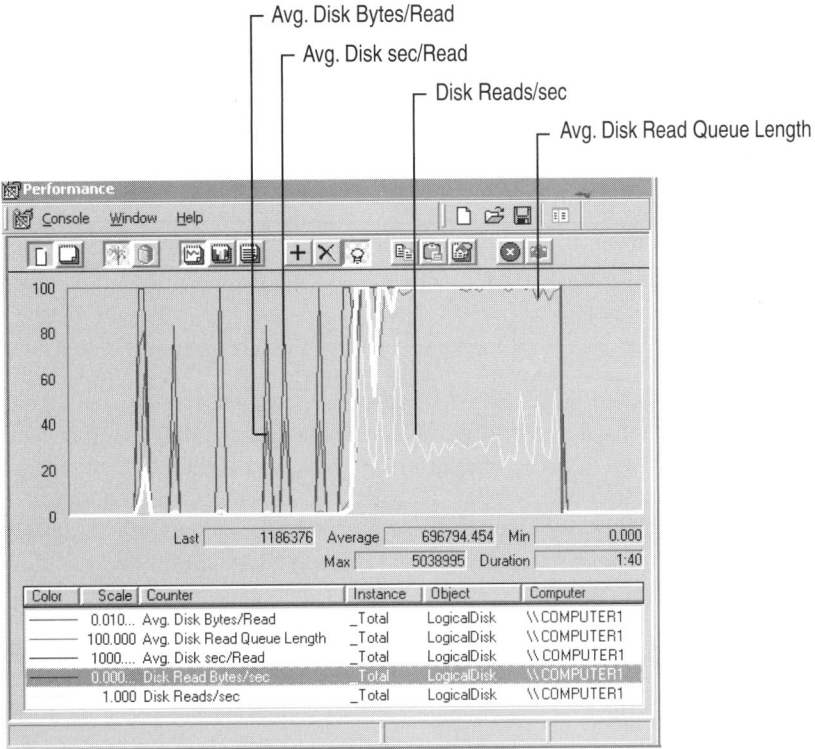

Figure 8.3   A Disk Reaching Maximum Throughput

After you determine the maximum throughput for your disk, you can adjust the load on your disk so it does not become a bottleneck.

Testing Reading vs. Writing

Some disks and disk configurations perform better when reading than when writing. You can compare the reading and writing capabilities of your disks by reading from a physical disk and then writing to the same physical disk. To measure reading from and writing to disk, log the Logical and Physical Disk objects in System Monitor, then chart the counters shown in Table 8.2.

Table 8.2   Counters for Measuring Reading and Writing

For information on	Counters for reads	Counters for writes
Average size of the request	Avg. Disk Bytes/Read	Avg. Disk Bytes/Write
Average duration of the request	Avg. Disk sec/Read	Avg. Disk sec/Write
Rate of transfer for the type of request	Disk Read Bytes/sec	Disk Write Bytes/sec
Rate at which requests are processed	Disk Reads/sec	Disk Writes/sec

You might see some variations in the time it takes to read from or write to disk on standard disk configurations. For example, disks with fast write caches can complete write operations very quickly if there is sufficient idle time between random writes. Also, if reads are sequential, read operations might also occur very quickly, provided the disk has had time to prefetch data. Prefetching data is the process whereby data that is expected to be requested is read ahead into the onboard cache.

On RAID 5 volumes and stripe sets, reading is faster than writing. When you read, you read only the data; when you write, you read, modify, and write the *parity*, as well as the data. The exception to this rule is full-stripe writes. If entire stripes are being written, there is no need to read the old data or parity.

Mirrored volumes also are usually faster at reading than writing, and are faster at writing than RAID 5 volumes. When a mirrored subsystem gets a read request, it chooses one of the two or more disk sources to service the request, in a round-robin fashion, or based on disk utilization.

When you start writing to the disk during a read operation that you are monitoring, you will notice some dips in the curves of graphed data for read activity. This is because the application doing the reads must stop briefly to allow the write operation to proceed and then, when the write is finished, the read operation resumes. You can observe this as Performance Logs and Alerts service logs data.

Figure 8.4 shows the effect of writing on the efficiency of the reads. Notice how the increase of reading activity is accompanied by a slight decrease in writing.

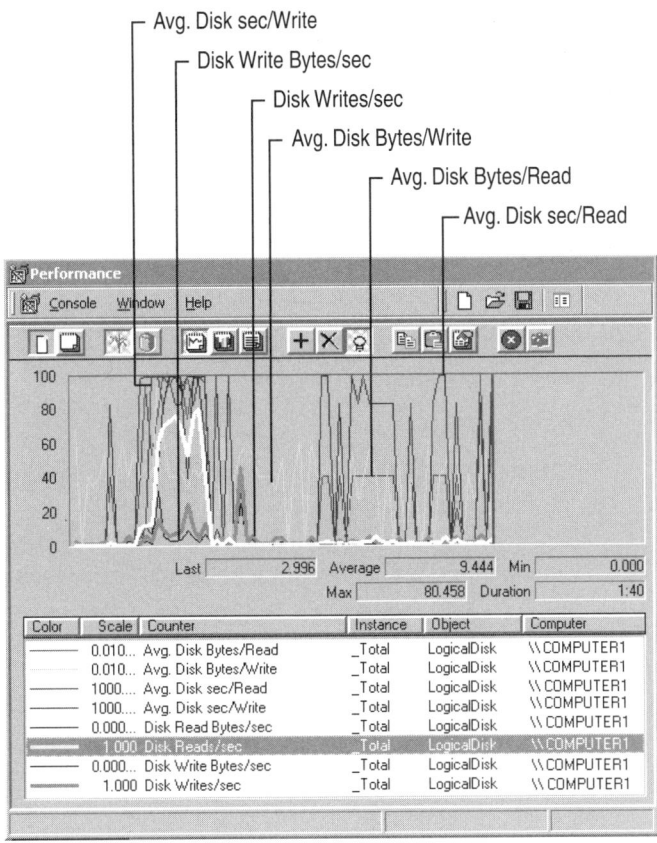

Figure 8.4   How I/O Operations are Affected by Competing Activity

Establishing a Baseline for Disk Usage

Start your disk monitoring process by establishing a *baseline*, which is the level of performance you can expect during typical usage and workloads. Establishing a baseline consists of collecting and analyzing data about typical disk usage under typical disk load.

Data Collection

Monitor disk counters along with counters from other objects. The following is a list of recommended counters.

- LogicalDisk\% Free Space
- PhysicalDisk\Disk Reads/sec
- PhysicalDisk\Disk Writes/sec
- PhysicalDisk\Avg.Disk Queue Length
- Memory\Available Bytes
- Memory\Cache Bytes
- Memory\Pages/sec
- Processor(*All_Instances*)\% Processor Time
- System\Processor Queue Length

For server computers add networking counters. These include the following:

- Network Segment\% Net Utilization (you must enable the Network Monitor Driver protocol to use this counter).
- Transmission counters such as Segments/sec, Datagrams/sec, or Frames/sec (for the object installed by the networking protocol in use).
- Application counters such as Server\Bytes Transmitted/sec or Server\Bytes Received/sec for the Server service

Figure 8.5 depicts a typical display for collecting overall system performance data.

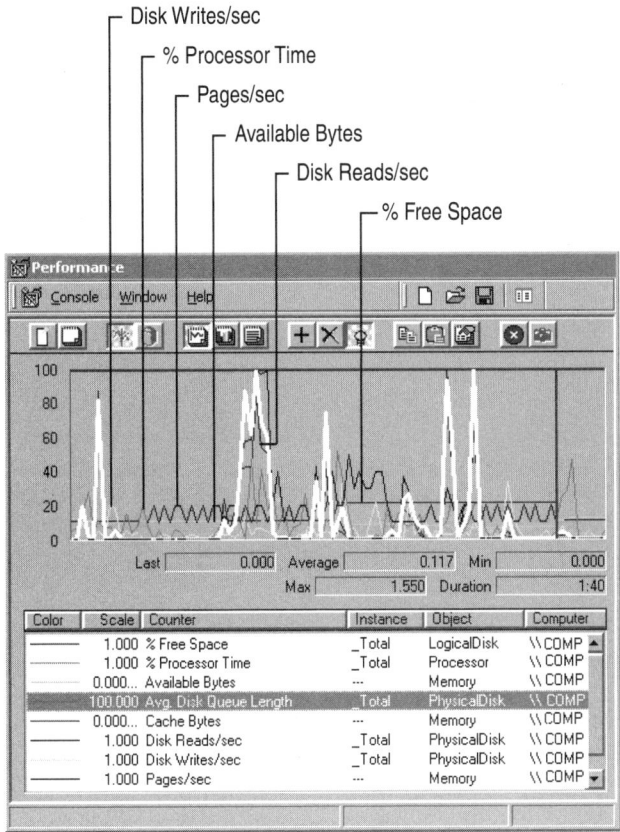

Figure 8.5   Counter Configuration for Baseline Monitoring

Observe activity at various times of day over a range of intervals, starting with one day, one week, one month, and so on. Over time a pattern develops, and you can see that the data tends to fall consistently within a particular range of values —that resulting range is your baseline.

You can monitor for short intervals such as two to five seconds, if your workload is characterized by random bursts of heavy activity. Otherwise 60-second intervals are adequate. If system demands fluctuate during the day, you might want to take shorter samples during periods of heaviest activity and longer samples when activity is tapering off.

For best results during monitoring, try to isolate the disk so that workload unrelated to your test does not affect your results. If you are logging performance to a disk that you are monitoring, values for the disk reflect a small amount of writing activity for that logging.

Data Analysis

While analyzing values at specific times, notice the type of work being performed on your system. Knowing the schedule and nature of your workload is important if you need to reschedule that work or distribute to other systems for better performance.

When interpreting log data, remember the limitations of the performance counters that report sums or that report disk time. The counters sum the totals rather than recalculate them over the number of disks. In addition, disk-time percentage counters cannot exceed 100 percent. Instead, use the Avg. Disk Queue Length, Avg. Disk Read Queue Length, and Avg. Disk Write Queue Length counters to display disk activity as a decimal, rather than a percentage, so that it displays values over 1.0 (100 percent). Then, remember to recalculate the values over the whole disk configuration.

Note Although disk-time percentage counters cannot exceed 100 percent by default, you can reset the registry to allow System Monitor to display percentages exceeding 100 percent if appropriate. For information about this adjustment and other aspects of performance data collection and reporting, see "Performance Objects" in "Overview of Performance Monitoring" in this book.

In general, you can exclude spiking values from your baseline, but make sure you understand what causes them. For example, if you run a weekly backup every Friday night it is acceptable to see out-of-range disk values during that time. But it is important that you know why the spikes are happening. If the pattern starts to shift or you feel that the baseline performance is not satisfactory, use additional counters to monitor disk activity and usage as described in the following sections. You might need to upgrade resources as described in "Resolving Disk Bottlenecks" later in this chapter. If you have access to source code for applications that are in use, you might want to fine-tune these for more efficient data access.

When counter values fall outside the range established for your baseline, follow the instructions contained in "Investigating Disk Performance Problems" later in this chapter. If you encounter a problem or need information about how to improve performance, see "Resolving Disk Bottlenecks" later in this chapter.

Investigating Disk Performance Problems

Several conditions must exist in order for you to determine that a disk bottleneck exists. These are a sustained rate of disk activity well above your baseline, persistent disk queues longer than two per disk, and the absence of a significant amount of paging. Without this combination of factors, it is unlikely that you have a bottleneck. However, if you suspect a disk-specific performance problem, monitor the following types of counters:

- Paging counters (under the Memory object): Pages/sec, Page Reads/sec, Page Writes/sec

- Usage counters: % Disk Time, % Disk Read Time, % Disk Write Time, % Idle Time, Disk Reads/sec, Disk Writes/sec, Disk Transfers/sec

- Queue-length counters: Avg. Disk Queue Length, Avg. Disk Read Queue Length, Avg. Disk Write Queue Length, Current Disk Queue Length

- Throughput counters: Disk Bytes/sec, Disk Read Bytes/sec, Disk Write Bytes/sec

---

Note   Although not reflected in disk activity, the rate of interrupt generation by your disk hardware can have a systemwide performance impact. Disk I/O can sometimes generate a sufficient number of interrupts to slow the performance of the processor. Although this does not constitute a "disk" bottleneck, it *is* a processor bottleneck caused by the disk system that can slow the responsiveness of the whole computer. For more information about monitoring disk interrupts and reducing their impact on system performance, see "Analyzing Processor Activity" in this book.

The following sections describe how you interpret the values of these counters to reveal or rule out a bottleneck.

Monitoring Paging

The symptoms of a memory shortage are very similar to those of a disk bottleneck. When physical memory is scarce, the system starts writing the contents of memory to disk and reading in smaller blocks more frequently (this process is called *paging*). The less memory you have, the more the disk is used, resulting in a greater load on the disk system. Therefore, it's important to monitor memory counters along with disk counters when you suspect a performance problem with your disk system.

Monitor paging activity along with disk reading and writing, using the following counters:

- Avg. Disk Queue Length
- Disk Reads/sec
- Disk Writes/sec
- Memory\Pages/sec
- Memory\Page Reads/sec
- Memory\Page Writes/sec

Figure 8.6 shows how a memory shortage can cause disk counters to indicate a problem.

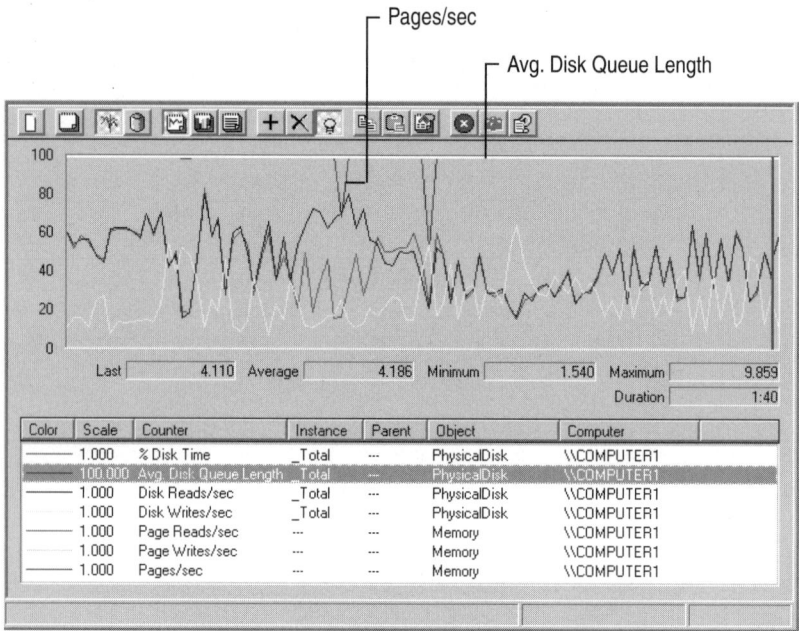

Figure 8.6   Paging Activity Compared with Disk Activity

Notice that this figure shows a long disk queue, accompanied by a high rate of paging. Compare the number of page reads against the number of disk reads to see how many times the system accessed the disk to retrieve pages that were not found in memory, or to write pages to free up memory for new data coming in from the disk. When these values are high, the system does not have sufficient memory. Without inclusion of the memory counters to reveal this behavior, you might have assumed that the disk was inadequate. Upgrading the disk in this situation would not have cured the problem.

For more information about measuring memory and identifying memory shortages, see "Evaluating Memory and Cache Usage" in this book.

Monitoring Usage

In general, a high-performance disk is capable of about 50 to 70 random or up to 160 sequential I/O operations per second. The components you are using, as well as the request size, bus speed, and other factors, determine your system's capacity. Judge the maximum acceptable usage that your system can sustain based on your experience. Disk-time values should not consistently exceed the rate you've established as your baseline for performance. Consistent values in the 70 percent to 85 percent range are a definite cause for concern. However, if a queue is developing, lower percentages might indicate a disk that is unable to handle the load. If you see extremely high rates of disk usage, investigate the factors that might be responsible. Monitoring Disk Transfers/sec (a counter with values equal to the sum of Disk Reads/sec and Disk Writes/sec) or the individual counters Disk Reads/sec and Disk Writes/sec can show you the number of requests for service by the disk; the values of these counters provide a measure of disk demand.

If your workloads consist of random bursts of high activity, you might see high activity rates followed by long periods of idle time. If you only look at the average counter values with these types of workload, it can appear that your disk isn't very busy even though it was bottlenecked during those bursts of high activity. To determine how well your disk system is handling these bursts, sample at short intervals when the activity occurs.

Note The disk time counters can yield inaccurate values when multiple disks are in use. You can compensate for this by monitoring % Idle Time and comparing its value with the values reported by the % Disk Time, % Disk Read Time, and % Disk Write Time counters.

Figure 8.7 depicts maximum disk usage and the development of a queue.

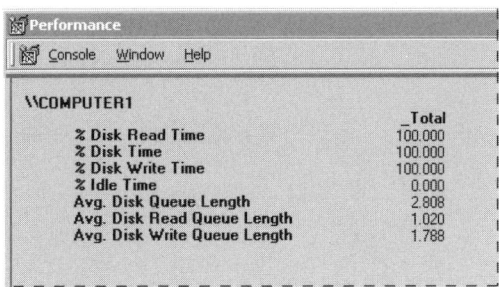

Figure 8.7   High Disk Time Values

Monitoring Queue Length

To determine the number of I/O requests queued for service, track Avg. Disk Queue Length for LogicalDisk or PhysicalDisk. Notice that this might overstate the true length of the queue, because the counter includes both queued and in-service requests. If the value of Avg. Disk Queue Length exceeds twice the number of spindles, then you are likely developing a bottleneck. With a volume set, a queue that is never shorter than the number of active physical disks indicates that you are developing a bottlcneck.

Figure 8.8 shows a disk bottleneck with high disk usage and a long queue.

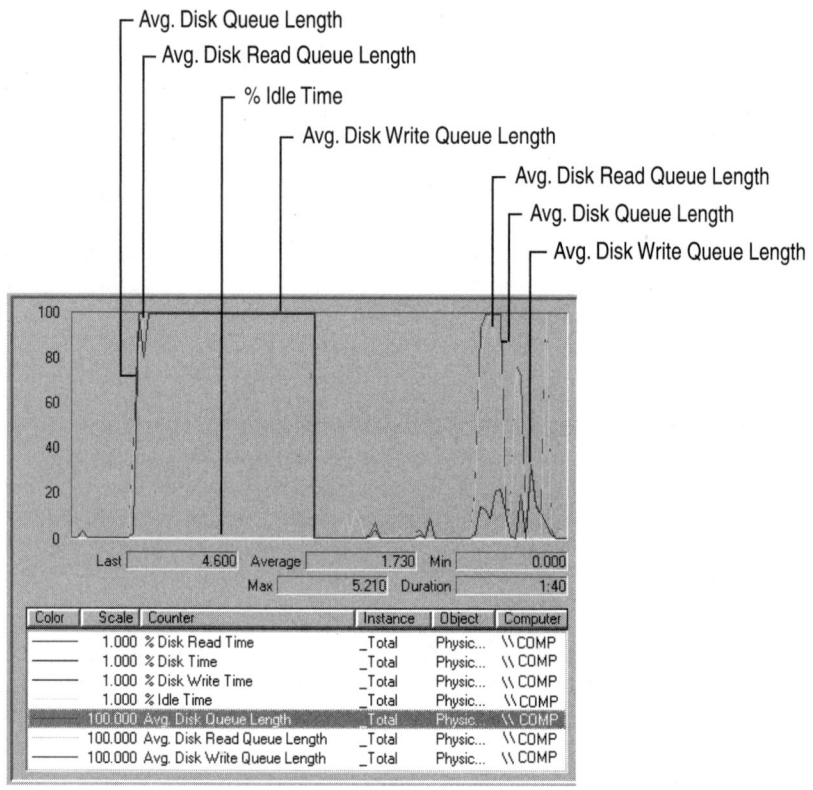

Figure 8.8   High Disk Usage and a Long Queue

Resolving Disk Bottlenecks

A disk that is developing a bottleneck might cause the entire system to slow. If you determine that disk resources are responsible for an overall decrease in system performance, you need to find a solution quickly. Although you might assume that installing another disk offers a quick fix, the right solution to your performance problem depends on the cause of the bottleneck.

Adding a disk is an appropriate solution if you can move files to a new disk, if you can create a stripe set, or if you are out of space. However, for disk-space problems only, you might want to compress your drive, provided that the processor has available cycle to handle the compression activity and that your disk requests are typically large. For a multiuser system, you can also implement disk quotas to restrict growth of user files.

If your disk system is too slow, consider the following alternative steps:

- Rule out a memory shortage. When memory is scarce, the Virtual Memory Manager writes more pages to disk, resulting in increased disk activity. Because low memory is a common cause of bottlenecks, make sure that this is not the source of the problem before adding hardware. Also, make sure to set the paging file to an appropriate size as described in "Evaluating Memory and Cache Usage" in this book.

- Defragment the disk using Disk Defragmenter. For information about using Disk Defragmenter, see Windows 2000 online Help.

- Use Diskpar.exe on the *Windows 2000 Resource Kit* companion CD to reduce performance loss due to misaligned disk tracks and sectors.

- Use stripe sets to process I/O requests concurrently over multiple disks. The type you use depends on your data-integrity requirements. If your applications are read-intensive and require fault tolerance, consider a RAID 5 volume. Use mirrored volumes for fault tolerance and good I/O performance overall. If you do not require fault tolerance, implement stripe sets for fast reading and writing and improved storage capacity. When stripe sets are used, disk utilization per disk should fall due to distribution of work across the volumes and overall throughput should increase.

  When using stripe sets, make sure to use the optimal size of stripe for your workload. In general, the stripe size should be a multiple of the size of the average request.

  If you find that there is no increased throughput when scaling to additional disks in a stripe set, you might be experiencing a bottleneck due to contention between disks for the disk adapter. You might need to add an adapter to better distribute the load.

- Place multiple drives on separate I/O buses, particularly if a disk has an I/O-intensive workload.

- Distribute workload among multiple drives. For example, for database applications, you might want to put transaction logs on a separate spindle from data. Notice that writing to a log file is a sequential operation and tends to be more efficient than the random operations typical of accessing data in a database.

  If you are unsure of a suitable distribution for network applications, track users and the files they work with in order to plan an efficient distribution by means of the auditing capability of the NTFS file system. This tells you which disks are getting the most usage and help you determine whether you should redistribute workloads. For more information about auditing, see Windows 2000 Server Help.

  Windows Clustering and Distributed File System provide solutions for load balancing on different drives. For more information about these technologies, see "Distributed File System" in the *Microsoft® Windows® 2000 Server Resource Kit Distributed Systems Guide*.

- Limit your use of file compression or encryption. These features can add some overhead and you should use them sparingly if not required by your enterprise and if performance is critical.

- When obtaining disk systems, use the most intelligent and efficient components available for your disk system, including controller, I/O bus, cabling, and the disk. Upgrade to faster-speed or wider-bandwidth components as necessary. These measures generally decrease transfer time and improve throughput. Use intelligent drivers that support interrupt moderation or interrupt avoidance to alleviate the interrupt activity for the processor due to disk I/O.

Evaluating Cache and Disk Usage by Applications

If you are an application developer, you might want to know if your programs read and write data efficiently to and from the disk, as well as how they utilize locality and manage the file-system cache. This section provides information to help you identify situations in which you can improve the I/O performance of applications.

Random and Sequential Data Access

Comparing random versus sequential operations is one way of assessing application efficiency in terms of disk use. Accessing data sequentially is much faster than accessing it randomly because of the way in which the disk hardware works. The seek operation, which occurs when the disk head positions itself at the right disk cylinder to access data requested, takes more time than any other part of the I/O process. Because reading randomly involves a higher number of seek operations than does sequential reading, random reads deliver a lower rate of throughput. The same is true for random writing. You might find it useful to examine your workload to determine whether it accesses data randomly or sequentially. If you find disk access is predominantly random, you might want to pay particular attention to the activities being done and monitor for the emergence of a bottleneck.

For workloads of either random or sequential I/O, use drives with faster rotational speeds. For workloads that are predominantly random I/O, use a drive with faster seek time.

For workloads that have high I/O rates, consider using stripe sets because they add physical disks, increasing the system's ability to handle concurrent disk requests. Notice, however, that stripe sets enabled in software can cause an increase in consumption of the processor. Hardware-enabled RAID sets eliminate this impact on the processor but increase the consumption of processing cycles on the hardware RAID adapter.

Note Even when an application reads records sequentially, if the file is fragmented throughout the disk or disks, the I/O will not be sequential. If the disk-transfer rate on a sequential or mostly sequential read operation deteriorates over time, run Disk Defragmenter on the disk and test again. When fragmentation occurs, data is not organized in contiguous clusters on the disk. Fragmentation slows performance because back-and-forth head movement is slow.

I/O Request Size

The size of requests and the rate at which they are sent are important for evaluating the way applications work with the disk. If you are an application developer, you can use the counters, such as Avg. Disk Bytes/Read, that reveal these types of information about I/O requests.

It is typically faster and more efficient to read a few large records than many small ones. However, transfer rates eventually peak due to the fact that the disk is moving blocks of data so large that each transfer occurs more slowly—although its total throughput is quite high. Unfortunately, it is not always easy to control this factor. However, if your system is used to transfer many small units of data, this inefficiency might help to explain, though not resolve, high disk use.

Requests should be at least 8 KB, and, if possible, 64 KB. Sequential I/O requests of 2 KB consume a substantial amount of processor time, which affects overall system performance. However, if you can be sure that only 2 KB of data is necessary, doing a 2 KB I/O is the most efficient, because a larger I/O wastes *direct memory access (DMA)* controller bandwidth. As the record size increases, the throughput increases and the transfer rate falls because it takes fewer reads to move the same amount data.

Using 64 KB requests results in faster throughput with very little processor time. Maximum throughput typically occurs at 64 KB, although some devices might have a higher maximum throughput size. When transferring data blocks greater than 64 KB, the I/O subsystem breaks the transfers into 64-KB blocks. Above 64 KB, the transfer rate drops sharply, and throughput levels off. Processor use and interrupts also appear to level off at 64 KB.

Investigating Disk Usage by Applications

Applications rarely read or write directly to disk. Instead, application code and data is typically mapped into the file system cache and copied from there into the working set of the application. When the application creates or changes data, the data is mapped into the cache and is then written back to the disk in batches. The disk is used only when an application requests a single write-through to disk or it instructs the file system not to use the cache at all for a file, usually because it is doing its own buffering. For this reason, tracking the cache and memory counters provides a way of investigating disk usage by your application. You can find information about monitoring cache and memory counters in "Evaluating Memory and Cache Usage" earlier in this book.

When monitoring disk usage by applications, you might find that applications that submit all I/O requests simultaneously tend to produce exaggerated values for the % Disk Time, % Disk Read Time, % Disk Write Time, and Avg. Disk sec/Transfer counters. Although throughput might be the same for applications that submit I/O requests intermittently, the values of counters that time requests will be much lower. It is important to understand your applications and factor their I/O methods into your analysis.

If you are writing your own tools to test disk performance, you might want to include the FILE_FLAG_NO_BUFFERING parameter in the open call for your test files. This instructs the Virtual Memory Manager to bypass the cache and go directly to disk.

CHAPTER 9

Monitoring Network
Performance

Communication across a network is increasingly important in the work
environment. Similar to processors or disks on your system, the behavior of the
network has an impact on the operation of your computer. Optimize your system's
performance by analyzing network performance, such as monitoring network
traffic and resource utilization that affects both hardware and software.

In This Chapter

Related Information in the Resource Kit

- For more information about the monitoring process, see "Overview of Performance Monitoring" in this book.

- For more information about monitoring memory and cache usage, see "Evaluating Memory and Cache Usage" in this book.

- For more information about monitoring processor performance, see "Analyzing Processor Activity" in this book.

- For more information about monitoring disk system activity, see "Examining and Tuning Disk Performance" in this book.

- For more information about diagnosing system problems, see "Troubleshooting Strategies" in this book.

- For information about the Transmission Control Protocol/Internet Protocol (TCP/IP), see "Introduction to TCP/IP" in the *Microsoft® Windows® 2000 Server Resource Kit TCP/IP Core Networking Guide.*

- For information about the Browser service, see "Windows 2000 Browser Service" in the *Microsoft® Windows® 2000 Server Resource Kit TCP/IP Core Networking Guide.*

- For information about the NetBEUI protocol, see "NetBEUI" in the *Microsoft® Windows® 2000 Server Resource Kit Internetworking Guide.*

Introduction to Network Performance Analysis

Network performance analysis is a follow-up to other monitoring and tuning efforts that are specific to a workstation or server computer. After you have tested and optimized the client or server system's resources, look at the performance of the network. For information about monitoring and tuning your system's memory, processor, and disk systems, see the optimization chapters of the *Microsoft® Windows® 2000 Server Resource Kit Server Operations Guide* before analyzing the network components.

Figure 9.1 illustrates the sequence for monitoring system performance.

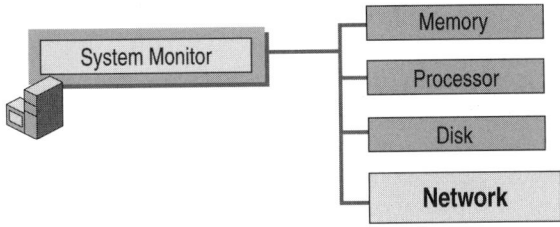

Figure 9.1   Sequence of Monitoring System Performance

When you are ready to examine your network's components, start by checking your networking hardware, including elements such as hubs, cables, routers, switches, and network adapters. For information about proper operation, see the manufacturer's documentation.

Use the most current network adapters and device drivers for your network components. In general, you want the widest bandwidth and highest-performing components possible for your entire system and budget. For example, to maximize the benefits of Windows 2000 networking performance enhancements, use adapters that support task offloading capabilities (checksum offloading, IP Security (IPSEC) offloading, or large send offloading) and interrupt moderation.

Note If you are using media-sense network adapters, Windows 2000 displays an icon in the Taskbar if the adapter becomes disconnected from the network medium. Because the driver supporting the adapter continues to run even when it is not processing traffic, the driver causes the system to continue to use resources unnecessarily. Therefore, you should attend to disconnected adapters when the system reports them. As soon as you see the icon, check the adapter connection. Reconnect the adapter if appropriate; otherwise disable or remove the adapter to avoid the waste of resources associated with this condition.

After you have checked the adapters and drivers, verify that your components are properly configured. Set adapters for speeds appropriate to the devices they are using. Notice that autodetection might not select the optimal speed for operation. For proper configuration, see the product documentation.

Tools for Monitoring Network Performance

Windows 2000 provides two primary utilities for monitoring network performance: System Monitor and Network Monitor. System Monitor, installed with both Windows 2000 Professional and Windows 2000 Server, tracks resource utilization and network throughput. Network Monitor, which you can install on Windows 2000 Server, tracks network throughput in terms of captured network traffic. Network Monitor monitors only local traffic. For monitoring traffic sent to or from any computer on the network, or for remotely capturing frames (for example, over a dial-up network connection) from other computers on the network, upgrade to the version of Network Monitor that ships with Microsoft® Systems Management Server version 2.0, Service Pack 1 or later. To monitor these types of traffic, the system from which you capture must have the Network Monitor driver installed (computers running Windows NT 4.0 must have the Network Monitor Agent version 2.0 installed). There is no support for the Network Monitor driver on Windows 95 or Windows 98.

Use the following tools to examine network traffic and system resource utilization. For information about using System Monitor, see "Overview of Performance Monitoring" in this book.

By default, only an administrator has sufficient privileges to install the Network Monitor driver on a computer to be monitored, to install Network Monitor on the computer used for monitoring, or to start Network Monitor.

System Monitor

The built-in Performance console provides the ability to monitor network activity along with the other performance data on the system. Treat network components as another set of hardware resources to observe as part of your normal performance-monitoring routine.

Network activity can influence the performance not only of your network components but also of your system as a whole. You should monitor other resources along with network activity, such as disk, memory, and processor activity. System Monitor enables you to track network and system activity using a single tool. Use the following counters as part of your normal monitoring configuration:

- Cache\Data Map Hits %
- Cache\Fast Reads/sec

- Cache\Lazy Write Pages/sec
- Logical Disk\% Disk Space
- Memory\Available Bytes
- Memory\Nonpaged Pool Allocs
- Memory\Nonpaged Pool Bytes
- Memory\Paged Pool Allocs
- Memory\Paged Pool Bytes
- Processor(_Total)\% Processor Time
- System\Context Switches/sec
- System\Processor Queue Length
- Processor(_Total)\Interrupts/sec

Monitoring network activity with System Monitor involves examining performance data at each network layer, as defined in the Open Systems Interconnect (OSI) model; for information about this model, see Appendix A, "OSI Model," in the *Windows 2000 Server Resource Kit TCP/IP Core Networking Guide*. System Monitor provides performance objects for collection of data that reflect transmission rates, packet queue lengths, and other network performance data.

Note Because of the overhead of the protocol headers, actual transmission rates might differ from the rates specified for the wire or line in use.

Table 9.1 illustrates the network layers and their associated performance objects.

Table 9.1   Network Layers and Related Performance Objects

OSI layer	Performance objects
Application, Presentation	Browser, Server, Redirector, and Server Work Queues
Session	NBT Connection (NBT is an abbreviation for NetBT, which means NetBIOS over TCP/IP; NetBIOS stands for network basic input/output system)
Transport	Protocol objects: TCP for the Transmission Control Protocol; UDP for the User Datagram Protocol, NetBEUI for NetBIOS, AppleTalk (installed by protocol)

(continued)

Table 9.1   Network Layers and Related Performance Objects *(continued)*

OSI layer	Performance objects
Network	Network Segment (installed when you install the Network Monitor driver), IP for the Internet Protocol, NWLink IPX/SPX for the Microsoft implementation of Internetwork Packet Exchange/Sequenced Packet Exchange (IPX/SPX). NWLink performance objects display only zeros for counters that report on frame activity.
	On systems running Windows NT version 4.0, installing the Network Monitor Agent installed the Network Segment counters.
Data Link, Physical	Network Interface
	These counters are maintained by the driver and can report inaccurate or zero values because of problems with implementation of counters by the driver.

Begin with the lowest-level components and work your way up as you monitor performance data for your network. Monitor the objects described in this chapter over periods of time ranging from days to weeks, to a month. Using this data, determine a performance baseline, the typical level of performance you expect under typical workloads and usage. A performance baseline gives you a point from which to compare performance over time to identify growth trends, changing demands, or the emergence of a bottleneck. If performance within the baseline range becomes unsatisfactory, tune the network as described in "Resolving Network Bottlenecks" later in this chapter.

As with other resources, establish a baseline for network performance. When performance data is incompatible with your baseline values, investigate the cause. Abnormal network counter values on a server often indicate problems with its memory, processor, or disks. For that reason, the best approach to monitoring a server is to watch network counters in conjunction with Processor\% Processor Time, PhysicalDisk\% Disk Time, and Memory\Pages/sec.

For example, if a dramatic increase in Pages/sec is accompanied by a decrease in Bytes Total/sec handled by a server, the computer is probably running short of physical memory for network operations. Most network resources, including network adapters and protocol software, use nonpaged memory. If a computer is paging excessively, it could be because most of its physical memory has been allocated to network activities, leaving a small amount of memory for processes that use paged memory. To verify this situation, check the computer's system event log for entries indicating that it has run out of paged or nonpaged memory. Also monitor the nonpaged pool memory and overall memory counters. For more information about monitoring memory and performance, see "Evaluating Memory and Cache Usage" in this book.

Network Counters

Starting from the physical layer and working up to the application layer of the OSI model, you will monitor the performance objects and their counters described in the following sections.

Network Interface Object

Use the Network Interface object to monitor transmissions starting at the physical layer. The Network Interface object is installed by Transmission Control Protocol/Internet Protocol (TCP/IP) and monitors activity of the IP protocol. The object reports transmissions over the network adapter. There are no separate objects to monitor the adapters over other networking protocols.

When you use the Network Interface object counters, note that the instances include the loopback address, the network adapter, the dial-out wide area network (WAN) wrapper for each device bound under the Routing and Remote Access service, and the dial-up WAN wrapper for each device. The wrapper is code that surrounds network driver interface specification (NDIS) device drivers, providing a uniform interface between protocol drivers and NDIS device drivers and support routines that make the development of an NDIS driver easier.

The instances typically list the loopback address 127.0.0.1 first, and the remaining instances should match the binding order of the TCP/IP protocol. (If Routing and Remote Access does not use IP for a device, its traffic is not counted.) To view the binding order for TCP/IP, in the **Network and Dial-up Connections** dialog box, on the **Connections** menu, click **Advanced**.

Monitor the following Network Interface object counters:

Network Interface\Output Queue Length

Use this counter to indicate the length of the output packet queue. The value should be low. Queues that are one or two items long constitute satisfactory performance; longer queues mean that the adapter is waiting for the network and cannot keep pace with server requests.

Network Interface\Packets Outbound Discarded

Use this counter to determine if the network is saturated. If this counter continuously increases, it might indicate that a network is so busy that the network buffers cannot keep up with the outbound flow of packets.

Network Interface\Bytes Total/sec

Use this counter to determine how the network adapter is performing. The Bytes Total/sec counter should report high values, to indicate a large number of successful transmissions. Compare this value with the value reported by the Network Interface\Current Bandwidth counter, reflecting each adapter's bandwidth. If you see the Bytes Total/sec rate approaching the maximum transfer rate, the probability of collisions on the network increases. This in turn impacts performance by increasing the latency of packet transfer on the network. In this case, you might want to consider increasing the bandwidth or segmenting the network. For example, if using 100 megabit/sec fast Ethernet, and the total rate of bytes transferred per second approaches 65 percent of the maximum network bandwidth, you can improve performance by using a gigabit or faster Ethernet switch to segment the network into smaller networks.

Network Segment Objects

Use this object to report statistics for the local network segment. To use this object, you must have already installed the Network Monitor driver on the computer where you will run System Monitor and on the computer from which you will collect data. For more information about installing Network Monitor, see "Installing Network Monitor" later in this chapter.

Monitor the following Network Segment object counters:

Network Segment\Broadcast Frames Received/sec

Use this counter to establish a baseline when monitored over time. To determine the cause of a problem, investigate large variations from the baseline. Because each computer processes every broadcast, frequent broadcasts mean lower performance. Determine what level of broadcasts is excessive based on past performance and your expectations for the local site.

Network Segment\% Network Utilization

Use this counter to reflect the percentage of network bandwidth used for the local network segment. Use it to monitor the effect of different network operations (such as logon validation or account synchronization). A low value is preferred. This counter should not report values that exceed the maximum recommended for the type of configuration. For example, 30 percent utilization is the maximum recommended for an unswitched Ethernet network. This means that a 10-megabyte (MB) Ethernet network becomes bottlenecked when its throughput exceeds 3 MB per second. If the value of the counter is above 40 percent, collisions can cause problems. You need to determine the appropriate maximum value for this counter based on your network design and topology, and ensure that % Network Utilization does not exceed this limit.

Network Segment\Total Frames Received/sec

Use this counter to indicate when bridges and routers might be saturated. If network traffic exceeds recommended local area network (LAN) capacity, performance typically suffers across the network. To prevent this situation, it is important to monitor network-wide traffic levels, particularly on larger networks with bridges and routers.

Network Protocol Objects

When monitoring protocol counters, you are likely to be most concerned with transmission rates. Monitor these rates using counters such as Bytes Total/sec, Datagrams Received/sec and Datagrams Sent/sec, or Frames Received/sec and Frames Sent/sec. When looking at transfer counters, consider the capacity of your network. The value of Bytes Total/sec should not be close to or matching the network capacity, or the network might already be saturated.

Following is a list of typical protocol objects. Monitor the ones that pertain to the network protocol in use.

- For the TCP/IP protocol, use the TCP, IP, UDP, and Internet Control Message Protocol (ICMP) objects. To monitor traffic at the network layer, use the IP object counters Datagrams Forwarded/sec, Datagrams Received/sec, Datagrams/sec, and Datagrams Sent/sec. To monitor activity at the transport layer, use the TCP object counters Segments Received/sec, Segments Retransmitted/sec, Segments/sec, and Segments Sent/sec. ICMP is used for maintaining route tables and diagnosing problems. UDP is used for DNS host name and IP address resolution and for NetBIOS name resolution by a WINS server.

   You should see high values for segments sent and received over the network. If not, reduce broadcast traffic. UDP\Datagrams/sec indicates the number of broadcasts sent and received. This value should be low. If the retransmission rate is high, there might be a hardware problem, so you need to investigate further with system counters such as the processor counters. Use baseline values to determine when these counters are out of range and might indicate a problem.

- For the NWLink protocol, use the following three objects to monitor: NWLink IPX for computers communicating over the IPX protocol, NWLink NetBIOS for computers communicating over the IPX protocol, and NWLink SPX for computers connecting over the SPX protocol.

   Each of these objects has the following counters that provide information about network transmissions:

   - Bytes Total/sec
   - Frame Bytes Sent/sec
   - Frame Bytes Received/sec
   - Frames Rejected/sec

- NWLink SPX for computers connecting over the SPX protocol.

  Each of these objects has the following counters that provide information about network transmissions:

  - Bytes Total/sec
  - Frame Bytes Sent/sec
  - Frame Bytes Received/sec
  - Frames Rejected/sec

  Bytes Total/sec should be high on an active network. Frames Rejected/sec should be low.

Note NWLink performance objects display only zeros for counters that report on frame activity.

- For the NetBEUI protocol, use the NetBEUI and NetBEUI resource objects. Monitor Bytes Total/sec and other transmission counters such as NetBEUI\Frame Bytes Received/sec and NetBEUI\Frame Bytes Sent/sec. In addition, track Frames Rejected/sec for increasing values. Also include NetBEUI Resource\Times Exhausted, which can indicate if resource buffers are being consumed. Information about the resource objects is also recorded in the event log.
- For the AppleTalk protocol, use the AppleTalk object counters.

For information about these counters, see the Performance Counter Reference on the *Windows 2000 Resource Kit* companion CD.

Improving performance over a slow WAN link under Windows 2000 Server

In general, Windows 2000 is self-tuning, and registry entries related to TCP/IP require no adjustment. If you are using a slow WAN link, adjusting registry entries for TCP/IP can improve performance; however, these changes can adversely affect computers that are short of memory. The following procedure describes how to edit the entries in the registry.

▶ **To edit TCP/IP entries in the registry**

1. On the **Start** menu, click **Run**.
2. In the **Run** dialog box, type **Regedt32**, and then click **OK**.

The following is a list of entries in HKEY_LOCAL_MACHINE\SYSTEM \CurrentControlSet\Services\Tcpip\Parameters that have an effect on performance when connecting by means of a slow WAN link. For information about these and other related registry settings, see "Technical Reference to the Windows 2000 Registry" on the *Windows 2000 Resource Kit* companion CD.

Caution Do not use a registry editor to edit the registry directly unless you have no alternative. The registry editors bypass the standard safeguards provided by administrative tools. These safeguards prevent you from entering conflicting settings or settings that are likely to degrade performance or damage your system. Editing the registry directly can have serious, unexpected consequences that can prevent the system from starting and require that you reinstall Windows 2000. To configure or customize Windows 2000, use the programs in Control Panel or Microsoft Management Console (MMC) whenever possible.

- **TcpMaxConnectRetransmissions**. The value of this entry can be increased to allow a connection over a slow WAN but should not be set so long that connection attempts never time out. The default is 2 and can range from 0 to 0xFF.

- **TcpMaxDataRetransmissions**. The value of this entry can be lengthened although this time-out is automatically doubled every time a transmission is re-attempted. The default is 5 and can range from 0 to 0xFFFFFFFF.

- **TcpWindowSize**. When modifying this entry, set it to the product of the bandwidth multiplied by the length of the "round trip" between the local computer and the server.

- **MaxUserPort**. The value of this entry can be changed to achieve higher throughput by allowing the creation of more sockets. The value can be set to 0xFFFE. The default is 0x1388. The minimum value is 0x400; values 0 to 0x3FF are reserved for services.

- **MaxHashTableSize**. The value of this entry can be changed to achieve higher throughput by allowing for faster look-up on connections. The default is 0x200 and can range from 0x40 to 0x10000. On a server in a multiprocessor environment, do not increase **MaxHashTableSize** beyond the estimated maximum number of concurrent connections.

- **NumTcbTablePartitions**. The value of this entry can be changed to partition the TCP control block (TCB) table to avoid contention. The default is 0x4; the value should be a power of two, that is, 2, 4, 8, 16, 32, and so on. On multiprocessor systems, change the number of partitions to four times the number of processors in your system.

NBT Connection Object

Use this object to track session-layer transmissions between computers. NBT stands for NetBT, an abbreviation for NetBIOS over TCP/IP. This feature provides the NetBIOS programming interface over the TCP/IP protocol. It is used for monitoring routed servers that use NetBIOS name resolution.

Application-Layer Objects

Finally, monitor services or applications at the presentation or application layers. By default, Setup installs the Browser, Redirector, Server, and Server Work Queues objects on computers running Windows 2000. These objects describe performance of file and print services using the Server Message Block (SMB) Protocol.

Note For detailed information about performance objects and counters, see the Performance Counter Reference on the *Windows 2000 Resource Kit* companion CD.

Browser Object

The primary function of the Browser service is to provide a list of computers sharing resources in a domain along with a list of other domain and workgroup names across the wide area network (WAN). This list is provided to clients that view network resources with My Network Places or the **net view** command. Active Directory replaces the computer browser service used in earlier versions of Windows to provide the Network Basic Input/Output System (NetBIOS) name resolution. The browser service in Windows 2000 provides backward compatibility with client computers that are running earlier versions of Windows.

The Browser performance object consists of counters that measure the rates of announcements, enumerations, and other browser transmissions. If your organization is maintaining domains under Windows NT Server version 4.0, use the counters in Table 9.2 for monitoring the Browser service.

Table 9.2   Browser Object Counters

Counter	Description
Browser\Mailslot Allocations Failed	The number of times the datagram receiver has failed to allocate a buffer to hold a user mailslot write.
Browser\Mailslot Opens Failed/sec	Indicates the rate of mailslot messages received by this workstation that were to be delivered to mailslots that are not present on this workstation.
Browser\Mailslot Receives Failed	Indicates the number of mailslot messages that could not be received due to transport failures.

(continued)

Table 9.2   Browser Object Counters *(continued)*

Counter	Description
Browser\Mailslot Writes Failed	The total number of mailslot messages that have been successfully received, but that were unable to be written to the mailslot.
Browser\Missed Mailslot Datagrams	The number of mailslot datagrams that have been discarded due to configuration or allocation limits.
Browser\Missed Server Announcements	The number of server announcements that have been missed due to configuration or allocation limits.
Browser\Missed Server List Requests	The number of requests to retrieve a list of browser servers that were received by this workstation, but could not be processed.
Browser\Server Announce Allocations Failed/sec	The rate of server (or domain) announcements that have failed due to lack of memory.

For information about the NTDS performance object that reports performance data for Active Directory, or about counters that report lightweight directory access protocol (LDAP) activity, see the Performance Counter Reference on the *Windows 2000 Resource Kit* companion CD.

Troubleshooting Performance Problems with the Browser Service

Improving the performance of computers running the Browser service relies primarily on reducing traffic. You can do this in several ways:

- Configure the computer so that it does not send announcements to browsers on the domain and thereby reduce traffic. Do this by editing the registry. Add the **Hidden** registry entry to HKEY_LOCAL_MACHINE\SYSTEM \CurrentControlSet\Services\lanmanserver\parameters with a data type of REG_DWORD and a value of 1 (hidden).

Caution Do not use a registry editor to edit the registry directly unless you have no alternative. The registry editors bypass the standard safeguards provided by administrative tools. These safeguards prevent you from entering conflicting settings or settings that are likely to degrade performance or damage your system. Editing the registry directly can have serious, unexpected consequences that can prevent the system from starting and require that you reinstall Windows. To configure or customize Windows, use the programs in Control Panel or Microsoft Management Console (MMC) whenever possible.

- Reduce the number of browser list entries. If a computer rarely shares network resources, configure it so that it doesn't become a browser server. This will reduce the size of the browse list that must be maintained and transferred upon request. Set the value of the **MaintainServerList** entry in HKEY_LOCAL_MACHINE\SYSTEM \CurrentControlSet\Services\Browser\Parameters to No. For more information about browser service configuration, see "Browser Service" in the *Windows 2000 TCP/IP Core Networking Guide.*

- Eliminate unnecessary network protocols. If a network uses three protocols, all browser announcements and elections will be repeated three times, one for each protocol. If you can reduce the number of protocols, it will have a large impact on reducing browser-related network traffic.

In addition, two registry entries can be configured to control the amount of network traffic generated by the browser. Add the following entries to the registry subkey HKEY_LOCAL_MACHINE\SYSTEM\CurrentControlSet\Services\Browser \Parameters.

- **MasterPeriodicity**. **MasterPeriodicity** specifies how frequently a master browser contacts the domain master browser. The default value is 720 seconds (12 minutes), with a minimum of 300 seconds (five minutes), and a maximum value of 0x418937 (4,294,967 seconds). This entry has the REG_DWORD data type, and can be changed without restarting the computer. Setting the value of this entry too low can increase traffic on the WAN traffic.

- **BackupPeriodicity**. **BackupPeriodicity** specifies how frequently a backup browser contacts the master browser. Add this entry to the registry with the REG_DWORD data type. You must restart Windows 2000 to make changes to this entry effective. The default value for **BackupPeriodicity** is 720 seconds. Changing this value to 1800 (30 minutes) reduces the frequency of browse list updates. This entry does not affect the WAN, because backup browsers always communicate with a local master browser, never with a remote one.

- Limit the number of workgroups on the network.

- Configure a system to be a preferred master browser on each subnet where no domain controller exists.

Redirector Object

Use the Redirector object counters for the Workstation service, and the Server and Server Work Queues objects for the Server service. The counters for these objects describe activity at the presentation layer of the networking architecture, as described in Table 9.3.

Table 9.3   Redirector Object Counters

Counter	Comments
Redirector\Bytes Total/sec	The rate at which the Redirector is processing data bytes. This includes all application and file data in addition to protocol information such as packet headers.
Redirector\Current Commands	The number of requests to the Redirector that are currently queued for service. If this number is much larger than the number of network adapters installed in the computer, you might want to increase the maximum allowance for pending net commands in the **MaxCmds** registry in HKEY_LOCAL_MACHINE\SYSTEM\CurrentControlSet \Services\lanmanserver\parameters. The default value is 5.
Redirector\Network Errors/sec	Serious unexpected errors that generally indicate the Redirector and one or more servers are having serious communication difficulties. For example, a Server Message Block (SMB) Protocol error generates a network error. Look in the system event log for results. You might need to increase the value of the **SessTimeout** registry entry in HKEY_LOCAL_MACHINE\SYSTEM \CurrentControlSet\Services\LanmanWorkstation \Parameters. The default is 45 seconds; values can range from 10 to 65535.
Redirector\Reads Denied/sec	The rate at which the server is unable to accommodate requests for Raw Reads. When a read is more than twice the negotiated buffer size of the server, the Redirector requests a raw read, which, if granted, would permit the transfer of the data without a lot of protocol overhead on each packet. To accomplish this, the server must lock out other requests, so the request is denied if the server is very busy.
Redirector\Server Sessions Hung	The number of active sessions that are timed out and unable to proceed due to a lack of response from the remote server.
Redirector\Writes Denied/sec	The rate at which the server is unable to accommodate requests for raw writes. When a write is much larger than the negotiated buffer size of the server, the Redirector requests a raw write, which, if granted, would permit the transfer of the data without a lot of protocol overhead on each packet. To accomplish this, the server must lock out other requests, so the request is denied if the server is very busy.

Server Object

The Server service supports file and print sharing and is important for communication between local and remote processes. Its companion, the Workstation service, provides network connections and communication. A computer uses the Workstation service to send requests to a server; the Server service responds to those requests. A server computer can run both services.

In general, memory and disk space are considerations on computers running the Server service, and overall server monitoring should include counters for these resources. Because many services might run on top of the Server service, you should also consider the requirements of those services when assessing server requirements. For more information about performance of the Server and Workstation services, monitor the computer using the counters in Table 9.4.

Table 9.4   Server Object Counters

Object\counter	Description
Server\Blocking Requests Rejected	The number of times the server has rejected blocking SMBs due to insufficient count of free work items. Indicates whether the MaxWorkItem or MinFreeWorkItems server entries might need tuning.
Server\Bytes Total/sec	The number of bytes the server has sent to and received from the network. Provides an overall indication of how busy the server is.
Server\Context Blocks Queued/sec	The rate at which work context blocks had to be placed on the server file system process queue to await server action.
	If this counter consistently averages higher than 50 milliseconds, the Server service is a bottleneck for all tasks on remote computers that are issuing remote I/O requests to the server.
Server\Errors System	The number of times an internal server error was detected. Unexpected errors usually indicate a problem with the server.
Server\Pool Nonpaged Failures	The number of times allocations from the nonpaged pool have failed. Indicates that the computer's physical memory is too small.
	If this number consistently increases, the server is running out of the paged or nonpaged pool it originally allocated. If this occurs, you might want to consider increasing the resource.
Server\Pool Nonpaged Peak	The maximum number of bytes of nonpaged pool that the server has had in use at any one point. Indicates how much physical memory the computer should have.

(continued)

Table 9.4   Server Object Counters *(continued)*

Object\counter	Description
Server\Pool Paged Failures	The number of times allocations from the paged pool have failed. Indicates that the computer's physical memory or page file are too small. If this number consistently increases, the server is running out of the paged or nonpaged pool it originally allocated. If this occurs, you might want to consider increasing the resource.
Server\Pool Paged Peak	The maximum number of bytes of nonpaged pool that the server has had in use at any one point. Indicates how much physical memory the computer should have.
Server\Sessions Errored Out	Reports auto-disconnects along with errored-out sessions. To get a more accurate value for errored-out sessions, obtain the value for Server\Sessions Timed Out and reduce the Server\Sessions Errored Out value by that amount.
Server\Work Item Shortages	The number of times that no work item was available or could be allocated to service the incoming request. A work item is the location where the server stores an SMB. The amount available fluctuates between a minimum and maximum value that is configured based on how the server is configured and the amount of memory on the computer. If work item shortages are occurring, it might be caused by an overloaded server. If the Work Item Shortages counter value increases, consider changing the **Maxworkitems** registry entry in HKEY_LOCAL_MACHINE\SYSTEM\ CurrentControlSet\Services\LanmanServer\Parameters. The value can range from 1 to 512. If the actual number of work items consistently matches the maximum set in the registry, the system consistently initiates flow control, which degrades performance.

Some additional counters, although not performance related, provide useful information about server security. These include:

- Server\Errors Access Permissions
- Server\Errors Granted Access
- Server\Errors Logon

Server Work Queues Object

The Server Work Queues performance object consists of counters that monitor the length of queues and objects in the queues. See Table 9.5.

Table 9.5   Server Work Queues Object Counters

Counter	Description
Bytes Transferred/sec	The rate at which the server is sending and receiving bytes with the network clients on this CPU. Use to determine how busy the server is.
Queue Length	The current length of the server work queue for this CPU. A sustained queue length greater than four can indicate microprocessor congestion. This is an instantaneous count, not an average over time.
Total Bytes/sec	The rate at which the server is reading and writing data to and from the files for the clients on this CPU. Use this counter to determine how busy the server is.
Total Operations/sec	The rate at which the server is performing file read and file write operations for the clients on this CPU. This value will always be zero (0) in the Blocking Queue instance. Use this counter to determine how busy the server is.
Work Item Shortages	The number of times that an inadequate number of work items was available. A work item is a request to the server from a client; the server maintains a pool of available work items per CPU to speed processing. A sustained value greater than zero indicates the need to increase MaxWorkItems for the Server service. This value will always be zero (0) in the Blocking Queue instance.

Troubleshooting Problems Involving the Server Service

In some cases, the Server service can be associated with performance problems, as described in this section.

Event log reports an event ID 2009.

An event ID 2009 might appear listed in the event log if the server could not expand an internal table because the table had reached the maximum size. These internal tables track active sessions, resource connections, open files, and open searches, so this error message can be generated by problems involving these activities.

Table 9.6 lists counters you can use to investigate these activities and possible related problems.

Table 9.6   Server Object Counters Used to Troubleshoot Event ID 2009 Events

Type of activity	Possible cause of event	Counters to monitor
Active sessions	No more user IDs (UIDs) exist to satisfy this SMB. This may be the result of maintaining unneeded user sessions on the server. This might include mapped drives in logon scripts or applications that automatically map drives to particular servers.	Redirector\Server Sessions Redirector\Server Sessions Hung
Resource connections	No more free tree IDs (TIDs) exist to satisfy a TreeConnect SMB.	Redirector\Connects Core Redirector\Connects Lan Manager 2.0 Redirector\Connects Lan Manager 2.1 Redirector\Connects Windows NT
Open files	No more file IDs (FIDs) could be allocated to process the various open file SMBs because of a shortage of available FIDs.	Server\Files Open Server\Files Opened Total

(continued)

Table 9.6   Server Object Counters Used to Troubleshoot Event ID 2009 Events *(continued)*

Type of activity	Possible cause of event	Counters to monitor
Open searches	Memory is allocated for search, find, and other SMB calls to store the current search state, but no additional memory could be allocated for storing search buffers. Because the Server service tends to allocate paged pool memory for storing search buffers, shortages of paged pool memory can cause this event.	Server\File Directory Searches Memory\Pool Paged Bytes Server Work Queues\Available Work Items

MS-DOS applications or older applications that do not make Win32 calls do not have a method for closing searches after they complete. In order to handle this situation, the Server service uses several search time parameters to clear the search handle and reclaim the memory allocated to the search buffers. If you want to adjust the search time parameters to avoid events, change the values for the following entries in HKEY_LOCAL_MACHINE\SYSTEM\ CurrentControlSet\Services\lanmanserver\parameters in the Windows 2000 registry:

Subkey	Comments
MaxGlobalOpenSearch	The value of the **MaxGlobalOpenSearch** entry determines the maximum number of open searches allowed by the LanmanServer service. The default value is 4096 with a maximum value of 65536. To allocate more search handles, increase the value of **MaxGlobalOpenSearch** to 16,000 (decimal).
MaxKeepSearch	The value of the **MaxKeepSearch** entry determines the maximum amount of time in seconds that a search will remain open. The default value is 1800 seconds (30 minutes). Decrease the value of **MaxKeepSearch** to 900 seconds (15 minutes).
MinKeepSearch	The value of the **MinKeepSearch** entry determines the minimum amount of time in seconds that a search will remain open. The default value is 480 seconds (8 minutes). Decrease the value of **MinKeepSearch** to 240 seconds (4 minutes).

Caution   Do not use a registry editor to edit the registry directly unless you have no alternative. The registry editors bypass the standard safeguards provided by administrative tools. These safeguards prevent you from entering conflicting settings or settings that are likely to degrade performance or damage your system. Editing the registry directly can have serious, unexpected consequences that can prevent the system from starting and require that you reinstall Windows. To configure or customize Windows, use the programs in Control Panel or Microsoft Management Console (MMC) whenever possible.

Trace Logs

The new trace log feature in Windows 2000 makes it possible to closely associate network input/output operations to the workload on a computer. Trace logs are a component of Performance Logs and Alerts. When configured to include Network TCP/IP activity, trace logs report TCP sends and receives as events, and measure the time required to complete these events, along with the bytes transmitted and other data. Using trace data, you can associate network traffic with the services or applications initiating it with the bandwidth utilization of the service or application. Note that trace logs are not output in readable format and must be parsed. The operating system does not provide a parser for trace logs. For information about creating and configuring trace logs, see Windows 2000 Help.

Network Monitor

Unlike System Monitor, which is used to monitor anything from hardware to software, Network Monitor focuses exclusively on network activity. To understand the traffic and behavior of your network components, install and use Network Monitor.

Network Monitor Features

Network administrators use Microsoft Windows 2000 Network Monitor to view and detect problems on local area networks (LANs). For example, as a network administrator, you can use Network Monitor to diagnose hardware and software problems when two or more computers cannot communicate. You can also copy a log of network activity into a file and then send the file to a professional network analyst or support organization.

Network application developers can use Network Monitor to monitor and debug network applications as they are developed.

Network Monitor monitors the network data stream, which consists of all information transferred over a network at any given time. Prior to transmission, this information is divided by the network software into smaller pieces, called frames or packets. Each frame contains:

- The source address of the computer that sent the message.
- The destination address of the computer that received the frame.
- Headers from each protocol used to send the frame.
- The data or a portion of the information being sent.

The process by which Network Monitor copies frames is referred to as capturing. You can use Network Monitor to capture all local network traffic or you can single out a subset of frames to be captured. You can also make a capture respond to events on your network. For example, you can make the network start an executable file when Network Monitor detects a particular set of conditions on the network.

After you have captured data, you can view it in the Network Monitor user interface. Network Monitor does much of the data analysis for you by translating the raw capture data into its logical frame structure.

For security reasons, Windows 2000 Network Monitor captures only those frames, including broadcast and multicast frames, sent to or from the local computer. Network Monitor also displays overall network segment statistics for broadcast frames, multicast frames, network utilization, total bytes received per second, and total frames received per second.

In addition, to help protect your network from unauthorized use of Network Monitor installations, Network Monitor can detect other installations of Network Monitor that are running on the local segment of your network. Network Monitor also detects all instances of the Network Monitor driver being used remotely (by either Network Monitor from Systems Management Server or the Network Segment object in System Monitor) to capture data on your network.

When Network Monitor detects other Network Monitor installations running on the network, it displays the following information:

- The name of the computer
- The name of the user logged on at the computer
- The state of Network Monitor on the remote computer (running, capturing, or transmitting)
- The adapter address of the remote computer
- The version number of Network Monitor on the remote computer

In some instances, your network architecture might prevent one installation of Network Monitor from detecting another. For example, if an installation is separated from yours by a router that does not forward multicasts, your installation cannot detect that installation.

Network Monitor uses a network driver interface specification (NDIS) feature to copy all frames it detects to its capture buffer, a resizable storage area in memory. The default size is 1 MB; you can adjust the size manually as needed. The buffer is a memory-mapped file and occupies disk space.

Note Because Network Monitor uses the local only mode of NDIS instead of promiscuous mode (in which the network adapter passes on all frames sent on the network), you can use Network Monitor even if your network adapter does not support promiscuous mode. Networking performance is not affected when you use an NDIS driver to capture frames. (Putting the network adapter in promiscuous mode can add 30 percent or more to the load on the CPU.)

Installing Network Monitor

To set up Network Monitor, perform two steps:

- Install the Network Monitor driver on any computer from which you want to capture data for analysis with Network Monitor.

- Install the Network Monitor utilities on a computer running Windows 2000 Server on which data will be captured.

You can install the driver on a computer running either Windows 2000 Professional or Windows 2000 Server. Installing the driver also installs the Network Segment object for use in System Monitor.

Installing the driver does not install Network Monitor itself. Instead, install the Network Monitor Tools on a computer running Windows 2000 Server to install Network Monitor.

▶ **To install the Network Monitor driver**

1. Click **Start**, point to **Settings**, click **Control Panel**, and then double-click **Network and Dial-up Connections**.

2. In **Network and Dial-up Connections**, right-click **Local Area Connection**, and then click **Properties**.

3. In the **Local Area Connection Properties** dialog box, click **Install**.

4. In the **Select Network Component Type** dialog box, click **Protocol**, and then click **Add**.

5. In the **Select Network Protocol** dialog box, click **Network Monitor Driver**, and then click **OK**.

If prompted for additional files, insert your Windows 2000 CD, or type a path to the location of the files on a network.

To display and analyze captured data, use the following procedure to install Network Monitor Tools on a computer running Windows 2000 Server. Network Monitor Tools installs Network Monitor along with the Network Monitor driver. If you are running Windows 2000 Server and are installing Network Monitor Tools, you can bypass the preceding procedure; you do not need to install the Network Monitor driver separately.

▶ **To install Network Monitor Tools**

1. Click **Start**, point to **Settings**, click **Control Panel**, and then double-click **Add/Remove Programs**.

2. In the **Add/Remove Programs** dialog box, double-click **Add/Remove Windows Components**.

3. In the **Windows Component Wizard** dialog box, click **Next**.

4. Under **Components**, click **Management and Monitoring Tools**, and then click the **Details** button.

5. Under **Subcomponents of Management and Monitoring Tools**, select the **Network Monitor Tools** check box, and then click **OK**.

6. Click **Next** to proceed with installation, and then click **Finish** and **Close** to exit.

▶ **To start Network Monitor on a computer running Windows 2000 Server**

1. Click **Start**, point to **Programs**, and point to **Administrative Tools**.

2. Under **Administrative Tools**, click **Network Monitor**.

For information about how to work with the Network Monitor user interface, see Windows 2000 Server Help.

Capturing Frame Data

When you've installed the Network Monitor driver on the computer from which to capture data (hereafter called the source computer) and installed Network Monitor Tools on the computer that will perform the capture (hereafter called destination computer), you can begin to capture data.

▶ **To capture data**

1. Open Network Monitor.

2. On the **Capture** menu, click **Start**.

   Or, click the **Capture** button on the toolbar.

As frames are captured from the network, statistics about the frames are displayed in the Network Monitor Capture window, as shown in Figure 9.2.

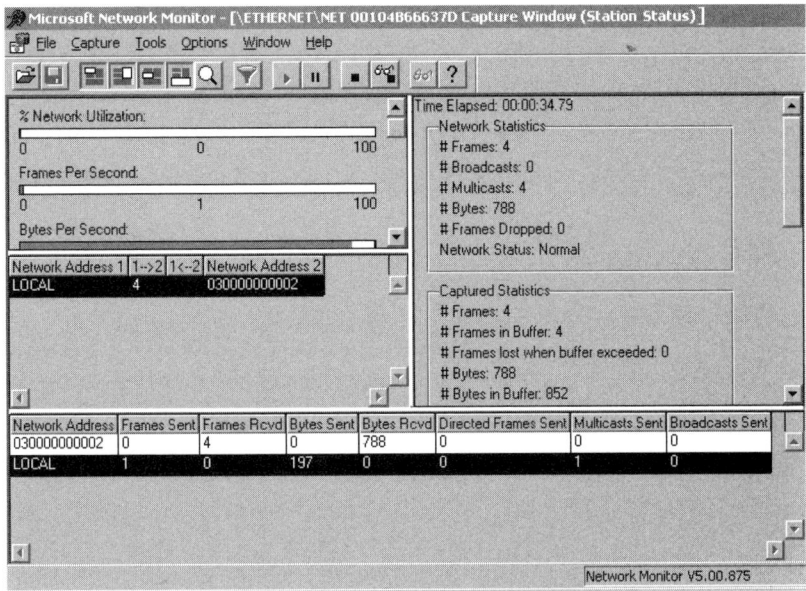

Figure 9.2   Network Monitor Capture Window

Network Monitor displays session statistics from the first 100 unique network sessions it detects. The Network Monitor Capture window includes the panes listed in Table 9.7.

Table 9.7   Description of Display Options for the Capture Pane

Pane	Displays
Graph	A graphical representation of the activity currently taking place on the network.
Session Stats	Statistics about individual sessions currently taking place on the network.
Station Stats	Statistics about the sessions participated in by the computer running Network Monitor.
Total Stats	Summary statistics about the network activity detected since the capture process began.

To reset statistics and see information on the next 100 network sessions detected, on the **Capture** menu, click **Clear Statistics**. To capture only those frames that originate with specific computers, determine the addresses of the computers on your network and associate the address with its DNS or NetBIOS name. After these associations are made, you can save the names to an address database (.adr) file that can be used to design capture filters and display filters. The capture filter allows you to specify criteria for inclusion in or exclusion from the capture. If the address is not available in the address database, try to capture all traffic and, after stopping and viewing the capture, use the **Find All Names** command on the **Display** menu to locate the address.

Note Capture filters can significantly increase the processor's workload because each packet must be processed through the filter and either saved or discarded. In some cases, using complex filters might result in missed frames.

An example of such a filter is an address pair, used to capture frames from specific computers on the network. An address pair consists of:

- The addresses of the computers between which you want to monitor traffic. Note that you can capture to a computer or to a router; however, you cannot select multiple address pairs with the **OR** operation. You must run multiple instances of Network Monitor to capture to either a computer or a router simultaneously. (An address is a hexadecimal number that identifies a computer uniquely on the network.)
- Arrows that specify the traffic direction you want to monitor.
- The INCLUDE or EXCLUDE keyword, indicating how Network Monitor should respond to a frame that meets a filter's specifications.

  Regardless of the sequence in which statements appear in the **Capture Filter** dialog box, EXCLUDE statements are evaluated first. Therefore, if a frame meets the criteria specified in an EXCLUDE statement in a filter containing both an EXCLUDE and INCLUDE statement, that frame is discarded. Network Monitor does not test that frame by INCLUDE statements to see if it meets that criterion also.

  For example, to capture all the traffic from Joe's computer *except* the traffic from Joe to Anne, use the following capture filter in the address section:

  ```
  include   Joe <----> Any
  exclude   Joe <----> Anne
  ```

  If there are no include lines, the default address
  your_computer_name – – – – Any
  is used by default.

Figure 9.3 shows the **Capture Filter** dialog box, accessed from the **Capture** menu or by pressing F8 in the Capture window.

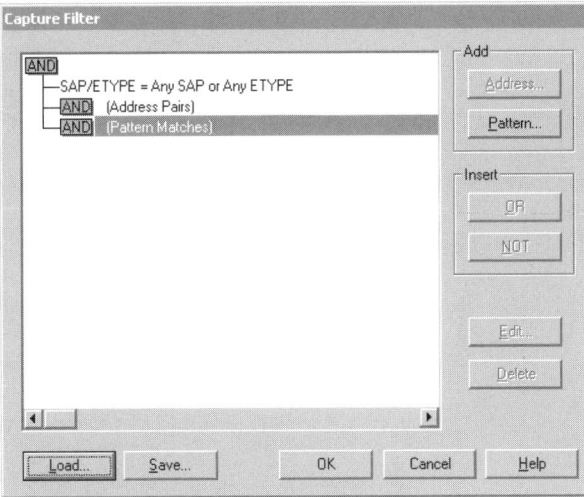

Figure 9.3   Capture Filter Dialog Box

To design a capture filter, specify decision statements in the **Capture Filter** dialog box. For information about display filters, see "Displaying Captured Data" later in this chapter.

By specifying a pattern match in a capture filter, you can:

- Limit a capture to only those frames containing a specific pattern of ASCII or hexadecimal data.

- Specify how many bytes into the frame the pattern must occur. This number of bytes is known as an offset.

  When you filter based on a pattern match, you must specify where the pattern occurs in the frame (how many bytes from the beginning or end). If your network medium has a variable size in the media access control protocol, such as Ethernet or Token Ring, specify to count from the end of the topology header.

- To capture frames sent using a specific protocol, specify the protocol on the capture filter SAP/ETYPE= line. Available protocols appear in the dialog box when you double-click the SAP/ETYPE= line. For example, to capture only IP frames, disable all protocols and then enable IP ETYPE 0x800 and IP SAP 0x6. By default, all of the protocols that Network Monitor supports are enabled.

- Use a capture trigger to automate actions to follow the capture. A trigger is a set of conditions that, when met, initiate an action. For example, before using Network Monitor to capture data from the network, you can set a trigger to stop the capture or to run a program or command file. You can also specify the conditions under which these actions will occur. One example of a trigger is a pattern match. You can save a trigger to the local computer if you save a capture filter. The default file path for saving filters is the \System32\Netmon\Captures directory in the root directory.

Table 9.8 describes the trigger types you can use to specify the condition that starts the trigger.

Table 9.8   Trigger Types for Network Monitor Captures

Trigger type	Description
Nothing	No trigger is initiated. This is the default.
Pattern Match	Initiates the trigger when the specified pattern occurs in a captured frame.
Buffer Space	Initiates the trigger when a specified amount of the capture buffer is filled.
Pattern Match Then Buffer Space	Initiates the trigger when the pattern occurs and is followed by a specified percentage of the capture buffer being filled.
Buffer Space Then Pattern Match	Initiates the trigger when the specified percentage of the capture buffer fills and is followed by the occurrence of the pattern in a captured frame.
No Action	No action is taken when a trigger condition is met. This is the default. Even though you select **No Action**, the computer beeps when the trigger condition is met.
Stop Capture	Stops the capture process when the trigger condition is met.
Execute Command Line	Runs a program or batch file when a trigger condition is met. If you select this option, provide a command or the path to a program or batch file.

If your computer uses multiple network adapters, use Network Monitor to collect data from multiple network adapters, and then either switch between the two adapters or run multiple instances of Network Monitor.

▶ **To switch between adapters**

- On the **Capture** menu, click **Networks**, and then select a different adapter.

Modem adapters appear as ETHERNET with a dial-up connection flag set to TRUE.

After capturing data, you might want to save it. For example, it is useful to save captures before starting another capture (to prevent loss of the captured data) if you think you might need to analyze the data later, or if you need to document network use or problems. When you save captured data, the data in the capture buffer is written to a capture (.cap) file.

Displaying Captured Data

To simplify data analysis, Network Monitor interprets raw data collected during the capture and displays it in the Frame Viewer window.

To display captured information in the Frame Viewer window, from the **Capture** menu, click **Stop and View** while the capture is running. You can also display captures by opening a file with the .cap extension.

Figure 9.4 shows the key elements in the Frame Viewer window.

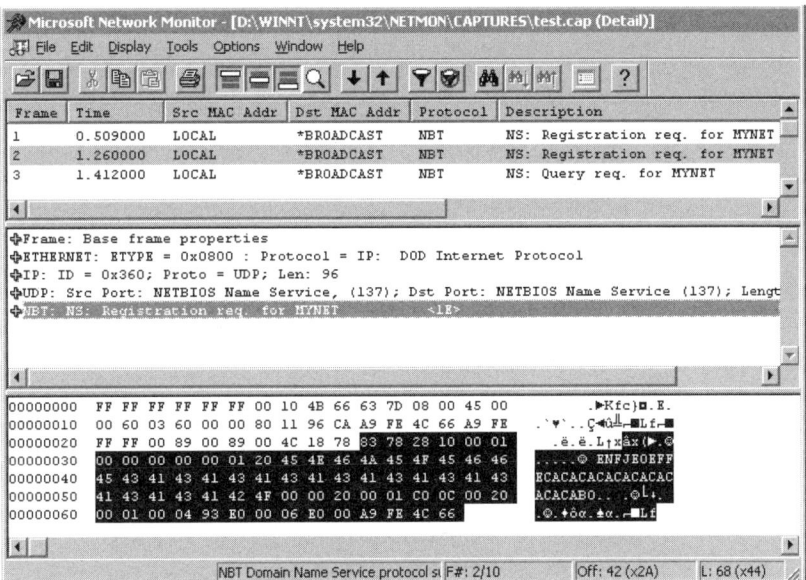

Figure 9.4   Frame Viewer Window

Table 9.9 lists Frame Viewer's panes.

Table 9.9   Frame Viewer Panes

Pane	Displays
Summary	General information about captured frames in the order in which they were captured.
Detail	The parsed contents of the frame's data.
Hex	A hexadecimal and ASCII representation of the captured data.

You can use a display filter to determine which frames to display. Like a capture filter, a display filter functions like a database query, allowing you to single out specific types of information. Because a display filter operates on data that has already been captured, it does not affect the contents of the Network Monitor capture buffer. You can filter a frame by:

- The frame's source or destination address.

- The protocols used to send the frame.

- The properties and values the frame contains. (A property is a data field within a protocol header. A protocol's properties, collectively, indicate the purpose of the protocol.)

Figure 9.5 shows the **Display Filter** dialog box, accessed from the **Display** menu or by pressing F8 in the Frame Viewer window.

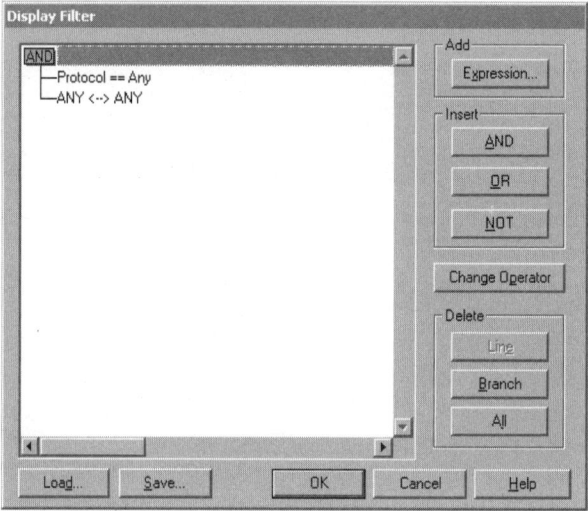

Figure 9.5   Display Filter Dialog Box

To design a display filter, specify decision statements in the **Display Filter** dialog box. Information in the **Display Filter** dialog box is in the form of a decision tree, which is a graphical representation of a filter's logic. When you modify display filter specifications, the decision tree reflects these modifications. Table 9.10 lists various types of filter items you can use.

Table 9.10   Filter Item Options

Filter item	Description
Protocol	Specifies the protocols or protocol properties.
Address Filter (default is ANY <– –> ANY)	Specifies the computer addresses on which you want to capture data.
Property	Specifies property instances that match your display criterion.

You must click **OK** to save the specified decision statement and add it to the decision tree before adding another decision statement.

Although capture filters are limited to four address filter expressions, display filters are not. With display filters, you can also use **AND**, **OR**, and **NOT** logic.

When you display captured data, all available information about the captured frames appears in the Frame Viewer window. To display only those frames sent by a specific protocol, edit the Protocol line in the **Display Filter** dialog box.

Protocol properties are information that defines a protocol's purpose. Because the purpose of protocols varies, properties differ from one protocol to another.

Suppose, for example, that you have captured a large number of frames using the SMB protocol but want to examine only those frames in which the SMB protocol was used to create a directory on your computer. In this instance, you can single out frames where the SMB command property is equal to **make directory**.

When you display captured data, all addresses from which information was captured appear in the Frame Viewer window. To display only those frames originating from a specific computer, edit the ANY <– –> ANY line in the **Display Filter** dialog box.

Reviewing Captured Data

Perform the steps in the following list as part of your routine for reviewing and analyzing captured data:

- Follow a session using source and destination IP address and port numbers.

- If you find a Reset, focus on the sequence numbers and acknowledgments that precede it.

- Try to understand the activity you are seeing:

  - Is the sender doing retries?

    If so, note the number of retries and the time elapsed. The default number of retries for TCP/IP is 5. This value might be different for other protocols.

- Did the sender back up and resend the previous packet?
- Is the receiver asking for a missed frame by acknowledging a previous sequence number?
- Does the size of the data being sent and received correspond to the size of the maximum transmit unit (MTU) of the hardware? If not, you might have the wrong network settings
- Is there a lengthy delay for receipt of acknowledgements or for transmission of subsequent packets? This could indicate that the destination computer has inadequate resources or that the application is performing inefficiently.

A reset can be caused by time-outs at the TCP layer or by time-outs of higher-layer protocols. Resets originating at the TCP layer should be easy to read from the trace. It might be more difficult to determine the cause of resets originating from higher-layer protocols such as the server message block (SMB).

For example, an SMB read might time out in 45 seconds and cause a reset of the session even though communications are slow but working at the TCP layer. The trace might only narrow down what component is at fault. From there you might need to use other troubleshooting methods to determine the cause.

To see TCP sequencing when higher-level protocols are present, start Network Monitor and edit the Expression dialog box, using the following steps. Figure 9.6 shows the **Expression** dialog box.

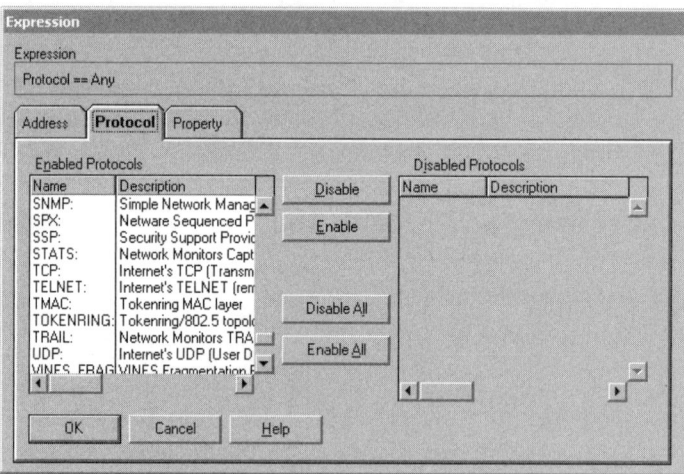

Figure 9.6   Expression Dialog Box

▶ **To see TCP sequencing**

1. Start Network Monitor.

2. Display captured data.

3. On the **Display** menu, click **Options**.

4. Select **Auto** (based on protocols in display filter), and then click **OK**.

5. Click **Display**, and then click **Filter**.

6. Double-click **Protocol=Any**.

7. Click the **Protocol** tab, and then click **Disable All**.

8. In the **Disabled Protocols** list box, click **TCP**.

9. Click **Enabled**, then click **OK**, and click **OK** again.

Network Monitor Performance Issues

Network Monitor creates a memory-mapped file for its capture buffer. For best results, make sure to create a capture buffer large enough to accommodate the traffic you need.

In addition, although you cannot adjust the frame size, you can store only part of the frame, thus reducing the amount of wasted capture buffer space. For example, if you are interested only in the data in the frame header, set the frame size (in bytes) to the size of the header frame. Network Monitor discards the frame data as it stores frames in the capture buffer, thereby using less capture buffer space.

Tip Windows Event Viewer shows start, stop, and connection events for Network Monitor. To verify Network Monitor operation, or as a first step in tracking down Network Monitor problems, examine the event log.

Resolving Network Bottlenecks

Typical causes for network bottlenecks are an overloaded server, an overloaded network, or a loss of network integrity. The following techniques can help to address some of these problems.

- If communicating over Token Ring, FDDI or switched Ethernet networks, attempt to balance network traffic by distributing client connections across multiple network adapters. When using multiple network adapters, make sure that the network adapters are distributed among the PCI buses. For example, if you have four network adapters with three PCI buses, one 64-bit and two 32-bit, allocate two network adapters to the 64-bit bus and one adapter to each 32-bit bus. Splitting the adapters across multiple Ethernet segments is an effective way to eliminate an overloaded network if the physical environment is switched Ethernet, and all adapters are on the same physical segment. For more information about adding network adapters, see "Adding Network Adapters" later in this chapter.

- Use adapters with the highest bandwidth available for best performance. Note that increasing bandwidth increases the number of transmissions that are taking place and in turn makes more work for your system, including more interrupts being generated. Remove unused network adapters to reduce overhead.

- Use adapters that support task offloading capabilities (checksum offloading, IPSEC offloading, and large send offloading).

- If your network uses multiple protocols, place each protocol on a different adapter. Make sure to use the most efficient protocols, especially ones that minimize broadcasts. Notice that reducing the number of protocols installed can increase performance.

- High rates of interrupts from network adapters can reduce performance. Using network adapters that batch interrupts by means of interrupt moderation can improve this performance problem, provided the adapter driver supports this capability. Another option is to bind interrupts arising from network adapters to a particular processor to improve performance. When using Interrupt Filter to bind a network adapter to a set of processors. For more information about processor affinity and Interrupt Filter, see "Measuring Multiprocessor System Activity" in this book. For more information about Interrupt Filter, see online Help on the *Windows 2000 Resource Kit* companion CD.

- Divide your network into multiple subnets or segments, attaching the server to each segment with a separate adapter. This reduces congestion at the server by spreading server requests.

- Although binding order is relevant on the client computer, there is no reason to reorder server bindings because the server accepts incoming connections based on the protocol used by the client computer.

- Use offline folders to work on network applications without being connected to a network. Offline folders make use of client-side caching, thereby reducing network traffic.

Adding Network Adapters

You need to disable some bindings to allow network adapters in the same computer on the same network segment to operate correctly when using NetBEUI. The reason for this is that, if you have two adapters on the same segment and install NetBEUI, the computer sees duplicate computer names due to the resulting NetBIOS name conflict, generates an error, and fails to start system services correctly. This also occurs on bridged or switched networks. In this case you also see the Event ID 2505 error in the event log, indicating a duplicate name on the network. The error might appear in the event log as either of the following messages:

- Event ID : 2505 The server could not bind to the transport/device/netbt_ *adapter_driver* because another computer on the network has the same name. The server could not start.

- Event ID : 2505 The server could not bind to the transport/device/nbf_*adapter_driver* because another computer on the network has the same name. The server could not start.

This problem does not affect routable protocols such as TCP/IP or AppleTalk because when you install or reconfigure them, you have to choose a network adapter, and this automatically disables the protocol's bindings to other adapters. In addition, the operating system treats NetBT as a namespace and need not be disabled. You can manually configure multiple network adapters in a computer by disabling NetBEUI bindings to network adapters other than the one you want to use for the NetBEUI protocol. To do this, disable the following bindings:

- Server to NetBEUI protocol to *adapter_driver* to *adapter*
- Workstation to NetBEUI protocol to *adapter_driver* to *adapter*
- NetBEUI protocol to *adapter_driver* to *adapter*
- NetBIOS interface to NetBEUI protocol to *adapter_driver* to *adapter*

When you have disabled all of these bindings, network operations can proceed.

In addition, if all clients have equal network access to any of the network adapters on the multihomed computer, and all of the client and server network adapters are on the same subnet, you can help to distribute the client connections between the server network adapters by adding the **RandomAdapter** registry entry in **HKEY_LOCAL_MACHINE\SYSTEM\CurrentControlSet \Services\Netbt\Parameters**. In this way, each network adapter will still respond to the name query, but each network adapter will choose the IP address randomly from all the network adapters on the server. This helps to distribute network sessions among the network adapters, but does not necessarily balance the load because network traffic might vary greatly between the sessions.

Caution Do not use a registry editor to edit the registry directly unless you have no alternative. The registry editors bypass the standard safeguards provided by administrative tools. These safeguards prevent you from entering conflicting settings or settings that are likely to degrade performance or damage your system. Editing the registry directly can have serious, unexpected consequences that can prevent the system from starting and require that you reinstall Windows 2000. To configure or customize Windows 2000, use the programs in Control Panel or Microsoft Management Console (MMC) whenever possible.

C H A P T E R   1 0

Measuring Multiprocessor System Activity

Managing the distribution of interrupt, thread, and deferred procedure call (DPC) activity for optimal performance means understanding factors that can limit and enhance the throughput on a symmetric multiprocessing (SMP) system.

In This Chapter

Related Information in the Resource Kit

- For more information about general monitoring procedures, see "Overview of Performance Monitoring" in this book.

- For more information about monitoring single-processor systems, see "Analyzing Processor Activity" in this book.

- For more information about system problems that can affect performance, see "Troubleshooting Strategies" in this book.

Overview of SMP Performance and Monitoring

Microsoft® Windows® 2000 is designed to implement symmetric multiprocessing (SMP). With symmetric multiprocessing, the operating system can run threads on any available processor. As a result, SMP makes it possible for applications to use multiple processors when additional processing power is required to increase the throughput capability of a system. Similarly, on Windows 2000, hardware interrupts and *deferred procedure calls* (DPCs), software interrupts at a low Interrupt Request Level (IRQL), can also run on any available processor determined by the hardware abstraction layer (HAL). Although most SMP systems running Windows 2000 dynamically distribute threads and hardware interrupts equally among all available processors, you might want to restrict threads and interrupts to one or more processors to improve processor cache locality and overall system throughput.

The following overview describes workloads that benefit most from scaling to an SMP system. This chapter also provides an overview of the steps involved in monitoring SMP systems and discusses the impact of SMP on system resources.

Benefits of Scaling

The process of adding processors to your system to achieve higher throughput is called *scaling*. Applications that benefit from multiprocessor configurations are typically those that are processor-intensive, such as database servers, Web servers, and active file and print servers. Processor-intensive applications that use multiple processes or are multithreaded with asynchronous execution are also well suited to multiprocessor systems. Systems requiring heavy computation capability, including detailed calculation for scientific or financial applications, complex graphic rendering, computer aided design (CAD)–based modeling, or electrical-engineering design might also demand multiprocessor systems.

To understand the degree of benefit you can attain from scaling to multiple processors, determine the *scale factor*. The scale factor is a measurement of the increase in throughput you can expect to achieve. You can determine the scale factor of the system by comparing the throughput of one processor to the throughput of multiple processors.

The formula for computing scale factor is:

```
Number of transactions per second on n processors ÷ Number of
transactions per second on 1 processor
```

For example, if a single-processor system is using 100 percent of the processor handling 100 transactions per second and, with the addition of three processors, the resulting four-processor system can handle 320 transactions per second, the scale factor of the system is 3.2.

Analyzing Performance on SMP Systems

You can monitor the activity of your SMP system by using the Performance console and its counters. To evaluate your system's performance, look at the following factors:

- Processor utilization and queue length. You might need to partition the workload so that a particular processor handles a particular workload to achieve better performance. For more information, see "Optimizing and Tuning Multiprocessor Installations" later in this chapter.

- Processor performance data, such as context switches, interrupts, threads, and processes. Activity rates and usage levels for these types of data that are higher than expected for a particular throughput can reveal inefficiencies in how your processors handle their workload. You might need to partition these types of activity. For more information, see "Optimizing and Tuning Multiprocessor Installations" later in this chapter.

- Overall resource utilization on your system. Scaling to multiple processors can increase the load on resources such as disks, memory, and network components, and it might be necessary to increase the capacity of these components. For more information, see "SMP Impact on System Resources" later in this chapter.

Note Application developers are in the best position to control how processes behave in an SMP environment. "Application Design and Multiprocessor Performance" later in this chapter provides guidelines for application developers who want to design programs that run well on multiprocessor systems.

SMP Impact on System Resources

The increased processing power and throughput on SMP systems can cause other system resources such as memory, the system bus, disks, and network to have a heavier load. For example, arbitration among shared resources increases memory latency. This is because code running on SMP systems needs to lock shared data to ensure data integrity, and locking shared data might result in contention for shared data structures. Further, the synchronization mechanisms used to lock shared data structures can increase the processor code path. As a result, when the number of processors on a system is scaled up, it is generally necessary to increase other resources on the system, such as memory, disks, and network components, as described in the following.

Processors. A large processor cache delivers the best performance. In multiprocessor configurations, the cache can reduce memory latency on the shared system bus thereby reducing resource contention and access.

Memory. It is recommended that your SMP system have more than 64 MB of memory because it is likely that it carries a heavier workload than a single-processor system, and runs more processes and threads. In general, it is recommended to scale memory with processors. For example, if a single-processor system requires 64 MB of memory and a second processor is added to increase the throughput, double the memory to 128 MB. Although multiprocessor systems do require additional memory because of their per-processor data structures, the additional memory required is minimal compared to the typical demand of the working sets for the additional processes and threads running in a multiprocessing environment.

Disk and network components. When adding processors to the system it is generally necessary to increase the disk and network capacity of the system.

For information about the adequacy of resources in your configuration, see the earlier chapters under the "Performance Monitoring" section of this book.

Monitoring Activity on Multiprocessor Systems

In addition to counters used to determine a baseline, as described in "Overview of Performance Monitoring" in this book, and processor-specific counters, as described in "Analyzing Processor Activity" in this book, the counters listed in Table 10.1 are useful for obtaining detailed information when evaluating the performance of multiprocessor systems.

Table 10.1   Multiprocessor System Counters and Descriptions

Object(Instance)\Counter	Description
Process(*process_name*)\Thread Counter	Shows the last observed value, not an average. You need to monitor it at various times to get an accurate picture of activity.
Processor\% DPC Time	Determines how much time the processor is spending processing DPCs. DPCs originate when the processor performs tasks requiring immediate attention, and then defers the remainder of the task to be handled at lower priority. DPCs represent further processing of client requests.
Processor\% Interrupt Time	Determines how much time the processor is spending processing interrupts. Interrupts are generated when a client requests a connection or sends data.
	If processor time is more than 90 percent and this value is greater than 15 percent, the processor is probably overburdened with interrupts.

(continued)

Table 10.1   Multiprocessor System Counters and Descriptions *(continued)*

Object(Instance)\Counter	Description
Processor\DPCs Queued/sec	Monitors the rate at which DPCs are queued on a particular processor. (This counter does not measure the number of DPCs in the queue.)
Processor\Interrupts/sec	Reflects the rate at which the processor is handling interrupts.
System\Context Switches/sec	Indicates that the kernel has switched the thread it is running on a processor. A context switch occurs each time a new thread runs, and each time one thread takes over from another. A large number of threads is likely to increase the number of context switches. Context switches allow multiple threads to share time slices on the processors, but they also interrupt the processor and might reduce overall system performance, especially on multiprocessor computers. You should also observe the patterns of context switches over time.
System\System calls/sec	Monitors the frequency of calls to Windows 2000 system service routines. These are the services exported to applications from the kernel.
Thread(*process_name*\Thread #)\% Processor Time	Monitors processor time usage by threads on the system.
Thread\Context Switches/sec	Monitors context switches generated by individual threads.

The following sections describe how to monitor and analyze the values reported in specific areas:

- Processor Time Data
- Processor Queue Lengths
- Interrupt and DPC Data
- Thread and Context Switching Data

Examining Processor Time Data

The Processor\% Processor Time counter reports CPU utilization on your system. It is important to monitor this counter on SMP systems just as it is on single-processor systems. Observe processor usage patterns for individual processors and for all processors over an extended period. Also consider the number of threads in the system's processor queue to determine if high processor usage is limiting the system's ability to accomplish work.

Figure 10.1 depicts a high rate of processor use on a multiprocessor system.

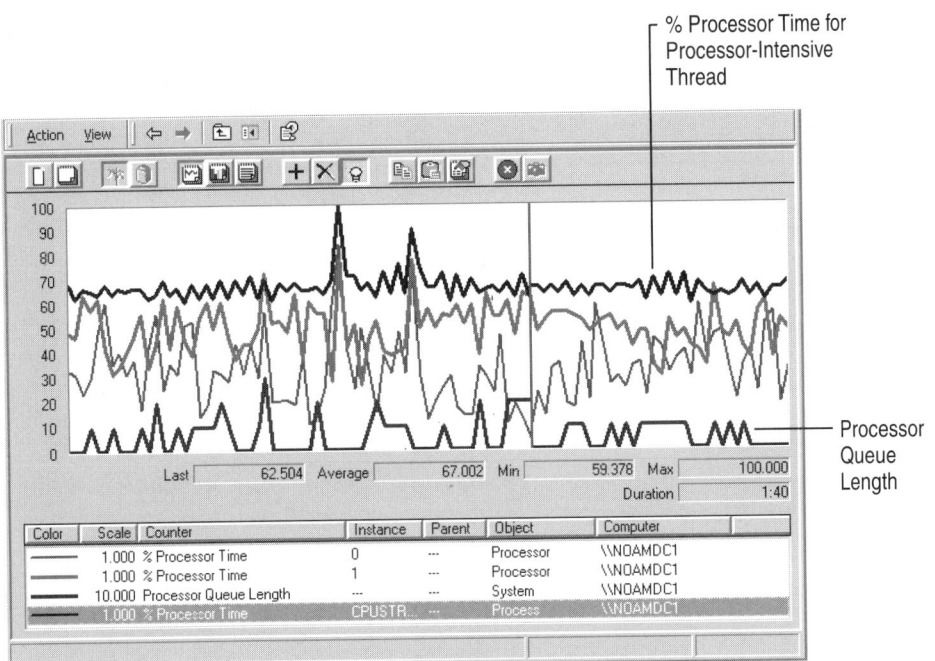

Figure 10.1   Example of High Rate of Processor Usage on an SMP System

On multiprocessor systems, the Processor\% Processor Time value reported by System Monitor will never exceed 100 percent for any particular processor or thread. On the other hand, the value of the % Processor Time reported for the Process object can report values over 100 percent; if such values occur, this could indicate that threads of the process are cumulatively using more than 100 percent of a processor. To get more detailed information, use the Thread object counters to analyze the processor time each thread within a process is using. Investigating other data described in this section, such as DPC activity or context switching, might help you to interpret high processor-time values.

Observing Processor Queue Length

The System\Processor Queue Length counter is a rough indicator of the number of threads each processor is servicing. The processor queue length, sometimes called processor queue depth, reported by this counter is an instantaneous value that is representative only of a current snapshot of the processor, so it is necessary to observe this counter over a long period of time. Also, the System\Processor Queue Length counter is reporting a total queue length for all processors, not a length per processor.

The optimal processor queue length can vary based on processor utilization or other factors as follows:

- For busy systems that experience processor utilization in the 80 to 90 percent range and use thread scheduling, the queue length should range from one to three threads per processor. For example, on a four-processor (4P) system, the expected range of processor queue length on a system with high CPU activity is 4 to 12.

- On systems with lower CPU utilization, the processor queue length is typically 0 or 1.

- For systems running services that use fiber scheduling, such as Microsoft® SQL Server™ version 7.0, the typical processor queue length will range between 0 and 1, because there is a single thread on each processor that schedules fibers within the thread. (Fiber scheduling is enabled when the lightweight pooling option is selected.)

If the processor queue length exceeds the value recommended in the preceding list, it generally indicates that there are more threads than the current processor can service in an optimal way. Reducing the number of threads or providing more CPU power, either by adding processors or upgrading to faster processors, are optional methods of shortening the processor queue.

Figure 10.2 shows a long queue that has developed over time, as processors have been working at capacity.

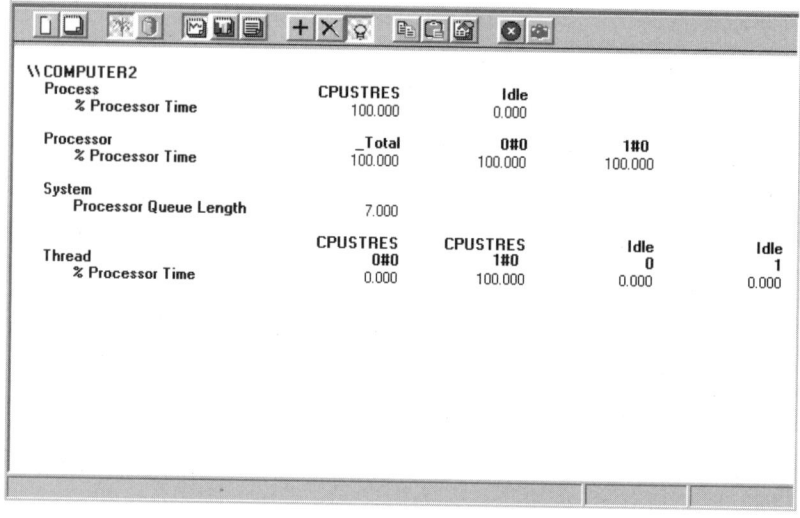

Figure 10.2   Example of Long Queue at High Processor Usage

When you begin to see longer queues, monitor additional counters for DPC and interrupt activity, as described in the following sections.

Analyzing Interrupt and DPC Activity

On a multiprocessor system, interrupt-activity rates on different processors indicate how your system is distributing its workload among the available processors. Similar to context-switching rates, interrupt-activity rates can reveal distribution of work in a way that is inefficient and costly in terms of overall performance.

Most SMP systems can distribute hardware interrupts for handling on any of the processors. This allows interrupts to be handled by all processors, rather than concentrating the load on a single processor. In general, distributing interrupts provides better throughput. However, this depends greatly on the workload being processed.

When interrupts are distributed, the DPCs that arise from those hardware interrupts might run on different processors as well, meaning that their shared data is not cached but must be rewritten and reread. In addition, the assignment of a DPC to run on a different processor causes an *interprocessor interrupt* (IPI). An IPI is a high-Interrupt Request Level (IRQL) interrupt. Although it has a relatively low cost in terms of performance, like any interrupt, it reduces the efficiency of the processor cache of the target processor because cache lines are displaced by the interrupt.

At times when the system is developing a long processor queue or experiencing high rates of processor usage, observe the proportion of the processor's time that is spent servicing interrupts and DPCs. Compare the values of the Processor\% Interrupt Time and Processor\% DPC Time counters to Processor\% Processor Time.

If interrupt and DPC processor-time values are high, you need to investigate further:

- Observe the rate of interrupts and DPCs for each processor.
- Note whether interrupts and DPCs are distributed equally among all processors or whether one or more processors are servicing all of the interrupts or DPCs.

In general, a very high rate of interrupts might indicate a disk or a network adapter that needs upgrading or replacing. Test your components and rule out a hardware problem before proceeding. However, on a multiprocessor computer, the most common interrupt-related problem is its distribution among processors. It might be necessary to redistribute interrupts or DPCs or upgrade to a faster processor to avoid a bottleneck.

For information about how to manage interrupt, DPC, and other activity for better SMP performance, see "Optimizing and Tuning Multiprocessor Installations" later in this chapter.

Monitoring Context Switches and Threads

When examining a multiprocessor system, monitor Thread\Context Switches/sec and Thread\% Processor Time to observe which threads are running on which processors, and to find out how frequently they switch between them to do the work of a particular process. This is important to know because there can be occasions when the switching of threads impedes optimal performance.

Typically, Windows 2000 uses a *soft affinity* algorithm that favors running a thread either on the last processor that serviced it or its *ideal processor,* a processor associated with a thread with a default value assigned by the system or optionally specified by the program developer in the application code. *Affinity* is the mechanism for associating threads of a process with a processor. With soft affinity, the association can vary between different processors; with hard affinity, the association is fixed to a set of one or more processors. In general, soft affinity is an optimal design that takes advantage of cache locality. However, when threads migrate from one processor to another processor, memory access to previously cached data may be slower. At worst, thread migration might cause false sharing because, to the cache coherency hardware of the CPU, it might appear that multiple processors are sharing a cache line.

Therefore, monitoring context-switching activity and thread processor usage is useful to application developers in understanding thread behavior.

Optimizing and Tuning Multiprocessor Installations

One way to get maximum performance from a system is to partition your workload so that a specific processor is servicing all threads, interrupts, and DPCs associated with that workload. This avoids the inefficiencies introduced when these items are distributed among processors, resulting in frequent context switching and loss of cache locality. *Full partitioning*, that is, partitioning threads and interrupts by processor, is extremely effective in providing linear scaling on SMP systems. Depending on your workload, you can use a combination of the partitioning strategies or implement one strategy at a time.

Strategies for managing threads, interrupts, and DPCs for better overall SMP performance are described in the following sections:

- Thread Partitioning.
- DPC (Software Interrupt) Partitioning.

- Hardware Interrupt Partitioning.
- Bypassing I/O Counts.

Note When using server applications, such as Microsoft SQL Server, Microsoft® Exchange Server, or Microsoft® Internet Information Services, consult the documentation provided with those servers, which might have built-in optimizations.

Thread Partitioning

Partitioning threads to specific processors is called setting a processor *affinity mask*. The affinity mask contains bits for each processor on the system, defining which processors a particular process or thread can use. When you set affinity for a process to a particular processor, all threads of the process inherit the affinity to the same processor.

Windows 2000 uses *soft* processor affinity, determining automatically which processor should service threads of a process. The soft affinity for a thread is the last processor on which the thread was run or the ideal processor of the thread. The Windows 2000 soft affinity thread scheduling algorithm enhances performance by improving the locality of reference. However, if the ideal or previous processor is busy, soft affinity allows the thread to run on other processors, allowing all processors to be used to capacity.

Windows 2000 also provides *hard affinity*, meaning that the processor affinity mask restricts the threads affected by the affinity mask to the processors specified by the mask. Threads restricted by a hard affinity mask will not run on processors that aren't included in the affinity mask. Hard affinity used with partitioning can improve performance of an SMP system substantially. However, be cautious when using hard affinity because it might cause the processors to have uneven loads. If processes that have had their affinity set to a specific processor are causing high CPU utilization on that processor while other processors on the system have excess processing capacity, the processes for which a hard affinity has been set might run slower because they cannot use the other processors.

If you want to ensure that a particular process or application doesn't have to share processing power with other tasks, you can use hard affinity to dedicate that process to one processor, leaving the remaining ones available for other work. This is easy to do using the **Set Affinity** command in Task Manager. For more information on Task Manager, see "Overview of Performance Monitoring" in this book.

Figure 10.3 shows the user interface for setting processor affinity.

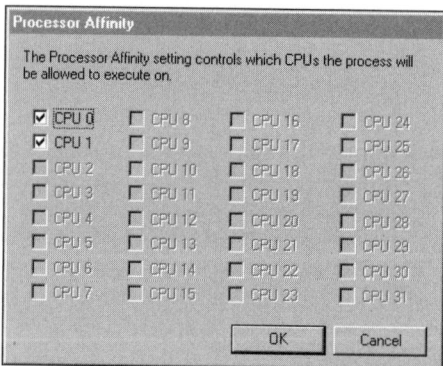

Figure 10.3   Processor Affinity Dialog Box in Task Manager

Another processor-partitioning option would be to divide discrete work items, such as tables in a database, among different processors. Consult the documentation accompanying your database software for information on partitioning databases for optimum performance.

Note Using functions in the Platform SDK, application developers who create applications using job objects can specify that all processes associated with the job object use the same processor affinity.

DPC (Software Interrupt) Partitioning

In an environment with a large volume of network processing, you might want to control DPCs that arise from interrupts generated by your network adapters. The default handling of these DPCs might not allow you to attain optimal performance for your SMP configuration if you have a network-intensive workload.

Depending on the processor platform detected by the HAL, the operating system might configure different default settings to handle DPC distribution. If Windows 2000 detects that your system supports symmetric interrupt distribution (this includes Pentium Pro or later processors), the network DPCs associated with an interrupt remain on the processor that handled the interrupt. By doing so, the system improves processor cache locality and reduces interprocessor interrupts.

Note *I/O completion ports* are synchronization mechanisms defined in the Microsoft® Win32 API that are used with asynchronous I/O to limit the number of active threads that service I/O on the completion port. By limiting the number of active threads, I/O completion ports allow a pool of threads to be used such that the number of threads that share memory or hold a lock are minimized, thereby improving SMP scaling. The value defining that limit is called the concurrency value. When the concurrency value is set to 0, the completion port allows the number of active threads to be equal to the number of processors on a system. When there is one active thread per processor, there is no need for context switching or memory sharing. If a thread becomes blocked, the completion port allows another thread to be activated. On completion of a work item, the thread returns to the completion port for more work, thereby reducing context switching and improving locality of reference.

On a system with a relatively light network load, keeping the DPC processing on a single processor will improve the cache locality for the network DPCs and prevent network interrupts from occurring while a running thread has a lock on most of the processors. However, this distribution does not work well on systems with significant amounts of network traffic.

You can also add network adapters so that you have one network adapter for each processor. Generally, you should only add a network adapter if you also need the bandwidth, because each additional network adapter has some intrinsic overhead.

However, if one of the processors is nearly always active (if Processor\% Processor Time consistently equals 100 percent) and more than half of its time is spent servicing DPCs (that is, if Processor\% DPC Time exceeds 50 percent), then adding a network card is likely to improve system performance.

If you are adding or upgrading network adapters, choose adapters with drivers that support interrupt moderation or interrupt avoidance. Interrupt moderation allows a processor to process interrupts more efficiently by grouping several interrupts to a single hardware interrupt. Interrupt avoidance allows a processor to continue processing interrupts without new interrupts queued until all pending interrupts are complete.

If your network adapter does not use NDIS miniport drivers, you cannot modify the distribution of DPCs for better performance. For this reason, and because other NDIS optimizations might be unavailable, you might want to consider upgrading your network adapter.

Note By default, DPCs for disk interrupts remain on the processor that took the interrupt.

Hardware Interrupt Partitioning

Some processor platforms can distribute interrupts across available processors; this capability is called *symmetric interrupt distribution*. These platforms typically include Pentium Pro and later processors; however, some Pentium processors also have this capability. Although symmetric interrupt distribution is designed as a way to balance interrupt activity, it can sometimes result in poor processor-cache performance. Partitioning interrupts to a specific processor is a strategy for addressing this problem. The Interrupt Filter tool on the *Windows 2000 Resource Kit* companion CD enables you to set the affinity for interrupts generated from disks or network adapters to a particular processor. This improves efficiency by taking advantage of cache locality, which can be lost when interrupts are serviced by any available processor. See Windows 2000 Professional Help for the Resource Kit tools for information about the requirements for using Interrupt Filter.

To help improve processor performance, some newer network adapter drivers provide an advanced feature known as *interrupt moderation* or *interrupt avoidance*. When the driver detects a high rate of interrupts from the network adapter, the interrupt-moderation code disables interrupts and accumulates the interrupts, sending them to the processor as a group of interrupts. Using a network adapter that supports interrupt moderation can provide better performance if your workload is network-intensive.

Bypassing I/O Counts

By default, Task Manager continuously measures data for process I/O operations that you can select and display under the Processes tab in Task Manager. In a multiprocessor environment, this data is shared by the processors on which the process runs. When a process that generates considerable disk and network I/O, such as a database service, runs on several processors, updating the shared measurements of process I/O and global I/O operations can slow the system. You can improve the performance of I/O-intensive operations on SMP systems if you configure the system to bypass the global I/O counters and Task Manager process I/O counters. To do so, add the **CountOperations** entry to the registry as a REG_DWORD in HKEY_LOCAL_MACHINE\SYSTEM\CurrentControlSet\Control\Session Manager\I/O System\. Set the entry value to 0. When so configured, Task Manager no longer provides per-process I/O measurements. For more information about Task Manager, see "Overview of Performance Monitoring" earlier in this book.

Upgrading or Adding Processors

If you cannot improve the efficiency of your SMP configuration through the preceding steps, you might want to add or upgrade system processors. When doing so, choose processors with a large secondary (L2) cache. File server applications, Web servers, and databases are a few examples of the many workloads that benefit from a large processor cache. A large processor cache, ranging from 512K to 4MB or larger, is recommended to improve performance on active servers running Web servers or other connection-intensive operations.

Application Design and Multiprocessor Performance

The design of applications and services has a significant influence on the performance of those programs in an SMP environment. This section is a brief summary of techniques that applications designers can implement to maximize the efficiency of their program on multiprocessing systems. More detailed discussions of writing applications that scale well to multiple processors appear on the Microsoft® Developer Network (MSDN).

Application developers can optimize application performance for SMP systems in the following ways:

- Keep the number of threads to a minimum. Generally, two to four application or server threads per processor works well.

- Limit processor queue depth. Keep the processor queue length (the number of ready threads waiting to run) in the range of two to three per processor. Depending on the characteristics of the application, such as the time a thread spends blocked or waiting for an I/O operation, the number of threads can be adjusted.

- Use a thread pool rather than one thread per client. It is more efficient to use a thread pool with an I/O completion port rather than to have a thread for each client, with the thread pool partitioned to each processor.

- Use I/O completion ports. I/O completion ports control the number of active threads to yield optimal throughput. Per-processor I/O completion ports can be implemented in an application or server to ensure completion of a work item from start to finish on the same processor.

- To minimize the cost of synchronization mechanisms, keep critical sections small and avoid shared data whenever possible. Synchronize shared data but do not try to synchronize code paths. Although critical sections— synchronization objects defined in the Win32 API— are a very fast method for mutual exclusion within a single multithreaded process, when contention arises, critical sections initiate context switching. Large numbers of critical section or spinlock acquisitions cause heavy data-access sharing and should be avoided.

Spinlocks are an extension of IRQL on SMP systems. They are used to synchronize kernel and driver data structures among interrupts, DPCs, or threads of execution running concurrently on an SMP computer. A thread acquires a spinlock before accessing protected resources. The spinlock keeps other processors from accessing the critical section (shared data) until the spinlock is released. A processor that is waiting for the spinlock loops until the spinlock is released.

Another characteristic of spinlocks is the associated IRQL. Attempted acquisition of a spinlock temporarily raises the IRQL of the requesting processor to the IRQL associated with the spinlock. This prevents all lower IRQL activity on the same processor from running until IRQL is lowered. Interrupts at a higher IRQL can preempt the executing thread. In a driver, if IRQL is already at the desired level, use the spinlock acquire-and-release APIs that don't change IRQL. For more information about spinlocks and associated IRQLs, see the Driver Development Kit link on the Web Resources page at http://windows.microsoft.com/windows2000/reskit/webresources.

- Avoid nested locks. Nesting locks can cause performance problems and reliability problems, such as deadlock. Always try to avoid nesting critical sections and spinlocks.

- Partition the workload, including interrupts. Whenever possible, partition the workload a server or application handles. Partitioning allows very effective use of system resources.

In addition, intensive memory access due to copying, zeroing (for C2 security), and checksum operations reduces the ability to scale effectively across multiple processors. You can identify some of these problems through profiling. For more information about profiling tools, see the Platform Software Development Kit (SDK) link on the Web Resources page at http://windows.microsoft.com/windows2000/reskit/webresources.

- Change applications to prevent data that might be used concurrently by threads on different processors from residing in the same cache block, or use processor affinity to force use of updated cache blocks only on a single processor.

- Use asynchronous, overlapped I/O. In overlapped mode, a server application can initiate multiple I/O requests without waiting for previous requests to complete, thereby enabling it to service multiple clients asynchronously using a single thread.

Network Load Balancing and Scaling

Another scaling solution is provided by Network Load Balancing. With Network Load Balancing, two or more computers are combined to provide availability and scalability benefits to mission-critical applications.

A concept called *shared nothing* supports scalability in clusters. Clusters that use shared nothing have their own system bus and access to disks and networks. This reduces the sharing issues of SMP systems because additional resources are available without extra arbitration. In general, shared nothing is similar to partitioning in an SMP environment except that the resource access latency is lessened. However, if cluster members need to communicate, the latency of communication is much larger than in an SMP system. In addition, if sharing is necessary (that is, the cluster is not a shared-nothing environment), the cost of sharing in a cluster is much higher than the cost of sharing in an SMP system.

P A R T   3

System Recovery

Preventative measures and strategic planning make computers running Microsoft®
Windows® 2000 more failure resistant. Part 3 describes how to reduce the
possibility of problems and recover from problems when they occur.

In This Part

C H A P T E R   1 1

Planning a Reliable Configuration

Planning a configuration well facilitates data backup and security, maintenance and record-keeping, and the prevention or handling of contingencies, such as system failure or natural disaster. The following discussion includes realistic scenarios and checklists that you can adapt to your organization.

In This Chapter

Related Information in the Resource Kit

- For more information about file systems, see "File Systems" in this book.

- For more information about recovery, see "Repair, Recovery, and Restore" in this book.

- For more information about security features and policies, see the *Microsoft® Windows® 2000 Server Resource Kit Distributed Systems Guide*.

Planning Considerations

When planning a configuration that includes computers running Microsoft® Windows® 2000 Server and Microsoft® Windows® 2000 Professional, consider the following questions:

- How many computers running Windows 2000 Server and how many computers running Windows 2000 Professional do you need for your company?

- Are there computers running operating systems other than Windows 2000 Server and Windows 2000 Professional in your enterprise?

- Where do the computers need to be located, and how do they need to be connected?

- How many single points of failure can you tolerate in your enterprise?

- What methods can you implement for fault tolerance—the ability of a system to function when a computer component fails?

- What data on the computers needs to be backed up, and what is your backup strategy?

- What records do you need to maintain to troubleshoot problems or recover from failures?

- Have you developed and tested solutions for emergencies such as fire, flood, or power outage?

For each computer that uses Windows 2000 Server or Windows 2000 Professional, consider the following questions:

- What file systems are appropriate?

- How many controllers and disks are needed, and how do they need to be configured?

- Does some data need to be configured on fault-tolerant volumes?

    - If so, does fault-tolerant hardware need to be used on a computer running Windows 2000 Professional or Windows 2000 Server?

    - Or do you want to use the fault-tolerant features available with Windows 2000 Server?

Climate Control

If the weather at the location of your company requires heating or cooling within the building to keep your computers and network devices within required operating temperatures, consider making the climate control system fault tolerant as well.

Software Failure

Find a vendor who can provide the support you need in case of software failure. If your company does not already have a technical support group to assist users when there are software problems, form one.

Power Control

Use an uninterruptible power supply (UPS) and battery backup to enhance fault tolerance. For more information about uninterruptible power supplies, see "Using an Uninterruptible Power Supply" later in this chapter.

Approaches to Planning

Three proven approaches to planning include: top-down execution and responsibility, bottom-up execution and responsibility, and top-down policy and bottom-up planning and execution. Whatever approach you use, ongoing improvement and updates are better than total revision when new information, policies, or procedures occur.

Top-down execution and responsibility One department in the company is responsible for planning and coordinating policies and procedures. A centralized operations staff might be responsible for all or most computers running Windows 2000 and for executing backups. This method allows for creating a specialized group to develop procedures, procure and install hardware, conduct tests, and train personnel. Two disadvantages to this approach are that the specialists might not understand how data from the various departments relates to the overall business, and each department might not get appropriate attention.

Bottom-up execution and responsibility Each department is responsible for developing and implementing its own plans. Each department might also be responsible for the computers that its members use and for developing backup procedures. It is the department manager who best understands the impact of data loss. However, this approach can be costly because each department must train its own personnel and do its own research.

Top-down policy and bottom-up planning and execution One department develops the planning policy, which includes overall planning guidelines. Each department is responsible for developing and implementing its own plans and procedures. This method offers a consistent approach, which helps to ensure that each department knows the important details for a successful operation.

System Maintenance

Routine, planned maintenance can prevent problems or minimize the effects when they occur. For example, if there are file system problems, you might not know about them until you restart the computer, when Chkdsk alerts you to the errors.

System administrators need to check both the system and application event logs daily. Impending file system problems can show up as errors in the system log before the file system is corrupted. Investigate any messages in the event log from FTDisk, Dmio, or disk device drivers.

Because disk fragmentation can cause performance problems, consider running a defragmentation program on a regular basis. You can use the Disk Defragmenter that is included with Windows 2000, or you can use a third-party defragmentation utility that runs under Windows 2000 and can defragment file allocation table (FAT) and NTFS file system volumes.

Planning for Security

It is important to minimize the possibility of human error or deliberate sabotage. If anyone can access a computer running Windows 2000 and restart it, security software cannot protect your data from being damaged or stolen.

You can implement procedures that restrict physical access to your entire facility or to certain areas to which various personnel need access. Some ways to protect data include keeping computers in secure offices and password-protecting screen savers. Run virus checks on floppy disks before using them or disable floppy disk drives, which can sometimes be done by using Basic Input/Output System (BIOS) options. You can also run virus checks on a computer or physically disconnect it.

Windows 2000 allows you to create a profile for each user and restrict user access to files and servers, but no amount of planning can anticipate all the ways that data or computers can be damaged. Therefore, backup is a crucial part of your security and storage procedures. For more information about planning backup and storage procedures, see "Backup" in this book.

Windows 2000 includes auditing software that writes information to a security log whenever there is an attempt to breach security. You can log access to files and all logon attempts, valid or invalid. Your audit policy determines the types of events that are recorded in the security log. For more information, see Windows 2000 Server Help.

Hardware and Software Upgrades

Even though you cannot avoid hardware and software upgrades, planning when and how to do them can minimize the time that an upgrade takes and can reduce the risk of failure.

When upgrading hardware or software keep the following in mind:

- Always back up important data files.
- Always back up the registry, master boot record (MBR), boot sector, and other critical system data.

- Maintain a current Emergency Repair Disk (ERD) for each computer.

- Maintain records about the computer configuration, such as jumper and DIP switch settings, interrupt requests (IRQs), and the hard disk configuration.

See the *Microsoft® Windows® 2000 Server Resource Kit Deployment Planning Guide* for more information about deploying Windows 2000.

Contingency Planning

There are several topics that you need to keep in mind during your contingency planning.

Disaster Planning

Just as every business needs to plan and budget for future growth, you need to plan for dealing with total or partial loss of business data. To determine what provisions to make for partial or complete loss of data, estimate the approximate cost in time and money to rebuild or replace critical data. Consider the following questions:

- Do you know the cost of reconstructing your company's financial, personnel, and other business data?

- Do you know if your business insurance would cover any or all of the cost of replacing data?

- Do you know how long it would take to reconstruct your business data? How might this affect future business?

- Do you know the cost per hour of computer downtime?

To prevent a natural disaster or sabotage from becoming a financial disaster for your business, test your plan for recovering and restoring critical data. Keep copies of your disaster recovery plan at on-site and off-site locations. Key personnel also need to keep a copy of critical data at home.

Because many books and magazine articles discuss disaster planning and recovery in detail, this section suggests topics to explore further instead of presenting detailed disaster plans to implement. Your insurance company can provide you with current and specific information for your situation.

The following are some important issues to consider when developing a comprehensive disaster plan to incorporate into your daily operations.

- What data do you need to back up, and how often do you need to do backups?

- What critical computer or other hardware configuration information, not saved during normal tape backups, needs to be saved?

- What data needs to be stored on-site or off-site, and how does it need to be stored?

- What training enables operators and administrators to respond quickly and effectively in an emergency?

Assessing the Probability of Failure

Mean time between failures (MTBF) information supplied by some equipment manufacturers is generally only helpful if you do extensive analysis and modeling based on your company's pattern of use. Thus, it is recommended that MTBF information be used only as a relative measure of reliability.

Maintaining a record of past failures and their causes can be very helpful. This information can help you categorize failures by type, such as:

- Hardware failure on a server, client, or network component.

- Software failure of the operating system or applications on a server or client.

- Administrative error.

- User error.

- Deliberate damage, such as sabotage or a virus.

The following questions can help you analyze failures and your procedures for handling them:

- What was done or can be done to solve the problem?

- How long would or did the solution take?

- What would or did the solution cost?

- What actions have you taken to reduce the recurrence of each recorded failure?

- What changes have you made that might affect the number of failures? Changes might include the size of local area networks (LANs) or wide area networks (WANs), or the number of:

  - Servers

  - Clients

  - Users

  - Administrators

  - Intermediary devices

  - External connections

Estimating Replacement Costs

There are several ways to measure the costs of recovering from problems. Some are easy to calculate, such as:

- Replacing file servers, mail servers, or print servers.
- Replacing servers running applications such as Microsoft® SQL Server™ or the Microsoft® Systems Management Server.
- Replacing gateway servers running Routing and Remote Access, Microsoft® SNA Server, Proxy Service, or Novell NetWare.
- Replacing workstations for personnel.
- Replacing computer components, such as hard disks and network adapters.
- Replacing products that have a set shelf life.

Far more difficult to measure, but just as devastating, are the invisible costs of computer downtime, such as lost sales, lost customer goodwill, lost productivity, increased costs for makeup time, missed contractual obligations, and loss of competitiveness.

If you have kept records of failures, you might find them useful in your contingency planning. You can investigate ways to avoid each failure, or to minimize the downtime associated with the failure. If you have cost information for the failures, you can then compare the cost of each failure to the cost of preventing or minimizing the failure. Table 11.1 describes two examples of failure, the costs related to each failure, and the effects of implementing solutions or workarounds to avoid future failures.

Table 11.1   Examples of the Effects of Failure

Category	Example One	Example Two
Failure description	File server in sales department down, network adapter failure	Router failure between development and testing department
Effect	Lost sales	Lost productivity of employees
Total downtime last year	Three hours	16 hours
Costs of failure per hour	$10,000	Average hourly wage of 10 affected employees is $18/hr
Annual downtime costs	$30,000	$2,880
Possible resolution or workaround	Three spare network adapters at $100 each	Put an alternate router in place or obtain a spare router

(continued)

Table 11.1   Examples of the Effects of Failure *(continued)*

Category	Example One	Example Two
Expected costs of resolution or workaround	$300	$500–$2,000
Estimated savings during first year with resolution in place	$29,700	$880–$2,380

Planning Tasks

Maintaining information about your hardware and software configurations, developing plans to deal with specific types of failure, and training personnel to handle recovery tasks can help minimize the effects on your systems and reduce costs incurred from downtime.

Maintaining Configuration and System Information

Hardware failures, power failures, and human errors can prevent Windows 2000 from starting successfully. Recovery is easier if you know the configuration of each computer and its history and if you back up critical system files when making changes to your Windows 2000 configuration.

Important If you have a clustered system and a disaster occurs, you need to recreate your disk structures and signatures. Write down this information and store it safely. If this information is not recorded, it cannot be recovered.

You can also use the DumpConfig command-line utility (Dumpcfg.exe) to output a computer's disk and volume configuration information to the command-line window or to a text file. In the event of disk failure, you can use this information to restore disk, partition, and volume configurations. When the Disk Management snap-in is displayed, you can record your disk configuration by printing the display or saving it to a file.

It is strongly recommended that you create a technical reference library for all hardware and software documentation. This library can also include other documentation related to your computers that you want to have in a central location. Useful materials to include in this library include:

- Vendor documentation, including manuals, receipts, warranties, proofs of purchase, and so on.
- Insurance policy and any claims.
- Information about any kits, tools, and add-ons that you have installed.

- All internal documentation that you have generated, including policies, procedures, and training guides.
- Hardware configuration information for each computer, including:
    - Location, cabling, intermediary devices, and external connections.
    - Computer type, and the models and serial numbers of system components.
    - Computer BIOS manufacturer, revision level, and BIOS modifications.
    - CMOS information.
    - For each component, information such as IRQ, direct memory access (DMA) addresses, and the input/output (I/O) port.
    - Amount of parity or nonparity random access memory (RAM).
    - Information about the video display and the video card.
    - Complete configuration of the disk subsystem, including the make, model, and serial number of each disk and controller, and their type, such as Small Computer System Interface (SCSI) or Enhanced Integrated Device Electronics (EIDE).
    - Configuration information for other storage media, such as tape, optical disk, or removable disk.
    - Types and configuration of network adapters.
    - Configuration information about any other adapters, such as multiple port adapters.
- Software configuration information and backups for each computer, including:
    - Disk map, noting location, type, and size of each partition, logical drive, and dynamic volume.
    - System state data backups.
    - The Windows 2000 Setup floppy disks created from the Windows 2000 Setup CD which can be used to start a disabled system.
    - Windows 2000 versions installed and the partitions on which they are installed.
    - User information, including which users are allocated disk space and what utilities and application programs they are using.
    - Applications and the volumes on which they are installed.
    - Licensing information.
    - Any service packs installed.
    - All hotfixes installed.
    - All Software Support Disks installed, when applicable.

- Updated contact information, including:
    - Appropriate personnel to respond to problems or emergencies.
    - Administrators.
    - Vendors and consultants.
    - Managers.
    - Critical users.

Developing a Recovery Plan

The skill and experience of support personnel is crucial in getting failed systems back online with minimal disruption to your business. They need to be trained to troubleshoot problems and to implement recovery procedures when problems occur.

In preparing a recovery plan, start by imagining some typical scenarios. Your plan needs to answer the following questions:

- Does each operator know how to restart the computer when the disk containing the operating system fails?
- Do you have a set of Windows 2000 Setup floppy disks that you can use to start a disabled Windows 2000 computer? Do you have a Windows 2000 startup floppy disk?
- When was the last time you tested the Windows 2000 Setup floppy disks or the Windows 2000 startup floppy disk?
- If a controller fails, how long will it take to replace the controller? Is the hardware configuration information immediately available?
- If a hard-disk drive fails, do you know how to replace it? If the drive was part of a fault-tolerant disk set, can you replace the disk and quickly fix the mirrored or RAID-5 volume?

Efficient recovery from system failures requires practice. Schedule drills several times a year that simulate computer crashes and disk failures.

Computers that have recently been taken out of service or are being prepared for production service can be used for training, or you can configure computers specifically for testing and training. Use training sessions and drills to update and document recovery procedures.

Testing Your System for Possible Problems

Testing is an important component of your contingency planning. You can use testing to try to predict failure situations and to practice recovery procedures. Be sure to stress test all functionality.

The following list identifies some of the failures that you need to test:

- Individual computer components, such as hard disks, controllers, processors, and RAM.
- External components such as routers, bridges, switches, cables, and connectors.

The following are some useful situations to simulate in your stress tests:

- Heavy network loads.
- Heavy disk I/O to the same disk.
- Heavy use of file, print, and applications servers.
- Large number of users simultaneously logging on.

Testing Recovery Procedures

Once you have created a set of Windows 2000 Setup floppy disks, a Windows 2000 startup floppy disk, and an ERD, and have backed up the system state data, use the floppy disks, ERD, safe mode and the Recovery Console to practice recovering from problems. This can help you to be diligent about making backups of the system state data and user data. This can also help you determine how long these procedures take to accomplish.

Your testing needs to help you determine the best recovery procedure for a particular situation. Determine when to use the set of Windows 2000 Setup floppy disks, the Windows 2000 startup floppy disk, safe mode, and the Recovery Console to restart your computer and when to use the ERD and Backup to replace files.

Your test computer needs to allow you to conduct the following tests:

- Look at the MBRs, partition tables, and boot sectors.
- Find the backup boot sector on an NTFS partition.
- Deliberately destroy and recover MBRs and boot sectors.
- Delete Windows 2000 system files and restore them by using the ERD.

Be sure to test recovery procedures before bringing a new computer or server into production. Every operator needs to have both primary and refresher training in recovering from the most common causes of unexpected downtime. Testing needs to include:

- Testing the UPS on the computer running Windows 2000 Server and on hubs, routers, and other network components.
- Testing the disaster plan.
- Restoring from your backups.
- Testing your ability to rebuild mirrored and RAID-5 volumes if you are running Windows 2000 Server and using software fault-tolerant volumes (a mirrored volume or a RAID-5 volume) or using hardware RAID arrays.

If a network adapter or other network component fails on the domain controller, the server operator needs to be familiar with the procedure for promoting a member server to be a domain controller, and demoting the failed server. Someone who is familiar with the procedure for reinstalling and reconfiguring the network adapter also needs to be available.

If a data volume fails, the operator must be able to restore the data from backup quickly and efficiently. The restore procedure needs to be tested frequently, both to ensure the skill of the operator and to test the quality of the backup tapes. The only way to test the quality of backup tapes is to do a full restore, which guarantees that the data is up-to-date and of consistent quality.

If your backup procedures involve the use of other computers running Windows 2000 Server or Windows 2000 Professional, verify that those backup and restore procedures work as expected.

Documenting Recovery Procedures

You need to develop step-by-step procedures for recovering from a variety of potential failures. You can use these procedures for:

- Testing a new computer before putting the computer into a production environment.
- Training new administrators and operators.
- Creating an operations handbook, including procedures for setting up new user accounts, conducting backups, maintaining ERDs, and completing other common administrative tasks.

Update your documentation when you make configuration changes to your computers or network, especially when you install a new operating system or change the utilities that you use to maintain your system.

Training Personnel for Recovery

Properly trained personnel can reduce the likelihood of failures and can reduce their severity when they do occur.

Effective training must start with the basics. Administrators and operators need to have a good understanding of Windows 2000 Server and Windows 2000 Professional. The Microsoft Certified Professional Program is a good starting point.

The following are several training and technical support options that can help you prepare to handle problems:

- Access Microsoft and vendor information through the Internet.
- Subscribe to TechNet.
- Have support personnel complete self-study programs.
- Enroll support personnel in vendor-approved or third-party courses.
- Enroll support personnel in certification courses in the use and troubleshooting of system hardware and software.
- Create a technical library that is available for personnel.
- Develop your own training courses.

You can also contract with Microsoft, hardware vendors, and third-party consultants for support. For more information about technical support options available to Microsoft customers, see "Troubleshooting Strategies" in this book.

Creating a Set of Windows 2000 Setup Floppy Disks

To prepare for the possibility of a system failure on a computer that cannot be started from the CD-ROM drive, you need to create a set of four Windows 2000 Setup floppy disks that you can use to start the computer.

Use the Windows 2000 Setup floppy disks under the following circumstances: starting setup, starting the Recovery Console, and starting the Emergency Repair Process. However, before deciding that a computer must be started from a CD-ROM or floppy disks, try starting the computer in safe mode. After you have started the disabled computer from the Windows 2000 Setup floppy disks, you can use either the Recovery Console or the ERD, if you have prepared one. For more information about safe mode, the Recovery Console and the Emergency Repair Process, see "Startup Process" and "Repair, Recovery, and Restore" in this book.

You can create floppy disks for starting a disabled system by using the Windows 2000 Setup CD on any computer that is running Windows 2000. You need four blank, formatted, 3.5-inch, 1.44-MB floppy disks. Label them as follows:

- Windows 2000 Setup Boot Disk
- Windows 2000 Setup Disk #2
- Windows 2000 Setup Disk #3
- Windows 2000 Setup Disk #4

The Windows 2000 Setup floppy disks must match the operating system on the computer that you want to start. You cannot use Windows 2000 Setup floppy disks created from the Windows 2000 Professional Setup CD to start a computer that is running Windows 2000 Server.

Note Recreate your Windows 2000 Setup floppy disks after installing any Windows 2000 service packs.

▶ **To create the Windows 2000 Setup floppy disks**

1. Insert a blank, formatted 1.44-MB disk into the floppy disk drive on a computer that is running Windows 2000.

2. Insert the Windows 2000 Server Setup CD.

3. Click **Start**, and then click **Run**.

4. In **Open**, type:

   d:\bootdisk\makebt32 a:

   Where **d:** is the drive letter assigned to your CD-ROM drive, and then click **OK**.

5. Follow the screen prompts.

Note Makebt32.exe runs under Windows 2000, Microsoft® Windows NT® version 4.0 and Microsoft® Windows NT® version 3.51. If you are using a computer that is running Microsoft® MS-DOS®, Microsoft® Windows®98, or Microsoft® Windows® 95 to create the Setup floppy disks, in Step 4, type:

d:\bootdisk\makeboot a:

Creating a Windows 2000 Startup Floppy Disk

You can use the Windows 2000 startup floppy disk to access a drive with a faulty startup sequence. This disk can access a drive that has either the NTFS, FAT16, or FAT32 file system installed. The Windows 2000 startup floppy disk can help with the following startup problems:

- Corrupted boot sector.

- Corrupted MBR.

- Virus infections.

- Missing or corrupt NTLDR or Ntdetect.com.

- Incorrect Ntbootdd.sys.

The Windows 2000 startup floppy disk can also be used to start from the surviving member of a mirrored volume. However, it might be necessary to modify the file Boot.ini first.

The Windows 2000 startup floppy disk cannot be used for the following problems:

- Incorrect or corrupted device drivers that have been installed into the Windows 2000 System directory.

- Startup problems that occur after the boot loader starts.

Use the emergency repair process to work around or fix these problems. On the **Windows 2000 Advanced Options** menu, choose **Last Known Good Configuration** or, if necessary, reinstall Windows 2000. For more information about the emergency repair process, see "Repair, Recovery, and Restore" in this book. For more information about the Last Known Good Configuration, see "Startup Process" in this book.

Note The Windows 2000 startup floppy disk must include the files NTLDR, Ntdetect.com, Boot.ini, and the correct device driver for your hard disk drive. NTLDR, Ntdetect.com, and Boot.ini usually have their file attributes set to system, hidden, and read-only. You do not need to reset these attributes for the Windows 2000 Startup disk to work properly.

▶ **To create a Windows 2000 startup floppy disk**

1. Insert a blank, formatted 1.44-MB disk into the floppy disk drive on a computer that is running Windows 2000.

2. Copy NTLDR, Ntdetect.com, and Boot.ini from the Windows 2000 Setup CD to the floppy disk.

3. If you have a SCSI system and the SCSI BIOS is not enabled, copy
   Ntbootdd.sys to the floppy disk.

Important Recreate your Windows 2000 startup floppy disk after the installation
of any Windows 2000 service pack.

If you are making a Windows 2000 startup floppy disk while your computer is
still functional, copy Boot.ini from the hard disk drive. If you have not yet made a
Windows 2000 startup floppy disk and you are encountering problems, you must
get the files from another Windows 2000 computer and modify Boot.ini to match
the configuration of the computer that is having problems.

For more information about creating and using a Windows 2000 startup floppy
disk, see the Microsoft Knowledge Base link on the Web Resources page at
http://windows.microsoft.com/windows2000/reskit/webresources.

Planning a Fault-Tolerant Disk Configuration

A redundant array of independent disks (RAID) is a fault-tolerant disk
configuration in which part of the physical storage capacity contains redundant
information about data stored on the disks. The redundant information is either
parity information (in the case of a RAID-5 volume), or a complete, separate copy
of the data (in the case of a mirrored volume). The redundant information enables
regeneration of the data if one of the disks or the access path to it fails, or a sector
on the disk cannot be read. Windows 2000 Server implements these fault-tolerant
configurations in its software. Use Disk Management, shown in Figure 11.1, to
configure mirrored volumes and RAID-5 volumes, and to reconstruct the volume
when there has been a failure.

Note You can also use hardware RAID arrays.

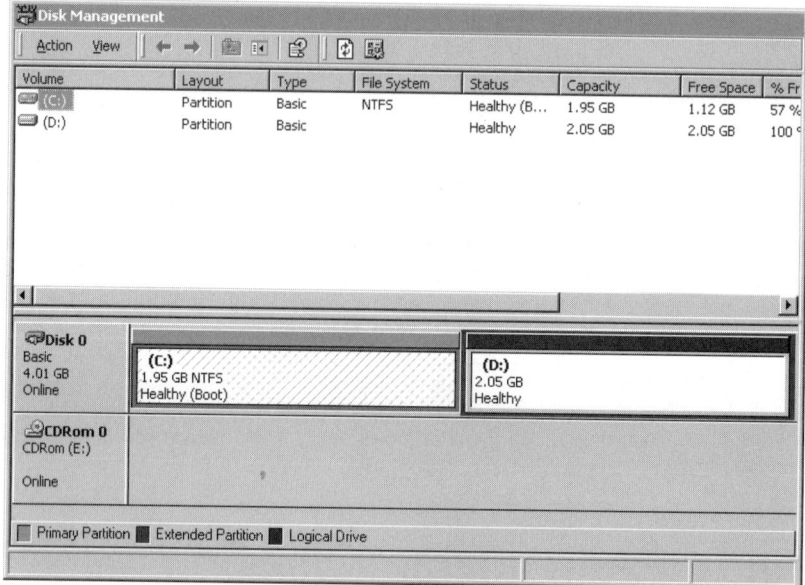

Figure 11.1 Disk Management

Table 11.2 shows the volume status descriptions that appear in the graphical view of the volume and in the Status column of the volume in List view.

Table 11.2 Disk Management Volume Status Descriptions

Volume Status	Description
Healthy	The volume is accessible and has no known problems. This is the normal volume status. No user action is required. Both dynamic volumes and basic volumes display the Healthy status.
Healthy (At Risk)	The dynamic volume is currently accessible, but I/O errors have been detected on the underlying disk. If an I/O error is detected on any part of a disk, all volumes on the disk display the Healthy (At Risk) status. Only dynamic volumes display the Healthy (At Risk) status.
Initializing	The dynamic volume is being initialized. Only dynamic volumes display the Initializing status.
Resynching	The volume's mirrors are being resynchronized so that volume mirrors contain identical data.
Regenerating	Data and parity are being regenerated for the RAID-5 volume.

(continued)

Table 11.2   Disk Management Volume Status Descriptions *(continued)*

Volume Status	Description
Failed Redundancy	The data on the volume is no longer fault tolerant because one of the underlying disks is not online. The Failed Redundancy status applies only to mirrored or RAID-5 volumes.
Failed Redundancy (At Risk)	The data on the volume is no longer fault tolerant and I/O errors have been detected on the underlying disk. If an I/O error is detected on any part of a disk, all volumes on the disk display the (At Risk) status. Only dynamic mirrored or RAID-5 volumes display the Failed Redundancy (At Risk) status.
Failed	The volume cannot be started automatically. Both dynamic and basic volumes display the Failed Status.
Missing	A dynamic disk is corrupted, powered down, or disconnected.

Certain disk subsystems implement RAID technology completely within the hardware. Some of these hardware implementations support hot swapping of disks, which enables you to replace a failed disk while the computer is still running Windows 2000 Server. A RAID array is a fault-tolerant disk subsystem where all of the fault tolerance is implemented by the hardware. For information about RAID arrays that are compatible with Windows 2000, see the Windows 2000 Hardware Compatibility List (HCL) link on the Web Resources page at http://windows.microsoft.com/windows2000/reskit/webresources.

All RAID disk configurations regenerate data to satisfy read requests when a disk or a path to a disk has failed. Regeneration involves reading data from other disks in the volume. RAID disk configurations also reconstruct the missing data onto the new disk when you have replaced the failed disk (or the path to it). When you have implemented a fault-tolerant volume, use Disk Management reconstruct the data. If you are using a RAID array, see the vendor's documentation for information about reconstructing data.

Configuring mirrored volumes and RAID-5 volumes is discussed later in this chapter. For more information about recovering from failures of mirrored volumes and RAID-5 volumes, see "Repair, Recovery, and Restore" in this book.

Dynamic Disks and Disk Groups

Windows 2000 uses a new disk layout that extends beyond disk partitioning. New to Windows 2000 are dynamic disks and Disk Groups. Dynamic disks allow more flexibility during configuration than basic disks. For example, dynamic disks allow you to increase the size of a volume or add a mirrored volume without restarting the computer. A Disk Group is a collection of disks managed as a collection that helps you organize dynamic disks and helps prevent data loss.

Disk Groups are unique to dynamic disks. Each disk in a Disk Group stores replicas of the same configuration data. This configuration data is stored in a 1-megabyte (MB) region at the end of each dynamic disk. Since this information is contained on each disk, you can move them to another computer or install another disk without losing this information. All dynamic disks in a computer are members of the same Disk Group and have the following characteristics:

- They overcome partitioning rules from Windows NT 4.0.

- They extend or create fault-tolerant sets without the need to restart the computer.

- They are not registry dependent: that is, disk information for both basic and dynamic disks and fault tolerance information for dynamic disks is kept on the disk in Windows 2000.

Note To simplify use with docking stations, you cannot use dynamic disks on portable computers. Also, you cannot use dynamic disks on removable media. This simplifies movement of media between machines.

Converting Basic Disks to Dynamic Disks

In Windows 2000, you can convert a basic disk to a dynamic disk. When you convert a disk, any existing partitions or fault tolerance structures on the disk are checked and then the disk is assigned a Disk Group identity and a copy of the current Disk Group configuration. Windows 2000 also adds dynamic volumes to the configuration.

Note By default, when you add a disk to an existing computer, it is considered a new disk. New disks are always dynamic disks.

Moving Disks

You can move basic and dynamic disks from one computer to another. For both basic and dynamic disks, you need to physically move the disk from the computer, and then either restart the computer or use the **Rescan Disks** command on the **Action** menu of Disk Management.

When you remove a dynamic disk from a computer, the remaining online dynamic disks retain information about it and its volumes. The removed disk is displayed in Disk Management as a **Dynamic/Offline** disk and assigned the status of "Missing."

You need at least one online dynamic disk to retain information about Missing disks and their volumes. When you remove the last dynamic disk, you lose the information, and the Missing disks are no longer displayed in Disk Management.

Note   When you move basic fault-tolerant sets from a computer running Windows NT 4.0, you need to save the configuration to a floppy disk, and then use Disk Management to restore the hard disk configuration. It is strongly recommended that you move all disks from the fault-tolerant set.

Connecting New Disks to a Computer

After you connect the disks to the new computer, from the Disk Management snap-in, select **Rescan Disks** on the **Action** menu. The New Signature Wizard is displayed. When you physically connect a dynamic disk, the rescan causes the disk to be displayed in Disk Management as **Dynamic/Foreign**. You might need to convert it to **Dynamic/Online**, and then activate the volumes. When you connect a new disk to a computer, or rescan the dynamic mirrored volume and move only one disk, it displays as **Dynamic/Offline**, and you need to manually activate it.

Note   When you connect a basic disk with existing partitions, you must select **Rescan Disks** from the Disk Management snap-in.

Importing Foreign Disks

If you move one or more disks from a Disk Group to another computer that contains its own Disk Group, the Disk Group you moved is marked as Foreign until you import it into the existing group.

To use Foreign/Dynamic disks, use the Import Foreign Disks operation associated with one of the disks. The manual operation lists one or more Disk Groups, identified by the name of the computer where they were created. If you expand the details on a Disk Group, it lists the locally-connected disks that are members. Click the appropriate Disk Group, and then click **OK**. You can then view the dialog box that lists volumes that were found in the Disk Group, along with some indication of the status of those volumes.

Since volumes can span multiple disks using simple disk spanning, striping, mirroring, or RAID-5 redundancy mechanisms, the display status of a volume in the **Import Foreign Disks** dialog box can become complicated if not all of the disks have been moved. Another complication can arise from moving a disk, and then later moving additional disks. This is supported, but can be complicated. For this reason, all fault tolerant and non-fault-tolerant volumes that span disks should be moved at the same time.

The state of a volume after import depends on whether the volume is simple, mirrored, RAID-5, or spans multiple disks (simple striping behaves like spanning in this respect). It also depends on if the whole or part of the volume is moved, and if the volume is moved incrementally. The state depends on whether changes to the configuration of a partially moved volume were made on the original or the new computer:

- When all disks that contain parts of a volume are concurrently moved from one computer to another, the state of the volume after the import is identical to the original state. All simple volumes on any moved disks are recovered to their original state.

- On a non-redundant volume that spans multiple disks, if only some disks are moved from one system to another, the volume is disabled during import: it also becomes disabled on the original system. As long as the volume is not deleted on either the original or the target system, the remaining disks can be moved later. When all disks are finally moved over, the volume is recovered to its original state.

- RAID-5 volumes can remain online if they are missing one disk. The status of the volume is displayed as either Failed Redundancy or Failed Redundancy (At Risk). If a disk is moved to a different computer, all or all but one of the disks must be moved. If all disks are moved, the status of the volume cycles from Regenerating to Healthy. If all but one of the disks are moved, the status of the volume is Failed Redundancy (At Risk). Whether the volume remains online depends on whether the data is known to be valid or can be regenerated from the parity and the data. Parity starts out as invalid when a RAID-5 volume is first created, since the parity blocks must be computed, which takes time. Parity is also marked as invalid after a system crash, because an in-progress write can leave a discrepancy between parity blocks and the corresponding data blocks. If the parity of a RAID-5 volume is valid, one disk can be missing and the RAID-5 volume still becomes (or remains) online. If parity is not valid, then all parts of the RAID-5 volume need to be available for the volume to become (or remain) online.

- If both halves of a mirrored volume are moved as a set, the volume functions normally and your data continues to be fault tolerant. If only one half of a mirrored volume is moved to another computer, and then you return it to the original computer, the two halves of the original mirrored volume do not function as a mirrored volume. To restore the mirrored volume, break the original mirrored volume and then recreate it.

- If one up-to-date mirror is moved first, the mirror on the resulting Missing disk (for the non-moved mirror) can be removed and reallocated to another disk. This leaves a fully mirrored volume on the target computer. In this case, if the second original mirror is moved over, it conflicts in a way that cannot be resolved readily. When this happens, the second mirror comes over as a new volume.

Warning   Note that when removing and moving disks with mirrored volumes, if one of the volumes becomes damaged during the move, your data is no longer fault tolerant.

It is better to remove all disks at the same time, and to add all disks at the same time. With SCSI disks, this is fairly easy: stop using the disks, and then defer the Rescan disks request until all disks are removed.

With any kind of disk, turn off the original system before removing the disks, and then turn off the target system before adding the disks.

For information about disk groups, see the Knowledge Base link on the Web Resources page at http://windows.microsoft.com/windows2000/reskit/webresources.

Simple Volumes

Simple volumes are the dynamic disk equivalent of primary partitions in Windows NT 4.0 and earlier versions. When you have only one dynamic disk, you can only create a simple volume. Simple volumes can be created on dynamic disks only. They cannot contain partitions or logical drives, and they can only be accessed by Windows 2000.

You can increase the size a simple volume to include unallocated space on the disk, but the volume must be formatted with the version of NTFS used in Windows 2000. You cannot increase the size of a simple volume that was converted from a basic disk partition. Increasing the size of a simple volume to include space on other disks of the same computer creates a spanned volume.

Spanned Volumes

Spanned volumes are created from unallocated space from between two and 32 dynamic disks. The areas of unallocated space used to create spanned volumes can be of different sizes. You can increase the size of a spanned volume, but the volume must be formatted with NTFS.

After a spanned volume is extended, no portion of it can be deleted without deleting the entire spanned volume. Spanned volumes cannot be mirrored or striped and do not offer fault tolerance. If one of the disks containing a spanned volume fails, the entire volume fails.

Note Only Windows 2000 can recognize a spanned volume. On a multiple-boot computer, spanned volumes are unusable by other operating systems.

Striped Volumes

Windows 2000 Server and Windows 2000 Professional provide software support for striped volumes, which are configured by using Disk Management. Striped volumes improve I/O performance by distributing I/O requests across disks. Striped volumes are composed of stripes of data of equal size written across each disk in the volume. They are created from equally sized, unallocated areas on up to 32 physical disks. For Windows 2000, the size of each stripe is 64 kilobytes (KB).

Conceptually, a striped volume is similar to a table in a document, where a disk is a column and a stripe is one of the entries in the table. A stripe includes all of the entries in one row. Table 11.3 illustrates the structure of a striped volume and shows the order in which data is written to the striped volume.

Table 11.3   Structure of a Striped Volume

Stripe Number	Disk 1	Disk 2	Disk 3	Disk 4
Stripe 1	1	2	3	4
Stripe 2	5	6	7	8
Stripe 3	9	10	11	12
Stripe 4	13	14	15	16
Stripe 5	17	18	19	20

In the preceding table, stripe 1 consists of the four stripes that are the first block on each of the four disks. Stripe 5 is made up of the stripes that are the last block on each disk.

When you write data to a striped volume, the data is written *across* the stripes in the volume. Thus, using Table 11.3 as an example, a file of 325 KB could occupy the following space:

- 64 KB on stripe 1 of disk 1
- 64 KB on stripe 1 of disk 2
- 64 KB on stripe 1 of disk 3

- 64 KB on stripe 1 of disk 4
- 64 KB on stripe 2 of disk 1
- 5 KB on stripe 2 of disk 2

The physical disks in a striped volume do not need to be identical, but there must be unused space available on each disk that you want to include in the volume. You cannot increase the size of a striped volume after it is created. To change the size of a striped volume, you must first complete the following steps:

- Back up the data.
- Delete the striped volume by using Disk Management.
- Create a new, larger, striped volume by using Disk Management.
- Restore the data to the new striped volume.

Striped volumes do not contain redundant information. Therefore, the cost per megabyte on a striped volume is identical to that for the same amount of storage configured from a contiguous area on a single disk. If one disk fails, the whole striped volume fails and no data can be recovered. The reliability for the striped volume is less than the least reliable disk in the set.

Stripe sets are used for performance reasons. In general, striped volumes work well when you need to distribute I/O operations. Access to the data on a striped volume is usually faster than access to the same data would be on a single disk, because the I/O is spread across more than one disk. Therefore, Windows 2000 can be seeking on more than one disk at the same time, and can have simultaneous read or write operations occurring.

A striped volume works well in the following situations:

- When users need rapid read access to large databases or other data structures.
- When storing program images, dynamic-link libraries (DLLs), or run-time libraries for rapid loading. Operating systems such as Windows 2000 that use memory mapped images can benefit from using striped volumes.
- When collecting data from external sources at very high transfer rates. This is especially useful when collection is done asynchronously.
- When multiple independent applications require access to data stored on the striped volume. When the operating system supports asynchronous multithreading, which helps load balance disk read and write operations.

Mirrored Volumes

A mirrored volume provides an identical twin of the selected volume. All data written to the mirrored volume is written to both volumes, which results in disk capacity of only 50 percent.

Note In this chapter, the terms original disk and original volume refer to the original volume that the data was written to, and shadow disk and shadow volume refers to the disk or volume that contains the copy.

Figure 11.2 shows a mirrored volume. To a user, only one read or write occurs to satisfy a request for data. For each user read request, Dmio.sys creates one read. For each user write request, Dmio.sys creates two writes.

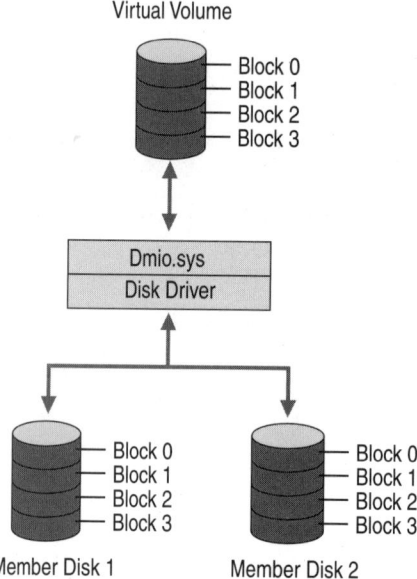

Figure 11.2   Mirrored Volume

If there is a read failure on one of the disks, Dmio reads the data from the other disk in the mirrored volume. If there is a write failure on one of the disks in the mirrored volume, the remaining disk is used for all accesses.

Because dual-write operations can degrade system performance, many mirrored volume configurations use duplexing, where each disk in the mirrored volume resides on its own disk controller.

Any volume can be mirrored, including the system and boot volumes. The disk that you select for the shadow volume does not need to be identical to the original disk in size, or in its number of tracks and cylinders. This means that you do not have to replace a failed disk with an identical model. The unused area that you select for the shadow volume cannot be smaller than the original volume. If the area that you select for the shadow volume is larger than the original, the extra space on the shadow disk can be configured as another volume.

Note As with striped volumes, you cannot add disk space to a mirrored volume to increase the size of the volume later.

When compared to a RAID-5 volume, a mirrored volume implementation:

- Has a lower entry cost because it requires only two disks, whereas a RAID-5 volume requires three or more disks, but does cost more per gigabyte.
- Requires less system memory.
- Provides very good overall performance.
- Does not show performance degradation during a failure. However, in the event of a single write error, redundancy is lost.
- Has a higher cost-per-megabyte.

Note The term system volume refers to the disk volume containing hardware-specific files needed to start Windows 2000 (such as the files NTLDR and Boot.ini). The boot volume contains the operating system files and support files. The boot volume and the system volume can be the same volume.

A mirrored volume works well in the following situations:

- When extremely high data reliability is required. A duplexed mirrored volume has the best data reliability because the entire I/O subsystem is duplicated.
- When simplicity is important. Mirrored volumes are simple to understand and easy to set up.

You might not want to use a mirrored volume if cost is a critical factor. Mirrored volumes are the most expensive solution based on the cost per unit of data storage.

Advantages of Mirrored Volumes

Random disk read operations on mirrored volumes are more efficient than on a single volume. Dmio has the capacity to load balance read operations across the physical disks. With current SCSI technology, two disk read operations can be done simultaneously.

Recovery from a disk failure is very rapid. Mirrored volumes offer the fastest data recovery, with the least impact on system performance, because the shadow volume contains all of the data. There is no data recomputation building needed to restore the system. When you configure your boot volume on a mirrored volume, you do not have to reinstall the Windows 2000 Server to be able to restart the computer.

Note If a mirrored system fails, you do not need to restart the computer. The system continues to run and, if your hardware supports it, you can replace the failed drive then resynchronize the mirror. Resynchronization is the process by which a mirrored volume's mirrors are made to contain identical data. During resynchronization, performance is affected because the computer is performing a lot of I/O operations.

It is not necessary to use identical physical disks or to have the same volumes on each disk, although it is recommended that you use identical disks if you put your system volume on a mirrored volume. However, sufficient unused space on the second disk is required to create the shadow volume.

Disadvantages of Mirrored Volumes

Disk write operations are less efficient. Because data must be written to both disks, there is a slight performance penalty. However, the penalty is not 100 percent. In many situations, a user-mode application is not affected by the extra disk update.

Mirrored volumes are the least efficient in terms of space utilization. Because the data is duplicated, the space requirements for a mirrored volume are higher than for a RAID-5 volume.

For information about recovering from the failure of a mirrored volume, see "Repair, Recovery, and Restore" in this book.

RAID-5 Volumes

A RAID-5 volume dedicates the equivalent of the space of one disk in the RAID-5 volume for storing the parity stripes, but distributes the parity stripes across all the disks in the group. The data and parity information are arranged on the volume so that they are always on different disks.

Table 11.4 shows the order in which data is written to a RAID-5 volume that consists of five stripes on five disks.

Table 11.4   Structure of a RAID-5 Volume

Stripe Number	Disk 1	Disk 2	Disk 3	Disk 4	Disk 5
Stripe 1	parity 1	1	2	3	4
Stripe 2	5	parity 2	6	7	8
Stripe 3	9	10	parity 3	11	12
Stripe 4	13	14	15	parity 4	16
Stripe 5	17	18	19	20	parity 5

The parity stripe is the exclusive OR (XOR) of all the data values for the data stripes in the stripe. If no disks in the RAID-5 volume have failed, the new parity for a write can be calculated without having to read the corresponding stripes from the other data disks. Thus, only two disks are involved in a write operation: the target data disk and the disk that contains the parity stripe. Figure 11.3 shows the steps that are involved in writing data to a RAID-5 volume.

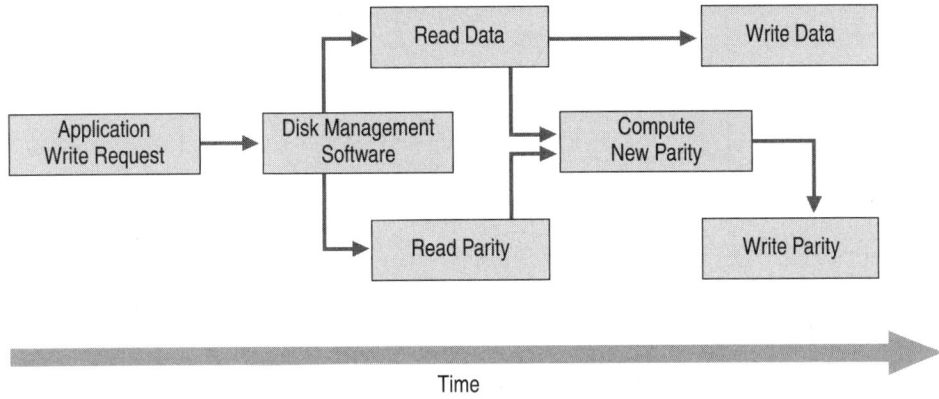

Figure 11.3   Writing Data to a RAID-5 Volume

Implementing a RAID-5 volume requires a minimum of three and a maximum of 32 disks in the set. The physical disks do not need to be identical. However, there must be equal size blocks of unused space available on each physical disk in the set. The disks can be on the same or different controllers. As with striped volumes, you cannot add disks to a RAID-5 volume if you need to increase the size of the volume later.

If one of the disks in a RAID-5 volume fails, none of the data is lost. When a read operation requires data from the failed disk, the system reads all of the remaining good data stripes in the stripe and the parity stripe. Each data stripe is subtracted (with XOR) from the parity stripe; the order is not important. The result is the missing data stripe.

When the system needs to write a data stripe to a disk that has failed, it reads the other data stripes and the parity stripe and backs them out of the parity stripe, leaving the missing data stripe. The modifications needed to the parity stripe can now be calculated and made. Because the data stripe is unavailable, it is not written; only the parity stripe is written.

There is no effect on a read operation when the disk that failed contains a parity stripe. (The parity stripe isn't needed for a read, unless there is a failure in a data stripe.) When the failed disk contains a parity stripe, the system does not compute or write the parity stripe when there is a change in a data stripe.

Advantages of RAID-5 Volumes

RAID-5 volumes are well suited for large sequential reads. Typically, RAID-5 is used in database mining. A RAID-5 volume also works well in the following situations:

- In large databases where reads occur much more often than writes. Performance degrades as the percentage of write operations increases. Database applications that read randomly work well with the built-in load balancing of a RAID-5 volume.

- Where a high degree of fault tolerance is required without the expense (incurred by the additional disk space required) of a mirrored volume. A RAID-5 volume is significantly more efficient than a mirrored volume when larger numbers of disks are used. The space required for storing the parity information is equivalent to 1/Number of disks, so a 10 disk array uses 1/10 of its capacity for parity information.

The utilization increases as the number of disks in the array increases.

Disadvantages of RAID-5 Volumes

In general, RAID-5 volumes are not well suited for any write intensive workload, since a single write is likely to generate a disk read of the parity and two writes (to update data and to parity).

A RAID-5 volume is not well suited for the following situations:

- Where applications that require high-speed data collection from a process are used. This type of application requires continuous high-speed disk writes, which do not work well with the asymmetrical I/O balance inherent in RAID-5 volumes and the extra I/Os required to write the parity stripe.

- In transaction processing database applications in which records are continually updated, such as in financial applications where balances are frequently updated.

- Where applications that require large sequential data transfers are used. These types of data transfer can prevent effective I/O load balancing.

Neither the system volume nor boot volume can be on a RAID-5 volume. If a disk that is part of a RAID-5 volume fails, read operations for data stripes on that disk are substantially slower than for a single disk. The software has to read all of the other disks in the set to calculate the data.

A RAID-5 volume requires more system memory than a mirrored volume.

Note On a computer running Windows 2000 Professional, 32 MB is the minimum amount of RAM; 64 MB is the minimum amount of RAM for a computer that is running Windows 2000 Server. You might want to add memory or use additional services when you configure disks as RAID-5 volumes.

Configuring and Using Mirrored Volumes and RAID-5 Volumes

This section discusses using features that are available in Windows 2000 Server software to implement mirrored volumes and RAID-5 volumes. It does not discuss configuring or using hardware RAID arrays.

Creating a Mirrored Volume or RAID-5 Volume

If you are using all SCSI disks, it is a good idea to use the same translation on all SCSI controllers on disks in a mirrored volume or RAID-5 volume. Disable translation when you do not need to multiple-boot with MS–DOS or have a system volume or boot volume larger than 1 gigabyte (GB).

When you create a mirrored or RAID-5 volume, Disk Management allocates unused space from each dynamic disk that you select.

For information about creating mirrored and RAID-5 volumes, see Windows 2000 Server Help.

Creating a Mirrored Volume

If you need to multiple-boot with MS–DOS, Windows 95, or Windows 98, you cannot mirror your system volume. If you need a boot volume larger than 1 GB, you need to enable translation.

When you want to create a mirrored volume, the original volume that you want to mirror must already exist. You must have an area of unused space on a dynamic disk at least as large as the original volume on another disk connected to the computer.

If the unused space that you select for the volume on the shadow disk is larger than the existing volume, the remaining space is unused and can be used to create other volumes.

Creating a RAID-5 Volume

To create a RAID-5 volume, you must have at least three unused areas on different dynamic disks connected to the computer. As with a mirrored volume, if the areas of unused space that you select for a RAID-5 volume are not all the same size, the space left over can also be used for other volumes.

When using a RAID-5 volume, performance is better if you put the operating system and page file on the volume and disks used for the RAID-5 volume. You can use different types of controllers for the operating system and the RAID-5 volume when you have them on separate controllers. For more suggestions, see "RAID-5 Volumes" earlier in this chapter.

Configuring the System Partition on a Mirrored Volume

If your system volume is on a SCSI disk, you need to have the BIOS enabled on the SCSI controller, or the system cannot find the MBR. If you have created a mirror of your system volume by using two SCSI controllers, make sure that you are using the same translation on both controllers.

Important Note that you cannot create a dynamic volume within Setup. If you must delete a dynamic volume from within Setup, delete all volumes on the disk. This reverts the drive to a basic drive and results in the loss of all data on that drive.

Use the translation feature on SCSI controllers to set the translation mode. Because you need to disable the BIOS on the second controller, Windows 2000 always translates the geometry of the shadow volume to 32 sectors per track and 64 heads per cylinder. Therefore, it is important to make sure that the SCSI controller for the original disk is using the same translation. When the BIOS is enabled, most SCSI controllers default to a large disk translation scheme if the disk is larger than 1 GB. The geometry for this translation is 255 heads and 63 sectors. Most SCSI controllers have a method to manually configure the controller to use the 32-sector, 64-head translation. Using 32 sectors and 64 heads on the controller for the original disk ensures that both disks are as close to a true sector-by-sector mirror image as possible. Recovery from failures of the original disk or its controller is *much* easier if the geometry of both disks is the same. The only disadvantage is that older controllers that do not support Interrupt 13 Extensions need the system volume to be within the first 1 GB, or 1024 cylinders, of the disk. Windows 2000 takes advantage of Interrupt 13 Extensions, which makes it possible for the system volume to reside on large volumes that exceed the 1024 cylinder limit

Disabling the controller BIOS is different from turning off translation. Problems occur because you need to have the BIOS enabled on the first controller to start the computer from the hard disk. If you do not turn off translation on both controllers, and the first controller fails, you need to enable the BIOS on the second controller. The translation on the second disk is now different than when you low-level formatted it, and you cannot use the disk.

Note If you disable the BIOS on both controllers, translation is automatically disabled as well. However, you cannot start up from the hard disk if the BIOS is disabled.

If you receive the message "Drive is too small" when you try to reconstruct the mirrored volume after the failure of the original disk, it is likely that the translation is not consistent.

Having two different SCSI controllers complicates restarting the computer in the event of a hardware failure. If you use two different SCSI controllers in your mirrored volume, you need to have a different SCSI device driver for each controller.

Note The term duplexed mirrored volume means that each disk in the mirrored volume has its own disk controller.

You can use Enhanced Integrated Drive Electronics (EIDE) controllers for a mirrored volume of the system volume. EIDE disks usually require motherboard BIOS support for logical block addressing (LBA), and each motherboard usually performs LBA in the same way for all EIDE disks.

Note If you are going to mirror an EIDE disk with a SCSI disk, do not mirror the system volume. However, you can mirror your boot volume.

When the shadow disk or controller fails, recovery is the same as recovering from any mirrored volume failure. Follow the guidelines for identical disks and controllers described earlier in this chapter. For more information about rebuilding the mirrored volume when you have replacement hardware, see "Repair, Recovery, and Restore" in this book and Windows 2000 Server Help.

When the original disk or controller fails, Windows 2000 seamlessly starts using the shadow disk for all accesses. For this reason, a problem can go undetected until you try to restart the computer. In this case, you might need to remove power from the failed disk or remove it from the SCSI bus before attempting to start from the shadow volume using the Windows 2000 startup floppy disk.

Important If you use a computer with an Extended Industry Standard Architecture (EISA) volume as the first volume on the primary system disk, you might find that the Windows 2000 startup floppy disk does not start the shadow drive. This is because the Boot.ini is pointing to volume(2) which is not the system volume on the shadow drive. On the shadow drive there is no EISA volume configured as the first volume on the shadow disk. Therefore, you need to change the volume parameter in the Boot.ini to volume(1) as well as changing the disk parameter to point to the shadow drive.

Important Try both startup paths before a failure, if possible. Also, you should always check Boot.ini if you are using mirrored volumes.

Guidelines for Configuring Mass Storage

When choosing a configuration for mass storage, you need to consider variables such as cost, performance, and the time required to completely rebuild a disk. Consider the relative advantages and disadvantages of mirrored volumes, RAID-5 volumes, or a combination of the two techniques.

In general, fault-tolerant configurations are only needed for information that must be readily available in case of hardware failure or unrecoverable disk errors. You do not need to have your page file on a fault-tolerant volume, and it is recommended that you not have the page file on a RAID-5 volume because of potential performance impacts.

You might not need to configure applications on a fault-tolerant volume. If you have applications and other common files on more than one computer running Windows 2000 Server, you can use replication to keep them consistent and to provide the redundancy. If you have applications on a single computer running Windows 2000 Server, you only need to configure them on a fault-tolerant volume if they must always be immediately available. Make sure that you back up the volume every time you install a new application or change default settings for an application.

Note Placing application data on a striped volume provides the fastest I/O performance for reading data.

If space is a consideration, format your application volume with NTFS (or convert a FAT volume to an NTFS volume), and use NTFS compression for folders and files on the volume.

Using Mirrored and RAID-5 Volumes

You need to consider the software and hardware constraints of fault-tolerant storage, as well as the cost and reliability of the system. Each vendor needs to have design guidelines for their system, whether you want a RAID array or want to use the fault-tolerant features provided in Windows 2000 Server.

In certain configurations and situations fault tolerance might not work as you might expect. Check that all of the disk hardware is on the Windows 2000 HCL. If any equipment is not included on the HCL, it might not work well.

If possible, use identical disks. Although this is not a requirement, there are several advantages to using identical hardware for fault-tolerant configurations:

- The performance of the disks are identical. Faster disks do not have to wait for slower disks.

- If you want to configure the entire disk for a mirrored volume or RAID-5 volume, the capacity is the same.

- There are fewer potential problems with configuration and compatibility.

Have a spare disk available and ready for use. When purchasing the disks, it is a good idea to purchase an extra disk for use as a spare. An identical disk guarantees that the spare disk is compatible, does not degrade the system performance, and can be easily installed. If you are using SCSI disks, check the disk documentation to see if you need to manually set the SCSI ID.

Having an available spare or warm spare (a disk that is powered at all times in the configuration and ready to be substituted) allows you to dynamically mirror or replace a member disk of a mirrored or RAID-5 volume in the event of a hardware failure on a spindle.

Have a backup controller available, or configure your disks with duplexed controllers. The system can continue operating when a disk fails, but not when a controller fails. System downtime can be minimized by having a preconfigured controller available. If the replacement controller is not the same as the original, you have to install a new driver, and your configuration becomes more complex.

Note If you have configured your system volume on a mirrored volume, use the same make and model of controller for your backup, and be sure to use the same translation for both the original and shadow volume.

Configuring Mirrored Volumes

To a large extent, how you configure your mirrored volumes depends on the number of disks and controllers that you want to have on the computer running Windows 2000 Server. Configuring your boot volume on a disk (and controller) that does not contain data sets results in better performance. There are also other considerations that are related to overall reliability.

When you use a mirrored volume for your system or boot partitions, the following issues must be kept in mind:

- You can make the configuration more fault tolerant by putting each disk member of the mirrored volume on separate controllers. This approach allows you to survive controller or disk failures. Putting each disk member of the mirrored volume on a separate channel of a multichannel controller does not make the controller fault tolerant. However, depending on the configuration, it might improve performance.

- Be sure to use the same disk translation for the disks in a mirrored volume of the system volume and to format both disks using the same controller.

Important Always try starting the computer from both mirrors *before* you have a failure.

Configuring RAID-5 Volumes

When configuring a RAID-5 volume, buy disks on the basis of cost per megabyte and performance, since storage efficiency increases with a larger number of disks. If you use high performance SCSI controllers, an array of six 9-GB disks provides more efficient storage than nine 6-GB disks. Smaller disks can also be rebuilt faster.

Keep the RAID-5 volume on a different controller and disk than your system and boot volume. Using separate controllers improves performance and can accelerate recovery from hardware failures. Remember that you cannot configure your system volume or your boot volume on a RAID-5 volume.

If the computer itself or the disk containing the boot volume fails (and the boot volume is not mirrored), it might be faster to move the RAID-5 volume to a different computer.

Fault-Tolerant Hardware Versus Software

The following are points to consider when deciding between a fault-tolerant hardware or software solution:

- Fault-tolerant software is available only on Windows 2000 Server.
- Hardware fault tolerance is faster.

- Software fault tolerance is less expensive.

- In a hardware fault tolerance implementation, some vendors support hot-swappable disks when there is a disk failure.

Regardless of whether you implement fault tolerance by using hardware or software, implementing fault tolerance does not reduce the need for backups.

Testing a Fault-Tolerant System

If the computer has software fault-tolerant volumes, test your configuration by simulating the failure and replacement of a disk.

Even though fault-tolerant volumes continue to work when one disk has failed, there is no fault tolerance until you install a replacement disk. A second disk failure during this interval will result in loss of data, because data redundancy was lost when the first failure occurred. If a backup disk is not readily available, significant business costs can result from the downtime.

If you have hardware RAID arrays, documentation provided by the vendor needs to describe how to recover from disk or controller failures. Make sure to test that their procedures work for your installation.

Important Fault tolerance is *not* an alternative to performing regular backups.

Avoiding Single Points of Failure

Although it is important to be prepared for problems, you can take steps to protect against certain failures, such as disk failures, component problems, network problems, and power failures. Hardware and software configurations can be implemented to help reduce the likelihood of problems that result in costly downtime and recovery processes.

Computers running Windows 2000 Server have fault tolerance features built into the operating system. Typically, fault tolerance applies to disk subsystems, but it can also apply to other parts of a system or an entire system. For example, a fully fault-tolerant computer system uses redundant disk controllers and a UPS as well as fault-tolerant disk subsystems.

Although data is always available and current in a fault-tolerant disk configuration, backups are always needed to protect data on a disk subsystem from failures caused by unpredictable occurrences such as user error, sabotage, or software malfunction, and catastrophes such as fires, earthquakes, or floods. Keeping replacement disks and controllers available on-site is cost-effective.

Disk fault tolerance is not an alternative to a backup strategy. Your backup strategy should include off-site storage.

Consider providing UPS protection for individual computers and the network itself, including hubs, bridges, and routers. Windows 2000 has UPS support on individual computers which typically provides power long enough for Windows 2000 to complete an orderly shutdown when power fails. If your company has a history of frequent or prolonged power outages, investigate alternative power sources besides the local power company for critical computers. It is important to remember that even a UPS for every computer on the network does not necessarily prevent data loss or corruption due to power fluctuations. The network is itself an electrical system. Intermediary devices such as routers, bridges, and hubs, require the same UPS protection to prevent loss of network functionality.

Avoiding Computer Component Failure

Typically, server failure is the most costly for a business, whether it is a file server, a print server, or an applications server. You need to consider the effects of individual components when deciding how to configure company computers and when to run diagnostic tests.

Motherboard and Central Processing Unit

Motherboards consist of electronics that can and do fail, although the motherboard and the CPU are generally reliable computer components. There is little that you can do to avoid a motherboard failure or CPU fault, except to run regular system checks to ensure that the components are functioning correctly. Some systems include built-in diagnostic tools that operate with Windows 2000.

RAM

The three major types of RAM that deal with error detection and correction are parity RAM, error-correction coding (ECC) RAM, and nonparity RAM.

Parity RAM Parity RAM contains an extra bit that indicates if each byte in the RAM is faulty. When parity RAM detects a parity difference, it signals the CPU through a nonmaskable interrupt (NMI). Depending on where and when detection happens, Windows 2000 determines if this is an I/O board parity error, memory bus error, or some other kind of parity error. Windows 2000 can also report I/O channel parity errors from cards in slots. This generates an error message in these cases, and sometimes the computer stops.

Error-correction coding RAM High-end systems often use ECC RAM, which can detect a two-bit failure and correct a single-bit failure in the system memory. Windows 2000 continues to run in spite of a single-bit failure. Depending on the hardware design, there might or might not be a report of this corrective action.

Nonparity RAM If you use nonparity RAM, Windows 2000 has no way to detect memory problems, and your computer might crash randomly. Nonparity RAM costs less than parity RAM, and parity RAM is not available for all computers. If you do not have parity RAM in your computers, ask your vendor if it can be installed or is supported by the computer.

Some vendors supply products that you can use to check the RAM in a computer.

Video Cards

Video cards drive the screen and render images for display. They rarely cause computer failures, but might cause the computer to behave erratically. More often, video cards cause screen painting problems, application page faults, and the like. Such problems are typically not critical enough to require you to shut down the computer. To minimize video problems, be sure that your computer is running the most recent release of a supported video driver.

Disks and Disk Controllers

You have many choices for your disk configuration, including fault tolerant configurations. EIDE and SCSI technologies each offer different benefits for fault tolerance and recovery. The MTBF gives you a measure of expected disk and controller reliability.

Be sure to run disk and controller diagnostics during every preventive maintenance check. Diagnostics are typically available from your hardware vendor. Windows 2000 automatically runs Chkdsk every time you start up the computer, and you can run a surface scan of the disks by specifying **chkdsk /r**. Chkdsk is also available from the Recovery Console.

Network Adapters

Asynchronous Transfer Mode (ATM) and other network adapters can have dual channel connections. If one channel fails, the other is automatically used.

Ethernet and Token Ring network adapters do not have dual channel capability. If the manufacturer provides a diagnostic program, it is recommended that you run it on the network adapterss during scheduled preventive maintenance or downtimes.

You can evaluate network segments with network packet trace programs, called sniffers. Network Monitor can check for the following problems:

- Invalid Cyclic Redundancy Checks (CRCs).
- Corrupted packets.
- Bandwidth saturation caused by a broadcast intensive network adapter.

Using an Uninterruptible Power Supply

An *uninterruptible power supply (UPS)* provides constant power to a computer system when a power fluctuation or power loss occurs. Built-in electronics constantly monitor line voltages: if the line voltage fluctuates above or below predefined limits, or fails entirely, the UPS supplies power to the computer system from built-in batteries. The UPS converts the direct current (DC) battery voltage into the alternating current (AC) voltage required by the computer system. The change to batteries must take place very rapidly to prevent data loss.

Most UPS devices are one of the following types:

- Online UPS. An online UPS is connected between the main power and the computer that constantly supplies power to your computer. The main power continuously charges the batteries which supply the power to the computer. Connecting it to the main power keeps its battery charged. This method provides power conditioning, which means that it removes spikes, surges, sags, and noise.

- Standby UPS. A device configured to provide either the main power or its own power source and to switch from one to the other as necessary. When main power is available, the UPS device connects the main power directly to the computer and monitors the main power voltage level. When the main power fails or the voltage falls below an acceptable level, the UPS device switches to its own power.

Use only UPS hardware that is included on the Windows 2000 HCL. Other options to consider include:

- Whether to use a separate UPS for each computer or have larger capacity, centralized UPSs that protect multiple computers.
- What type of UPS you want to use.
- How big the UPS needs to be to protect your computer systems.
- How long the UPS needs to run before automatically shutting down.
- What other features your UPS needs to have, such as:
  - Continuous conditioning of the incoming power to provide clean, steady power.
  - Software that produces statistics or logs UPS information to the event log.
  - Software for testing the integrity and reliability of the UPS battery.

For robust resistance to power failures, use UPS hardware connected to the computer and software that handles power failures, including shutting down the system before the UPS batteries are depleted. Without such software, human intervention is needed to shut down the system.

Windows 2000 has built-in UPS functionality that takes advantage of the features included with many UPS systems, such as ensuring the integrity of data on the system by providing for an orderly shutdown of the computer system if a power failure lasts long enough to deplete the UPS batteries. In addition, users connected to a computer running Windows 2000 Server can be notified that a shutdown will occur, and new users are prevented from connecting. Finally, damage to the hardware from a sudden, uncontrolled shutdown can be prevented.

Some vendors also provide a user interface for configuring the UPS, which you can use instead of the one provided in Windows 2000.

To fully protect your network, you also need to install a UPS on network devices such as routers, hubs, and bridges. For the best protection, install UPS systems on the cables that connect your computer to your modem, telephone, printer, and network equipment. Most UPS systems have built-in surge protection.

In Control Panel, click **Power Options** to configure the Windows 2000 UPS service.

▶ **To configure the UPS service in Windows 2000**

1. In Control Panel, select the **Power Options** option.

2. Select the **UPS** tab, and then click the **Select** button.

3. From the **UPS Select** dialog box, select the manufacturer and model of the UPS unit you are using.

4. In the **On port** field, select the port to which the UPS is connected, and then click **Finish**.

5. On the UPS page of the **Power Options Properties** dialog box, click the **Configure** button.

6. From the **UPS Configuration** dialog box, select the configuration options that best suit your needs.

7. Click **OK**.

8. On the **UPS** page of the **Power Options Properties** dialog box, click **OK** or **Apply** to commit the new settings.

The remaining information depends upon your specific UPS and its use.

When selecting the signals to use in the **UPS Configuration** group box, the interface voltages indicate the active state for the signal. For example, if you select a negative interface voltage for the power failure signal, the normally positive signal becomes negative when a power failure occurs.

Use the following procedure to configure the Windows 2000 UPS service to run a command file when a power failure occurs.

▶ **To configure the UPS service in Windows 2000 to run a command file when a power failure occurs**

1. In the **UPS Configuration** dialog box, select the **When the alarm occurs, run this program** check box, and then click **Configure**.

2. In the **UPS System Shutdown Program** dialog box, select the **Task** tab.

3. Type the name of the file in the **Run** field.

4. If you want the scheduled task to run at a specified time, select the **Enabled (scheduled task runs at specified time)** check box and continue this procedure.

5. Select the **Schedule** tab, and then select the frequency and start time of the task.

6. For further schedule settings, click the **Settings** tab.

7. Choose from options in the **Scheduled Task Completed**, **Idle Time** and **Power Management** areas of the **Settings** tab, then click **OK**.

8. In the **Set Account Information** dialog box, type the **Run as** and password information, and then click **OK**.

Note The command file must reside in %SystemRoot%\System32 and have a file name extension such as .exe, .com, .bat, or .cmd.

Avoiding Disruptions to Network Connections

If users cannot connect to the computers in a configuration that is running Windows 2000 Server, that configuration is not fault tolerant. You need to consider what can fail in the connections between computers as well as within an individual computer.

Network Cabling

If your company is growing, the connections between the computers that make up your configuration could become saturated with network traffic. It is recommended that you evaluate network traffic regularly to determine your need to upgrade by adding equipment. You can also use newer technologies, such as ATM, Fast Ethernet 100 BaseT, or GB Ethernet.

Intermediary Devices

Devices that connect different segments of your network, such as routers, bridges, hubs, and switches can also cause bottlenecks and failures. Intermediary devices need to be protected with a UPS.

Determine the level of vendor support available for each device, as well as the standards supported by each device, and whether the vendor has a migration path for new standards. You also need to find out if there are frequent software changes.

External Network Connections

If you lease an X.25 connection, an Integrated Services Digital Network (ISDN), Asymmetric Digital Subscriber Line (ADSL), or T1 line to connect to another building, branch, or subsidiary of your company, verify that your line vendor has adequate recovery procedures in place.

Additional Resources

- For more information about RAID volumes, see Windows 2000 Server Help.
- For more information about mirrored and RAID-5 volumes, see Windows 2000 Server Help.

CHAPTER 12

Backup

Backing up system state data, files, and other data on your system is an important aspect of planning a reliable configuration. If you do not back up your data, you might not be able to recover important information or settings when problems occur. Microsoft® Windows® 2000 provides a backup utility that you can use to make sure that up-to-date copies of your data can be readily restored.

In This Chapter

Related Information in the Resource Kit

- For more information about planning considerations, see "Planning a Reliable Configuration" in this book.

- For more information about restoring from backups, see "Repair, Recovery, and Restore" in this book.

- For more information about data storage options, see "Data Storage and Management" in this book.

Overview of Backups

Regular backup of servers and local hard disks prevents data loss and damage caused by disk drive failures, power outages, virus infection, and many other possible computer problems. Backup operations based on careful planning and reliable equipment make file recovery easier and less time consuming.

Backup Types

Backup can perform several types of backups:

- A normal backup copies all selected files and marks each as having been backed up. With normal backups, you need only the most recent copy of the backup file to restore all of the files.

- An incremental backup backs up only those files created or changed since the last normal or incremental backup. It marks files as having been backed up. If you use a combination of normal and incremental backups, you need the last normal backup set as well as all the incremental backup sets to restore your data.

- A differential backup copies files created or changed since the last normal or incremental backup. It does not mark files as having been backed up. If you are doing normal and differential backups, you must have the last normal and last differential backup sets to restore.

- A copy backup copies all selected files but does not mark each file as having been backed up. Copying is useful to back up files between normal and incremental backups, because it does not affect other backup operations.

- A daily backup copies all selected files that have been modified on the day that the daily backup is performed. The backed up files are not marked as having been backed up.

Note Perform regular backups when the fewest people are using the network. If many files are in use, the backup might not accurately reflect your network.

Storage Devices and Media

Windows 2000 can back up files to a variety of storage devices, including a tape drive. Data can be backed up to a logical drive, removable disk, network share, or a library of disks or tapes organized into a media pool and controlled by a robotic changer. If you do not have a separate storage device, you can back up to another hard disk or to a floppy disk.

Storage Devices

Storage technology changes rapidly, so it is important to research the merits of various media before you make a purchase. Consider drive and media costs, as well as reliability and capacity, when selecting a storage device. Ideally, a storage device has more than enough capacity to back up your largest server and can also detect and correct errors during backup-and-restore operations. For information about supported storage devices, see the Windows 2000 Hardware Compatibility List (HCL) link on the Web Resources page at http://windows.microsoft.com/windows2000/reskit/webresources.

Tip The best way to make sure that your storage devices and media are working correctly is to verify your backups by performing test restores.

Media Types

The most common type of medium is magnetic tape. The primary tape drives used for backup include a quarter-inch cartridge (QIC), digital audio tape (DAT), 8mm cassette, and digital linear tape (DLT). High-capacity, high-performance tape drives typically use SCSI controllers. Other types of media include magnetic disks, optical disks and CD-ROMs (CD-R and CD-RW).

Backup Strategies

A good backup strategy is the best defense against data loss. The following are three common backup strategies with questions to consider when determining what is appropriate for your computer system.

Network backup or server only Do you plan to back up your entire network, or do you have storage devices attached to certain servers where users copy their important files?

Individual or local computer backup Does each computer need a storage device? Is each user responsible for backing up his or her data?

Server and computer backup Does each department have a storage device and a designated user to back up all data for that department?

You can physically connect your storage device to a local computer or to a server. Table 12.1 lists some advantages and disadvantages of each configuration.

Table 12.1   Comparison of Server-Only and Local Computer Backups

Backup Type	Advantages	Disadvantages
Server-only	Fewer storage devices are needed. There is less media to manage because shared media stores multiple backups. If each server has more than one client computer, server-only backup costs less than backing up individual computers.	Registries and event logs of remote computers are not backed up. Backups and restorations are slower, due to network throughput. Backups and restorations require greater planning and preparation. They must be scheduled when network traffic is low or when critical information can be backed up as quickly as possible.
Local computer	Fewer network resources are committed to lengthy backup procedures. File recovery is quicker.	Using more storage devices costs more.

Backups that include computers running both Microsoft® Windows® 2000 Server and Microsoft® Windows® 2000 Professional combine the advantages and disadvantages of server-only and local computer backups. Additional considerations include the following:

- If you run backups from a server, you can back up and restore that server quickly. However, if your network has more than one server, the speed advantage is lost.

- Servers typically operate 24 hours a day, so it is possible to run backups during less busy hours. However, if a problem with backup hardware occurs, you might have to turn off the server.

- As a rule, if data is primarily on one server, it is better to run backups from that server.

Note Whether you run remote backups from a local computer or a server, it makes sense to place the storage device on the portion of your network with the greatest bandwidth or highest transmission frequency. You might also consider keeping the storage device in a secure room.

Figure 12.1 illustrates local computer and server-only backup options for a tape drive.

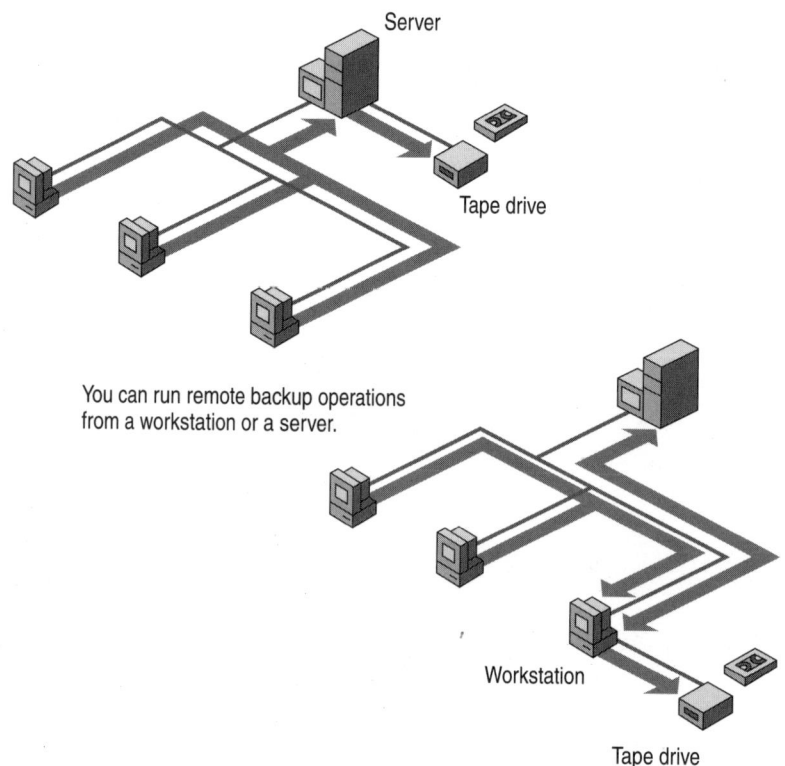

Figure 12.1   Server-Only and Local Computer Backup Configurations

Caution Backups protect data against viruses. Because some viruses take weeks to appear, it is recommended that you keep normal backup tapes for at least a month to make sure that you can restore a system to its uninfected status.

Security Considerations

There are several steps that you can take to enhance the security and operation of your backup-and-restore operations. You should also take steps to secure your backup media.

When you form a backup plan, consider implementing the following methods:

- Secure both the storage device and the backup media. Data from stolen media can be accessed and restored to another server.

- Back up an entire volume in case of a disk failure. It is more efficient to restore the entire volume in one operation.

- Always back up the system state data on a domain controller to prevent the loss of user accounts and security information.
- Keep three current copies of backup media. Store at least one copy off-site in a properly controlled environment.

Backup and Restore Rights

Backup and restore rights are independent of each other. However, you can grant both rights together.

Important You must have administrative privileges to restore the system, but only restore privileges are required to restore files.

If you are the system administrator, extend backup and restore rights only to persons responsible for backing up your network. In a minimum-security or medium-security network, grant one user backup rights and another user restore rights. Train personnel with restore rights to perform all restore tasks in the event that you are unavailable. In a high-security network, only you should restore files.

Caution A person who does not have permission to write to a file might have permission to restore the file. During restoration, such permission conflicts are ignored, and the existing file can be overwritten.

Granting Rights at Large Sites

Large sites might have two groups of backup operators: one with backup rights only; and the other with restore rights. It is recommended that you implement the following guidelines:

- Grant backup-only rights by creating a local group named Backup Operators and give members **Backup files and directories** user rights. Then, create a global group named Backup Only and add it to the local group.
- Grant restore-only rights by creating a local group named Restore Operators and give members **Restore files and directories** user rights. Then, create a global group named Restore Only and add it to the local group.

File Permissions

In Windows 2000, access to NTFS files is limited by NTFS file permissions, share permissions, and file attributes. You cannot back up or restore NTFS files to which you do not have access right unless:

- You belong to the permissions group of administrators, backup operators, or restore operators.

- You have been granted user rights to **Backup files and directories** (if you are backing up) and **Restore files and directories** (if you are restoring).

Note Neither the FAT16 nor the FAT32 file systems provide file permissions.

Storing Backup Media

Some kinds of information need to be stored near your computers to be readily available; store some data off-site to be available in the event of a disaster or for long-term storage.

Caution Backup media lasts longer in cool, humidity-controlled locations. Your storage area should also be free of magnetic fields, such as those near the backs of computer terminals and analog telephone equipment.

On-Site Storage

Some data needs to be stored on-site and readily available in the event of a failure.

Daily backups, whether full or incremental Store media in a fireproof safe or cabinet. Secure storage protects against natural disaster, theft, and sabotage.

Copies of the media If more than one copy of a software program is purchased, store one off-site if possible. If you have only one copy, you can back it up to media and label it as a backup of the application. If you need to reinstall software, you can restore from media to a computer running Windows 2000. You can then run the application setup program over the network and delete the software from the server.

Off-Site Storage

For highly confidential data that must be stored off-site, consider assistance from a company that specializes in secure data storage. Such companies lease space in underground vaults that remain impervious to most threats. If the cost or logistics of such protection is too great, use an alternative solution, such as a safe-deposit box or an off-site fireproof safe designed to protect magnetic media.

It is recommended that you store the following items off-site:

- A full backup of the entire system, best performed weekly.
- Original software installed on computers (only copies kept on site).
- Documents required for processing an insurance claim, such as purchase orders or receipts for computer hardware and software. (Pertinent information is available from your business insurance agent.)

- Information required to get network hardware reinstalled or reconfigured.
- Information required to reconfigure your storage subsystem.

Tip Make sure that your off-site storage location is bonded.

Establishing a Backup Plan

When developing your backup plan, keep the following in mind:

- Be sure to have spare hardware in case of a failure in your backup device.
- Test backed up data regularly to verify the reliability of your backup procedures and equipment.
- Include stress testing of backup hardware (storage drives, optical drives, and controllers) and software (backup program and device drivers).

Backup Scenarios

There is a wide range of system configurations that can affect your backup strategies. At one extreme is a small, simple network with a computer that must be backed up and also be available 24 hours a day, seven days a week; at the other is a computer with a large amount of data that needs to be backed up. This section discusses backup strategies for these two situations.

Caution Backup does not back up files on computers running Microsoft® MS-DOS®. Consider reserving some space on the server so that users of MS-DOS and Microsoft® Windows version 3.1 can copy important files. Those files can be backed up during regular server backups.

Small and Medium LANs

The following scenario illustrates a possible approach for backing up a small network comprised of a computer that is running Windows 2000 Server and 20 client computers:

The situation The clients are a mix of computers running MS-DOS, Microsoft® Windows® for Workgroups, Microsoft® Windows® 95, Microsoft® Windows® 98, Microsoft® Windows NT®, and Windows 2000. You plan to purchase one tape drive and a controller card and to use Backup.

An approach   You can work out a backup solution by following these four steps:

1. Research and select a tape drive for its reliability, speed, capacity, cost, and compatibility with Windows 2000. The drive should support tape cartridges with more than enough space to back up your entire server.

2. Install the tape controller card in the server. If you are using SCSI, put the tape drive on its own controller.

3. Connect your tape drive to the server so that you can back up the server system state data and so that server backups are most efficient. If you are using a SCSI tape driver, turn on the tape drive before turning on the server so that the SCSI tape driver can be loaded properly. From the server, you can back up user files on remote computers that are running Windows for Workgroups, Windows 95, Windows 98, Windows NT, and Windows 2000.

4. Establish a tape rotation schedule for backing up computers running Windows for Workgroups, Windows 95, Windows 98, Windows NT, and Windows 2000 Professional. To conserve tapes, back up clients less frequently than the server and encourage users to copy critical files to the server at the end of the day. Figure 12.2 shows one possible tape rotation schedule.

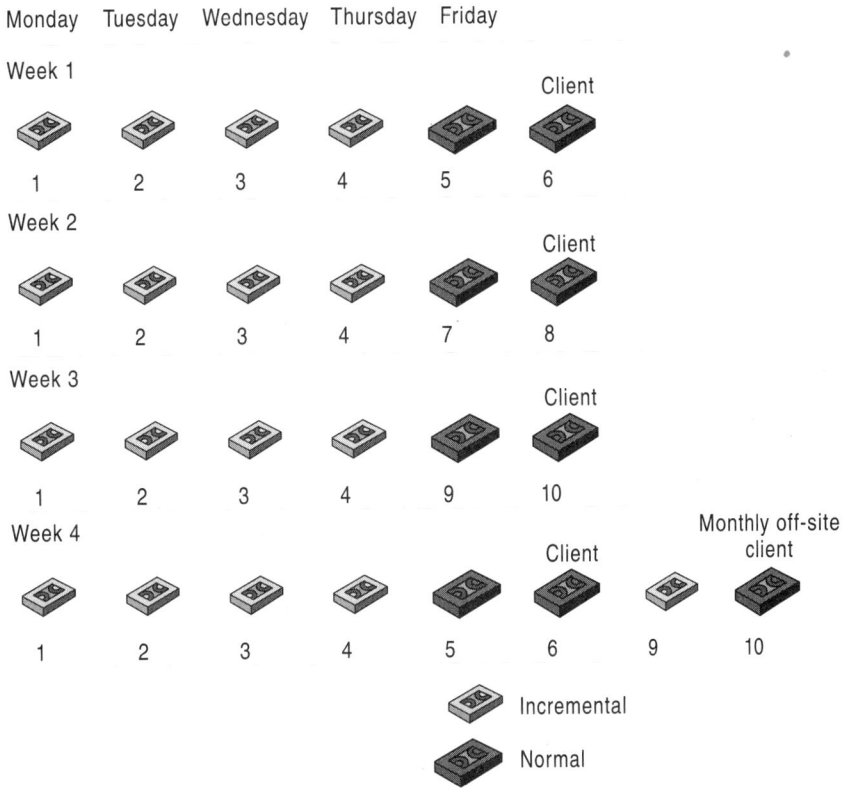

Figure 12.2   Possible Rotation Schedule for Backup

Methods for 24-Hour Operations or Very Large Backups

If you need to back up a lot of data, such as a Microsoft® SQL Server™ database or a number of large graphics files, it can take a long time. When the time available for backups is short, approaches that work for small and medium-sized local area networks (LANs) become inadequate. It is helpful if you use a backup utility that can back up while the application remains available to clients.

You can configure the disks that require daily backup separately from the Windows 2000 system disks. For critical data, use host-based or hardware-based redundant array of independent disks (RAID). For very critical data, you can even implement a software mirror of two separate hardware-controlled RAID arrays. With this configuration, if either a disk or an entire array fails, operations continue. If a component such as a network adapter, video device, IDE adapter, or power supply fails, it can easily be replaced. It is recommended that you have a spare computer with Windows 2000 Server installed as a backup for data. For more information about RAID arrays, see "Planning a Reliable Configuration" in this book.

Important   Hardware reliability does not replace the need for regular backups. Backing up data protects you against software problems as well as human error.

In the descriptions of the following methods, the computer that contains the data to be backed up is called Data. The computer that runs the backup is called Target. Unlike the Methods One and Two, Method Three allows users to continue to access Data while it is being backed up.

Method One

Back up Data locally to disk. Use a networked backup or Xcopy to move the resulting backup file to Target. Make sure to regularly run a backup verification pass comparing the data on Data and Target. Do not use Compare when you are using the Active Directory™ directory service because comparing data takes about twice as long as copying it. Typically, Ethernet or Token Ring transfer speeds are 1 megabyte (MB) per second if the network is not busy. You can use this transfer rate and the total amount of data being transferred to estimate the transfer time. You might need to use a faster network connection or a different backup method.

Method Two

Back up Data over the network to Target. Copy the data that you want to back up to another disk or disks on Data. Bring Data online, and copy the data using a backup device connected to Data. You can also back up Data over the network to Target. Whether to perform the backup from Data or from Target depends on the following factors:

- The availability of a target computer.

- Any backup policies requiring that backups be performed on designated computers.

- The time and cost of performing the backup from Data versus transferring the files to Target.

Method Three

Use hardware mirroring and third-party utilities that can mirror data across the network to another computer running Windows 2000 while the files are being used on Data. For more information about two-site backups, refer to the documentation provided by your hardware or software vendor. Mirroring data is best when you cannot risk losing data because a disk or RAID array fails or when you must protect against loss of an entire site. While there might be some downtime while moving data from the mirror computer to Data after a failure on Data is fixed, it is preferable to losing all data created or changed since the last backup.

Important   Backup file servers often. If the data is critical, it must be mandatory for users to close their files at the end of the day.

Establishing a Backup Schedule

The frequency with which you create backups depends on how often your data changes and how valuable your data is. You can perform a weekly backup, a monthly backup, and an archive backup. The archive backup can be a simple copy.

Twelve-Week Schedule

The 12-week schedule uses a different backup tape each day for two weeks, with the first tape being used again at the beginning of every third week. Incremental backups are performed Monday through Thursday, and normal backups are performed Friday, with the most recent normal backup stored on-site, as illustrated in Figure 12.3. The normal backup of the preceding week is stored off-site. At the end of 12 weeks, the cycle starts again with a new set of tapes.

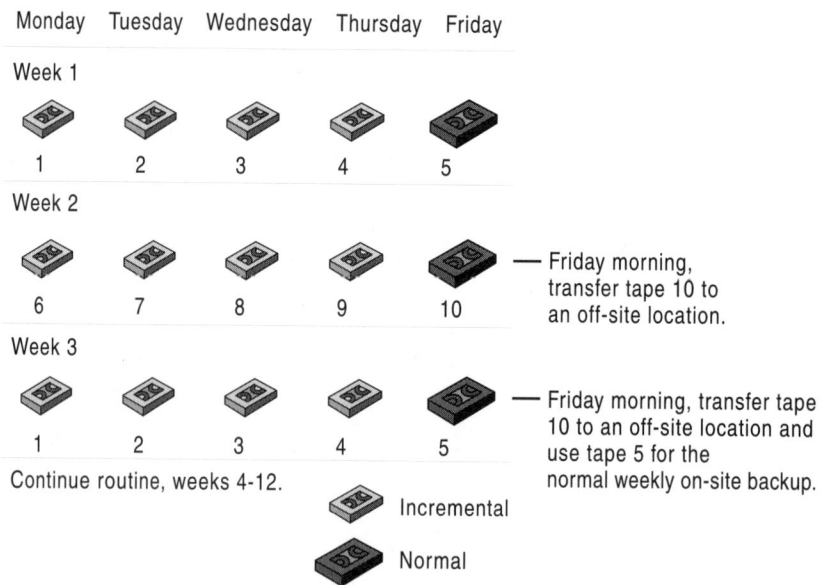

Figure 12.3 Backup Rotation for a 12-Week Schedule

Twelve-Month Schedule

One popular tape-alternation schedule uses 19 tapes over the course of one year. Four tapes are used Monday through Thursday for incremental backups, and three tapes are used for the normal backups performed each Friday. Figure 12.4 shows one month of the 12-month schedule. The remaining 12 tapes are used for monthly normal backups that are stored off-site.

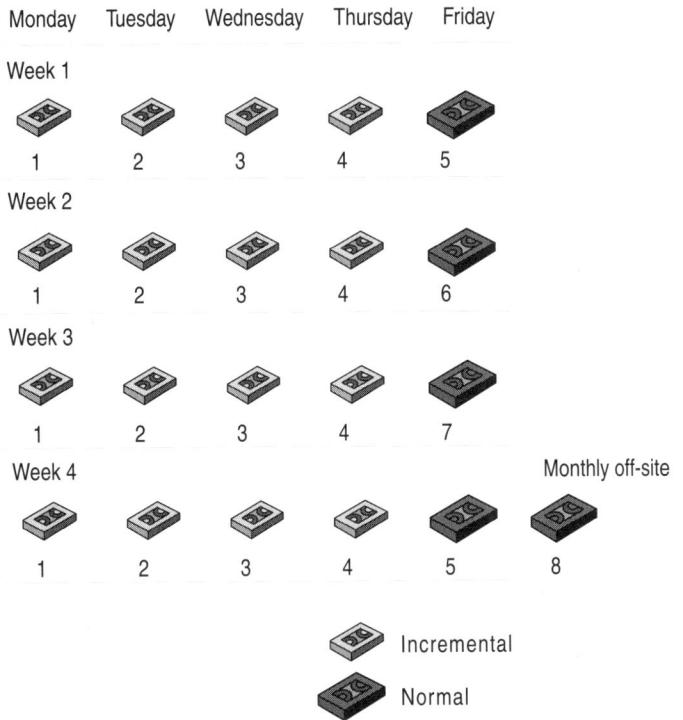

Figure 12.4   Backup Rotation for One Month in a 12-Month Schedule

Note   You can lower backup costs by alternating backup media. The life cycle of a tape depends on the manufacturer and on storage conditions.

Developing Backup and Restore Procedures

Backup specifics and procedures vary according to the needs of a company. After you develop your procedures based on the considerations discussed in this section, it is important to test, document, and verify them. Periodically reviewing your backup-and-restore process is a key part of ensuring data security.

Considerations for Developing Procedures

This section offers a series of checklists—suggestions and questions—to serve as flexible guidelines when you develop a comprehensive backup-and-restore process for your company.

Delegation of Tasks

It is critical that reliable personnel perform your backup and restore operations. Consider the following questions when deciding how to delegate these tasks:

- Who makes the policy that determines what files and computers are backed up, and how is the policy made known?
- Who is responsible for performing backups?
- If backups occur automatically, who handles interruptions such as error messages?
- Who does the backup when the assigned backup operator is unavailable?
- To whom is the success or failure of a backup reported? Who notifies the users if a backup fails?

Time-Sensitive Backup Questions

In addition to determining when and how often backups take place, it is important to know how long it takes to retrieve backup media and perform a restore. To determine this, ask the following questions:

- Do all backups, both full and partial, occur outside of regular business hours?
- Should backups occur immediately after or before regular business hours?
- How often do you perform full and incremental backups?
- How long does it take to retrieve backups or copies from a local or remote storage area? Can the remote copies be obtained at any time or only during business hours?
- How long does it take to perform a full restore if the computer fails?

In the Event of a Backup Problem

Make sure to take certain issues into consideration before a backup problem occurs:

- Determine who is notified if a problem or backup failure occurs, and what process they follow.
- If backup fails because of hardware problems, is standby hardware on-site or available on loan from your vendor? Determine how long it takes to replace failed hardware.
- Determine the availability of hardware and software technical support.
- Does your technical support staff have configuration information about computers running Windows 2000? If not, you need to determine how to make the information available in the event of a problem.
- How does support from hardware or software vendors affect how long fixes take?

- If trained personnel monitor overnight backups, are they also scheduled to work the next day? Who covers their other duties while they troubleshoot backup problems or restore data?

Security Considerations

The security of your backup operations, as well as the security of the storage location, is of paramount importance. Take the following questions into consideration when planning for the security of company data:

- Where are the backup tapes stored?
- What has been done to make the backup location secure in the event of fire, flood, theft, or another disaster?
- How is the backup location monitored?
- Are the tapes that are stored on-site always accessible to the people who need them?
- If there are copies of backup media, where are they stored?
- Is the backup location bonded?

Policy Considerations

Developing a backup-and-restore process and deciding what to back up requires that you either set or comply with company policy. Keep the following issues in mind when determining your backup plans:

- What is the policy for backup, and how is your plan in compliance?
- Are all modified files to be backed up, or does company policy specify only critical files or the files of certain users, groups, departments, or divisions?
- Are any disks or volumes on the computer not to be backed up?
- Are users responsible for backing up their own client systems?
- Is there a charge-back system for the amount of storage used?
- How is the backup process validated?

Technical Considerations

You also need to determine how your backups are performed. For instance, determine the following:

- Does the system have to meet certain conditions before the backup starts?
- How is the backup started—from the command line, from an icon, or by batch?
- Are logs created and are they correct?
- If the path is long, the file name odd, the file size very large, or the number of files large, does the backup still work? Can you restore files that have these characteristics?

- Is the backup done to a local tape drive, remotely over the LAN, or remotely over the wide area network (WAN)?

- Does the tape verify that the backed-up data is correct?

- How are the connections between a data source and the storage device verified before the backup begins?

- Are computers equipped for power outages if operators are not present when backups take place?

- Do backups occur on schedule?

- What is the process in place for dealing with unforeseen occurrences during a backup or restore?

Testing Backup-and-Restore Procedures

Complete verification of the entire backup-and-restore process is critical. Develop backup-and-restore strategies with appropriate resources and personnel, and then test them. Testing backup strategies also demonstrates how much time is required to restore data. A good plan ensures fast recovery of lost data.

Try performing a trial restoration periodically to verify that your files are properly backed up. A trial restoration can uncover hardware problems that do not show up with software verifications.

After a backup strategy has been designed, test it thoroughly with as many simulated failures as possible. For example, if you use disk mirroring, simulate a disk failure by removing or powering down one of the mirrors and ensure that remaining mirror continues to operate without interruption. Again, while RAID is effective, it does not eliminate the need for backups. A data recovery plan based on disk mirroring alone offers no protection if a computer is stolen.

The following questions can help you assess your verification strategy.

- Has every option that you expect to use been tested?

- Do automated backup instructions work?

- Does the backup-and-restore process work properly?

- After you make changes to the operating system (such as installing a service pack), or the backup program, does the backup-and-restore process work properly?

- After you make hardware changes (such as installing a new controller or tape drive, or changing the BIOS on the motherboard) does the backup-and-restore process work properly?

- When you change the hardware or software involved in a backup, how do you verify that you can use the old tapes?

Documenting Backup-and-Restore Procedures

Keeping accurate backup records is essential to finding missing information quickly, particularly if you have accumulated a large number of high-volume media. Thorough records include media labels, catalogs, and online log files and log books.

Media labels Labels should contain a date, the type of backup (normal, incremental, or differential), and a list of contents. If you are restoring from differential or incremental backups, you need to locate the last normal backup and either the last differential backup or all incremental backups created since the last normal backup. Alternately, you can label media sequentially and keep a log book of media content.

Catalogs Most backup software includes a mechanism for cataloging backup files. Backup stores backup catalogs on the backup media and temporarily loads them into memory. Catalogs are created for each backup set, or collection of backed up files from one drive.

Log files Log files include the names of all backed up and restored files and directories. A log file is useful when restoring data because you can print or read it from any text editor. Keeping printed logs in a notebook makes it easier to locate specific files. For example, if the tape containing the catalog of the backup set is corrupt, you can use the printed logs to locate a file.

Conducting Verify Operations

A verify operation compares the files on disk to the files on backup media. It occurs after all files are backed up or restored, and it takes about as long as the backup procedure. It is recommended that you perform a verify operation after every backup, especially if you back up to a set of media for long-term storage. A verify operation is also recommended after file recovery.

Note If a verify operation fails for a given file, check the date that the file was last modified. If the file changes between a backup and a verify operation, the verify operation fails.

Backing Up System State Data

System state data is comprised of the following files:

- Boot files, including the system files, and all files protected by Windows File Protection (WFP).
- Active Directory (on a domain controller only).
- Sysvol (on a domain controller only).

- Certificate Services (on certification authority only).
- Cluster database (on a cluster node only).
- The registry.
- Performance counter configuration information.
- Component Services Class registration database.

The system state data can be backed up in any order. Restoration of the system state replaces boot files first and commits the system hive of the registry as a final step in the process.

System state backup and restore operations include all system state data: you cannot choose to backup or restore individual components due to dependencies among the system state components. However, you can restore system state data to an alternate location in which only the registry files, Sysvol directory files, and system boot files are restored. The Active Directory database, Certificate Services database, and Component Services Class Registration database are not restored to the alternate location.

Although you cannot change which components of the system state are backed up, you can back up all protected system files with the system state data by setting advanced backup options.

▶ **To set advanced backup options**

1. In the **Backup** dialog box, click the **Backup** tab, and then select the files and folders that you want to back up.
2. Click **Start Backup**.
3. In the **Backup Job Information** dialog box, click **Advanced**.
4. Set the advanced backup options that you want, and then click **OK**.

The advanced backup options are described in Table 12.2.

Table 12.2   Advanced Backup Options

Option	Description
Back up data that is in Remote Storage	Backs up data that has been designated for Remote Storage. You can restore Remote Storage data only to an NTFS volume that is used with Windows 2000.
Verify data after backup	Verifies that the backed up data is exactly the same as the original data. This could substantially increase the time it takes to perform a backup.

(continued)

Table 12.2   Advanced Backup Options *(continued)*

Option	Description
If possible, compress the backup data to save space	Compresses the data you are backing up so you can save more data on a tape. If this option is disabled, you do not have a tape drive on your computer or your tape drive cannot compress data.
Automatically back up system protected files with the system state	Backs up all of the system files that are in your %SystemRoot% directory in addition to the boot files that are included with the system state data. Substantially increase the size of your backup job.

Note If you have more than one domain controller in your organization, and Active Directory is replicated to any of these other servers, you might have to authoritatively restore any Active Directory data that you want to restore. For more information about authoritative restores, see the *Microsoft® Windows® 2000 Server Resource Kit Distributed Systems Guide*.

▶ **To back up system state data**

1. Start Backup.

2. Click the **Backup** tab, and then select the **System State** check box.

   This backs up the system state data along with any other data that you have selected for the current backup operation.

Keep the following in mind when you are backing up system state data:

- You must be an administrator or a backup operator to back up files and folders.

- You can only back up the system state data on a local computer. You cannot back up the system state data on a remote computer.

- You can also use the Backup wizard to back up system state data.

If you are backing up the system state data to a tape, and the Backup program indicates that there is no unused media available, you might have to use Removable Storage to add your tape to the Backup media pool. For more information about Removable Storage, see "Data Storage and Management" in this book.

Boot and System Files

Backup considers the functionality of WFP when backing up and restoring boot and system files. System files are backed up and restored as a single entity. The Window File Protection service catalog file, located in the folder %SystemRoot%\system32\ catroot\{F750E6C3-38EE-11D1-85E5-00C04FC295EE}, is backed up with the system files.

In Windows NT 4.0 and earlier, backup programs could selectively backup and restore operating system files as they would data files, allowing for incremental backup and restore operations of most operating system files. Windows 2000, however, does not allow incremental restoration of operating system files.

The Advanced Backup option **Automatically back up system protected files with the System State** backs up all system files that are in your %SystemRoot% directory, in addition to the startup files that are included with the system state data.

Active Directory

A directory service provides a way to locate and identify users and resources available in a distributed system. Windows 2000 Server includes Active Directory to manage the enterprise directory information for distributed networks. The information in this directory must be considered within your overall backup and restore strategy.

The directory service can be backed up either online or offline, but the restoration process can be completed only when the directory is offline, similar to Microsoft® Exchange Server. The Active Directory database can only be backed up completely; incremental backup is not supported.

Directory information can be replicated, so the system administrator needs to formulate a recovery plan. One option is to restore a replica of the directory and then propagate changes that occurred since the backup from other replicas in the domain. The domain controller can also be restored from tape backup. This assumes that other replicas are not corrupted. If the other replicas are corrupted, you might need to do an authoritative restore. For more information about Active Directory backups, see the *Distributed Systems Guide*.

Certificate Services Information

Windows 2000 includes a certificate server service that can be installed and configured to provide X.509 certificates for clients. A full backup of the Certificate Services database must exist before it can be restored.

Cluster Database

System state data includes the cluster database. For more information about backing up and restoring clusters, see the *Distributed Systems Guide*.

Registry

The contents of the registry are backed up and restored when you back up and restore system state data.

When you back up the system state data, a copy of your registry files is also saved in the folder %SystemRoot%\Repair\Regback. If your registry files become corrupted or are accidentally erased, you can use these files to repair the registry without performing a full restore of the system state data. This method of repairing the registry is only recommended for advanced users.

Important It is important that you have current, reliable backup copies of the registry. Make sure to back up the registry as part of your regular backup routine and before you edit the registry. If you select the **System State** check box on the **Backup** tab in Backup, the registry is automatically backed up.

Performance Counter Configuration

The performance counter configuration files are also backed up and restored as part of the boot data.

Component Services Class Registration Database

The Component Object Model (COM) is a binary standard for writing component software in a distributed systems environment. The Component Services Class Registration Database is backed up and restored with the system state data.

Component Services have special backup and restore considerations. There are two Component Services elements on each system: the component binaries, including dynamic-link libraries (DLLs) and executable files (EXEs), and the Component Services database. The components are backed up as a part of normal file enumeration. The Component Services database, however, is backed up and restored as a part of the system state data.

Using Backup

Backup is a graphical tool used with a variety of storage media to back up and restore files on either NTFS or file allocation table (FAT) volumes. Backup also simplifies archiving and allows you to use the Windows 2000 Job Scheduler for automating backup jobs.

Tasks such as mounting and dismounting a tape or disk are done by Removable Storage. It tracks and controls backup media, usually organized into pools, on storage devices, and allows applications such as Backup to share robotic changers and media libraries. Once started, Removable Storage is transparent to the data path, so you only need to access it when changing media, not when performing a backup or restore operation.

Note You can back up to a file or a tape without using Removable Storage as long as the backup medium is not part of a media pool.

Selecting Backup Type

There are several factors to consider when deciding what backup to use, including the following issues:

- The normal backup type is best when a large amount of data changes between backups or to provide a baseline for the other backup types.
- The incremental backup type is best to record the progression of frequently changed data.
- The differential backup type simplifies the process for restoring files.
- To provide for long-term storage with fewer media, you can use a combination of a normal backup plus either incremental or differential backups.

Some backup types use backup markers, also known as archive attributes, to track when a file has been backed up. When the file changes, Windows 2000 marks the file to be backed up again. Files or directories that have been moved to a new location are not marked for backup. Backup allows you to choose to back up only files with this marker set, and you can choose whether or not to mark files as having been backed up.

Table 12.3 lists the main advantages and disadvantages associated with common types of backup.

Table 12.3   Advantages and Disadvantages of Backup Types

Backup type	Advantages	Disadvantages
Normal	Files are easy to find because they are always on a current backup of your system or on one medium. File recovery requires only one medium or set of media.	Most time-consuming. If files do not change frequently, backups are redundant.
Incremental	Least data storage space required. Least time-consuming.	Files can be difficult to find, because they can be on several media.
Differential	Recovery requires only the last normal backup medium and last differential medium. Less time-consuming than normal backups.	Recovery takes longer than if files were on a single medium. If large amounts of data change daily, backups can consume more time than incremental backups.

Selecting Backup Media

Backup displays a list of all available storage devices in **Backup** destination the **Backup** tab. If no external devices are detected, you can back up to disk. If you want to back up to media not managed by Removable Storage, make sure that the disk or tape is loaded in a stand-alone storage device.

Note If you are backing up to media managed by Removable Storage, you must first start Removable Storage in the Services snap-in. To back up to new media, you must first make the media available in the media scratch pool. If you want to back up to an existing media pool, the media must be loaded in the library. For more information about using Removable Storage, see "Data Storage and Management" in this book.

Files Skipped During Backup

Backup skips the following file types during the backup and restore processes:

- Files that are held open by other applications.
- Files that are skipped by default by Backup.

Files Skipped by Default

Backup skips certain files by default, including the following:

- Files that you do not have permission to read. Only users with backup rights can copy files that they do not own.

- Files that are temporary in nature, such as Pagefile.sys, Hiberfil.sys, Win386.swp, 386spart.par, Backup.log, and Restore.log. These files are neither backed up nor restored by Backup. The list of skipped files is embedded into Backup and cannot be changed.

- Registry files on remote computers. Windows 2000 backs up only local registry files.

Locked Files

Windows 2000 lets you back up local files that are exclusively locked by the operating system, such as event logs and registry files; however, Backup skips those files held open by other processes.

Encrypted Files

If encrypted files exist on backup tapes, it is important to ensure that user keys, particularly the recovery agent keys, are also stored safely on backup media. Certificate Services provides methods to export keys to floppy disks, or other removable media so that they can be secured in a trusted location.

For more information about Encrypting File System (EFS), see "Encrypting File System" in the *Distributed Systems Guide*.

Backing Up Files on Your Local Computer

Backup lets you back up any file on your local disk system. This section describes various files on your local computer that it is recommended to back up.

Logon Scripts

Logon scripts are files that can be assigned to user accounts. Each time a user logs on, the assigned logon script is run. You can use logon scripts to configure user working environments by creating network connections and starting applications. Logon scripts are useful when you want to affect the user work environment without managing all aspects of it. A logon script is always downloaded from the computer running Windows 2000 Server that validates a user's logon request.

On Windows 2000 Server domains, any domain controller can authorize a user's logon attempt. To ensure that logon scripts always work, make sure that logon scripts for all user accounts in a domain exist on every domain controller.

To ensure that logon scripts are always available and consistent, use the Active Directory Replicator service. In replication, copies of the files are sent across the network to other computers. A domain controller sends the logon scripts to the other computers in the domain.

Note Only use replication for critical information that must be available because replicating files puts a large load on the network. For example, use replication for such critical data as the DHCP and WINS databases. For more information, see the *Microsoft® Windows® 2000 Server Resource Kit TCP/IP Core Networking Guide*.

User Data

Most changes on a server occurs in the users' folders. Users constantly add, modify, or delete files from the computer. It is recommended that you back up changes to users' folders daily.

Some users keep most of the files that they want backed up on file servers. Other users require that data on local computers be backed up. Your backup procedures need to consider both situations.

Application Programs

Network users primarily use applications, such as Microsoft® Word. You can reinstall the executable files from the original distribution media, but the time and productivity lost make this approach less than ideal. Additionally, if you have customized the applications to suit the needs of your organization, then reproducing those settings can be more difficult than reloading the programs themselves. Since the applications rarely change, backing them up as part of your backup procedure ensures that the latest version is always available without using a lot of offline storage space.

Archived Data

Backup can back up data that has been archived using Remote Storage. If the archived files are on your local disk, the backup operation works the same as any other. If the archived files are offline or remote, only placeholders on your local disk for the archived data are backed up. If you elect to back up the remote archived data, do so by direct media copy (tape to tape).

Backing Up Files on Remote Computers

You can use Backup to back up files on any computers to which you can connect remotely. This allows a single media drive to be shared across an entire network and one backup policy to be in effect for the entire network.

Note Backup does not recognize MS-DOS or computers that are running Windows 3.1.

Backing Up Windows 2000 Services and NTFS Features

Windows 2000 includes a number of system services and NTFS features that require special handling of descriptive catalog, metadata, or logging data stores. The binaries of these extensions and services are backed up during normal file backup. Temporary files or other files that can be skipped are registered to be excluded.

Remote Storage Considerations

Implement Remote Storage should be implemented within a well-planned primary backup scheme. Remote Storage media are standard Microsoft Tape Format (MTF) tapes. MTF-compliant backup applications can catalog the tapes and restore migrated files from Remote Storage media.

Important Do not confuse Remote Storage media with primary backup media or view Remote Storage as a substitute for primary backups. Remote Storage migrates data that is used infrequently. Busy data that needs to be restored immediately after a primary storage catastrophe, is less likely to be present on Remote Storage media.

Remote Storage enhances system usability by ensuring a steady supply of free space on file server volumes. It also enhances backup procedures because infrequently used data is no longer present on the volume, and this data doesn't need to be included in a full backup. It is not meant to protect data the way that backup applications do.

Where backup and Remote Storage share a single tape changer that only has one tape drive, backups of this type cannot be created because they would be contending for use of the single tape drive. Remote Storage uses Removable Storage to arbitrate its access to secondary storage. If Backup also uses Removable Storage, then under normal conditions the backup application and Remote Storage can share devices. However, Remote Storage recalls cannot preempt backup jobs, so it is necessary to ensure that backups do not cause recalls when only a single tape drive is available.

When writing to tape media, Remote Storage uses the MTF. When files cannot be recovered from regular backups, Backup uses MTF tapes to restore the Remote Storage data from the Remote Storage tapes.

For more information about Remote Storage, see "Data Storage and Management" in this book.

Backing Up Remote Storage Databases

Remote Storage requires that the Remote Storage database files be backed up during Backup operations. If the database files are corrupted or lost, stop all Remote Storage services, restore the database files, and then restart the service. If the files in %SystemRoot%\system32\NtmsData are backed up, Remote Storage functions properly after they are restored. Make sure that the system directories are assigned to the same path, including drive letter and directory structure. For example, if the system path is D:\Winnt\system32 prior to the recovery of Windows 2000, after recovery operations the drive letter is still D and the path is still Winnt\system32.

Protecting Remote Storage Media

Administrators can make up to three copies of each Remote Storage medium. This ensures that tape media, which is less durable than other types of media, is available to the administrator for multiple purposes, including rotating media to off-site storage and having data redundancy in case a tape becomes no longer usable. Media sets can be removed from changers to provide shelf storage of infrequently used data. Media sets can also be added to the backup sets to provide a full set of managed data for recovery.

Using the Remote Storage snap-in, the administrator can identify the copy state of each Remote Storage medium, request that copies be created or updated, and request that media be recreated from copies. Media copies should be part of the normal backup procedure for a Remote Storage volume.

A minimum of two drive changers and three tapes of equal length are needed to create media copies.

Once Remote Storage data has been moved to the media, a copy set of all Remote Storage media can be produced.

▶ **To make media copies**

1. In the Remote Storage snap-in, set the number of needed media copies on the general properties tab. You need enough media within the changer to be able to create copies of each medium that is within the Remote Storage media list.

2. In the media context menu, start the Submit Synchronize Media Copies Now wizard. This will submit a one-time-only scheduled job to provide a copy of the media.

Note The schedule can be updated under the scheduled task manager to provide an update of the copy set regularly. Only use this option if media sets are not being rotated out of the changer.

▶ **To add a media copy to the Backup set for recovery**

1. After performing the media copy procedure, right-click the media set that is going to be used as part of the backup set.

   The copy must be in the Remote Storage pool before it can be deleted from the Remote Storage databases. By deleting the media copy, you set the tape to Idle, Available.

2. In the Remote Storage pool, right-click the appropriate media, and then click **Copy**.

3. In the Remote Storage pool, right-click the wanted media pool, and then click **Paste**.

   This allows the media copy to become part of the Backup set. This medium can subsequently be removed from the changer. A medium that is created by Backup does not carry an on tape catalog and requires significantly more time to restore than media produced from Remote Storage. Use multiple media copies to recover the media from a standard media copy. The deleted media copies can be recreated. Copies that are deleted from the database are not available for Remote Storage recovery but can be recovered using Backup.

Remote Storage Self-Backup

Although Remote Storage requires that managed files be backed up, it also copies critical structured storage and Jet database information on Remote Storage media.

Exchange Database

Although the Exchange directory and information store services are independent of each other, they are built on top of Jet databases.

Backing up Exchange

The Exchange services are backed up online with the data divided into two parts: the database, and the transaction logs and patch files. The transaction logs can be backed up independently from the database during an incremental backup. Backup determines which services are running on the specified server.

Note To restore, the Exchange service needs the database and a sequential list of transaction logs. If circular logging is enabled on Exchange services, it is not possible to perform a no-loss restore. A no-loss restore uses the log files that reside on the system prior to the restore along with the restored log files to bring the system data to a state just before the crash. Thus if circular logging is enabled, then the existing logs must be deleted. After the restore, the system data is at the state it was just after the backup.

If the log file path is not set, a new log is created on the default directory. Otherwise, the existing log files are used.

Restoring Exchange

Exchange services are restored offline. To perform the restoration, Backup stops the associated services. The Win32 Service Manager functions are used to control the services.

SQL Database Backup

Microsoft® SQL Server™ should not be backed up using Backup. SQL Server has a built-in backup capability. A separate process should be in place to ensure that SQL Server is properly backed up.

Logical Volume Information

In Windows 2000, the Fault Tolerant Disk state is stored on disk in hidden sectors. This is a change from Windows NT, which stored this information in the registry. Backup applications do not save or restore Fault Tolerant Disk configuration information in Windows 2000. It is up to the operator to reconfigure the disks to the original configuration (including stripe sets, mirrors, and volume sets) prior to restore.

CHAPTER 13

Repair, Recovery, and Restore

No computer is failure proof, but preventative measures and strategic planning can make a computer running Microsoft® Windows® 2000 more failure resistant. Developing plans and procedures for recovering from failures before they occur can also minimize damage and time lost. Maintaining records about your hardware and software configurations, and regularly backing up data and system configurations can help you recover from serious failures.

In This Chapter

Related Information in the Resource Kit

- For more information about planning before failures occur, see "Planning a Reliable Configuration" in this book.

- For more information about creating backups to use during recovery, see "Backup" in this book.

- For more information about common disk problems, see "Disk Concepts and Troubleshooting" in this book.

Repairing a Windows 2000 Installation

Windows 2000 provides you with the option of fixing problems by using either the Recovery Console or the Emergency Repair Process. During Setup you are asked if you want to set up Windows 2000, repair a Windows 2000 installation, or quit Setup. When you select the Repair option by pressing R, the following information is displayed on your screen:

```
Windows 2000 repair options:
    To repair a Windows 2000 installation by using
    the recovery console, press C.
    To repair a Windows 2000 installation by using
    the Emergency Repair Process, press R.
```

Using each of these options to repair a Windows 2000 installation is discussed in the following sections.

Important If the repair options do not work, it might be necessary to perform an in-place upgrade. For more information about this option, see "If the Emergency Repair Process Does Not Fix Your System" later in this chapter.

Using the Recovery Console

The Recovery Console is a text-mode command interpreter that is separate from the Windows 2000 command prompt and allows the system administrator to gain access to the hard disk of a computer running Windows 2000, regardless of the file format used, for basic troubleshooting and system maintenance. Since starting Windows 2000 is not a prerequisite for using the Recovery Console, it can help you recover when your Windows 2000–based computer does not start properly or at all. The Recovery Console allows you to obtain limited access to NTFS, file allocation table (FAT), (FAT16 and FAT32) volumes without starting the graphical interface. The Recovery Console allows administrators and Microsoft Product Support Services technicians to start and stop services, and repair the system in a very granular way. It can also be used to repair the master boot record (MBR) and boot sector and to format volumes. The Recovery Console prevents unauthorized access to volumes by requiring the user to enter the system administrator password.

Note If you are using software mirroring or if you are running the Recovery Console using a Remote Install Server, see the Microsoft Knowledge Base link on the Web Resources page at http://windows.microsoft.com/windows2000/reskit/webresources.

Starting the Recovery Console

To start the Recovery Console, start the computer from the Windows 2000 Setup CD or the Windows 2000 Setup floppy disks. If you do not have Setup floppy disks and your computer cannot start from the Windows 2000 Setup CD, use another Windows 2000–based computer to create the Setup floppy disks. For more information about creating the Windows 2000 Setup floppy disks, see "Planning a Reliable Configuration" in this book or Windows 2000 Server Help.

If the Recovery Console was installed on the local hard disk, it can also be accessed from the Windows 2000 startup menu. However, if the MBR or the system volume boot sector has been damaged, you need to start the computer using either the Windows 2000 Setup floppy disks or the Windows 2000 Setup CD to access the Recovery Console.

To add the Recovery Console to existing installations of Windows 2000, on the **Start** menu, click **Run**, and then type:

```
F:\I386\Winnt32.exe /cmdcons
```

where **F** is the CD-ROM drive letter.

This installation requires approximately 7 megabytes (MB) of disk space on your system partition.

Important You cannot preinstall the Recovery Console on a computer that contains a mirrored volume. First break the mirror, then install the Recovery Console. After the Recovery Console is installed, you can re-establish the mirrored volume. For more information, see the Microsoft Knowledge Base link on the Web Resources page at http://windows.microsoft.com/windows2000/reskit/webresources.

Start the computer and enter Windows 2000 Setup. Press ENTER at the "Setup Notification" screen. Press R to repair a Windows 2000 installation, and then press C to use the Recovery Console.

When the Recovery Console is started, the following information is displayed:

```
Microsoft Windows 2000(TM) Recovery Console.

The Recovery Console provides system repair and recovery
functionality.

Type EXIT to quit the Recovery Console and restart the computer.

1: C:\WINNT

Which Windows 2000 installation would you like to log onto
(To cancel, press ENTER)?
```

Important If there is more than one installation of Windows 2000 or Microsoft®
Windows NT® 4.0 or earlier, they are also shown in the Recovery Console startup
menu.

Mirrored volumes appear twice in the Recovery Console startup menu, but each
entry has the same drive letter so they are actually the same drive.

Changes made in the Recovery Console to mirrored volumes are mirrored.

To access the disk by using the Recovery Console, press the number key
representing the Windows 2000 installation that you want to repair, and then press
ENTER. The Recovery Console then prompts you for the administrator password.
If you press ENTER without typing a number, the Recovery Console exits and
restarts the computer.

Note To use the Recovery Console, you must know the password for the local
Administrator account. If you do not have the correct password, Recovery
Console does not allow access to the computer. If an incorrect password is entered
three times, the Recovery Console quits and restarts the computer. However, you
can use either the Group Policy snap-in or the Security Configuration and
Analysis snap-in to specify automatic administrative logon.

Once the password has been validated, you have full access to the Recovery
Console, but limited access to the hard disk. You can only access the following
folders on your computer:

- %SystemRoot%. If you have multiple Windows installations, this is on the
  partition that contains Boot.ini and other Windows files required to start the
  system.

- %Windir% and subfolders of the Windows 2000 installation that you are currently logged on to.
- %SystemRoot%\Cmdcons and its subfolders.

Note With the **set** command enabled, you can copy files to removable media and access all paths on the system. The **set** command is an optional Recovery Console command that can be enabled by either the Group Policy snap-in or the Security Configuration and Analysis snap-in. For more information about the **set** command, see "Supported Commands" later in this chapter.

The Recovery Console prevents access to other folders such as Program Files or Documents and Settings, as well as to folders containing other installations of Windows 2000. However, you can use the **logon** command to access an alternate installation. Alternatively, you can gain access to other installation folders by restarting the Recovery Console, choosing the number representing that installation, and then entering the administrator password for that installation.

You cannot copy a file from the local hard disk to a floppy disk, but you can copy a file from a floppy disk or a CD-ROM to any hard disk, and from a hard disk to another hard disk. However, with the **set** command enabled, you can copy files to a floppy disk. The Recovery Console displays an "Access is denied" error message when it detects invalid commands.

Important The **set** command makes use of Recovery Console environment variables to enable, among other options, disk write access to floppy disks. To enable the user to modify the restricted default Recovery Console environment variables, a policy setting must be made. For more information about enabling the **set** command in Recovery Console, see the procedure later in this section.

The Recovery Console buffers previously entered commands and makes them available to the user with the up and down arrow keys. To edit a previously entered command, use **backspace** to move the cursor to the point of the edit and retype the remainder of the command. At any point, you can quit the Recovery Console and restart the computer by typing **exit** at the command prompt.

Important The Recovery Console might not map disk volumes with the same drive letters that they have in Windows 2000. If you are having trouble copying files from one location to another, use the **map** command from the Recovery Console to make sure that the drive mappings for both the source and the target locations are correct.

Several of the Recovery Console commands are not fully functional to users who have converted to dynamic disks. For more information about dynamic disks, see the chapter "Disk Concepts and Troubleshooting" in this book.

Supported Commands

Table 13.1 lists the commands that are supported by the Recovery Console. You can use the **help** command to list the commands supported by the Recovery Console.

Note The switch **/?** works with every Recovery Console command to display a help screen offering a description of the command, its syntax, definitions of its parameters, and other useful information.

Table 13.1   Available Recovery Console Commands

Command	Explanation
attrib	Changes attributes on one file or directory. `ATTRIB -R │ +R │ -S │ +S │ -H │ +H │ -C │ +C  filename` `+` Sets an attribute. `-` Clears an attribute. `R` Read-only file attribute. `S` System file attribute. `H` Hidden file attribute. `C` Compressed file attribute. More than one attribute can be set or cleared at a time. To view attributes, use the **dir** command.
batch	Executes commands specified in a text file. `BATCH Inputfile [Outputfile]` `Inputfile` Specifies the text file that contains the list of commands to be executed. `Outputfile` If specified, contains the output of the specified commands. If not specified, the output is displayed on the screen. Batch cannot be one of the commands included in the Inputfile.

continued

Table 13.1   Available Recovery Console Commands *(continued)*

Command	Explanation
cd/chdir	Displays the name of the current directory, or switches to a new directory. CHDIR [path] CHDIR [..] CHDIR [drive:] CD [path] CD [..] CD [drive:] CD .. Specifies that you want to change to the parent directory. Type **CD [drive:]** to display the current directory in the specified drive. Type **CD** without parameters to display the current drive and directory. The **chdir** command treats spaces as delimiters. Use quotation marks around a directory name containing spaces. For Example: **cd "\winnt\profiles\username\programs\start menu"** **Chdir** operates only within the system directories of the current Windows installation, removable media, the root directory of any hard disk partition, or the local installation sources.

chkdsk	Checks a disk and displays a status report,
	
	chkdsk [drive:] [/p] | [/r]
	
	[drive:] Specifies the drive to check.
	/p Check even if the drive is not flagged dirty.
	           bad.
	/r Locates bad sectors and recovers readable
	           information (implies /p).
	
	Chkdsk may be used without any parameters, in which case the current drive is checked with no switches. You can specify the listed switches.
	
	Chkdsk requires the Autochk.exe file. **Chkdsk** automatically locates Autochk.exe in the startup (boot) directory. If it cannot be found in the startup directory, **chkdsk** attempts to locate the Windows 2000 Setup CD. If the installation CD cannot be found, **chkdsk** prompts for the location of Autochk.exe.

cls	Clears the screen.

continued

Table 13.1   **Available Recovery Console Commands** *(continued)*

Command	Explanation
copy	Copies a single file to another location. `copy source [destination]` `source` Specifies the file to be copied. `Destination` Specifies the directory and/or file name for the new file. The source might be removable media, any directory within the system directories of the current Windows installation, the root of any drive, the local installation sources, or the cmdcons directory. The destination might be any directory within the system directories of the current Windows installation, the root of any drive, the local installation sources, or the cdirectory. The destination cannot be removable media. If a destination is not specified, it defaults to the current directory. **Copy** does not support replaceable parameters (wild cards). **Copy** prompts if the destination file already exists. A compressed file from the Windows 2000 Setup CD is automatically decompressed as it is copied.

del/delete	Deletes one file.
	
	`del     [drive:][path]filename`
	`delete  [drive:][path]filename`
	
	`[drive:][path]filename` Specifies the file to delete.
	
	Delete only operates within the system directories of the current Windows installation, removable media, the root directory of any hard disk partition, or the local installation sources.
	
	Del and **delete** do not support replaceable parameters (wild cards).

dir	Displays a list of files and subdirectories in a directory. `dir [drive:][path][filename]` `[drive:][path][filename]` Specifies drive, directory, and/or files to list. **Dir** lists all files, including hidden and system files. Files might have the following attributes: `a` Files ready for archiving `h` Hidden `c` Compressed `p` Reparse Point `d` Directory `r` Read-only `e` Encrypted `s` System file

continued

Table 13.1   Available Recovery Console Commands *(continued)*

Command	Explanation
disable	Disables a Windows system service or driver.

```
disable servicename
```

servicename	The name of the service or driver to be disabled.

Disable prints the old start_type of the service before resetting it to SERVICE_DISABLED. You should make a note of the old start_type, in case you need to enable the service again.

The start_type values that the **disable** command displays are:

```
SERVICE_DISABLED
SERVICE_BOOT_START
SERVICE_SYSTEM_START
SERVICE_AUTO_START
SERVICE_DEMAND_START
```

Command	Explanation
diskpart	Manages the partitions on your hard disk volumes.

```
diskpart [/add | /delete] [device-name | drive-name |
partition-name] [size]
```

/add	Create a new partition
/delete	Delete an existing partition
device-name	Device name for creating a new partition (such as \Device\HardDisk0)
drive-name	Drive-letter based name for deleting an existing partition (such as D:)
partition-name	Partition-based name for deleting an existing partition and can be used in place of the drive-name argument (such as \Device\HardDisk0\Partition1)
size	Size of the new partition, in megabytes

If no arguments are used, a user interface for managing your partitions appears.

Warning

This command can damage your partition table if the disk has been upgraded to dynamic disk. Always use Disk Management to modify the structure of dynamic disks.

continued

Table 13.1   Available Recovery Console Commands *(continued)*

Command	Explanation
enable	Enables a Windows system service or driver.

```
enable servicename [start_type]
```

servicename	Name of the service or driver to be enabled.
start_type	How the service or driver is scheduled to be started. Valid start-type values are:

```
SERVICE_BOOT_START
SERVICE_SYSTEM_START
SERVICE_AUTO_START
SERVICE_DEMAND_START
```

Enable prints the old start_type of the service before resetting it to the new value. Note the old value, in case it is necessary to restore the start_type of the service. If you do not specify a new start_type, **enable** prints the old start_type.

Command	Explanation
exit	Quits the Recovery Console and restarts your computer.
expand	Expands a compressed file.

```
EXPAND source [/F:filespec] [destination] [/Y]
EXPAND source [/F:filespec] /D
```

source	Specifies the file to be expanded. May not include wildcard (* and ?) characters.
Destination	Specifies the directory for the new file. Default is the current directory.
/y	Do not prompt before overwriting an existing file.
/f:filespec	If the source contains more than one file, this parameter is required to identify the specific file(s) to be expanded. May include wildcards.
/d	Do not expand; only display a directory of the files which are contained in the source.

The destination might be any directory within the system directories of the current Windows installation, the root of any drive, the local installation sources, or the Cmdcons directory. The destination cannot be removable media. The destination file cannot be read-only. Use the **attrib** command to remove the read-only attribute. **Expand** prompts if the destination file already exists unless /**Y** is used.

continued

Table 13.1   Available Recovery Console Commands *(continued)*

Command	Explanation
fixboot	Writes a new boot sector onto the system partition. `fixboot [drive:]` drive: Specifies the drive to which a boot sector will be written, overriding the default choice of the system boot partition.

fixmbr	Repairs the master boot code of the boot partition.
	
	`fixmbr [device-name]`
	
	`device-name   Optional name that specifies the device that`
	`              needs a new MBR. If this is left blank then`
	`              the boot device is used.`
	
	If **fixmbr** detects an invalid or nonstandard partition table signature, it prompts you before rewriting the MBR.
	
	Warning
	
	This command can damage your partition table if a virus is present or a hardware problem exists and causes partitions to become inaccessible. It is recommended that you run antivirus software before using this command.
	
	Windows 2000 includes the antivirus software AvBoot. For more information about AvBoot, see "Troubleshooting Strategies" in this book.

format	Formats a disk for use with Windows 2000.
	
	`format [drive:] [/q] [/fs:file-system]`
	
	`[drive:]          Specifies the drive to format.`
	`/q                Performs a quick format.`
	`/fs:file-system   Specifies the file system to use (FAT,`
	`                  FAT32, or NTFS)`

help	Displays information about commands supported by the Recovery Console.
	
	`help [command]`
	`command      Any Recovery Console command.`
	
	If command is not specified, all of the commands supported by the Recovery Console are listed. The command parameter is used to see the help for a specific command.

listsvc	Lists all available services and drivers on the computer.
logon	Lists the detected installations of Windows 2000, and requests the local administrator password for those installations.

continued

Table 13.1   Available Recovery Console Commands *(continued)*

Command	Explanation

map	Lists the drive letter to physical device mappings that are currently active.
	
	`map [arc]`
	
	`arc     Tells MAP to use ARC paths instead of Windows 2000`
	`        device paths.`

md/mkdir	Creates a directory.
	
	`md    [drive:]path`
	`mkdir [drive:]path`
	
	Mkdir only operates within the system directories of the current Windows installation, removable media, the root directory of any hard disk partition, or the local installation sources.

more/type	Displays a text file to the screen.
	
	`more [filename]`
	`type [filename]`
	
	More or **type** displays a text file.

rd/rmdir	Removes (deletes) a directory.
	
	`rd    [drive:]path`
	`rmdir [drive:]path`
	
	Rmdir only operates within the system directories of the current Windows installation, removable media, the root directory of any hard disk partition, or the local installation sources.

ren/rename	Renames a single file.
	
	`ren [drive:][path]filename1 filename2`
	`rename [drive:][path]filename1 filename2`
	
	You cannot specify a new drive or path for your destination file.
	
	Rename only operates within the system directories of the current Windows installation, removable media, the root directory of any hard disk partition, or the local installation sources.

continued

Table 13.1   Available Recovery Console Commands *(continued)*

Command	Explanation

set	Displays and sets Recovery Console environment variables.
	
	`set variable = parameter`
	`set AllowWildCards = TRUE`
	
	The following environment variables are supported:
	
	`AllowWildCards` Enable wildcard support for some commands, such as DEL, that do not otherwise support them.
	`AllowAllPaths` Allow access to all files and folders on the computer.
	`AllowRemovableMedia` Allow files to be copied to removable media, such as floppy disks.
	`NoCopyPrompt` Do not prompt when overwriting file.
	
	To display the list of current environment variable settings, type **set** without parameters.
	
	The **set** command is an optional Recovery Console command that can be enabled by using either the Group Policy snap-in or the Security Configuration and Analysis snap-in.

systemroot	Sets the current directory to %SystemRoot%.

Often it is useful to enable the **set** command to make full use of the Recovery Console. To do this, a local policy must be enabled.

▶   **To enable full functionality of the set command using Group Policy**

> **Note** If Group Policy has already been added to your MMC, skip to step 8.

1. From the **Start**, click **Run**, and then type

   mmc

2. Press **ENTER**.

3. In the **Console1** dialog box, click **Console**, select **Add/Remove Snap-in**, and then click **Add**.

4. Select **Group Policy,** and then click **Add**.

5. In the **Select Group Policy Object** list box, choose **Local Computer**, and then click **Finish**.

6. In the **Add Standalone Snap-in** dialog box, click **Close**.

7. In the **Add/Remove Snap-in** dialog box, click **OK**.

8. Expand **Local Computer Policy**, **Computer Configuration**, **Windows Settings**, **Security Settings**, and then **Local Policies**. Click **Security Options**.

9. Double-click the policy **Recovery Console: Allow floppy copy and access to all drives and folders**.

10. In the **Local Security Policy Setting** dialog box, select **Enabled**, and then click **OK**.

▶ **To enable full functionality of the set command using the Security Configuration and Analysis snap-in**

> **Note** If Security Configuration and Analysis snap-in has already been added to your MMC, skip to step 7.

1. From the **Start**, click **Run**, and then type

   mmc

2. Press ENTER.

3. In the **Console1** dialog box, click **Console**, select **Add/Remove Snap-in**, and then click **Add**

4. Select **Security Configuration and Analysis**, click **Add**, and then click **Close**. In the **Add/Remove Snap-in** dialog box, click **OK.**

5. In the **Console1** dialog box, double click **Security Configuration and Analysis**. Follow the instruction to either open an existing database or create a new database.

6. In the **Console1** dialog box, follow the instructions to configure your computer and analyze your computer security settings.

7. In the **Security Configuration and Analysis** snap-in, double click **Security Configuration and Analysis**.

8. Expand Local Policies, and then click **Security Options**.

9. Double-click the policy **Recovery Console: Allow floppy copy and access to all drives and folders**.

10. In the **Analyzed Security Policy Setting** dialog box, select **Enabled**, and then click **OK**.

> **Note** You can also use the Group Policy snap-in and the Security Configuration and Analysis snap-in to select the policy **Recovery Console: Allow automatic administrative logon.**

Replacing the Registry Using the Recovery Console

If you are having problems with the registry, you can use the **copy** command to replace individual registry files by copying them from either the %sSystemRoot%\Repair folder or the %SystemRoot%\Repair\RegBack folder.

Important If you copied the files from %SystemRoot%\Repair\RegBack, your registry settings reflect those that were in effect when you selected the **System State** option during Backup operations.

If you copied the files from %SystemRoot%\Repair, your registry settings reflect those that were in effect when you installed Windows 2000.

Recreating Boot.ini Using the Recovery Console

You can use the Emergency Repair Process to replace a missing or corrupted Boot.ini file. Alternatively, you can use the **map** command to determine the location of the disks. With this information, you can create a Boot.ini file on another computer, and then use a floppy disk to transfer the Boot.ini file to the original computer.

Using the Emergency Repair Disk

If your system does not start, and using safe mode or the Recovery Console has not helped, you can try using the Emergency Repair Disk (ERD) option of Backup. Backup includes a wizard to help you create an ERD. If a system failure occurs, you can start the system using the Windows 2000 Setup CD or the Windows 2000 Setup floppy disks which can be created by running Makeboot.exe from the Bootdisk folder on the Windows 2000 Setup CD. Then use the Emergency Repair Process to restore core system files.

Make sure to create an ERD when your computer is functioning well so that you are prepared if you need to repair system files. The ERD allows you to make only basic system repairs, such as to the system files, boot sector, and startup environment. The ERD does not back up data, programs, or the registry and is not a replacement for regular system backups.

Important The Windows 2000 ERD, unlike the ERD used with Windows NT, does not contain a copy of the registry files. The backup registry files are in the folder %SystemRoot%\Repair. However, these files are from the original installation of Windows 2000. In the event of a problem, they can be used to return your computer to a usable state.

When you back up system state data, a copy of your registry files is placed in the folder %SystemRoot%\Repair\Regback. If your registry files become corrupted or are accidentally erased, use the files in this folder to repair your registry without performing a full restore of the system state data. This method is recommended for advanced users only and can also be accomplished by using the Recovery Console commands.

Creating the Emergency Repair Disk

When the ERD is created, the files listed in Table 13.2 are copied from %SystemRoot%\Repair to a floppy disk.

Table 13.2   Contents of the Repair Directory Created by Windows 2000 Setup

File Name	Contents
Autoexec.nt	A copy of %SystemRoot%\System32\Autoexec.nt, which is used to initialize the MS-DOS environment.
Config.nt	A copy of %SystemRoot%\System32\Config.nt, which is used to initialize the MS-DOS environment.
Setup.log	A log of which files were installed files, and Cyclic Redundancy Check (CRC) information for use during the Emergency Repair Process. This file has the read-only, system, and hidden attributes, and it is not visible unless you have configured My Computer to show all files.

Create the ERD after Windows 2000 is installed. Recreate the ERD after each service pack, system date, or updated driver is installed. Be sure to make a copy of your current ERD and store it in a secure location, perhaps off-site.

Note The ERD is not a replacement for backups!

For more information about the %SystemRoot%\Repair and %SystemRoot%\System32\Config folders and the ERD, see the Knowledge Base link on the Web Resources page http://windows.microsoft.com/windows2000/reskit/webresources.

Emergency Recovery Process

If you have prepared an ERD, you can use it to help repair system files after starting the computer using either the Windows 2000 Setup CD or the Windows 2000 Setup floppy disks. However, the Windows 2000 Setup CD is required for replacing any damaged files.

The ERD must include current configuration information. Make sure that you have an ERD for each installation of Windows 2000 on your computer, and never use an ERD from another computer.

Note   You cannot repair all disk problems by using the ERD.

When you start the Emergency Repair Process, the following information is displayed on the screen:

This operation will attempt to repair your Windows 2000 system.

Depending on the type of damage present, this operation might or might not be successful. If the system is not successfully repaired, restart Setup and choose the option to recover a destroyed system or system disk.

Select one of the following repair options:

- Manual Repair. To choose from a list of repair options, press M.
- Fast Repair. To perform all repair options, press F.

If you select **Manual Repair**, the registry files are not checked. If you select **Fast Repair,** and if the folder %SystemRoot%\Repair is accessible, the registry files are checked. If the folder %SystemRoot%\Repair is inaccessible (for example, due to file system corruption) the registry files are not checked.

- **Manual Repair**. It is recommended that only advanced users or administrators choose this option. Using it, you can repair system files, boot sector problems, and startup environment problems.

- **Fast Repair**. This is the easier option to use, and does not require user input. If you choose this option, the Emergency Recovery Process attempts to repair problems related to system files, the boot sector on your system disk, and your startup environment (if your computer has more than one operating system installed). This option also checks and repairs the registry files by loading and unloading each registry key. If a key is not successfully checked, it is automatically copied from the repair directory to the folder %SystemRoot%\System32\Config.

If you choose Fast Repair, all repair options are performed. Manual Repair allows you to select from the following three options:

Inspect Startup Environment   Inspect Startup Environment verifies that the Windows 2000 files in the system partition are correct. If any of the files that are needed to start Windows 2000 are missing or corrupted, Repair replaces them from the Windows 2000 Setup CD. These include NTLDR and Ntdetect.com. If Boot.ini is missing, it is recreated.

Verify Windows 2000 System Files   Verify Windows 2000 System Files uses a checksum to verify that each installed file is good and that it matches the file that was installed from the Windows 2000 Setup CD. If the recovery process determines that a file on the disk does not match what was installed, it displays a message that identifies the file and asks if you want to replace it. The Emergency Repair Process also verifies that startup files, such as NTLDR and Ntoskrnl.exe, are present and valid.

Inspect Boot Sector   Inspect Boot Sector verifies that the boot sector on the system partition still references NTLDR. The Emergency Repair Process can only replace the boot sector for the system partition on the first hard disk. The Emergency Repair Process can also repair the boot sector for the system partition on the startup disk.

If you choose Fast Repair, all repair options are performed.

If the Emergency Repair Process Does Not Fix Your System

If you have performed the Emergency Repair Process and the computer still does not operate normally, you can use the Windows 2000 Setup CD to perform an in-place upgrade over the existing installation. This is a last resort before reinstalling the operating system. Note that the time required to complete the following procedure is equal to the time it takes to reinstall the operating system.

▶ **To perform an in-place upgrade of Windows 2000**

1. Mount the Windows 2000 Setup CD.

2. Press **Enter** to install a copy of Windows 2000.

3. When you are prompted to repair the existing Windows 2000 installation, press R.

Note Windows 2000 Setup performs an in-place upgrade of your existing installation. However, you might lose some customized settings of your system files.

Restoring System State Data

In Microsoft® Windows® 2000 Server, system state data comprises the registry, COM+ Class Registration database, system startup files, and the Certificate Services database (if the server is a certificate server). If the server is a domain controller, Active Directory™ directory services and the Sysvol directory are also contained in the system state data. If the server is running the Cluster service, the system state data also includes resource registry checkpoints and the quorum resource recovery log, which contains the most recent cluster database information.

When you restore the system state data, all system state data that is relevant to your computer is backed up or restored: you cannot back up or restore individual components of the system state data. This is due to dependencies among the system state components. However, you can restore the system state data to an alternate location, and only the registry files, Sysvol directory files, Cluster database information files, and system startup files are restored to the alternate location. The Active Directory database, Certificate Services database, and COM+ Class Registration database are not restored if you designate an alternate location when you restore the system state data.

Note You can only back up and restore the system state data on a local computer: you cannot back up and restore the system state data on a remote computer.

▶ **To restore system state data**

1. Start Backup.

2. Click the **Restore** tab, and then select the check box for any drive, folder, or file that you want to restore.

3. Click the box next to **System State** to restore the system state data along with any other data you have selected for the current restore operation.

> **Caution** If you restore the system state data, and you do not designate an alternate location for the restored data, Backup erases the system state data that is currently on your computer and replaces it with the system state data you are restoring.

You must be an administrator or a backup operator to restore files and folders. For more information about restoring the system state data to a domain controller and about authorative restores, see the *Microsoft® Windows® 2000 Server Resource Kit Distributed Systems Guide*.

Restoring the Registry

When you back up the system state data, a copy of your registry files is also saved in %SystemRoot%\Repair\Regback. If your registry files become corrupted or are accidentally erased, you can use these files to repair the registry without performing a full restore of the system state data. This method is recommended only for advanced users.

> **Note** Backup does not allow you to restore only the registry files. If you use Backup to restore lost data to the registry, all system state data is replaced.

You can also use Backup to restore lost data to the registry. The system must be stable enough for you to open Backup. If your computer cannot start, you might be able to repair the operating system using an ERD. The **Fast Repair** option of the Emergency Repair Process checks and, if necessary, replaces each registry key by copying it from the repair directory to the folder %SystemRoot%\Config.

If you cannot fix the problem with the registry by performing the Emergency Repair Process or by selecting **Last Known Good Configuration** from the **Windows 2000 Advanced Options** menu, it might be necessary to reinstall the operating system and device drivers and to reconfigure the system before you can restore the data.

Restoring Data

If files, the registry, or directory services are not accessible, you need to restore them. Restore operations are only possible if you have used Backup or another program to backup the files on your computer. Backup allows you to restore the entire backup medium, one or more backup sets, or individual files. After the restore operation starts, you have the option of restoring the local registry and directory service as well.

All catalog information is normally maintained on the corresponding medium for that backup set.

When you insert a backup medium to restore information, only information about the first backup set is displayed. To restore the entire medium, load the catalog first. Otherwise, when you select a medium, you are selecting only the displayed sets.

Restoring Files from Third-Party Backup Programs

You can use Backup to restore data from a tape that was backed up with a program other than Backup if the tape is in the Microsoft tape format (MTF). Although the tape might not have the full on-tape catalog (OTC) information that Backup produces, it should have equivalent information. Also, some older tape backup devices might not support creating full OTCs with Backup. Contact the vendor if you suspect that your tape backup device does not support creating a full OTC.

Restoring File Security Settings

Backup preserves permissions, ownership, and audit flags on files restored to NTFS volumes but not on files restored to FAT volumes. It is not possible to secure information on FAT volumes.

When you restore files to a new computer or hard disk, you do not have to restore security information. The files inherit the permissions of the directory in which they are placed. If the directory has no permissions, the file retains its previous permissions, including ownership.

Recovering Your Disk Configuration

In case of a disaster, you can recreate your disk structures and signatures by using the Disk Signature information displayed when you used the Dir command.

You can restore disk, partition, and volume configurations by using the results from the DumpConfig command-line tool (Dumpcfg.exe).

Recovering a Mirrored or RAID-5 Volume

The process of error detection and recovery for software fault-tolerant volumes is similar for both mirrored volumes and RAID-5 volumes. The Windows 2000 response to the problem depends on when the problem occurred. For recovery of a hardware fault-tolerant volume, see the documentation for the controller that you are using.

Note Marking a mirror as failed does not occur during a read, only during a write. The read cannot affect the data on the disks, so performing mirror error processing is not necessary.

The operating system usually continues to work normally. Users accessing resources over the network usually are not affected.

Be sure to back up important data immediately, because the volume is no longer fault tolerant. Use a new tape for backup, not an existing tape. Replace the failed disk and begin the recovery of the mirrored volume or RAID-5 volume as soon as possible.

During system initialization, if the system cannot locate a partition in a mirrored volume or a RAID-5 volume, it logs a severe error in the event log, marks the volume as Failed Redundancy and uses the remaining portions of the mirrored volume or RAID-5 volume. The system continues to function by using the fault-tolerant capabilities inherent in such volumes. For more information about the status of volumes displayed in the Disk Management snap-in, see "Planning a Reliable Configuration" in this book.

Recovering a Mirrored Volume

A mirrored volume is provides fault tolerance by duplicating data on two disks. If one disk fails, the data on the failed disk becomes unavailable, but the system continues to operate using the unaffected disk.

If the failure of a mirrored volume did not cause any disruption in service, you can continue running in a non-fault-tolerant configuration and schedule a time to reconstruct the mirrored volume. This activity can occur during a normally scheduled maintenance period or during a less busy time. However, if you have a spare disk in the configuration, you can reconstruct the mirror immediately.

Note The failed disk can be replaced with any disk that is the same size or larger.

It is a good idea to use a disk as similar to the remaining disk as possible.

When you move or replace a disk that was at the end of a SCSI bus, be sure that you terminate only the disk that is now at the end of the bus.

When a member of a mirrored volume is orphaned, you need to break the mirrored volume to expose the remaining volume as a separate volume. The remaining member of the mirrored volume receives the drive letter that was assigned to the complete mirrored volume. The orphaned volume receives the next available drive letter or a new letter assigned to it.

You can then create a new mirrored volume from unused free space on another disk. When you restart the computer, the data from the working volume is copied to the new member of the mirrored volume.

Note In Windows NT 4.0 and earlier, mirrored volumes were known as mirror sets. Disk Management renames all mirror sets to Mirrored Volume. These mirrored volumes reside only on basic disks.

Repairing a Basic Mirrored Volume

When you follow the procedure to repair a basic mirrored volume, the status of the mirrored volume changes to Regenerating and then Healthy. If the volume does not return to the Healthy status, right-click the volume, and then click **Resynchronize Mirror**.

Note If a basic disk containing part of a mirrored volume is disconnected or fails, the status of the mirrored volume becomes Failed Redundancy and the disk status remains Online. If this happens, you can try to repair the volume.

When you repair a mirrored volume on a basic disk, Disk Management creates a new mirror on a healthy disk and then resynchronizes the new mirror.

Repairing a mirrored volume on a basic disk requires another basic disk with sufficient free space for the new mirror. If an additional disk is not available, the **Repair Volume** option is unavailable and you cannot repair the volume.

You must use a basic disk to repair a basic mirrored volume (mirror set). You cannot use a dynamic disk.

Replacing a Failed Mirror

If the disk containing part of the mirrored volume cannot be reactivated and the volume does not return to the Healthy status, replace the failed mirror with a new mirror on another disk.

▶ **To replace the failed mirror with a new mirror on another disk**

1. Open Disk Management.

2. Right-click the mirror on the missing or offline disk, and then click **Remove Mirror**. Follow the instructions on your screen.

3. Right-click the volume to be remirrored, and then click **Add Mirror**. Follow the instructions on your screen.

To replace a mirror in the mirrored volume, you need a dynamic disk with unallocated space that is at least as large as the region to repair. If you don't have a dynamic disk with enough unallocated space, the Add Mirror command is unavailable.

Breaking a Mirrored Volume

Breaking the mirrored volume results in two independent partitions or logical drives. No information is deleted, but the data is no longer redundant. Back up the volume before breaking a mirrored volume.

Deleting Mirrored Volumes on a Basic Disk

Deleting a mirrored volume deletes all the data contained in the volume as well as the partitions that make up the volume. You can delete only entire mirrored volumes.

Resynchronizing Mirrored Volumes

Resynchronize a mirrored volume when data on one disk becomes stale. For example, if one disk of a mirrored volume is disconnected, data is written to the remaining disk, but the volume is no longer fault tolerant. If you reconnect the disk, the data on the reconnected disk is stale. To make the mirrored volume fault tolerant again, resynchronize the mirrored volume to update the information on the reconnected disk.

In most cases, mirrored volumes on dynamic disks are resynchronized automatically. However, you need to use the Resynchronize Mirror command for mirrored volumes on basic disks.

Removing Mirrored Volumes

Once you remove a mirror from a mirrored volume, that mirror becomes unallocated space; the remaining mirror becomes a simple volume and is no longer fault tolerant. All data on the removed mirror is deleted.

Recovering a RAID-5 Volume

When a member of a mirrored or RAID-5 volume fails, it becomes an orphan. The operating system determines that it can no longer be used and directs reading and writing all new data to the remaining members of the fault-tolerant volume.

When a member of a RAID-5 volume fails, you can reconstruct the data for the failed member from the remaining members. In Disk Management, select a new area of free space that is the same size as or larger than the other members of the RAID-5 volume, and then regenerate the data. If you are required to restart the computer, the volume manager reads the information from the stripes on the other member disks and then reconstructs the data of the missing member and writes it to the new member.

To regenerate a RAID-5 volume, the volume must be locked by the operating system. All network connections to the volume are lost when a volume is regenerated.

Note Do not put your page file on a RAID-5 volume because it degrades performance. If you want your page file on a fault-tolerant volume, use a mirrored volume instead.

Replacing a Stripe in the RAID-5 Volume

To replace a stripe in the RAID-5 volume, you need a dynamic disk with unallocated space that is at least as large as the stripe to repair. If you don't have a dynamic disk with enough unallocated space, the **Repair Volume** command is unavailable.

When a member of a RAID-5 volume fails in a severe manner (such as a loss of power or a hard disk failure), it becomes an orphan. If this happens, you can regenerate the data for the orphaned member from the remaining members of the RAID-5 volume.

If the RAID-5 failure is due to a power or cabling failure on a single device, you can regenerate the data within the orphaned member of the RAID-5 volume once the hardware state is restored.

Note The RAID-5 volume does not display the Healthy status in Disk Management until regeneration is complete.

Deleting a RAID-5 Volume on a Basic Disk

Deleting a RAID-5 volume deletes all the data contained in the volume as well as the partitions that make up the RAID-5 volume. You can delete only entire RAID-5 volumes.

Note In Windows NT 4.0 and earlier, RAID-5 volumes were known as stripe sets with parity. Disk Management renames all stripe sets with parity to RAID-5 Volumes. In Windows 2000, you can delete RAID-5 volumes that were created in Windows NT 4.0 or earlier, but you cannot create RAID-5 volumes on basic disks.

Repairing a RAID-5 Volume on a Basic Disk

If a basic disk containing part of a RAID-5 volume is disconnected or fails, its status becomes Failed Redundancy and the disk status remains Online. If this happens, you can try to repair the volume. The RAID-5 status of the volume should change to Regenerating and then Healthy.

When you repair a RAID-5 volume on a basic disk, Disk Management relocates part of the RAID-5 volume to a healthy disk, regenerates the parity, and then returns the status to Healthy.

Repairing a RAID-5 volume on a basic disk requires an additional basic disk with sufficient free space for part of the RAID-5 volume. If an additional disk is not available, the **Repair Volume** option is not available and you cannot repair the volume. If the disk containing part of the RAID-5 volume cannot be reactivated and the volume does not return to the Healthy status, replace the failed stripe in the RAID-5 volume.

Note You must use a basic disk to repair a basic RAID-5 volume: you cannot use a dynamic disk.

Recovering Data in Remote Storage

Remote Storage maintains data critical for operation in three areas: the reparse data that exists on each managed file; the Remote Storage database files; and the Remote Storage media. If Remote Storage data becomes corrupted or is damaged by a virus, you need to implement recovery procedures.

Using Rstore.exe

Periodically, the Remote Storage engine makes a backup of the Jet databases. Each time a file is copied or migrated to tape, these databases are automatically backed up. If required, this data might be used to restore the Jet database. The Registry Restore utility Rstore.exe is provided with Remote Storage to recover the Jet database from the backup files.

Note This data cannot simply be copied from the EngDb.bak subdirectory to the EngDb subdirectory. The files need to be restored to the same system path, including drive letter and directory structure. For example, if the system path is D:\Winnt\System32\Remotestorage\Engdb before the recovery, then after the recovery the path is still D:\Winnt\System32\Remotestorage\Engdb. This is a requirement based on the Jet database recovery mechanisms, which only recovers the Jet database to the original path location.

▶ **To use Rstore**

1. Using an MS-DOS window, change directories to the %SystemRoot%\System32\Remotestorage\Engdb subdirectory.

2. Delete the contents of this subdirectory.

3. Run Rstore.exe from the %SystemRoot%\System32\Remotestorage\Engdb subdirectory. Rstore.exe requires one parameter which identifies the location of the backup subdirectory. Typically, the following command is entered:

   Rstore %SystemRoot%\System32\Remotestorage\Engdb.bak

Restoring the Remote Storage and Removable Storage Databases

There are two reasons for restoring the Remote Storage database, each with its own restore procedure. Use the appropriate method to restore the Remote Storage database in the following circumstances:

- After completely reinstalling Windows 2000, you need to restore the Remote Storage database files before you can recall files from offline storage.

- The Remote Storage database is damaged.

Note If you try to access a file in offline storage when the Remote Storage service is not installed, you might receive the following error message:

path and file name The file can not be accessed by the system.

If Remote Storage is installed but does not start you might receive the following error message:

Path and file name The remote storage service was not able to recall the file.

Restoring the Removable Storage Databases

After completely reinstalling Windows 2000, restore the Removable Storage databases before you restore the Remote Storage database. Each time Remote Storage migrates data to tape, these databases are automatically backed up to the media containing the migrated data. It is recommended that the databases on this media be used since they will contain the most recent copy of the Removable Storage database. Use the following procedure to restore the Removable Storage databases.

Note For the following procedure, you need to reinstall Windows 2000 into the same folder and drive previously used. If Windows 2000 is installed to a different folder, the restore operation cannot return the databases to their original location.

▶ **To restore the Removable Storage databases**

Caution This procedure can cause you to lose changes to the Removable Storage database made after Remote Storage was backed up and before it was restored.

1. Verify that your tape or storage device is online and functioning. Start the Computer Management snap-in by right-clicking **My Computer**. Click **Manage**, double-click the **Storage** branch to expand it, and then click **Removable Storage**.

2. Open the **Media** pools and look in the **Import** pool. Locate the most recent tape used to store the Remote Storage migrated files. The default name for Remote Storage media is "RS" appended with the computer name and an incremental number (for example, "RS-MachineX-1"). The media with the highest number contains the most recent database backup. If the Remote Storage media spans two or more tapes, catalog these tapes using Backup (temporarily move these tapes to the **NTBackup Media** pool) and check the dates of the Remote Storage databases. Use the one with the most recent date.

3. Move this media to the **NTbackup Media** pool. If the pool does not exist, start Backup, and it is created automatically.

4. Use Backup to catalog the tape to find the latest copy of the Removable Storage and Remote Storage databases. These databases are stored on tape in the folders %windir%\system32\Ntmsdata and %windir%\system32\RemoteStorage. Check the dates of the files to determine the most recent copies.

5. Select the most current versions of the NtmsData and RemoteStorage folders to be restored. Make sure that all files below these sub-folders are also selected.

6. In the **Restore files to** box, click **alternate location**, and then click the drive that contains the Windows folder.

Caution If the previous step is not performed, the databases are restored to the Remote Storage managed volume instead of the Windows 2000 operating system partition.

---

7. Click **Start Restore**, and then click **Advanced**. Click **Restore Removable Storage Database**, click **OK**, and then click **OK**.

8. After this process finishes, restart your computer.

Restoring the Remote Storage Database After Completely Reinstalling Windows 2000

Before restoring the Remote Storage database, reinstall Windows 2000 to the same drive and folder as the previous installation. During Setup, do not add the Remote Storage component. If this component was added accidentally or automatically, remove it, and then restart your computer.

Important The following procedure assumes that you have completely reinstalled Windows 2000; that volumes that contain Remote Storage managed data are still intact; and that you have already performed the procedure to restore the Removable Storage databases.

▶   **To restore the Remote Storage database after completely reinstalling Windows 2000**

1. Start the Removable Storage snap-in and verify that the databases have been restored. You can do this by looking to see if all of your media pools are present and the media are in their appropriate pools.

2. In Control Panel, use **Add/Remove Programs** to add Remote Storage .

3. Restart your computer, log on, and then using the Computer Management snap-in, expand the **Services And Applications** branch, and then click **Services**. Verify that the following services are stopped:

   - Remote Storage Engine
   - Remote Storage File
   - Remote Storage Media
   - Remote Storage Notification

4. At a command prompt, change to the %SystemRoot%\System32\RemoteStorage\Engdb folder, and then verify that this folder is empty by moving the files to another folder.

5. Use the **Rstore**.exe tool to run the following command from the Engdb folder. Type:

   Rstore %systemroot%\system32\RemoteStorage\engdb.bak

6. In the Computer Management snap-in, expand **Services And Applications**, and then click **Services**. Locate and start the following services:

   - Remote Storage Engine
   - Remote Storage File
   - Remote Storage Media

7. Open the Remote Storage snap-in and verify that your managed volumes appear and that all settings are correct. You may also want to test by recalling a few of the migrated files before putting the server back into production.

Restoring a Damaged Remote Storage Database

The following procedure assumes that the Removable Storage database is intact and that you are only restoring the Remote Storage database. For detailed information about restoring the Removable Storage database, see "Restoring the Removable Storage Databases" earlier in this chapter.

▶ **To restore a damaged Remote Storage database**

1. In the Computer Management snap-in, expand **Services And Applications**, and then click **Services**. Verify that the following services are stopped:

   - Remote Storage Engine
   - Remote Storage File
   - Remote Storage Media
   - Remote Storage Notification

2. Using Removable Storage, open the **Media** pools and view in the **Import** pool. Locate the most recent tape used to store the Remote Storage migrated files. The default name for Remote Storage media is "RS" appended with the computer name and an incremental number. For example, RS-MachineX-1. The media with the highest number contains the most recent backup of the databases.

3. Move this media to the **NTbackup** media pool. If the pool does not exist, start Backup.

4. Using Backup, catalog the tape to find the latest copy of the Remote Storage database on tape in the %Windir%\System32\RemoteStorage folder. Check the dates of the files to find the most recent copies.

> **Note** If the Remote Storage media spans two or more tapes, catalog these tapes using Backup (temporarily move these tapes to the **NTBackup Media** pool). Check the dates of the Remote Storage databases and use the most recent one.

5. Select the most current RemoteStorage folder to be restored, and make sure that all files under this folder are also selected.

6. In the **Restore files to** dialog box, click **Alternate location**, and then click the drive that contains the Windows folder.

> **Caution** If the previous step is not performed, the databases are restored to the Remote Storage managed volume instead of the Windows 2000 operating system partition.

7. After the restoration finishes, at the command prompt, type:

   %systemroot%\system32\RemoteStorage\engdb

> **Note** Make sure that this folder is empty by moving any existing files to another folder.

8. Use the **Rstore**.exe tool to run the following command from the Engdb folder. Type:

   Rstore %systemroot%\system32\RemoteStorage\engdb.bak

9. After this command finishes, place the Remote Storage media used during the restoration in the RemoteStorage media pool.

10. In the Computer Management snap-in, expand **Services And Applications**, and then click **Services**. Locate and start the following services:

    - Remote Storage Engine
    - Remote Storage File
    - Remote Storage Media

11. Open the Remote Storage snap-in and verify that your managed volumes appear and that all settings are correct. You might also want to test by recalling some migrated files before putting the server back into production.

Recovering Managed Files

Remote Storage data is stored in the MTF format. To recover managed files from the system backup, perform the same restore operations that you would use to restore files that are not managed by Remote Storage. Remote Storage detects when restore operations have occurred and schedules a validate job to run against the restored volume. The restore function on a Backup tape restores the reparse points and all files that are not managed by Remote Storage. By default, when Backup backs up files in Remote Storage, the reparse data (not the full file) is backed up. For this reason you still need the Remote Storage media with the Remote Storage databases to recall the files from the reparse point and fully recover a managed volume.

If the volume was destroyed and you have backups of the reparse point data, you can recover by either restoring the reparse point data from tape or restoring the Remote Storage and Removable Storage databases from the Remote Storage media. For more information, see "Restoring the Remote Storage Database" earlier in this chapter.

Caution As a last resort (for example, if remote storage recovery was not successful), use Backup to restore data from the Remote Storage media.

Using Backup to restore data from the Remote Storage media can cause problems under the following circumstances:

- More than one version of the file exists on the Remote Storage media. For example, if a file was migrated, recalled, modified, and then migrated again, the wrong version of the file might be restored.

- A user has deleted a file that no longer needs to be archived. The file still resides on the tape even though the reparse point to it is severed.

▶ **To recover Remote Storage files**

Remote Storage does not recall files while they are being recovered.

1. Open the Removable Storage snap-in, and then locate the Remote Storage tapes in the import media pool or the Remote Storage pool.

2. Open Backup to create a media pool in Removable Storage.

3. Right-click the appropriate media, click **Copy**, right-click the Backup pool, and then click **Paste**.

–Or–

Highlight the media, and then drag it to the Backup pool.

Note Backup needs to have been opened before a pool can be created in Removable Storage. Backup then needs to be restarted before it can recognize the media that is pasted into its pool. This needs to be done with care, because this temporarily prevents recalls from occurring if Remote Storage is installed and running.

---

4. After recovering the needed files, cut and paste the media back into the Remote Storage media pool.

Use the Backup restore function to catalog and view the available directories and files to be restored. The tape contains the directory names and the date of the Remote Storage and Removable Storage database files.

Each set needs to be individually cataloged to produce a listing of all files on the tape. All files and directories that were managed are visible in the right pane after expanding the directory associated with the file. The restore function allows the restoration of files to the same directory as well as to alternative locations. If you want the file to be able to be recalled from the managed placeholder, restore it to an alternative location. The restore operation returns the file to the state that the file was in at time of management.

Recovering from Bad Media

Tape media can wear out, become unstable, or become unusable. If this happens, you can make a media copy and recover using the media copy set. This process ensures that the managed data is safe for a longer period of time. If you cannot make a media copy because only one drive is available or no tapes are available, set the write-protect tab on the medium. Only use this procedure if the medium is unstable or unusable.

If a master medium becomes unusable, use the following procedure to recreate the master media for Remote Storage recall use.

▶ **To recreate the master media**

- In the Remote Storage snap-in, on the individual media property page, submit a recreate master from the recovery page, using the latest media copy.

There is a potential for lost data because the copy was older than the master that was in place. This allows for the recovery of the data up to the point where the media copy was last updated. At this point, the original master is marked "bad" and all data is accessed through the recreated master.

Additional Resources

- For more information about using tools such as the ERD and the Recovery Console, see Windows 2000 Server Help.

PART 4

Troubleshooting

Troubleshooting strategies include methods, checklists, and hints to find and correct problems with a computer running Microsoft® Windows® 2000. A wide range of troubleshooting tools are included with the operating system and the *Windows 2000 Resource Kit*. Part 4 includes general troubleshooting data and information that can be used to troubleshoot specific problems.

In This Part

CHAPTER 14

Troubleshooting Strategies

If a problem occurs while running Microsoft® Windows® 2000, you can use the general troubleshooting methods and tools provided with the operating system to isolate and fix a wide range of problems. Information in the registry can be used to determine why services are not working correctly. General troubleshooting methods can isolate the problem, as can isolating services or drivers that are not working properly; following the specific troubleshooting examples in this chapter can help solve problems with Windows 2000. If you are unable to solve the problem yourself, find out as much information as possible before contacting Microsoft Product Support Services.

In This Chapter

Related Information in the Resource Kit

- For more information about messages generated by the Windows 2000 Executive, see "Windows 2000 Stop Messages" in this book.

- For more information about the Event Messages, see the Windows 2000 Error and Event Messages Help on the *Microsoft® Windows® 2000 Resource Kit* companion CD.

- For more information about using the registry to troubleshoot problems, see the Technical Reference to the Windows 2000 Registry (Regentry.chm) on the *Windows 2000 Resource Kit* companion CD.

Technical Support and Services

Microsoft offers technical support and services ranging from self-help tools to direct assistance with a Microsoft Product Support Services engineer. Service categories include:

- Business customer support
- Education customer support
- Software or Web developer support
- IT professional
- Personal users

These services are available in the United States and Canada only. Features of some support options differ in Canada, while services outside the United States and Canada might vary. For information on support for products obtained outside the United States and Canada, please contact the Microsoft subsidiary in your area. For a list of worldwide Microsoft subsidiaries see the Support Options link on the Web Resources page at http://windows.microsoft.com/windows2000/reskit/webresources.

Note Customers who are deaf or hard of hearing can reach Microsoft text telephone (TT/TDD) services at (800) 892-5234 in the United States.

Support services are subject to current prices, terms, and conditions, which are subject to change without notice. For information about specific technical support options, see the Personal Online Support link on the Web Resources page at http://windows.microsoft.com/windows2000/reskit/webresources.

Note To provide the highest quality of support possible, it is sometimes necessary to end support for discontinued products and apply those resources to supporting the latest developments and technologies that Microsoft has to offer.

Project Ascent

Project Ascent is at the core of Microsoft support offerings. Through Project Ascent, support processes are further tuned to meet customer requirements, and processes are integrated more tightly. In addition, Project Ascent stresses the sharing of skills, resources, and infrastructure in emerging areas and creates continual learning opportunities for people to stay current on rapidly changing products and technologies.

Other Resources

Personal Online Support makes it easy to find answers to a variety of questions. The search engine uses a natural language query, allowing you to type your question in your own words and search the vast collection of problem-solving tools and technical information, including Frequently Asked Questions.

- Submitting questions on the Internet. In the United States and Canada, you can submit your Pay-Per-Incident or Priority Annual support questions on the Internet with Web Response.

- Microsoft Certified Support Centers. Success and the ability to meet the demands of the competitive market depend on high-quality and well-defined product support in environments that integrate various combinations of hardware, software, and operating systems from multiple vendors. Central to this support is provided by Microsoft Certified Support Centers (MCSCs). MCSCs are industry leading, multi-vendor support providers who have a special relationship with Microsoft that helps ensure that they deliver high quality technical support for Microsoft products.

- MSDN Online. MSDN Online and MSDN Online Support allow you to search Microsoft developer support information, including the Knowledge Base, troubleshooters, white papers, and downloadable files. For more information about MSDN Online Support, see the MSDN link on the Web Resources page at http://windows.microsoft.com/windows2000/reskit/webresources.

- Microsoft TechNet. TechNet CDs are packed with valuable and accessible technical information, and monthly editions provide updated information, including Knowledge Base articles, resource kits, the Software Library, Microsoft Services Directory, educational materials, and other useful software and information. For more information about subscribing to TechNet, see the Microsoft TechNet link on the Web Resources page http://windows.microsoft.com/windows2000/reskit/webresources.

- Technical Newsgroups. Technical newsgroups offer peer support for common computer problems. You can post persistent problems on an appropriate online forum. Other users might have already discovered, reported, and found solutions and workarounds for your problem. Suggestions from others can save you time in tracking down the source of the problem and provide direction for your troubleshooting tasks.

Troubleshooting Tools for Windows 2000

The Windows 2000 Setup CD and the *Windows 2000 Resource Kit* companion CD contain many software tools to help you manage TCP/IP, networks, the registry, security, remote administration, configuration, batch files, and other areas of the operating system. Several of these tools can be used for troubleshooting. These tools can help you maintain your system in the following ways:

- Keep your system running smoothly
- Isolate problem areas
- Diagnose problems
- Fix problems
- Seek further assistance

System Information

System Information is located under **System Tools** in the Computer Management snap-in. System Information collects and displays configuration information to help support personnel diagnose and correct problems. This tool displays the required data to resolve problems, including information about hardware, system components, and the software environment. More specifically, the tool can be used to gather information about the following:

- **Hardware Resources** displays hardware resource settings such as direct memory access (DMA), interrupt requests (IRQs), input/output (I/O) addresses, and memory addresses.

- **Components** displays information about the Windows 2000 configuration and is used to determine the status of peripheral devices, ports, and universal serial bus (USB) connections.

- **Software Environment** displays a snapshot of drivers, environment variables, tasks, and services loaded into computer memory. This information can be used to see if a process is still running or to check version information.

Note You can use the **View** menu of the Computer Management snap-in to switch between the display of Basic and Advanced information. The Advanced view shows the information in the Basic view and additional information that might be of interest to more advanced users or to Product Support Services.

System Information Categories

The information displayed by System Information is divided into five categories: System Summary, Hardware Resources, Components, Software Environment, and Internet Explorer 5. The categories and subcategories displayed in System Information can be used for troubleshooting.

Note Hardware information is not available in safe mode. While System Information can run in safe mode, it is limited to displaying system components and the software environment.

System Information allows you to save, export, and print system information.

System Summary

System Summary provides general information about your computer system. This includes information about the version of Windows that you are running, including the installation folder, the amount of physical and virtual memory, the locale and local time zone, and information about system hardware, including basic input/output system (BIOS), central procesing unit (CPU), memory, and other system resources. Use this information at the beginning of the troubleshooting process to develop a basic picture of the environment in which the problem occurs.

Hardware Resources

Hardware Resources displays hardware-specific settings, such as assigned or used IRQs, I/O addresses, and memory addresses. Table 14.1 describes the information provided in Hardware Resources.

Table 14.1   Hardware Resources

Section	Definition
Conflicts/Sharing	Identifies resource conflicts between Industry Standard Architecture (ISA) devices or Peripheral Component Interconnect (PCI) devices. Use this information to help you identify hardware conflicts or troubleshoot a nonworking device.
DMA	Reports the DMA channels in use, the devices using them, and those free for use.
Forced Hardware	Lists hardware devices that have user-specified resources as opposed to system-specified resources. This information is useful when troubleshooting Plug and Play resource conflicts.
I/O	Lists all I/O port ranges in use and the devices using each range.
IRQs	Summarizes IRQ usage, identifying the devices using the IRQs and showing free IRQs.
Memory	Lists memory address ranges in use by devices.

Components

Components displays information about your Windows 2000 system configuration, including information about the status of peripheral devices, ports, and USB connections. There is also a summary of problem devices. Table 14.2 defines some of the items that can be listed in Components.

Table 14.2   Component Item Definitions

Section	Definition
Multimedia	Lists sound card information, audio and video codecs loaded, and drive letter and model of the CD-ROM drive. With a data CD-ROM in the drive, MSInfo also performs a data transfer test.
Display	Lists video card information and current video configuration.
Infrared	Lists infrared device information.
Input	Lists keyboard and pointer device information.
Modem	Lists modem information.
Network	Lists network adapter, protocol, and Winsock information.
Ports	Lists serial and parallel port information.
Storage	Lists information on hard disk drives, floppy disk drives, removable storage, and controllers.
Printing	Lists installed printers and printer drivers.
Problem Devices	Lists devices with problems. Each device flagged in Device Manager is displayed with the corresponding status information.
USB	Lists USB controllers and drivers installed.

Software Environment

Software Environment displays a snapshot of the software installed on the computer. Table 14.3 defines some of the software components that can be listed in Software Environment.

Table 14.3   Software Environment

Section	Definition
Drivers	Lists all drivers loaded, if they are currently running, and their status.
Environment Variables	Lists all system environment variables and their values.
Jobs	Lists all open jobs, including print jobs.
Network Connections	Lists all mapped network connections.

(continued)

Table 14.3   Software Environment *(continued)*

Section	Definition
Running Tasks	Lists all processes currently running on the system.
Loaded Modules	Lists loaded system-level dynamic-link libraries (DLLs) and programs, along with their version numbers, size, file date, and path. This is for debugging software problems, such as application faults.
Services	Lists all system services available to the system, showing current run status and start mode.
Program Groups	Lists all existing program groups for all known users of the system.
Startup Programs	Lists programs started automatically from the registry, the **Startup** menu, or Win.ini.
OLE Registration	Lists object linking and embedding (OLE) file associations that are controlled by the registry.

Internet Explorer 5

The information provided by Internet Explorer 5 includes Summary, File Versions, Connectivity, Cache, and Content.

Tools Menu

The **Tools** menu lists several key support tools that can be used for troubleshooting. The **Tools** menu is available in the Computer Management snap-in.

Disk Cleanup

Sometimes Windows 2000 uses files for a specific operation and then retains them in a folder designated for temporary files. You might also have previously installed Windows 2000 components that you are no longer using. To avoid running out of space on your hard disk drive, you can reduce the number of files on your disk, or create more free space. Disk Cleanup searches your drive and shows you files that you can safely delete. You can choose to delete some or all of those files.

Dr. Watson for Windows 2000

Dr. Watson for Windows 2000 detects errors in programs, diagnoses errors, and logs diagnostic information. The Dr. Watson for Windows 2000 log file, drwtsn32.log, can be sent to support personnel to help diagnose problems. If a program error occurs, Dr. Watson for Windows 2000 starts automatically. To start Dr. Watson manually, click Dr. Watson in the **Tools** menu. For more information about Dr. Watson for Windows 2000, see Windows 2000 Server Help.

DirectX Diagnostic

The DirectX Diagnostic Tool is a Windows-based DirectX tool that presents information about the components and drivers of the Microsoft® DirectX® application programming interface (API) installed on your system. The DirectX Diagnostic Tool helps you test the functionality of DirectX, diagnose problems, and configure your system to optimize DirectX performance. Administrators and users can test sound and graphics output, test DirectPlay service providers, and disable some hardware acceleration features. You can use the DirectX Diagnostic Tools to gather information for a support technician.

Hardware Wizard

If a device is not Plug and Play, you might have to use the Hardware wizard in the **Tools** menu to tell Windows 2000 what type of device you are installing. After the device is detected or you identify the device using the Hardware wizard, Windows 2000 might ask you to insert the Windows 2000 Setup CD or the manufacturer's disk so it can load the proper device drivers. After the device drivers are loaded onto your system, Windows 2000 configures the properties and settings for the device.

Important   Allow Windows 2000 to configure the device properties and settings, don't do it yourself, unless absolutely necessary. If you manually configure properties and settings, the settings become fixed, and Windows 2000 cannot modify them in the future if a problem arises or if there is a conflict with another device.

You must be logged on as an administrator or a member of the Administrators group to configure a device using the Hardware wizard.

Network Connections

Network Connections opens the Network and Dial-up Connections folder which contains network connections for your computer and a wizard to help you create a new connection. From this folder, you can open a connection, create a new connection, access the settings and components of a connection, identify your computer on the network, and add additional networking components.

Backup

Backup protects data from accidental loss in the event of hardware or storage media failure. You can use Backup to create a duplicate copy of the data on your hard disk and archive the data on another storage device such as a hard disk or a tape. If the original data on your hard disk is accidentally erased or overwritten, or becomes inaccessible because of a hard disk malfunction, you can easily restore the data from the archived copy.

For more information about using Backup and creating a backup plan, see Windows 2000 Help and "Backup" in this book.

File Signature Verification Utility

If system files are overwritten by unsigned or incompatible versions, system instability can result. The system files provided with Windows 2000 have a digital signature which indicates that the files are original, unaltered system files or that they have been approved by Microsoft for use with Windows 2000. The file signature verification utility ensures system integrity by detecting changes to critical system files digitally signed by Microsoft. The Advanced option in the **File Signature Verification** dialog box allows you to save the file signature verification results to a log file and to search using the following criteria:

- System files that are not signed.
- Other files that are not digitally signed.

Update Wizard Uninstall

Update Wizard Uninstall is a tool that you can use to remove a patch, driver, or system file that was installed from Windows Update and to restore the previous version of the file.

You can also remove a patch, driver, or system file and restore the previous version of the file by connecting to the Windows Update Web page and following instructions to uninstall. However, if you do not have an Internet connection when you want to restore a previous version of the file, you can use Update Wizard Uninstall to accomplish the task instead.

Windows Report Tool

The Windows Report Tool collects information about your computer that can be used by support personnel to diagnose and troubleshoot problems. This tool provides a description of the problem, the expected results, and the steps required to reproduce the problem. The Windows Report Tool collects system files to help technicians make their diagnoses. You can also change system file selections.

The Windows Report Tool takes a snapshot of your computer settings and selected system and application files. This snapshot can be submitted to a computer manufacturer, software vendor, or support personnel, such as by e-mail.

Device Manager

In Windows 2000, Device Manager is located under System Tools in the Computer Management snap-in. Device Manager is a Windows-based tool for managing installed hardware. It works with both Plug and Play and devices supported by Microsoft® Windows NT® version 4.0. With Device Manager, you can check if a hardware device installed is improperly configured or is inoperable. From the **View** menu, you can sort the installed devices and system hardware resources by type or connection. You can use Device Manager to disable, uninstall, or update individual device drivers and troubleshoot problematic devices.

Important Changing resource settings improperly can disable your hardware and cause your computer to malfunction or become inoperable. It is recommended that only users who have expert knowledge of computer hardware and hardware configurations change resource settings.

You must be logged on as an administrator or a member of the Administrators group to change resource settings. If your computer is connected to a network, network policy settings might also prevent you from completing this procedure.

For Plug and Play–compliant devices, there are no true default settings. Instead, Windows 2000 identifies devices and their resource requests, and then arbitrates requests among them. If no other device requests the same resources as another device, its resource settings do not change. If another device requests its resources, the settings might change to accommodate the request. Consequently, never change resource settings for a Plug and Play–compliant device unless absolutely necessary. Doing so makes its resource settings permanently fixed, and Windows 2000 cannot grant requests from other devices to use that resource. Fixed resource settings on Plug and Play devices can be brought back to their original state: in the **Device Properties** dialog box, on the **Resources** tab, check the **Use automatic settings** check box.

All devices supported by Windows NT 4.0 have fixed resource settings, which are defined either while upgrading from a previous configuration, or later by using the Add New Hardware Wizard in Control Panel.

Certain circumstances might require users to change resource settings after they have been configured. For example, Windows 2000 might not be able to configure one device without creating conflicts with another. In such a case, a message usually appears to explain what you can do about the problem—for example, turn off a device to make room for the new device, disable the new device, or reconfigure a device from Windows NT 4.0.

The best place for resolving conflicts that might occur is the Hardware troubleshooter in Windows 2000 online Help. If you manually change a device configuration, Device Manager helps you avoid errors that can result from editing registry entries directly. If you need or want to resolve device conflicts manually, you can use Device Manager and try the following strategies:

- Identify a free resource, and assign the device to use that resource.
- Disable a conflicting Plug and Play–compliant device to free its resources.
- Disable a legacy device to free its resources, by removing the legacy device card and not loading the device drivers.
- Rearrange resources used by other devices to free needed resources.
- Change jumpers on your hardware to match the new settings.

AVBoot

The program InoculateIT AntiVirus AVBoot V1.1is a virus scanner that scans the computer memory, master boot record (MBR), and boot sectors on all physical disks installed for memory resident and boot sector viruses. If a virus is found, AVBoot can remove the virus. To create a startup floppy disk, insert an empty floppy disk and run Makedisk.bat from the folder Valueadd\3rdparty\CA_antiv of the Windows 2000 Setup CD. To scan for viruses, insert the AVBoot startup floppy disk into drive A and restart your computer. AVBoot runs automatically. For more information about AVBoot, see the readme file in the folder Valueadd\3rdparty\CA_antiv of the Windows 2000 Setup CD.

Important It is extremely important that you regularly update your antivirus program. In most cases antivirus programs are unable to reliably detect and clean viruses of which they are unaware. False negative reports can result when using an out-of-date virus scanner. Most commercial antivirus software manufacturers offer monthly updates. Take advantage of the latest download to ensure that your system is protected with the latest virus defenses.

Whether you use a third-party antivirus program or AVBoot, regularly update the virus signature files. Once you install an antivirus program, immediately update the signature files, usually through an Internet connection. Check with the software manufacturer's documentation for specific instructions. AVBoot includes update instructions in the installation folder and on the AVBoot floppy disk.

System File Checker

System File Checker (SFC) is a command-line tool that scans all protected system files and replaces incorrect versions with correct versions. It is part of the Windows File Protection (WFP) feature of Windows 2000.

The WFP feature provides protection for system files using two mechanisms. The first mechanism runs in the background. The WFP feature is implemented when it is notified that a file in a protected folder is modified. Once this notification is received, WFP determines which file was changed. If the file is protected, WFP looks up the file signature in a catalog file to determine if the new file is the correct version. If it is not, the file is replaced from the %SystemRoot%\System32\Dllcache folder or the distribution media. By default, WFP displays the following message to an administrator:

```
A file replacement was attempted on the protected system file <file
name>. To maintain system stability, the file has been restored to the
correct Microsoft version. If problems occur with your application,
please contact the application vendor for support.
```

The second WFP mechanism is SFC, which gives an administrator the ability to scan all protected files to verify their versions. SFC also checks and repopulates the Dllcache folder. The administrator can initiate a full scan of all system files, using either the **/scanonce** or **/scanboot** switches on SFC. If the Dllcache folder becomes damaged or unusable, you can use SFC with **the /purgecache** switch to remove the contents of the Dllcache folder, and copy the files from the Windows 2000 Setup CD again. All SYS, DLL, EXE, TTF, FON, and OCX files included on the Windows 2000 Setup CD are protected. By default, all versions of Windows 2000 Server cache all system files by default to ensure server reliability. Again, all versions of Windows 2000 Professional cache only the most critical system files.

The syntax for SFC is as follows:

```
sfc [/scannow] [/scanonce] [/scanboot] [/cancel] [/enable] [/purgecache]
[/cache size=x] [/quiet]
```

The SFC switches are listed in Table 14.4.

Table 14.4   SFC Switches

Switch	Description
/scannow	Scans all protected system files immediately.
/scanonce	Scans all protected system files once at the next boot.
/scanboot	Scans all protected system files at every restart.
/cancel	Cancels all pending scans of protected system files.
/quiet	Replaces all incorrect file versions without prompting the user.
/enable	Enables WFP for normal operation.
/purgecache	Purges the file cache and scans all protected system files immediately.
/cachesize=*x*	Sets the file cache size in bytes. This change does not take effect until you restart the computer.
/?	Displays this list.

Windows Update

Windows Update is an online extension of Windows 2000. It provides a central location to find customized files and product enhancements, such as service packs, device drivers, and new features, that have been specifically selected by Windows Update to work with your computer's configuration.

When Windows 2000 is installed, an Internet shortcut to the Windows Update is created on the **Start** menu. Windows Update uses Active Setup and Microsoft® ActiveX® controls to provide product enhancements. The ActiveX controls are downloaded and installed on your system when you connect to the Windows Update Web page. Once the controls are installed, they automatically compare device drivers installed on your computer with a database of updated drivers on the server. If any drivers are found to be newer than your current set, they are offered to you to install.

Note   Windows Update requires an Internet browser that supports ActiveX controls.

Device drivers, system patches, or hot fixes can be uninstalled using the Restore page on the Web site. If you are unable to connect to the Windows Update Web site, you can uninstall the latest updates by using Update Wizard Uninstall. Existing files and drivers are automatically backed up before new ones are installed.

When you select **Start**, Windows Update scans your system, generates a list of items that can be updated, and then installs the files for the items you choose to update.

For system administrators who want to closely control the types of updates that users download to their computers, Windows Update offers a number of options, including the following:

- Corporate IT Catalog. Windows Update provides a searchable catalog of updates, drivers, and more. System administrators can select which downloads are available to users, download them to a server behind a firewall, and make them available over an intranet.

- Restricting Access to Windows Update. You can use Group Policy to restrict access to Windows Update. System administrators can control access to updates to ensure that Windows 2000 configurations remain consistent across all desktops. Use the following check boxes in System Policy Editor to restrict access:
  - **Override Local Web Page** redirects the user to a specified Web page the first time that Windows Update is launched.
  - **Override Windows Update Site URL** redirects the user to a specified URL when Windows Update is launched.
  - **Disable Windows Update** disables all access to Windows Update and removes its shortcut from the **Start** menu.

NetDiag

NetDiag is a command-line, diagnostic tool included with the Support Tools on the Windows 2000 Setup CD that helps isolate networking and connectivity problems by performing a series of tests to determine the state of your network client. NetDiag diagnoses network problems by checking all aspects of a host computer's network configuration and connections. Beyond troubleshooting TCP/IP issues, it also examines a host computer's Internetwork Packet Exchange (IPX) and NetWare configurations.

IPConfig

IPConfig is a command-line tool that displays the current configuration of the installed IP stack on a networked computer. Run IPConfig whenever you need to know the status of a computer's TCP/IP configuration. Start IPConfig from the command prompt rather than from Windows Explorer to see the resulting display.

Since the results fill more than one normal command prompt screen when you use the **/all** switch, you might wish to redirect the output to a text file which can be viewed later in Notepad. To redirect IPConfig's screen output to a text file type:

ipconfig /all > ipconfig.txt

Run IPConfig whenever you need to know the status of a computer's TCP/IP configuration. When used with the **/all** switch, it displays a detailed configuration report for all interfaces, including any configured wide area networks (WAN) miniports (typically used for remote access or VPN connections). The following is a sample report:

```
Windows 2000 IP Configuration

        Host Name . . . . . . . . . . . . : TESTPC1
        Primary Domain Name . . . . . . . : reskit.com
        Node Type . . . . . . . . . . . . : Hybrid
        IP Routing Enabled. . . . . . . . : No
        WINS Proxy Enabled. . . . . . . . : No
        DNS Suffix Search List. . . . . . : ntcorpdc1.reskit.com
                                            dns.reskit.com
                                            reskit.com


Ethernet adapter Local Area Connection:

        Connection-specific DNS Suffix  . : dns.microsoft.com
        Description . . . . . . . . . . . : Acme XL 10/100Mb Ethernet NIC
        Physical Address. . . . . . . . . : 00-CC-44-79-C3-AA
        DHCP Enabled. . . . . . . . . . . : Yes
        Autoconfiguration Enabled . . . . : Yes
        IP Address. . . . . . . . . . . . : 172.16.245.111
        Subnet Mask . . . . . . . . . . . : 255.255.248.0
        Default Gateway . . . . . . . . . : 172.16.240.1
        DHCP Server . . . . . . . . . . . : 172.16.248.8
        DNS Servers . . . . . . . . . . . : 172.16.55.85
                                            172.16.55.134
                                            172.16.55.54
        Primary WINS Server . . . . . . . : 172.16.248.10
        Secondary WINS Server . . . . . . : 172.16.248.9
        Lease Obtained. . . . . . . . . . : Friday, March 05, 1999 2:21:40 PM
        Lease Expires . . . . . . . . . . : Sunday, March 07, 1999 2:21:40 PM
```

A number of other useful switches for IPConfig include **/flushdns**, which deletes the DNS name cache; **/registerdns**, which refreshes all Dynamic Host Configuration Protocol (DHCP) leases and re-registers DNS names; and **/displaydns** which displays the contents of the DNS resolver cache.

The **/release** *<adapter>* and **/renew** *<adapter>* options release and renew the DHCP-allocated IP address for a specified adapter. If no adapter name is specified, the DHCP leases for all adapters bound to TCP/IP are released or renewed. Table 14.5 lists all IPConfig switches.

Table 14.5   IPConfig Switches

Switch	Effect
/all	Produces a detailed configuration report for all interfaces.
/release *<adapter>*	Releases the IP address for a specified adapter.
/renew *<adapter>*	Renew the IP address for the specified adapter.
/flushdns	Removes all entries from the DNS Resolver Cache.
/registerdns	Refreshes all DHCP leases and reregisters DNS names.
/displaydns	Displays the contents of the DNS Resolver Cache.
/showclassid *adapter*	Displays all the DHCP class IDs allowed for the adapter specified.
/setclassid *adapter*	Modifies the DHCP class ID for the adapter specified.
/?	Displays this list.

Caution Many of the advanced features of IPConfig must not be used on a client system without the assistance of a network administrator or support personnel. Using these commands incorrectly can cause problems with the client system's connection to the server.

NBTStat

NBTStat is a command-line tool that is designed to help troubleshoot NetBIOS name over TCP/IP resolution problems. It displays protocol statistics and current TCP/IP connections using NetBIOS over TCP/IP (NetBT). When a network is functioning normally, NetBT resolves NetBIOS names to IP addresses. Start NBTStat from the command prompt rather than from Windows Explorer to see the resulting display.

PathPing

PathPing is a command-line route tracing tool that combines features of the tools Ping and TraceRt with additional information. PathPing sends packets to each router on the way to a final destination over a period of time, and then computes results based on the packets returned from each hop. PathPing shows the degree of packet loss at any given router or link, allowing you to pinpoint which routers or links might be causing network problems. Start PathPing from a command prompt rather than from Windows Explorer to see the resulting display.

IPSecMon

The IP Security Monitor (IPSecMon) is a Windows-based tool used to confirm whether your secured communications are successful by displaying the active security associations on local or remote computers. IPSecMon can be run locally or remotely if you have a network connection to the remote computer. IPSecMon displays an entry for each active security association. Use **Options** to set the refresh rate.

Troubleshooting Options

Several troubleshooting options that are built into Windows 2000 allow you to troubleshoot and resolve problems. Some problems are accompanied by an error message or display box. Windows 2000 troubleshooting options include:

- Stop Messages
- Event Viewer
- Windows 2000 Error and Event Messages Help
- Troubleshooters
- Troubleshooting Tools for Windows 2000
- Knowledge Base
- Windows 2000 registry

Stop Messages

Windows 2000 generates Stop messages when it detects an error condition from which it cannot recover. These messages must be interpreted and appropriate action taken to resolve the problems.

Stop messages are used to identify and debug hardware and software problems that occur while loading or running Windows 2000. When a mission-critical operating system fails, it is preferable to generate an obvious error message, such as a Stop message, rather than to fail in an invisible manner and possibly corrupt data. The Stop error consists of a blue screen, the actual Stop message, the text translation, the addresses of the violating call, and the drivers loaded at the time of the Stop error. The Stop message provides information to help in locating and identifying problem areas. Stop messages indicate where the error has occurred at both the address and driver levels.

The Stop message identifies the type of exception, and the exception indicates where the problem occurred; that is, whether it involved user-mode operating system software or kernel-mode (involving operating system, third-party drivers, or hardware) operations. The third and fourth lines describe which components were immediately involved and at what addresses.

The Stop messages that appear when the system fails are documented in the Error and Event Messages Help. For information about accessing information about Stop messages, see "Troubleshooting Stop Messages" later in this chapter. For more information about troubleshooting Stop messages see "Windows 2000 Stop Messages" in this book.

Event Viewer

Event Viewer allows you to monitor events in your system. It maintains logs about program, security, and system events on your computer. You can use Event Viewer to view and manage the event logs, gather information about hardware and software problems, and monitor Windows 2000 security events. The Event Log service starts automatically when you start Windows 2000. All users can view application and system logs.

To access Device Manager, on the **Start** menu, click **Programs**, point to **Administrative Tools**, and then click **Event Viewer**.

Event logs consist of a header, a description of the event (based on the event type), and, optionally, additional data. Most Security log entries consist of the header and a description.

Event Viewer displays events from each log separately. Each line shows information about a single event, including date, time, source, event type, category, Event ID, user account, and computer name.

For more information about Event Viewer, see Windows 2000 Server Help.

Event Logs

You can use Event Viewer to view and manage the System, Application, and Security event logs.

System Log. The System log records events logged by the Windows 2000 system components. For example, the failure of a driver or other system component to load during startup is recorded in the System log. The event types logged by system components are predetermined by Windows 2000.

Application Log. The Application log records events logged by programs. For example, a database program might record a file error in the Application log. Program developers decide which events to monitor.

Security Log. The Security log records security events, such as valid and invalid logon attempts, and events related to resource use, such as creating, opening, or deleting files or other objects. The Security Log helps track changes to the security system and identify any possible breaches to security. For example, attempts to log on the system might be recorded in the Security log, if logon and logoff auditing are enabled.

Note You can view the Security log only if you are an administrator for a computer.

By default, security logging is turned off, but you can use Group Policy to enable security logging. To control the types of security events that are audited, in Group Policy, go to Computer Configuration\Windows Settings\Security Settings\Local Policies\Audit Policy. To control the auditing of files and folders, display the properties of a file or folder. An administrator can also set auditing policies in the registry that cause the system to halt when the security log is full.

Event Descriptions

The format and contents of event descriptions vary, depending on the event type. The description indicates what happened or the significance of the event. Table 14.6 lists the five types of events recorded by the event logs.

Table 14.6   Event Types and Definitions

Event Type	Definition
Error	A significant problem, such as loss of data or loss of functionality.
Warning	An event that might not be significant, but might indicate a future problem.
Information	An event that describes the successful operation of an application, driver, or service.
Success Audit	An audited security access attempt that succeeds.
Failure Audit	An audited security access attempt that fails.

Viewing Events

After you select a log in Event Viewer, you can search, filter, sort, and view details about events.

Search for Events Searches can be useful when you are viewing large logs. For example, you can search for all Warning events related to a specific application, or search for all Error events from all sources. To search for events that match a specific type, source, or category, on the **View** menu, click **Find**.

Filter Events   Event Viewer lists all events recorded in the selected log. However, you can filter events using specified criteria. Filtering the events that occur on your network can help you pinpoint the source of problems. All events are logged continually, whether the filter is active or not. If you archive a log from a filtered view, all records are saved, even if you select a text format or comma-delimited text format file. Filtering has no effect on the actual content of the log; it changes only the view.

Sort Events   By default, Event Viewer sorts events by date and time from the newest to the oldest. When a log is archived, the default sort order is saved. You can also sort events to assess their sequence, filter events for specific characteristics, and search for events based on specific criteria.

View Details About Events   The **Event Properties** dialog box shows a text description of the selected event and any available binary data. Binary data, which appears in hexadecimal format, is generated by the program that is the source of the event record. A support technician familiar with the source program can interpret its meaning. Not all events generate binary data. For more information about an event, highlight the event, and then click it.

If you archive a login log file format, you can reopen it in Event Viewer. Logs saved as event log files have an EVT file name extension and retain the binary data for each event recorded. Logs archived in text or comma-delimited format have TXT and CSV file name extensions, respectively. Such logs can be reopened in most word-processing or spreadsheet applications. Logs saved in text or comma-delimited format do not retain the binary data. When you archive a log file, the entire log is saved, regardless of filtering options.

Error and Event Messages Help

The Error and Event Messages Help is another source of troubleshooting information. Here, thousands of error messages are documented, with corresponding explanations and recommended user actions. In particular, the kernel Stop messages that appear when the system fails are documented in the Error and Event Messages Help.

The Error and Event Messages Help gives you quick access to message string definitions so that you can resolve system and network problems within a minimum amount of time. Messages are normally followed by a description of the circumstances that might generate the message and, if appropriate or needed, by a suggested user action.

Sometimes the suggested user action is to obtain help from a technical support group. If this is the case, collect the following information before contacting Product Support Services:

- The type of hardware you are using, including network hardware, if applicable.
- The exact content of the message that appears on the screen.
- A description of what happened and what you were doing when the problem occurred.

System Monitor

System Monitor is a tool that can be used to track system resources usage. System Monitor can be used to test an application's usage of system resources. Common objects that a user can log are memory, CPU, network, and disk activity.

For more information about performance monitoring see "Overview of Performance Monitoring" in this book.

Troubleshooters

The troubleshooters are self-serve utilities to help you easily pinpoint problems and identify solutions. You can use the troubleshooters to quickly solve routine glitches, or common network configuration or interoperability problems without contacting a support specialist. Troubleshooters are included in Windows 2000 Help. They ask a series of questions and provide detailed information on troubleshooting the problem.

Use the Troubleshooters to diagnose and solve technical problems with the following system components and events:

- Client Service for NetWare
- Dynamic Host Configuration Protocol (DHCP)
- Display
- Group Policy and Active Directory
- Domain Name System
- Hardware
- Internet connections
- Modem
- Microsoft® MS-DOS® programs
- Multimedia and games
- Networking (TCP/IP)

- Print
- Routing and Remote Access
- Remote Installation Services
- Sound
- Startup and Shutdown
- Stop Errors
- System setup
- Server Management
- Microsoft® Windows® 3.*x* programs
- Windows Internet Name Service (WINS)

Knowledge Base

The Knowledge Base is an excellent source of information about all aspects of using and maintaining Windows 2000. The Knowledge Base is a database of tips, hints, and solutions to known problems. It contains thousands of articles written by support professionals at Microsoft. Articles are added and updated daily.

You can search the Knowledge Base by keyword or you can specify a driver, downloadable tool, or troubleshooting tool. You can also ask a question using free-text query or you can search for specific Knowledge Base articles by referencing the unique article ID assigned to each article. An article ID is assigned in the form of the letter "Q," followed by a number. Use the keyword **kbprb** to search for problem resolutions.

To search for Knowledge Base articles, see the Knowledge Base link on the Web Resources page at http://windows.microsoft.com/windows2000/reskit/webresources.

Windows 2000 Registry

The Windows 2000 registry is a database repository for information about a computer's configuration. The registry contains information that Windows 2000 continually references during operations, such as:

- Profiles for each user.
- The programs installed on the computer and the types of documents that each can create.
- Property settings for folders and program icons.
- What hardware exists on the system.
- Which ports are being used.

The registry is organized hierarchically as a tree and consists of subtrees, keys, subkeys, and entries. The registry has five predefined keys through which all registry subkeys and assigned values are accessed.

Note When accessing the registry of a remote computer, only the registry keys HKEY_USERS and HKEY_LOCAL_MACHINE appear.

The five subtrees, through which all registry keys, subkeys and assigned values are accessed, are defined in Table 14.7.

Table 14.7   Registry Subtrees

Subtree	Definition
HKEY_CURRENT_USER	Contains the root of the configuration information for the user who is currently logged on. The user's folders, screen colors, and Control Panel settings are stored here. This information is referred to as a user's profile.
HKEY_USERS	Contains the root of all user profiles on the computer. HKEY_CURRENT_USER is an alias for a key in the HKEY_USERS subtree.
HKEY_LOCAL_MACHINE	Contains configuration information particular to the computer (for any user).
HKEY_CLASSES_ROOT	Contains two types of data: data that associates file types with programs, and configuration data for COM objects.
HKEY_CURRENT_CONFIG	Contains information about the hardware profile used by the local computer at system startup.

Registry Editors

A registry editor is an advanced, Windows-based tool for changing settings in your system registry, which contains information about how your computer runs. Windows 2000 stores its configuration information in a database (the registry) that is organized in a tree format. Although the registry editors Regedit and Regedt32 allow you to inspect and modify the registry, normally you do not need to do so, and making incorrect changes can break your system. An advanced user who is prepared to edit and restore the registry can safely use a registry editor for such tasks as eliminating duplicate entries or deleting entries for programs that have been uninstalled or deleted.

Folders represent subtrees, keys, and subkeys in the registry and are shown in the left pane that is displayed when you use the registry editors. In the topic pane, the entries in a key or subkey are displayed. When you double-click an entry name, it opens an editing dialog box.

Warning Do not use a registry editor to edit the registry directly unless you have no alternative. The registry editors bypass the standard safeguards provided by administrative tools. These safeguards prevent you from entering conflicting settings or settings that are likely to degrade performance or damage your system. Editing the registry directly can have serious, unexpected consequences that can prevent the system from starting and require that you reinstall Windows 2000. To configure or customize Windows 2000, use the programs in Control Panel or Microsoft Management Console (MMC) whenever possible.

Edit your registry only if it is absolutely necessary. If there is an error in your registry and your computer ceases to function properly, you can restore the registry to its state when you last successfully started your computer. To do this, either select **Last Known Good Configuration** from the **Hardware Profile/Configuration Recovery** menu that is displayed during the startup process, or press F8 during Setup and select **Last Known Good Configuration** from the **Windows 2000 Advanced Options** menu. For more information about the **Windows 2000 Advanced Options** menu, which includes three safe mode options, see "Startup Process" in this book.

You can use a registry editor to add or delete keys and subkeys, and to add, delete, or change the values of entries. Entries that appear in the registry editors consist of three components. For example, in the following registry entry:

```
RefCount : REG_DWORD : 0x1
```

RefCount is the entry name, REG_WORD is the data type, and 0x1 is the value of the entry.

Updating Registry Information

Regedt32 and Regedit provide the following ways to update registry information:

- **Auto Refresh** (on the **Options** menu) automatically updates the registry when a change is made to registry data.

- **Refresh All** (on the **View** menu) updates all of the information in all registry editor windows.

- **Refresh Active** (on the **View** menu) updates only the information in the active registry editor window.

Note When **Auto Refresh** is in effect, a check mark appears next to the command and both **Refresh All** and **Refresh Active** on the **View** menu are unavailable.

You cannot use **Auto Refresh** while displaying the registry from a remote computer. If you click **Auto Refresh** while displaying a remote registry, the manual refresh options (**Refresh All** and **Refresh Active**) are not available. Although **Auto Refresh** appears to be working as it would if a local registry window were displayed, the contents of the remote window are not automatically refreshed.

For more information about using a registry editor to save a portions of the registry as files, and about printing, importing, and exporting registry data, see Windows 2000 Server Help and the Technical Reference to the Windows 2000 Registry (Regentry.chm) on the *Windows 2000 Resource Kit* companion CD.

Troubleshooting with the Registry

Many problems can be traced to services, device drivers, or startup control data. The Windows 2000 registry subtree HKEY_LOCAL_MACHINE contains this configuration information, so it is a good place to look for information to solve these types of problems.

Caution Do not use the registry editor to edit the registry directly unless you have no alternative. The registry editors bypass the standard safeguards provided by administrative tools. These safeguards prevent you from entering conflicting settings or settings that are likely to degrade performance or damage your system. Editing the registry directly can have serious, unexpected consequences that can prevent the system from starting and require that you reinstall Windows 2000. To configure or customize Windows 2000, use the programs in Control Panel or Microsoft Management Console (MMC) whenever possible.

Most of the examples in this section use the Regedt32.exe registry editor.

Table 14.8 briefly describes the registry keys for the HKEY_LOCAL MACHINE subtree.

Table 14.8   Registry Keys in the HKEY_LOCAL_MACHINE Subtree

Key	Description
HARDWARE	Describes the physical hardware in the computer, how device drivers use the hardware, and mappings and related data that link kernel-mode drivers with various user-mode code.
SAM	Contains security information for user and group accounts.
SECURITY	Contains local security policy, such as specific user rights.
SOFTWARE	Describes the software installed on each computer.
SYSTEM	Controls system startup, device driver loading, Windows 2000 services, and operating system behavior.

The SYSTEM key is the most useful for troubleshooting.

The registry information and examples in this section use the Transmission Control Protocol/Internet Protocol (TCP/IP) network protocol, which uses a DHCP server to get IP addresses. If your computer has a different configuration, or has third-party device drivers or services installed, the registry contains different information.

HKEY_LOCAL_MACHINE\SYSTEM

The HKEY_LOCAL_MACHINE\SYSTEM key contains information that controls system startup, device driver loading, Windows 2000 services, and operating system behavior. All startup-related data that must be stored (rather than computed during startup) is saved in the SYSTEM key.

Some of the most important troubleshooting information in the registry key HKEY_LOCAL_MACHINE\SYSTEM is the information in the control sets. A control set contains system configuration information, such as which device drivers and services to load and start. There are at least two control sets, and sometimes more, depending on how often you change system settings or have problems with the settings you choose:

- Clone
- ControlSet001
- ControlSet002
- CurrentControlSet

The registry subkey HKEY_LOCAL_MACHINE\SYSTEM\Select identifies how the control sets are used, and determines which control set is used at startup. This subkey contains the following entries:

- **Current**. Identifies which control set is the CurrentControlSet. When you use Control Panel options or a registry editor to change the registry, you are changing information in the CurrentControlSet.

- **Default**. Identifies which control set is used the next time you start Windows 2000, unless you either select the Last Known Good Configuration from the **Hardware Profile/Configuration Recovery** menu that is displayed during the startup process, or press F8 during Setup and select **Last Known Good Configuration** from the **Windows 2000 Advanced Options** menu.

- **Failed**. The control set that was pointed to by Default when a user last started the computer by selecting the **Last Known Good Configuration** option.

- **LastKnownGood**. The control set that is a clean copy of the last control set that actually worked. After a successful logon, the Current control set is copied to create the Clone control set, which is referenced by the LastKnownGood control set.

Note The Windows 2000 Advanced Options menu is displayed in safe mode. For more information about safe mode, see "Startup Process" in this book.

Using the LastKnownGood Configuration

You can start your computer in either of the following configurations:

- Default. The configuration that was saved when you shut down the computer.

- LastKnownGood. The configuration that was saved when you last successfully logged on to your computer. This configuration is invoked when you do the following:

  - Select **Last Known Good Configuration** from the **Hardware Profile/Configuration Recovery** menu that is displayed during startup.

  - Press F8 during Setup and select **Last Known Good Configuration** from the Windows 2000 Advanced Options menu.

The configurations are stored as control sets in the registry key HKEY_LOCAL_MACHINE\SYSTEM. If you made changes to your configuration when you were last logged on, such as adding drivers, changing services, or changing hardware, the two control sets contain different information. As soon as you log on, however, the information in these control sets is the same. Therefore, if you are having problems with startup and think the problems might be related to changes in your configuration, do not log on. Instead, restart the computer, and start safe mode by pressing F8 when prompted. Select the **Last Known Good Configuration** option when the **Windows 2000 Advanced Options** menu is displayed. The **Last Known Good Configuration** option can help you recover from the following types of problems:

- You install a new device driver, restart Windows 2000, and the system stops responding. The LastKnownGood control set contains no reference to the new, faulty driver set and enables you to start.

- You install a new video driver and are able to restart the system. However, you cannot see anything, because the new video resolution is incompatible with your video adapter. Do not try to log on. If you have the option to shut down the computer without logging on, do so. If that option is not available, turn off the computer or use the reset button. Wait for all disk activity to stop before restarting, especially if the computer has FAT volumes.

- You accidentally disable a critical device driver. Windows 2000 is not able to start and automatically reverts to the LastKnownGood control set.

Using the LastKnownGood control set does not help in the following situations:

- Any problem that is not related to changes in control set information, such as information like user profiles and file permissions.

- Once you have logged on after making changes. The LastKnownGood control set has already been updated to include the changes made during the previous session.

- Switching between different hardware profiles. The LastKnownGood control set can only switch between configuration information in the registry. Use Hardware Profiles to correct this problem.

- Startup failures caused by hardware failures or corrupted files.

- Copying a new driver over an old one while the old one is active.

Select Subkey

The values for the entries in the Select subkey identify which control set is **Current**, **Default**, **Failed**, and **LastKnownGood**. For example, a value of 0x00000001 indicates ControlSet001 (Current).

ControlSet001 is modified when you make any changes using options in Control Panel. ControlSet001 will be used for the Default control set the next time you start the computer.

ControlSet002 is the LastKnownGood control set. If you choose this control set to start the computer, Windows 2000 uses ControlSet002.

Finding Service and Device Dependencies

This section describes using information in the Control and Services subkeys to troubleshoot problems with your computer.

When you install Windows 2000, it creates the Control and Services subkeys for each control set subkey in the HKEY_LOCAL_MACHINE\SYSTEM key. Some information, such as which services belong to which group, and the order in which to load the groups, is the same for all Windows 2000 computers. Other information, such as which devices and services to load when you start your computer, is based on the hardware and the network software installed on your computer.

Each control set has four subkeys:

- *Control*. Contains startup data for Windows 2000, including the maximum size of the registry.
- *Enum*. Contains the Plug and Play hardware tree.
- *Hardware Profiles*. Enables you to define different configurations for your computer and select the one you want to use at startup.
- *Services*. Lists all kernel device drivers, file system drivers, and Microsoft® Win32® service drivers that can be loaded by the boot loader, the I/O (Input/Output) Manager, and the Service Control Manager. It also contains subkeys describing which drivers are attached to which hardware devices, as well as the services that are installed on the system.

Note The Control and Services subkeys can be used for troubleshooting startup and device driver problems, respectively.

Services Subkey

The registry subkey HKEY_LOCAL_MACHINE\SYSTEM\CurrentControlSet \Services contains information that controls how services are loaded. This section describes some of the entries for this subkey, with an explanation of their values.

ServiceGroupOrder Subkey

You can see the order in which device drivers must be loaded and initialized by viewing the registry subkey HKEY_LOCAL_MACHINE\SYSTEM \CurrentControlSet\Control\ServiceGroupOrder.

Service Groups

Many device drivers are arranged in groups to make startup easier. When device drivers and services are being loaded, Windows 2000 loads the groups in the order defined by the ServiceGroupOrder subkey.

DependOnGroup Entry

When a subkey in the Services subkey has a value for the **DependOnGroup** entry, at least one service from the group must be loaded before this service is loaded.

DependOnService Entry

The **DependOnService** entry identifies specific services that must be loaded before this service is loaded.

By knowing the dependencies, you can troubleshoot problems more effectively. If a service is stopped, the services that depend on that service are also stopped. When you start a service, the Service Control Manager automatically starts services on which the selected service is dependent.

If any of the files that are part of a service are missing or corrupt, an error occurs when you try to start the service.

ErrorControl Entry

The **ErrorControl** entry controls whether an error during the startup of this driver causes the system to switch to the LastKnownGood control set. If the value of this entry is 0 (Ignore, no error is reported) or 1 (Normal, error reported), startup proceeds. If the value is 2 (Severe) or 3 (Critical), an error is reported and the LastKnownGood control set is used.

If the value of the **ErrorControl** entry is 0x1, an error is logged in the event log, but Windows 2000 completes startup.

ImagePath Entry

The **ImagePath** entry identifies the driver path and file name. You can use My Computer to verify the existence of the named file. The value of the **ImagePath** entry is %SystemRoot%\System32\Services.exe.

Start Entry

The **Start** entry determines when services are loaded during system startup. If a service is not starting, you need to determine when and how it should be starting, and then look for the services that should have been loaded prior to this service. Table 14.9 describes the values of the **Start** entry that determine when services are to be loaded.

Table 14.9   Values for the Start Entry

Value	Meaning	Description
0	Boot	Loaded by the boot loader (NTLDR or OSLOADER) during the startup sequence.
1	System	Loaded at kernel initialization during the load sequence.
2	Auto Load	Loaded or started automatically at system startup.
3	Load On Demand	Driver is manually started by the user or another process.
4	Disabled	Driver is not to be started. If a driver is accidentally disabled, reset this value by using the **Services** option in Control Panel. However, file system drivers are loaded even if they have a start value of 4.

TypeEntry

The **Type** entry shows where the service fits within the Windows 2000 architecture. Table 14.10 lists a few possible values for the **Type** entry.

Table 14.10   Sample Values for the Type Entry

Value	Description
0x1	Kernel device driver.
0x2	File system driver, which is also a kernel device driver.
0x4	Set of arguments for an adapter.
0x10	A Win32 program that can be started by the Service Controller and that obeys the service control protocol. This type of Win32 service runs in a process by itself.
0x20	A Win32 service that can share a process with other Win32 services.

Many of the services that have a **Type** value of 0x20 are part of Services.exe.

Troubleshooting Suggestions

Reference materials, such as hardware and software installation records, notes about your configuration and problems experienced with it, and documentation provided with hardware and software products, can be valuable troubleshooting tools.

Keep Records

It is recommended that you record all hardware and software details in a notebook. If possible, note the order in which you set up the software, and list the software operating system and all of the software applications that are installed on the computer. When identifying your system, consider the following details:

- Number of CPUs.
- Processor class and speed of each CPU.
- Amount of RAM on each computer.
- Amount of hard disk drive space on each computer.
- Operating system, including versions and any service pack installations, hotfixes, or driver updates on each computer.
- Brand and model name of each computer.
- All software loaded on each computer.

Careful record keeping is essential to successful troubleshooting. Make sure to maintain records of your network layout, cabling, previous problems and their solutions, dates of installation of hardware and software, and so on, and keep them readily accessible.

Keep Notes

When troubleshooting a system, it is important to keep careful notes of your installation and of any troubleshooting attempts to correct the problem. You will find it valuable to read through your notes whenever a new problem occurs. The methods previously used to pinpoint other problems can also help you to handle new ones. Use a notebook to take notes as you install or set up a test scenario.

Refer to Documentation

Many problems occur when users begin a process without first familiarizing themselves with important concepts, issues, and guidelines. If you are having a problem:

- Read all the documentation.
- Check the Knowledge Base and search for information about the issue in the documentation provided in the Windows 2000 Resource Kit.
- Refer to the readme files and release notes provided with Windows 2000.

Finding Information About the Problem

Use the following checklist to find specific information about the problem:

- Check to see if the Emergency Repair Disk (ERD), backup data sets, or Disk Configuration backup is available.
- Does the computer work with another operating system?
- Try reinstalling the software to eliminate the problem.
- Determine if the system works with standard VGA.
- Is there IRQ or DMA sharing in WinMSD?
- Are any third-party services running?
- Are there terminate-and-stay-residents (TSRs) in the Task List, such as programs that are loaded with the startup group, or loaded in the registry?
- Are there any errors in Event Log? What is the exact text of the Event message?
- Search for related information in the Knowledge Base.
- Removed any nonessential cards.
- Where appropriate, contact third-party vendors for help.

Setting up the System for Further Troubleshooting

You can set up your computer to assist you in troubleshooting by configuring it to write information about errors to files that can be viewed or sent to a support engineer for analysis.

Local Stop File Creation

Setting up a system to write Stop information to a local Memory.dmp file is useful for servers that are extremely mission critical in nature and that must be backed up and running quickly. When you enable the System Recovery options to create the Memory.dmp file, the system writes the debugging information on your local hard disk drive. The Memory.dmp file on your hard disk drive can be sent to Product Support Services engineers for later analysis, and the server can be restarted. The System Recovery options in Control Panel are enabled by default on computers running Windows 2000 Server but not on computers running Windows 2000 Professional.

Sending the Dump File to Product Support Services

Compress the file, then send your file to support engineers by one of the following methods:

- Upload the file to an FTP server.

- Backup the file to tape and send the tape.

- Use Dumpflop.exe to backup the dump file onto floppy disks and send the disks.

Troubleshooting Techniques

There are several standard techniques that can be used to troubleshoot problems. Using the tools and documentation provided with your hardware and software is a good starting place. Once you have familiarized yourself with these materials, you can begin identifying the problem and testing the affected features to determine the exact cause. Problems can be caused by issues as diverse as incompatible hardware, outdated drivers, loose connections, incorrect configurations, or other issues. You can use a variety of resources to isolate the problem and determine if it is a known issue with a documented solution.

There are several basic troubleshooting tips and procedures that you can follow as a standard approach to solving problems:

- Follow the system checklist.

- Analyze symptoms and factors.

- Check to see if the problem is a common issue.

- Isolate the source of the problem.

- Define an action plan.

- Consult technical support resources.

Follow the System Checklist

Refer to the following checklist when you encounter a problem with the installation or operation of Windows 2000:

- Make sure no physical connections are loose.
- If there are any network connections, make sure they are all connected. If they are, restart the computer in case you have temporarily lost connection. Use the ping protocol to test whether client and server computers are connected.
- Even if you're not connected, restart your computers and make sure you still have the problem.
- Check Event Viewer for the system and the application events that might explain the problem. For information about using Event Viewer and the event logs, see Windows 2000 Help.
- Try a few tests of the affected feature to see if there are other problems you have not yet encountered. For more information about running test on features, see "Isolating the Source of the Problem" later in this chapter.
- Uninstall and reinstall the feature that is having a problem. Make sure the problem persists after reloading.

Analyzing Symptoms and Factors

Start troubleshooting by gathering information. Develop a clear understanding of the symptoms and collect pertinent system information to understand the environment in which they occur. Identify the exact problem to make it easier and faster for Product Support Services to solve your problem. Precisely what is not working correctly? Under what conditions does the problem occur? Which aspects of the operating system control those conditions? Is the problem specific to an application, or is it specific to a subsystem (networks, video, and so on)?

Has what you are trying to do ever worked on this computer before? If so, something might have changed that affects it. Have you changed hardware or installed new software? Has somebody else been using the computer, and could that person have made changes you do not know about?

If this program or functionality has never worked on this computer, compare the setup and configuration on this computer with the same program on another computer to identify differences.

The following questions are used by Product Support Services when troubleshooting problems. These questions can help you analyze the problem you are having.

1. Have you read the documentation?
   - If the answer is no, read the documentation to become familiar with important concepts, issues, and guidelines.
   - If the answer is yes, continue with the next step.

2. Can you install Windows 2000 on your computer using the Windows 2000 Setup program?
   - If the answer is no, contact Product Support Services.
   - If the answer is yes, continue with the next step.

3. Have you upgraded to Windows 2000 from the latest version of Windows NT? Did you apply the latest Service Pack? Are you using the latest versions of third-party drivers? Releases contain fixes to known software problems.
   - If the answer is no, install the latest version, service pack, or driver. If the problem persists, continue with the next step.
   - If the answer is yes, continue with the next step.

4. Have you installed new hardware or software recently?
   - If the answer is no, continue with the next step.
   - If the answer is yes, revert to the previous configuration. If the problem persists, continue with the next step.
   - If the error is the result of the recent change, call Product Support Services.

5. Was an error message displayed? Have you looked it up in the Error and Event Messages Help and the Knowledge Base? What is the probable cause and recommended user action?
   - If no error message was displayed, continue with the next step.
   - If you have implemented the user action recommended by the Error and Event Messages Help, and the problem still occurs, continue with the next step.

6. Check the Event Logs (System, Application, and Security, as appropriate) for any errors or warnings and search the Knowledge Base and the Error and Event Messages Help for their Event IDs.
   - If no errors or warnings were displayed, continue with the next step.
   - If you have implemented the user action recommended by the Error and Event Messages Help, and the problem still occurs, continue with the next step.

7. Did the task ever work? What happened just before it stopped working? For example, was new software installed? Did the network crash? Did the computer crash?

   ▪ If the problem occurred after you installed new software or changed a configuration setting, reverse the activity you performed. If the problem still occurs, continue with the next step.

8. Are any files missing or have any been accidentally deleted?

9. If you are troubleshooting an installation problem, examine your notes to see if you can identify where the problem might have occurred. Did you receive any error messages during the installation process?

10. Is this a new system or an established system? If it's a new system, how is it different from earlier systems where this problem did not occur?

    View **System Information** in the **Computer Management** snap-in to compare the hardware, software, and configuration of the computer you were using when the problem occurred with the hardware, software, and configuration of a computer where the problem did not occur.

11. Can you reproduce this problem on a different computer that has the same hardware?

    ▪ If the answer is yes, the problem involves software.

    ▪ If the answer is no, check the hardware on the computer you were using when the problem first occurred.

12. What happens in safe mode? For more information about safe mode, see "Startup Process" in this book.

Checking for Common Issues

Check to see if the problem is a common issue by reviewing Windows 2000 Server Help, and other document files included on the Windows 2000 Setup CD. For example, check Read1st.txt and Readme.doc in the root folder and the files in the Setuptxt folder.

Use the Troubleshooters in Windows 2000 Server Help to diagnose and solve technical problems. For a list of troubleshooters available with Windows 2000, see "Troubleshooters" earlier in this chapter.

Isolating the Source of the Problem

Identify the variables that could affect the problem. As you troubleshoot the problem, change only one of these variables at a time. If you must escalate your issue to a support provider, your detailed notes provide valuable information to the technician who is helping you solve your problem.

For example, if your computer does not complete startup, you need to identify exactly where it fails, and write down any error messages. If you get an error such as **Missing operating system** from the system BIOS when you start your computer, the problem is very different than if startup fails after the boot loader (NTLDR) starts. You know that the NTLDR has started when you see the message:

```
Starting Windows . . .
```

followed by a bar graph. When the bar graph turns solid, the text mode switches to the graphical mode (as represented by the display of the Microsoft Windows 2000 Server Family screen).

For more information about troubleshooting startup problems, see "Startup Process" in this book.

Eliminating variables can help determine the cause of a problem. Do symptoms manifest themselves when you run the system in safe mode? If not, check the programs that run when the system is started normally. Look at the icons stored in the Startup group located in the folder Documents and Settings*username*\Start Menu\Programs\Startup. Pointers to other programs executed at system startup are located in the registry at HKEY_LOCAL_MACHINE\SOFTWARE\Microsoft \Windows\CurrentVersion\Run.

Caution Do not use the registry editor to edit the registry directly unless you have no alternative. The registry editors bypass the standard safeguards provided by administrative tools. These safeguards prevent you from entering conflicting settings or settings that are likely to degrade performance or damage your system. Editing the registry directly can have serious, unexpected consequences that can prevent the system from starting and require that you reinstall Windows 2000. To configure or customize Windows 2000, use the programs in Control Panel or Microsoft Management Console (MMC) whenever possible.

Troubleshooting Ideas

The following are several troubleshooting techniques to help you isolate problems. These include, but are not limited to, hardware and driver compatibility verification, software compatibility verification, and error message analysis:

- If the problem is the result of a recent change to the system, undo that change. Device Manager lists the device drivers installed on the system. If a device fails and its driver had been recently updated, replace it with the original driver and retest.

- If an update installed from the Windows Update Web site fails to meet your expectations, restore the original files by running the **Update Wizard Uninstall** from the **Tools** menu.

- If you had no problems the last time the system was started, enter safe mode by restarting the computer and pressing F8 at the Starting Windows screen. When the **Windows 2000 Advanced Options** menu is displayed, select **Last Known Good Configuration** to restore the system configuration to the last known working version. Restoring a previous system configuration results in the loss of any changes made in the interim.

- If you find that there are additional programs executed at startup that are not listed in either of these locations, your computer might be controlled by Group Policies. For more information about policies, see Windows 2000 Server Help. If the computer is on a network, logon scripts or system management applications might also start programs on your computer as you log on to the network.

Caution   The Plug and Play specification allows an operating system to disable devices at the hardware level. For example, if you disable a COM port in Device Manager, you might be required to enter the CMOS or system setup to re-enable it.

Test each modification individually to see if it solved the problem. Make note of all modifications and their effect. This information is useful when troubleshooting problems with support personnel, and it provides an excellent reference for future troubleshooting.

Hardware and Driver Compatibility

Make sure that all hardware and drivers are compatible with Windows 2000. Many problems are related to defective or incompatible motherboards, memory, drives, and drivers. Before adding hardware or drivers to your Windows 2000 system, follow the guidelines listed here:

- For new hardware and new drivers, install Windows 2000 on a single system by running the Windows 2000 Setup CD. Test all hardware for complete functionality on this single system before preinstalling multiple computers.

- See the Hardware Compatibility List (HCL) and "Designed for Microsoft Windows" hardware logo program information. For more information, see the HCL link on the Web Resources page at http://windows.microsoft.com/windows2000/reskit/webresources.

- The safest, most reliable drivers to use with Windows 2000 are those that have been tested and signed by Windows Hardware Quality Lab (WHQL). For information about driver signing, see the Windows Hardware Quality Lab link on the Web Resources page at http://windows.microsoft.com/windows2000/reskit/webresources.

- See the hardware-related readme files provided on the Windows 2000 Setup CD.

Software Compatibility

Make sure that all preinstalled software is compatible with Windows 2000. Certain problems can be related to software that doesn't work well with Windows 2000 or that has an installation routine that is not easily adapted to the preinstallation process.

Install Windows 2000 on a single system by running Windows 2000 Setup from the product CD. Install and test all software for complete functionality on this single system before preinstalling on multiple computers.

Viruses and Error Messages

Check for viruses and see error message documentation. Many problems are related to unexpected errors or system failures. For example, the computer stalls, general protection faults occur, and so on.

- If protection faults are occurring or the system is failing with Stop messages, check the Knowledge Base for documentation about error messages.

- Run virus-checking software on the reference system, network reference system, and target computers. It is recommended that regular virus checks be scheduled for all systems as a preventative measure. For more information about virus protection, see "AVBoot" earlier in this chapter.

Test the Affected Feature

Sometimes a single component is behaving incorrectly, such as giving error messages whose origin is cryptic or failing under conditions that cannot be duplicated. If you cannot pinpoint the problem, you might want to try a few tests on the component to gather additional information. Following are examples of tests that can help pinpoint a problem with a component:

- Make sure the component gives correct responses for valid inputs.

- Make sure the component gives incorrect responses for invalid inputs.

- Follow the data. As the data moves from one component to another, examine the inputs and outputs to see if you can determine where the error happens.

- Use a different set of inputs to see if the problem still occurs. Put together a file that produces a simple known output, and try the test again.

- If there is more than one computer involved, use independent means to test whether the computers are connected.

- If you can, check the installation to make sure communication is established between processes.

Developing an Action Plan

It is a good idea to outline your troubleshooting plan on paper. Decide what steps you want to take, and what you expect to do based on the results of each step. Then do the steps in order, and follow your plan.

If you see a result for which you have no plan:

- Return to the isolation phase.

- Determine what happens in similar situations.

- Define another plan.

Contacting Technical Support Services

Do as much as you can to troubleshoot your system, and carefully document your attempts. If you have followed the guidelines discussed in this chapter and the problem persists, contact Product Support Services.

Gather the following information before contacting Product Support Services:

- The version of operating system that you are running.

- The service packs and hotfixes that you have applied.

- The top four lines of any Stop message displayed.

- The frequency nature and the trap.

- Information about any third party drivers or services that are installed.
- A detailed hardware list, including configuration information:
  - Computer make and model
  - Hard disk type and size
  - Disk controllers installed
  - Amount of memory installed
  - Tape drive model
  - CD-ROM drive model
  - Network adapter
  - Serial ports
  - Other adapters

Troubleshooting Hardware Problems

Certain problems can arise when incompatible hardware is used with software, when hardware is configured incorrectly, when cables and other connections are not working properly, or from other hardware-related issues.

Hardware Compatibility List

The Hardware Compatibility List (HCL) is a compilation of computers and system hardware that have been extensively tested with Windows 2000 for stability and compatibility. It is the guide used by Product Support Services to determine if a computer is supported for use with the Windows 2000 operating system.

The most common cause of hardware problems is the use of hardware that is not listed on the HCL. To avoid problems, make sure that you are using a device make and model that is listed on the HCL.

It is especially important to refer to the HCL if you plan to use modems, tape backup units, or SCSI adapters. If your system component is not included on the list, contact Microsoft for an updated Windows 2000 HCL.

Even if several models from a manufacturer are included in the HCL, only those models that are included in the list are supported: a slightly different model might cause problems. Where special criteria are required for a model to be supported (for example, if a particular version of a driver is required), this information is described as a footnote in the HCL. As additional hardware is tested, including device drivers and other system components, the HCL is updated. The updated list and software are available through the electronic services listed at the end of the HCL.

If the system is not on the HCL or if components not on the HCL, such as hard disk drive controllers, net cards or video, appear to be involved in the problem, Product Support Services might not be able to fully support and diagnose the problem.

For the latest HCL, see the Hardware Compatibility List link on the Web Resources page at http://windows.microsoft.com/windows2000/reskit/webresources.

Tip Use System Information to determine the hardware configuration of the computer that you are troubleshooting. Print the hardware information and save it to a file, keeping the report and file with the other configuration information for your computer. You can use the report when planning to change the configuration.

Other Approaches to Troubleshooting Hardware Problems

If your hardware components are listed on the HCL, and you are still having problems, check that the physical connections are secure.

If you are using a SCSI device, check its termination. Even if you are sure the termination is correct, and you are having problems that could be due to incorrect termination, open the computer case and check again. Whenever possible use active rather than passive terminators.

Note Terminators are used to provide the correct impedance at the end of a cable. If the impedance is too high or too low, internal signal reflections can take place. These echoes represent noise on the cable and can corrupt subsequent signals, which can result in degraded performance or data loss.

Passive terminators are resistors with the appropriate resistance value for the characteristic impedance of the cable. Active terminators are slightly more sophisticated electronics that are able to better maintain the correct impedance necessary to eliminate signal reflection.

Verify that the SCSI cables are not longer than they need to be. If a two-foot cable is long enough to connect the device to the controller, do not use a three-foot cable. The acceptable lengths vary depending on such factors as whether you are using basic SCSI, SCSI-2, wide SCSI, ultra-wide SCSI, or differential SCSI; the quality of the termination; and the quality of the devices being used. Consult your hardware documentation for this information.

Check your hardware configuration. I/O and interrupt conflicts that went unnoticed with another operating system must be resolved when you switch to Windows 2000. Likewise, you must pay close attention to CMOS and Extended Industry Standard Architecture (EISA) configuration parameters when using Windows 2000.

The Knowledge Base is a good source of information for hardware problems. There are several articles about memory problems, memory parity errors, SCSI problems, and other hardware information in the Knowledge Base.

If your computer crashes randomly and inconsistently, you might have memory problems. You can use the **/maxmem** switch in the Boot.ini file to troubleshoot memory problems. For more information about the **/maxmem** switch, see "Startup Process" in this book.

Troubleshooting Specific Problems

Certain problems are common and have known solutions. If you can isolate the cause of a problem, or determine what actions seem to cause the problem, you can refer to documentation and troubleshooting articles to help you find a solution.

Troubleshooting Setup

During the GUI portion of Setup, Windows 2000 installs drivers, creates accounts, configures the network settings, and builds the system tree. If there are hardware problems or conflicting hardware settings, Windows 2000 probably will not succeed in installing or upgrading.

Problems after the final reboot of Windows 2000 Setup are normally due to incorrect information either in the Boot.ini file or in the hardware configuration. For more information about troubleshooting startup problems, see "Startup Process" in this book.

Many problems can be avoided with routine virus checks. Be sure to check for viruses before installing or upgrading to Windows 2000 on a computer that is already in use.

Troubleshooting Stop Messages

Information about troubleshooting Stop messages is provided in Windows 2000 Help and there is a Stop Errors troubleshooter. For detailed information about gathering information about and troubleshooting Stop messages see "Windows 2000 Stop Messages" in this book.

Troubleshooting the Startup Process

The following are the phases of a successful startup process:

- Initial phase
- Boot loader phase
- Kernel phase
- Logon phase

Any one of these startup phases can prevent the computer from starting successfully and might require troubleshooting. Troubleshooting might require examining the Boot.ini file, verifying drivers, or replacing damaged or missing files. You might also need to refer to the following steps:

- Identify the phases of a successful Windows 2000 startup.
- Identify the events of the initial phase of the startup process.
- Identify the events of the boot loader phase of the startup process.
- Identify the events of the kernel phase of the startup process.
- Identify the events of the logon phase of the startup process.
- Identify the contents and switches of Boot.ini.
- Verify which drivers were successfully loaded.
- Replace missing or damaged files.

Windows 2000 provides a variety of options that you can use when a computer does not start, including safe mode, the Windows 2000 setup floppy disks, the Recovery Console and the Emergency Repair Disk (ERD).

For more information about using the Windows 2000 startup floppy disks to start your computer, see "Planning a Reliable Configuration" in this book. For more information about troubleshooting startup problems and using safe mode, see "Startup Process" in this book. For more information on using the Recovery Console and the emergency repair process see "Repair, Recovery, and Restore" in this book.

Troubleshooting Networking Problems

Isolating the problem allows your problem report to be as informative as possible and greatly speeds up the investigation process. Refer to the following troubleshooting steps when you suspect that you have a network problem:

- Check your hardware (hub, cables, and so on).
- Check your network adapters and drivers.
- Use the ipconfig.exe tool. At the command line type:

  ipconfig /all

Scan through the output from ipconfig.exe, and try to answer the following questions:

- Do you have an IP address?
- Do you have a default gateway?
- Do you have a DHCP server?

Try to ping the default gateway and DHCP server. Attach the output to your mail, and then type:

ipconfig /all > c:\mail_attachment1.txt

Use the Netdiag.exe tool. At the command line type:

netdiag.exe

Scan through the output looking for words like "FATAL."

Make sure the domain controller is working properly by pinging the domain controller.

DHCP might be the problem. Try releasing your IP address, restarting DHCP and getting an IP address again.

If you can't get an address, do a network sniff of *all* traffic to and from your computer and to and from the DHCP server from which you usually get addresses. If you can't connect (even though you have a valid address), a network sniff of the connection attempt could be useful.

Note   Use Nbtstat and Nslookup for name resolution and to report problems.

For more information about troubleshooting network problems, see the *Microsoft® Windows® 2000 Server Resource Kit TCP/IP Core Networking Guide*.

Troubleshooting Video Problems

If your screen stays black or is skewed after a restart, either the video device is not resetting correctly during the restart or the video is sharing an IRQ.

Turn the power off and restart. If the video works, you probably need to turn the power off each time you restart Windows 2000. This problem is related to the video and system-BIOS.

If the video is still not working properly after shutting the power down and restarting, check for IRQ and memory conflicts with other cards on your system.

If you have installed a new video driver, or used the **Display** option in Control Panel to change the display type, you might have created an incompatibility between the driver and the video device. If you get a black screen instead of the logon message when you restart Windows 2000 this is likely the case.

Turn off your computer or use the reset button to restart your computer. In safe mode, select the **Last Known Good Configuration** option from the **Windows 2000 Advanced Options** menu. For more information about troubleshooting problems using safe mode, see "Startup Process" in this book.

Another option is to start your computer in safe mode and select **Enable VGA mode** from the **Windows 2000 Advanced Options** menu. Windows 2000 uses the standard VGA driver to start up. You can then use the **Display** option to reconfigure your video device.

Note Windows 2000 requires new video and printer drivers. Microsoft® Windows NT® version 3.51 and Microsoft® Windows NT® version 4.0 drivers for these devices do not work correctly when you are running Windows 2000.

Troubleshooting Services and Drivers

Some services are configured to start automatically on Windows 2000. The specific services depend on your computer configuration and which network services and protocols you are using.

To view which services should start automatically (and which did start), click **Start**, click **Administrative Tools**, click **Computer Management**, and then select **Services and Applications**.

Sometimes, if a file that is needed to load or run Windows 2000 becomes corrupt or is deleted, the system displays a message about a problem with the file. You might also get information logged in the event log. Either of these clues can help you find the problem.

Not all executable files (EXEs) or dynamic-link libraries (DLLs) report missing or corrupt files, and the symptoms of a missing file can be unpredictable. However, it is recommended that all Windows 2000 EXEs and DLLs be protected by System File Protection (SFP).

What do you do if there is no indication of an error, but you think that a component did not start correctly? To check the files, at the command prompt type:

SFC /Scannow

SFC scans all your protected System files immediately. You can check to see if all the Windows 2000 system files exist and appear to be uncorrupted. Symptoms of corruption include a file that is an unusual size (for example, zero bytes or larger than its original size), or having a date or time that does not match the Windows 2000 installation date or dates on service packs that you have installed. You can use Windiff.exe, which is included with the Support Tools on the Windows 2000 Setup CD to compare files in your %SystemRoot%\System32 folder and subfolders with files in these folders on another computer that is running Windows 2000.

Note   SFP protects DLL, EXE, OCX, and SYS operating system files, as well as several TrueType and System Font files.

If you can log on to your computer, you can use the Drivers utility on the *Windows 2000 Resource Kit* companion CD to display information about the device drivers that were loaded. If you have previously printed the output from the Drivers utility (by redirecting the output to a printer or a file), you can compare the previous output with one produced when you think that drivers are not loading. Another method of determining if there are drivers missing from the list is to run the Drivers utility on a similar computer and compare the results.

Table 14.11 describes the output from the Drivers utility. The most important field is **ModuleName**, which is the name of the component.

Table 14.11   Drivers Utility Output

Column	Definition
ModuleName	The driver's file name.
Code	The nonpaged code in the image.
Data	The initialized static data in the image.
Bss	The uninitialized static data in the image. This is data that is initialized to 0.
Paged	The size of the data that is paged.
Init	Data not needed after initialization.
LinkDate	The date that the driver was linked.

Troubleshooting Problems with Portable Computers

Hardware profiles are especially useful for troubleshooting problems with portable computers. You can have one hardware profile for running your portable computer when it is in the docking station, and another one for the undocked situation. When you have more than one hardware profile defined, select the one that you want to use during startup from the **Hardware Profile/Configuration Recovery** menu.

To set up the hardware profiles, install Windows 2000 Professional when your portable computer is docked. Windows 2000 Setup installs the network software that you need to use your docking station and creates a hardware profile called Original Configuration (Current). You can copy this hardware profile and customize the new hardware profile.

You can also use the undocked hardware profile to set a different video resolution for your portable computer. For example, the Original Configuration can have the video resolution set to 1024x768 to run on your monitor, and you can change your undocked configuration to use a resolution of 640x480 or 800x600 as appropriate.

Additional Resources

- For more information about troubleshooting tasks, see Windows 2000 Server Help.

- For more information about the Microsoft AnswerPoint Information Services, see the *Windows 2000 Server Start Here* book.

- For more information about troubleshooting techniques, see the Knowledge Base link on the Web Resources page at http://windows.microsoft.com/windows2000/reskit/webresources.

C H A P T E R   1 5

Startup Process

Understanding each step in the startup process is important for troubleshooting problems that can occur while starting up or that can prevent the computer from starting at all. Microsoft® Windows® 2000 also provides tools that you can use to identify and repair startup problems when they occur.

In This Chapter

Related Information in the Resource Kit

- For more information about recovery, see "Repair, Recovery, and Restore" in this book.

- For more information about using the registry to troubleshoot problems, see the Technical Reference to the Windows 2000 Registry (Regentry.chm) on the *Microsoft® Windows® 2000 Resource Kit* companion CD.

Windows 2000 Startup Requirements

The data contained in the system files is required to start the Windows 2000 operating system. During the startup process, various screens and messages are displayed on your screen.

The Windows 2000 startup process requires the following steps:

1. Power-on self test (POST) processing
2. Initial startup process
3. Bootstrap loader process
4. Selecting the operating system
5. Detecting hardware
6. Selecting a configuration
7. Loading and initializing the kernel (Ntoskrnl.exe)
8. Logging on

You can begin startup by one of the following methods:

- Turn on the computer.
- In the **Shut Down Windows** dialog box, select **Restart**.

Important Windows 2000 might not start or operate correctly if any hardware components do not initialize correctly. Startup fails if any of the files that are required to start Windows 2000 are not present in the correct folder, or if any of the files has been corrupted.

When you see **Press Ctrl+Alt+Delete to begin** in the **Welcome to Windows** dialog box, the loading and much of the initialization of Windows 2000 is complete. However, startup is complete only when you can successfully log on using the **Welcome to Windows** dialog box.

Starting Windows 2000

Table 15.1 describes specific files that are required to start Windows 2000.

Table 15.1   Files Required to Start Windows 2000

File	Location
NTLDR	Active Partition
Boot.ini	Active Partition
Bootsect.dos (required only for multiple booting)	Active Partition
Ntdetect.com	Active Partition
Ntbootdd.sys (Required only if you are using a SCSI-controlled boot partition, and the SCSI adapter does not have a SCSI BIOS enabled).	Active Partition
Ntoskrnl.exe	%SystemRoot%\System32
Hal.dll	%SystemRoot%\System32
SYSTEM key	%SystemRoot%\System32\Config
Device drivers	%SystemRoot%\System32\Drivers

Note The string %SystemRoot% is replaced by the directory in the boot partition that contains the Windows 2000 system files.

Power-On Self Test Process

When you turn on or restart a computer, it begins a POST routine. The POST routine determines the available amount of real memory and verifies the presence of required hardware components, such as the keyboard.

After the computer runs its POST routine, each adapter card with a basic input/output system (BIOS) runs its own POST routine. The computer and adapter card manufacturers determine what appears on the screen during POST processing.

Initial Startup Process

After the successful execution of the POST, the system BIOS then checks the first hard disk that is powered up.

When the hard disk is the startup disk, the system BIOS reads the master boot record (MBR) and loads it into memory. The system BIOS then transfers the execution of the startup process to the MBR. After the MBR loads a copy of the active partition's boot sector into memory, the boot sector code starts the operating system as defined by the operating system.

Bootstrap Loader Process

NTLDR is the bootstrap loader for the Windows 2000 operating system, and is responsible for the following operations:

- Enabling the user to select an operating system to start.
- Loading the operating system files from the boot partition.
- Controlling the operating system selection process and hardware detection prior to the Windows 2000 kernel initialization.

Before you can start the operating system, NTLDR and the following files must be in the active partition of your startup disk:

- Ntdetect.com
- Boot.ini
- Bootsect.dos (if you plan to boot more than one operating system on your computer)

Signature() Syntax

The signature() syntax is equivalent to the SCSI() syntax, but is used instead to support the Plug and Play architecture in Windows 2000. The SCSI controller number might vary each time you start Windows 2000, especially if you add new SCSI controller hardware after Setup is finished. Using the signature() syntax instructs NTLDR to locate the drive whose disk signature matches the value in the parentheses, no matter which SCSI controller number the drive is connected to. The following is an example of a Boot.ini file with a signature() entry:

```
signature(8b467c12)disk(1)rdisk(0)partition(2)\winnt="description"
```

Note If multiple preexisting Boot.ini entries use scsi() they are maintained and not converted to signature() syntax.

Advanced RISC Computing (ARC) path entries in the Boot.ini file start with "signature()" syntax in the following situations:

- The partition on which you installed Windows 2000 is larger than 7.8 gigabytes (GB) in size, or the ending cylinder number is higher than 1024 for that partition.
- The drive on which you installed Windows 2000 is connected to a SCSI controller whose BIOS is disabled, so INT13 BIOS calls cannot be used during the startup process.

Because the signature() syntax replaces the scsi() syntax, the same requirement applies in that a file named Ntbootdd.sys is required in the root folder of the system partition to address the SCSI controller at startup. This file is the specific SCSI miniport device driver for the SCSI adapter from which you are booting, renamed to Ntbootdd.sys, and placed in the root folder of the system drive.

Note If multiple pre-existing Boot.ini entries use scsi() syntax, they are maintained and not converted to signature() syntax.

For more information about signature() syntax, see the Microsoft Knowledge Base link on the Web Resources page at http://windows.microsoft.com/windows2000/reskit/webresources.

NTLDR

When NTLDR runs, it clears the screen and displays the bootstrap loader message:

```
OS Loader V5.0
```

NTLDR then performs the following steps:

- Switches the processor into the 32-bit flat memory mode. When a computer first starts, it runs in real mode, like an 8088 or 8086 CPU. Because NTLDR is mostly a 32-bit program, it must switch the processor to 32-bit flat memory mode before it can perform any other functions.

- Starts the appropriate minifile system. The code to access files on file allocation table (FAT) file system and NTFS file system volumes is built into NTLDR. This code enables NTLDR to read, access, and copy files.

- Reads the Boot.ini file, and displays the operating system selections. This screen is referred to as the bootstrap loader screen.

- Allows you to select an operating system from the bootstrap loader screen.

   If you select an operating system other than Windows 2000, NTLDR loads Bootsect.dos and passes control to it. The operating system then starts up as normal, because Bootsect.dos contains the boot sector that was on the primary partition before you installed Windows 2000.

   If you select Windows 2000, NTLDR runs Ntdetect.com to gather information about currently installed hardware.

- Allows you to choose between starting the computer in the configuration in use when Windows 2000 was last shut down (Default), or selecting troubleshooting and advanced startup options by pressing F8. For more information on safe mode, see "Safe Mode" later in this chapter.

- Loads and starts Ntoskrnl.exe. NTLDR passes the hardware information collected by Ntdetect.com to Ntoskrnl.exe.

Selecting the Operating System

NTLDR displays the bootstrap loader screen, where you can select an operating system to start. This screen is based upon the information in the Boot.ini file. The screen display is similar to the following:

```
Please select the operating system to start:

  Windows 2000 Advanced Server

Use ↑ and ↓ to move the highlight to your choice.
Press ENTER to choose.

Seconds until highlighted choice will be started automatically: 29

For troubleshooting and advanced startup options for Windows 2000, press
F8.
```

If you do not select an entry before the counter reaches zero, NTLDR loads the operating system specified by the default parameter in the Boot.ini file. Windows 2000 Setup sets the default entry to the most recently installed copy of Microsoft® Windows NT® version 4.0 or earlier. You can edit the Boot.ini file if you want to change the default to either an earlier version of Windows 2000 or to another operating system.

Windows 2000 Setup places the Boot.ini file in the active partition. NTLDR uses information in the Boot.ini file to display the bootstrap loader screen from which you select the operating system.

The following is an example of a Boot.ini file:

```
[boot loader]
timeout=30
default=multi(0)disk(0)rdisk(0)partition(1)\WINNT
[operating systems]
multi(0)disk(0)rdisk(0)partition(1)\WINNT="Windows 2000 Server"
/fastdetect
```

The Boot.ini file has two sections, [boot loader] and [operating systems]. You can use the parameters in the [boot loader] section to customize startup, as described in Table 15.2.

Table 15.2   Bootstrap Loader Parameters

Parameter	Description
Time-out	The time that the user has to select an operating system from the bootstrap loader screen before NTLDR loads the default operating system. If the time-out value is 0, NTLDR immediately starts the default operating system without displaying the bootstrap loader screen. If you set this value to –1, NTLDR waits indefinitely for you to make a selection. You must edit the Boot.ini file directly because –1 is an illegal value for the **System** option in **Control Panel**.
Default	The ARC pathname to the default operating system.

Each entry in the [operating systems] section includes the ARC pathname to the boot partition for the operating system, the string to display on the bootstrap loader screen, and optional parameters. The bootstrap loader screen presented earlier in this chapter is an example of the use of this section of the Boot.ini file.

You can use the Boot.ini file to start multiple versions of the Windows 2000 operating system, as well as one other operating system, including Microsoft® MS-DOS®, Microsoft® Windows® 95, and Microsoft® Windows® 98.

Boot.ini Switches

The switches listed in Table 15.3, which can be added to the end of the [operating system] section of the Boot.ini file, are not case sensitive. For more information about the **/MAXMEM** and **/SOS** switches, see "Problem Occurs After the Bootstrap Loader Starts" later in this chapter. The switch you want to add must be placed on a separate line of the Boot.ini file.

Table 15.3   Boot.ini Switches

Switch	Description
/BASEVIDEO	The computer starts up using the standard VGA video driver. If you have installed a new video driver and it is not working correctly, you can select the Windows 2000 entry with this switch to start the computer and change to a different driver.
/BAUDRATE=nnnn	Specifies the baud rate to be used for debugging. The default baud rate is 9600 if a modem is attached, and 19200 for a null-modem cable. Including this switch in the Boot.ini file causes the **/DEBUG** switch to activate.

(continued)

Table 15.3   Boot.ini Switches *(continued)*

Switch	Description
/CRASHDEBUG	The debugger is loaded when you start Windows 2000, but remains inactive unless a kernel error occurs. This switch is useful if you are experiencing random kernel errors.
/DEBUG	The debugger is loaded when you start Windows NT, and can be activated at any time by a host debugger connected to the computer. Use this switch when you are debugging problems that are regularly reproducible.
/DEBUGPORT= com$x$	Specifies the communications port to use for debugging, where x is the communications port that you want to use. Including this switch in the Boot.ini file causes the **/DEBUG** switch to activate.
/MAXMEM:n	Specifies the maximum amount of RAM that Windows 2000 can use. Use this switch if you suspect that a memory chip is bad.
/NODEBUG	No debugging information is being used.
NUMPROC=x	Allows you to force a multiprocessor computer to start up with < n processors.
/FASTDETECT =[COMx | COMx,y,z...]	Turns off serial and bus mouse detection in NTDETECT. Use this switch if you have a component other than a mouse attached to a serial port during the startup process. If you use **/FASTDETECT** without specifying a communications port, serial mouse detection is disabled on all communications ports.
/SOS	Displays the device driver names as they are being loaded. Use this switch when startup fails (while loading drivers), to determine which driver is triggering the failure.
/PAE	Specify the /PAE switch with the corresponding entry in Boot.ini to allow a computer that supports physical address extension (PAE) mode to start normally. In safe mode, the computer starts using normal kernels even if the /PAE switch is specified.

Editing Boot.ini

When you install Windows 2000, the read-only, system, and hidden attributes of the Boot.ini file are set. Regardless of the value of these attributes, you can edit the timeout and default parameters in the Boot.ini file using the **System** option in Control Panel.

To edit the Boot.ini file with a text editor, you need to make the file visible and turn off the read-only attribute. You can change file attributes using My Computer or at the command prompt.

▶ **To change file attributes using My Computer**

1. On the **Tools** menu, click **Folder Options**.

2. On the **View** tab, double-click **Hidden files and folders**.

3. Select either **Do not show hidden files and folders** or **Show hidden files and folders**.

4. Click **OK**.

Important If you change the path to the Windows 2000 boot partition, make sure to edit both the default path and operating system path entries. If you change one but not the other, a new choice is designated as the default selection and added to the bootstrap loader screen.

Detecting Hardware

Ntdetect.com detects installed hardware during the Windows 2000 startup sequence. Ntdetect.com passes this information to NTLDR and places a list in the registry. Ntdetect.com detects the following components:

- Computer ID
- Bus/adapter type
- SCSI adapters
- Video adapters
- Keyboard
- Communication ports
- Parallel ports
- Floppy disks
- Mouse/pointing device
- Floating-point coprocessor

Ntdetect.com runs after you select an operating system on the bootstrap loader screen (or the timer times out). NTLDR has started when you see the message:

```
Starting Windows . . .
```

followed by a bar graph. When the bar graph becomes solid, the text mode switches to the graphical mode, and the Microsoft® Windows® 2000 Server Family screen is displayed.

Loading and Initializing the Kernel

After you choose a hardware profile or configuration, or when NTLDR automatically makes the selection for you, the kernel load phase of the Windows 2000 startup process begins. During this process, NTLDR performs the following operations:

- Loads the Windows 2000 kernel (Ntoskrnl.exe) and the hardware abstraction layer (Hal.dll) into memory (NTLDR does not initialize these programs yet).

- Loads the registry key HKEY_LOCAL_MACHINE\SYSTEM from %SystemRoot%\System32\Config\System.

- Selects a Configuration. The first hardware profile is highlighted by default. If you have created other hardware profiles, use the DOWN ARROW key to select the one that you want to use.

- Selects the control set that it uses to initialize the computer.

- Loads device drivers that have a Start value of 0x0.

Important Do not change the values in the folder %SystemRoot%\System32\Config\System.

For more information about hardware profiles, use see Windows 2000 Server Help.

Selecting the Control Set

The values of the entries in the HKEY_LOCAL_MACHINE\SYSTEM\Select subkey determine which control set to use.

If you did not press F8 when the OS Loader V5.0 screen was displayed, or if you have only one hardware profile, NTLDR uses the control set identified by the value of the Default entry in the subkey HKEY_LOCAL_MACHINE\SYSTEM \Select. However, if you chose **Last Known Good Configuration** from the **Windows 2000 Advanced Options** menu that is displayed when you pressed F8 *and* you selected **Last Known Good Configuration** from the **Hardware Profile/Configuration Recovery** menu, the value of the LastKnownGood entry in the subkey HKEY_LOCAL_MACHINE\SYSTEM\Select specifies the control set.

Based on your actions and the value of the corresponding Select subkey entry, NTLDR determines which ControlSet00x to use. NTLDR sets the Current value of the subkey HKEY_LOCAL_MACHINE\SYSTEM\Select to the number of the control set it will use.

Note The two registry editors, Regedt32.exe and Regedit.exe, are included on the Windows 2000 Setup CD. You can use either one to view the registry. For more information about the registry, see the Technical Reference to the Registry on the *Windows 2000 Resource Kit* companion CD.

Loading Device Drivers

NTLDR scans the driver-specific registry subkeys in HKEY_LOCAL_MACHINE\SYSTEM\CurrentControlSet\Services for **Start** entries with a value of 0x0. This value indicates that the device drivers should be loaded, but not initialized. Device drivers are loaded into memory by using BIOS calls in real mode or by Ntbootdd.sys.

Next, Ntoskrnl.exe initializes the kernel. If the Boot.ini ARC path entry contains the /SOS switch, text similar to the following is displayed:

```
Microsoft (R) Windows 2000 (TM) Version 5.0 (Build xxxx)
1 System Processor (16 MB Memory)
```

Upon successful initialization, Ntoskrnl.exe:

- Creates the Clone control set by making a copy of the control set pointed to by the value of Current.

- Creates the HKEY_LOCAL_MACHINE\HARDWARE key using the information that was passed from NTLDR. This key contains the hardware data that is detected and computed at each system startup. The data includes information about hardware components on the system board and about the interrupts hooked by specific hardware devices.

Initializing Device Drivers

Ntoskrnl.exe initializes the low-level device drivers with a start value of 0x0, which were loaded during the Kernel load phase. Ntoskrnl.exe then scans the subkey HKEY_LOCAL_MACHINE\SYSTEM\CurrentControlSet\Services for device drivers with a Start value of 0x1, which are initialized as soon as they are loaded. They are not loaded by BIOS, but by the device drivers loaded during the kernel load phase and that have already been initialized.

Error Processing

If an error occurs during the loading and initializing of a device driver, the action taken is based on the value of the **ErrorControl** entry in the registry subkey HKEY_LOCAL_MACHINE\SYSTEM\CurrentControlSet\Services for the device driver that has a problem.

Logging On to Windows 2000

The Windows 2000 subsystem automatically starts Winlogon.exe, which starts the Local Security Administration, Lsass.exe. The **Welcome to Windows** dialog box appears, containing the text **Press Ctrl+Alt+Delete to begin**. Although Windows 2000 might still be initializing network device drivers, you can log on.

Next, the Service Controller (Screg.exe) checks the subkey HKEY_LOCAL_MACHINE\SYSTEM\CurrentControlSet\Services for services with a Start value of 0x2, which are loaded automatically.

Services are loaded in parallel, based on their dependencies. The dependencies are described in the **DependOnGroup** and **DependOnService** entries in the subkey HKEY_LOCAL_MACHINE\SYSTEM\CurrentControlSet\Services.

Note Windows 2000 startup is not considered complete until a user successfully logs on to the system. After a successful logon, the Clone control set is copied to the LastKnownGood control set.

Troubleshooting Startup Problems

If your computer fails to complete startup, it might stop, or it might display an error message. This section discusses ways to troubleshoot problems that can prevent Windows 2000 from starting.

The first step in figuring out what causes a startup problem is to determine if the problem occurs before or after the operating system takes control. If you do not see the bootstrap loader screen, the problem might be due to hardware failure. Possible causes also include a faulty MBR or partition table, or a damaged boot sector.

Damage can have several causes, including viruses. Viruses use BIOS calls to install themselves, so they are operating-system independent. Windows 2000 traps BIOS calls while it is running, but cannot protect itself when the computer is multiple-booted by using MS-DOS. For more information about protecting your computer from viruses and recovering from problems with viruses, see the Microsoft Knowledge Base link on the Web Resources page at http://windows.microsoft.com/windows2000/reskit/webresources.

If the problem occurs after selecting Windows 2000 from the bootstrap loader screen, files that are needed by the operating system might be missing or corrupt. For more information, see "Options to Use When a System Does Not Start" later in this chapter.

Problem Occurs Before the Bootstrap Loader Starts

This section describes the problems that might occur between the time you turn the computer on until you see the bootstrap loader screen. Symptoms of problems in this group include the following:

- The computer hangs immediately after the power-on self test (POST).
- You do not see the bootstrap loader screen.
- You receive messages such as:
  - Missing operating system.
  - A disk read error occurred.
  - Insert a system diskette and restart the system.
  - Invalid partition table.
  - Hard disk error.
  - Hard disk absent/failed.

Table 15.4 lists symptoms, possible trouble causes and sources of more detailed information.

Table 15.4   Startup Problems

If You See Messages About or Suspect a Problem with . . .	Possible Problem	Source for More Information
POST routine	The POST routine is inaccessible.	"Hardware Problems" later in this chapter.
System partition	There is no system partition on the first hard disk.	"Disks Concepts and Troubleshooting" in this book.
Master boot record	The MBR is corrupt.	"Disks Concepts and Troubleshooting" in this book.
Partition table	The partition table is invalid.	"Disks Concepts and Troubleshooting" in this book.
Multiple-booting between Windows 2000 and MS-DOS	Bootsect.dos must be restored.	Windows 2000 Server Help.

(continued)

Table 15.4   Startup Problems *(continued)*

If You See Messages About or Suspect a Problem with . . .	Possible Problem	Source for More Information
Boot.ini	The Boot.ini file is missing.	"Problem Occurs after the Bootstrap Loader Starts" later in this chapter.
Bootstrap loader screen	NTLDR, is missing or corrupt.	"Problem Occurs after the Bootstrap Loader Starts" later in this chapter.
CMOS	The CMOS is corrupt, or the CMOS battery is run down.	"Disks Concepts and Troubleshooting" in this book.
Hardware	If you have installed new hardware or new drivers, they could be causing the problem, or a hardware component has malfunctioned.	"Hardware Problems" later in this chapter.

You might not be able to start your computer to troubleshoot the problem. If all of your volumes are formatted by using NTFS, you cannot use MS-DOS-based utilities.

Problem Occurs After the Bootstrap Loader Starts

This section describes problems that might occur after NTLDR starts executing until you successfully log on to Windows 2000.

Using Checked Version of NTDETECT

NTDETECT detects installed hardware components.

There is a debug version of Ntdetect.com on the *Windows 2000 Resource Kit* companion CD, called Ntdetect.chk. If Ntdetect.com fails to detect all of the hardware that you think it should find, you can use Ntdetect.chk to help isolate the problem. Typically, a mouse or a disk controller is the cause of the problem.

▶ **To use the debug version of Ntdetect:**

1. Rename Ntdetect.com to Ntdetect.bak in the root folder of your system partition.

2. Copy Ntdetect.chk from Support\Debug\I386 to the root folder.

3. Rename Ntdetect.chk to Ntdetect.com.

The utility Installd, included on the *Windows 2000 Resource Kit* companion CD, performs the same functions.

Ntdetect.com has the hidden, system, and read-only attributes set when you install Windows 2000. Clear these attributes to make the file visible.

After Ntdetect.chk displays information about the components, press ENTER to continue. Ntdetect.chk next displays information about the current nodes for the controllers and peripherals. Press ENTER at the end of each screen.

When you have finished using Ntdetect.chk, rename Ntdetect.com to Ntdetect.chk and rename Ntdetect.bak to Ntdetect.com.

Using the /MAXMEM Switch

The Boot.ini file has a **/MAXMEM** switch which you can use specify the maximum amount of RAM that Windows 2000 can use. You can use this switch to troubleshoot memory parity errors, mismatched SIMM speeds, and other memory-related problems. To use this switch, the memory must be contiguous. Never specify a value less than 32 for Windows 2000 Professional.

Include this switch at the end of the ARC path specified in the [operating systems] section of the Boot.ini file. In the following example Windows 2000 Professional is restricted to using only the first 32 MB RAM.

```
[operating systems]
multi(0)disk(0)rdisk(0)partition(1)\winnt="Windows 2000 Professional"
/fastdetect  /MAXMEM=32
```

Note For Windows 2000 Server, use a minimum of 64 MB.

For more information about troubleshooting memory problems, see "Troubleshooting Strategies" in this book.

Using the /SOS Switch

You can add the /SOS switch to the Boot.ini file to have NTLDR display the kernel and device driver names while they are being loaded. Use this switch if Windows 2000 does not start up and you think a driver is missing or corrupted. For information about changing Boot.ini switches, see "Boot.ini Switches" earlier in this chapter.

Hardware Problems

If a device fails to initialize during the POST routine, you might not be able to gain access to it. If you have not changed or added devices since the last startup, check for the following:

- Controller cards are seated properly.
- Cables are properly connected.
- Disks are turned on.

If you have changed hardware or device drivers since the last startup, the problem might be with the new configuration. You should check that:

- SCSI devices are terminated properly.
- There are no IRQ conflicts.
- The BIOS is enabled on only the first SCSI controller (if at all).

During the startup process, the **Hardware Profile/Configuration Recovery** menu provides options for using alternative configurations. If you have checked the above items and Windows 2000 does not complete startup, try using one of the other configuration options listed in the **Hardware Profile/Configuration Recovery** menu.

For more information about hardware problems, see "Troubleshooting Strategies" in this book, or see the Microsoft Knowledge Base link on the Web Resources page at http://windows.microsoft.com/windows2000/reskit/webresources.

Note On NTFS volumes, you need to use Windows 2000-based utilities, such as DiskProbe, to examine information on the volume. DiskProbe is a low-level disk editor that you can use to examine and change individual disk sectors.

If you use the Windows 2000 Setup floppy disks, try using the following utilities:

- The Computer Management snap-in in Administrative Tools where you can view system information.
- The DiskProbe tool, a low-level disk editor that you can use to examine and change individual disk sectors.

Options to Use When a System Does Not Start

Windows 2000 provides a variety of options that you can use when a computer does not start, including safe mode, the Recovery Console, and the Emergency Repair Disk (ERD). You can use safe mode to start the computer with only minimal necessary services. Safe mode options, including Last Known Good Configuration, are especially useful if a newly-installed driver is causing the problems.

If safe mode does not start the computer, you can use the Recovery Console. Using the Recovery Console is recommended only for advanced users or administrators. You can access the Recovery Console to start the system by using the Windows 2000 Setup CD or the Setup floppy disks that you created from the CD. The Recovery Console is a command-line interface that allows you to perform tasks such as starting and stopping services and accessing the local drive.

The ERD provides another option if safe mode and the Recovery Console do not start the system. If you have already created an ERD, you can start the system with the Windows 2000 Setup CD or the Setup floppy disks, and then use the ERD to restore core system files.

Safe Mode

Safe mode is a diagnostic tool for troubleshooting problems that can occur with starting and running Windows 2000. It is only accessible when the computer is started. As part of the **Windows 2000 Advanced Options** menu, safe mode allows the user to specifically control how the computer starts Windows 2000.

If the computer fails to startup properly, on the next restart, Windows 2000 displays the **Windows 2000 Advanced Options** menu, containing several startup troubleshooting options. You can also manually prompt Windows 2000 to display the **Windows 2000 Advanced Options** menu.

When starting Windows 2000 in safe mode, only essential drivers and system services are loaded, including the mouse, keyboard, CD-ROM and standard VGA device drivers, and the Event Log, Plug and Play, Remote Procedure Call (RPC), and the Logical Disk Manager system services. This makes safe mode useful for isolating and resolving error conditions that are caused by faulty applications, system services, and device drivers that are started automatically.

Although a computer started in safe mode has only a minimum of necessary services, you can access all partitions on functioning physical disks. Use safe mode for system startup in situations such as the following:

- If Windows 2000 seems to stall for an extended period of time.
- If Windows 2000 does not work correctly or has unexpected results.
- If your video display does not work correctly.
- If your computer suddenly slows down.
- If you need to test an intermittent error condition.

Once in safe mode, you can disable or delete a system service, a device driver, or automatically started application that is preventing the computer from starting normally.

To use a safe mode option, restart your computer, and then press F8 when you see the **Boot** menu. The **Windows 2000 Advanced Options** menu appears:

```
Windows 2000 Advanced Options Menu
Please select an option:
    Safe Mode
    Safe Mode with Networking
    Safe Mode With Command Prompt

    Enable Boot Logging
    Enable VGA Mode
    Last Known Good Configuration
    Directory Services Restore Mode (Windows 2000 domain controllers
only)
    Debugging Mode
    Boot Normally

Use ↑ and ↓ to move the highlight to your choice.
Press Enter to choose.
```

Select an option, and then press ENTER. The **Boot** menu is displayed again, with the words "Safe Mode" displayed in red at the bottom. Select the operating system installation that you want to start, and then press ENTER.

Important   When you select the operating system installation to start, you must choose a version of Windows 2000. Do not choose another Windows-based operating system.

When you use one of the safe mode options the environment variable Safeboot_Option is set to either Network or Minimal.

The default Microsoft VGA driver is used for display (640 x 480 x 16 colors). You must log on in all modes (either by a domain or the local SAM, depending on which safe mode option you choose).

Table 15.5 describes the **Windows 2000 Advanced Options** menu.

Table 15.5   Windows 2000 Advanced Options Menu

Option	Description
Safe Mode (Safeboot_Option=Minimal)	Starts Windows 2000 using basic files and drivers only, without networking. The drivers and files used are for mouse, monitor, keyboard, mass storage, base video, and default system services.
Safe Mode with Networking (Safeboot_Option= Network)	Similar to standard safe mode, but also adds essential services and drivers needed to start networking.
Safe Mode with Command Prompt (Safeboot_Option= Minimal)	Similar to standard safe mode but loads the command interpreter instead of Explorer.exe as the user shell.
Enable Boot Logging	Creates a log file, Ntbtlog.txt, during startup where the names and status of all drivers loaded into memory are recorded. The log file is stored in the %SystemRoot% folder.
Enable VGA Mode	Starts the computer in basic VGA mode in cases of corruption or incompatibility of currently installed video driver. The basic video driver is always used when you start Windows 2000 in any kind of safe mode.
Last Known Good Configuration	Starts Windows 2000 using the settings (registry information) that Windows saved at the last shutdown. Use Last Known Good Configuration only in cases of incorrect configuration. It does not solve problems caused by corrupted or missing drivers or files. All system setting changes made after the last successful startup are lost.
Directory Service Restore Mode	Allows restores of Active Directory on a domain controller. This option is not available on computers that are running Windows 2000 Professional or on member servers.
Debugging Mode	Starts Windows 2000 in kernel debug mode, which allows a debugger to access the kernel for troubleshooting and system analysis.
Boot Normally	Starts Windows 2000, loading all normal startup files and registry values.

If you are using, or have used, Remote Install Services to install Windows 2000 on your computer, the advanced startup options might include options related to restoring or recovering your system using Remote Install Services, in addition to the options described above.

If you plan to start the computer in safe mode and then use Backup with Removable Storage, the only safe mode options you can use are **Enable VGA Mode**, **Last Known Good Configuration**, and **Directory Services Restore Mode**.

When the computer is started with any of the safe mode options except **Last Known Good Configuration**, a boot log of devices and services that are loading is created. The log is saved to the file Ntbtlog.txt in the folder in which Windows 2000 is installed (typically \Winnt).

If the problem was caused by a newly-installed driver, you might be able to start the computer using the **Last Known Good Configuration** option so you can research the problem with the driver. If there were other causes, after starting the computer in safe mode, you can use Event Viewer, System Information, Control Panel, Backup, and other tools to try to diagnose and correct the problem.

Recovery Console

The Recovery Console is a command-line console designed to help you recover when your Windows 2000-based computer does not start. You can use the Recovery Console after starting the computer with the Windows 2000 Setup CD or the Setup floppy disks. You can use the Recovery Console to obtain limited access to NTFS, FAT, and FAT32 volumes without starting the graphical interface.

To use the Recover Console, you must be logged on as an administrator.

Caution The Recovery Console is powerful. It is recommended that you use Recovery Console only if you are an advanced user or administrator who can use basic commands to identify and locate problem drivers and files.

Each time you use Backup to back up the system state data, a copy of the registry is placed on the local system partition in a subfolder of %SystemRoot%\Repair\RegBack. You can use the Recovery Console to copy files from %SystemRoot%\Repair\RegBack to %SystemRoot%\System32\Config (the location of the registry). After you do this, the registry contains the information it had when the system state was last backed up. Changes made after that time are lost.

Caution Do not use a registry editor to edit the registry directly unless you have no alternative. The registry editors bypass the standard safeguards provided by administrative tools. These safeguards prevent you from entering conflicting settings or settings that are likely to degrade performance or damage your system. Editing the registry directly can have serious, unexpected consequences that can prevent the system from starting and require that you reinstall Windows 2000. To configure or customize Windows 2000, use the programs in Control Panel or Microsoft Management Console (MMC) whenever possible.

For more information about the Recovery Console, including a list and description of available commands, see "Repair, Recovery, and Restore" in this book.

Emergency Repair Disk

If your system does not start, and neither safe mode nor the Recovery Console has helped, you can try using the Emergency Repair Disk option in Backup. If you have prepared an ERD beforehand, you can use it to repair system files (after you start the system using the Windows 2000 Setup CD or Setup floppy disks).

The ERD can make only basic system repairs, such as to the system files, the boot sector, and the startup environment. The ERD does not back up data or programs, and it is not a replacement for regular system backups.

For more information about the ERD, see "Repair, Recovery, and Restore" in this book.

If you cannot fix the problem by using one of the options described above, try removing the disk from the computer and installing it as a second disk on another computer that is running Windows 2000. You can then use Windows 2000-based utilities for troubleshooting. For more information about using disk troubleshooting utilities, see the Windows 2000 Resource Kit Tools Help.

Caution Moving disks between computers is not recommended because problems can arise if the disk controllers on the two systems are incompatible or are configured differently. However, if the two computers have the same configuration, you might be able to identify and correct the problem.

Additional Resources

- For more information about troubleshooting startup problems, see the Microsoft Knowledge Base link on the Web Resources page at http://windows.microsoft.com/windows2000/reskit/webresources.

C H A P T E R   1 6

Windows 2000 Stop Messages

When Microsoft® Windows® 2000 detects an error condition from which it cannot recover, it generates a variety of system messages including Stop messages and hardware malfunction messages, commonly referred to as blue screen messages. Interpreting the meaning of various Stop messages and taking appropriate action to resolve the problems that generated the errors are critical skills in a production environment. In addition, it is vital that technical support personnel and power users know how to handle system hardware failure correctly. This chapter contains general information and troubleshooting tips about these types of errors as well as specific information about the twelve most common Stop messages seen by callers to Microsoft Product Support.

In This Chapter

System Messages

The two types of system messages generated by Windows 2000 depend on the event being reported. Both are generated in character mode.

Stop messages occur when the Windows 2000 kernel detects a condition from which it cannot recover.

Hardware malfunction message occur when the processor detects a hardware condition from which the system cannot recover.

These messages were created to cover everything that might happen to halt the system, so you are unlikely to see most of them. For example, the Stop message 0x0000003E, or "Multiprocessor Configuration Not Supported" is displayed only if multiple but asymmetric central processing unit (CPU) types, such as a Pentium and a Pentium III, are installed on the same system.

To diagnose and resolve Stop messages, many users also need technical assistance from a person who has been trained to support Windows 2000. In some circumstances, running a kernel debugger on the faulty system might be required.

Stop Messages

Stop messages are always displayed on a full screen in character mode, as shown in Figure 16.1, rather than in a window. Each message is uniquely identified by a hexadecimal number and a string indicating the error's symbolic name. In addition, Stop messages are usually followed by a series of up to four additional hexadecimal numbers, shown in parentheses, which identify error parameters, as shown in the following example:

```
*** STOP: 0x0000001E (0xC0000005, 0xFDE38AF9, 0x00000001, 0x7E8B0EB4)
KMODE_EXCEPTION_NOT_HANDLED ***
```

To a trained support technician, the content of the symbolic name string might suggest which part of the system is affected by the error that left the kernel no recourse but to stop. However, it is also possible that the cause might be in another part of the system. Figure 16.1 is an example of a complete Stop message screen generated by Windows 2000.

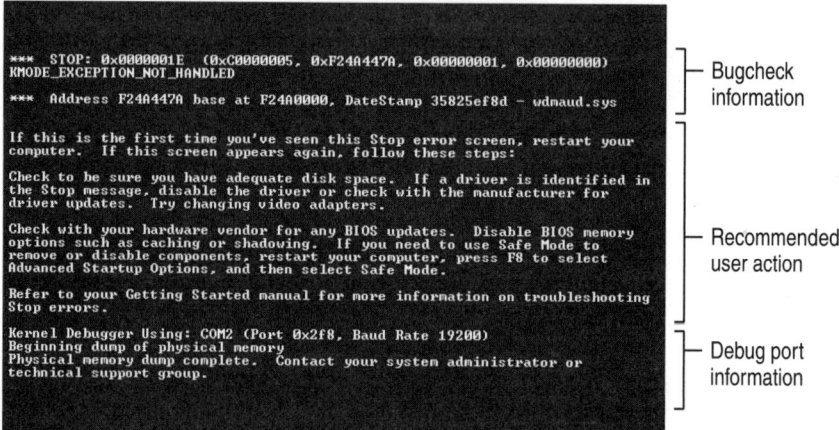

Figure 16.1   Stop Message Screen

Stop Message Screen Sections

As shown in Figure 16.1, a Windows 2000 Stop message screen contains three major sections: bugcheck information, recommended user action, and debug port information. Whenever a Stop message is displayed, first examine the bugcheck information section for assistance with troubleshooting. Second, examine the recommended user action section for troubleshooting information; Windows 2000 now incorporates troubleshooting tips, including some custom tips relevant to the particular error detected. Finally, check the debug port information section to see whether or not a memory dump file was saved for later use by a debugger.

Bugcheck Information

The bugcheck information section includes the Stop error code, also known as the bugcheck code, which contains up to four developer-defined parameters, enclosed in parentheses, and the symbolic name of the error. In Figure 16.1, the Stop error code is 0x0000001E and its symbolic name is KMODE_EXCEPTION_NOT_HANDLED.

The bugcheck information section frequently, but not always, includes a line that lists the specific hexadecimal memory address of the problem's source, along with the name of the particular driver or device in question. The type of problem detected determines whether or not this information is displayed.

Under some conditions, the kernel displays only the first line of the Stop message. This can occur if vital services needed for the display have been affected by the error.

Recommended User Action

The recommended user action section provides a list of suggestions for recovering from the error. In some cases, a simple restart might be all that is necessary because the problem is not likely to recur. In other cases, even after restarting, the Stop message returns and you are faced with getting back to an operable state. Often, this means either backing out of a recent change or, in the case of Windows 2000 setup, pinpointing and eliminating the source of the problem.

Tip A generic list of troubleshooting tips is displayed when no specific text for a Stop message exists. For some Stop messages, tips specific to the problem are listed.

Debug Port Information

The debug port information section provides confirmation of the communications parameters (COM port and bits per second data transmission rate) used by the kernel debugger on the computer, if the kernel debugger is enabled. It also indicates whether a memory dump file was saved (the dump file indicator will be displayed only if that feature is enabled).

Types of Stop Messages

Stop messages generally fall into one of four categories:

- Messages that appear during general use of Windows 2000.
- Messages that appear during the installation of Windows 2000.
- Messages that appear only during the relatively short Phase 4 period of the Windows 2000 Executive initialization sequence.
- Messages that can be traced to a software condition, called a *software trap*, detected by the processor.

General Stop Messages

The most common Stop messages are generated during regular operations. Even in a complex and robust operating system such as Windows 2000, catastrophic problems sometimes cause the system to stop responding and display a Stop message. In Windows 2000, a driver or the file system can generate a Stop message by introducing an unhandled error (exception) in the code or by performing some illegal operation.

For information about troubleshooting Stop messages, including detailed information about the most common errors, see "Troubleshooting Stop Messages" later in this chapter.

For the most comprehensive list of Stop messages in Windows 2000, along with useful information about diagnosing and troubleshooting these messages, refer to the Microsoft Knowledge Base article Q103059, titled "Descriptions of Bug Codes for Windows NT."

Stop Messages During Installation

An unsuccessful attempt to install Windows 2000 can result in a Stop message. When this happens, first check that the computer and all of its peripheral hardware are compatible with Windows 2000. To do this, refer to the latest Windows 2000 Hardware Compatibility List (HCL). Microsoft compiles the HCL through rigorous component and compatibility testing of computers and peripheral hardware to determine if they work well with Windows 2000. For more information about the HCL, see "Additional Resources" at the end of this chapter.

If the hardware you use is not included on the Windows 2000 HCL, contact the hardware manufacturer as a first-line resource for available information, newly tested hardware, and Basic Input/Output System (BIOS) and firmware revisions. Reducing the number of hardware components by removing nonessential peripherals and devices can help you pinpoint installation conflicts as well.

Stop Messages That Occur Only at Executive Initialization

Some Stop messages occur only during the relatively short Phase 4 period of the Windows 2000 startup sequence. Initialization of the *Windows 2000 Executive*, a family of software components that provides basic operating system services, is one step during Phase 4. Executive initialization can be further broken down into two phases: Phase 0 and Phase 1. During Phase 0, interrupts are disabled and only a few Executive components, such as the hardware abstraction layer (HAL), are initialized. During Phase 1 of Executive initialization, the system is fully operational, and the Windows 2000 subcomponents go through a full initialization.

Phase 0 Initialization Stop Messages

If you receive one of the Phase 0 initialization Stop messages listed in Table 16.1, run the hardware diagnostics provided by your system manufacturer.

Note In many situations, hardware failures manifest themselves as errors that generate Stop messages. This is why troubleshooting many of the Stop messages includes running hardware diagnostics on the system.

If no hardware problems are found, reinstall Windows 2000 and try to initialize it again. If you get the same message, contact a support technician.

Table 16.1   Phase 0 Initialization Stop Messages

Message ID	Symbolic Name
0x31	PHASE0_INITIALIZATION_FAILED
0x5C	HAL_INITIALIZATION_FAILED
0x5D	HEAP_INITIALIZATION_FAILED
0x5E	OBJECT_INITIALIZATION_FAILED
0x5F	SECURITY_INITIALIZATION_FAILED
0x60	PROCESS_INITIALIZATION_FAILED

Phase 1 Initialization Stop Messages

If you receive one of the Phase 1 initialization Stop messages listed in Table 16.2, reinstall Windows 2000 and try to initialize it again. If you get the same message, contact a support technician.

Table16.2   Phase 1 Initialization Stop Messages

Message ID	Symbolic Name
0x32	PHASE1_INITIALIZATION_FAILED
0x61	HAL1_INITIALIZATION_FAILED
0x62	OBJECT1_INITIALIZATION_FAILED
0x63	SECURITY1_INITIALIZATION_FAILED
0x64	SYMBOLIC_INITIALIZATION_FAILED
0x65	MEMORY1_INITIALIZATION_FAILED
0x66	CACHE_INITIALIZATION_FAILED
0x67	CONFIG_INITIALIZATION_FAILED
0x68	FILE_INITIALIZATION_FAILED
0x69	IO1_INITIALIZATION_FAILED
0x6A	LPC_INITIALIZATION_FAILED
0x6B	PROCESS1_INITIALIZATION_FAILED
0x6C	REFMON_INITIALIZATION_FAILED
0x6D	SESSION1_INITIALIZATION_FAILED
0x6E	SESSION2_INITIALIZATION_FAILED
0x6F	SESSION3_INITIALIZATION_FAILED
0x70	SESSION4_INITIALIZATION_FAILED
0x71	SESSION5_INITIALIZATION_FAILED

Stop Messages Caused by Software Traps

Erroneous software conditions detected by the processor, called software traps, can also generate Stop messages. A software trap occurs when a processor detects a problem with executing an instruction, which causes it to stop. For example, a processor does not carry out an instruction whose variables contains invalid data types.

When you receive one of these messages, first write down the information displayed in the bugcheck information section of the Stop message, and then restart the computer. If the message recurs, you have four options for diagnosing the Stop error, all of which should be handled by a trained support technician at your own site:

- Diagnose the problem by using the information and troubleshooting tips displayed in the Stop message. For more information see "Troubleshooting Stop Messages" later in this chapter and in the Windows 2000 Error and Event Messages Help, where message explanations and recommended user actions for the most common Stop messages are listed. This file is located on the *Microsoft® Windows® 2000 Resource Kit* companion CD.

- Contact your own or another technical support group to discuss the information in the Stop message. They might recognize a familiar pattern in the information and be able to offer assistance.

Important If you use either of the following options, be sure Windows 2000 is in debug mode before you restart your computer.

- Set up the Windows 2000 kernel debugger to gather more information about the problem.

- Contact your own or another technical support group for assistance in the remote use of the Windows 2000 kernel debugger.

Troubleshooting Stop Messages

Many problems can be resolved through troubleshooting procedures, such as verifying instructions, reinstalling key components, and verifying file dates. Also, diagnostic tools such as Winmsd, Network Monitor, and Network General Sniffer, and those found on the *Windows 2000 Resource Kit* companion CD might isolate and resolve these issues.

Generic Troubleshooting Procedures

For general troubleshooting of Windows 2000 Stop messages, follow these suggestions:

- If new hardware has been added to the system recently, remove it or replace it to see if that resolves the error. Also, try running hardware diagnostics supplied by the system manufacturer. Check with the manufacturer to see if an updated system BIOS or firmware is available. Make sure that any expansion boards are properly seated and all cables are completely connected.

- Confirm that any new hardware is listed on the Windows 2000 Hardware Compatibility List (HCL). For more information about the HCL, see "Additional Resources" at the end of this chapter.

- If new device drivers or system services have been added recently, remove them or update them to see if the problem is resolved. You need to use Safe Mode to remove or disable components, since Safe Mode loads only the minimum required drivers and system services during the startup of Windows. To enter Safe Mode, restart your computer, and press F8 at the character-mode screen that displays the prompt "For troubleshooting and advanced startup options for Windows 2000, press F8." At the resulting Windows 2000 Advanced Options menu, choose Safe Mode. For more information about Safe Mode, see chapter "Startup Process" in this book.

- Check the computer with an up-to-date virus scanner program that is compatible with Windows 2000. Viruses can infect all types of Windows-formatted hard disks, and resulting disk corruption can generate system stop messages. Make sure the virus scanner checks the master boot record for infections.

- Verify that any recently added software is listed as compatible with Windows 2000. If it is not, check with the manufacturer to see if an update or a patch is available. Otherwise, remove the program to see if this resolves the error.

- Verify that the system has the latest Service Pack installed. To check which Service Pack, if any, is installed on your system, click **Start**, click **Run**, type **winver,** and then press ENTER. The **About Windows 2000** dialog box displays the Windows version number and the version number of the Service Pack, if one has been installed. For information about downloading the latest Service Packs, see "Additional Resources" at the end of this chapter.

- Disable BIOS memory options such as caching or shadowing.

- Check the System Log and Application Log in Event Viewer to see if any additional error messages have been logged recently. These might pinpoint the cause of the error.

- Check the Microsoft Knowledge Base link using the keywords **winnt** and the full Stop error code, such as the example in Figure 16.1, **0x0000001E**. For information about the Microsoft Knowledge Base link , see "Additional Resources" at the end of this chapter.

Kernel debugging is especially helpful when other troubleshooting techniques have failed, or when a problem repeats often. In these cases, it is possible to pinpoint the failing code in a driver or an application by using a kernel debugger. For kernel debugging, it is important to capture the exact text in the bugcheck information section of the error message. Also, in order to isolate a complex problem and develop a viable workaround or a program replacement, it is essential to record the exact steps leading to the failure.

Troubleshooting Common Stop Messages

For the most commonly encountered Stop messages, troubleshooting tips and recommendations have been gathered together to help you resolve the problem on your own. If the error persists after you have tried all of the recommendations listed both here and within the Stop message display, contact your technical support group for further assistance.

Stop 0x0000000A or IRQL_NOT_LESS_OR_EQUAL

This Stop message, also known as Stop 0xA, indicates that a kernel-mode process attempted to access a portion of memory at an Interrupt Request Level (IRQL) that was too high. A kernel-mode process can only access other processes that have an IRQL lesser than or equal to its own.

Interpreting the Message

The four parameters listed in the Stop 0xA message are defined in order of appearance as follows:

1. Memory address referenced
2. IRQL
3. Type of access (0 = read operation, 1 = write operation)
4. Address that referenced memory in parameter 1

If the third parameter is the same as the first parameter, a special condition exists in which a system worker routine, executed by a worker thread to handle background tasks known as work items, returned at a raised IRQL. In that case, the parameters are defined as follows:

1. Address of the worker routine
2. IRQL
3. Address of the worker routine
4. Address of the work item

Resolving the Problem

Buggy device driver, system service or BIOS. The error that generates Stop 0xA usually occurs after the installation of a buggy device driver, system service, or BIOS. To resolve it quickly, restart your computer, and press F8 at the character-mode screen that displays the prompt "For troubleshooting and advanced startup options for Windows 2000, press F8." At the resulting Windows 2000 Advanced Options menu, choose the **Last Known Good Configuration** option. This option is most effective when only one driver or service is added at a time.

Incompatible device driver, system service, virus scanner or backup tool. If you encounter Stop 0xA while upgrading to a newer version of Windows, it might be caused by a device driver, a system service, a virus scanner, or a backup tool that is incompatible with the new version. If possible, remove all third-party device drivers and system services and disable any virus scanners prior to upgrading. Contact the software manufacturers to obtain updates of these tools.

For additional error messages that might help pinpoint the device or driver that is causing the error, check the System Log in Event Viewer. Disabling memory caching of the BIOS might also resolve this error. You should also run hardware diagnostics supplied by the system manufacturer, especially the memory scanner. For details on these procedures, see the owner's manual for your computer.

If your system has small computer system interface (SCSI) adapters, contact the adapter manufacturer to obtain updated Windows 2000 drivers. Try disabling sync negotiation in the SCSI BIOS, checking the cabling and the SCSI IDs of each device, and confirming proper termination. For enhanced integrated device electronics (EIDE) devices, define the onboard EIDE port as Primary only. Also, check each EIDE device for the proper master/slave or stand-alone setting. Try removing all EIDE devices except for hard disks.

If the message appears during an installation of Windows 2000, make sure that the computer and all installed peripherals are listed on the Microsoft Windows 2000 Hardware Compatibility List (HCL). For more information about the HCL, see "Additional Resources" at the end of this chapter.

Microsoft periodically releases a package of product improvements and problem resolutions called a Service Pack. Because many problems are resolved by installing the latest Service Pack, it is recommended that all users install them as they become available. To check which Service Pack, if any, is installed on your system, click **Start**, click **Run**, type **winver,** and then press ENTER. The **About Windows 2000** dialog box displays the Windows version number and the version number of the Service Pack, if one has been installed. For information about installing the latest Service Pack, see "Additional Resources" at the end of this chapter.

Occasionally, remedies to specific problems are developed after the release of a Service Pack. These remedies are called hotfixes. Microsoft does not recommend that you install a post-Service Pack hotfix unless the specific problem it addresses has been encountered. Service Packs include all of the hotfixes released since the release of the previous Service Pack. The status of hotfix installations is not indicated in the **About Windows 2000** dialog box. For information about downloading hotfixes and Service Packs, see "Additional Resources" at the end of this chapter.

For more troubleshooting information about the 0xA Stop message, refer to the Microsoft Knowledge Base link , using the keywords **winnt** and **0x0000000A**. For information about this resource, see "Additional Resources" at the end of this chapter.

Stop 0x0000001E or KMODE_EXCEPTION_NOT_HANDLED

This Stop message, also known as Stop 0x1E, indicates that a kernel-mode process tried to execute an illegal or unknown processor instruction. This error handler is a default error handler that catches errors not associated with other specific error handlers.

Interpreting the Message

The four parameters listed in the message are defined in order of appearance as follows:

1. Exception code that was not handled
2. Address at which the exception occurred
3. Parameter 0 of the exception
4. Parameter 1 of the exception

The first parameter is a Windows 2000 error code, which is defined by the type of error encountered in the file Ntstatus.h of the Windows 2000 Device Driver Kit (DDK). For information about the DDK, see "Additional Resources" at the end of this chapter. The second parameter identifies the address of the module in which the error occurred. Frequently, the address points to an individual driver or piece of faulty hardware, which is generally listed on the third line of the Stop message. Always make a note of this address, as well as the link date of the driver or image that contains it. The last two parameters vary, depending upon the exception that has occurred. You can typically find a description of the parameters that are included with the name of error code in Ntstatus.h. If the error code has no parameters, the last two parameters are listed as 0x00000000.

Resolving the Problem

Hardware incompatibility. First, make sure that any new hardware installed is listed on the Windows 2000 Hardware Compatibility List (HCL). For more information about the HCL, see "Additional Resources" at the end of this chapter.

Buggy device driver or system service. In addition, a buggy device driver or system service might be responsible for this error. Hardware issues, such as memory conflicts and IRQ conflicts, can also generate this error.

If a driver is listed by name within the Stop message, disable or remove that driver. Disable or remove any drivers or services that were recently added. If the error occurs during the startup sequence, restart the computer using Safe Mode to rename or delete the file. If the driver is used as part of the system startup process in Safe Mode, you need to start the computer by using the Recovery Console to access the file. For more information about Safe Mode, see chapter "Startup Process" in this book. For more information about the Recovery Console, see chapter "Repair, Recovery, and Restore" in this book.

If the problem is associated with Win32k.sys, the source of the error might be a third-party remote control program. If such software is installed, the service can be removed by starting the system using the Recovery Console and disabling the offending system service.

Check the System Log in Event Viewer for additional error messages that might help pinpoint the device or driver that is causing Stop 0x1E. Disabling memory caching of the BIOS might also resolve the error. You should also run hardware diagnostics, especially the memory scanner, supplied by the system manufacturer. For details on these procedures, see the owner's manual for your computer.

One type of this kind of error displays exception code 0x80000003. This error indicates a hard-coded breakpoint or assertion was hit, but the system was started with the /NODEBUG switch. This problem should rarely occur. If it occurs repeatedly, make sure a kernel debugger is connected and the system is started with the /DEBUG switch.

The error that generates this message can occur after the first restart during Windows 2000 Setup, or after setup is finished. A possible cause of the error is lack of disk space for installation and system BIOS incompatibilities. For problems during Windows 2000 installation that are associated with a lack of disk space, reduce the number of files on the target hard disk. Check for and delete any unneeded temporary files, Internet cache files, application backup files, and CHK files containing saved file fragments from disk scans. You can also use another hard disk with more free space for the installation. BIOS problems can be resolved by upgrading the system BIOS version.

For more troubleshooting information about the 0x1E Stop message, refer to the Microsoft Knowledge Base link , using the keywords **winnt** and **0x0000001E**. For information about this resource, see "Additional Resources" at the end of this chapter.

Stop 0x00000024 or NTFS_FILE_SYSTEM

This Stop message, also known as Stop 0x24, indicates that a problem occurred within Ntfs.sys (the driver file that allows the system to read and write to NTFS drives).

Interpreting the Message

The four parameters listed in the message are defined in order of appearance as follows:

1. Source file and line number
2. A non-zero value contains the address of the exception record
3. A non-zero value contains the address of the context record
4. A non-zero value contains the address where the original exception occurred

All Stop messages due to problems with the file system have encoded in their first parameter the source file and the line number within the source file that generated the Stop. The high 16 bits (the first four hex digits after the 0x) identify the source file number, while the lower 16 bits (the last four hex digits of the parameter) identify the source line in the file where the stop occurred.

Resolving the Problem

Disk Corruption. Corruption in the NTFS file system or bad blocks (sectors) on the hard disk can induce this error. Corrupted SCSI and EIDE drivers can also adversely affect the system's ability to read and write to disk, thus causing the error.

Check Event Viewer for error messages from SCSI and FASTFAT (System Log) or Autochk (Application Log) that might help pinpoint the device or driver that is causing the error. Try disabling any virus scanners, backup programs, or disk defragmenter tools that continually monitor the system. You should also run hardware diagnostics supplied by the system manufacturer. For details on these procedures, see the owner's manual for your computer. Run **Chkdsk /f /r** to detect and resolve any file system structural corruption. You must restart the system before the disk scan begins on a system partition. If you cannot start the system due to the error, use the Recovery Console and run **Chkdsk /r**. For more information about the Recovery Console, see chapter "Repair, Recovery, and Restore" in this book.

Warning If your system partition is formatted with the file allocation table (FAT16) file system, the long file names used by Windows 2000 can be damaged if Scandisk or another MS-DOS-based hard disk tool is used to verify the integrity of your hard disk from an MS-DOS prompt. (An MS-DOS prompt is typically derived from an MS-DOS startup disk or from starting MS-DOS on a multiboot system.) Always use the Windows 2000 version of Chkdsk on Windows 2000 disks.

Depletion of nonpaged pool memory. If you create a Services for Macintosh volume on a large partition (7 gigabytes or larger) with a large number of files (at least 100,000) while the AppleTalk driver Apf.sys is loaded, the indexing routine consumes a large amount of nonpaged pool memory. If the nonpaged pool memory is completely depleted, this error can stop the system. However, during the indexing process, if the amount of available nonpaged pool memory is very low, another kernel-mode driver requiring nonpaged pool memory can also trigger this error. To resolve this error, either increase the amount of installed random access memory (RAM), which increases the quantity of nonpaged pool memory available to the kernel, or reduce the number of files on the Services for Macintosh volume.

Microsoft periodically releases a package of product improvements and problem resolutions called a Service Pack. Because many problems are resolved by installing the latest Service Pack, it is recommended that all users install them as they become available. To check which Service Pack, if any, is installed on your system, click **Start**, click **Run**, type **winver,** and then press ENTER. The **About Windows 2000** dialog box displays the Windows version number and the version number of the Service Pack, if one has been installed.

Occasionally, remedies to specific problems are developed after the release of a Service Pack. These remedies are called hotfixes. Microsoft does not recommend that you install a post-Service Pack hotfix unless the specific problem it addresses has been encountered. Service Packs include all of the hotfixes released since the release of the previous Service Pack. The status of hotfix installations is not indicated in the **About Windows 2000** dialog box. For more information about Service Packs and hotfixes, see "Additional Resources" at the end of this chapter.

For more troubleshooting information about the 0x24 Stop message, refer to the Microsoft Knowledge Base link , using the keywords **winnt** and **0x00000024**. For information about this resource, see "Additional Resources" at the end of this chapter.

Stop 0x0000002E or DATA_BUS_ERROR

This message, also known as Stop 0x2E, typically indicates that a parity error in system memory has been detected. This error is almost always caused by a hardware problem—either a configuration issue, defective hardware or incompatible hardware. The exception is when a device driver has accessed an address in the 0x8xxxxxxx range that does not exist (that is, does not have a physical address mapping).

Interpreting the Message

The four parameters listed in the message are defined in order of appearance as follows:

1. Virtual address that caused the fault
2. Physical address that caused the fault
3. Processor status register (PSR)
4. Faulting instruction register (FIR)

Resolving the Problem

Hardware problem. The most common cause of this error is a hardware problem, usually related to defective RAM, Level 2 (L2) RAM cache, or video RAM.

Stop 0x2E usually occurs after the installation of faulty hardware or when existing hardware fails. If hardware has recently been added to the system, remove it to see if the error recurs. If existing hardware has failed, remove or replace the faulty component. You should run hardware diagnostics supplied by the system manufacturer to determine which hardware component has failed. For details on these procedures, see the owner's manual for your computer. Check that all the adapter cards in the computer, including memory modules, are properly seated. Use an ink eraser or an electrical contact treatment, available at electronics supply stores, to ensure adapter card contacts are clean. Be sure to wipe the cleaned contacts off, removing all cleaning debris, before reinstalling the adapter card into the computer. If compressed air is available, use it to clear out the adapter card slot.

If the problem occurs on a newly installed system, check the availability of updates for BIOS revisions on the motherboard, SCSI controllers, or network cards. Updates of this kind are typically available on the Web site or BBS of the hardware manufacturer.

If the error occurs after installing a new or updated device driver, the driver should be removed or replaced. If, under this circumstance, the error occurs during startup, restart the computer using Safe Mode to rename or delete the file. If the driver is used as part of the system startup process in Safe Mode, you need to start the computer using the Recovery Console in order to access the file. For more information about Safe Mode, see chapter "Startup Process" in this book. For more information about the Recovery Console, see chapter "Repair, Recovery, and Restore" in this book.

For additional error messages that might help pinpoint the device or driver that is causing the error, check the System Log in Event Viewer. Disabling memory caching of the BIOS might also resolve this error. In addition, check the system for viruses, using any up-to-date, commercial virus scanning software that examines the Master Boot Record of the hard disk. All Windows 2000 file systems can be infected by viruses.

Disk corruption. This error can also be a result of hard disk corruption. Run **Chkdsk /f /r** on the system partition. You must restart the system before the disk scan begins. If you cannot start the system due to the error, use the Recovery Console and run **Chkdsk /r**. For more information about the Recovery Console, see chapter "Repair, Recovery, and Restore" in this book.

Warning If your system partition is formatted with the FAT16 file system, the long file names used by Windows 2000 can be damaged if Scandisk or another MS-DOS-based hard disk tool is used to verify the integrity of your hard disk from an MS-DOS prompt. (An MS-DOS prompt is typically derived from an MS-DOS startup disk or from starting MS-DOS on a multiboot system.) Always use the Windows 2000 version of Chkdsk on Windows 2000 disks.

Microsoft periodically releases a package of product improvements and problem resolutions for Windows 2000 called a Service Pack. Because many problems are resolved by installing the latest Service Pack, it is recommended that all users install them as they become available. To check which Service Pack, if any, is installed on your system, click **Start**, click **Run**, type **winver,** and then press ENTER. The **About Windows 2000** dialog box displays the Windows version number and the version number of the Service Pack, if one has been installed.

Occasionally, remedies to specific problems are developed after the release of a Service Pack. These remedies are called hotfixes. Microsoft does not recommend that you install a post-Service Pack hotfix unless the specific problem it addresses has been encountered. Service Packs include all of the hotfixes released since the release of the previous Service Pack. The status of hotfix installations is not indicated in the **About Windows 2000** dialog box. For more information about Service Packs and hotfixes, see "Additional Resources" at the end of this chapter.

Finally, if all the above suggestions fail to resolve the error, take the system motherboard to a repair facility for diagnostic testing. A crack, a scratched trace, or a defective component on the motherboard can also cause this error.

For more troubleshooting information about the 0x2E Stop message, refer to the Microsoft Knowledge Base link , using the keywords **winnt** and **0x0000002E**. For information about this resource, see "Additional Resources" at the end of this chapter.

Stop 0x00000050 or PAGE_FAULT_IN_NONPAGED_AREA

This Stop message, also known as Stop 0x50, occurs when requested data is not found in memory. The system generates a fault, which normally indicates that the system looks for data in the paging file. In this circumstance, however, the missing data is identified as being located within an area of memory that cannot be read to disk. The system faults, but cannot find, the data and is unable to recover. Faulty hardware, a buggy system service, antivirus software, and a corrupted NTFS volume can all generate this type of error.

Interpreting the Message

The four parameters listed in the message are defined in order of appearance as follows:

1. Virtual address which caused the fault

2. Type of access (0 = read operation, 1 = write operation)

3. If not zero, the instruction address which referenced the address in parameter 1

4. Opaque information about the stop, interpreted by the kernel

Resolving the Problem

Faulty hardware. Stop 0x50 usually occurs after the installation of faulty hardware or in the event of failure of installed hardware (usually related to defective RAM, be it main memory, L2 RAM cache, or video RAM). If hardware has been added to the system recently, remove it to see if the error recurs. If existing hardware has failed, remove or replace the faulty component. You should run hardware diagnostics supplied by the system manufacturer. For details on these procedures, see the owner's manual for your computer.

Buggy system service. Often, the installation of a buggy system service is a culprit. Disable the service and confirm that this resolves the error. If so, contact the manufacturer of the system service about a possible update. If the error occurs during system startup, restart your computer, and press F8 at the character-mode screen that displays the prompt "For troubleshooting and advanced startup options for Windows 2000, press F8." At the resulting Windows 2000 Advanced Options menu, choose the **Last Known Good Configuration** option. This option is most effective when only one driver or service is added at a time.

Antivirus software. Antivirus software can also trigger this error. Disable the program and confirm that this resolves the error. If it does, contact the manufacturer of the program about a possible update.

Corrupted NTFS volume. A corrupted NTFS volume can also generate this error. Run **Chkdsk /f /r** to detect and repair disk errors. You must restart the system before the disk scan begins on a system partition. If you cannot start the system due to the error, use the Recovery Console and run **Chkdsk /r**. For more information about the Recovery Console, see chapter "Repair, Recovery, and Restore" in this book. If the hard disk is SCSI, check for problems between the SCSI controller and the disk.

Warning If your system partition is formatted with the FAT16 file system, the long file names used by Windows 2000 can be damaged if Scandisk or another MS-DOS-based hard disk tool is used to verify the integrity of your hard disk from an MS-DOS prompt. (An MS-DOS prompt is typically derived from an MS-DOS startup disk or from starting MS-DOS on a multiboot system.) Always use the Windows 2000 version of Chkdsk on Windows 2000 disks.

Finally, check the System Log in Event Viewer for additional error messages that might help pinpoint the device or driver that is causing the error. Disabling memory caching of the BIOS might also resolve this error.

Microsoft periodically releases a package of product improvements and problem resolutions for Windows 2000 called a Service Pack. Because many problems are resolved by installing the latest Service Pack, it is recommended that all users install them as they become available. To check which Service Pack, if any, is installed on your system, click **Start**, click **Run**, type **winver,** and then press ENTER. The **About Windows 2000** dialog box displays the Windows version number and the version number of the Service Pack, if one has been installed.

Occasionally, remedies to specific problems are developed after the release of a Service Pack. These remedies are called hotfixes. Microsoft does not recommend that you install a post-Service Pack hotfix unless the specific problem it addresses has been encountered. Service Packs include all of the hotfixes released since the release of the previous Service Pack. The status of hotfix installations is not indicated in the **About Windows 2000** dialog box. For more information about Service Packs and hotfixes, see "Additional Resources" at the end of this chapter.

For more troubleshooting information about the 0x50 Stop message, refer to the Microsoft Knowledge Base link , using the keywords **winnt** and **0x00000050**. For information about this resource, see "Additional Resources" at the end of this chapter.

Stop 0x00000077 or KERNEL_STACK_INPAGE_ERROR

This Stop message, also known as Stop 0x77, indicates that the requested page of kernel data from the paging file could not be read into memory.

Interpreting the Message

The four parameters listed in the message are defined in order of appearance as follows:

1. 0 (zero)
2. Value found in stack where signature should be
3. 0 (zero)
4. Address of signature on kernel stack

The first set of definitions apply only if the first and third parameters are both zero. Otherwise, the following definitions are applicable:

1. Status code
2. I/O status code
3. Page file number
4. Offset into page file

Frequently, the cause of this error can be determined from the second parameter, the I/O status code. Examples include:

- 0xC000009A, or STATUS_INSUFFICIENT_RESOURCES, is caused by lack of nonpaged pool resources.
- 0xC000009C, or STATUS_DEVICE_DATA_ERROR, is generally due to bad blocks (sectors) on the hard disk.
- 0xC000009D, or STATUS_DEVICE_NOT_CONNECTED, indicates defective or loose cabling, termination, or the controller not seeing the hard disk.
- 0xC000016A, or STATUS_DISK_OPERATION_FAILED, is also caused by bad blocks (sectors) on the hard disk.
- 0xC0000185, or STATUS_IO_DEVICE_ERROR, is caused by improper termination or defective cabling on SCSI devices, or two devices attempting to use the same IRQ.

These codes are the most common ones for which specific causes have been determined. For information about other possible status codes that can be returned, see the file Ntstatus.h of the Windows 2000 Device Driver Kit (DDK). For information about the DDK, see "Additional Resources" at the end of this chapter.

Resolving the Problem

Bad block. Stop 0x77 is caused by a bad block (sector) in a paging file or a disk controller error. In extremely rare cases, it is caused when nonpaged pool resources run out.

If the first and third parameters are zero, the stack signature in the kernel stack was not found. This error is caused by defective hardware. If the I/O status is C0000185 and the paging file is on a SCSI disk, the disk cabling and SCSI termination should be checked for problems.

Viruses. In addition, check your computer for viruses using any up-to-date, commercial virus scanning software that examines the Master Boot Record of the hard disk. All Windows 2000 file systems can be infected by viruses.

An I/O status code of 0xC000009C or 0xC000016A normally indicates that the data could not be read from the disk due to a bad block (sector). If you can restart the system after the error, Autochk runs automatically and attempts to map the bad sector to prevent its further use. If Autochk does not scan the hard disk for errors, you can manually start the disk scanner. Run **Chkdsk /f /r** on the system partition. You must restart the system before the disk scan begins. If you cannot start the system due to the error, use the Recovery Console and run **Chkdsk /r**. For more information about the Recovery Console, see chapter "Repair, Recovery, and Restore" in this book.

Warning If your system partition is formatted with the FAT16 file system, the long file names used by Windows 2000 can be damaged if Scandisk or another MS-DOS-based hard disk tool is used to verify the integrity of your hard disk from an MS-DOS prompt. (An MS-DOS prompt is typically derived from a MS-DOS startup disk or from starting MS-DOS on a multiboot system.) Always use the Windows 2000 version of Chkdsk on Windows 2000 disks.

Failing RAM. Another common cause of this error message is failing RAM. You should run hardware diagnostics supplied by the system manufacturer, especially the memory scanner. For details on these procedures, see the owner's manual for your computer.

Also, check that all the adapter cards in the computer, including memory modules, are properly seated. Use an ink eraser or an electrical contact treatment, available at electronics supply stores, to ensure adapter card contacts are clean. Be sure to wipe the cleaned contacts off, removing all cleaning debris, before reinstalling the adapter card into the computer. If compressed air is available, use it to clear out the adapter card slot.

In addition, check the System Log in Event Viewer for additional error messages that might help pinpoint the device that is causing the error. Disabling memory caching of the BIOS might also resolve this error.

Finally, if all the above steps fail to resolve the error, take the system motherboard to a repair facility for diagnostic testing. A crack, a scratched trace, or a defective component on the motherboard can also cause this error.

For more troubleshooting information about the 0x77 Stop message, refer to the Microsoft Knowledge Base link , using the keywords **winnt** and **0x00000077**. For information about this resource, see "Additional Resources" at the end of this chapter.

Stop 0x00000079 or MISMATCHED_HAL

This message, also known as Stop 0x79, is displayed when the hardware abstraction layer (HAL) and the kernel or the computer type do not match. This error most often occurs when single-processor and multiprocessor configuration files are mixed on the same system.

Interpreting the Message

The types of mismatch parameters are defined in order of appearance in the sets as follows. The first parameter determines which set is applicable.

1. If this parameter is 1, the processor control block (PRCB) release levels mismatch (something is out of date).
2. Major PRCB level of Ntoskrnl.exe.
3. Major PRCB level of Hal.dll.
4. 0 (zero).

   –Or–

1. If this parameter is 2, the build types mismatch.
2. Build type of Ntoskrnl.exe.
3. Build type of Hal.dll.
4. 0 (zero).

   (Build Types: 0 = free, multiprocessor-enabled build; 1 = checked, multiprocessor-enabled build; and 2 = free, single-processor build)

Resolving the Problem

Stop 0x79 can occur if either the Ntoskrnl.exe or Hal.dll files have been manually updated. The error can also indicate that one of those two files is out of date (that is, the HAL is designed for Microsoft® Windows NT® version 4.0 and the kernel is for Windows 2000). Additionally, the computer might erroneously have a multiprocessor HAL and a single-processor kernel installed, or vice versa.

The kernel file Ntoskrnl.exe is for single-processor systems and Ntkrnlmp.exe is for multiprocessor systems. However, these file names correspond to the files on the installation media; after Windows 2000 has been installed, the file is renamed to Ntoskrnl.exe, regardless of the source file used. The HAL file also uses the name Hal.dll after installation, but there are several possible HAL files on the installation media.

To resolve this error, restart the computer using either the product CD or the four Setup disks and enter Windows 2000 Setup. Press ENTER at the "Setup Notification" screen to go to the "Welcome to Setup" screen. Press R to repair a Windows 2000 installation, and then press C to use the Recovery Console. Use the **Copy** command to copy either the correct HAL or kernel file from the original CD into the appropriate folder on the hard disk. The **Copy** command detects whether the file to be copied is in the Microsoft compressed file format. If so, it automatically expands the file copied on the target drive, although you will need to specify the correct filename extension as part of the command. These files can also be located within the Driver.cab file. If so, use the **Expand** command to extract them from the CAB and copy them to the hard disk. For more information about the Recovery Console, see chapter "Repair, Recovery, and Restore" in this book.

For more troubleshooting information about the 0x79 Stop message, refer to the Microsoft Knowledge Base link , using the keywords **winnt** and **0x00000079**. For information about this resource, see chapters under "Additional Resources" at the end of this chapter.

Stop 0x0000007A or KERNEL_DATA_INPAGE_ERROR

This Stop message, also known as Stop 0x7A, indicates that the requested page of kernel data from the paging file could not be read into memory.

Interpreting the Message

The four parameters listed in the message are defined in order of appearance as follows:

1. Lock type that was held (value 1, 2, 3, or Page Table Entry [PTE] address).
2. I/O status code.
3. Current process (virtual address for lock type 3, or PTE).
4. Virtual address that could not be read into memory.

For information about all possible status codes that might be returned, see the file Ntstatus.h of the Windows 2000 Device Driver Kit (DDK). For information about the DDK, see "Additional Resources" at the end of this chapter.

Resolving the Problem

Stop 0x7A is usually caused by a bad block (sector) in a paging file, a virus, a disk controller error, or failing RAM. In rare cases, it is caused when nonpaged pool resources run out. It is also caused by defective hardware.

SCSI problems. If the I/O status is C0000185 and the paging file is on a SCSI disk, check the disk cabling and SCSI termination for problems.

Viruses. Check your computer for viruses, using any up-to-date, commercial virus scanning software that examines the Master Boot Record of the hard disk. Any Windows 2000 file system can be infected by viruses.

Bad block. An I/O status code of 0xC000009C or 0xC000016A normally indicates the data cannot be read from the disk due to a bad block (sector). If you can restart the system after the error, Autochk runs automatically and attempts to map out the bad sector. If Autochk does not scan the hard disk for errors, you can manually launch the disk scanner. Run **Chkdsk /f /r** on the system partition. You must restart the system before the disk scan begins. If you cannot start the system due to the error, use the Recovery Console and run **Chkdsk /r**. For more information about the Recovery Console, see chapter "Repair, Recovery, and Restore" in this book.

Warning If your system partition is formatted with the FAT16 file system, the long file names used by Windows 2000 can be damaged if Scandisk or another MS-DOS-based hard disk tool is used to verify the integrity of your hard disk from an MS-DOS prompt. (An MS-DOS prompt is typically derived from a MS-DOS startup disk or from starting MS-DOS on a multiboot system.) Always use the Windows 2000 version of Chkdsk on Windows 2000 disks.

Failing RAM. Another common cause of this error message is failing RAM. Run hardware diagnostics supplied by the system manufacturer, especially the memory scanner. For details on these procedures, see the owner's manual for your computer.

Also, check that all the adapter cards in the computer, including memory modules, are properly seated. Use an ink eraser or an electrical contact treatment, available at electronics supply stores, to ensure adapter card contacts are clean. Be sure to wipe the cleaned contacts off, removing all cleaning debris, before reinstalling the adapter card into the computer. If compressed air is available, use it to clear out the adapter card slot.

Check the System Log in Event Viewer for additional error messages that might help pinpoint the device that is causing the error. Disabling memory caching of the BIOS might also resolve it.

Microsoft periodically releases a package of product improvements and problem resolutions for Windows 2000 called a Service Pack. Because many problems are resolved by installing the latest Service Pack, it is recommended that all users install them as they become available. To check which Service Pack, if any, is installed on your system, click **Start**, click **Run**, type **winver,** and then press ENTER. The **About Windows 2000** dialog box displays the Windows version number and the version number of the Service Pack, if one has been installed.

Occasionally, remedies to specific problems are developed after the release of a Service Pack. These remedies are called hotfixes. Microsoft does not recommend that you install a post-Service Pack hotfix unless the specific problem it addresses has been encountered. Service Packs include all of the hotfixes released since the release of the previous Service Pack. The status of hotfix installations is not indicated in the **About Windows 2000** dialog box. For more information about Service Packs and hotfixes, see "Additional Resources" at the end of this chapter.

Finally, if all the above steps fail to resolve the error, take the system motherboard to a repair facility for diagnostic testing. A crack, a scratched trace, or a defective component on the motherboard can also cause this error.

For more troubleshooting information about the 0x7A Stop message, refer to the Microsoft Knowledge Base link , using the keywords **winnt** and **0x0000007A**. For information about this resource, see "Additional Resources" at the end of this chapter.

Stop 0x0000007B or INACCESSIBLE_BOOT_DEVICE

This Stop message, also known as Stop 0x7B, indicates that Windows 2000 lost access to the system partition during the startup process. This error always occurs while the system is starting and cannot be debugged because it generally occurs before the operating system has loaded the debugger.

Interpreting the Message

The four parameters listed in the message are defined in order of appearance as follows:

1. Address of a Unicode string data structure representing the Advanced RISC Computing (ARC) specification name of the device from which the startup was being attempted

2. Pointer to ARC name string in memory

3. 0 (zero)

4. 0 (zero)

The first parameter typically contains two separate pieces of data. For example, if the parameter is 0x00800020, 0x0020 is the actual length of the Unicode string and 0x0080 is the maximum name string length. The next parameter contains the address of the buffer. This address is in system space, so the high-order bit is set.

If the file system that is supposed to read the boot device failed to initialize or simply did not recognize the data on the boot device as a file system structure, the following parameter definition applies:

1. Address of the device object that could not be mounted
2. 0 (zero)
3. 0 (zero)
4. 0 (zero)

The value of the first argument determines whether the argument is a pointer to an ARC name string (ARC names are a generic method of identifying devices within the ARC environment) or a device object, because a Unicode string never has an odd number of bytes, and a device object always has a Type code of 0003.

Resolving the Problem

Failed boot device. During I/O system initialization, the boot device driver might have failed to initialize the boot device (typically a hard disk). File system initialization might have failed because it did not recognize the data on the boot device.

Also, repartitioning the system partition or installing a new SCSI adapter or disk controller might induce this error. If this happens, the Boot.ini file must be edited. For additional information about the Boot.ini file, see "Additional Resources" at the end of this chapter.

Incompatible disk hardware. If the error occurred at the initial setup of the system, the system might have been installed on an unsupported disk or SCSI controller. Some controllers are supported only by drivers that are in the Windows Driver Library (WDL), which requires the user to use a custom driver during installation. If upgrading the computer to Windows 2000, you might see a prompt to press F6 to use a custom driver. If doing a clean installation of Windows 2000, press F6 when the message "Setup is inspecting your computer's hardware configuration..." is displayed. You will be prompted later for the new driver. If Setup autodetected the controller, you might need to skip detection and use a specific manufacturer's diskette to load the driver. Also, check the availability of updates for the system BIOS and SCSI controller firmware. Updates of this kind are typically available on the Web site or BBS of the hardware manufacturer.

Remove any recently added hardware, especially hard disks or controllers, to see if the error is resolved. If the offending piece of hardware was a hard disk, the disk firmware version might be incompatible with Windows 2000. Contact the manufacturer for updates. If the removal of another piece of hardware resolved the error, IRQ or I/O port conflicts likely exist. Reconfigure the new device according to the manufacturer's instructions.

Confirm that all hard disks, hard disk controllers, and SCSI adapters are listed on the Microsoft Windows 2000 Hardware Compatibility List (HCL). For more information about the HCL, see "Additional Resources" at the end of this chapter.

If a driver was recently added, restart your computer, and press F8 at the character-mode screen that displays the prompt "For troubleshooting and advanced startup options for Windows 2000, press F8." At the resulting Windows 2000 Advanced Options menu, choose the **Last Known Good Configuration** option. This option is most effective when only one driver or service is added at a time.

In addition, check your computer for viruses using any up-to-date, commercial virus scanning software that examines the Master Boot Record of the hard disk. All Windows 2000 file systems can be infected by viruses.

This error can also be a result of hard disk corruption. Run **Chkdsk /f /r** on the system partition. You must restart the system before the disk scan begins. If you cannot start the system due to the error, use the Recovery Console and run **Chkdsk /r**. For more information about the Recovery Console, see chapter "Repair, Recovery, and Restore" in this book.

Warning If your system partition is formatted with the FAT16 file system, the long file names used by Windows 2000 can be damaged if Scandisk or another MS-DOS-based hard disk tool is used to verify the integrity of your hard disk from an MS-DOS prompt. (An MS-DOS prompt is typically derived from a MS-DOS startup disk or from starting MS-DOS on a multiboot system.) Always use the Windows 2000 version of Chkdsk on Windows 2000 disks.

If your system has SCSI adapters, contact the adapter manufacturer to obtain updated Windows 2000 drivers. Try disabling sync negotiation in the SCSI BIOS, checking the cabling and the SCSI IDs of each device, and confirming proper termination. For EIDE devices, define the onboard EIDE port as Primary only. Also check each EIDE device for the proper master/slave/stand alone setting. Try removing all EIDE devices except for hard disks.

For more troubleshooting information about the 0x7B Stop message, refer to the Microsoft Knowledge Base link , using the keywords **winnt** and **0x0000007B**. For information about this resource, see "Additional Resources" at the end of this chapter.

Stop 0x0000007F or UNEXPECTED_KERNEL_MODE_TRAP

This Stop message, also known as Stop 0x7F, means that one of two types of problems occurred in kernel-mode, either a kind of condition that the kernel is not allowed to have or catch (a *bound trap*), or a kind of error that is always fatal. Occasionally, this message can be caused by software problems, but the most common cause is hardware failure.

Interpreting the Message

The four parameters listed in the message are defined in order of appearance as follows:

1. Processor exception code
2. 0 (zero)
3. 0 (zero)
4. 0 (zero)

The first and most important parameter (0x0000000x) can have several different values. The cause of this error can vary, depending on the value of this parameter. All conditions that cause a Stop 0x7F can be found in any x86 microprocessor reference manual because they are specific to the x86 platform. Here are some of the most common exception codes:

- 0x00000000, or Divide by Zero Error, is caused when a DIV instruction is run and the divisor is 0. Memory corruption, other hardware problems, or software failures can cause this error.

- 0x00000004, or Overflow, occurs when the processor executes a call to an interrupt handler when the overflow (OF) flag is set.

- 0x00000005, or Bounds Check Fault, is generated when the processor, while executing a BOUND instruction, finds that a variable's assigned value exceeds the specified limits. A BOUND instruction is used to ensure that a signed array index is within a certain range.

- 0x00000006, or Invalid Opcode, is generated when the processor attempts to run an invalid instruction. This is generally caused when the instruction pointer has become corrupted and is pointing to the wrong location. The most common cause of this is hardware memory corruption.

- 0x00000008, or Double Fault, is when an exception occurs while trying to call the handler for a prior exception. Normally, the two exceptions can be handled serially. However, there are several exceptions that cannot be handled serially, and in this situation the processor signals a double fault. This is almost always caused by hardware problems.

Other exception codes are defined as follows:

- 0x00000001—A system-debugger call.
- 0x00000003—A debugger breakpoint.
- 0x00000007—A hardware coprocessor instruction with no coprocessor present.
- 0x0000000A—A corrupted Task State Segment.
- 0x0000000B—An access to a memory segment that was not present.
- 0x0000000C—An access to memory beyond the limits of a stack.
- 0x0000000D—An exception not covered by some other exception; a protection fault that pertains to access violations for applications.

Resolving the Problem

Hardware failure or incompatibility. Stop 0x7F usually occurs after the installation of faulty or mismatched hardware (especially memory) or in the event that installed hardware fails. If hardware was recently added to the system, remove it to see if the error recurs. If existing hardware has failed, remove or replace the faulty component. Run hardware diagnostics supplied by the system manufacturer, especially the memory scanner, to determine which hardware component has failed. For details on these procedures, see the owner's manual for your computer. Check that all the adapter cards in the computer, including memory modules, are properly seated. Use an ink eraser or an electrical contact treatment, available at electronics supply stores, to ensure adapter card contacts are clean. Be sure to wipe the cleaned contacts off, removing all cleaning debris, before reinstalling the adapter card into the computer. If compressed air is available, use it to clear out the adapter card slot.

If the error appears on a newly installed system, check the availability of updates for BIOS revisions on the motherboard, SCSI controllers, or network cards. Updates of this kind are typically available on the Web site or BBS of the hardware manufacturer.

Confirm that all hard disks, hard disk controllers, and SCSI adapters are listed on the Windows 2000 Hardware Compatibility List (HCL). For more information about the HCL, see "Additional Resources" at the end of this chapter.

If the error occurred after the installation of a new or updated device driver, the driver should be removed or replaced. If, under this circumstance, the error occurs during the startup sequence, restart the computer using Safe Mode to rename or delete the file. If the driver is used as part of the system startup process in Safe Mode, you need to start the computer using the Recovery Console in order to access the file. For more information about Safe Mode, see chapter "Startup Process" in this book. For more information about the Recovery Console, see chapter "Repair, Recovery, and Restore" in this book.

Also try restarting your computer, and press F8 at the character-mode screen that displays the prompt "For troubleshooting and advanced startup options for Windows 2000, press F8." At the resulting Windows 2000 Advanced Options menu, choose the **Last Known Good Configuration** option. This option is most effective when only one driver or service is added at a time.

Overclocking. Setting the CPU to run at speeds above the rated specification (known as *overclocking* the CPU) can cause this error. If this has been done to the computer experiencing the error, return the CPU to the default clock speed setting.

Check the System Log in Event Viewer for additional error messages that might help pinpoint the device or driver that is causing the error. Disabling memory caching of the BIOS might also resolve it.

If you encountered this error while upgrading to Windows 2000, it might be caused by a device driver, a system service, a virus scanner, or a backup tool that is incompatible with the new version. If possible, remove all third-party device drivers and system services and disable any virus scanners prior to upgrading. Contact the software manufacturer to obtain updates of these tools.

Microsoft periodically releases a package of product improvements and problem resolutions for Windows 2000 called a Service Pack. Because many problems are resolved by installing the latest Service Pack, it is recommended that all users install them as they become available. To check which Service Pack, if any, is installed on your system, click **Start**, click **Run**, type **winver,** and then press ENTER. The **About Windows 2000** dialog box displays the Windows version number and the version number of the Service Pack, if one has been installed.

Occasionally, remedies to specific problems are developed after the release of a Service Pack. These remedies are called hotfixes. Microsoft does not recommend that you install a post-Service Pack hotfix unless the specific problem it addresses has been encountered. Service Packs include all of the hotfixes released since the release of the previous Service Pack. The status of hotfix installations is not indicated in the **About Windows 2000** dialog box. For more information about Service Packs and hotfixes, see "Additional Resources" at the end of this chapter.

Finally, if all the above steps fail to resolve the error, take the system motherboard to a repair facility for diagnostic testing. A crack, a scratched trace, or a defective component on the motherboard can also cause this error.

For more troubleshooting information about the 0x7F Stop message, refer to the Microsoft Knowledge Base link , using the keywords **winnt** and **0x0000007F**. For information about this resource, see "Additional Resources" at the end of this chapter.

Stop 0xC000021A or STATUS_SYSTEM_PROCESS_TERMINATED

This Stop message occurs when a user-mode subsystem, such as Winlogon or the Client Server Runtime Subsystem (CSRSS), is fatally compromised and security can no longer be guaranteed. The operating system switches into kernel-mode and generates this error. Because Windows 2000 cannot run without Winlogon or CSRSS, this is one of the few situations where the failure of a user-mode service can bring down the system. Running the kernel debugger is not useful in this situation because the actual error occurred in a user-mode process.

Interpreting the Message

The first three parameters listed in the message are defined in order of appearance as follows:

1. Status code
2. 0 (zero)
3. 0 (zero)

For information about all possible status codes that might be returned, see the file Ntstatus.h of the Windows 2000 Device Driver Kit (DDK). For information about the DDK, see "Additional Resources" at the end of this chapter.

Resolving the Problem

Device drivers, system services, and third-party applications. Because Stop 0xC000021A occurs in a user-mode process, the most common culprits are third-party applications. If the error occurred after the installation of a new or updated device driver, system service or third-party application, the new software should be removed or disabled. Contact the manufacturer of the software about a possible update.

If the error occurs during system startup, restart your computer, and press F8 at the character-mode screen that displays the prompt "For troubleshooting and advanced startup options for Windows 2000, press F8." At the resulting Windows 2000 Advanced Options menu, choose the **Last Known Good Configuration** option. This option is most effective when only one driver or service is added at a time. If this does not resolve the error, try manually removing the offending software by restarting the computer in Safe Mode and renaming or uninstalling the faulty software. If the faulty software is used as part of the system startup process in Safe Mode, you need to start the computer using the Recovery Console in order to access the file. For more information about Safe Mode, see chapter "Startup Process" in this book. For more information about the Recovery Console, see chapter "Repair, Recovery, and Restore" in this book. If a newly installed piece if hardware is suspected, remove it to see if this resolves the issue.

Try running the Emergency Recovery Disk (ERD) and allow the system to repair any errors that it detects. For more information about the ERD, see chapter "Repair, Recovery, and Restore" in this book.

Mismatched system files. Mismatched system files can also cause this error. If you can successfully start the computer using Safe Mode, try using the System File Checker (SFC) to correct the problem. Open up the Run dialog box, type **sfc /scannow** and press ENTER. If SFC does not correct the problem, try running a full system restore from tape might generate this error (some restore programs might skip restoring system files they determine are in use). Check if there is an updated version of the Backup/Restore program available from the manufacturer.

Microsoft periodically releases a package of product improvements and problem resolutions for Windows 2000 called a Service Pack. Because many problems are resolved by installing the latest Service Pack, it is recommended that all users install them as they become available. To check which Service Pack, if any, is installed on your system, click **Start**, click **Run**, type **winver,** and then press ENTER. The **About Windows 2000** dialog box displays the Windows version number and the version number of the Service Pack, if one has been installed.

Occasionally, remedies to specific problems are developed after the release of a Service Pack. These remedies are called hotfixes. Microsoft does not recommend that you install a post-Service Pack hotfix unless the specific problem it addresses has been encountered. Service Packs include all of the hotfixes released since the release of the previous Service Pack. The status of hotfix installations is not indicated in the **About Windows 2000** dialog box. For more information about Service Packs and hotfixes, see "Additional Resources" at the end of this chapter.

For more troubleshooting information about the 0xC000021A Stop message, refer to the Microsoft Knowledge Base link , using the keywords **winnt** and **0xC000021A**. For information about this resource, see "Additional Resources" at the end of this chapter.

Stop 0xC0000221 or STATUS_IMAGE_CHECKSUM_MISMATCH

This Stop message indicates that a driver or a system DLL has been corrupted. Typically, the name of the damaged file is displayed as part of the message.

Resolving the Problem

To resolve this error, restart the computer using either the product CD or the four Setup disks and enter Windows 2000 Setup. Press ENTER at the "Setup Notification" screen to go to the "Welcome to Setup" screen. Press R to repair a Windows 2000 installation, then press R to start the Emergency Repair Process, and then press F to run the Fast Repair option. You will be prompted for the Emergency Recovery Disk (ERD). Allow the system to repair or replace the missing or damaged driver file on the system partition. For more information about the ERD, see chapter "Repair, Recovery, and Restore" in this book.

If you can successfully start the computer using Safe Mode, try using the System File Checker (SFC) to correct the problem. Open up the Run dialog box, type **sfc /scannow** and press ENTER.

If a specific file was identified in the Stop message as being corrupted, you can try replacing that individual file manually. Restart the system, then press F8 at the character-mode screen that displays the prompt "For troubleshooting and advanced startup options for Windows 2000, press F8." At the resulting Windows 2000 Advanced Options menu, choose Safe Mode with Command Prompt. From there, copy a fresh version of the file from the original source onto the hard disk. If the file is used as part of the system startup process in Safe Mode, you need to start the computer using the Recovery Console in order to access the file. For more information about Safe Mode, see chapter "Startup Process" in this book. For more information about the Recovery Console, see chapter "Repair, Recovery, and Restore" in this book. If these methods fail, try reinstalling Windows 2000 and then restoring the system from a backup.

Note Some files are located in the Driver.cab located on either on the product CD or in the %SystemRoot%\Driver cache\I386 folder. Files inside the CAB file need to be extracted before they can be used. If you can successfully start the computer with Safe Mode, they can be extracted by double-clicking the CAB file in Explorer and copying the files to the target location. If you cannot start the computer, use the Recovery Console. Use the **Expand** command to extract them from the CAB and copy them to the hard disk. If the original file from the product CD is not in a CAB file but has a file name extension ending in an underscore, the file needs to be uncompressed before it can be used. The Recovery Console's **Copy** command automatically detects compressed files and expands them as they are copied to the target location, although you will need to specify the correct filename extension as part of the command. For more information about the Recovery Console, see chapter "Repair, Recovery, and Restore" in this book..

Disk errors can be a source of file corruption. Run **Chkdsk /f /r** to detect and resolve any file system structural corruption. You must restart the system before the disk scan begins on a system partition. If you cannot start the system due to the error, use the Recovery Console and run **Chkdsk /r**. For more information about the Recovery Console, see chapter "Repair, Recovery, and Restore" in this book.

Warning If your system partition is formatted with the FAT16 file system, the long file names used by Windows 2000 can be damaged if Scandisk or another MS-DOS-based hard disk tool is used to verify the integrity of your hard disk from an MS-DOS prompt. (An MS-DOS prompt is typically derived from an MS-DOS startup disk or from starting MS-DOS on a multiboot system.) Always use the Windows 2000 version of Chkdsk on Windows 2000 disks.

If the error occurred immediately after RAM was added to the system, the paging file might be corrupted or the new RAM itself might be either faulty or incompatible.

▶ **To determine if newly added RAM is causing a Stop message**

1. Return the system to the original RAM configuration.

2. Use the Recovery Console to access the partition containing the paging file and delete the file Pagefile.sys. For more information about the Recovery Console, see chapter "Repair, Recovery, and Restore" in this book.

3. While still in the Recovery Console, run **Chkdsk /r** on the partition that contained the paging file.

4. Restart the system.

5. Set the paging file to an optimal level for the amount of RAM added.

6. Shut down the system and add your RAM.

   The new RAM must meet the system manufacturer's specifications for speed, parity, and type (that is, fast page mode [FPM] vs. extended data out [EDO] vs. synchronous dynamic random access memory [SDRAM]). Try to match the new RAM to the existing installed RAM as closely as possible. RAM can come in many different capacities, and more importantly, in different formats (single inline memory modules [SIMMs] or dual inline memory modules [DIMMs]). The electrical contacts can be either gold or tin and it is not wise to mix these contact types.

If you experience the same error message after reinstalling the new RAM, run hardware diagnostics supplied by the system manufacturer, especially the memory scanner. For details on these procedures, see the owner's manual for your computer.

When you can log on to the system again, check the System Log in Event Viewer for additional error messages that might help pinpoint the device or driver that is causing the error. Disabling memory caching of the BIOS might also resolve this error.

For more troubleshooting information about the 0xC0000221 Stop message, refer to the Microsoft Knowledge Base link , using the keywords **winnt** and **0xC0000221**. For information about these resources, see "Additional Resources" at the end of this chapter.

Hardware Malfunction Messages

Hardware malfunction messages are another form of Stop messages. Like Stop messages, they are character-mode messages. They are caused by a hardware condition detected by the processor. The first one or two lines of the hardware malfunction message on one computer might differ from those on a different computer, even with the same failed component, depending upon the hardware abstraction layer (HAL) that is loaded at startup. However, these lines always convey the same idea, as shown in the following example:

```
Hardware malfunction.
Call your hardware vendor for support.
```

The installed HAL also determines how additional lines in each system's message differ in format and content. Therefore, before doing what the hardware malfunction message recommends, contact a support technician within your own organization to run hardware diagnostics on your computer. The information provided after the first two lines in the message helps your support technician decide which hardware diagnostics to run. For example, for ISA bus computers, this information indicates whether it is a memory-parity error or a bus-data error. On EISA computers, if the hardware problem is in an adapter, the adapter slot number on the system board is displayed.

Important In many situations, hardware failures first manifest themselves as Stop errors. Software using the failing hardware can detect problems because of unexpected results before the hardware itself has been identified as faulty. This is why troubleshooting many of the Stop messages includes running hardware diagnostics on the system.

Under rare circumstances, hardware malfunction messages can be generated by software bugs—specifically driver problems. For example, if a problematic driver writes to the wrong I/O port, the actual device at the targeted port might generate a hardware malfunction message. However, most errors of this sort are detected and debugged before the software is released to the public.

If you need help from outside your organization to interpret the information on the screen, contact the hardware manufacturer for your specific brand of computer, adapter, or peripheral device.

Additional Resources

- For more information about individual Stop messages, see the Microsoft Knowledge Base link on the Web Resources page at http://windows.microsoft.com/windows2000/reskit/webresources.

- The Microsoft Hardware Compatibility List (HCL) is available on the *Microsoft® Windows® 2000 Resource Kit* companion CD. See the Microsoft Hardware Compatibility List on the Web Resources page at http://windows.microsoft.com/windows2000/reskit/webresources.

- The latest Service Packs and hotfixes for Windows 2000 are available from Microsoft Update. Click **Start** and click **Windows Update** to see a list of components, if any, that are available as downloads for your system.

- For more information about Windows 2000 status code definitions in the file Ntstatus.h of the Windows 2000 Device Driver Kit (DDK), see the Device Driver Kit (DDK) link on the Web Resources page at http://windows.microsoft.com/windows2000/reskit/webresources.

Glossary

A

access control entry (ACE) An entry in an access control list (ACL) containing a security identifier (SID) and a set of access rights. A process with a matching security identifier is either allowed access rights, denied rights, or allowed rights with auditing.

access control list (ACL) The part of an object's security descriptor that grants or denies permission to specific users and groups to access the object. Only the owner of an object can change permissions in an ACL; thus access to the object is at the owner's discretion. See also discretionary access control list (DACL); system access control list (SACL).

ACE See access control entry.

ACL See access control list.

Active Directory The directory service included with Windows 2000 Server. It stores information about objects on a network and makes this information available to users and network administrators. Active Directory gives network users access to permitted resources anywhere on the network using a single logon process. It provides network administrators with an intuitive hierarchical view of the network and a single point of administration for all network objects. See also directory; directory service.

ActiveX A set of technologies that enables software components to interact with one another in a networked environment, regardless of the language in which the components were created.

ActiveX control A reusable software component that incorporates ActiveX technology.

ADSL See Asymmetric Digital Subscriber Line.

affinity mask A value that contains bits for each processor on the system, defining which processors a process or thread can use.

allocate To mark media for use by an application. Media in the available state may be allocated.

allocated state A state that indicates media are in use and assigned to application media pools.

AppleTalk The Apple Computer network architecture and network protocols. A network that has Macintosh clients and a computer running Windows 2000 Server with Services for Macintosh functions as an AppleTalk network.

AppleTalk Protocol The set of network protocols on which the AppleTalk network architecture is based. The AppleTalk Protocol stack must be installed on a computer running Windows 2000 Server so that Macintosh clients can connect to it. See also AppleTalk.

application media pool A data repository that determines which media can be accessed by which applications and that sets the policies for that media. There can be any number of application media pools in a Removable Storage system. Applications create application media pools.

application programming interface (API)
A set of routines that an application uses to request and carry out lower-level services performed by a computer's operating system. These routines usually carry out maintenance tasks such as managing files and displaying information.

Asymmetric Digital Subscriber Line (ADSL)
A high-bandwidth digital transmission technology that uses existing phone lines and also allows voice transmissions over the same lines. Most of the traffic is transmitted downstream to the user, generally at rates of 512 Kbps to about 6 Mbps.

attribute (object) In Active Directory, a single property of an object. An object is described by the values of its attributes. For each object class, the schema defines what attributes an instance of the class must have and what additional attributes it might have.

authoritative In the Domain Name System (DNS), the use of zones by DNS servers to register and resolve a DNS domain name. When a DNS server is configured to host a zone, it is authoritative for names within that zone. DNS servers are granted authority based on information stored in the zone.

automatic file truncation A process that converts premigrated files into a remote storage identifier or placeholder to reclaim space on the managed volume. Automatic file truncation is initiated on a managed volume whenever the amount of free space is less than the desired free space as defined by the administrator.

available state A state in which media can be allocated for use by applications.

averaging counter A type of counter that measures a value over time and displays the average of the last two measurements over some other factor (for example, PhysicalDisk\Avg. Disk Bytes/Transfer).

B

bad block A disk sector that can no longer be used for data storage, usually due to media damage or imperfections.

bar code A machine-readable label that identifies an object, such as physical media.

baseline A range of measurements derived from performance monitoring that represents acceptable performance under typical operating conditions.

basic disk A physical disk that contains primary partitions or extended partitions with logical drives used by Windows 2000 and all versions of Windows NT. Basic disks can also contain volume, striped, mirror, or RAID-5 sets that were created using Windows NT 4.0 or earlier. As long as a compatible file format is used, basic disks can be accessed by MS-DOS, Windows 95, Windows 98, and all versions of Windows NT.

basic input/output system (BIOS)
The set of essential software routines that tests hardware at startup, is involved with starting the operating system, and supports the transfer of data among hardware devices. The BIOS is stored in read-only memory (ROM) so that it can be executed when the computer is turned on. Although critical to performance, the BIOS is usually invisible to computer users.

bindery A database in Novell NetWare 2.*x* and 3.*x* that contains organizational and security information about users and groups.

BIOS   See basic input/output system.

BIOS parameter block (BPB)   A series of fields containing data on disk size, geometry variables, and the physical parameters of the volume. The BPB is located within the boot sector.

boot partition   The volume that contains the operating system and its support files. The boot partition can be (but does not have to be) the same as the system partition. Both a primary partition and a logical drive in an extended partition can be used as a boot partition.

boot sector   A critical disk structure for starting your computer located at sector 1 of each volume or floppy disk. It contains executable code and data that is required by the code, including information used by the file system to access the volume. The boot sector is created when you format the volume.

bottleneck   A condition, usually involving a hardware resource, that causes the entire system to perform poorly.

bound trap   In programming, a problem in which a set of conditions exceeds a permitted range of values that causes the microprocessor to stop what it is doing and handle the situation in a separate routine.

C

C2 level of security   U.S. government security level that designates a system that has controls capable of enforcing access limitations on an individual basis. In a C2 system, the owner of a system resource has the right to decide who can access it, and the operating system can detect when data is accessed and by whom.

cache   For DNS and WINS, a local information store of resource records for recently resolved names of remote hosts. Typically, the cache is built dynamically as the computer queries and resolves names; it helps optimize the time required to resolve queried names. See also cache file; naming service; resource record.

cache file   A file used by the Domain Name System (DNS) server to preload its names cache when service is started. Also known as the "root hints" file because resource records stored in this file are used by the DNS service to help locate root servers that provide referral to authoritative servers for remote names. For Windows DNS servers, the cache file is named Cache.dns and is located in the %SystemRoot%\System32\Dns folder. See also authoritative; cache; systemroot.

caching   For DNS, the ability of DNS servers to store information about the domain namespace learned during the processing and resolution of name queries. In Windows 2000, caching is also available through the DNS client service (resolver) as a way for DNS clients to keep a cache of name information learned during recent queries. See also caching resolver.

caching resolver   For Windows 2000, a client-side Domain Name System (DNS) name resolution service that performs caching of recently learned DNS domain name information. The caching resolver service provides system-wide access to DNS-aware programs for resource records obtained from DNS servers during the processing of name queries. Data placed in the cache is used for a limited period of time and aged according to the active Time To Live (TTL) value. You can set the TTL either individually for each resource record (RR) or default to the minimum TTL set in the start of authority RR for the zone. See also cache; caching; expire interval; minimum TTL; resolver; resource record; Time To Live (TTL).

capture buffer The maximum size of the capture file. When the capture file reaches the maximum size, the oldest frames are removed to make room for newer frames (FIFO queue).

change journal A feature new to Windows 2000 that tracks changes to NTFS volumes, including additions, deletions, and modifications. The change journal exists on the volume as a sparse file.

changer The robotic element of an online library unit.

checkpoint In a server cluster node's registry, a snapshot of the cluster hive or of an application key; the checkpoint is written to the quorum disk when certain events take place, such as a node failure. See also cluster database; cluster hive.

child object An object that resides in another object. For example, a file is a child object that resides in a folder, which is the parent object. See also object; parent object.

Client Service for NetWare A service included with Windows 2000 Professional that allows clients to make direct connections to resources on computers running NetWare 2.*x*, 3.*x*, 4.*x*, or 5.*x* server software.

cluster database The database of configuration data (cluster objects and their settings) pertinent to the cluster. This database is the product of the cluster hive checkpoint and the changes recorded in the quorum log. A local copy of this database is maintained by all the nodes of the cluster hive in the registry. See also checkpoint; cluster hive.

cluster hive In the system registry of a server cluster node, the local copy of the cluster database; the portion of the system registry on each node that contains the configuration data of a cluster. When all the cluster nodes are up, changes to the cluster hive are synchronized on all cluster nodes, and the cluster hive is identical with the cluster database. While a node is down, that node's cluster hive is not updated with cluster configuration changes, but the changes are recorded on the quorum log. At startup, the local copy might have out-of-date information. If so, it is recreated using the last checkpoint and the change records in the quorum log. See also checkpoint; cluster database.

Cluster service Clussvc.exe, the primary executable of the Windows Clustering component that creates a server cluster, controls all aspects of its operation, and manages the cluster database. Each node in a server cluster runs one instance of the Cluster service.

COM See Component Object Model.

complementary metal-oxide semiconductor (CMOS) The battery-packed memory that stores information, such as disk types and amount of memory, used to start the computer.

completed state A state that indicates that media can no longer be used for write operations.

Component Object Model (COM) An object-based programming model designed to promote software interoperability; it allows two or more applications or components to easily cooperate with one another, even if they were written by different vendors, at different times, in different programming languages, or if they are running on different computers running different operating systems. COM is the foundation technology upon which broader technologies can be built. Object linking and embedding (OLE) technology and ActiveX are both built on top of COM.

console tree The tree view pane in a Microsoft Management Console (MMC) that displays the hierarchical namespace. By default it is the left pane of the console window, but it can be hidden. The items in the console tree (for example, Web pages, folders, and controls) and their hierarchical organization determines the management capabilities of a console. See also Microsoft Management Console (MMC); namespace.

container object An object that can logically contain other objects. For example, a folder is a container object. See also noncontainer object; object.

context switch An event that occurs when the kernel switches the processor from one thread to another, for example, when an I/O operation causes a thread to be blocked and the operating system selects another thread to run on the processor.

cyclical redundancy check (CRC)
A procedure used in checking for errors in data transmission. CRC error checking uses a complex calculation to generate a number based on the data transmitted. The sending device performs the calculation before transmission and sends its result to the receiving device. The receiving device repeats the same calculation after transmission. If both devices obtain the same result, it is assumed that the transmission was error-free. The procedure is known as a redundancy check because each transmission includes not only data but extra (redundant) error-checking values. Communications protocols such as XMODEM and Kermit use cyclical redundancy checking.

D

Data Link Control (DLC) A protocol used primarily for IBM mainframe computers and printer connectivity.

deallocate To return media to the available state after they have been used by an application.

decommissioned state A state that indicates that media have reached their allocation maximum.

deferred procedure call (DPC) A kernel-defined control object type that represents a procedure that is to be called later. A DPC runs at DISPATCH_LEVEL IRQL. A DPC can be used when a timer event occurs or when an ISR needs to perform more work but should do so at a lower interrupt request level than the one at which an ISR executes. In an SMP environment, a DPC might run immediately on a processor other than the current one, or might run after another interrupt has run on the current processor.

desired free space The amount of free space that should be maintained on a volume at all times during normal use.

device fonts Fonts that reside in your printer. They can be built into the printer itself or provided by a font cartridge or font card. See also printer fonts.

Dfs See Distributed file system.

DHCP See Dynamic Host Configuration Protocol.

direct memory access (DMA) Memory access that does not involve the microprocessor. DMA is frequently used for data transfer directly between memory and a peripheral device, such as a disk drive.

directory An information source that contains information about computer files or other objects. In a file system, a directory stores information about files. In a distributed computing environment (such as a Windows 2000 domain), the directory stores information about objects such as printers, applications, databases, and users.

directory service   Both the directory information source and the service that make the information available and usable. A directory service enables the user to find an object given any one of its attributes. See also Active Directory; directory.

disconnected placeholder   A placeholder whose file contents have been removed from remote storage. A disconnected placeholder could have been restored from backup after the space in remote storage was reclaimed, or the data within remote storage is physically unavailable (for example, because of a media failure).

discretionary access control list (DACL)
The part of an object's security descriptor that grants or denies specific users and groups permission to access the object. Only the owner of an object can change permissions granted or denied in a DACL; thus access to the object is at the owner's discretion. See also access control entry; object; system access control list; security descriptor.

disk bottleneck   A condition that occurs when disk performance is reduced to the extent that overall system performance is affected.

disk quota   The maximum amount of disk space available to a user.

Distributed file system (Dfs)   A Windows 2000 service consisting of software residing on network servers and clients that transparently links shared folders located on different file servers into a single namespace for improved load sharing and data availability.

DNS server   A computer that runs DNS server programs containing name-to-IP address mappings, IP address-to-name mappings, information about the domain tree structure, and other information. DNS servers also attempt to resolve client queries.

domain controller   For a Windows NT Server or Windows 2000 Server domain, the server that authenticates domain logon requests and maintains the security policy and the master database for a domain. Both servers and domain controllers are capable of validating a user's logon request, but password changes must be made by contacting the domain controller.

domain local group   A Windows 2000 group only available in native mode domains and can contain members from anywhere in the forest, in trusted forests, or in a trusted pre-Windows 2000 domain. Domain local groups can only grant permissions to resources within the domain in which they exist. Typically, domain local groups are used to gather security principals from across the forest to control access to resources within the domain.

dots per inch (DPI)   The standard used to measure screen and printer resolution, expressed as the number of dots that a device can display or print per linear inch. The greater the number of dots per inch, the better the resolution.

DVD decoder   A hardware or software component that allows a digital video disc (DVD) drive to display movies on your computer screen. See also DVD disc; DVD drive.

DVD disc   A type of optical disc storage technology. A digital video disc (DVD) looks like a CD-ROM disc, but it can store greater amounts of data. DVD discs are often used to store full-length movies and other multimedia content that requires large amounts of storage space. See also DVD decoder; DVD drive.

DVD drive   A disk storage device that uses digital video disc (DVD) technology. A DVD drive reads both CD-ROM and DVD discs; however, a DVD decoder is necessary to display DVD movies on your computer screen. See also DVD decoder; DVD disc.

dynamic disk A physical disk that is managed by Disk Management. Dynamic disks can contain only dynamic volumes (that is, volumes created by using Disk Management). Dynamic disks cannot contain partitions or logical drives, nor can they be accessed by MS-DOS. See also dynamic volume; partition.

Dynamic Host Configuration Protocol (DHCP) A networking protocol that provides safe, reliable, and simple TCP/IP network configuration and offers dynamic configuration of Internet Protocol (IP) addresses for computers. DHCP ensures that address conflicts do not occur and helps conserve the use of IP addresses through centralized management of address allocation.

dynamic priority The priority value to which a thread's base priority is adjusted to optimize scheduling.

dynamic volume A logical volume that is created using Disk Management. Dynamic volumes include simple, spanned, striped, mirrored, and RAID-5 volumes. Dynamic volumes must be created on dynamic disks. See also dynamic disk; volume.

dynamic-link library (DLL) A feature of the Microsoft Windows family of operating systems and the OS/2 operating system. DLLs allow executable routines, generally serving a specific function or set of functions, to be stored separately as files with .dll extensions, and to be loaded only when needed by the program that calls them.

E

EFS See Encrypting File System.

emergency repair disk (ERD) A disk, created by the Backup utility, that contains copies of three of the files stored in the %SystemRoot%/Repair folder, including Setup.log that contains a list of system files installed on the computer. This disk can be used during the Emergency Repair Process to repair your computer if it will not start or if your system files are damaged or erased.

Encrypting File System (EFS) A Windows 2000 feature that enables users to encrypt files and folders on an NTFS volume disk to keep them safe from access by intruders. In the registry, a feature that allows the file system to automatically encrypt and decrypt file data as it is read and written to the disk, which prevents users from being able to start under MS-DOS or another operating system and then use a low-level disk editing utility to view data stored on an NTFS volume. See also NTFS file system.

Enhanced Integrated Drive Electronics (EIDE) An extension of the IDE standard, EIDE is a hardware interface standard for disk drive designs that houses control circuits in the drives themselves. It allows for standardized interfaces to the system bus, while providing for advanced features, such as burst data transfers and direct data access.

event logging The Windows 2000 process of recording an audit entry in the audit trail whenever certain events occur, such as services starting and stopping or users logging on and off and accessing resources. You can use Event Viewer to review Services for Macintosh events as well as Windows 2000 events.

expire interval For DNS, the number of seconds that DNS servers operating as secondary masters for a zone use to determine if zone data should be expired when the zone is not refreshed and renewed.

Extended Industry Standard Architecture (EISA) A 32-bit bus standard introduced in 1988 by a consortium of nine computer-industry companies. EISA maintains compatibility with the earlier Industry Standard Architecture (ISA) but provides for additional features.

F

failback (v., fail back) In a server cluster, the moving of a failed-over group to the next node on the group's Preferred Owners list. See also failover; node; resource.

failover (v., fail over) In a server cluster, the means of providing high availability. Upon failure, either of a resource in a group or of the node where the group is online, the cluster takes the group offline on that node, and then brings it online on another node. See also node; resource.

FAT See file allocation table.

fault tolerance The assurance of data integrity when hardware failures occur. On the Windows NT and Windows 2000 platforms, fault tolerance is provided by the Ftdisk.sys driver.

FIFO First in, first out.

file allocation table (FAT) A file system based on a file allocation table (FAT) maintained by some operating systems, including Windows NT and Windows 2000, to keep track of the status of various segments of disk space used for file storage.

file system In an operating system, the overall structure in which files are named, stored, and organized. NTFS, FAT, and FAT32 are types of file systems.

File Transfer Protocol (FTP) A protocol that defines how to transfer files from one computer to another over the Internet. FTP is also a client/server application that moves files using this protocol.

foreground boost A mechanism that increases the priority of a foreground application.

FTP See File Transfer Protocol.

G

global group For Windows 2000 Server, a group that can be used in its own domain, in member servers and in workstations of the domain, and in trusting domains. In all those places a global group can be granted rights and permissions and can become a member of local groups. However, a global group can contain user accounts only from its own domain. See also group; local group.

globally unique identifier (GUID) A 16-byte value generated from the unique identifier on a device, the current date and time, and a sequence number. A GUID is used to identify a particular device or component.

graphical user interface (GUI) A display format, like that of Windows, that represents a program's functions with graphic images such as buttons and icons. GUIs allow a user to perform operations and make choices by pointing and clicking with a mouse.

group   A collection of users, computers, contacts, and other groups. Groups can be used as security or as e-mail distribution collections. Distribution groups are used only for e-mail. Security groups are used both to grant access to resources and as e-mail distribution lists. In a server cluster, a group is a collection of resources, and the basic unit of failover. See also domain local group; global group.

Group Policy   An administrator's tool for defining and controlling how programs, network resources, and the operating system operate for users and computers in an organization. In an Active Directory environment, Group Policy is applied to users or computers on the basis of their membership in sites, domains, or organizational units.

H

HAL   See hardware abstraction layer.

hard affinity   A mechanism by which a thread can only run on a set of processors.

hardware abstraction layer (HAL)

A thin layer of software provided by the hardware manufacturer that hides, or abstracts, hardware differences from higher layers of the operating system. Through the filter provided by the HAL, different types of hardware all look alike to the rest of the operating system. This allows Windows NT and Windows 2000 to be portable from one hardware platform to another. The HAL also provides routines that allow a single device driver to support the same device on all platforms. The HAL works closely with the kernel.

Hardware Compatibility List (HCL)

A list of the devices supported by Windows 2000, available from the Microsoft Web site.

hardware malfunction message   A character-based, full-screen error message displayed on a blue background. It indicates the microprocessor detected a hardware error condition from which the system cannot recover.

HCL   See Hardware Compatibility List.

heartbeat   In a server cluster or Network Load Balancing cluster, a periodic message sent between nodes to detect system failure of any node.

heartbeat thread   A thread initiated by the Windows NT Virtual DOS Machine (NTVDM) process that interrupts every 55 milliseconds to simulate a timer interrupt.

high performance file system (HPFS)

The file system designed for the OS/2 version 1.2 operating system.

HTML   See Hypertext Markup Language.

HTTP   See Hypertext Transfer Protocol.

Hypertext Markup Language (HTML)

A simple markup language used to create hypertext documents that are portable from one platform to another. HTML files are simple ASCII text files with embedded codes (indicated by markup tags) to indicate formatting and hypertext links. HTML is used for formatting documents on the World Wide Web.

Hypertext Transfer Protocol (HTTP)

The protocol used to transfer information on the World Wide Web. An HTTP address (one kind of Uniform Resource Locator [URL]) takes the form: http://www.microsoft.com

I

ideal processor A processor associated with a thread containing a default value assigned by the system, or specified by the program developer in the application code. In Windows 2000, the scheduler favors running a thread on the ideal processor that is assigned to the thread as part of the soft affinity algorithm.

import media pool A repository where Removable Storage puts media when it recognizes the on-media identifier (OMID), but does not have the media cataloged in the current Removable Storage database.

imported state A state that indicates media whose label types are recognized by Removable Storage, but whose label IDs are not cataloged by Removable Storage.

inaccessible state A state that indicates that a side of a multi-cartridge drive is in a drive, but is not in the accessible state.

incompatible state A state that indicates that media are not compatible with the library in which they were classified. This media should be immediately ejected from the library hardware unit.

independent software vendors (ISVs) A third-party software developer; an individual or an organization that independently creates computer software.

input/output (I/O) port A channel through which data is transferred between a device and the microprocessor. The port appears to the microprocessor as one or more memory addresses that it can use to send or receive data.

instantaneous counter A type of counter that displays the most recent measurement taken by the Performance console.

Integrated Services Digital Network (ISDN) A type of phone line used to enhance WAN speeds. ISDN lines can transmit at speeds of 64 or 128 kilobits per second, as opposed to standard phone lines, which typically transmit at 28.8 kilobits per second. An ISDN line must be installed by the phone company at both the server site and the remote site. See also wide area network (WAN).

Internet Information Services (IIS) Software services that support Web site creation, configuration, and management, along with other Internet functions. Internet Information Services include Network News Transfer Protocol (NNTP), File Transfer Protocol (FTP), and Simple Mail Transfer Protocol (SMTP). See also File Transfer Protocol (FTP); Network News Transfer Protocol (NNTP); Simple Mail Transfer Protocol (SMTP).

Internetwork Packet Exchange (IPX) A network protocol native to NetWare that controls addressing and routing of packets within and between LANs. IPX does not guarantee that a message will be complete (no lost packets). See also Internetwork Packet Exchange/Sequenced Packet Exchange (IPX/SPX).

Internetwork Packet Exchange/Sequenced Packet Exchange (IPX/SPX) Transport protocols used in Novell NetWare and other networks.

interprocess interrupt A high Interrupt-Request Level (IRQL) interrupt that can send an interrupt from one processor to another, allowing processors to communicate.

interrupt avoidance A feature of device adapters that allows a processor to continue processing interrupts without new interrupts being queued until all pending interrupts are complete.

interrupt moderation A feature of device adapters that allows a processor to process interrupts more efficiently by grouping several interrupts to a single hardware interrupt.

interrupt request (IRQ) A signal sent by a device to get the attention of the processor when the device is ready to accept or send information. Each device sends its interrupt requests over a specific hardware line, numbered from 0 to 15. Each device must be assigned a unique IRQ number.

IP address A 32-bit address used to identify a node on an IP internetwork. Each node on the IP internetwork must be assigned a unique IP address, which is made up of the network ID, plus a unique host ID. This address is typically represented with the decimal value of each octet separated by a period (for example, 192.168.7.27). In Windows 2000, the IP address can be configured manually or dynamically through DHCP. See also Dynamic Host Configuration Protocol (DHCP); node.

ISDN See Integrated Services Digital Network.

J

job object A feature in the Win32 API set that makes it possible for groups of processes to be managed with respect to their processor usage and other factors.

K

kernel The core of layered architecture that manages the most basic operations of the operating system and the computer's processor for Windows NT and Windows 2000. The kernel schedules different blocks of executing code, called threads, for the processor to keep it as busy as possible and coordinates multiple processors to optimize performance. The kernel also synchronizes activities among Executive-level subcomponents, such as I/O Manager and Process Manager, and handles hardware exceptions and other hardware-dependent functions. The kernel works closely with the hardware abstraction layer.

L

library A data-storage system, usually managed by Removable Storage. A library consists of removable media (such as tapes or discs) and a hardware device that can read from or write to the media. There are two major types of libraries: robotic libraries (automated multiple-media, multidrive devices) and stand-alone drive libraries (manually operated, single-drive devices). A robotic library is also called a jukebox or changer. See also Removable Storage.

library request A request for an online library or stand-alone drive to perform a task. This request can be issued by an application or by Removable Storage.

Line Printer Daemon (LPD) A service on the print server that receives documents (print jobs) from line printer remote (LPR) tools running on client systems. See also Line Printer Remote (LPR).

Line Printer Remote (LPR) A connectivity tool that runs on client systems and is used to print files to a computer running an LPD server. See also Line Printer Daemon (LPD).

local area network (LAN) A communications network connecting a group of computers, printers, and other devices located within a relatively limited area (for example, a building). A LAN allows any connected device to interact with any other on the network. See also wide area network (WAN).

local group For computers running Windows 2000 Professional and member servers, a group that is granted permissions and rights from its own computer to only those resources on its own computer on which the group resides. See also global group.

local printer A printer that is directly connected to one of the ports on your computer.

local storage For Windows 2000 Server, NTFS disk volumes used as primary data storage. Such disk volumes can be managed by Remote Storage by copying infrequently accessed files to remote, or secondary, storage. See also Remote Storage.

LocalTalk The Apple networking hardware built into every Macintosh computer. LocalTalk includes the cables and connector boxes to connect components and network devices that are part of the AppleTalk network system. LocalTalk was formerly known as the AppleTalk Personal Network.

logical printer The software interface between the operating system and the printer in Windows 2000. While a printer is the device that does the actual printing, a logical printer is its software interface on the print server. This software interface determines how a print job is processed and how it is routed to its destination (to a local or network port, to a file, or to a remote print share). When a document is printed, it is spooled (or stored) on the logical printer before it is sent to the printer itself. See also spooling.

M

Master Boot Record (MBR) The data structure that starts the process of booting the computer. The most important area on a hard disk. The MBR contains the partition table for the disk and a small amount of executable code.

master file table (MFT) The database that tracks the contents of an NTFS volume. The MFT is a table whose rows correspond to files on the volume and whose columns correspond to the attributes of each file.

media access control A layer in the network architecture of Windows NT and Windows 2000 that deals with network access and collision detection.

media label library A dynamic-link library (DLL) that can interpret the format of a media label written by a Removable Storage application.

memory address A portion of computer memory that can be allocated to a device or used by a program or the operating system. Devices are usually allocated a range of memory addresses.

memory leak A condition that occurs when applications allocate memory for use but do not free allocated memory when finished.

metadata Stored data that describes and controls the functioning of the Remote Storage system.

Microsoft Management Console (MMC)

A framework for hosting administrative consoles. A console is defined by the items on its console tree, which might include folders or other containers, World Wide Web pages, and other administrative items. A console has one or more windows that can provide views of the console tree and the administrative properties, services, and events that are acted on by the items in the console tree. The main MMC window provides commands and tools for authoring consoles. The authoring features of MMC and the console tree might be hidden when a console is in User Mode. See also console tree.

migration The process of copying an object from local storage to remote storage.

minimum TTL A default Time To Live (TTL) value set in seconds for use with all resource records in a zone. This value is set in the start of authority (SOA) resource record for each zone. By default, the DNS server includes this value in query answers to inform recipients how long it can store and use resource records provided in the query answer before they must expire the stored records data. When TTL values are set for individual resource records, those values will override the minimum TTL. See also Time To Live (TTL).

mirrored volume A fault-tolerant volume that duplicates data on two physical disks. The mirror is always located on a different disk. If one of the physical disks fails, the data on the failed disk becomes unavailable, but the system continues to operate by using the unaffected disk. A mirrored volume is slower than a RAID-5 volume in read operations but faster in write operations. Mirrored volumes can only be created on dynamic disks. In Windows NT 4.0, a mirrored volume was known as a mirror set. See also dynamic disk; dynamic volume; fault tolerance; redundant array of independent disks (RAID); volume.

MMC See Microsoft Management Console.

N

namespace A set of unique names for resources or items used in a shared computing environment. The names in a namespace can be resolved to the objects they represent. For Microsoft Management Console (MMC), the namespace is represented by the console tree, which displays all of the snap-ins and resources that are accessible to a console. For Domain Name System (DNS), namespace is the vertical or hierarchical structure of the domain name tree. For example, each domain label, such as "host1" or "example," used in a fully qualified domain name, such as "host1.example.microsoft.com," indicates a branch in the domain namespace tree. For Active Directory, namespace corresponds to the DNS namespace in structure, but resolves Active Directory object names.

naming service A service, such as that provided by WINS or DNS, that allows friendly names to be resolved to an address or other specially defined resource data that is used to locate network resources of various types and purposes.

NetBEUI See NetBIOS Enhanced User Interface.

NetBIOS Enhanced User Interface (NetBEUI)
A network protocol native to Microsoft
Networking, that is usually used in local area
networks of one to 200 clients. NetBEUI uses
Token Ring source routing as its only method of
routing. It is the Microsoft implementation of the
NetBIOS standard.

NetBIOS over TCP/IP (NetBT) A feature that
provides the NetBIOS programming interface
over the TCP/IP protocol. It is used for
monitoring routed servers that use NetBIOS name
resolution.

NetWare Core Protocol (NCP) The file-sharing
protocol that governs communications about
resource (such as disk and printer), bindery, and
NDS operations between server and client
computers on a Novell NetWare network.
Requests from client computers are transmitted by
the IPX protocol. Servers respond according to
NCP guidelines. See also bindery; Internetwork
Packet Exchange (IPX); Novell Directory
Services (NDS).

network administrator A person responsible for
setting up and managing domain controllers or
local computers and their user and group
accounts, assigning passwords and permissions,
and helping users with networking issues.
Administrators are members of the Administrators
group and have full control over the domain or
computer.

network data stream The total amount of data
transferred over a network at any given time.

Network News Transfer Protocol (NNTP)
A member of the TCP/IP suite of protocols, used
to distribute network news messages to NNTP
servers and clients, or news-readers, on the
Internet. NNTP is designed so that news articles
are stored on a server in a central database, and
the user selects specific items to read. See also
Transmission Control Protocol/Internet Protocol
(TCP/IP).

NNTP See Network News Transfer Protocol.

node In tree structures, a location on the tree that
can have links to one or more items below it. In
local area networks (LANs), a device that is
connected to the network and is capable of
communicating with other network devices. In a
server cluster, a server that has Cluster service
software installed and is a member of a cluster.
See also local area network (LAN).

noncontainer object An object that cannot
logically contain other objects. A file is a
noncontainer object. See also container object;
object.

Novell Directory Services (NDS) On networks
running Novell NetWare 4.x and NetWare 5.x, a
distributed database that maintains information
about every resource on the network and provides
access to these resources.

NTFS file system A recoverable file system
designed for use specifically with Windows NT
and Windows 2000. NTFS uses database,
transaction-processing, and object paradigms to
provide data security, file system reliability, and
other advanced features. It supports file system
recovery, large storage media, and various
features for the POSIX subsystem. It also supports
object-oriented applications by treating all files as
objects with user-defined and system-defined
attributes.

NWLink An implementation of the Internetwork Packet Exchange (IPX), Sequenced Packet Exchange (SPX), and NetBIOS protocols used in Novell networks. NWLink is a standard network protocol that supports routing and can support NetWare client/server applications, where NetWare-aware Sockets-based applications communicate with IPX/SPX Sockets-based applications. See also Internetwork Packet Exchange (IPX).

O

object An entity, such as a file, folder, shared folder, printer, or Active Directory object, described by a distinct, named set of attributes. For example, the attributes of a File object include its name, location, and size; the attributes of an Active Directory User object might include the user's first name, last name, and e-mail address. For OLE and ActiveX objects, an object can also be any piece of information that can be linked to, or embedded into, another object. See also attribute; container object; noncontainer object; parent object; child object.

object linking and embedding (OLE)
A method for sharing information among applications. Linking an object, such as a graphic, from one document to another inserts a reference to the object into the second document. Any changes you make in the object in the first document will also be made in the second document. Embedding an object inserts a copy of an object from one document into another document. Changes you make in the object in the first document will not be updated in the second unless the embedded object is explicitly updated. See also ActiveX.

offline media Media that are not connected to the computer and require external assistance to be accessed.

offset When defining a pattern match within a filter using Network Monitor, the number of bytes from the beginning of the frame where the pattern occurs in a frame.

on-media identifier (OMID) A label that is electronically recorded on each medium in a Removable Storage system. Removable Storage uses on-media identifiers to track media in the Removable Storage database. An application on-media identifier is a subset of the media label.

online library A robotic library unit, sometimes referred to as a jukebox.

operator request A request for the operator to perform a task. This request can be issued by an application or by Removable Storage.

original equipment manufacturer (OEM)
The maker of a piece of equipment. In making computers and computer-related equipment, manufacturers of original equipment typically purchase components from other manufacturers of original equipment and then integrate them into their own products.

overclocking Setting a microprocessor to run at speeds above the rated specification.

P

page-description language (PDL)
A computer language that describes the arrangement of text and graphics on a printed page. See also printer control language (PCL); PostScript.

paper source The location (such as Upper Paper Tray or Envelope Feeder) of the paper at the printer.

parent object   The object in which another object resides. A parent object implies relation. For example, a folder is a parent object in which a file, or child object, resides. An object can also be both a parent and a child object. See also child object; object.

partition   A logical division of a hard disk. Partitions make it easier to organize information. Each partition can be formatted for a different file system. A partition must be completely contained on one physical disk, and the partition table in the Master Boot Record for a physical disk can contain up to four entries for partitions.

pattern match   In Network Monitor, specific pattern of ASCII or hexadecimal data. A pattern match can be used in setting a filter or capture trigger. See also offset.

paused   The state of a node that is a fully active member in the server cluster but cannot host groups. The paused state is provided for an administrator to perform maintenance. See also; failback; failover; node.

performance counter   In System Monitor, a data item associated with a performance object. For each counter selected, System Monitor presents a value corresponding to a particular aspect of the performance that is defined for the performance object. See also performance object.

Performance Monitor   A Windows NT administrative tool that monitors performance on local or remote machines. Performance Monitor is replaced by the Performance console in Windows 2000. See also System Monitor.

performance object   In System Monitor, a logical collection of counters that is associated with a resource or service that can be monitored. See also performance counter.

peripheral component interconnect (PCI)
A specification introduced by Intel Corporation that defines a local bus system that allows up to 10 PCI-compliant expansion cards to be installed in the computer.

physical media   A storage object that data can be written to, such as a disk or magnetic tape. A physical medium is referenced by its physical media ID (PMID).

placeholder   A Remote Storage identifier for an NTFS volume. See also Remote Storage.

Plug and Play   A set of specifications developed by Intel that allows a computer to automatically detect and configure a device and install the appropriate device drivers.

port   A mechanism that allows multiple sessions. A refinement to an IP address. In Device Manager, a connection point on a computer where devices that pass data in and out of a computer can be connected. For example, a printer is typically connected to a parallel port (also known as an LPT port), and a modem is typically connected to a serial port (also known as a COM port).

port monitor   A device that controls the computer port that provides connectivity to a local or remote print device.

Portable Operating System Interface for UNIX (POSIX)
An IEEE (Institute of Electrical and Electronics Engineers) standard that defines a set of operating-system services. Programs that adhere to the POSIX standard can be easily ported from one system to another. POSIX was based on UNIX system services, but it was created in a way that allows it to be implemented by other operating systems.

POSIX See Portable Operating System Interface for UNIX.

PostScript A page-description language (PDL) developed by Adobe Systems for printing with laser printers. PostScript offers flexible font capability and high-quality graphics. It is the standard for desktop publishing because it is supported by imagesetters, the high-resolution printers used by printing services for commercial typesetting. See also printer control language (PCL); page-description language (PDL).

PostScript printer A printer that uses the PostScript page-description language (PDL) to create text and graphics on the output medium, such as paper or overhead transparency. See also page-description language (PDL); PostScript.

power-on self test (POST) A set of routines stored in read-only memory (ROM) that tests various system components such as RAM, the disk drives, and the keyboard, to see if they are properly connected and operating. If problems are found, these routines alert the user with a series of beeps or a message, often accompanied by a diagnostic numeric value. If the POST is successful, it passes control to the bootstrap loader.

premigrated file An object that has been copied to remote storage in preparation for truncation, but remains on the managed volume. When it is truncated, it will become a placeholder for the file.

print device A hardware device used for printing that is commonly called a printer. See also logical printer.

print processor A PostScript program that understands the format of a document's image file and how to print the file to a specific printer or class of printers. See also PostScript.

print server A computer that is dedicated to managing the printers on a network. The print server can be any computer on the network.

Print Server for Macintosh A Services for Macintosh service that enables Macintosh clients to send and spool documents to printers attached to a computer running Windows 2000 Server, and allows clients to send documents to printers on an AppleTalk network. Print Server for Macintosh is also called MacPrint.

print server service A service that receives print jobs from remote print clients. Different services are provided for different clients.

Print Services for UNIX A print server service for UNIX clients. See also print server service.

print spooler Software that accepts a document sent to a printer and then stores it on disk or in memory until the printer is ready for it. This collection of dynamic-link libraries (DLLs) receives, processes, schedules, and distributes documents for printing. The term spooler is an acronym created from "simultaneous print operations online." See also spooling.

printer control language (PCL) The page-description language (PDL) developed by Hewlett Packard for their laser and inkjet printers. Because of the widespread use of laser printers, this command language has become a standard in many printers. See also page-description language (PDL); PostScript.

printer driver A program designed to allow other programs to work with a particular printer without concerning themselves with the specifics of the printer's hardware and internal language. By using printer drivers that handle the subtleties of each printer, programs can communicate properly with a variety of printers. See also printer control language (PCL); PostScript.

printer fonts Fonts residing in or intended for a printer. A printer font, usually located in the printer's read-only memory (ROM), can be internal, downloaded, or on a font cartridge. See also font.

printer job language (PJL) The printer command language developed by Hewlett Packard that provides printer control at the print-job level. Using PJL commands, default printer settings such as the number of copies to print can be changed. PJL commands also permit switching printer languages between print jobs without action by the user. If bi-directional communication is supported, a PJL-compatible printer can send information such as printer model and job status to the print server. See also printer control language (PCL); page-description language (PDL); PostScript.

printer permissions Permissions that specify the type of access that a user or group has to a printer. The printer permissions are Print, Manage Printers, and Manage Documents.

printers folder The folder in Control Panel that contains the Add Printer wizard and icons for all the printers installed on your computer.

priority inversion The mechanism that allows low-priority threads to run and complete execution rather than being preempted and locking up a resource such as an I/O device.

pruning A process that removes unavailable printers from Active Directory listing. An orphan pruner program running on the domain controller periodically checks for orphaned printers, that is, printers that are offline or powered down, and deletes the printer objects of the printers it cannot find.

pull partner A Windows Internet Name Service (WINS) feature that pulls in replicas from its push partner by requesting them and then accepting the pushed replicas. See also push partner.

push partner A Windows Internet Name Service (WINS) feature that sends replicas to its pull partner upon receiving a request from the pull partner. See also pull partner.

Q

quantum A feature of a network adapter that supports its detection of all frames sent on the network.

queue A list of programs or tasks waiting for execution. In Windows 2000 printing terminology, a queue refers to a group of documents waiting to be printed. In NetWare and OS/2 environments, queues are the primary software interface between the application and print device; users submit documents to a queue. In Windows 2000, however, the printer is that interface; the document is sent to a printer, not a queue.

quorum resource A quorum-capable resource (usually a Physical Disk resource) that has been configured to manage the quorum log and cluster database checkpoints, which comprise the configuration data necessary for recovery of the cluster.

R

RAID See redundant array of independent disks.

RAID-5 volume A fault-tolerant volume with data and parity striped intermittently across three or more physical disks. Parity is a calculated value that is used to reconstruct data after a failure. If a portion of a physical disk fails, you can recreate the data that was on the failed portion from the remaining data and parity. Also known as a striped volume with parity.

recall An operation that retrieves the removed, unnamed data attribute from remote storage and places it on the managed volume. The placeholder is replaced on the managed volume with a copy of the file from remote storage. Upon completion of the recall, the file becomes a premigrated file.

redundant array of independent disks (RAID)
A method used to standardize and categorize fault-tolerant disk systems. Six levels gauge various mixes of performance, reliability, and cost. Windows 2000 provides three of the RAID levels: Level 0 (striping) which is not fault-tolerant, Level 1 (mirroring), and Level 5 (striped volume with parity). See also fault tolerance; mirrored volume; RAID-5 volume; striped volume.

registry In Windows 2000, Windows NT, Windows 98, and Windows 95, a database of information about a computer's configuration. The registry is organized in a hierarchical structure and consists of subtrees and their keys, hives, and entries.

registry key An identifier for a record or group of records in the registry.

remote procedure call (RPC) A message-passing facility that allows a distributed application to call services that are available on various machines in a network. Used during remote administration of computers.

Remote Storage A hierarchical storage management application that migrates data from primary storage to secondary storage. Hierarchical storage management makes sure that data is stored in the most cost-effective method possible. Frequently accessed data is stored on high-performance disks, while data that is not accessed as often is migrated to cheaper media until it is needed again.

remote storage For Windows 2000 Server, removable tapes in a library used for secondary data storage. Specified tapes used for secondary data storage are managed by Remote Storage and contain data that is either stored on, or has been removed from, local storage to free up disk space. See also local storage.

Removable Storage A service used for managing removable media (such as tapes and discs) and storage devices (libraries). Removable Storage allows applications to access and share the same media resources. See also library.

reparse points New NTFS file system objects that have a definable attribute containing user-controlled data and are used to extend functionality in the input/output (I/O) subsystem.

replication The process of copying data from a data store or file system to multiple computers that store the same data for the purpose of synchronizing the data. In Windows 2000, replication of Active Directory occurs through the Directory Replicator Service and replication of the file system occurs through Dfs replication.

Request for Comments (RFC) A document that defines a standard. RFCs are published by the Internet Engineering Task Force (IETF) and other working groups.

reserved state A state that indicates that a side is the second side of a two-sided medium. It is unavailable for allocation to all but the application that has already allocated the first side.

resolver DNS client programs used to look up DNS name information. Resolvers can be either a small "stub" (a limited set of programming routines that provide basic query functionality) or larger programs that provide additional lookup DNS client functions, such as caching. See also caching, caching resolver.

resource Any part of a computer system or network, such as a disk drive, printer, or memory, that can be allotted to a program or a process while it is running. For Device Manager, any of four system components that control how the devices on a computer work. These four system resources are: interrupt request (IRQ) lines, direct memory access (DMA) channels, input/output (I/O) ports, and memory addresses. In a server cluster, an instance of a resource type; the Cluster service manages various physical or logical items as resources. See also direct memory access (DMA); input/output (IO) port; interrupt request (IRQ) lines; memory address.

resource record (RR) Information in the DNS database that can be used to process client queries. Each DNS server contains the resource records it needs to answer queries for the portion of the DNS namespace for which it is authoritative.

response time The amount of time required to do work from start to finish. In a client/server environment, this is typically measured on the client side.

RFC See Request for Comments.

S

scaling The process of adding processors to a system to achieve higher throughput.

secondary storage A storage device used to store data that has been migrated from managed volumes. Secondary storage includes the part of the hard disk that is used for a migration staging area.

security descriptor A set of information attached to an object that specifies the permissions granted to users and groups, as well as the security events to be audited. See also discretionary access control list (DACL); object; system access control list (SACL).

security identifier (SID) A unique name that identifies a user who is logged on to a Windows NT or Windows 2000 security system. A security identifier can represent an individual user, a group of users, or a computer.

Server Message Block (SMB) A file-sharing protocol designed to allow networked computers to transparently access files that reside on remote systems over a variety of networks. The SMB protocol defines a series of commands that pass information between computers. SMB uses four message types: session control, file, printer, and message.

shared nothing A scalability concept in clusters and SMP systems whereby a workload is partitioned among available hardware resources. These resources are used on the workload independently, without sharing of processors, disks, or other hardware resources.

shared printer A printer that receives input from more than one computer. For example, a printer attached to another computer on the network can be shared so that it is available for many users. Also called a network printer.

Simple Mail Transfer Protocol (SMTP)
A protocol used on the Internet to transfer mail. SMTP is independent of the particular transmission subsystem and requires only a reliable, ordered, data stream channel.

Simple Network Management Protocol (SNMP)
A network management protocol installed with TCP/IP and widely used on TCP/IP and Internet Package Exchange (IPX) networks. SNMP transports management information and commands between a management program run by an administrator and the network management agent running on a host. The SNMP agent sends status information to one or more hosts when the host requests it or when a significant event occurs.

Small Computer System Interface (SCSI)
A standard high-speed parallel interface defined by the X3T9.2 committee of the American National Standards Institute (ANSI). A SCSI interface is used for connecting microcomputers to peripheral devices, such as hard disks and printers, and to other computers and local area networks.

SMTP See Simple Mail Transfer Protocol.

SNMP See Simple Network Management Protocol.

soft affinity A mechanism designed to optimize performance in a multiprocessor environment. Soft affinity favors scheduling threads on the processor in which they recently ran or the ideal processor for the thread. With soft affinity, the efficiency of the processor cache is higher because threads often run on the processor on which they previously ran. Soft affinity does not restrict a thread to run on a given processor.

software trap In programming, an event that occurs when a microprocessor detects a problem with executing an instruction, which causes it to stop.

sparse file A file that is handled in a way that requires less disk space than would otherwise be needed by allocating only meaningful non-zero data. Sparse support allows an application to create very large files without committing disk space for every byte.

spooling A process on a server in which print documents are stored on a disk until a printer is ready to process them. A spooler accepts each document from each client, stores it, and sends it to a printer when the printer is ready.

Standard TCP/IP Port Monitor A port monitor that connects a Windows 2000 print server to network-interface printers that use the TCP/IP protocol. It replaces LPRMON for TCP/IP printers connected directly to the network through a network adapter. Printers connected to a UNIX or VAX host that requires RFC 1179 compliance may still require LPRMON on the print server.

Stop error A serious error that affects the operating system and that could place data at risk. The operating system generates an obvious message, a screen with the Stop message, rather than continuing on and possibly corrupting data. Also known as a fatal system error. See also Stop message.

Stop message   A character-based, full-screen error message displayed on a blue background. A Stop message indicates that the Windows 2000 kernel detected a condition from which it cannot recover. Each message is uniquely identified by a Stop error code (a hexadecimal number) and a string indicating the error's symbolic name. Stop messages are usually followed by up to four additional hexadecimal numbers, enclosed in parentheses, which identify developer-defined error parameters. A driver or device may be identified as the cause of the error. A series of troubleshooting tips are also displayed, along with an indication that, if the system was configured to do so, a memory dump file was saved for later use by a kernel debugger. See also Stop error.

storage hierarchy   A directed cyclic graph of linked storage pools.

storage pool   A unit of storage administered by Removable Storage and composed of homogenous storage media. A storage pool is a self-contained storage area with homogenous characteristics (for example, random access, sequential access, read/write, and write-once).

stream   A sequence of bits, bytes, or other small structurally uniform units.

striped volume   A volume that stores data in stripes on two or more physical disks. Data in a striped volume is allocated alternately and evenly (in stripes) to these disks. Striped volumes offer the best performance of all volumes available in Windows 2000, but they do not provide fault tolerance. If a disk in a striped volume fails, the data in the entire volume is lost. You can create striped volumes only on dynamic disks. Striped volumes cannot be mirrored or extended. In Windows NT 4.0, a striped volume was known as a stripe set. See also dynamic disk, dynamic volume, fault tolerance, volume.

symmetric interrupt distribution   A mechanism for distributing interrupts across available processors.

system access control list (SACL)
The part of an object's security descriptor that specifies which events are to be audited per user or group. Examples of auditing events are file access, logon attempts, and system shutdowns. See also access control entry (ACE); discretionary access control list (DACL); object; security descriptor.

System Monitor   A tool that supports detailed monitoring of the use of operating system resources. System Monitor is hosted, along with Performance Logs and Alerts, in the Performance console. The functionality of System Monitor is based on Windows NT Performance Monitor, not Windows 98 System Monitor.

System State   A collection of system-specific data that can be backed up and restored. For all Windows 2000 operating systems, the System State data includes the registry, the class registration database, and the system boot files. For Windows 2000 Server, the system state data also includes the Certificate Services database (if the server is operating as a certificate server). If the server is a domain controller, the system state data also includes Active Directory and the Sysvol directory. See also Active Directory; domain controller; Sysvol.

systemroot   The path and folder name where the Windows 2000 system files are located. Typically, this is C:\Winnt, although a different drive or folder can be designated when Windows 2000 is installed. The value %systemroot% can be used to replace the actual location of the folder that contains the Window 2000 system files. To identify your systemroot folder, click Start, click Run, and then type %systemroot%.

Sysvol A shared directory that stores the server's copy of the domain's public files, which are replicated among all domain controllers in the domain. See also domain controller.

T

T1 A wide-area carrier that transmits data at 1.544 Mbps.

TCP/IP See Transmission Control Protocol/Internet Protocol.

thread A type of object within a process that runs program instructions. Using multiple threads allows concurrent operations within a process and enables one process to run different parts of its program on different processors simultaneously. A thread has its own set of registers, its own kernel stack, a thread environment block, and a user stack in the address space of its process.

thread state A numeric value indicating the execution state of the thread. Numbered 0 through 5, the states seen most often are 1 for ready, 2 for running, and 5 for waiting.

Time To Live (TTL) A timer value included in packets sent over TCP/IP-based networks that tells the recipients how long to hold or use the packet or any of its included data before expiring and discarding the packet or data. For DNS, TTL values are used in resource records within a zone to determine how long requesting clients should cache and use this information when it appears in a query response answered by a DNS server for the zone.

Token Ring A type of network media that connects clients in a closed ring and uses token passing to allow clients to use the network. See also LocalTalk.

total instance A unique instance that contains the performance counters that represent the sum of all active instances of an object.

Transmission Control Protocol/Internet Protocol (TCP/IP)
A set of software networking protocols widely used on the Internet that provide communications across interconnected networks of computers with diverse hardware architectures and operating systems. TCP/IP includes standards for how computers communicate and conventions for connecting networks and routing traffic.

TrueType fonts Fonts that are scalable and sometimes generated as bitmaps or soft fonts, depending on the capabilities of your printer. TrueType fonts are device-independent fonts that are stored as outlines. They can be sized to any height, and they can be printed exactly as they appear on the screen. See also font.

truncate To remove files that are in remote storage from local storage, reclaiming space in local storage. When a premigrated file is truncated it is converted to a remote storage identifier or placeholder.

U

UNC See Universal Naming Convention.

Unicode A fixed-width, 16-bit character-encoding standard capable of representing the letters and characters of the majority of the world's languages. Unicode was developed by a consortium of U.S. computer companies.

Uniform Resource Locator (URL)
An address that uniquely identifies a location on the Internet. A URL for a World Wide Web site is preceded with http://, as in the fictitious URL http://www.example.microsoft.com/. A URL can contain more detail, such as the name of a page of hypertext, usually identified by the file name extension .html or .htm. See also HTML; HTTP; IP address.

Universal Naming Convention (UNC)
A convention for naming files and other resources beginning with two backslashes (\), indicating that the resource exists on a network computer. UNC names conform to the \\SERVERNAME\SHARENAME syntax, where SERVERNAME is the server's name and SHARENAME is the name of the shared resource. The UNC name of a directory or file can also include the directory path after the share name, with the following syntax: \\SERVERNAME\SHARENAME\DIRECTORY\FILENAME.

Universal Serial Bus (USB)   A serial bus with a bandwidth of 1.5 megabits per second (Mbps) for connecting peripherals to a microcomputer. USB can connect up to 127 peripherals, such as external CD-ROM drives, printers, modems, mice, and keyboards, to the system through a single, general-purpose port. This is accomplished by daisy chaining peripherals together. USB supports hot plugging and multiple data streams.

unnamed data attribute   The default data stream of an NTFS file, sometimes referred to as $DATA.

unprepared state   A state that indicates a side of a medium that is not claimed or used by any application, but which does not have a free label on it. Applications cannot allocate unprepared media. This is a temporary state.

unrecognized media pool   A repository of blank media and media that are not recognized by Removable Storage.

unrecognized state   A state that indicates that the label types and label IDs of a medium are not recognized by Removable Storage.

V

value bar   The area of the System Monitor graph or histogram display that shows last, average, minimum and maximum statistics for the selected counter.

virtual memory   The space on the hard disk that Windows 2000 uses as memory. Because of virtual memory, the amount of memory taken from the perspective of a process can be much greater than the actual physical memory in the computer. The operating system does this in a way that is transparent to the application, by paging data that does not fit in physical memory to and from the disk at any given instant.

volume   A portion of a physical disk that functions as though it were a physically separate disk. In My Computer and Windows Explorer, volumes appear as local disks, such as drive C or drive D.

volume decommission   A process that occurs when a managed volume is no longer accessible. The data in remote storage is no longer associated with a placeholder or a premigrated file. This space is available for space reclamation.

volume mount points   New system objects in the version of NTFS included with Windows 2000 that represent storage volumes in a persistent, robust manner. Volume mount points allow the operating system to graft the root of a volume onto a directory.

W

WAN See wide area network.

wide area network (WAN) A communications network connecting geographically separated computers, printers, and other devices. A WAN allows any connected device to interact with any other on the network. See also local area network (LAN).

WINS database The database used to register and resolve computer names to IP addresses on Windows-based networks. The contents of this database are replicated at regular intervals throughout the network. See also push partner, pull partner, replication.

working set For a process, the amount of physical memory assigned to a process by the operating system.

Index

Comprehensive
information and tools—
straight from the
Windows 2000 Server team!

Deploy, manage, and optimize Microsoft's next-generation operating system with expertise from those who know the technology best—the Microsoft Windows 2000 Server development team. This RESOURCE KIT gives you seven comprehensive guides—thousands of pages packed full of technical details—plus hundreds of tools and utilities on CD. It's the complete kit you need to help maximize system performance and reduce ownership and support costs. Get seven volumes of authoritative Windows 2000 Server drill down, straight from the source!

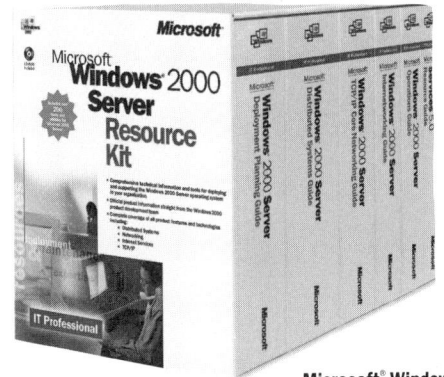

Microsoft® Windows® 2000 Server Resource Kit
ISBN: 1-57231-805-8

Also available in
separate volumes!

These powerhouse guides—available separately and distilled from the MICROSOFT WINDOWS 2000 SERVER RESOURCE KIT—make it easy to find the exact technical information you need to optimize system performance and reduce costs.

Microsoft® Windows® 2000 Server Deployment Planning Guide
ISBN: 0-7356-1794-5

Microsoft Windows 2000 Server Distributed Systems Guide
ISBN: 0-7356-1795-3

Microsoft Windows 2000 Server Operations Guide
ISBN: 0-7356-1796-1

Microsoft Windows 2000 Server Internetworking Guide
ISBN: 0-7356-1797-X

Microsoft Windows 2000 Server TCP/IP Core Networking Guide
ISBN: 0-7356-1798-8

Microsoft®
microsoft.com/mspress

In-depth. Focused.
And
ready for work.

Get the technical drilldown you need to deploy and support Microsoft products more effectively with the MICROSOFT TECHNICAL REFERENCE series. Each guide focuses on a specific aspect of the technology—weaving in-depth detail with on-the-job scenarios and practical how-to information for the IT professional. Get focused—and take technology to its limits—with MICROSOFT TECHNICAL REFERENCES.

Data Warehousing with Microsoft® SQL Server™ 7.0 Technical Reference
U.S.A. $49.99
Canada $76.99
ISBN 0-7356-0859-8

Microsoft SQL Server 7.0 Performance Tuning Technical Reference
U.S.A. $49.99
Canada $76.99
ISBN 0-7356-0909-8

Building Applications with Microsoft Outlook® 2000 Technical Reference
U.S.A. $49.99
Canada $72.99
ISBN 0-7356-0581-5

Microsoft Windows NT® Server 4.0 Terminal Server Edition Technical Reference
U.S.A. $49.99
Canada $72.99
ISBN 0-7356-0645-5

Microsoft Windows® 2000 TCP/IP Protocols and Services Technical Reference
U.S.A. $49.99
Canada $76.99
ISBN 0-7356-0556-4

Active Directory™ Services for Microsoft Windows 2000 Technical Reference
U.S.A. $49.99
Canada $76.99
ISBN 0-7356-0624-2

Microsoft Windows 2000 Security Technical Reference
U.S.A. $49.99
Canada $72.99
ISBN 0-7356-0858-X

Microsoft Windows 2000 Performance Tuning Technical Reference
U.S.A. $49.99
Canada $72.99
ISBN 0-7356-0633-1

mspress.microsoft.com

Practical, *portable* guides for
IT administrators

For immediate answers that will help you administer Microsoft products efficiently, get ADMINISTRATOR'S POCKET CONSULTANTS. Ideal at the desk or on the go from workstation to workstation, these hands-on, fast-answers reference guides focus on what needs to be done in specific scenarios to support and manage mission-critical products.

Microsoft® Windows® 2000 Administrator's Pocket Consultant
ISBN 0-7356-0831-8

Microsoft Windows NT® Server 4.0 Administrator's Pocket Consultant
ISBN 0-7356-0574-2

Microsoft SQL Server™ 2000 Administrator's Pocket Consultant
ISBN 0-7356-1129-7

Microsoft Exchange 2000 Server Administrator's Pocket Consultant
ISBN 0-7356-0962-4

Microsoft Windows 2000 and IIS 5.0 Administrator's Pocket Consultant
ISBN 0-7356-1024-X

Microsoft®
mspress.microsoft.com

Get a **Free**
e-mail newsletter, updates,
special offers, links to related books,
and more when you

register on line!

Register your Microsoft Press® title on our Web site and you'll get a FREE subscription to our e-mail newsletter, *Microsoft Press Book Connections*. You'll find out about newly released and upcoming books and learning tools, online events, software downloads, special offers and coupons for Microsoft Press customers, and information about major Microsoft® product releases. You can also read useful additional information about all the titles we publish, such as detailed book descriptions, tables of contents and indexes, sample chapters, links to related books and book series, author biographies, and reviews by other customers.

Registration is easy. Just visit this Web page and fill in your information:

http://www.microsoft.com/mspress/register

Microsoft®

Proof of Purchase

Use this page as proof of purchase if participating in a promotion or rebate offer on this title. Proof of purchase must be used in conjunction with other proof(s) of payment such as your dated sales receipt—see offer details.

Microsoft® Windows® 2000 Server Operations Guide
0-7356-1796-1

CUSTOMER NAME

Microsoft Press, PO Box 97017, Redmond, WA 98073-9830

END-USER LICENSE AGREEMENT FOR MICROSOFT SOFTWARE

Microsoft WINDOWS 2000 RESOURCE KIT

IMPORTANT-READ CAREFULLY: This Microsoft End-User License Agreement ("EULA") is a legal agreement between you (either an individual or a single entity) and Microsoft Corporation for the Microsoft software identified above, which includes computer software and may include associated media, printed materials, additional computer software applications, and "online" or electronic documentation ("SOFTWARE"). By downloading, installing, copying, or otherwise using the SOFTWARE, you agree to be bound by the terms of this EULA. If you do not agree to the terms of this EULA, do not install or use the SOFTWARE. This print EULA supercedes any End User License Agreement found on the CD.

SOFTWARE LICENSE

The SOFTWARE is protected by copyright laws and international copyright treaties, as well as other intellectual property laws and treaties. **The SOFTWARE is licensed, not sold.**

1. **GRANT OF LICENSE.** This EULA grants you the following rights:

   a. **SOFTWARE.** Except as otherwise provided herein, you, as an individual, may install and use copies of the SOFTWARE on an unlimited number of computers, including workstations, terminals or other digital electronic devices ("COMPUTERS"), provided that you are the only individual using the SOFTWARE. If you are an entity, you may designate one individual within your organization to have the right to use the SOFTWARE in the manner provided above. The SOFTWARE is in "use" on a COMPUTER when it is loaded into temporary memory (i.e.. RAM) or installed into permanent memory (e.g., hard disk, CD-ROM, or other storage device) of that COMPUTER.

   b. **Client/Server Software.** The SOFTWARE may contain one or more components which consist of both of the following types of software: "Server Software" that is installed and provides services on a COMPUTER acting as a server ("Server"); and "Client Software" that allows a COMPUTER to access or utilize the services provided by the Server Software. If the component of the SOFTWARE consists of both Server Software and Client Software which are used together, you may also install and use copies of such Client Software on COMPUTERS within your organization and which are connected to your internal network.

   Such COMPUTERS running this Client Software may be used by more than one individual.

2. **DESCRIPTION OF OTHER RIGHTS AND LIMITATIONS.**

   a. **Limitations on Reverse Engineering, Decompilation, and Disassembly.** You may not reverse engineer, decompile, or disassemble the SOFTWARE, except and only to the extent that such activity is expressly permitted by applicable law notwithstanding this limitation.

   b. **Rental.** You may not rent, lease, or lend the SOFTWARE.

   c. **Support Services.** Microsoft does not support the SOFTWARE, however, in the event Microsoft does provide you with support services related to the SOFTWARE ("Support Services"), use of such Support Services is governed by the Microsoft policies and programs described in the user manual, in "online" documentation, and/or in other Microsoft-provided materials. Any supplemental software code provided to you as part of the Support Services shall be considered part of the SOFTWARE and subject to the terms and conditions of this EULA. With respect to technical information you provide to Microsoft as part of the Support Services, Microsoft may use such information for its business purposes, including for product support and development. Microsoft will not utilize such technical information in a form that personally identifies you.

   d. **Software Transfer.** You may permanently transfer of all of your rights under this EULA, provided you retain no copies, you transfer all of the SOFTWARE (including all component parts, the media and printed materials, any upgrades, this EULA, and, if applicable, the Certificate of Authenticity), **and** the recipient agrees to the terms of this EULA. If the SOFTWARE is an upgrade, any transfer must include all prior versions of the SOFTWARE.

   e. **Termination.** Without prejudice to any other rights, Microsoft may terminate this EULA if you fail to comply with the terms and conditions of this EULA. In such event, you must destroy all copies of the SOFTWARE and all of its component parts.

3. **UPGRADES.** If the SOFTWARE is labeled as an upgrade , you must be properly licensed to use a product identified by Microsoft as being eligible for the upgrade in order to use the SOFTWARE. SOFTWARE labeled as an upgrade replaces and/or supplements the product that formed the basis for your eligibility for the upgrade. You may use the resulting upgraded product only in accordance with the terms of this EULA. If the SOFTWARE is an upgrade of a component of a package of software programs that you licensed as a single product, the SOFTWARE may be used and transferred only as part of that single product package and may not be separated for use on more than one computer

4. **INTELLECTUAL PROPERTY RIGHTS.** All title and intellectual property rights in and to the SOFTWARE (including but not limited to any images, photographs, animations, video, audio, music, text and "applets" incorporated into the SOFTWARE), and any copies you are permitted to make herein are owned by Microsoft or its suppliers. All title and intellectual property rights in

and to the content which may be accessed through use of the SOFTWARE is the property of the respective content owner and may be protected by applicable copyright or other intellectual property laws and treaties. This EULA grants you no rights to use such content. If this SOFTWARE contains documentation which is provided only in electronic form, you may print one copy of such electronic documentation. You may not copy the printed materials accompanying the SOFTWARE.

5. **U.S. GOVERNMENT LICENSE RIGHTS**. SOFTWARE provided to the U.S. Government pursuant to solicitations issued on or after December 1, 1995 is provided with the commercial license rights and restrictions described elsewhere herein. SOFTWARE provided to the U.S. Government pursuant to solicitations issued prior to December 1, 1995 is provided with "Restricted Rights" as provided for in FAR, 48 CFR 52.227-14 (JUNE 1987) or DFAR, 48 CFR 252.227-7013 (OCT 1988), as applicable.

6. **EXPORT RESTRICTIONS**. You agree that you will not export or re-export the SOFTWARE (or portions thereof) to any country, person or entity subject to U.S. export restrictions. You specifically agree not to export or re-export the SOFTWARE (or portions thereof): (i) to any country subject to a U.S. embargo or trade restriction; (ii) to any person or entity who you know or have reason to know will utilize the SOFTWARE (or portion thereof) in the production of nuclear, chemical or biological weapons; or (iii) to any person or entity who has been denied export privileges by the U.S. government. For additional information see http://www.microsoft.com/exporting/.

7. **DISCLAIMER OF WARRANTIES. To the maximum extent permitted by applicable law, Microsoft and its suppliers provide the SOFTWARE and any (if any) Support Services *AS IS AND WITH ALL FAULTS,* and hereby disclaim all warranties and conditions, either express, implied or statutory, including, but not limited to, any (if any) implied warranties or conditions of merchantability, of fitness for a particular purpose, of lack of viruses, of accuracy or completeness of responses, of results, and of lack of negligence or lack of workmanlike effort, all with regard to the SOFTWARE, and the provision of or failure to provide Support Services. ALSO, THERE IS NO WARRANTY OR CONDITION OF TITLE, QUIET ENJOYMENT, QUIET POSSESSION, CORRESPONDENCE TO DESCRIPTION OR NON-INFRINGEMENT, WITH REGARD TO THE SOFTWARE. THE ENTIRE RISK AS TO THE QUALITY OF OR ARISING OUT OF USE OR PERFORMANCE OF THE SOFTWARE AND SUPPORT SERVICES, IF ANY, REMAINS WITH YOU.**

8. **EXCLUSION OF INCIDENTAL, CONSEQUENTIAL AND CERTAIN OTHER DAMAGES. TO THE MAXIMUM EXTENT PERMITTED BY APPLICABLE LAW, IN NO EVENT SHALL MICROSOFT OR ITS SUPPLIERS BE LIABLE FOR ANY SPECIAL, INCIDENTAL, INDIRECT, OR CONSEQUENTIAL DAMAGES WHATSOEVER (INCLUDING, BUT NOT LIMITED TO, DAMAGES FOR LOSS OF PROFITS OR CONFIDENTIAL OR OTHER INFORMATION, FOR BUSINESS INTERRUPTION, FOR PERSONAL INJURY, FOR LOSS OF PRIVACY, FOR FAILURE TO MEET ANY DUTY INCLUDING OF GOOD FAITH OR OF REASONABLE CARE, FOR NEGLIGENCE, AND FOR ANY OTHER PECUNIARY OR OTHER LOSS WHATSOEVER) ARISING OUT OF OR IN ANY WAY RELATED TO THE USE OF OR INABILITY TO USE THE SOFTWARE, THE PROVISION OF OR FAILURE TO PROVIDE SUPPORT SERVICES, OR OTHERWISE UNDER OR IN CONNECTION WITH ANY PROVISION OF THIS EULA, EVEN IN THE EVENT OF THE FAULT, TORT (INCLUDING NEGLIGENCE), STRICT LIABILITY, BREACH OF CONTRACT OR BREACH OF WARRANTY OF MICROSOFT OR ANY SUPPLIER, AND EVEN IF MICROSOFT OR ANY SUPPLIER HAS BEEN ADVISED OF THE POSSIBILITY OF SUCH DAMAGES.**

9. **LIMITATION OF LIABILITY AND REMEDIES. Notwithstanding any damages that you might incur for any reason whatsoever (including, without limitation, all damages referenced above and all direct or general damages), the entire liability of Microsoft and any of its suppliers under any provision of this EULA and your exclusive remedy for all of the foregoing shall be limited to the greater of the amount actually paid by you for the SOFTWARE or U.S.$5.00. The foregoing limitations, exclusions and disclaimers shall apply to the maximum extent permitted by applicable law, even if any remedy fails its essential purpose.**

10. **NOTE ON JAVA SUPPORT**. THE SOFTWARE MAY CONTAIN SUPPORT FOR PROGRAMS WRITTEN IN JAVA. JAVA TECHNOLOGY IS NOT FAULT TOLERANT AND IS NOT DESIGNED, MANUFACTURED, OR INTENDED FOR USE OR RESALE AS ONLINE CONTROL EQUIPMENT IN HAZARDOUS ENVIRONMENTS REQUIRING FAIL-SAFE PERFORMANCE, SUCH AS IN THE OPERATION OF NUCLEAR FACILITIES, AIRCRAFT NAVIGATION OR COMMUNICATION SYSTEMS, AIR TRAFFIC CONTROL, DIRECT LIFE SUPPORT MACHINES, OR WEAPONS SYSTEMS, IN WHICH THE FAILURE OF JAVA TECHNOLOGY COULD LEAD DIRECTLY TO DEATH, PERSONAL INJURY, OR SEVERE PHYSICAL OR ENVIRONMENTAL DAMAGE. Sun Microsystems, Inc. has contractually obligated Microsoft to make this disclaimer.

11. **APPLICABLE LAW.** If you acquired this SOFTWARE in the United States, this EULA is governed by the laws of the State of Washington. If you acquired this SOFTWARE in Canada, unless expressly prohibited by local law, this EULA is governed by the laws in force in the Province of Ontario, Canada; and, in respect of any dispute which may arise hereunder, you consent to the jurisdiction of the federal and provincial courts sitting in Toronto, Ontario. If this SOFTWARE was acquired outside the United States, then local law may apply.

12. **ENTIRE AGREEMENT. This EULA (including any addendum or amendment to this EULA which is included with the SOFTWARE) is the entire agreement between you and Microsoft relating to the SOFTWARE and the Support Services (if any) and it supersedes all prior or contemporaneous oral or written communications, proposals and representations with respect to the SOFTWARE or any other subject matter covered by this EULA. To the extent the terms of any Microsoft policies or programs for Support Services conflict with the terms of this EULA, the terms of this EULA shall control.**

13. **QUESTIONS?** Should you have any questions concerning this EULA, or if you desire to contact Microsoft for any reason, please contact the Microsoft subsidiary serving your country, or write: Microsoft Sales Information Center/One Microsoft Way/ Redmond, WA 98052-6399.

SI VOUS AVEZ ACQUIS VOTRE PRODUIT MICROSOFT AU CANADA, LA GARANTIE LIMITÉE SUIVANTE VOUS CONCERNE :

RENONCIATION AUX GARANTIES. Dans toute la mesure permise par la législation en vigueur, Microsoft et ses fournisseurs fournissent le PRODUIT LOGICIEL et tous (selon le cas) Services d'assistance TELS QUELS ET AVEC TOUS LEURS DÉFAUTS, et par les présentes excluent toute garantie ou condition, expresse ou implicite, légale ou conventionnelle, écrite ou verbale, y compris, mais sans limitation, toute (selon le cas) garantie ou condition implicite ou légale de qualité marchande, de conformité à un usage particulier, d'absence de virus, d'exactitude et d'intégralité des réponses, de résultats, d'efforts techniques et professionnels et d'absence de négligence, le tout relativement au PRODUIT LOGICIEL et à la prestation ou à la non-prestation des Services d'assistance. DE PLUS, IL N'Y A AUCUNE GARANTIE ET CONDITION DE TITRE, DE JOUISSANCE PAISIBLE, DE POSSES-SION PAISIBLE, DE SIMILARITÉ À LA DESCRIPTION ET D'ABSENCE DE CONTREFAÇON RELATIVEMENT AU PRODUIT LOGICIEL. Vous supportez tous les risques découlant de l'utilisation et de la performance du PRODUIT LOGICIEL et ceux découlant des Services d'assistance (s'il y a lieu).

EXCLUSION DES DOMMAGES INDIRECTS, ACCESSOIRES ET AUTRES. Dans toute la mesure permise par la législation en vigueur, Microsoft et ses fournisseurs ne sont en aucun cas responsables de tout dommage spécial, indirect, accessoire, moral ou exemplaire quel qu'il soit (y compris, mais sans limitation, les dommages entraînés par la perte de bénéfices ou la perte d'information confidentielle ou autre, l'interruption des affaires, les préjudices corporels, la perte de confidentialité, le défaut de remplir toute obliga-tion y compris les obligations de bonne foi et de diligence raisonnable, la négligence et toute autre perte pécuniaire ou autre perte de quelque nature que ce soit) découlant de, ou de toute autre manière lié à, l'utilisation ou l'impossibilité d'utiliser le PRODUIT LOGICIEL, la prestation ou la non-prestation des Services d'assistance ou autrement en vertu de ou relativement à toute disposition de cette convention, que ce soit en cas de faute, de délit (y compris la négligence), de responsabilité stricte, de manquement à un contrat ou de manquement à une garantie de Microsoft ou de l'un de ses fournisseurs, et ce, même si Microsoft ou l'un de ses fournisseurs a été avisé de la possibilité de tels dommages.

LIMITATION DE RESPONSABILITÉ ET RECOURS. Malgré tout dommage que vous pourriez encourir pour quelque raison que ce soit (y compris, mais sans limitation, tous les dommages mentionnés ci-dessus et tous les dommages directs et généraux), la seule responsabilité de Microsoft et de ses fournisseurs en vertu de toute disposition de cette convention et votre unique recours en regard de tout ce qui précède sont limités au plus élevé des montants suivants : soit (a) le montant que vous avez payé pour le PRODUIT LOGICIEL, soit (b) un montant équivalent à cinq dollars U.S. (5,00 $ U.S.). Les limitations, exclusions et renonciations ci-dessus s'appliquent dans toute la mesure permise par la législation en vigueur, et ce même si leur application a pour effet de priver un recours de son essence.

LÉGISLATION APPLICABLE.. Sauf lorsqu'expressément prohibé par la législation locale, la présente convention est régie par les lois en vigueur dans la province d'Ontario, Canada. Pour tout différend qui pourrait découler des présentes, vous acceptez la compétence des tribunaux fédéraux et provinciaux siégeant à Toronto, Ontario.

Si vous avez des questions concernant cette convention ou si vous désirez communiquer avec Microsoft pour quelque raison que ce soit, veuillez contacter la succursale Microsoft desservant votre pays, ou écrire à: Microsoft Sales Information Center, One Microsoft Way, Redmond, Washington 98052-6399.